D1035558

JOURNAL FOR THE STUDY OF THE NEW TESTAMENT SUPPLEMENT SERIES

68

JSOT Press
Sheffield

Jeremiah in Matthew's Gospel

The Rejected-Prophet Motif in Matthaean Redaction

Michael Knowles

Journal for the Study of the New Testament
Supplement Series 68

For Eleanor Grace

Published by JSOT Press
JSOT Press is an imprint of
Sheffield Academic Press Ltd
343 Fulwood Road
Sheffield S10 3BP
England

Typeset by Sheffield Academic Press
and
Printed on acid-free paper in Great Britain
by Biddles Limited
Guildford

British Library Cataloguing in Publication Data

Knowles, Michael
Jeremiah in Matthew's Gospel: Rejected-
Prophet Motif in Matthaean Redaction.—
(JSNT Supplement Series, ISSN 0143-5108;
No. 68)
I. Title II. Series
226.2

ISBN 1-85075-344-X

And indeed the prophets, along with other things which they predicted, also foretold this, that all those on whom the Spirit of God should rest...should suffer persecution, and be stoned and slain. For the prophets prefigured in themselves all these things, because of their love to God, and on account of his word. For since they themselves were members of Christ...every one of them, in his special place as a member...shadowed forth beforehand that particular working of Christ which was connected with that member.

(Irenaeus, *Adversus Haereses* 4.33.10)

But those who said that Jesus was Jeremiah, and not that Jeremiah was a type of the Christ, were perhaps influenced by what is said in the beginning of Jeremiah about Christ, which was not fulfilled in the prophet at that time, but was beginning to be fulfilled in Jesus, whom 'God set up over nations and kingdoms to root up, and to break down, and to destroy, and to build up, and to transplant,' having made him to be a prophet to the Gentiles to whom he proclaimed the word.

(Origen, *Commentariorum in Matthaeum* 12.9 [on 16.14])

Contents

PREFACE

This study reproduces, with some modification, the substance of a doctoral dissertation presented to the Faculty of Wycliffe College, Toronto, and the Biblical Department of the Toronto School of Theology in the Spring of 1991. I would like to thank my doctoral supervisor, Dr Richard N. Longenecker, for his gracious direction and consistent encouragement throughout the course of a long programme of studies, as well as for his fine sensitivity to language, which improved the presentation of my argument immeasurably. I am also grateful for the assistance and helpful criticism offered by Dr Schuyler Brown, Dr John Kloppenborg, Dr Peter Richardson and Dr Michael Steinhauser (all of Toronto), as well as by Dr Graham Stanton of King's College, University of London. In addition, my fellow doctoral students provided invaluable encouragement, companionship, reassurance and good humor along the way; especially Ann, Brad, Douglas, Grant, John, Paul, Terry and Van.

Special thanks are due to the congregation of the Church of the Messiah, Toronto, for their many kindnesses; among them in particular Rob Alloway, Betty and Tom Gracie, Dick and Nina Hillier, Dorothy McBride, and Judy and Richard Tanner, who alone know the contribution they each have made. Above all, my debt of gratitude to my wife Janette for her love, patience, support and faith in me over many difficult years cannot be expressed in words or ever hope to be repaid.

The generous financial support of Wycliffe College and of the Social Sciences and Humanities Research Council of Canada for the programme of doctoral studies represented by this monograph is also gratefully acknowledged.

Printed quotations of the Greek New Testament are from the *Novum Testamentum Graece*, Nestle-Aland 26th edition, accessed via GramGreek 1.11 in conjunction with the GramCord Grammatical Concordance System from the GramCord Institute/Trinity Evangelical Divinity School, 2065 Half Day Road, Deerfield, Illinois 60015.

ABBREVIATIONS

AB	Anchor Bible
AnBib	Analecta biblica
ANTF	Arbeiten zur neutestamentlichen Textforschung
AOAT	Alter Orient und Altes Testament
ASNU	Acta seminarii neotestamentici upsaliensis
ASTI	*Annual of the Swedish Theological Institute*
ATANT	Abhandlungen zur Theologie des Alten und Neuen Testaments
ATR	*Anglican Theological Review*
AusBR	*Australian Biblical Review*
AUSS	*Andrews University Seminary Studies*
BAGD	W. Bauer, W.F. Arndt, F.W. Gingrich and F.W. Danker, *Greek-English Lexicon of the New Testament*
BDB	F. Brown, S.R. Driver and C.A. Briggs, *Hebrew and English Lexicon of the Old Testament*
BDF	F. Blass, A. Debrunner and R.W. Funk, *A Greek Grammar of the New Testament*
BETL	Bibliotheca ephemeridum theologicarum lovaniensium
BEvT	Beiträge zur evangelischen Theologie
BFCT	Beiträge zur Förderung christlicher Theologie
Bib	*Biblica*
BJRL	*Bulletin of the John Rylands University Library of Manchester*
BJS	Brown Judaic Studies
BKAT	Biblischer Kommentar: Altes Testament
BNTC	Black's New Testament Commentaries
BR	*Biblical Research*
BTB	*Biblical Theology Bulletin*
BWANT	Beiträge zur Wissenschaft vom Alten und Neuen Testament
BZ	*Biblische Zeitschrift*
BZNW	Beihefte zur *ZNW*
CBC	Cambridge Bible Commentary
CBQ	*Catholic Biblical Quarterly*
CBQMS	*Catholic Biblical Quarterly*, Monograph Series
CNT	Commentaire du Nouveau Testament
CRINT	Compendia rerum iudaicarum ad novum testamentum
DBSup	*Dictionnaire de la Bible, Supplément*
DJD	Discoveries in the Judaean Desert

EBib	Etudes bibliques
EKKNT	Evangelisch-Katholischer Kommentar zum Neuen Testament
EncJud	*Encyclopaedia Judaica*
ETL	*Ephemerides theologicae lovanienses*
EvQ	*Evangelical Quarterly*
ExpTim	*Expository Times*
FRLANT	Forschungen zur Religion und Literatur des Alten und Neuen Testaments
GKC	*Gesenius' Hebrew Grammar*, ed. E. Kautzsch, trans. A.E. Cowley
HeyJ	*Heythrop Journal*
HNT	Handbuch zum Neuen Testament
HTKNT	Herders theologischer Kommentar zum Neuen Testament
HTR	*Harvard Theological Review*
HUCA	*Hebrew Union College Annual*
IB	*Interpreter's Bible*
IBS	*Irish Biblical Studies*
ICC	International Critical Commentary
IDB	G.A. Buttrick (ed.), *Interpreter's Dictionary of the Bible*
IDBSup	*IDB*, Supplementary Volume
JBL	*Journal of Biblical Literature*
JJS	*Journal of Jewish Studies*
JQR	*Jewish Quarterly Review*
JR	*Journal of Religion*
JRS	*Journal of Roman Studies*
JSHRZ	Jüdische Schriften aus hellenistisch-römischer Zeit
JSJ	*Journal for the Study of Judaism in the Persian, Hellenistic and Roman Period*
JSS	*Journal of Semitic Studies*
JTS	*Journal of Theological Studies*
LD	Lectio divina
LTP	*Laval théologique et philosophique*
LumVie	*Lumière et Vie*
MNTC	Moffatt NT Commentary
N-A^{26}	Nestle–Aland, *Novum Testamentum Graece*
NCB	New Century Bible
NICNT	New International Commentary on the New Testament
NICOT	New International Commentary on the Old Testament
NovT	*Novum Testamentum*
NovTSup	*Novum Testamentum* Supplements
NTAbh	Neutestamentliche Abhandlungen
NTD	Das Neue Testament Deutsch
NTS	*New Testament Studies*
NTTS	New Testament Tools and Studies
OBO	Orbis biblicus et orientalis

OTL	Old Testament Library
PG	J. Migne (ed.), *Patrologia graeca*
PL	J. Migne (ed.), *Patrologia latina*
RevQ	*Revue de Qumran*
RevScRel	*Revue des sciences religieuses*
RHPR	*Revue d'histoire et de philosophie religieuses*
RNT	Regensburger Neues Testament
RSR	*Recherches de science religieuse*
RTL	*Revue théologique de Louvain*
SBLDS	SBL Dissertation Series
SBLMS	SBL Monograph Series
SBLSBS	SBL Sources for Biblical Study
SBLSCS	SBL Septuagint and Cognate Studies
SBLTT	SBL Texts and Translations
SBS	Stuttgarter Bibelstudien
SBT	Studies in Biblical Theology
SC	Sources chrétiennes
SE	*Studia Evangelica*
SJT	*Scottish Journal of Theology*
SNTSMS	Society for New Testament Studies Monograph Series
SPB	Studia postbiblica
SSS	Semitic Study Series
ST	*Studia theologica*
STDJ	Studies on the Texts of the Desert of Judah
Str–B	[H. Strack and] P. Billerbeck, *Kommentar zum Neuen Testament aus Talmud und Midrasch*
SUNT	Studien zur Umwelt des Neuen Testaments
SVTP	Studia in Veteris Testamenti pseudepigrapha
TCGNT	B.M. Metzger, *A Textual Commentary on the Greek New Testament*
TDNT	G. Kittel and G. Friedrich (eds.), *Theological Dictionary of the New Testament*
THKNT	Theologischer Handkommentar zum Neuen Testament
TS	*Theological Studies*
TU	Texte und Untersuchungen
TWNT	G. Kittel and G. Friedrich (eds.), *Theologisches Wörterbuch zum Neuen Testament*
UBSGNT	United Bible Societies' *Greek New Testament*
VSpir	*Vie spirituelle*
VT	*Vetus Testamentum*
WMANT	Wissenschaftliche Monographien zum Alten und Neuen Testament
WUNT	Wissenschaftliche Untersuchungen zum Neuen Testament
ZNW	*Zeitschrift für die neutestamentliche Wissenschaft*
ZTK	*Zeitschrift für Theologie und Kirche*

INTRODUCTION

Matthew is the only Evangelist to mention the prophet Jeremiah by name. In 2.17-18 the Bethlehemites' lamentation over the slaughter of their children is likened, by appeal to Jer. 31.15, to Rachel weeping for her children. In the Caesarea Philippi encounter of 16.13-20, when Jesus asks his followers 'Who do men say the Son of man is?', Matthew inserts the enigmatic reply, 'Jeremiah or one of the prophets' (v. 14). Then in 27.9-10 the words of 'the prophet Jeremiah' comment on the purchase of the 'Field of Blood' with Judas's thirty pieces of silver.

Yet each of these passages poses difficulties for interpreters. For example, 2.17 and 27.9 both employ fulfillment formulae that differ significantly from the remainder of those in Matthew's Gospel, possibly indicating some distinct role or purpose for these two references. And whereas Rachel's sorrow serves in Jeremiah to introduce a prophecy of consolation, Matthew takes the passage in just the opposite sense. As B.M. Nolan declares, 'no exegete has satisfactorily elucidated Matthew's intention in 2.18'.[1] Likewise, according to G.M. Soares Prabhu, 'The formula quotation of Mt 2, 17f. is surely among the most problematic of all those in Mt's Gospel'.[2]

Even more problematic is the ascription τὸ ῥηθὲν διὰ Ἰερεμίου τοῦ προφήτου of 27.9, since most agree that the primary reference here is to Zech. 11.12-13. Unless the ascription to Jeremiah is simply

1. B.M. Nolan, *The Royal Son of God: The Christology of Matthew 1–2 in the Setting of the Gospel* (OBO, 23; Fribourg: Editions Universitaires; Göttingen: Vandenhoeck & Ruprecht, 1979), p. 136.

2. G.M. Soares Prabhu, *The Formula Quotations in the Infancy Narratives of Matthew: An Enquiry into the Tradition History of Mt. 1–2* (AnBib, 63; Rome: Pontifical Biblical Institute, 1976), p. 253; cf. M.D. Goulder (*Midrash and Lection in Matthew* [London: SPCK, 1974], p. 239), 'of all the citations in the Gospel, this is the most clearly artificial', R. Schnackenburg (*Matthäusevangelium*, [Die Neue Echter Bibel; Würzburg: Echter, 1985], I, p. 27), 'weit hergeholt'.

an error, the most widely accepted explanation is that Matthew intends a reference to Jeremiah's purchase of a field from Hanamel ben Shallum (Jer. 32.6-15). But again, whereas in Jeremiah this episode constitutes a sign of hope and return from exile, it appears to have quite the opposite purpose for Matthew.

The most difficult of Matthew's three references to Jeremiah, however, is that found in the Caesarea Philippi episode. For a start, it is not clear whether the various opinions cited in response to Jesus' question—including the possibility that Jesus himself bears some resemblance to Jeremiah—are alternatives to be rejected or anticipations of Peter's response, 'You are the Christ'. Unlike 2.17 and 27.9, here the reference is to Jeremiah himself or to some thematic relevance that he bears for Matthew, rather than to a specific quotation from the canon.

This investigation into the meaning and interrelationship of these three references must therefore operate on at least two levels. First, the two fulfillment quotations must be understood within the context of Matthew's use of fulfillment quotations generally. For only when we have gained some sense of how these specifically designated textual and/or thematic correspondences function in Matthew, and in what sense they constitute 'fulfillment', shall we be able to evaluate the particular significance of 2.17-18 and 27.9-10. Specifically, we must investigate the way in which these two passages, together with other less obvious textual allusions, contribute to Matthew's portrayal of Jesus and his mission. But secondly, the mention of Jeremiah in 16.14 is so closely associated with the question of Jesus' identity that we must necessarily consider some sort of typological reference on the part of the Evangelist. Accordingly, this reference must be compared to Matthew's use of other OT figures such as Abraham, David, Moses, Jonah and Moses, so as to illuminate particular aspects of Jesus' messianic identity.

Thus my investigation will seek first to discover the degree to which the two fulfillment quotations and the introduction of 'Jeremiah' into the pivotal discussion of Jesus' messiahship are governed by a unified redactional purpose (Chapter 1). I will then attempt to account for this redactional outlook on the basis of the literary sources from which Matthew has drawn his material (Chapter 2), and to evaluate the findings in light of further redactional evidence. Such evidence will include references or allusions to Jeremiah that are both textual

(Chapter 3) and typological (Chapter 4) in character. Matthew's treatment of Jeremiah and Jeremiah material will also be compared to the various traditions associated with the prophet within first-century Judaism and Christianity (Chapter 5). Having thus surveyed Matthew's various references to the prophet and his work, and the redactional outlook that they reveal, I will propose some explanation of how this feature of the Evangelist's endeavor might have served the community for which he wrote (Chapter 6). Because they employ similar fulfillment formulae and raise similar problems of context, the references in Matthew 2 and 27 will be examined first, following which I will turn to the more enigmatic reference in 16.14.

Chapter 1

MATTHEW'S THREE EXPLICIT REFERENCES TO JEREMIAH

A. *Formula Quotations in the Gospel of Matthew*

1. *Background and Purpose*

The study of OT quotations in the NT, particularly those in Matthew's Gospel, has been conducted on the basis of a variety of different viewpoints and with a number of different purposes in mind.[1] As distinct from studies that look to these quotations to shed light on such matters as MT or LXX textual questions, the Synoptic Problem, or the original language of the Evangelists, this investigation will focus primarily upon 'the function and significance of the quotations from the Scriptures'.[2] This means that I will, in the main, leave to one side the complex and controverted issue of the sources, whether written or oral, 'targumic' or testimonial, of Matthew's formula quotations.[3]

1. For a survey of recent scholarly discussion, see I.H. Marshall, 'An Assessment of Recent Developments', in D.A. Carson and H.G.M. Williamson (eds.), *It is Written: Scripture Citing Scripture: Essays in Honour of Barnabas Lindars* (Cambridge: Cambridge University Press, 1988), pp. 1-21. More generally, a comprehensive and invaluable introduction to the use of Scripture in this period is provided by J.M. Mulder (ed.), *Mikra: Text, Translation, Reading and Interpretation of the Bible in Ancient Judaism and Early Christianity* (CRINT, 2.1; Assen: Van Gorcum; Philadelphia: Fortress Press, 1988).

2. K. Stendahl, *The School of St Matthew and its Use of the Old Testament* (ASNU, 20; Lund: Gleerup, 2nd edn, 1968), p. 42.

3. For summaries of scholarly discussion on this point, see R.H. Gundry, *The Use of the Old Testament in St Matthew's Gospel, with Specific Reference to the Messianic Hope* (NovTSup, 18; Leiden: Brill, 1967), pp. 151-71; M.P. Miller, 'Targum, Midrash, and the Use of the Old Testament in the New Testament', *JSJ* 2 (1971), pp. 64-71; D.M. Smith, 'The Use of the Old Testament in the New', in J.M. Efird (ed.), *The Use of the Old Testament in the New and Other Essays: Studies in Honor of William Franklin Stinespring* (Durham, NC: Duke University Press, 1972), pp. 25-35, cf. pp. 43-45.

Certain of these considerations will, of course, necessarily arise as we examine individual texts; yet my primary emphasis will not be on questions of provenance in and of themselves, but rather on the literary, thematic and theological function of these references within Matthew's Gospel.

In attempting to understand Matthew's use of Scripture, we must recognize at the outset that the early Church was constrained by opposing theological and socioreligious exigencies. On the one hand, they were as 'Christian' believers convinced that the God of Israel had acted anew in history in the person of Jesus of Nazareth. This conviction set them increasingly apart from their communities of origin, particularly so in the case of Christians of Jewish background. On the other hand, these same Christians reveal a frequent concern to demonstrate, whether for apologetic or polemical reasons, the continuity between themselves and Judaism. 'By what authority do you do these things?' (Mt. 21.23) is a question that appears to have echoed loudly through the conscience and self-consciousness of the early Church (cf. Acts 5.7). Out of this creative tension between discontinuity and continuity, between the assertion of distinct identity and the appeal to authoritative origins, emerged the conscious reappropriation of texts and conceptual paradigms from what would increasingly be understood as the 'Old Testament'.[1]

Christians and Jews alike held to the inspired nature and authoritative status of 'the law and the prophets', which conveyed the record of God's dealings with his creation. Insofar as Scripture made plain the intimate connection between world history and the divine purpose, it was only natural that exegetes seek to clarify that connection—even for those features of their history not explicitly dealt with by the sacred text. As T.W. Manson observed:

> The task of faith was thus twofold: (1) to study the oracles of God in order to understand better the nature of the divine purpose; (2) to study the course of events in order to discover any indication that the divine purpose was working itself out in history... When Scripture rightly interpreted

1. Similarly, R.A. Greer (in J.L. Kugel and R.A. Greer, *Early Biblical Interpretation* [Philadelphia: Westminster Press, 1986], p. 116) describes this tension in terms of competing tendencies within the early Christian community either to remain a Jewish sect, or, at the other extreme, to embrace an ahistorical Gnosticism.

coincided with event rightly understood, then you had the argument from prophecy.[1]

For the Christian exegete, of course, the particular events on which their study focused, and to which Scripture was to be related, were the life, death and resurrection of Jesus.[2] Such an outlook is succinctly captured by the opening words of the writer to the Hebrews: 'In many and various ways God spoke of old to our fathers by the prophets; but in these last days he has spoken to us by a Son' (Heb. 1.1-2). In other words, the 'history' to which Scripture was now to be related was not history of the customary sort, but rather, specifically 'messianic' history. Given the premise that the messiah was newly manifest, the fact of his advent and the details of his presence had become a new locus of revelation, a fundamental revelatory datum to which the sacred writings must now be seen to point.

Yet precedents for such a startling approach to Scripture are widely available in Second Temple Judaism. Midrashic exegesis, for example, constituted an 'actualization' of Scripture, applying scriptural premises and precepts to the life of the contemporary community. As R. Bloch points out, 'It always has to do with a living Word addressed personally to the people of God'.[3] In particular, midrashic exegesis

1. T.W. Manson, 'The Argument from Prophecy', *JTS* 46 (1945), pp. 129, 130.

2. Cf. B. Lindars, *New Testament Apologetic: The Doctrinal Significance of the Old Testament Quotations* (London: SCM Press, 1961), pp. 24-28; M. Wilcox, 'On Investigating the Use of the Old Testament in the New Testament', in E. Best and R.M. Wilson (eds.), *Text and Interpretation: Studies in the New Testament Presented to Matthew Black* (Cambridge: Cambridge University Press, 1979), pp. 241-43. A systematic exploration of this thesis is provided by D. Juel, *Messianic Exegesis: Christological Interpretation of the Old Testament in Early Christianity* (Philadelphia: Fortress Press, 1988). But as J. Barr notes (*Old and New in Interpretation: A Study of the Two Testaments* [London: SCM Press, 1966], pp. 118-29), further elements such as a heightened awareness of predictive prophecy, the rise of 'apocalyptic', increased emphasis upon Torah, and the gradual development of a Jewish 'canon' also had a significant effect on scriptural interpretation in the early Church. See also C.H. Dodd, *According to the Scriptures: The Substructure of New Testament Theology* (London: Nisbet, 1952), pp. 127-33; Lindars, *NT Apologetic*, pp. 282-86.

3. R. Bloch, 'Midrash', *DBSup* V, col. 1266. Cf. A.G. Wright, 'The Literary Genre Midrash', *CBQ* 28 (1966), pp. 133-34 ('The aim of the midrash is to comment on the Scriptures, to make them religiously relevant to the contemporaries of the interpreter'), pp. 137-38; R. Kasher, 'The Interpretation of Scripture in Rabbinic Literature', in Mulder (ed.), *Mikra*, p. 577. Although Wright ('Midrash', p. 441)

legitimized post-biblical cultural traditions and customs by deriving a warrant for their practice from the sacred text.[1]

D. Patte notes that halakhic/midrashic exegesis was accomplished 'either by scrutinizing Scripture in the light of the new cultural situation or by scrutinizing Tradition in the light of Scripture'.[2] So as the community of God's people sought to embody the divine will in their practical obedience to Scripture, their own praxis became a source of divine revelation. Indeed, Patte contends that, particularly in the case of targumic exegesis, the experience of the community became as much a locus of revelation as the sacred text, both by means of the members' halakhic or 'moral' actualization of Scripture, and in their worship, which was the liturgical embodiment of their covenant identity.[3] More precisely,

> revelation, far from being contained in Scripture, occurred in the tension among Scripture, the worshipping community, and the history of cultural changes.[4]

Likewise in the literature of apocalyptic Judaism there is a rewriting of biblical history in such a way as to incorporate contemporary events, with these events perceived as inaugurating the end-time. Contemporary history was thus interpreted according to biblical types and patterns, in light of which that history was understood to reflect providential design.[5] This is evident both in the apocalyptists' periodizations of history (e.g. *1 Enoch* 93; *4 Ezra* 11–12; *2 Baruch* 53, 56–74) and in their deliberate incorporations of specific scriptural themes and language—whether in terms of (1) a broad narrative structure (e.g. *Jubilees* as a contemporizing of Genesis and Exodus, or the many views of national history as a recurrent pattern of sin, judgment, repentance and restoration), or (2) the evocation of specific scriptural

specifies that 'a proof or fulfillment text is not a midrash' insofar as it fails to demonstrate how the scriptural text is applied to the new situation, my intention is simply to demonstrate the similarity of approach in terms of an accommodational or contemporizing exegesis.

1. So D. Patte, *Early Jewish Hermeneutic in Palestine* (SBLDS, 22; Missoula, MT: Scholars Press, 1975), p. 118.
2. Patte, *Early Jewish Hermeneutic*, p. 124.
3. Patte, *Early Jewish Hermeneutic*, pp. 80-81, 85-86.
4. Patte, *Early Jewish Hermeneutic*, p. 126.
5. Patte, *Early Jewish Hermeneutic*, pp. 160-67.

passages through the use of common vocabulary.[1] Here, even more strongly than in the exegesis of classical Judaism, contemporary experience was a locus of revelation. In the eyes of the apocalyptists God was active in contemporary history, revealing to the elect new and crucial aspects of his purpose.[2]

The Qumran covenanters similarly believed that they had been granted the key to the 'mystery' or 'mysteries of God', thereby enabling them to understand the divine purposes for history, including contemporary history, so as to bring about the messianic age. Once again, this revelation was seen to emerge from a proper interpretation of Scripture and history alike. For example, contemporary events were used to interpret the biblical text in 1QpHab and portions of the Damascus Document (e.g. CD 3.19–4.5), rather than vice versa, as might be expected.[3] An even more radical example can be seen in the community's conviction of its own elect and chosen identity, with the divine presence in their midst, which self-understanding reduces Scripture to a merely supporting role in portions of the Hodayot (1QH) and the Manual of Discipline (1QS).[4]

Yet however much they may originally have formed the basis of the community's self-understanding, both Scripture and contemporary history in the DSS are ultimately subject to a more fundamental revelational claim: that God had made known to the 'Teacher of Righteousness', the leader or leaders of the sect, 'all the secrets of the words of his servants the prophets'.[5] And it is this claim, above all,

1. See examples, Patte, *Early Jewish Hermeneutic*, pp. 185-99. Cf. J.H. Charlesworth, 'The Pseudepigrapha as Biblical Exegesis', in C.A. Evans and W.F. Stinespring (eds.), *Early Jewish and Christian Exegesis: Studies in Memory of William Hugh Brownlee* (Atlanta: Scholars Press, 1987), pp. 144-48, on the (contemporizing) use of Scripture as 'framework' in *4 Ezra*, *2 Baruch* and the various pseudepigraphical Testaments.

2. Cf. Patte, *Early Jewish Hermeneutic*, pp. 205-207.

3. Patte, *Early Jewish Hermeneutic*, pp. 242-44; cf. J. Neusner, *What is Midrash?* (Guides to Biblical Scholarship, New Testament Series; Philadelphia: Fortress Press, 1987): 'The self-evident purpose of the [Qumran] exegete is to allow for further inquiry into the near future. For once Scripture has made its statement about the future that the later exegete thinks has taken place, the exegete finds solid ground for listening for yet further messages from the same scriptural prophetic passages.'

4. Patte, *Early Jewish Hermeneutic*, pp. 251-69, 278-79.

5. 1QpHab 7.4-5, cited in Patte, *Early Jewish Hermeneutic*, p. 216; cf.

that presents the closest analogy to the circumstances of early Christian scriptural exegesis.[1]

Accommodational exegesis—the adaptation of the sacred text to a concrete situation in the immediate experience of the exegete or his community—was, in fact, widespread in Second Temple Judaism. Indeed, as Manson observes,

> accurate reproduction of the traditional wording of the Divine oracles took second place to publication of what was held to be their essential meaning and immediate application.[2]

For Christian as well as for Jewish exegetes, their adaptation of the sacred text, because it conformed to the revelation contained in recent events, constituted the 'true' meaning of the original text, however much it might vary in detail from previous text forms.[3]

Such an approach to the biblical text naturally applied *a fortiori* to the question of the original or contextual meaning of the reappropriated passage, for, as Barr observes,

pp. 226-27; 1QH 11.3-18; and G. Vermes, 'The Qumran Interpretation of Scripture in its Historical Setting', in J. MacDonald (ed.), *The Annual of Leeds University Oriental Society*. VI. *Dead Sea Scrolls Studies 1969* (Leiden: Brill, 1969), pp. 90-93. On exegetical method at Qumran, see J.A. Fitzmyer, 'The Use of Explicit Old Testament Quotations in Qumran Literature and in the New Testament', *NTS* 7 (1960–61), pp. 306-30; for a series of examples detailing the complex interplay of text and interpretation, see G.J. Brooke, 'The Biblical Texts in the Qumran Commentaries: Scribal Errors or Exegetical Variants?', in Evans and Stinespring (eds.), *Early Jewish and Christian Exegesis*, pp. 85-100.

1. Indeed, rather than treating them as separate categories, Neusner (*What is Midrash?*, pp. 37-40) argues that the historically focused exegesis of both Qumran and Matthew's Gospel constitutes a distinctive variety of midrash.

2. 'Argument', p. 136; cf. Gundry, *Use of the OT*, pp. 173-76, and the comment of Jerome ('Letter to Aglasias' [*Ep.* 121.2; *PL* 22.1011]; cited by W. Rothfuchs, *Die Erfüllungszitate des Matthäus-Evangeliums: Eine biblische-theologische Untersuchung* [BWANT, 88; Stuttgart: Kohlhammer, 1969], pp. 9-10): 'ubicumque de veteri Instrumento Evangelistae et Apostoli testimonia protulerunt, diligentius observandum est: non eos verba secutos esse, sed sensum' (cf. *Ep.* 57.9; *PL* 22.576). Similar explanations of the wide variety of text forms in both allusions and quotations are offered by Stendahl, *School of St Matthew*, pp. 150-51, 205; Gundry, *Use of the OT*, pp. 149-50; Rothfuchs, *Erfüllungszitate*, p. 89.

3. Cf. R.N. Longenecker, *Biblical Exegesis in the Apostolic Period* (Grand Rapids: Eerdmans, 1975), pp. 38-39; Kugel and Greer, *Early Biblical Interpretation*, pp. 126, 133.

> the Old Testament material relates itself to the Christ not so much through the meanings directly intended by the original writers of passages, but through the combinations and alterations which these meanings produce when they are associated with other elements under the conditions which actually obtained in post-Biblical Judaism.[1]

That is to say, recognition of Christ as the key to the meaning of sacred Scripture provided Christian exegetes, no less than their counterparts at Qumran, with a considerable degree of interpretative freedom. Or, as Rothfuchs notes,

> On the basis of the New Testament event, which has been handed down and understood as a Christological event, the original Old Testament associations become comparatively unimportant.[2]

Thus the use of OT quotations in the NT must be understood not so much in terms of their original contexts, but 'against the context of what the early Christians were doing with them'.[3]

To return to the example of Qumran, Fitzmyer finds that the sectarian exegetes quoted the sacred text in a number of ways: (1) literally, in the same sense as the biblical source and with due respect to its original context; (2) in a modernizing sense, with the original meaning reapplied to an analogous contemporary situation (so 'typologically'); (3) by accommodation, with the scriptural text 'obviously wrested from its original context, modified or deliberately changed...in order to adapt it to a new situation or purpose'; and (4) eschatologically, with an eschatological threat or promise being understood to apply to the new eschaton of Qumran theology.[4] As examples of similar modernizing or typological exegesis in Matthew Fitzmyer cites 4.15-16, 8.17, 11.10, 13.35, 15.8 and 21.42; of accommodational exegesis, 3.3 (on Isa. 40.3, as in 1QS 8.13-16) and 12.32 (on

1. *Old and New*, p. 27; cf. p. 30.
2. Rothfuchs, *Erfüllungszitate*, pp. 114-15, cf. pp. 91-94; so also R.S. McConnell, *Law and Prophecy in Matthew's Gospel: The Authority and Use of the Old Testament in the Gospel of Saint Matthew* (Basel: Friedrich Reinhardt, 1969), pp. 136-38, cf. pp. 108-109.
3. Barr, *Old and New*, p. 143.
4. Fitzmyer, 'Old Testament Quotations', pp. 306-307. While deeming this classification insufficiently 'flexible or complex', M. Fishbane ('Use, Authority, and Interpretation of Mikra at Qumran', in Mulder [ed.], *Mikra*, p. 348, cf. p. 347 n. 25) concurs that 'the original sense of the prooftext must be disregarded in order to understand how the writer has exegetically appropriated it'.

Exod. 3.6, 15-16).[1] Such a recognition that scriptural texts were treated in a range of different ways both at Qumran and in the NT indicates the necessity of a case-by-case comparison of text and context—both original and as reappropriated—in order to discover the principles at work in any given passage.[2]

With respect to the Matthaean formula quotations, McConnell concludes that Matthew consistently either selects from variant textual traditions or reshapes the OT passages in question 'so that they demonstrate something that Matthew wants to be regarded as fore-ordained in prophecy'.[3] Nor were all the texts that Matthew uses originally 'prophetic' in character. Rather, it is a text's potential applicability to the life of Jesus that determines whether it is to be regarded as prophetic, and so fulfilled in him.[4] That is to say, christological confession is for Matthew as much a presupposition as a product of exegesis.[5] Thus, whatever criticisms have been levelled on formal grounds against Stendahl's comparison of Matthew's exegetical methods and pesher exegesis at Qumran, it nonetheless remains true that both demonstrate an exegesis of accommodation, or, as Stendahl calls it, 'text interpretation of an actualizing nature'.[6]

Even when isolated from the remainder of the Gospel, Matthew's formula quotations provide, in the Evangelist's application of them, a basic outline of Jesus' life and ministry prior to the Passion.[7] It is not

1. 'Old Testament Quotations', pp. 315-18, 324.

2. Fitzmyer, 'Old Testament Quotations', pp. 332-33.

3. McConnell, *Law and Prophecy,* pp. 215-16.

4. McConnell, *Law and Prophecy*; cf. S.L. Edgar, 'New Testament and Rabbinic Messianic Interpretation', *NTS* 5 (1958–59), pp. 52-53; Kugel and Greer, *Early Biblical Interpretation,* p. 135.

5. Juel, *Messianic Exegesis,* pp. 171-73; E.E. Ellis, 'Biblical Interpretation in the New Testament Church', in Mulder (ed.), *Mikra,* p. 704.

6. *School of St Matthew,* p. 200; cf. Miller, 'Targum, Midrash', p. 69; McConnell, *Law and Prophecy,* pp. 139-41; Soares Prabhu, *Formula Quotations,* pp. 85, 104. To underscore further the similarity to Matthew, W.H. Brownlee (*The Midrash Pesher of Habakkuk* [SBLMS, 24; Missoula, MT: Scholars Press, 1979], pp. 26-27) indicates that pesher exegesis (at least in 1QpHab) itself strongly implies the 'prophetic fulfillment' of the text in question (so also Fishbane, 'Use, Authority and Interpretation', pp. 351, 373-75). The article by M. Black, 'The Theological Appropriation of the Old Testament by the New Testament' (*SJT* 39 [1986], pp. 1-17) represents a detailed attempt to trace pesher exegesis in the Synoptic material.

7. Although 27.9-10 bears on the initial circumstances of the Passion, Jesus' statements in Mt. 26.54, 56 (// Mk 14.49b; cf. Mt. 26.31 // Mk 14.27) indicate a

simply that these quotations provide illustrative or 'pictorial details' in order to flesh out a biographical sketch of Jesus.[1] This could have been accomplished without any recourse to Scripture or its 'fulfillment'.[2] Rather, the underlying purpose of the formula quotations seems to be to show that the basic elements of Jesus' origin, identity, ministry—and even his betrayal—were already providentially set out in the inspired text and so conform to 'the divinely ordained plan for the Messiah'.[3] Or, to quote Rothfuchs,

> [Matthew] takes these words of the prophets as God's 'commentary' on the story of Jesus, which they thus exegete. By means of the fulfillment citations Matthew thereby proclaims what has been handed down about Jesus as Messiah.[4]

more general fulfillment of Scripture in the final events of his life. This may account for the surprising infrequency of fulfillment formulae in the final section of the Gospel, and renders 27.9-10 all the more noteworthy from a redactional point of view.

1. So Lindars, *NT Apologetic*, pp. 260-65; G. Strecker, *Der Weg der Gerechtigkeit: Untersuchungen zur Theologie des Matthäus* (FRLANT, 82; Göttingen: Vandenhoeck & Ruprecht, 1971), p. 85.

2. Still less do the OT quotations form the basis on which 'biographical' details were adumbrated, for as Gundry (*Use of the OT*, pp. 194-96) points out, 'the looseness with which many Matthaean citations from the OT are appended shows that the direction is from tradition to prophecy, not vice versa... The citations from Hos. 11.1 and Jer. 31.15 [for example] are so obscure that no one would have thought of them as bases for invention of the stories to which Mt. relates them'. So G. Stanton, 'Matthew', in Carson and Williamson, *It is Written*, p. 215. For fuller discussion, and a similar conclusion, see Soares Prabhu, *Formula Quotations*, pp. 162-70.

3. McConnell, *Law and Prophecy*, pp. 133-34. Indeed, such a unique view of history accounts for a corresponding lack of fulfillment formulae either in the Mishnah (so B.M. Metzger, 'The Formulas Introducing Quotations of Scripture in the New Testament and in the Mishnah', *JBL* 70 [1951], pp. 306-307) or at Qumran (so Fitzmyer, 'Old Testament Quotations', pp. 303-304; cf. McConnell, *Law and Prophecy*, pp. 140-41).

4. Rothfuchs, *Erfüllungszitate*, p. 92, cf. pp. 119-21; so Stanton, 'Matthew', p. 217, and the similar conclusions of R. Hummel, *Die Auseinandersetzung zwischen Kirche und Judentum im Matthäusevangelium* (Munich: Chr. Kaiser Verlag, 1966), pp. 134-35; Gundry, *Use of the OT*, p. 234; A. Sand, *Das Gesetz und die Propheten: Untersuchungen zur Theologie des Evangeliums nach Matthäus* (Biblische Untersuchungen, 11; Regensburg: Pustet, 1974), pp. 153-56; Soares Prabhu, *Formula Quotations*, p. 300.

Therefore simply by highlighting the feature of messianic 'fulfillment', the fulfillment quotations of the First Gospel reflect a significant feature of Matthaean theology.[1] The basic principle governing Matthew's understanding of Scripture is articulated in the dominical word placed at the beginning of Jesus' 'Sermon on the Mount':

> Μὴ νομίσητε ὅτι ἦλθον καταλῦσαι τὸν νόμον ἢ τοὺς προφήτας· οὐκ ἦλθον καταλῦσαι ἀλλὰ πληρῶσαι (5.17).

Granted, the immediate context of vv. 17-20—indeed of all of vv. 17-48—emphasizes and outlines in detail the fulfillment of only the first of these categories, ὁ νόμος.[2] This might suggest that ἢ τοὺς προφήτας is merely a generalizing expansion referring to the halakhic content of the prophetic books. Yet ὁ νόμος καὶ οἱ προφῆται (see also 7.12; 11.13; 22.40) typically designate for Matthew the whole of Scripture in its halakhic as well as its prophetic aspects.[3] Furthermore, Matthew's use of πληρόω suggests that this statement refers more widely to the messianic fulfillment of Scripture in the events of Jesus' life. For throughout Matthew's Gospel πληρόω consistently conveys a theologically pregnant sense of messianic fulfillment,[4] particularly so where it serves as the key term in the

1. Although Mark does not resort to fulfillment formulae in the same manner as Matthew (despite a few references to scriptural fulfillment, e.g., Mk 1.2-3; 4.12; 7.6-7; 9.11-13; 11.17; 12.10-11; 14.27, 49), a similarly apologetic and transformative—or fulfillment-oriented—use of Scripture is, according to H.C. Kee ('The Function of Scriptural Quotations and Allusions in Mark 11-16', in E.E. Ellis and E. Gräber [eds.], *Jesus und Paulus: Festschrift für Werner Georg Kümmel zum 70. Geburtstag* [Göttingen: Vandenhoeck & Ruprecht, 1975], pp. 173-88), already present in Mark's Passion account, accounting for each significant feature of the last week of Jesus' ministry. Matthew's contribution has been to underscore the general scriptural background of the Passion narrative (so 26.54, 56), as well as to provide an explicitly scriptural foundation for the earlier part of Jesus' ministry.

2. Cf. McConnell, *Law and Prophecy*, pp. 22-30. For a survey of the various interpretations of 5.17, see E.P. Blair, *Jesus in the Gospel of Matthew* (New York: Abingdon Press, 1960), pp. 117-24.

3. McConnell, *Law and Prophecy*, pp. 11-14.

4. Some indication of the significance of πληρόω is provided by its relative frequency in the Synoptic Gospels: Matthew 16×; Mark 3×; Luke 9×. It is essential to bear in mind that word frequencies must be related to the percentage of material supplied by each Evangelist within the larger comparison group, in this case the sum of occurrences in all three Synoptic Gospels. R. Morgenthaler (*Statistik des Neutestamentliches Wortschatzes* [Zürich: Gotthelf, 1958], p. 164) provides the

fulfillment formulae.[1] That is to say, 'the law and the prophets' come to fulfillment in Jesus not only through his obedience to and promulgation of (albeit reinterpreted) Torah, but even more so in the sense that the events of his life and ministry constitute a realization and enactment of a divinely foreordained plan recorded in Scripture. Whatever the present context of 5.17 fails to emphasize in this regard is amply made up for in the remainder of the Gospel. Or, observing Moule's distinctions more carefully, what 5.17 declares in all-encompassing terms—that is, that Jesus fulfills the divine purpose *in toto*—the fulfillment passages are left to work out in detail by relating particular scriptural promises or 'prophecies' to the life of Jesus.

2. *The Fulfillment Formulae*

In all, Matthew has fourteen fulfillment quotations: 1.22, 2.5, 2.15, 2.17, 2.23, 3.3 (// Lk. 3.4), 4.14, 8.17, 12.17, 13.14 (cf. Jn 12.38, 39-40), 13.35, 21.4, 26.56 (// Mk 14.49, cf. Mt. 26.54) and 27.9, although the use of the introductory formula is not uniform in all fourteen cases. Of these, the ten that both use an unambiguous citation formula (so excepting 2.5, 3.3 and 13.14) and refer to a specific

following figures for the Synoptic Gospels in the Nestle-Aland 21st edition, as well as his own count, which differs slightly:

	NA21	Morgenthaler	Percentage
Matthew	18305	18278	37.4
Mark	11242	11229	22.9
Luke	19428	19404	39.7
	48975	48911	100

Only with these percentages in mind can an adequate statistical comparison be made of word frequency totals. That is to say, a word such as κατά (Matthew 37×; Mark 23×; Luke 44×), or better, λέγω (Matthew 475×; Mark 289×; Luke 515×; which amount to 37.1%, 22.6%, and 40.3% respectively), cannot be said to occur twice as frequently in Luke or Matthew as in Mark, but, proportionately, with virtually equivalent frequency in all three Synoptic Gospels.

1. McConnell (*Law and Prophecy*, pp. 18-19 [cf. pp. 14-17]) correctly observes that context and use of the term must take precedence over purely linguistic arguments as to the meaning of πληρόω in Matthew's Gospel. On the different levels at which 'fulfillment' functions in the NT, see C.F.D. Moule, 'Fulfilment-Words in the New Testament: Use and Abuse', *NTS* 14 (1967–68), pp. 293-320 (on Mt. 5.17 in particular, pp. 316-18).

passage of Scripture (so excepting Mt. 25.56) all occur in uniquely Matthaean material.[1]

Indeed, 'the formula that introduces the quotations is unmistakably redactional'.[2] It can be summarized as follows:

1. (τοῦτο δὲ [ὅλον] γέγονεν)
2. ἵνα/ὅπως πληρωθῇ (τότε ἐπληρώθη)
3. τὸ ῥηθέν (ὑπὸ κυρίου [2×])
4. διὰ ('Ησαΐου/'Ιερεμίου) τοῦ προφήτου λέγοντος[3]

The above synthesis, however, should not obscure the fact that Matthew is not uniform in his wording of fulfillment citations, for apart from 2.17 and 27.9 only 4.14 and 12.17 share identical formulae (ἵνα πληρωθῇ τὸ ῥηθὲν διὰ 'Ησαΐου τοῦ προφήτου λέγοντος).

Element 1 occurs only in 1.22, 21.4 and 26.56, serving to clarify an otherwise less-than-obvious connection between the citation and its narrative context. Yet beneath this narrative or stylistic purpose lies a deeper theological intent, which is to stress both the 'historical-biographical facticity of the events themselves and the providential direction and unity of history revealed by means of reference to the sacred text'.[4] Thus, to expand the phrase, 'all *this* [and nothing else, since "this" conforms to the divine plan] *happened* [in the life of Jesus, revealing the historical foundation for the claims made about him]'.

The significance of the congruence between Scripture and messianic history is made explicit by element 2 of the fulfillment formula. Both ἵνα (*sexto*) and ὅπως (*ter*), which may be considered equivalent in meaning, specify the purposive intent of the subjunctive πληρωθῇ.[5]

1. Soares Prabhu (*Formula Quotations*, pp. 25-41) concludes that none of the five (i.e. including 26.54) passages thus omitted are properly to be classified as 'formula citations', although 2.5 has been 'redactionally assimilated' to their form.

2. M.J.J. Menken, 'The References to Jeremiah in the Gospel according to Matthew (Mt 2,17; 16,14; 27,9)', *ETL* 60 (1984), p. 7, together with the consensus of scholarly opinion cited in n. 8.

3. Cf. the detailed discussion of this formula in R. Pesch, 'Der Gottessohn im matthäischen Evangelienprolog (Mt 1-2): Beobachtungen zu den Zitationsformeln der Reflexionzitate', *Bib* 48 (1967), pp. 398-408; Rothfuchs, *Erfüllungszitate*, pp. 33-46; Soares Prabhu, *Formula Quotations*, pp. 46-63.

4. Strecker, *Weg*, p. 85, cited by Rothfuchs, *Erfüllungszitate*, p. 36; cf. T. Zahn, *Das Evangelium nach Matthäus* (Kommentar zum NT, 1; Leipzig: Deichert; Erlangen: Scholl, 1922), pp. 82-83.

5. Cf. BDF §369.

Here, again, the events Matthew relates are to be seen not as random, but as having occurred specifically in order to fulfill the words of Scripture and so to reveal God at work within them.

The primary component of element 3, τὸ ῥηθέν, is unique to Matthew, although not limited to the fulfillment formulae. In addition to ten occurrences of τὸ ῥηθέν in 1.22, 2.15, 17, 23, 4.14, 8.17, 12.17, 13.35, 21.4, and 27.9, Matthew employs the masculine participle in 3.3 (οὗτος γάρ ἐστιν ὁ ῥηθεὶς διὰ Ἠσαΐου τοῦ προφήτου λέγοντος, cf. Lk. 3.4, ὡς γεγράπται), then returns to the neuter aorist passive when referring to the word of God in 22.31 (τὸ ῥηθὲν ὑμῖν ὑπὸ τοῦ θεοῦ λέγοντος, cf. Mk 12.26, εἶπεν) and in 24.15 (τὸ ῥηθὲν διὰ Δανιὴλ τοῦ προφήτου, cf. Mk 13.14). Nowhere else in the Gospels does τὸ ῥηθέν appear, although Luke–Acts has a similar formulation with the neuter perfect passive participle of εἰπεῖν (Lk. 2.24; Acts 2.16, τὸ εἰρημένον διὰ τοῦ προφήτου Ἰωήλ; 13.40; cf. Rom. 4.18).

Also to be observed is that the concurrence of τὸ ῥηθέν with λέγοντος lays stress on the verbal aspect of the prophetic word (as distinct from, for example, γέγραπται in 2.5, 26.31; cf. 26.54, 56), and that the passive voice of the participle underscores the divine agency behind the prophecy.[1] This latter consideration is confirmed both by the addition of ὑπὸ κυρίου in 1.22 and 2.15[2] and by the force of the ensuing διά.

Finally, the Evangelist indicates the source of the quotation by means of element 4. Isaiah is named in 4.14, 8.17, 12.17 and 13.35 (so ℵ* Θ f^1 f^{13} *al.*) and Jeremiah in 2.17 and 27.9, although no specific source is mentioned in 1.22, 2.15, 2.23 or 21.4. The designation προφήτης is characteristic of Matthew (Matthew:Mark:Luke = 37:6:29; cf. προφητεία 1:0:0; προφητεύω 4:2:2). And the role of the προφήτης is signalled by λέγοντος, for over and above its merely recitative function this participle emphasizes that the word spoken by God (τὸ ῥηθέν) is nonetheless mediated by the word of the prophet.[3]

1. Cf. Rothfuchs, *Erfüllungszitate*, pp. 41-42.

2. This is not to deny that in these two quotations this insertion may carry other nuances as well, particularly in association with the theme of divine sonship; so Pesch, 'Gottessohn', pp. 408-19; see also W.D. Davies and D.C. Allison, *The Gospel according to Saint Matthew*. I. *Introduction and Commentary on Matthew I–VII* (ICC; Edinburgh: T. & T. Clark, 1988), p. 212.

3. Cf. Rothfuchs, *Erfüllungszitate*, p. 44. While I have chosen to examine the

Rothfuchs has observed that the four fulfillment formulae that specifically mention Isaiah are bound by a common redactional interest, and since his observation bears on our investigation into the unitary purpose of the two 'Jeremiah' passages, it is worth considering here. Although it is not clear that 4.14, 8.17, 12.17 and 13.35 themselves provide a 'summary' of Jesus' messianic works,[1] yet they do, as Rothfuchs contends, highlight the messiah's proclamation of salvation both to Israel and to the Gentiles. At least this can be maintained for 4.14-16 (Isa. 9.1-2), which declares that a 'great light' has shone forth in the land of Zebulun and Naphtali, where Jesus now dwells; for 8.17 (Isa. 53.4), which recapitulates Jesus' work of healing and exorcism; and for 12.17 (Isa. 42.1-4), which makes Jesus the hope of the Gentiles. Thus, according to Rothfuchs, 'It is this salvific proclamation to Israel of the works of Jesus that the evangelist has deliberately linked with the name of the prophet Isaiah'.[2]

Such an interpretation, however, is more difficult to maintain for 13.35, both because the reference to Isaiah is textually uncertain—all the more so because the passage cited is from Ps. 78.2—and because it comments on Jesus' preaching in parables. For parabolic proclamation is in Matthew's Gospel a 'two-edged sword', as likely to conceal as to reveal, a point made explicitly in 13.14 by reference to Isa. 6.9-10 (καὶ ἀναπληροῦται...ἡ προφητεία 'Ησαΐου; cf. Mk 4.12; 8.17b-18). Van Segbroeck argues for the authenticity of διὰ 'Ησαΐου in 13.35 as Matthew's way of emphasizing the spiritual obduracy of Israel described in 13.14-15 (Isa. 6.9-10). In his view, Isaiah is 'the prophet of obduracy and unbelief' (cf. Acts 28.26-27.

various elements of the formula for their individual meaning in the present context, it must also be borne in mind that as a whole they likely reflect various OT, intertestamental and rabbinic precedents; *Erfüllungszitate*, pp. 44-54.

1. While such a contention can be defended for 8.17, it would be more accurate to say, stressing the redactional function of the context in which the fulfillment quotations occur, that with the exception of 21.5 and 27.9-10 'les citations concernant l'activité publique de Jésus se trouvent uniquement dans les sommaires [rédactionels] et ont trait... à l'ensemble de l'activité de Jésus' (F. van Segbroeck, 'Les citations d'accomplissement dans l'évangile selon Matthieu d'après trois ouvrages récents', in M. Didier [ed.], *L'évangile selon Matthieu: Rédaction et théologie* [BETL, 29: Gembloux: Duculot, 1972], p. 119).

2. *Erfüllungszitate*, p. 43.

[Isa. 6.9-10]; Jn 12.27-31 [Isa. 6.10; 53.1]; Rom. 9.30 [Isa. 53.1]).[1] As he states elsewhere, the fact that 'no Old Testament prophet is as preoccupied as Isaiah with the salvation of Israel, even while emphasizing in his preaching the fruitlessness of this task' may account for all such references to the prophet.[2] But even apart from the textual difficulties associated with this particular passage, van Segbroeck does not take sufficient account of Matthew's remaining references to Isaiah, which Rothfuchs has highlighted.

Furthermore, there are two other explicit references to Isaiah in Matthew's Gospel, even though they do not occur in 'fulfillment' quotations of the sort under consideration: 3.3 (Isa. 40.3, from Mk 1.2-3) which proclaims the coming of John the Baptist; and 15.7-9 (Isa. 29.13, from Mk 7.6), which condemns the Pharisees and their scribes as 'hypocrites'. On balance, it would appear that while Matthew generally follows his Markan source in employing references to Isaiah that have more negative associations, the three unambiguous references that he himself introduces indeed convey more positive, salvific overtones.

It remains to be seen, however, whether any similarly unitary redactional purpose can be discerned in the Evangelist's references to the book of Jeremiah. It is, therefore, to an examination of the particular aspects of 'messianic history' highlighted by the formula quotations of 2.17-18 and 27.9-10 that we must now turn.

B. *Matthew 2.17-18*

17 τότε ἐπληρώθη τὸ ῥηθὲν διὰ Ἰερεμίου τοῦ προφήτου λέγοντος·
18 φωνὴ ἐν Ῥαμὰ ἠκούσθη, κλαυθμὸς καὶ ὀδυρμὸς πολύς· Ῥαχὴλ κλαίουσα τὰ τέκνα αὐτῆς, καὶ οὐκ ἤθελεν παρακληθῆναι, ὅτι οὐκ εἰσίν.[3]

1. F. van Segbroeck, 'Le scandale de l'incroyance: La signification de Mt. XIII,35', *ETL* 41 (1965), p. 370.

2. Van Segbroeck, 'Citations', p. 127.

3. κλαυθμός ℵ B Z 0250 f^{1} lat $syr^{p,pal}$ $cop^{sa,bo}$ *et al.*; the text has been brought into closer conformity to LXX^{A} Jer. 38.15 through the insertion of θρῆνος καί by C D K L W Δ f^{13} 𝔐 $syr^{c,s,h}$ Origen *et al.*

1. *The Fulfillment Formula of 2.17*

Of note first of all in Mt. 2.17—and 27.9—is the substitution of τὸτε (Matthew 90×; Mark 6×; Luke 15×) for ἵνα/ὅπως in all the remaining fulfillment formulae of Matthew's Gospel. Matthew uses τότε primarily to describe the temporal course of events in Jesus' life, and so to locate each event at a precise point within the larger narrative/historical concatenation.[1] Here τότε serves to specify the moment in messianic history when this particular Scripture came to fulfillment. Thus τότε, first, binds 'prophecy' to fulfillment-event, and, second, places both into their proper narrative context and chronological sequence.

More significant from our point of view is the fact that τότε (followed by the passive ἐπληρώθη) specifically avoids the purposive intent of ἵνα/ὅπως (followed by the subjunctive) of all the other fulfillment formulae. There is a consensus of scholarly opinion that since 2.17-18 and 27.9-10 describe mortal opposition to the Christ, Matthew has sought in this manner to avoid direct ascription of evil consequences to divine providence, as would normally be indicated by a fulfillment formula.[2] For although the purpose of fulfillment

1. Cf. Rothfuchs, *Erfüllungszitate*, p. 39. See also D.P. Senior, *The Passion Narrative According to Matthew: A Redactional Study* (BETL, 39; Leuven: Leuven University Press, 1975), p. 22 n. 6, pp. 364-66 and n. 65 ['A close examination of τότε in Matthew uncovers a careful effort to link events in the gospel sequence on a temporal-causal basis'], and further, *idem*, 'The Passion Narrative in the Gospel of Matthew', in Didier (ed.), *L'évangile selon Matthieu*, p. 351 n. 28; Strecker, *Weg*, pp. 90-91. (Senior's monograph incorporates as an appendix [pp. 343-397] his earlier article, 'The Fate of the Betrayer: A Redactional Study of Matthew XXVII, 3-10', *ETL* 48 [1972], pp. 372-46, reference to which, below, will cite the monograph pagination.)

2. Cf. A.B. Bruce, 'The Synoptic Gospels', in W.R. Nicholl (ed.), *Expositor's Greek Testament* (London: Hodder & Stoughton, 1901), I, pp. 75-76; A. Plummer, *An Exegetical Commentary on the Gospel according to St Matthew* (London: Stock, 1910), p. 18; Zahn, *Matthäus*, p. 109; A.H. M'Neile, *The Gospel according to St Matthew: The Greek Text with Introduction, Notes and Indices* (London: Macmillan, 1915), p. 19; M.-J. Lagrange, *Evangile selon Matthieu* (Paris: Lecoffre, 1927), p. 34; G. Friedrich, 'προφήτης κτλ', *TWNT*, VI, p. 833 n. 343 [*TDNT*, p. 832 n. 343]; Strecker, *Weg*, p. 59 n. 5; J. Schmid, *Das Evangelium nach Matthäus* (RNT, 1; Regensburg: Pustet, 1965), p. 51; Hummel, *Auseinandersetzung*, pp. 131-32; E. Lohmeyer, *Das Evangelium nach Matthäus* (Kritisch-exegetischer Kommentar über das NT; ed. W. Schmauch; Göttingen: Vandenhoeck & Ruprecht, 1967), p. 29; R. Pesch, 'Gottessohn', p. 399; E. Nellessen, *Das Kind und seine Mutter: Struktur und Verkündigung des 2. Kapitels im Matthäusevangelium* (SBS,

quotations in general is to demonstrate a divinely ordained pattern of redemptive history, here, it seems, Matthew wishes to say that it was not the divine intent that King Herod and his forces should slaughter innocent children in order to forestall a potential threat to his throne—nor, as in 27.9-10, that one of the chosen Twelve should sell the messiah for a paltry sum to those who sought his life. To have used ἵνα/ὅπως πληρωθῇ in this context would have risked setting Scripture itself against the divine plan.

Yet, paradoxically, even human opposition is part of messianic history and so must be accounted for within the providence of God. Hence Matthew substitutes the more nuanced and circumspect τότε ἐπληρώθη, which affirms scriptural fulfillment while avoiding the suggestion of divine initiative. The introductory formulae of 2.17 and 27.9 affirm, therefore, that even human initiative that sets itself in opposition to God's messianic purpose can be explained by scriptural precedent.[1]

39; Stuttgart: Katholisches Bibelwerk, 1969), p. 39 n. 39; W. Grundmann, *Das Evangelium nach Matthäus* (THKNT, 1; Berlin: Evangelische Verlaganstalt, 1971), p. 85; E. Klostermann, *Das Matthäusevangelium* (HNT, 4; Tübingen: Mohr [Paul Siebeck], 1971), p. 18; S. van Tilborg, *The Jewish Leaders in Matthew* (Leiden: Brill, 1972), p. 86-87; E. Schweizer, *Das Evangelium nach Matthäus* (NTD, 2; Göttingen: Vandenhoeck & Ruprecht, 1973), pp. 10, 19; Senior, *Passion Narrative*, p. 366; J.-M. van Cangh, 'La Bible de Matthieu: Les citations de l'accomplissement', *RTL* 6 (1975), pp. 209-10; Soares-Prabhu, *Formula Quotations*, pp. 50-51; R.E. Brown, *The Birth of the Messiah: A Commentary on the Infancy Narratives in Matthew and Luke* (Garden City, NY: Doubleday, 1977), p. 205; Nolan, *Royal Son of God*, p. 136; J.P. Meier, *Matthew* (New Testament Message, 3; Wilmington, DE: Michael Glazier, 1980), pp. 14, 339; J. Gnilka, *Das Matthäusevangelium* (HTKNT, 1; Freiburg: Herder, 1986, 1988), I, p. 52, II, p. 548; Contrary: Gundry, *Use of the OT*, p. 213 n. 4 (although in *Matthew: A Commentary on his Literary and Theological Art* [Grand Rapids: Eerdmans, 1982], p. 35, he affirms the majority opinion).

This interpretation receives some support from the similar substitution of ὅτι for ἵνα (Mk 4.12) at Mt. 13.13 (so Strecker, *Weg*, p. 106 n. 2), together with the use of the passive voice (ἀναπληροῦται) in the following verse, again so as to avoid the suggestion of *praedestinatio ad malum*. Conversely, Jesus' reference in 26.56 to his own betrayal combines ἵνα with the passive (so 26.54) in words that seem to echo the fulfillment formulae: τοῦτο δὲ ὅλον γέγονεν ἵνα πληρωθῶσιν αἱ γραφαὶ τῶν προφητῶν. Cf. Jn 17.12; Acts 1.16, 20.

1. According to Rothfuchs (*Erfüllungszitate*, p. 39 n. 39), following Gnilka it is this human initiative and opposition that Matthew intends to designate by the

2. *The Text of 2.18*

The fact that Matthew does not reproduce any of the extant texts of Jer. 31[38].15, but rather chooses elements from each, suggests that he was guided more by redactional concerns than by a desire for fidelity to any specific text. Accordingly, a review of the Evangelist's text will highlight its distinctive features in comparison to other extant forms:

Matthew	LXX[1]	MT
φωνὴ ἐν Ῥαμὰ ἠκούσθη,	φωνὴ ἐν Ῥαμὰ ἠκούσθη B ἐν τῇ ὑψηλῇ A ℵ^{txt} Aq *Tg*	קול ברמה נשמע
κλαυθμὸς καὶ ὀδυρμὸς[2]	θρήνου καὶ κλαυθμοῦ καὶ ὀδυρμοῦ	נהי בכי תמרורים
πολύς·		[תמרורים ?]
Ῥαχὴλ κλαίουσα	Ῥαχὴλ ἀποκλαιουμένη(ς A)	רחל מבכה
τὰ τέκνα αὐτῆς,	ἐπὶ τῶν υἱῶν αὐτῆς A	על־בניה
καὶ οὐκ ἤθελεν	(A καὶ) οὐκ ἤθελεν	מאנה להנחם
παρακληθῆναι	παρακληθῆναι, A B^{mg}	
	παύσασθαι ἐπὶ τοῖς υἱοῖς αὐτῆς B ℵ	על־בניה
ὅτι οὐκ εἰσίν.	ὅτι οὐκ εἰσίν	כי איננו

The phrase φωνὴ ἐν Ῥαμὰ ἠκούσθη echoes LXX^{B} exactly, while in κλαυθμὸς καὶ ὀδυρμὸς πολύς Matthew deletes the noun θρήνος/נהי and appears to have rendered תמרורים (the adjectival construct meaning 'bitter'; cf. Jer. 6.26; 31.21; Hos. 12.15) by πολύς.[3] The net effect is to abbreviate and intensify Rachel's cry of sorrow, giving κλαυθμός a prominence that anticipates, whether intentionally or not, the sentence of judgment ἐκεῖ ἔσται ὁ κλαυθμὸς καὶ ὁ βρυγμὸς τῶν ὀδόντων (originally derived from Q: Mt. 8.12 = Lk. 13.28) that

change in formula, rather than wishing to avoid the ascription of evil to God. Davies and Allison (*Matthew*, p. 266) consider either this or the majority explanation 'equally possible'.

1. An exhaustive textual apparatus for LXX Jeremiah is found in J. Ziegler, *Ieremias, Baruch, Threni, Epistula Ieremiae* (Göttingen: Vandenhoeck & Ruprecht, 1976), *in loc.* Stendahl (*School of St Matthew*, p. 102) cites the full texts of both LXX^{A} and LXX^{B}.

2. Again we note that the Matthaean text has been brought into closer conformity to LXX through the insertion of θρῆνος καί by C D K L W Δ f^{13} 𝔐 syr^{c,s,h} Origen *et al.*

3. Cf. Lagrange, *Matthieu*, p. 36; Lohmeyer and Schmauch, *Matthäus*, p. 29 n. 1; Rothfuchs, *Erfüllungszitate*, p. 63; Gundry, *Use of the OT*, p. 95.

Matthew repeatedly inserts into his narrative (cf. 13.42, 50; 22.13; 24.51; 25.30). Or, to state the matter differently, Matthew's distinctive use of κλαυθμός (Matthew 7×; Mark 0×; Luke 1×) in association with punishment and eschatological judgment lends sinister overtones to Rachel's weeping, underscoring its gravity. This is so whether or not the original intent of the term was to depict self-reproach.[1] Likewise, Matthew's κλαίουσα (Matthew 2×; Mark 4×; Luke 11×) is simpler and more direct than the LXX compound ἀποκλαιουμένη(ς) (cf. *piel* מבכה).[2]

Of more significance, however, is the substitution of τέκνα for υἱοί/בניה (or παῖδες, 2.16; cf. 2.13), since in Matthew's Gospel τέκνα often has the sense of 'posterity' or 'descendants' (3.9; 23.37; 27.25; cf. 22.24). So Rachel's lament for her τέκνα seems to anticipate the fate of those descendants both in 23.37 and, more pointedly, in 27.25, where the crowd at Jesus' trial call down blood upon themselves and τὰ τέκνα ἡμῶν. For in 2.18 and 27.25, if not 23.37 as well,

> the appalling consequences for all the people, which the evangelist sees as arising from the enmity of the popular authorities against the Messiah, provide the focus of attention.[3]

This substitution, therefore, whether a selective reading from Matthew's sources or a conscious interpretative alteration, suggests a correspondence between Jesus' treatment by the authorities at the beginning and at the end of his life. Not only is he opposed, rejected and threatened with death, but the fact that this is so entails sorrowful consequences, in Matthew's view, for the children of Israel. And it is for the innocent blood thus shed that Matthew's Rachel weeps.

The presence of τὰ τέκνα αὐτῆς coincides (in substance if not in detail) with LXX[A], as do also the subsequent καὶ, the verb

1. B. Schwanke, 'Dort wird Heulen und Zähneknirschen sein', *BZ* 16 (1972), p. 122; cf. K.H. Rengstorf, 'κλαυθμός', *TWNT*, III, p. 725 (= *TDNT*, pp. 724-25).

2. The only other occurrence of this verb in Matthew (26.75) is derived from Mk 14.72. Mt. 9.23-24 omits κλαίειν as found in Mk 5.38-39, and substitutes ἐκόψασθε (11.17) for ἐκλαύσετε as in Lk. 7.32. 'This indicates that κλαίειν was a word which the evangelist sought to avoid' (G.D. Kilpatrick, *The Origins of the Gospel according to Saint Matthew* [Oxford: Clarendon Press, 1946], p. 15).

3. Rothfuchs, *Erfüllungszitate*, pp. 64-65; cf. Gundry, *Use of the OT*, p. 36; *idem*, *Matthew*, p. 36; A. Vögtle, 'Die matthäische Kindheitsgeschichte', in Didier (ed.), *L'évangile selon Matthieu*, p. 173; Davies and Allison, *Matthew*, p. 270.

παρακληθῆναι, and the omission of the second reference to 'sons' (cf. MT/LXX[B]). Finally, ὅτι οὐκ εἰσίν follows the LXX against the incomprehensible singular איננו of the MT. Thus while there are notable similarities between Matthew and the LXX, the Evangelist appears to offer an independent rendering of the MT, doubtless influenced by redactional considerations.[1]

3. *Jeremiah 31.15 and its OT Context*

In citing Jer. 31.15, Matthew has chosen the one verse in Jeremiah 31 that is negative in outlook. Indeed, in its original context its force is immediately denied. For not only does v. 15 follow a lengthy and jubilant description of the consolation God will bestow upon the returning exiles (31.1-14), but that same consolation proves Rachel's weeping to be mistaken and unnecessary.

> Thus says the Lord: 'Keep your voice from weeping, and your eyes from tears; for your work shall be rewarded, says the Lord, and they shall come back from the land of the enemy' (31.16).

Thus the report of lamentation in v. 15 merely serves as a foil to introduce the ensuing proclamation of restoration. Although Rachel laments for her children and refuses to be comforted because she is convinced 'they are not', the Lord specifically contradicts her: 'they shall come back from the land of the enemy'; and again in v. 17, 'your children shall come back to their own country'. Jewish inter-

1. So Zahn, *Matthäus*, p. 111 n. 11; J.J. O'Rourke, 'The Fulfillment Texts in Matthew', *CBQ* 24 (1962), p. 396; Stendahl, *School of the St Matthew*, p. 102; Gundry, *Use of the OT*, p. 97; Strecker, *Weg*, pp. 58-59; F.W. Beare, *The Gospel according to Matthew* (New York: Harper & Row, 1981), p. 83; P. Bonnard, *L'évangile selon Saint Matthieu* (CNT, 1; Geneva: Labor et Fides, 1982), p. 29. C.C. Torrey (*Documents of the Primitive Church* [New York: Harper & Brothers, 1941], pp. 51-52) chooses to ignore the evidence of LXX variants in order to preserve his thesis of an Aramaic Matthew. As C. Wolff (*Jeremia im Frühjudentum und Urchristentum* [TU, 118; Berlin: Akademie Verlag, 1976], pp. 157-58) observes, the text demonstrates 'am Anfang stärkere Berührung mit dem masoretischen Text, während der Schluß mit LXX[A] wörtlich übereinstimmt'. But Wolff does not believe the naming of Jeremiah betrays any direct interest in that prophet on the part of the Evangelist (*Jeremia*, p. 159). Lohmeyer and Schmauch (*Matthäus*, pp. 28-29), on the other hand, suggest that Matthew's text gives evidence of an alternative Hebrew original. According to Strecker (*Weg*, p. 59), however, the citation is taken over from pre-Matthaean tradition. But even if this is so Matthew's use of it remains the same.

pretation of Jer. 31.15, as indicated by *Mek.* on Exod. 12.1 (Str-B 1.89-90), is positive in outlook.[1] To this may be compared *Gen. R.* 70.10 (on Gen. 29.4-6); *Lam. R.* Proem 24 and 1.2.23 (on Lam. 1.2), where 'Rachel's protestations have become the cause of the return from exile'.[2] In these passages Jer. 31.16-17 is cited as God's countermanding of v. 15. More broadly, Jer. 31.2-20 was read as Haftara to Gen. 22.1-9 on the second day of Rosh Hashanah.[3] A positive interpretation for the whole passage is suggested by 31.2 ('The people who survived the sword found grace in the wilderness'), which highlights the theme of the passage and suggests its likely connection in the Torah reading to the *Akedah Isaac* or 'Binding of Isaac'.[4] Moreover, of the sixteen or so instances in which readings from Jeremiah formed part of the ancient triennial synagogue lectionary, no fewer than eight were taken from chs. 31–32 (with two more from chs. 33–34), with the focus being on themes of restoration, redemption and/or the 'new' covenant.[5] All of this, of course, denotes a positive reading of these chapters in early Jewish tradition.

By contrast, the verse evidently appeared to Matthew so applicable to the fate of Herod's victims that he ignored its original intent. As for the children of Bethlehem, he declares, 'they are not', regardless of whether such an estimation had proven premature in the original context of Jeremiah 31. So glaring, in fact, is the contradiction between the contextual significance of Jer. 31.15 and Matthew's application of it that many scholars have suspected an implicit reference to the remainder of Jeremiah 31. For example, as B.F.C. Atkinson explains:

1. Cf. Davies and Allison, *Matthew*, p. 269.

2. R.T. France, 'The Formula Quotations of Matthew 2 and the Problem of Communication', *NTS* 27 (1980–81), p. 246 n. 31; cf. Zahn, *Matthäus*, p. 111 n. 111; Schlatter, *Matthäus*, p. 44.

3. Cf. Goulder, *Midrash and Lection*, pp. 312-13; R. Hayward (trans.), *The Targum of Jeremiah: Translated, with a Critical Introduction, Apparatus, and Notes* (Aramaic Bible, 12; Wilmington, DE: Michael Glazier, 1987), pp. 1-2; see also *b. Meg.* 31a.

4. The anomalous v. 15 could have been skipped (cf. Patte, *Early Jewish Hermeneutic*, p. 40, on *m. Meg.* 4.4) in order to produce a thematically uniform reading, since the Haftara was often limited to ten or so verses (*b. Meg.* 23a-b).

5. Cf. C. Perrot, 'The Reading of the Bible in the Ancient Synagogue', in Mulder (ed.), *Mikra*, pp. 141-43.

> The evangelist quotes only the tragic opening of the passage (Jer. xxxi.15; Mt. ii.18), but it is scarcely possible that he does not intend to send us back to Jeremiah to complete the prophecy. When we read it in full we find a promise of resurrection for the murdered children (Jer. xxxi.16,17 in the light of Mt. ii.16-18).[1]

Thus, according to Gundry,

> 2.18 rests on the correspondence between Judah's captivity and Herod's massacre, in both of which the future of the nation is threatened and Jewish mothers mourn, but the very disaster heralds a joyful future.[2]

The most thorough-going exposition of such a position is that of C.H. Dodd, according to whom the independent citation by NT authors of particular sections of Scripture indicates that

1. B.F.C. Atkinson, *The Christian's Use of the Old Testament* (London: Inter-Varsity Press, 1952), p. 83. This position is argued most forcefully by Zahn (*Matthäus*, pp. 109-10); so also M.M. Bourke, 'The Literary Genus of Matthew 1-2', *CBQ* 22 (1960), pp. 171-72; R.V.G. Tasker, *The Gospel according to Matthew: An Introduction and Commentary* (Leicester: Inter-Varsity Press; Grand Rapids: Eerdmans, 1961), pp. 43-44; W.F. Albright and C.S. Mann, *Matthew, Introduction, Translation and Notes* (AB, 26; Garden City, NY: Doubleday, 1971), p. lxiii; D. Hill, *The Gospel of Matthew* (NCB; London: Marshall, Morgan & Scott, 1972), p. 86; H.B. Green, *The Gospel according to Matthew in the Revised Standard Version* (Oxford: Oxford University Press, 1975), p. 60; Brown, *Birth*, p. 217; Nolan, *Royal Son*, p. 137 n. 4.

Lindars (*NT Apologetic*, pp. 217-18) distinguishes between the proper understanding of the earliest church, which selected this text 'as a prophecy of the reversal of grief', since Herod's designs would be defeated and Jesus would return to live in Galilee, and Matthew's subsequent 'misunderstanding' (p. 260) whereby he thinks only of the grief. But Matthew himself relates Jesus' safe return, in which case Lindars would have the Evangelist 'misunderstand' the immediate context of his own narrative. S.L. Edgar ('Respect for Context in Quotations from the Old Testament', *NTS* 9 [1962–63], pp. 55-62) has argued that the Evangelist's use of the OT (citing, *inter alia*, Mt. 2.18 and 27.9) can be distinguished by its lack of regard for original context from the more literal OT citations of Jesus, but this view has been strongly challenged (e.g. R.T. Mead, 'A Dissenting Opinion about Respect for Context in Old Testament Quotations', *NTS* 10 [1963–64], pp. 279-89).

2. *Use of the OT*, p. 211; also 'Just as the mourning of the Israelite mothers for the Babylonian exiles preluded a brighter future through divine preservation in a foreign land and restoration to Palestine, so the mourning by the mothers of the Bethlehem innocents is a prelude to the Messianic future through divine preservation of the infant Messiah in a foreign land and his later restoration to Palestine (2.18)' (*Use of the OT*, p. 210).

these sections were understood as *wholes*, and particular verses or sentences were quoted from them rather as pointers to the whole context than as constituting testimonies in and for themselves.[1]

So Dodd believes the whole context of Jer. 31[38].31-34 to be in view in Mt. 26.28, 1 Cor. 11.25, 2 Cor. 3.2-14, and Heb. 8.8-12, as well as possibly Jn 4.42 and 1 Jn 2.12-14, where some or all of Jer. 31.15 is quoted or alluded to.[2] With somewhat less certainty, he suggests that since Matthew quotes Jer. 31.15 explicitly, and the remainder of Jeremiah 31 speaks of redemption in terms that anticipate NT theology, the whole chapter may have influenced the vocabulary of the early Christians.[3] But even if a wider influence of Jer. 31.10-34 can be demonstrated in Matthew's Gospel, its relevance remains to be seen in the present context. Dodd himself admits that 'the actual meaning discovered in a given passage will seldom... coincide precisely with that which it had in its original context'.[4]

In the case of Mt. 2.16-18, however, references to the context of Jeremiah 31 prove altogether elusive. For while it is true that the threat to Jesus' life fails, so that he returns in safety to Galilee (so Lindars), this event is referred (however enigmatically) not to Jeremiah but to the collective word of the prophets in 2.23, 'He shall

1. *According to the Scriptures*, p. 126; summarized in his shorter work, *The Old Testament in the New* (Philadelphia: Fortress Press, 1963), and followed by, for example, Lindars (*NT Apologetic*, pp. 16-17) and Gundry (*Use*, pp. 205-208). J.A.E. van Dodewaard ('La force évocatrice de la citation mise en lumière en prenant pour base l'évangile de S. Matthieu', *Bib* 36 [1955], pp. 486-87) demonstrates that in some instances the citation of the opening of a verse is intended to recall its conclusion (e.g. Ps. 8.3 in Mt. 21.16 or Ps. 22.1 in 27.46). This citation of *pars pro toto* is widely evident in Talmudic literature.

2. *According to the Scriptures*, pp. 46-47.

3. *According to the Scriptures*, pp. 85-86. For example, the gathering (συνάγειν) of God's people in Jer. 31.10, so Mk 13.27, Jn 11.32; with Israel depicted as God's flock, so Jn 10.9, 21.17; Israel's redemption (λυτροῦν) in Jer. 31.11; the feeding of the hungry both in Jer. 31.12 (cf. Lk 6.21, Jn 6.35, Rev. 7.16) and in 31.14 (ἐμπλησθήσεται; so Jn 6.12, ἐνεπλήσθησαν).

4. *According to the Scriptures*, p. 130. So also G.W. Buchanan ('The Use of Rabbinic Literature for New Testament Research', *BTB* 7 [1977], p. 119): 'The wide belief among rabbis that all scripture prophesies only for the days of the Messiah ([*b. Ber.*] 34b; 1QpHab 2.5-6; 7.1-12) shows that the OT passages quoted in the NT out of context and with distorted meanings were not out of order, according to the standards of NT times'. By way of illustration, Buchanan cites the use of the OT in Mt. 1–2, although he sees Mt. 2.18 as a reference to Gen. 35.19!

be called a Nazarene'. Yet even apart from this consideration, the force of Matthew's introductory τότε (2.17) is retrospective, limiting the scope of fulfillment to the massacre at Bethlehem. Nowhere is there any reference by the Evangelist to a future resurrection for the murdered children, nor any immediate indication of a 'joyful future' for the nation as a whole. On the contrary, Matthew's Gospel has in view a series of coming disasters: the punishment of 'this generation' for 'all the righteous blood shed on earth' from Abel to Zechariah (23.35-36), the destruction of Jerusalem (22.7; 23.38; 24.2), and the removal of the kingdom from Israel (21.43).

Lohmeyer offers an alternative version of Dodd's thesis, suggesting that allusions to Jeremiah 31 are scattered throughout Matthew's infancy narrative and beyond. This is based on the premise that Matthew depicts Jesus as the messiah of Ephraim, whom later interpreters also saw in Jer. 31.9 (Str–B 1.67.*r*; 2.288-90). Accordingly, Lohmeyer asks whether Mt. 1.21 (αὐτὸς γὰρ σώσει τὸν λαὸν αὐτοῦ) might not recall LXX Jer. 38.7, ἔσωσεν κύριος τὸν λαὸν αὐτοῦ; likewise Mt. 2.13 (the angel orders Joseph to flee Herod's wrath) Jer. 38.11, ἐξείλατο αὐτὸν ἐκ χειρὸς στερεωτέρων αὐτοῦ; and Mt. 2.20 (the command to return to the land of Israel) the rabbinic interpretation of Jer. 31.20 as describing the messiah's return from obscurity. Lohmeyer also refers LXX Jer. 37.21, καὶ ὁ ἄρχων αὐτοῦ ἐξ αὐτοῦ ἐξελεύσεται, and 38.10, φυλάξει αὐτὸν ὡς ὁ βόσκων τὸ ποίμνιον αὐτοῦ, to Matthew 26 in general, presumably highlighting the image of Jesus as a shepherd in 26.31-32.[1]

But even apart from the tenuous nature of Lohmeyer's premise, only 1.21 might offer a substantial parallel to Jer. 38.7, were it not already amply accounted for both etymologically (ישוע from הושיע, 'to deliver', 'save') and scripturally (Isa. 7.14 in Mt. 1.23). The remainder of Lohmeyer's suggested parallels are too general to substantiate his thesis, with the final pair so vague as to be altogether obscure.

More nuanced is the argument of Davies and Allison, who propose that both the general eschatological character and many of the specific details of Jeremiah 31 'would have caught [Matthew's] attention' as he read them with the story of Jesus in mind. Common elements would have included reference to a παρθένος returning from exile (LXX Jer. 38.4, 21; cf. Mt. 1.23), to God's υἱὸς ἀγαπητός (Jer. 38.20; cf.

1. Lohmeyer and Schmauch, *Matthäus*, p. 29 n. 3.

Mt. 3.17; 17.5; also 2.15), and to God's declaration 'I am a father to Israel, and Ephraim is my first-born' (Jer. 31.9; cf. Mt. 11.25-27). Also compared in this analysis are (1) the return from exile of 'the woman with child' (so RSV Jer. 31.8; but MT הרה, 'pregnant woman'; LXX τεκνοποιήσῃ) and Mt. 2.11, 14, 20-21, (2) the declaration that 'your children shall come back to their own country' (Jer. 31.17) and Mt. 2.19-21, (3) the promise of salvation in Jer. 31.7 and Mt. 1.22, and (4) the prospect of a 'new covenant' (Jer. 31.31-33 with Mt. 26.28). Less obvious, however, are the parallels these commentators see between Jer. 31.35, where God has fixed 'the stars for light by night', and the star of the Magi (Mt. 2.1-12); or between the promises of spiritual replenishment in Jer. 31.25 and Mt. 5.6, respectively. Davies and Allison conclude:

> In the light of all this, and given the typological equation of Jesus with Israel... the evangelist could readily have seen in Jeremiah's prophecy of Israel's return from the exile and of the new things promised for thereafter a transparent cipher or prototype for the Messiah's return to Israel and subsequent ministry.[1]

So Davies and Allison propose that this series of similarities would have led Matthew to the one proof-text he required, that is, to Jer. 31.15. But they do not insist that Matthew's use of this verse was intended to convey the optimistic overtones of its context: 'Whether or not such was Matthew's expectation we have no way to decide'.[2] Thus, although a number of Matthaean parallels to Jeremiah 31 will require more detailed examination later on, in general the conclusion still holds: Matthew's use of Jer. 31.15 does not take account either of its biblical context or of its predominant interpretation in the Jewish schools and synagogues.

4. *Jeremiah 31.15 and its Matthaean Context*

This conclusion is borne out by an examination of 2.16-18 within the narrative of the first two chapters of Matthew's Gospel. Whatever structure is assigned to the Matthaean infancy narratives as a whole,[3] 2.16-18 corresponds both formally and thematically to 2.1-12. For

1. Davies and Allison, *Matthew*, p. 267.
2. *Matthew*, p. 269.
3. For brief summaries of the question, see Nellesen, *Das Kind und seine Mutter*, pp. 25-27, and Soares Prabhu, *Formula Quotations*, pp. 10-12 (together with his own proposal, pp. 171-72).

both episodes 'describe the futile efforts of the enemies of Jesus to put him to death'[1] and both are united by a common interest in Herod, the Magi and the consequences of their encounter. Their presence, in fact, sets the earliest history of the messiah's life against a backdrop of contrasting responses to his advent. On the one hand, there is the response of the messiah's own people: 'Herod the king...and all Jerusalem with him' are 'troubled (ἐταράχθη)' by the news of his birth (2.3). None of these, nor indeed any of 'the chief priests and scribes of the people' (2.3), either acclaim or welcome him. The Gentile Magi, on the other hand, declare that they have 'come to worship him (ἤλθομεν προσκυνῆσαι αὐτῷ)' (2.2), and with their worship offer the new-born messiah wealthy gifts that befit his rank (2.11).[2] Herod's offer to 'worship' is, by contrast, cynical and treacherous (2.8), as his later actions demonstrate.

This contrast between the responses of Jews and Gentiles, of adoration and murderous rejection, 'deftly foreshadows the opposition between faith and worship...and unbelief and persecution...that permeates the whole Gospel'.[3] For, as we have already seen, the fate of the 'innocents' anticipates yet graver consequences that will, in Matthew's view, come upon the heads of *all* those who reject the messiah. But nothing could be further from Jeremiah's own use of 31.15.

In addition, as we also saw, Matthew's exegesis does not focus in the first instance on the text at hand, but rather, beginning with the revelatory event of Jesus' life, seeks a scriptural text that will reaffirm what is, in effect, already known. That is to say, Scripture does not provide the interpretative key to the meaning of Jesus' life; rather, Jesus' life provides the interpretative key to the meaning of the sacred

1. Soares Prabhu, *Formula Quotations*, p. 176, cf. p. 188. The redactional character of the chapter as a whole is demonstrated by Nellesen, *Das Kind und seine Mutter*, pp. 35-57.

2. The highly significant προσκυνεῖν (Mt. 13×; Mk 2×; Lk. 3×) describes 'in the imperfect (8,2; 9,18; 15,25; also 18,26) a suppliant's plea to, in the aorist (14,33; 20,20; 28,9; also 4,9.10) a disciple's adoration of, the all-powerful saving Lord' (Soares Prabhu, *Formula Quotations*, p. 274); cf. H. Greeven, 'προσκυνέω', *TWNT*, VI, pp. 764-65 (= *TDNT*, p. 763-64); Pesch, 'Gottessohn', pp. 414-15; W. Schenk, *Die Sprache des Matthäus: Die Text-konstituenten in ihren makro-und mikrostrukturellen Relationen* (Göttingen: Vandenhoeck & Ruprecht, 1987), pp. 421-23.

3. Nolan, *Royal Son*, p. 132.

text. This preliminary analysis will now be tested in greater detail as we examine more closely the Evangelist's own application of the text.

5. *Ramah, Bethlehem and Rachel's Lament*
Stendahl has argued that a geographical interest underlies the formula quotations of Matthew 2, by means of which the Evangelist treats, in turn, Bethlehem (2.5-6), Egypt (2.13-15), Ramah (2.18) and Nazareth (2.23).[1] Yet whereas each of the other three passages mentions the relevant geographical term in both the Scriptural quotation and its immediate narrative context, 'Ramah' appears only in v. 18 and seems to be associated with 'Bethlehem' in 2.16. As R.T. France complains, 'in this chapter of formula-quotations with clearly geographical motivation, this one is conspicuous for its geographical inappropriateness—Ramah is not Bethlehem'.[2] Why, then, is Rachel associated with Ramah, and what connection does this have to Bethlehem?

There were two rival traditions as to the location of Rachel's tomb. According to 1 Sam. 10.2 her burial place was to be found 'in the territory of Benjamin at Zelzah', near the Ramah of Jer. 31.15 some five miles north of Jerusalem (cf. Judg. 19.13). Gen. 35.19 and 48.7, on the other hand, declare that Rachel was buried 'on the way to Ephrath[ah], (that is, Bethlehem)'. Here, six miles to the south of Jerusalem, Islamic tradition still venerates her tomb (cf. MT Mic. 5.1, 'Bethlehem Ephrathah', and *Jub.* 32.34). Even in Genesis there is indirect attestation of competing traditions, for the final parentheses appear to be explanatory glosses occasioned by the clan of Ephrath[ah] having taken up residence in the area of Bethlehem (cf. Ruth 1.2, 1 Sam. 17.12).[3]

Matthew appears to have conflated the two traditions, so that

1. 'Quis et Unde: An Analysis of Matthew 1–2', in W. Eltester (ed.), *Judentum, Urchristentum, Kirche* (Berlin: Töpelmann, 1960), repr. G. Stanton (ed.), *The Interpretation of Matthew* (London: SPCK; Philadelphia: Fortress Press, 1983), pp. 57-59.

2. 'Herod and the Children of Bethlehem', *NovT* 21 (1979), p. 104. For France's own solution, not unlike that proposed here, see 'Formula Quotations', p. 245.

3. Brown, *Birth*, p. 185 n. 18, p. 205. See further S.V. Fawcett, 'Rachel's Tomb', *IDB*, IV, p. 5, and M. Tsevat, 'Rachel's Tomb', *IDBSup*, pp. 724-25. In this connection, M. Oberweis ('Beobachtungen zum AT-Gebrauch in der Matthäischen Kindheitsgeschichte', *NTS* 35 [1989], p. 136) sees here a specific reference to 1 Sam. 10.2.

Rachel's lament becomes the common factor justifying the association of Ramah in Jer. 31.15 with the Bethlehem of Jesus' birth. That is to say, he acknowledges the one tradition of Rachel's tomb at Ramah by choosing to see in Jer. 31.15 a geographical place name[1] (as opposed to LXX^{A} Aquila *Tg* Vulg); but by τότε ἐπληρώθη he affirms the greater validity of the alternative tradition, so that Jeremiah's reference to Ramah is 'fulfilled' by Herod's persecution of Jesus in Bethlehem. It is not a question of whether Matthew is 'mistaken',[2] since from his point of view the conflation of Ramah with Bethlehem is confirmed, via Jer. 31.15, by the Holy Family's flight from there.[3] Moreover, Matthew is careful to specify, perhaps as a redactional addition to his traditional material,[4] that Herod's deadly order was carried out not only in Bethlehem itself, but also ἐν πᾶσι τοῖς ὁρίοις αὐτῆς (2.16). Thus he anticipates the fulfillment quotation by ensuring that the area of Rachel's tomb, north of Bethlehem on the Jerusalem road, is included in the slaughter.

For whom, then, does Rachel weep? Jeremiah envisages the shade of Rachel rising up from her grave to lament the descendants of Ephraim, her grandson (Jer. 31.6, 9, 18, 20), one of the main tribes of the Northern Kingdom. In other words, Rachel's lament was originally for the exiles of 721, not 587.[5] On the other hand,

1. There are at least five villages by the name of Ramah recorded in the OT (see, e.g., Josh. 19.8, 29, 36; 1 Sam. 1.19; further, s.v: 'Ramah', *IDB*, IV, pp. 7-9), although geographical miscalculation does not appear to underlie Matthew's exegesis. More significant, according to Davies and Allison (*Matthew*, p. 269) is the fact that in addition to its being the departure point for the exile, Isa. 10.29, Jer. 31.15 and Hos. 5.8 all associate Ramah with disaster, suggesting that 'Ramah might be regarded as a city of sadness par excellence'.

2. So Brown, *Birth*, p. 205; U. Luz, *Das Evangelium nach Matthäus*. I. *Mt 1-7* (EKKNT, 1.1; Zürich: Benzinger; Neukirchen–Vluyn: Neukirchener Verlag, 1985), p. 130 n. 27.

3. The same conflation is found in *Gen. R.* 82.10 (on Gen. 35.19): 'What was Jacob's reason for burying Rachel on the way to Ephrath? Jacob foresaw that the exiles would pass on from thence: therefore he buried her there so that she might pray for mercy for them. Thus it is written... [Jer 31.15-17]'. This confirms (1) the Bethlehem tradition ('Ephrath'), (2) the Ramah tradition (the citation of Jer. 31.15), and (3) the association of both with the exile of the Southern Kingdom ('the exiles would pass on from there', referring to Jer. 40.1).

4. Cf. Soares Prabhu, *Formula Quotations*, p. 259.

5. Cf. J. Bright, *Jeremiah: Introduction, Translation, and Notes* (AB, 21; Garden City, NY: Doubleday, 1965), pp. 281-82; J.A. Thompson, *The Book of*

Jer. 40.1 designates the same Ramah as the assembly point for the forced march to Babylon by the captives of the Southern Kingdom, in addition to which Jer. 31.23-24 makes clear reference to Judah and the הר הקדש of Jerusalem.[1] Matthew could therefore have taken Jer. 31.15 as referring to either expulsion or, as is more likely, to both. In any event, the focus of his quotation is not on the events of the past but on their fulfillment in the present. In Matthew's eyes Rachel weeps above all for the slaughtered children of Bethlehem, among whose number Jesus was intended to be. He has used the quotation, in the first instance, to clarify an incident that has come to him via tradition.[2]

At the same time, the fact that Rachel mourns for *exiles* probably suggested to Matthew a further connection with Jesus, himself on his way into exile. According to Stendahl, Jer. 31.15 serves merely as a 'prophetic alibi' in order to explain Jesus' removal from Bethlehem and eventual residence in Nazareth.[3] Yet the infancy narrative as a whole seems to intend a larger correspondence between Jesus and Israel in general, as well as Moses in particular.[4] Quite striking are the resemblances between Moses, who alone escapes the slaughter of the Israelite children, and the infant Jesus (cf. ἀναχωρεῖν and ἀναίρειν in LXX Exod. 2.15 and Mt. 2.16). Furthermore, Philo's *De*

Jeremiah (NICOT; Grand Rapids: Eerdmans, 1980), p. 573; Soares Prabhu, *Formula Quotations*, p. 256 and nn. 156, 157; cf. W.L. Holladay, *A Commentary on the Book of the Prophet Jeremiah* (ed. P.D. Hanson; Minneapolis: Augsburg–Fortress, 1986, 1989), II, pp. 186-87. For the suggestion that Jeremiah repeats an earlier, traditional lament by way of commentary on the second deportation, see B. Lindars, '"Rachel Weeping for her Children"—Jeremiah 31.15-22', JSOT 12 (1979), pp. 52-53.

1. Cf. R.P. Carroll, *Jeremiah: A Commentary* (OTL; Philadelphia: Westminster Press, 1986), p. 598. By way of comparison, *Targ. Jer.* 31.15 explicitly connects this verse with 'Nebuzaradan, the chief of the killers' from 40.1, in which case it is understood to refer to the Babylonian exile.

2. Cf. Strecker, *Weg*, p. 59.

3. 'Quis et Unde', p. 58; *School of St Matthew*, pp. vii-viii.

4. It has been argued that Matthew's typological interest begins with the correspondences between Joseph the patriarch and Joseph the husband of Mary. For Joseph, Jesus's earthly father who consistently receives divinely inspired dreams (Mt. 1.20; 2.12, 13, 19, 22), reminds one of the 'man of dreams' of Gen. 37.19, and, like his namesake but alone in the NT, sojourns in Egypt. It may even be relevant that the guardian of Jesus plays the same role as the patriarch in leading Jesus/Israel to safety there.

Vita Mosis and Josephus's *Antiquities of the Jews* (2.205-37) include such additional details as a prophecy from one of Pharaoh's scribes of a Hebrew whose birth threatens the Egyptian kingdom, filling the nation with fear; a warning in a dream to Moses' father; and a promise that the child would deliver his people from their bondage.[1] In each of these details, parallels to Matthew's infancy narrative appear obvious.

In larger terms, Matthew's citation of Hos. 11.1, 'Out of Egypt have I called my son', suggests that Jesus recapitulates the history of the nation as a whole. For not only does he undergo an 'Exodus' of sorts, but he also spends forty days and forty nights in the desert—an echo of Israel's forty years of wandering—before assuming his ministry.[2] Thus Matthew appears to 'telescope' a series of incidents in the redemptive history of Israel into one: the suffering in Egypt (both that of Moses and that of the nation as a whole); the Assyrian/ Babylonian Exile (cf. 1.11-12); and, *de novo*, the persecution of the messianic 'Son'. Indeed, as Brown observes, the first three formula citations of ch. 2, by focusing in turn on 'Bethlehem, the city of David, Egypt, the land of the Exodus, and Ramah, the mourning-place

1. Set out in detail by R. Bloch, 'Quelques aspects de la figure de Moïse dans la tradition rabbinique', in *Moïse, L'homme de l'alliance* (Paris: Desclée, 1955), pp. 164-66; Nellesen, *Das Kind und seine Mutter*, pp. 63-67; Brown, *Birth*, pp. 111-16; Davies and Allison, *Matthew*, pp. 192-93. Cf. the cautious affirmation by W.D. Davies, *The Setting of the Sermon on the Mount* (Cambridge: Cambridge University Press, 1966), pp. 78-83. Yet a further typological correspondence between the flights to Egypt by Jesus and Jacob/Israel, the latter following persecution by Laban, is proposed by D. Daube, *The New Testament and Rabbinic Judaism* (London: Athlone Press, 1956), pp. 189-92; *idem*, 'The Earliest Structure of the Gospels', *NTS* 5 (1958–59), pp. 184-86; Bourke, 'Literary Genus', pp. 160-75; and C.H. Cave, 'St Matthew's Infancy Narrative', *NTS* 9 (1962–63), pp. 382-90. Cf. the negative estimations of Nellesen, *Das Kind und seine Mutter*, pp. 69-72; Brown, *Birth*, pp. 544-55; France, 'Herod and the Children', pp. 105-108; and Nolan, *Royal Son*, pp. 36-37, 83-89.

2. So, e.g., H. Milton, 'The Structure of the Prologue to St Matthew's Gospel', *JBL* 81 (1962), p. 179; Nellesen, *Das Kind und seine Mutter*, pp. 67-68; R.T. France, *Jesus and the Old Testament: His Application of Old Testament Passages to himself and his Mission* (Grand Rapids: Baker, 1982), pp. 50-59; Brown, *Birth*, p. 215; D.C. Allison, 'The Son of God as Israel: A Note on Matthean Christology', *IBS* 9 (1987), pp. 79, 76-77 (with transposed pagination).

of the Exile, offer a theological history of Israel in geographical miniature'.[1]

But there is potential here for further significant thematic resonances. For, according to the canonical record, Jeremiah accompanied the exiles on their way to Babylon only as far as Ramah, whence he returned to dwell in Jerusalem with the remnant of the people (Jer. 39.14; 40.16). Only later does he accompany another group—against his will—into Egypt (Jer. 42–43). There is an alternative tradition, however, attested in such early second-century works as *2 Baruch* (10.2; 33.2) and *Paraleipomena Jeremiou* (4.6), that Jeremiah too went into exile in Babylon.[2]

Also to be considered is the evidence of *Targ. Jer.* 31.15, according to which God 'in the height (ברום) of the world' hears the voice of (1) 'the house of Israel[3] who weep and lament after Jeremiah the prophet, when Nebuzaradan, the chief of the killers, sent him from Ramah, with a dirge'; (2) 'those who weep for the bitterness of Jerusalem'; and (3) Jerusalem herself 'as she weeps for her children...because they have gone into exile'.[4] Although here, of course, the exiles lament for Jeremiah because he is returning without them to Jerusalem, it is significant that Jer. 31.15 in particular is seen as tying together the sorrowful fate of prophet, people and city alike, with the result being that lament for one is lament for the others.

In similar terms, Matthew's Rachel laments the Bethlehemite children whose fate anticipates that of the nation as a whole. Included in the latter consideration from Matthew's perspective would, of course, be the fate of Jerusalem in particular.[5] And because Rachel's lament

1. Brown, *Birth*, p. 217; cf. Schnackenburg, *Matthäusevangelium*, p. 27.

2. Cf. LXX Bar. 1.1, which places Jeremiah's scribe in Babylon, as well as *Pes.R.* 26.6; *Lam. R.* Proem 24; *Midr. Ps.* 137.2 and *S.'Ol. R.* 26, which have Jeremiah travelling as far as the Euphrates, then returning. See further, L. Ginzberg, *The Legends of the Jews* (Philadelphia: Jewish Publication Society, 1913, 1928), IV, pp. 310-12; VI, pp. 399-400.

3. Here Rachel represents Israel; so also *Gen. R.* 71.2; 82.1; *Pes. K.* 141b (Simeon b. Yoḥai, c. 150); cf. *4 Ezra* 5.26.

4. כדנן אמר יוי קלא ברום עלמא אשתמע בית ישראל דבכן ומתאנחין בתר ירמיה נביא כד שלח יתיה נבוזראדן רב קטוליא מרמתא אליא ודבכן במרר ירשלים בכיא על בנהא מסרבא לאתנחמא על בנהא ארי גלו.

The ET is taken from Hayward, *Targum of Jeremiah*, which indicates specific targumic interpolations by the use of italics.

5. But there is nothing to support the suggestion of Nolan (*Royal Son*, p. 138)

focuses as well on the exiled messiah, Matthew's use of Jer. 31.15 suggests an analogy between Jesus and Jeremiah.

The antiquity of specific targumic traditions is difficult to verify. The case for this latter correspondence cannot, therefore, rest on *Targum Jonathan* alone. Nonetheless, the similarity of its exegesis of Jer. 31.15 to Matthew's use of the text may help explain why Matthew declared this passage to have been 'fulfilled' in the persecution of the infant Messiah and the attendant suffering of the Jewish τέκνα.[1]

that Rachel's lament is for the unbelief of her descendants. J. Schniewind (*Das Evangelium nach Matthäus* [NTD, 2; Göttingen: Vandenhoeck & Ruprecht, 1964], p. 20) sees in this episode an inauguration of the time of messianic eschatological tribulation. Grundmann (*Matthäus*, p. 84), concurring, observes a more specific parallel: 'Um das Jesuskind zu retten, müssen unschuldige Kinder sterben; Jesus wird selbst sterben, um sein Volk vom Sünden zu retten (1.21; 26.28)'; so also Zahn, *Matthäus*, p. 112; Green, *Matthew*, p. 60.

1. *Targ. Jer.* 31.15 is rendered all the more striking by the fact that its exegesis runs counter not only to the tenor of the chapter as a whole, but also to the dominant interpretation of the passage available to us from alternative Jewish sources.

Regarding the dating of *Targum Jeremiah*, while 'there are indications that Tg. [Jer] is aware of a number of old exegetical traditions known also to LXX', as well as having 'some points of contact with the Qumran literature' (*Targum of Jeremiah*, pp. 26-27), Hayward believes that it 'reached something like its present form by the beginning of the fourth century AD' (*Targum of Jeremiah*, p. 35; see also P.S. Alexander, 'Jewish Aramaic Translations of Hebrew Scriptures', in Mulder (ed.), *Mikra*, p. 223). S.H. Levey ('The Date of Targum Jonathan to the Prophets', *VT* 21 [1971], pp. 186-96), however, sets the *terminus a quo* of *Targum Jonathan* in 'the period between 200 and 150 BC, comparable to the time of the emergence of LXX', and its *terminus ad quem* 'at some time subsequent to the Arab conquest of Babylonia, that is, after 640-41', perhaps as late as the time of Saadia Gaon (pp. 892-942). See the critique of Levey with regard to the latter date by B. Chilton, *Targumic Approaches to the Gospels: Essays in the Mutual Definition of Judaism and Christianity* (Lanham, MD: University Press of America, 1986), p. 106 n. 9. Authorship of *Targum Jonathan* has traditionally been ascribed to Jonathan ben-Uzziel, a first-century disciple of Hillel (*b. Meg.* 3a; cf. B.J. Roberts, *The Old Testament Text and Versions: The Hebrew Text in Transmission and the History of the Ancient Versions* [Cardiff: University of Wales Press, 1951], p. 208).

Because the Targumim represent a cumulative exegetical process, 'it follows... that although a Targum text may be late it will often contain a great deal of very early material' (J. Bowker, *The Targums and Rabbinic Literature: An Introduction to Jewish Interpretations of Scripture* [Cambridge: Cambridge University Press, 1969], p. 16). Indeed, such evidence as geographical knowledge (particularly where it reflects points of contact with *Targum Neofiti*); references to the

At the heart of Matthew's use of Jer. 31.15 is a synthetic, conflational or 'telescoping' view of sacred history. This conflation is at once geographical (Ramah/Bethlehem), temporal (Exodus/Exile), and individual (Rachel; the two Josephs; Moses/Jeremiah/Jesus). Such a synthetic use of sacred Scripture and history is typical of contemporary Jewish exegesis, and particularly the Targumim. Indeed, it represents the essence of typology, for on such a view, as D. Patte points out,

> history is a synthetic unity, and... its different periods are closely interrelated. Because of this... the meaning of an event is to be understood together with similar events which occurred before and after it... the unity or basic identity between these events is to be found in that they are all considered as Act or Word (*dabar* in both cases) of God, the God who is One.[1]

Jerusalem priesthood, and to 'Edom' and 'Babylon' as ciphers for Rome; and, more tentatively, exegetical features, together '[seem] to provide sufficient grounds for discerning the origins of Tg. Jeremiah in the land of Israel during, or slightly before, the first century AD' (Hayward, *Targum of Jeremiah*, p. 38). Again, as Alexander concludes on linguistic grounds, 'given their dialect, it is hardly likely that Onk[elos] and Yon[atan] (at least as to their basic text) could have originated after 135 CE' (*Mikra*, p. 247).

This brings *Targum Jeremiah* into a sphere of exegetical activity roughly contemporary with Matthew, encouraging us to make use of its traditions where such comparison seems warranted. But as we saw earlier, this should not be taken to necessitate direct lines of dependence: 'The coincidence of a NT reading with one or other... Targumic authority represents not so much the use of that particular Targum or its putative ancestor as the preservation by both the NT and the Targumic authority of early Jewish exegetical tradition' (Wilcox, 'On Investigating the Use of the OT in the NT', p. 239). As Chilton (*Targumic Approaches*, p. 116) affirms, 'When a Targumic passage parallels or appears to provide the logical antecedent to a New Testament passage, the natural inference is that the Targum in question informs us of the basis on which the New Testament tradents were operating'.

For a general introduction to Targumic literature, see Roberts, *OT Text and Versions*, pp. 197-213; on Targumic method, see R. LeDéaut, 'La tradition juive ancienne et l'exégèse chrétienne primitive', *RHPR* 51 (1971), pp. 44-49; also Patte, *Early Jewish Hermeneutic*, pp. 55-57, 65-81. For a valuable discussion of the relevance of Targumic interpretation to the NT—not least as a precedent for the latter's free handling of the OT text—see LeDéaut, *Tradition juive*, pp. 31-39.

1. Patte, *Early Jewish Hermeneutic*, pp. 69, 71; also p. 73; cf. A. Schlatter, *Der Evangelist Matthäus: Seine Sprache, sein Ziel, seine Selbständigkeit* (Stuttgart: Calwer Verlag, 1982), pp. 43-44. These observations on the hermeneutical principles underlying Matthew's exegesis will prove instructive when we return in

In summary, Matthew invokes Jer. 31.15 to indicate that even the suffering of the infant Christ was in accord with the divine plan, although his introductory τότε avoids ascribing such evil directly to God's foreordination and will. Matthew's interpretation and application of this 'prophecy' operates simultaneously in a variety of related ways. Ignoring altogether the original context of the passage, he uses Rachel's lament to suggest a correspondence between the suffering of the children of Israel in Exile (as well as of the infants in Egypt, on the analogy of Moses' infancy) and the suffering of the children of Israel under Herod. In Matthew's eyes the mother of Israel weeps for all these victims. Indeed, she laments not only for the slaughtered innocents, but also for the messiah who, as representative of the nation, recapitulates its historical destiny by himself departing into exile. Matthew's forced conflation of traditions, whereby he places Rachel's tomb in both Ramah and Bethlehem, underscores this latter correspondence. Finally, it must not be forgotten that the entire episode arises because the Jewish authorities, here represented by Herod (cf. 2.3, 'Herod...and all Jerusalem with him'), chose to reject and persecute the messiah foretold by Scripture.[1] More precisely, Rachel's 'wailing and loud lamentation' is occasioned by the fact that the innocent infants of Bethlehem, designated as τέκνα in anticipation of later events, bear on their own heads the tragic consequences of this rejection.

C. *Matthew 27.9-10*

9 τότε ἐπληρώθη τὸ ῥηθὲν διὰ ⸀Ἰερεμίου τοῦ προφήτου λέγοντος· καὶ ἔλαβον τὰ τριάκοντα ἀργύρια, τὴν τιμὴν τοῦ τετιμημένου ὃν ἐτιμήσαντο ἀπὸ υἱῶν Ἰσραήλ, 10 καὶ ⸀ἔδωκαν αὐτὰ εἰς τὸν ἀγρὸν τοῦ κεραμέως, καθὰ συνέταξέν μοι κύριος.[2]

Chapter 4 to a closer examination of Matthaean typology.

1. Cf. Rothfuchs, *Erfüllungszitate*, p. 64; Vögtle, 'Kindheitsgeschichte', pp. 173-74; Menken, 'Jeremiah', p. 10; Nellesen, *Das Kind und seine Mutter*, pp. 89-90.

2. 9 ⸀Ἰερεμίου ℵ A B C L X W Γ Δ Θ Π lat vg syr[hpt] cop[sa,bo] | Ζαχαρίου 22 syr[hmg] | Ἠσαΐου 21 lat[1] | omit Φ 33 157 lat[a,b] syr[s,p] cop[bopt] 10 ⸀ἔδωκαν A[c] B* C L X Δ Θ 064 0133 f^1 f^{13} 𝔐 it vg cop | ἔδωκεν A*[vid] ἔδωκα ℵ B[2vid] | W 2174 *pc* syr.

1. *The Fulfillment Formula of 27.9*

The introductory formula of Mt. 27.9, as noted earlier, is identical in every respect to that of 2.17. Furthermore, it shares with all the Matthaean fulfillment formulae the basic purpose of demonstrating the accomplishment of scriptural prophecy in the life of the messiah. At the same time, the fact that both 2.17 and 27.9 substitute τότε ἐπληρώθη (aorist passive) for the customary ἵνα/ὅπως with the subjunctive and refer the fulfillment quotation to 'Jeremiah the prophet' suggests a common redactional purpose in these two passages. In both passages the more circumspect τότε is appropriate to the dire circumstances in which Scripture is seen to be fulfilled: here in 27.9 the remorse and suicide of one of the Twelve following his betrayal of the messiah. But the particular relevance of Jeremiah in this context remains to be explored.

2. *The Source of Matthew's Quotation: Zechariah 11.12-13*

The primary source of Matthew's quotation in 27.9 is easily identifiable. In response to Judas Iscariot's question, 'What will you give me if I deliver him to you?' Matthew relates that τοῦς ἀρχιερεῖς... ἔστησαν αὐτῷ τριάκοντα ἀργύρια (26.14-15). The wording of the response, both in its description of the sum and its use of ἱστάναι (for שׁקל) with the sense of 'to weigh out money,'[1] clearly reflects LXX Zech. 11.12, καὶ ἔστησαν τὸν μισθόν μου τριάκοντα ἀργυροῦς [MT וישׁקלו את־שׂכרי שׁלשׁים כסף]. The thirty pieces of silver are not mentioned again until 27.3, 5-6, when the remorseful Judas brings them back in an effort to absolve himself of the blood-guilt that they entail.

In Zechariah 11 the 'shepherd of the flock doomed to slaughter' (11.4, 7) delivers up the sheep to destruction by symbolically annulling his covenant with them (11.9-11). He then confronts the false shepherds and demands the wages due him for his previous care of the flock. They weigh out for him thirty shekels of silver (11.12), the value of a slave (Exod. 21.32) or a woman (Lev. 27.4). Matthew's use of the ensuing verse may be set out as follows.

1. BAGD *s.v.* I.2.c prefers the sense 'to set, establish (a price)', although the frequency of LXX ἱστάναι for MT שׁקל (e.g. 2 Kgdms [Sam.] 14.26; 18.12; Job 6.2; 28.15; 31.6; Isa. 40.12; 46.6; Jer. 39[32].9, 10, etc.) favours the Hebraic meaning in the present context. Cf. Senior, *Passion Narrative*, p. 46; Gnilka, *Matthäusevangelium*, II, p. 391.

Mt. 27.9-10	Zech. 11.13
καὶ ἔλαβον τὰ τριάκοντα ἀργύρια,	(D) καὶ ἔλαβον τοὺς τριάκοντα ἀργυροῦς ואקחה שלשים הכסף
τὴν τιμὴν τοῦ τετιμημένου	(C) καὶ σκέψομαι εἰ δόκιμόν ἐστίν אדר היקר
ὃν ἐτιμήσαντο ἀπὸ υἱῶν Ἰσραήλ,	ὅν τρόπον ἐδοκιμάσθη ὑπὲρ αὐτῶν. אשר יקרתי מעליהם
καὶ ἔδωκαν αὐτὰ εἰς τὸν ἀγρὸν τοῦ κεραμέως, καθὰ συνέταξέν μοι κύριος.	(A) καὶ εἶπεν κύριος πρὸς μέ· וימר יהוה אלי (B) κάθες αὐτοὺς εἰς τὸ χωνευτήριον, השליכהו אל־היוצר (E) καὶ ἐνέβαλον αὐτοὺς εἰς τὸν οἶκον κυρίου εἰς τὸν χωνευτήριον ואשליך אתו בית יהוה אל־היוער

Matthew's text seems to reflect features found in both the MT and the LXX, leading Stendahl to conclude that he presents us with an independent rendering of the Hebrew.[1] For while Matthew has retained the major thematic components of the Lord's command (A),[2]

1. *School of St Matthew*, p. 124; so also Strecker, *Weg*, p. 78; Senior, *Passion Narrative*, p. 356.

2. Cf. Stendahl, *School of St Matthew*, p. 123. C.C. Torrey ('The Foundry of the Second Temple at Jerusalem', *JBL* 55 [1936], p. 252) and P. Benoit ('La Mort de Judas', in *Exégèse et Théologie* [Paris: Cerf, 1961], II, p. 351 n. 2) believe this element to derive instead from Jer. 32.6, 8 (see further below), whereas A. Baumstark ('Die Zitate des Mt.-Evangeliums aus dem Zwölfprophetenbuch', *Bib* 37 [1956], pp. 302-303) proposes that it represents a reading of ביד יהוה (i.e. at the command of...') for בית יהוה. But this last solution fails to consider the fact that even in the examples Baumstark himself cites (Exod. 38.21; Num. 7.8; 10.13) ביד designates intermediate human agency, and in this sense is not directly predicated of God (see BDB *s.v.* יד 5.d).

Matthew likely reworded the final clause in accordance with the καθὰ συνέταξε κύριος of, for example, LXX Exod. 9.12, although to see here a connection between LXX Zech. 11.13 χωνευτήριον and the furnace from which Moses in this passage takes ashes to produce a plague of boils (so Lindars, *NT Apologetic*, p. 121) is too 'ingenious' to be plausible. In any event, the same phrase is found in LXX Exod. 36.8, 12, 14, 28, 33; 37.20; 39.10; 40.19; Lev. 16.34 B*; 24.23; Num. 8.3, 22 AB^c; 9.5; 15.36; 17.26; 20.9, 27; 27.11; 31.31, 41. Cf. Josh. 24.31a. While the influence of this formula is confirmed by the presence of the valuation of the subject of the text (C), and his receipt of thirty silver coins (D), several features suggest that the Evangelist has adapted the quotation to the context of his narrative. These include: (1) the confusion of singular and plural verb forms; (2) the use of ἀργύρια for the LXX ἀργυροῦς; (3) the language of valuation; (4) the specification ἀπὸ υἱῶν Ἰσραήλ for the more general LXX ὑπὲρ αὐτῶν and MT מעליהם; and (5) the much-contested question of where the thirty pieces of silver were deposited (B, E).

In Zechariah the text begins with the first person singular subject καὶ ἔλαβον/ואקחה, although Matthew probably understood the Greek as a third person plural. The latter better suits the Matthaean context, with the temple priests as its immediate subjects—as does also the reading ἔδωκαν of 27.10 (A^c B* C L X Δ Θ 064 0133 f^1 f^{13} 𝔐 it vg cop) against the first person singular ἔδωκα (א B^{2vid} W 2174 *pc syr*).[1] By the same token, Matthew's ἀργύρια for the LXX ἀργυροῦς appears to reflect either ἀργύριον from Mk 14.11 or a simple editorial preference (Matthew 9×; Mark 1×; Luke 4×).[2] Again, the pleonastic τὴν τιμὴν τοῦ τετιμημένου[3] ὃν ἐτιμήσαντο departs from both MT and LXX traditions in emphasizing the estimation of the messiah's worth implied by this sum (i.e., as equivalent to that of a

καθά (only here in the NT), Matthew's inserted μοί is dependent upon Zech. 11.13a (so D.J. Moo, *The Old Testament in the Gospel Passion Narratives* [Sheffield: Almond Press, 1983], p. 197).

1. This may have resulted by assimilation to the ensuing μοι. See Stendahl, *School of St Matthew*, p. 125; Gundry, *Use of the OT*, p. 126; Lohmeyer and Schmauch, *Matthäus*, p. 378; Senior, *Passion Narrative*, p. 353 n. 17; Gnilka, *Matthäusevangelium*, II, p. 448 n. 29.

2. Mt. 27.15 substitutes the plural ἀργύρια for the singular ἀργύριον of Mk 14.11. Cf. Stendahl, *School of St Matthew*, p. 124 n. 1; Senior, 'Passion Narrative', p. 354. Note that in Matthew's Gospel ἀργύριον has consistent negative overtones, being associated in turn with the 'wicked and slothful servant' of 25.18, 27 [// Lk. 19.23]; Judas, 26.15 [// Mk 14.11]; 27.3, 5, 6, 9; and the bribe paid to the guards, 28.12, 15.

3. Whereas MT has אֶדֶר הַיְקָר ('magnificence of price'), Matthew's τετιμημένου vocalizes the consonantal text as הַיָּקָר ('the precious one') instead of הַיְקָר ('the price'), while τιμήν has the double sense of both 'price' and 'honour'. See C.C. Torrey, 'Foundry', p. 251; Stendahl, *School of St Matthew*, p. 125; Gundry, *Use of the OT*, p. 126; Senior, 'Passion Narrative', pp. 354-55; Moo, *Gospel Passion Narratives*, pp. 192-93; cf. JB, 'the sum at which the *precious* One was priced' (emphasis added).

slave),[1] while the concluding specification ἀπὸ υἱῶν Ἰσραήλ serves to focus responsibility for the betrayal that the money represents.[2]

By far the most problematic aspect of Matthew's use of Zech. 11.13, however, is his exploitation of the text so as to explain the return of the silver to the Temple and its ultimate use in purchasing a field. Since Wellhausen,[3] scholars have noted that Matthew's narrative seems to make use of two alternative textual variants from Zech. 11.13. According to the MT, the Lord commands the shepherd to 'Cast the money אל־היוצר', that is, 'to the potter', and so he throws the thirty shekels בית יהוה אל־היוצר.[4] The Syriac, however, with *bēth gazzā'*, seems to reflect a reading that has Zechariah's silver being cast not אל־היוצר, that is, 'to the potter', but rather אל־האוצר, 'to the treasury'.[5]

1. But this does not imply a low estimation of worth, as is commonly held. As J.S. Kloppenborg observes, 'in ancient economies, slaves were not insignificant properties...thirty shekalim is in fact a sizeable amount of money in first century currency' (personal communication).

2. According to Senior (*Passion Narrative*, p. 355 and n. 27), this latter alteration 'reflects Matthew's tendency to replace indefinite with definite subjects'. At the same time, similar expansion via the addition of בני ישראל is typical of the Palestinian targums (Baumstark, 'Zitate', p. 308), and thus may be here no more than an explanatory addition. Stendahl (*School of St Matthew*, p. 126 n. 1; followed by McConnell, *Law and Prophecy*, p. 133; and further discussion by Senior, *Passion Narrative*, p. 355 n. 28) takes ἀπό as equivalent to the partitive מן, meaning that '*some* of the sons of Israel'—specifically, the leaders and therefore not the whole people—are responsible for this estimation of the messiah.

3. J. Wellhausen, *Das Evangelium Matthaei* (Berlin: Georg Reimer, 1904), pp. 144-45. Although this work has not been available to me, the relevant passage is cited by Torrey, 'Foundry', p. 253; cf. Stendahl, *School of St Matthew*, p. 124. Wellhausen is followed by W.C. Allen, *A Critical and Exegetical Commentary on the Gospel According to St Matthew* (ICC; Edinburgh: T. & T. Clark, 1907), p. 288; M'Neile, *Matthew*, p. 408; Kilpatrick, *Origins*, p. 104; S.E. Johnson, 'The Gospel according to St Matthew', *IB*, VII, p. 592; Lohmeyer and Schmauch, *Matthäus*, p. 379; Klostermann, *Matthäusevangelium*, p. 219; Beare, *Matthew*, p. 256.

4. The LXX renders this as εἰς τὸν οἶκον κυρίου τὸ χωνευτήριον ('furnace, foundry'). For the second of these elements Aquila gives πλάστης ('potter'? cf. Rom. 9.20, 21), while targum reads אמרכלא ('[temple] official'); see also the text as cited by *b. Ḥul.* 92a, which has היוצר.

5. Torrey ('Foundry', pp. 255-57) rejects the theory of a double reading in Matthew, arguing that the יוצר of Zech. 11.13 was a 'moulder', whose responsibility was to melt down and mould the precious metals offered as gifts to the Temple. The readings of LXX (χωνευτήριον [foundry]), Aquila (πλάστης [moulder]), *Targ. Jon.* (אמרכלא [temple official]; on which see further pp. 257-58)

In Matthew's narrative Judas returns the money to the Temple:

> ἔστρεψεν τὰ τριάκοντα ἀργύρια... καὶ ῥίψας[1] τὰ ἀργύρια εἰς τὸν ναὸν ἀνεχώρησεν... οἱ δὲ ἀρχιερεῖς λαβόντες τὰ ἀργύρια εἶπαν· οὐκ ἔξεστιν βαλεῖν αὐτὰ εἰς τὸν κορβανᾶν... (27.3-6).

Judas's return of the money to the temple (εἰς τὸν ναόν) can be accounted for on the basis of a common MT/LXX tradition (בית יהוה/εἰς τὸν οἶκον κυρίου). It is, however, Matthew's portrayal of the authorities' concern not to place the money εἰς τὸν κορβανᾶν that possibly reflects a variant tradition represented by the Syriac. If so, then Matthew's treatment of the text here is similar to his treatment of Jer. 31.15 in 2.17-18: that while he acknowledges both variants, the circumstances he reports affirm one over the other, so that the money is not returned אל־האוצר ('to the treasury') but rather אל־היוצר ('to the potter').

Such a reading depends, in the first place, on understanding Matthew's κορβανᾶν as being equivalent to the putative האוצר of

and Vulgate (*statuarius* [maker of statues (!)]) are adduced in support of this view. But Torrey's argument only succeeds in demonstrating the appropriateness of the putative reading, since it bears out the connection to the Temple indicated by κορβανᾶς: 'Both in the Peshitta and Matthew the word אוצר was probably in the minds of the translators, even if it was not in the text' (Stendahl, *School of St Matthew*, p. 25). As for the reference to a potter, κεραμεύς is the normal LXX rendering of היוצר (cf. 2 Sam. 17.28; 1 Chron. 4.23; Ps. 2.9; Isa. 29.16; 30.14; 41.25; 45.9; Jer. 18.2, 3, 6; 19.1; Lam. 4.2). Gundry (*Use of the OT*, p. 123; followed by Moo, 'Tradition', p. 163 n. 41; *idem*, *Gospel Passion Narratives*, pp. 202-204) objects that the linguistic evidence does not support Torrey's interpretation and insists that the priests' refusal to accept the money into the treasury obviates any fulfillment of the putative variant. But this demands too rigid an understanding of Matthew's use of prophetic fulfillment (so Senior, *Passion Narrative*, p. 357 n. 34). Finally, Strecker (*Weg*, p. 76-82) argues that the literal sense of 'potter' in the quotation, as opposed to the expanded sense of 'treasury' in the narrative context, can be taken as evidence for the original independence of these elements, rather than for a double interpretation on the part of the Evangelist. See the response of D.P. Senior ('A Case Study in Matthean Creativity: Matthew 27.3-10', *BR* 19 [1974], pp. 26-36; *Passion Narrative*, pp. 370-73).

1. According to Lindars (*NT Apologetic*, p. 118 n. 1) and Senior (*Passion Narrative*, p. 382 n. 128), Matthew's choice of this verb could reflect the text of Aquila (καὶ εἶπε κύριος πρὸς μέ· ῥίψον αὐτὸ πρὸς τὸν πλάστην) or that of Symmachus (ῥίψον αὐτὸ εἰς τὸ χωνευτήριον).

Zechariah, in support of which may be cited Josephus, *War* 2.175.[1] Even here, however, the money itself, rather than its resting place, may be intended,[2] in which case the priests would simply be objecting to placing the tainted τιμὴ αἵματός together with other money dedicated (κορβᾶν) to God.[3]

Far more significant, however, is Matthew's adaptation of the phrase אל־היוצר. For he inserts the crucial element τὸν ἀγρὸν [τοῦ] into the fulfillment quotation (καὶ ἔδωκαν αὐτὰ εἰς τὸν ἀγρὸν τοῦ κεραμέως, καθὰ συνέταξέν μοι κύριος, 27.10), evidently in order to conform the whole more closely to the circumstances he reports: that the Temple authorities purchased τὸν ἀγρὸν τοῦ κεραμέως with Judas's silver (27.7). According to Baumstark, this addition represents '[a] purely formal targumic expansion' on the part of Matthew's source, whereby in place of the potter himself 'the plot of land that provides the clay for his work' is introduced.[4]

Baumstark provides examples from the Targums of similar expansions via the introduction of a genitive subordinate clause. In addition, he points out that this substitution of an abstract for a personal object finds a close parallel in LXX Zech. 11.13 (i.e. εἰς τὸν χωνευτήριον rather than πρὸς τὸν χωνευτήν, 'to the foundry man').[5] Wolff, on the other hand, considers Baumstark's thesis of an Aramaic Matthaean *Urtext*, behind which lay a Targum wherein Matthew's text of Zechariah was already present, 'unconvincing'.[6]

The reference to the 'field' almost certainly comes to the Evangelist from tradition.[7] For just as Matthew speaks of τὸν ἀγρὸν τοῦ κεραμέως εἰς ταφὴν τοῖς ξένοις called ἀγρὸς αἵματος ἕως τῆς

1. Josephus: τὸν ἱερὸν θησαυρόν, καλεῖται δὲ κορβωνᾶς. Cf. BAGD *s.v.* κορβανᾶς; K.H. Rengstorf, 'κορβᾶν, κορβανᾶς', *TWNT*, III, p. 860, pp. 864-65 (= *TDNT*, pp. 861, 865). Wolff (*Jeremia*, p. 160) notes that the usual LXX term for אוצר is θησαυρός, but never κορβανᾶς.

2. Cf. Albright and Mann, *Matthew*, p. 341.

3. As in Mk 7.10: ὅ ἐστιν Δῶρον; cf. Senior, *Passion Narrative*, pp. 385-86.

4. So already Zahn, *Matthäus*, p. 709.

5. Baumstark, 'Zitate', p. 309.

6. *Jeremia*, p. 163 n. 3.

7. Cf. Benoit, 'Mort de Judas', p. 352; P. Nepper-Christensen, *Das Matthäusevangelium: Ein judenchristliches Evangelium?* (Acta Theologica Danica, 1; Aarhus: Universitetsforlaget, 1958), pp. 160-61; and the non-Matthaean vocabulary noted by Kilpatrick, *Origins*, p. 45; Strecker, *Weg*, p. 77; van Tilborg, *Jewish Leaders*, p. 84.

σήμερον (27.7-8), so Acts 1.19 informs us of a location associated with Judas's death that was 'known to all the inhabitants of Jerusalem' and called Ἀκελδαμάχ, τουτ' ἔστιν χωρίον αἵματος.

The differing accounts of Judas's death according to Matthew and Luke are, of course, difficult to reconcile.[1] So their agreement on this point—including their joint testimony that such was common knowledge—is all the more significant. Presumably this was one of the details of 'messianic history' that the fulfillment quotations were meant to explain. Yet Matthew could hardly have inserted such a detail into the text of Zechariah simply on the basis of received tradition and then declared his conveniently emended text duly 'fulfilled'. Much less would he have been likely to ascribe the quotation as a whole to 'Jeremiah' without intending some identifiable reference to that prophet. Indeed, the difficulty involved in accounting for this ascription is itself a telling argument against the view that Matthew simply composed his narrative on the basis of certain OT texts!

Such an understanding, however, hardly brings us closer to discerning what Matthew intended by the quotation of Zech. 11.13 in 27.9-10, for even in its original context the meaning of Zech. 11.13 is almost entirely obscure.[2] Not least among the difficulties is that of explaining the presence of a 'potter' (היוצר is the *lectio difficilior* and therefore likely to be original) in the Temple precincts.[3] Presumably the salient feature for Matthew was the return of the thirty pieces of silver both to the Temple and to the potter (whatever the latter term means). But beyond these formal similarities, little thematic continuity between Zechariah and Matthew here seems evident. Furthermore,

1. See the foundational study by K. Lake, 'The Death of Judas', in F.J.F. Jackson and K. Lake (eds.), *The Beginnings of Christianity. Part I: The Acts of the Apostles* (London: Macmillan, 1933), V, pp. 22-30, which traces the attempts at harmonization in patristic literature.

2. Rabbinic literature takes the thirty pieces of silver to represent, *inter alia*, the few who worship God, a record of whose faith is deposited in the Temple (*Targ. Zech.* 11.13); the thirty precepts the messiah will teach the Gentiles (or Israel); or the thirty righteous men whom God maintains in the world (*b. Ḥul.* 92a; *Gen. R.* 98.9).

3. Gundry (*Use of the OT*, p. 124; followed by J.A. Upton, 'The Potter's Field and the Death of Judas', *Concordia Journal* 8 [1982], pp. 214-216) suggests: 'Perhaps it is best to think that the prophet was to throw the money to the potter who sold vessels for offerings of grain, wine, and oil in the Temple precincts', although this is a less plausible solution than that of Torrey cited above.

recourse to Zech. 11.12-13 fails to account either for the crucial reference to the 'field of blood' or for the mention of Jeremiah.

3. *The Source of Matthew's Quotation: 'Jeremiah'*

The question as to why Matthew ascribes this passage to Jeremiah when, in fact, he quotes from Zechariah, has generated a variety of attempted solutions. These may be set out as follows.

a. *Transcriptional Error*

The earliest of these attempted solutions appears in the textual apparatus to Mt. 27.9. For although the reading Ἰερεμίου is firmly attested by the consensus of, *inter alia*, the Alexandrian codices ℵ, B and L, the Byzantine A, W and Π, and the Western Latin tradition, as well as by the fact that this is without doubt the *lectio difficilior*, a few witnesses propose either Ζαχαρίου (22 syr^{hmg}) or Ἠσαΐου (21 lat^{1}). The former is readily explicable by the clear reference in the text to Zech. 11.13; the latter is probably best explained as a copyist's insertion of the only other name that Matthew employs with any frequency in his fulfillment formulae. A number of witnesses (Φ 33 157 lat^{a,b} syr^{s,p} cop^{bopt}) simply omit the name altogether, presumably because they consider it erroneous.[1] In the last analysis, however, the reading Ἰερεμίου best accounts for all the others as attempts to clarify an obscure reference. Conversely, since the allusion to Zechariah is obvious, it is virtually impossible to envisage any widespread insertion at a later date of a reference that caused such difficulties.

b. *Mental Error on the Part of Matthew*

The possibility that this is simply a mistake on the part of the Evangelist is one that commended itself first to Origen (see c, below), then to Eusebius (*Demonstratio Evangelica* 10.4.13) and Augustine (*De*

1. Augustine rejected this solution after careful consideration (*de Consensu Evangelistarum* 3.7.29 [*PL* 34.1174-75]. It is, however, championed by A.S. Lewis, *Light on the Four Gospels from the Sinai Palimpsest* (London: Williams, 1913), pp. 61-63 [cited in Gundry, *Use of the OT*, p. 125 n. 3]. On the basis of the Syriac text here and in 2.15 (naming Isaiah), Nepper-Christensen (*Matthäusevangelium*, p. 149 n. 46) proposes 'dass die keinen Prophetennamen enthaltenden Formulierungen in dem Sinne sekundär sein können, dass sie in einen früheren Gestalt einen Prophetennamen enthielten, der später gestrichen wurde, weil man gemeint hat, er sei verkehrt gewesen'.

Consensu Evangelistarum 3.7.30). It is likewise the view taken by a number of modern scholars. Stendahl, for example, concludes that 'the reference to Jeremiah is somewhat arbitrary and we had better take it to be a slip or rather a confusion of memory'.[1] Jeremias is more specific in assigning a cause for the error: 'This is probably a slip of memory occasioned by recollection of Jer. 32.9 (the purchase of the field)'.[2] According to Lindars, the error can be blamed on a previous exegete at some earlier stage of composition, and so Matthew, who 'had no interest in the connection with Jeremiah...may perhaps be forgiven for leaving the false attribution untouched'.[3]

In 2.17-18, however, as we have seen, Matthew is very deliberate about his use of Jeremiah. As Senior points out, the passage quoted 'shows evidence of receiving the author's close attention'.[4] This fact, coupled with the unusual fulfillment formula in both 2.17 and 27.9, makes it unlikely that Matthew was merely mistaken in his attribution.[5] Furthermore, since the prophecies of Zechariah have already

1. *School of St Matthew*, p. 123.

2. ''Ιερεμίας', *TWNT*, III, p. 220. Likewise, *inter alia*, Plummer, *Matthew*, p. 386; M'Neile, *Matthew*, pp. 407-408; Zahn, *Matthäus*, p. 708 (occasioned by Jer. 18.2-12; 19.1-15); B.T.D. Smith, *The Gospel according to St Matthew* (Cambridge: Cambridge University Press, 1927); Lagrange, *Matthieu*, pp. 515-16; J. Finegan, *Die Überlieferung der Leidens- und Auferstehungsgeschichte Jesu* (BZNW, 15; Giessen: Töpelmann, 1934), p. 26; K. Staab, *Das Evangelium nach Matthäus* (Würzburg: Echter Verlag, 1951), p. 152; Nepper-Christensen, *Matthäusevangelium*, p. 157; A.W. Argyle, *The Gospel according to Matthew: Commentary* (Cambridge: Cambridge University Press, 1963), p. 211; Schmid, *Matthäus*, p. 369; Klostermann, *Matthäusevangelium*, p. 219; H.M. Shires, *Finding the Old Testament in the New* (Philadelphia: Westminster Press, 1974), p. 17.

3. *NT Apologetic*, p. 119.

4. Senior, *Passion Narrative*, p. 367; cf. Stendahl, *School of St Matthew*, p. 125.

5. It can be shown, the evidence of 2.23 notwithstanding, that Matthew tends to be precise in his naming of sources. For whereas Mk 1.2-3 quotes Mal. 3.1 and Isa. 40.3 as a composite quotation ascribed as a whole to Isaiah, Mt. 3.3 carefully deletes the Malachi passage (inserting it instead at 11.10) so that the ascription to Isaiah, which he also takes over, is now rendered correct. In other words, Matthew's naming of sources is conscious, even if sometimes obscure.

The difficult textual situation of 13.35 could be taken as evidence to the contrary, for according to ℵ* Θ f^1 f^{13} 33 *et al.*, Matthew erroneously ascribes a passage from Psalms to Isaiah. But the insertion of 'Isaiah' is a scribal attempt to explain the reading διὰ τοῦ προφήτου (ℵ^c B C D K L W X Δ Π it^{mss} vg syr^{c,s,p,h} cop^{sa,bo} *et*

played a significant role in Matthew's Passion narrative (cf. 21.4-5 [Zech. 9.9]; 26.31 [Zech. 13.7) and since Zech. 11.12-13 has already been introduced in 26.15, it is hardly likely that the Evangelist would have confused his sources.

Alternative forms of the 'error' thesis are offered by Toy and Baumstark.[1] According to Toy, Matthew mistook Ζριου for Ιριου. According to Baumstark, Ἰερεμίου represents a misreading of the introductory formula ביד נביא [= διὰ τοῦ προφήτου] as ביר נביא [= διὰ Ἰερεμίου τοῦ προφήτου], in which יר would have served as an abbreviation of the prophet's name. But these are highly conjectural solutions that, in view of more soundly based approaches, hardly merit further attention.

c. *A Jeremiah Apocryphon*

According to Origen[2] and Jerome,[3] the source of Matthew's quotation in 27.9-10 is an apocryphal book wherein the passage is ascribed to Jeremiah. Strecker argues in favour of this thesis on the grounds that καθὰ συνέταξέν μοι κύριος and ἀπὸ υἱῶν Ἰσραήλ cannot be traced to any extant version of Zech. 11.13.[4]

Both of these expressions, however, as we have seen, are susceptible of alternative explanations. Indeed, whatever source Jerome was shown, according to Jeremias,

al.) by ascribing it to a more specific prophetic source. In 22.43 Matthew refers to Δαυὶδ ἐν πνεύματι, suggesting that this is the προφήτης to whom he was referring in 13.35 (so Stendahl, *School of St Matthew*, pp. 78, 118).

1. C.H. Toy, *Quotations in the New Testament* (New York: Charles Scribner's Sons, 1884), p. 71; Baumstark, 'Zitate', p. 301 n. 1.

2. *Comm. in Mt.*, ad 27.9 [*PG* 13.1770a]: 'Si quis autem potest scire, ostendat ubi sit scriptum; suspicor aut errorem esse Scripturae, et pro Zacharia positum Jeremiam, aut esse aliquam secretam Jeremiae scripturam in qua scribitur'.

3. *Comm. in Mt.*, ad 27.9-10 [*PL* 26.205b] (as cited in *TWNT*, III, p. 219 n. 4 [= *TDNT*, p. 218 n. 4]): 'Legei nuper in quodam Hebraico volumine, quod Nazaraenae sectae mihi Hebraeus obtulit, Jeremiae apocryphum, in quo haec ad verbum scripta reperi'. Also quoted, with tentative affirmation, by Grundmann, *Matthäus*, p. 551.

4. *Weg*, pp. 80-81, although he admits (pp. 76-77) the influence of Jer. 18.3 and LXX 39.9.

> This work was probably of Jewish-Christian origin, and arose out of a desire to have a text of Jeremiah containing the quotation from Zechariah erroneously ascribed to Jeremiah in Mt. 27.9.[1]

Therefore the creation of such a work by Jewish Christians to fill an obvious need is more plausible than its compilation prior to Matthew, for which some further explanation would have to be found.[2] Since almost the entire quotation can be traced to Zechariah, postulating such an additional source (apart, as we shall see, from canonical Jeremiah) is simply unnecessary.

d. *A 'Testimony' Ascribed to Jeremiah*

In the first volume of his *Testimonies*, J. Rendel Harris observed that the Syriac writer Bar Ṣalibi, in a series of testimonies to the Passion and betrayal of Christ, quotes both Zech. 11.12 and a text attributed to Jeremiah that matches 27.9-10. Although the quoted text conforms exactly to the Syriac version of Matthew 27, it does not, according to Harris, 'follow that it was originally taken from Matthew, for in the Syriac version the name of the prophet is wanting'.[3] Thus Matthew

1. Jeremias, ''Ἱερεμίας', *TWNT*, III, p. 219 [*TDNT*, pp. 218-19]. According to P. Vaccari ('Le versioni arabe dei Profeti', *Bib* 3 [1922], pp. 420-23), followed by Benoit ('La Mort de Judas', p. 351 n. 4), such an Apocryphon has apparently survived in Coptic, Ethiopic and Arabic, the last being perhaps the earliest. A Latin translation is supplied by A. Resch, *Agrapha: Aussercanonische Schrift-Fragmenta* (TU, 15; Leipzig: Hinrichs, 1906), pp. 317-18, cf. pp. 23-24; a German translation by Wolff, *Jeremia*, p. 165.

2. Resch (*Agrapha*, pp. 317-18), following Michaelis, postulates the existence of an 'altchristliche Jeremiabuch' (in addition to canonical Jeremiah), arguing that the expansions of the apocryphal text betray no dependence on Mt. 27.9—indeed that the text's omission of τοῦ τετιμημένου ὃν ἐτιμήσαντο argues against such dependence. Similar is Lohmeyer's thesis (*Matthäus*, pp. 378-79) that the patristic sources give evidence of a pre-Matthaean text already adapted from Zech. 11.13 yet ascribed to Jeremiah on the analogy of Jer. 32.1–33.13. Lohmeyer (p. 380) further proposes that the sentence 'they paid him thirty pieces of silver' (26.15) derives from the same apocryphal source.

3. *Testimonies* (Cambridge: Cambridge University Press, 1916), I, p. 59. Using an argument similar to that of Resch (see previous note), Harris (*Testimonies*, p. 68) interprets the textual variations between the Greek of Mt. 27.9-10 and the similar quotation ascribed to Jeremiah in the Armenian translation of Irenaeus's *Proof of Apostolic Preaching*, §81 (Patrologia Orientalis 12, pp. 718-19) as evidence that Irenaeus's text is not dependent on Matthew. Also subscribing to the testimony explanation are J.A. Findlay, *Jesus in the First Gospel* (London: Hodder &

would have employed a Greek form of the testimony source preserved in Syriac, quoting first the Zechariah text (at 26.15) and then that ascribed to Jeremiah. The 'error', in other words, derives from a testimony-book rather than from the Evangelist.

This solution, however, merely re-poses at an earlier stage the dual problem of why the texts of Zechariah and Jeremiah were brought together in the first place, and why the author ascribed the final product to 'Jeremiah'. Furthermore, as Benoit succinctly points out with regard to the evidence of Bar Ṣalibi:

> Such collections are hypothetical, and in this particlar instance the testimonies that are called upon to demonstrate this prior combination are too late for us to be able to claim to reconstruct a literary source for Matthew.[1]

e. *General Reference to the Prophetic Corpus*

According to one talmudic tradition (*b. B. Bat.* 14b [*Baraita*]), the book of Jeremiah is to be placed at the head of the latter prophets: 'Our Rabbis taught: The order of the prophets is, Joshua, Judges, Samuel, Kings, Jeremiah, Ezekiel, Isaiah and the Twelve Minor Prophets'. This tradition is confirmed by an Aramaic list in Greek transliteration found in the Byrennios MS of the Didache, which mentions the prophets in the following order: Jeremiah, the Twelve, Isaiah, Ezekiel, Daniel.[2]

Stoughton, [1925]), pp. 21-22; *idem*, 'The First Gospel and the Book of Testimonies', in H.G. Wood (ed.), *Amicitiae Corolla: A Volume of Essays Presented to James Rendel Harris, D. Litt., on the Occasion of his Eightieth Birthday* (London: University of London, 1933), p. 65; T.H. Robinson, *The Gospel of Matthew* (New York: Doubleday, 1928), p. 225; F.F. Bruce, 'The Book of Zechariah and the Passion Narrative', *BJRL* 43 (1960–61), p. 341; and, tentatively, N. Hillyer, 'Matthew's Use of the Old Testament', *EvQ* 36 (1964), p. 22.

1. 'Mort de Judas', p. 352; cf. n. 1; so Lagrange, *Matthieu*, p. 516.

2. So J. P. Audet, 'A Hebrew-Aramaic List of Books of the Old Testament in Greek Transcription', *JTS* NS 1 (1950), p. 136; C.C. Torrey, 'The Aramaic Period of the Nascent Christian Church', *ZNW* 44 (1952-53), p. 222. Similarly, C.D. Ginsburg (*Introduction to the Massoretico-critical Edition of the Hebrew Bible* [London: Trinitarian Bible Society, 1897], pp. 4-6) lists three Hebrew MSS that place the books in the order Jeremiah, Ezekiel and Isaiah, and two more that have Jeremiah immediately before Isaiah (cited by J. Carmignac, 'Pourquoi Jérémie est-il mentionné en Matthieu 16,14?', in G. Jeremias (ed.), *Tradition und Glaube: Das*

Taking this approach, H.F.D. Sparks contends that Matthew 'regarded Jeremiah as the typical prophet... [because] he was accustomed to a Canon of the later Prophets in which the book of Jeremiah stood first'.[1] While Sparks accepts this conclusion for Mt. 16.14, Sutcliffe applies it to 27.9, and so argues that since the name of Jeremiah 'stood at the head of the later prophets...its mention was equivalent to writing "in the prophets"'.[2] Even apart from the fact that the order represented in these lists 'varies widely...from all canons known to us',[3] this theory is undercut by the observation that when in 2.23 and 26.56 Matthew refers to the prophets in general, he does so without need of recourse to a particular prophet's name. Furthermore, since Matthew does not find it necessary to name the source of his quotations in 1.22, 2.5, 2.15 or 21.4, the fact that he does so here favours a more substantial redactional motive —all the more so if a similarly unitary purpose can be discerned behind the references to Isaiah. In addition, since the one other ascription of a formula quotation to 'Jeremiah' (in 2.17-18) is clearly to the canonical work of the prophet, a more general reference here seems highly improbable.

f. *Confused Identification*

M. Gaster proposed that the association of a text from Zechariah with the name of Jeremiah results from Matthew's confusion ('Verwechslung') of the death of Zechariah (ben Jehoiada) by stoning (e.g. 2 Chron. 24.21; *b. Giṭ.* 57b; *b. Sanh.* 96b) with the similar death of Jeremiah (*Par. Jer.* 9.21-32; *Vit. Proph.* 2.1).[4] Of course, this

frühe Christentum in seiner Umwelt (Festgabe K.G. Kuhn) [Göttingen: Vandenhoeck & Ruprecht, 1971], p. 290).

1. H.F.D. Sparks, 'St Matthew's References to Jeremiah', *JTS* NS 1 (1950), p. 155.

2. E.F. Sutcliffe, 'Matthew 27,9', *JTS* 3 (1952), p. 227. So also Str–B, I, p. 1030; P. Gaechter, *Das Matthäusevangelium* (Innsbruck: Tyrolia, 1963), p. 901; Soares Prabhu, *Formula Quotations*, p. 53-54. This solution apparently originates with J. Lightfoot, *Horae Hebraicae et Talmudicae Impensae... In Evangelium S. Matthaei* (1658), p. 308 (cited in Carmignac, 'Jérémie', p. 287 n. 15).

3. Stendahl, *School of St Matthew*, p. 123 n. 3. Carmignac ('Jérémie', p. 290 n. 27) cites a series of canonical lists from Origen, Jerome, Melito of Sardis, Epiphanius and early copies of the LXX, all of which have Jeremiah following Isaiah.

4. M. Gaster, *Studies and Texts in Folklore, Magic, Medieval Romance, Hebrew Apocrypha, and Samaritan Archaeology* (London: Maggs, 1925–28), II,

conflation depends in turn on the prior identification of ben Jehoiada the martyr with Zechariah ben Berechiah, specified in Zech. 1.1 as the author of that work. But Matthew has already made that association in 23.35: 'the blood of Zechariah the son of Berechiah, whom you murdered between the sanctuary and the altar'.[1]

Whether Matthew's references to the stoning of the prophets (21.35, 23.37) contain allusions to the fate of Jeremiah will be investigated later. It is difficult, however, to see what purpose such an allusion would serve in the context of Matthew 27. For the tradition of Jeremiah's death by stoning sees him as a martyr, which is the very opposite of Judas, to whom the fulfillment quotation refers. Moreover, this explanation does nothing to clarify those features of Matthew's text that cannot be traced to Zech. 11.13.

g. *Thematic Reference*

More compelling is the suggestion of van Segbroeck that Matthew's references to Jeremiah (or Isaiah) are not meant to evoke any one text or literary source; rather, that the Evangelist intends a wider theological or thematic allusion:

> does he simply wish to point out that the cited text has a certain affinity with the person named, yet without ascribing to him the quotation's literary paternity? In other words, is it not simply a matter of indicating the spirit in which the text is to be read?. . . Matthew does not mean to refer in the first instance to a literary source, but rather to his 'theological' source.[2]

Although van Segbroeck does not explore the possible associations such a reference to 'Jeremiah' might entail, the question invites further discussion. But it must also be asked whether a reference to the 'spirit' in which the passage is to be read necessarily precludes any more specific reference. The definite textual reference in 2.17-18, linked to 27.9-10 by a common fulfillment formula, suggests rather that here too Matthew had an actual text or combination of texts in mind.

pp. 1292-93. On the death of Jeremiah, see Wolff, *Jeremia*, pp. 89-95 (with a response to Gaster, pp. 89-90).

1. On the identification/confusion of the two, see S.H. Blank, 'The Death of Zechariah in Rabbinic Literature', *HUCA* 12-13 (1937–38), pp. 327-46.

2. 'Scandale', p. 371; cf. Soares Prabhu, *Formula Quotations*, p. 54; Rothfuchs, *Erfüllungszitate*, pp. 43-44.

h. *Topographical Reference*

P. Benoit believes that since textual links to Jeremiah in Matthew 27 (e.g. chs. 18–19 and 32) are tenuous and evidence for specific literary sources weak, the one unifying factor in this 'strange amalgam of various biblical texts' is 'topographical folklore'. He argues, not implausibly, that this fulfillment quotation refers to a popular tradition that linked the name of Jeremiah with the 'Potter's Quarter' (cf. Jer. 19.2) located at the confluence of the Kidron, Tyropoeon and Hinnom Valleys, with which was already associated the Temple foundry (hence the Matthaean wordplay), a common cemetery, 'and above all an atmosphere of dread and malediction, of impiety and damnation' evoked by the name 'Topheth'. All such associations would have prepared the way for locating Judas' 'Field of Blood' there, in support of which the scriptural texts would later have been adduced.[1] But even if Benoit's analysis should prove correct on purely tradition-historical grounds, the association of Jeremiah with a particular locale is not sufficient to explain the insertion of the prophet's name into the fulfillment formula, for which some more substantial explanation must yet be sought.

i. *Canonical Jeremiah*

If a reference to the canonical book(s) of Jeremiah is intended, 27.9-10 would provide a further example of a mixed quotation in Matthew's Gospel.[2] As is already evident, however, this quotation is singular in the obscurity of its components.

1. *Jeremiah 18.1-2 and/or 32.6-9.* The most widely-held view in modern scholarship is that Matthew intended to refer the reader to Jer. 18.1-2 and/or 32.6-9.[3] In Jer. 18.1-2 the Lord commands

1. 'Mort de Judas', pp. 352-59; cf. Zahn, *Matthäus*, p. 709.

2. Other instances include Mt. 11.10 // Mk 1.2 (Mal. 3.1 + Exod. 23.20 [+ Isa. 40.3 in Mark]; see Stendahl, *School of St Matthew*, pp. 49-53); Mt. 21.5 (Isa. 62.11 + Zech 9.9); and Mt. 21.13 // Mk 11.17 (Isa. 56.7 + Jer. 7.11).

3. So E. Hühn, *Die alttestamentlichen Citate und Reminiscenzen im Neuen Testament* [= *Die messianischen Weissagungen des israelitischjudischen Volkes bis zu den Targumim*, II] (Tübingen: Mohr [Paul Siebeck], 1900), p. 36; W. Dittmar, *Vetus Testamentum in Novo: Die alttestamentlichen Parallelen des Neuen Testament im Wortlaut mit der Urtexte und der Septuaginta. 1. Hälfte: Evangelien und Apostelgeschichte* (Göttingen: Vandenhoeck & Ruprecht, 1899), pp. 66-67; Allen, *Matthew*, pp. lxii, 289; C.G. Montefiore, *The Synoptic Gospels* (London:

Jeremiah to 'go down to the house of the potter [בית היוצר = εἰς οἶκον τοῦ κεραμέως]' to hear his word. There the Lord uses the example of the potter and his clay as a metaphor for his own sovereign right to deal freely with Israel according to the nation's obedience or rebellion (18.5-11; cf. Rom. 11.20-24). In Jer. 32.6-9 Jeremiah recounts the redemption of his ancestral patrimony, a field at Anathoth. He pays his cousin Hanamel seventeen silver shekels for the property, then seals the deed of purchase in a clay jar (בכלי־חרש = ἀγγεῖον ὀστράκινον) as a testimony for the future (32.9-15).[1] The coincidence of a potter's house and a potter's vessel in the respective passages is thought

Macmillan, 1927), II, p. 342; Torrey, 'Foundry', pp. 250, 252; *idem*, *Documents*, pp. 86-88; Johnson, 'Matthew', p. 593; Atkinson, *The Christian's Use of the OT*, pp. 86-87; Stendahl, *School of St Matthew*, p. 122; Lindars, *NT Apologetic*, p. 120 (at a pre-Matthaean stage); J.C. Fenton, *The Gospel of St Matthew* (Harmondsworth: Penguin Books, 1963), p. 432; Schniewind, *Matthäus*, p. 265; McConnell, *Law and Prophecy*, p. 132; Rothfuchs, *Erfüllungszitate*, pp. 84-86, 175; Albright and Mann, *Matthew*, p. 341; F.V. Filson, *A Commentary on the Gospel according to St Matthew* (London: A. & C. Black, 1971), p. 288; Klostermann, *Matthäusevangelium*, p. 219; Strecker, *Weg*, p. 77; Hill, *Matthew*, p. 349; Schweizer, *Matthäus*, p. 329; Beare, *Matthew*, p. 526; S.T. Lachs, *A Rabbinic Commentary on the New Testament: The Gospel of Matthew, Mark, and Luke* (Hoboken, NJ: Ktav; New York: Anti-defamation League of the B'nai B'rith, 1987), p. 423; Holladay, *Jeremiah*, II, p. 94. And indirectly (i.e. in association with the testimonia hypothesis) Robinson, *Matthew*, p. 225; Bruce, 'Zechariah and the Passion Narrative', p. 341. Cf. Grundmann, *Matthäus*, p. 551.

Jer. 32 alone is credited by Tasker, *Matthew*, pp. 258-59 (against his earlier citation [*The Old Testament in the New Testament* (London: SCM Press, 1954), p. 46] of Jer. 18.3); O'Rourke, 'Fulfillment Texts', p. 401; E. Haenchen, *Der Weg Jesu: Eine Erklärung des Markus-Evangeliums und der kanonischen Parallelen* (Berlin: Töpelmann, 1966), p. 516; Lohmeyer and Schmauch, *Matthäus*, p. 379; A. Descamps, 'Rédaction et christologie dans le récit matthéen de la Passion', in Didier (ed.), *L'évangile selon Matthieu*, p. 389; Soares Prabhu, *Formula Quotations*, p. 53; Wolff, *Jeremia*, pp. 164-66; Schlatter, *Matthäus*, p. 770. Augustine (*De Consensu Evangelistarum* 3.7.31) also proposed a reference to Jer. 32 as an alternative solution.

1. Curiously, the same contextual dislocation as obtained earlier with regard to Jer. 31.15 in Mt. 2.17-18 is operative in this instance, for whereas the field and purchase deed serve as signs of hope and return from exile in Jer. 32, their reappropriation by Matthew (if substantiated) is in quite an opposite sense. Cf. Wolff, *Jeremia*, p. 166.

sufficient to account for their collocation with Zechariah 11 in the mind of the Evangelist.[1]

But neither Jer. 18.1-2 nor Jer. 32.6-9 is entirely satisfactory as the text for Matthew's quotation in 27.9-10. As Gundry succinctly notes, 'In Jer. 18 a potter is mentioned, but no field; in Jer. 32 a field, but no potter'.[2] Torrey solves this difficulty by having Matthew identify Hanamel of Jeremiah 32 with the potter of Jeremiah 18, since the deed of purchase is placed into a potter's vessel.[3] But there is no obvious warrant for connecting either Hanamel or the 'earthen vessel' with the potter or a 'potter's field'.[4] Yet both the 'potter' and the 'field' are essential if a link to Matthew is to be demonstrated—the one providing a verbal similarity, the other supplying the essential element lacking from Zech. 11.13.

2. *Jeremiah 19.1-13*. A number of commentators have proposed Jer. 19.1-13 as the source of Matthew's reference to Jeremiah.[5] Here

1. F. Vouga ('La seconde passion de Jérémie', *LumVie* 32, 165 [1983], p. 75) proposes that Matthew refers the potter's destruction of the faulty vessel (Jer. 18.2-3) to the crucifixion, 'et probablement aussi, par télescopage, la destruction du Temple', seeing the potter's moulding of a new pot as a sign of 'la disqualification d'Israël et de ses prophètes' and the universal enfranchisement of the disciples consequent upon Jesus' death. But this demands too much of an already tentative allusion.

2. *Use of the OT*, p. 124.

3. Torrey, 'Foundry', p. 352. Cf. Lindars, *NT Apologetic*, p. 120; Stendahl, *School of St Matthew*, p. 122.

4. Cf. Gundry, *Use of the OT*, p. 124; Lagrange (*Matthieu*, p. 517): 'Expliquer la pensée de Mt. d'après le champs acheté par Jérémie en figure du retour de la captivité, c'est fantaisie pure'.

5. Among the earliest is A. Edersheim, *The Life and Times of Jesus the Messiah* (London: Longmans, Green, 1883), II, p. 596, followed by Plummer, *Matthew*, p. 386 (with 18.2); Gundry, *Use of the OT*, pp. 124-25; O.L. Cope, *Matthew: A Scribe Trained for the Kingdom of Heaven* (CBQMS, 5; Washington: Catholic Biblical Association, 1976), pp. 88-89; Senior, *Passion Narrative*, pp. 359-61; J.P. Meier, *The Vision of Matthew: Christ, Church, and Morality in the First Gospel* (New York: Paulist Press, 1979), p. 195 n. 234; *idem*, *Matthew*, p. 339; F. Manns, 'Un midrash chrétien: Le récit de la mort de Judas', *RevScRel* 54 (1980), p. 202 (19.4 with 32.10-14); Upton, 'Potter's Field', pp. 216-17; D.J. Moo, 'Tradition and Old Testament in Mt. 27.3-10', in R.T. France and D. Wenham (eds.), *Gospel Perspectives*. III. *Studies in Midrash and Historiography* (Sheffield: JSOT Press, 1983), p. 159-60; *idem*, *Gospel Passion Narratives*, pp. 195-96;

the Lord commands Jeremiah to 'Go, buy a potter's earthen flask [בקבק יוער חרש = βικὸν πεπλασμένον ὀστράκινον]' and to lead the chief priests and elders into the Hinnom Valley at the entry of the Potsherd Gate, there to proclaim to them the word of the Lord. Jeremiah then proclaims a word of judgment against the kings of Judah and the inhabitants of Jerusalem because, in addition to their idolatry, 'they have filled this place with the blood of innocents'. As a result, he says, 'this place shall no longer be called Topheth, or the Valley of the son of Hinnom, but the Valley of Slaughter' (19.6). Having specified in 19.2 that the valley is τὸ πολυάνδριον υἱῶν τῶν τέκνων αὐτων, the LXX adds the explanation that its name will no longer be Διάπτωσις καὶ Πολυάνδριον υἱοῦ 'Εννομ, ἀλλ' ἤ Πολυάνδριον τῆς σφαγῆς. Finally, the Lord commands: 'You shall break the flask...[for] so will I break this people and this city, as one breaks a potter's vessel. . . Men shall bury in Topheth because there will be no place else to bury' (19.10-11).

This passage offers several close parallels to Matthew's narrative. First, while there is no mention of a specific 'field', the key term היוצר is present, providing the essential verbal link to Zech. 11.13.[1] Secondly, the locations in question derive their respective significance from their use as burial places (LXX πολυάνδριον).[2] As a result,

Menken, 'References to Jeremiah', pp. 10-11.

A reference to all three of Jer. 18, 19, and 32 is favoured by Benoit, 'Mort de Judas', p. 349; *idem*, *L'évangile selon Saint Matthieu* (Paris: Cerf, 1950), p. 157; Goulder, *Midrash and Lection*, pp. 446-47; Green, *Matthew*, p. 218-19; J.D.G. Dunn, *Unity and Diversity in the New Testament: An Inquiry into the Character of Earliest Christianity* (London: SCM Press; Philadelphia: Westminster Press, 1977), pp. 93, 96; G. Maier, *Matthäus-Evangelium* (Neuhausen: Hänssler, 1980), II, pp. 423-24; Bonnard, *Matthieu*, p. 395; Vouga, 'Seconde passion', pp. 74-75; Gnilka, *Matthäusevangelium*, II, pp. 447-49. J.W. Doeve (*Jewish Hermeneutics in the Synoptic Gospels and Acts* [Assen: Van Gorcum, 1954], pp. 185-86) sees a reference here to Jer. 19, 26 and 32.

1. Note, however, that the LXX paraphrases יוצר as πεπλασμένος; cf. Moo, *Gospel Passion Narratives*, p. 196.

2. Senior (*Passion Narrative*, pp. 388-89) draws attention to the final phrase of MT Jer. 19.11, 'Men shall bury in Topheth because there will be no place else to bury', as a key factor in suggesting the appropriateness of Jer. 19 to the Evangelist. On the LXX rendering of this passage, see W. McKane, *A Critical and Exegetical Commentary on Jeremiah*. I. *Introduction and Commentary on Jeremiah I-XXV* (Edinburgh: T. & T. Clark, 1986), pp. 444-46. In addition, compare with Mt. 27.7 (εἰς ταφὴν τοῖς ξένοις) the burial of Uriah in Jer. 26[33].23: καὶ ἔρριψεν αὐτὸν

thirdly, whereas both were formerly associated with potters, they now carry names connoting bloodshed ('Valley of Slaughter'; 'Field of Blood').[1] Fourthly, the prophetic action in both cases involves interaction with the chief priests and elders of the people. Fifthly, and most significantly, judgment is pronounced in both instances against the shedding of 'innocent blood'—judgment which, sixthly, anticipates destruction on Jerusalem as a whole.[2]

While the first three points are self-evident, the final three require more detailed examination. Matthew characteristically designates the opponents of Jesus as οἱ ἀρχιερεῖς καὶ οἱ πρεσβύτεροι [τοῦ λαοῦ] (21.23; 26.3, 47; 27.1, 3, 12, 20; 28.11-12; cf. 16.21; 26.57; 27.41). He arrives at this formula either by inserting οἱ πρεσβύτεροι into his Markan source (e.g. 26.3 [// Mk 14.1]; 27.12, 20 [// Mk 15.3, 11]; cf. 27.41 [// Mk 15.31) or by deleting Mark's third group, οἱ γραμματεῖς (e.g. 21.23 [// Mk 11.27]; 26.47 [// Mk 14.43]; 27.1 [// Mk 15.1]).[3] More specifically, although Luke refers once to τὸ πρεσβυτέριον τοῦ λαοῦ (22.66), the fuller designation πρεσβύτεροι τοῦ λαοῦ is unique to Matthew (21.23; 26.3, 47; 27.1).[4]

εἰς τὸ μνῆμα υἱῶν λαοῦ αὐτοῦ = וישלך את־נבלתו אל־קברי בני העם.

1. Matthew could have modeled 27.8 on the wording of Jer. 19.6 as follows (with the Gospel text in brackets): διὰ τοῦτο [διὸ] ἰδοῦ ἡμέραι ἔρχονται, [ἕως σήμερον], λέγει κύριος, καὶ οὐ κληθήσεται [ἐκλήθη] τῷ τόπῳ τούτῳ... [ὁ ἄγρος ἐκεῖνος] Πολυάνδριον τῆς σφαγῆς [ἀγρὸς αἵματος] (so Senior, *Passion Narrative*, p. 361, noting that a comparison of the two texts must allow for their different temporal perspectives; cf. Green, *Matthew*, p. 219).

2. That Matthew intended a verbal parallel or word-play between the death of Ἰούδας and Jeremiah's polemic against the ἄνδρες Ἰούδα (LXX 19.2) who will be buried in Topheth is unlikely. The contention of Manns ('Midrash chrétien', p. 203) that a common 'allusion à la maison de Juda' links 'la fin de Judas' with Zech. 11 (11.14; the 'house of Judah' [although Manns cites this as 11.3]), Jer. 19 (v. 4; the 'kings of Judah'), and Jer. 32 (v. 12; היהודים), is tenuous at best.

3. Matthew is inconsistent in the latter regard (e.g. 16.21 // Mk 8.31; 26.57 // Mk 14.53) and frequently pairs Φαρισαῖοι καὶ γραμματεῖς as opponents (12.38; 15.1; cf. 5.20), particularly with the telling epithet ὑποκριταί (23.2, 13, 15, 23, 25, 27, 29), indicating that he is not motivated by any deference to scribes (cf. 13.52)!

4. Cf. Senior ('Passion Narrative', p. 351 n. 29), who observes that whereas elsewhere in Matthew the Pharisees and others 'represent a united front of opposition to Jesus... within the passion narrative the role of opposition falls to the Priests and the Elders of the people', thereby presenting 'the enemies of Jesus as representatives of official Judaism and of the Jewish people'. Again, 'because the events of the Passion are connected with Jerusalem, the designation of the enemies of Jesus shifts

Of the ten instances of this phrase in the LXX, only two occur in conjunction with 'priests': Jer. 19.1 and 1 Macc. 7.33.[1] Any connection between Matthew and 1 Macc. 7.33, however, is unlikely, for 1 Macc. 7.33 has to do with Nicanor's treachery against Judas (!) Maccabaeus.[2] Jeremiah, on the other hand, leads forth into the Hinnom Valley ἀπὸ τῶν πρεσβυτέρων τοῦ λαοῦ καὶ ἀπὸ (τῶν πρεσβυτέρων A) τῶν ἱερέων (MT ומזקני חעם ומזקני הכהנים), to which may be compared Mt. 27.1, πάντες οἱ ἀρχιερεῖς καὶ οἱ πρεσβυτέροι τοῦ λαοῦ (cf. 27.3 τοῖς ἀρχιερεῦσιν καὶ πρεσβυτέροις).[3] Both in Jeremiah 19 and in Matthew 27, therefore, the two groups share the same role: that of opponents to the Lord's prophet (cf. Jer. 18.18).

Furthermore, the theme of 'innocent' or 'righteous blood' is prominent in Matthew's Gospel.[4] In the diatribe of Matthew 23 the Evangelist invokes 'the blood of the prophets' (23.30; cf. Q 11.47) and 'all the righteous blood (πᾶν αἷμα δίκαιον) shed on earth, from the blood of righteous Abel (τοῦ αἵματος Ἄβελ τοῦ δικαίου) to the blood of Zechariah' (23.35, expanding Q 11.50-51). In 23.35, in fact, he coordinates the present passive participle ἐκχυννόμενον (cf. Lk. 11.50 ἐκκεχυμένον, perfect passive) with the words of institution αἷμα...ἐκχυννόμενον in Mt. 26.28 (cf. Mk 14.24 //

from the teaching group... to the Priests and Elders' who are based there (*Passion Narrative*, p. 376 n. 108).

1. Cf. Exod. 17.5; 19.7; Num. 11.16, 24; Ruth 4.4; 3 Kgdm 12.24; Isa. 3.14; 1 Macc. 12.35. For their role in Matthew, see Gnilka, *Matthäusevangelium*, II, p. 216: 'Für sie ist characteristisch, daß sie in der Passionsgeschichte in den Vordergrund tritt und so als der Hauptinitiator im Vorgehen gegen Jesus in das Blickfeld rückt (vgl. 26,3.47; 27,1.3.12.20; 28.11f.).'

2. 1 Macc. 7.33: καὶ ἐξῆλθον ἀπὸ τῶν ἱερέων ἐκ τῶν ἁγίων καὶ ἀπὸ τῶν πρεσβυτέρων τοῦ λαοῦ ἀσπάσασθαι εἰρηνικῶς.

3. Matthew's specification that these are '*chief* priests' could depend upon LXX, MT, or, as seems most likely, his Markan source (e.g. 15.1, 3, 10, 11, 31, etc.). The phrase πρεσβύτεροι τῶν ἱερέων occurs elsewhere only in 4 Kgdm 19.2 and Isa. 37.2.

4. The shedding of innocent blood is among the most heinous of crimes in the OT; see Lohmeyer and Schmauch, *Matthäus*, p. 375 n. 3. Matthew's treatment of this theme no doubt builds upon, and is rendered all the more significant by the widespread use of, the 'blood of Christ' motif in the early Christian community to signify the (atoning) death of the messiah; see E. Löhse, *Märtyrer und Gottesknecht: Untersuchungen zur urchristlichen Verkündigung vom Sühntod Jesu Christi* (FRLANT, NS 46; Göttingen: Vandenhoeck & Ruprecht, 1963), pp. 138-41.

Lk. 22.20) to suggest that the shed blood of this 'prophet' too is innocent. Likewise, the theme of innocent blood is central to 27.3-10, for it is the priests' refusal to accept the τιμὴ αἵματος (27.6) and their subsequent purchase of the ἀγρὸς αἵματος that calls forth the fulfillment quotation under discussion.[1] Finally, ironically echoing the words of Judas (ἥμαρτον παραδοὺς αἷμα ἀθῷον, 27.4),[2] Pilate declares ἀθῷός εἰμι ἀπὸ τοῦ αἵματος τούτου,[3] to which the crowd replies τὸ αἷμα αὐτοῦ ἐφ' ἡμᾶς (27.24-25).

In Jer. 19.3-4 the prophet declares that the people and 'kings of Judah...have filled this place with the blood of innocents (ἔπλησεν τὸν τόπον τοῦτον αἱμάτων ἀθῴων [MT דם נקים])'. Although this expression is by no means unique to Jeremiah, its presence in Mt. 27.4 (αἷμα ἀθῷον) and nowhere else in the NT can be taken as yet one more indication of Matthew's indebtedness to Jeremiah 19.[4]

1. Cf. Senior (*Passion Narrative*, p. 386): 'The intertwining notion of innocent blood and the price of blood is one of the key structural supports which carries the account to its completion'.

2. ἀθῷον ℵ A B* C K W X Δ Π f^{1} f^{13} 33 892 1241 syr^{p,h,hgr} cop^{sams,boms} Origen, Eusebius, etc. δίκαιον B^{2mg} L Θ it^{pt} vg syr^{pal} cop^{sa,bo} Origen, Cyprian, etc. τοῦ δικαίου syr^{s} Diatessaron^{1}. Being both early and widespread, 'the weight of the external evidence here is strongly in support of ἀθῷον' (*TCGNT in loc.*).

3. Or possibly, τοῦ δικαίου τούτου (ℵ K L W Π f^{1} f^{13} 33 892 1241 cop^{bo} etc.) or τούτου τοῦ δικαίου (A Δ 1230 it^{mss} syr^{p,pal} etc.). Cf. J.A. Fitzmyer, 'Anti-Semitism and the Cry of "All the People" (Mt. 27.25)', *TS* 26 (1965), p. 668 ('Pilate's action and words allude to Dt. 21.1-9 and are clearly a theologoumenon to express his religious innocence in the blood to be shed [cf. Ps. 26.6; 73.13]'); and further, W. Trilling, *Das wahre Israel: Studien zur Theologie des Matthäus-Evangeliums* (Munich: Kösel, 1964), pp. 69-70.

4. Cf. (in most instances representing the same Hebrew phrase) LXX Deut. 27.25; 1 Kgdms 19.5; 25.26, 31; 2 Kgdms 3.28; 3 Kgdms 2.5; 4 Kgdms 21.16; 24.4 [2×]; 2 Chron. 36.5d [2×]; Est. 8.12e; Ps. 93.21; 105.38; Jer. 2.34; 7.6; 19.4; 22.3, 17; 33.15; 1 Macc. 1.37; 2 Macc. 1.8; cf. Sus. 46. Also Philo, *Spec. Leg.* 1.5.204; *T. Zeb.* 2.2; *T. Levi* 16.3; *Prot. Jas.* 14.1, 23.3. Note that the expression is more frequent in Jeremiah than in any other single work (cf. Thompson, *Jeremiah*, p. 278 n. 25; McKane, *Jeremiah*, p. 452).

W.C. van Unnik ('The Death of Judas in Saint Matthew's Gospel', in M.H. Shepherd and E.C. Hobbs [eds.], *Gospel Studies in Honor of Sherman Elbridge Johnson* [ATR Supplement Series, 3; Evanston, IL: Anglican Theological Review, 1974], pp. 49-55) reviews these passages briefly, favoring a primary reference to Deut. 27.25, 'Cursed be he who takes gifts [bribes], to take the life of innocent blood' (as does Doeve, *Jewish Hermeneutics*, p. 185). Van Unnik argues that Judas, having accepted money to betray Jesus, falls under this curse. Failing to

For the fate of Judas in this passage, it would seem, is intended to anticipate the fate of the people as a whole.[1] By his own admission, Judas's death is due to his betrayal of innocent blood. So if the people call down that same blood upon themselves, and Jesus has already declared that 'all the righteous blood shed on earth...will come upon this generation' (23.35-36), surely disaster awaits them too—which is precisely the tone of Jer. 19.3-15.

Such a solution in explanation of the reference to Jeremiah in 27.9, however, is not without its difficulties. The verbal link both to Zechariah 11 (which Matthew apparently quotes according to a Hebrew version) and to the context of Matthew 27 is dependent upon the Hebrew term היוצר, whereas allusions to αἷμα ἀθῷον and the ἱερεῖς καὶ πρεσβύτεροι τοῦ λαοῦ seem to reflect the LXX as much

undo the curse by returning the money, his suicide is an attempt to make propitiation for his sin, on the analogy of the hanging of the seven sons of Saul in 2 Sam. 21. Thereby he accepts the sentence of Deut. 21.23, 'Accursed by God is everyone who is hanged', and 'in doing away with himself, he does away with the curse' (pp. 56-57). But it is hardly likely that the account, or Judas's own thinking, is to be understood in such complex terms: he is motivated simply by remorse. If anything the attempt to return the money, rather than the hanging, reflects his desire to atone; the latter is a gesture of despair and self-condemnation, not propitiation. Cf. J. Jeremias, *Jerusalem in the Time of Jesus: An Investigation into the Economic and Social Conditions during the New Testament Period* (Philadelphia: Fortress Press, 1969), pp. 139-40.

S. van Tilborg (*Jewish Leaders*, pp. 88-89) is not convinced by the parallels to Jer. 19. Taking the remorse of Judas (27.4) as the focus of the passage and 'the betrayal of innocent blood as a ἁμαρτία' to be its central theme, he discerns a primary reference to Jer. 2.34-35, which 'speaks of confession and non-confession of sin and this precisely in the presence of innocent blood'. But the focus of 27.3-10 is on the purchase of the field and the price of innocent blood it represents, which vitiates any reference to Jer. 2, in addition to which 'Jeremiah' in 27.9 refers not to 27.4, as van Tilborg seems to suggest (cf. p. 89 n. 1), but to the fulfillment quotation it introduces.

1. So Gundry, *Use of the OT*, p. 125; Senior, *Passion Narrative*, p. 380, and the literature cited in n. 116. Some indication of the gravity of Judas's betrayal and of the words of the crowd is provided by *m. Sanh.* 4.5 (= *b. Sanh.* 37a): 'In capital cases the witness is answerable for the blood of him [that is wrongfully condemned] and the blood of his posterity [that should have been born to him] to the end of the world' (cf. Manns, 'Midrash chrétien', p. 201; also H. Kosmala, '"His Blood on us and on our Children" [The Background of Mat. 27,24-25]' *ASTI* 7 [1970], pp. 108-109).

as the MT. Moreover, Jeremiah 19 fails to account explicitly for the all-important potter's 'field'.

Nonetheless, such features may be traced to different stages of exegesis. It may be that in the interests of demonstrating scriptural fulfillment, Matthew began with Zech. 11.12-13, since this text best paralleled circumstances in the life of the messiah for which he had to account. These were, primarily, that the messiah was betrayed for money, but also that the attempted return of that money resulted in the purchase of a plot of land that—apparently—had some previous association with potters. To this end, Zechariah 11 provided references both to the money and to the potter. Yet since the text of Zechariah neither includes an allusion to '[innocent] blood', which is a key feature of the received tradition, nor accounts for the association of the potter with the plot of land, the Evangelist was forced to look further. The Hebrew term היוצר provides the crucial exegetical link to Jeremiah 19, from which chapter details can be supplied that are lacking in Zechariah: the references to burial, bloodshed and innocent blood, the chief priests and elders, and the prospect of judgment. These latter features, however, as opposed to those from Zechariah 11, give evidence of dependence on a Greek text, albeit at a subsequent stage of the exegetical process.

Finally, the specific addition of τὸν ἀγρὸν τοῦ [κεραμέως] may simply be an expansion of the text occasioned by the prophecy in Jer. 19.11 that Hinnom/Topheth will become a place for burial. But we cannot dismiss the possibility that the central function of a potter's vessel as a symbol of destruction in Jeremiah 19 draws into consideration the similar vessel of Jeremiah 32. This vessel, fortuitously, is associated both with the only mention of 'shekels' in Jeremiah and with the only actual purchase we ever see the prophet making: that of his family's ancestral 'field'. Such a combination would have been facilitated by verbal similarities between Jer 19.1, 10 (בקבק יוצר חרש = βικὸν πεπλασμένον ὀστράκινον), or better, 19.11 (את־כלי היוצר = ἄγγος ὀστράκινον), on the one hand, and 32.14 (בכלי־חרש = ἀγγεῖον ὀστράκινον), on the other.[1]

1. Again, these correspondences are most evident in Greek: while ἄγγος occurs some six times in the LXX, the combination ἄγγος ὀστράκινον is found only in Jer. 19.11 and Ezek. 4.9 [2×], while ἀγγεῖον ὀστράκινον occurs at Lev. 14.5; Num. 5.17; Isa. 30.14; Jer. 39[32].14; and Lam. 4.2. The infrequency of these terms within the works ascribed to Jeremiah would invite assimilation. Schlatter

But as a further, albeit tenuous possibility, the vocabulary of Lam. 4.2 (בני ציון היקרים...נחשבו לנבלי־חרש מעשׂה ידי יוצר = υἱοὶ Σιὼν οἱ τίμιοι...ἐλογίσθησαν εἰς ἀγγεῖα ὀστράκινα, ἔργα χειρῶν κεραμέως) is remarkably similar to Matthew's citation of Zech. 11.13. For in common with that passage, Lam. 4.2 includes (1) mention of the potter (היוצר/κεραμεύς), (2) a description of valuation (היקרים/οἱ τίμιοι...ἐλογίσθησαν) that, like Matthew's τὴν τιμὴν τοῦ τετιμημένου ὃν ἐτιμήσαντο, uses the vocalization הַיְקָר (see p. 55 n. 3, above), and (3) a reference to 'sons of Sion' (cf. υἱῶν Ἰσραήλ). But it also mentions, in concert with Jer. 32.14, ἀγγεῖα ὀστράκινα. This suggests that Lam. 4.2—which is also τὸ ῥηθὲν διὰ Ἰερεμίου τοῦ προφήτου—could have provided the common term joining the potter's vessel(s) of Jer. 19.11 and 32.14, and so linking them both to Zech. 11.13. But even without the intermediary function of this verse, exegetical conflation of the two similar objects in Jeremiah 19 and 32 alone would have provided the Evangelist sufficient grounds for inserting τὸν ἀγρὸν τοῦ [κεραμέως] into his text of Zech. 11.13.

What this amounts to, then, is 'fulfillment' in verbal detail from Zechariah, but 'fulfillment' in thematic substance from Jeremiah—or, to use Gundry's terms, fulfillment of 'two separate prophecies, one typical and one explicit'.[1] According to Senior,

> The explicit details which have been fulfilled are spelled out in the words of [Zechariah], but it is the tragic tone of Jeremiah's prophecy that colors the accomplishment of God's will in a moment of betrayal and death.[2]

It would appear, therefore, that Matthew refers to Jeremiah by name

(*Matthäus*, p. 738) sees an allusion to Jer. 32.9 already at Mt. 26.15.

Doeve (*Jewish Hermeneutics*, pp. 184-85) sees here a process whereby the exegete first relates the 'innocent blood' mentioned in Mt. 27.5 to that of Jer. 26.15. The judgment against Jerusalem also described in Jer. 26 would then have suggested the similar judgments of Jer. 19 and 32. And these in turn would have been linked to Zech. 11.12-13 by means of the catchword יוצר (in common with Jer. 19.1) and the verbal roots כסף and שקל (as in Jer. 32.9). But while Jer. 26 indeed figures in the thought of the Evangelist, as we shall see in Chapter 3, Moo ('Tradition', p. 159 and n. 17) is correct in objecting that the contacts provided by the phrase 'innocent blood', the theme of judgment against Jerusalem, and by כסף and שקל (which are common roots), do not of themselves provide a sufficient foundation for joining the various passages.

1. *Use of the OT*, p. 125.
2. Senior, *Passion Narrative*, p. 369.

in his introductory formula as a means of drawing attention to an important allusion that could otherwise easily be overlooked.[1] So if Scripture has been been fulfilled according to Zechariah, how much more so, the Evangelist wishes to say, according to Jeremiah.

4. *Summary*

In 27.9-10 Matthew sees in what is probably the most perfidious act of opposition to the messiah in his Gospel—Jesus' betrayal by one of his closest disciples—not only the fulfillment of prophecy in general but also a link to the words of Jeremiah in particular. Indeed, the fact that the entire fulfillment quotation is given under the name of Jeremiah characterizes the whole as typical of that prophet. Without question, the fulfillment quotation provides the climax and focal point for Matthew's narrative: the messiah is sold for the price of a slave, with Judas's belated attempt to redress the wrong demonstrating both a recognition of his own guilt and the complicity of those who refuse what they themselves acknowledge to be 'the price of blood'. In this way Matthew demonstrates Jesus' innocence at the expense of the other participants' guilt and responsibility.[2] And all this is seen to be fulfilled in the words ascribed deliberately, albeit enigmatically, to the prophet Jeremiah.

In this respect, 27.9-10 closely parallels the fulfillment quotation of 2.17-18.[3] Not only are they identical in terms of their introductory formulae, but they are similar in tone and outlook. For both envisage mortal opposition to the messiah on the part of those who, according to the Evangelist, should have received him.[4] Furthermore, both depict the consequences of that opposition falling on the nation of

1. So Gundry, *Use of the OT*, p. 125; Senior, *Passion Narrative*, p. 369; Moo, *Gospel Passion Narratives*, pp. 197-98; cf. Torrey, *Documents*, pp. 85-86: 'the lack of any passage that could be quoted verbally from Jer. would certainly cause the prediction to be unrecognized, in the absence of such definite ascription by the evangelist' (albeit with reference to chs. 18 and 32); also *idem*, 'Foundry', p. 252.

2. Wolff (*Jeremia*, pp. 161-64) sums up Matthew's purpose in this passage as apologetic (Jesus' innocence), etiological ('Field of Blood') and edifying (emphasis on Jesus' blood).

3. Soares Prabhu (*Formula Quotations*, p. 54) accounts for the διὰ Ἰερεμίου of 27.9 primarily as 'a more or less conscious assimilation to the already closely parallel Mt. 2,17'!

4. Cf. Menken, 'Jeremiah', p. 9.

Israel: in the first instance, the children of Bethlehem; in the second, Judas and, ultimately, all those who accept responsibility by calling down on their own heads the innocent blood he has helped to shed.[1] Thus the fateful cry of the crowd, 'His blood be on us and on τὰ τέκνα ἡμῶν' (27.25), is not only anticipated but already proleptically fulfilled in the slaughter of the Bethlehemites, as Rachel's lament for τὰ τέκνα αὐτῆς (2.18) indicates.[2]

We are now in a better position to appreciate the larger pattern of linguistic and thematic links between the Infancy and the Passion narratives to which these passages make an essential contribution. With regard to Christology, first in 2.2 (M) and not again until 27.11 (// Mk 15.2), Gentiles inquire into Jesus' identity as ὁ βασιλεὺς τῶν Ἰουδαίων. Then in 27.29 Jesus is mocked as such (// Mk 15.18), and in 27.37 the same designation is written on the *titulus* of his cross (// Mk 15.26). Thus in both the Magi pericopes and Pilate's first question to Jesus, the title 'King of the Jews' introduces episodes of hostility towards the messiah.[3]

But in 27.17 and 22 Matthew replaces Mark's two remaining references to 'King of the Jews' by Ἰησοῦν τὸν λεγόμενον Χρίστον (cf. Mk 15.9, 12), which echoes the same phrase in the genealogy at 1.16 and in the reference of 2.4 to the 'Christ' in relation to Herod's deadly inquiries.[4] Matthew similarly transforms the crowd's mocking epithet in Mk 15.32, ὁ Χριστὸς ὁ βασιλεὺς Ἰσραήλ, into the separate titles βασιλεὺς Ἰσραήλ and θεοῦ...υἱός (27.42-43), the latter recalling with 27.40 ('If you are the Son of God...') the theme of sonship in Jesus' sojourn in Egypt (2.15; cf. 14.33, 16.16). Likewise, although here the evidence is less uniform, the titles 'Christ' and 'Son' focus

1. Cf. Vögtle, 'Kindheitsgeschichte', pp. 172-73; Nolan, *Royal Son*, p. 136. Kosmala ('His Blood on us' *passim*) attempts to avoid the force of Mt. 27.25 as indicating self-incrimination upon Israel (e.g. πᾶς ὁ λαός can only refer to the crowd who were actually present; the cry 'His blood on us' is relevant only to the circumstances of a judicial process). While such objections are valid, the passage must nonetheless be interpreted as part of a wider redactional motif within the context of Matthew's Gospel.

2. Cf. A. Vögtle, *Messias und Gottessohn: Herkunft und Sinn der matthäischen Kindheitsgeschichte* (Düsseldorf: Patmos, 1971), p. 69 [= *idem*, 'Kindheitsgeschichte', p. 173]: the citation from Jeremiah 'keine Voraussage, sondern eine Notiz zur Geschichte Israels ist' (following Rothfuchs, *Erfüllungszitate*, p. 64).

3. Cf. Senior, *Passion Narrative*, p. 226.

4. Cf. Nolan, *Royal Son*, p. 104.

attention in both the Infancy and the Passion narratives on the messiah's identity as a means of emphasizing responsibility for his rejection.[1]

Similarly, the secular leaders together with the chief priests and scribes (or elders) of the people respond in 2.4 and throughout the Passion narrative by gathering to take counsel against Jesus.[2] Not only Herod and his court, but πᾶσα Ἱεροσόλυμα μετ' αὐτοῦ are 'troubled' at the thought of a newborn king (2.3; cf. 21.10), even as πᾶς ὁ λαός (27.25, only here in Matthew) are said to take responsibility for Jesus' condemnation.[3] By the same token, as Senior points out, 'the flight into Egypt and the slaying of the innocents are threatening portents of Jewish rejection of the messiah eventually confirmed in the Passion account'—which means, in other words, that Jesus is persecuted from infancy.[4] Such reactions, however, are in

1. Cf. Senior, *Passion Narrative*, pp. 226-27, with p. 227 n. 1; Nolan, *Royal Son*, p. 105.

2. So Nolan (*Royal Son*, p. 88, cf. p. 106): 'The συνάγειν of 2.4 later describes the gatherings of his enemies against Jesus during his Jerusalem ministry and passion—22.34, 41; 26.3, 57; 27.62; 28.12'. In addition to a general use of this verb of 'a gathering of persons', Matthew 'also uses the term in a more narrow sense for a gathering of persons for a formal consultation or judgment' (Senior, *Passion Narrative*, p. 23).

3. Fitzmyer, 'Anti-Semitism', pp. 669-70; J.D. Kingsbury, *Matthew: Structure, Christology, Kingdom* (Philadelphia: Fortress Press, 1975), p. 48; Brown, *Birth*, p. 183. The force of Matthew's designation γραμματεῖς τοῦ λαοῦ (2.4, unique in the NT) is that the scribes act in solidarity with the people (in contrast to Lk. 19.47 and Acts 6.12, where 'scribes' and 'people' are clearly distinguished). Cf. Matthew's favourite πρεσβύτεροι τοῦ λαοῦ (see p. 71, above). The further emphasis on dreams (κατ' ὄναρ; in the NT only at 1.20; 2.12, 13, 19, 22, and 27.19 [Pilate's wife and her counsel at the trial]) noted by Senior (*Passion Narrative*, pp. 245-46) stresses the element of divine intervention on behalf of the δίκαιος (esp. 1.19, 27.19; albeit, in the latter case, to no avail).

4. Senior, *Passion Narrative*, p. 226. Cf. H.B. Green, 'The Structure of St Matthew's Gospel', *SE*, IV, p. 57; M. Hengel and H. Merkel, 'Die Magier aus dem Osten und die Flucht nach Ägypten (Mt 2) im Rahmen der Antiken Religionsgeschichte und der Theologie des Matthäus', in P. Hoffmann (ed.), *Orientierung an Jesus: Zur Theologie der Synoptiker. Für Josef Schmid.* (Freiburg: Herder, 1973), p. 165; Menken, 'References to Jeremiah', p. 9-10; R.A. Edwards, *Matthew's Story of Jesus* (Philadelphia: Fortress Press, 1985), p. 21, and especially Vögtle (*Messias und Gottessohn*, p. 70 [= 'Kindheitsgeschichte', p. 173]): 'Indem der Evangelist eine der Stammütter Israels, die spätere Generationen als Fürbitterin für ganz Israel ansehen, ihre Nachkommen beweinen und beklagen und untröstlich

marked contrast to those of Gentiles: the adoration of the Magi (2.11), the judicial exoneration by Pilate (27.24), and the confessions of faith by the centurion and his companions (27.54).[1] Finally, as a result of Jerusalem's persecution, Jesus takes refuge in Nazareth of Galilee (2.22-23). His place of residence figures again in the account of his final return to Jerusalem (21.11, 26.71), and when that city finally triumphs over him, he once again goes before his disciples to Galilee, where they join him (26.32, 28.7, 10, 16-17).[2] So it is to be noted that distinctive features of Matthew's vocabulary and narrative underscore the contrast both at the outset and at the conclusion of Jesus' life between his identity as the Christ, on the one hand, and the response of many who persecute him, on the other—together with the grave responsibility such rejection entails in the eyes of the Evangelist.

The persecution of the Messiah, in turn, is part of a larger emphasis on innocent suffering and 'innocent blood' that we have already observed in Matthew's Gospel. Indeed, the 'innocent blood' of the children of Bethlehem is the first to be spilled in Matthew's account. Their fate, intended for the infant messiah, foreshadows the much greater suffering that will ensue when opposition to him finally succeeds. As Soares Prabhu rightly observes,

> The confrontation between Herod and Jesus...which dominates his Infancy Narrative, is seen by Matthew as a continuation of the age-old persecution of the 'just' which reaches back to the beginning of history (ἀπὸ τοῦ αἵματος Ἄβελ τοῦ δικαίου: 23.35); and as a foretaste of the growing opposition which will develop between the Jewish leaders and Jesus.[3]

The climax of that opposition and the supreme example of innocent suffering is, of course, the otherwise inexplicable rejection of the messiah by his own people, culminating in his crucifixion. This Matthew emphasizes by means of repeated references to Jesus' inno-

sein läßt, "weil sie nicht (mehr) sind", will er das Schicksal der bethlehemitischen Knäblein gewissermaßen als Voranzeige der entsetzlichen Folge der ungläubigen Ablehnung, ja der Verurteilung des Messias Jesus verstanden haben'.

1. So Green, 'Structure', p. 58; Nellesen, *Das Kind und seine Mutter*, p. 91; Hengel and Merkel, 'Magier', p. 144.

2. Cf. Green, 'Structure', p. 58; Nolan, *Royal Son*, p. 105. Further possible parallels between chs. 1–2 and 28 are noted by Nolan, *Royal Son*, pp. 107-108, and by those authors cited on p. 104 n. 1.

3. *Formula Quotations*, p. 300.

cence and 'innocent blood'. And this same fate is apparently shared by the 'prophets and wise men and scribes' of Matthew's community, who no doubt concur with him in the view that 'all the righteous blood shed on earth' has come upon their opponents in the present day (23.35-36; 27.25).

The two fulfillment quotations that appeal to 'Jeremiah', therefore, contribute to the thematic correspondences between the Infancy and the Passion narratives, as well as to the more widespread theme of innocent suffering. For both of these redactional emphases underscore, with apologetic and polemical intent, the rejection of the messiah by his own people. The references to Rachel weeping for her children and to the purchase of a field with the fruits of betrayal are united by a common introductory formula and by a common redactional purpose. As Rothfuchs observes, Matthew sees 'in Jeremiah the prophet who foretold the enmity of the Jewish authorities towards the messiah of Israel, and the disaster that ensued for Israel as a result'.[1] Whether the name of Jeremiah carries similar thematic or theological overtones into the remainder of the Gospel will provide the focus for an investigation into the third such reference in 16.14.

D. *Matthew 16.14*

> 13 Ἐλθὼν δὲ ὁ Ἰησοῦς εἰς τὰ μέρη Καισαρείας τῆς Φιλίππου
> ἠρώτα τοὺς μαθητὰς αὐτοῦ λέγων· τίνα λέγουσιν οἱ ἄνθρωποι
> εἶναι τὸν υἱὸν τοῦ ἀνθρώπου; 14 οἱ δὲ εἶπαν· οἱ μὲν Ἰωάννην τὸν
> βαπτιστήν, ἄλλοι δὲ Ἠλίαν, ἕτεροι δὲ Ἰερεμίαν ἢ ἕνα τῶν
> προφητῶν. 15 λέγει αὐτοῖς· ὑμεῖς δὲ τίνα με λέγετε εἶναι; 16 ἀπο-
> κριθεὶς δὲ Σίμων Πέτρος εἶπεν· σὺ εἶ ὁ χριστὸς ὁ υἱὸς τοῦ θεοῦ τοῦ
> ζῶντος.[2]

The reference to Jeremiah in 16.14, as noted earlier, is of a different nature from the formula quotations of 2.17-18 and 27.9-10, since here a thematic rather than a textual allusion is in view. Having led his disciples into the predominantly Gentile territory of Caesarea

1. *Erfüllungszitate*, pp. 43-44; so also Meier, *Matthew*, p. 339: 'Jeremiah, the prophet of national tragedy and judgement'; Menken, 'Jeremiah', p. 10; Davies and Allison, *Matthew*, p. 266-67.

2. The textual variants in this passage (e.g. the insertion of με at various junctures by C D W K L X Δ Π f^1 f^{13} etc.) do not affect, for our purposes, the basic meaning of the passage.

Philippi, Jesus poses the theologically pregnant question: τίνα λέγουσιν οἱ ἄνθρωποι εἶναι τὸν υἱὸν τοῦ ἀνθρώπου (16.13). This introduces Jesus' final challenge, ὑμεῖς δὲ τίνα με λέγετε εἶναι, to which Peter replies, σὺ εἶ ὁ χριστός... (Mt. 16.16 // Mk 8.29).[1]

Theologically, this passage marks a watershed in Matthew's Gospel. To this point, both demons (4.3; 8.29) and disciples (14.33) have acclaimed Jesus as 'Son of God', and he has been designated the 'Christ' in redactional contexts (1.1, 16, 17, 18; 2.4; 11.2). But this is the first place—indeed, the only place in Matthew's Gospel—where the disciples explicitly acknowledge Jesus' messianic identity.

To such a highly significant passage Matthew makes a curious addition. For into the three alternatives reported by Mark as examples of popular opinion concerning Jesus (οἱ δὲ εἶπαν αὐτῷ λέγοντες [ὅτι] Ἰωάννην τὸν βαπτιστήν, καὶ ἄλλοι, Ἠλίαν, ἄλλοι δὲ ὅτι εἷς τῶν προφητῶν, Mk 8.28), Matthew inserts a fourth: Ἰερεμίαν (16.14). Several of the explanations that have been offered for this insertion are similar to those proposed for 27.9, and so need only to be reviewed here.[2] Others, however, will require more extensive treatment.

1. *Explanations for the Redactional Insertion*

a. *Jeremiah as a 'Typical' Prophet*

At first glance, Matthew's emendation seems almost arbitrary: not simply 'one of the prophets', but '*Jeremiah* or one of the prophets'. Carmignac's survey of references to Jeremiah in the Babylonian Talmud, Dead Sea Scrolls and Christian literature indicates that in all three the prophet Isaiah was cited with considerably greater frequency than Jeremiah, and so would probably have come more readily to mind.[3] Matthew himself, in fact, explicitly mentions Isaiah in his Gospel twice as often as Jeremiah (3.3; 4.14; 8.17; 12.17; 13.14; 15.7), so making it unlikely that Jeremiah would serve here as an example of a 'typical' prophet.

1. Menken ('References', p. 12-13) provides a fuller review of the Matthaean redactional context.

2. These proposals have been well summarized by Carmignac ('Jérémie', pp. 284-93) and Menken ('References', pp. 12-23), to whose studies the present review is indebted.

3. 'Jérémie', pp. 284-85.

b. *Jeremiah as Representative of the Prophetic Corpus*

Closely related to this first explanation is that which appeals to the few sources in which Jeremiah's name stands at the head of the list of Latter Prophets.[1] That is, Jeremiah is cited as a representative of the prophetic corpus, or more specifically, as Sparks suggests, 'Jeremiah was added to Elijah as the representative "writing" prophet'.[2] But as we have already seen, Jeremiah does not function elsewhere in Matthew's Gospel as a 'representative' prophet. Furthermore, the ancient authorities in question merely testify to the unsettled order of the canon at this early date. Indeed, as Carmignac points out, the very notion of a 'prophetic canon' may be premature at the time of Matthew's Gospel.[3] Notwithstanding the classification suggested by Lk 24.44 ('the law of Moses and the Prophets and the Psalms'), there was a tendency in Jewish circles to insist on the independent integrity of each prophetic book. This is attested by the enduring Jewish preference for separate scrolls over unifying codices, as witness the opinion cited in *b. B. Bat.* 13b, in which same context (*b. B. Bat.* 14b; cf. *m. B. Bat.* 1.6) the anomalous list with Jeremiah at its head is reported:

> Our Rabbis taught: It is permissible to fasten the Torah, the Prophets, and the Hagiographa together. This is the opinion of R. Meir. R. Judah, however, says that the Torah, the Prophets, and the Hagiographa should each be in a separate scroll; while the Sages say that each book should be separate.

It is therefore not possible to establish the pre-eminence or representative status of Jeremiah with respect to the rest of the prophetic corpus in the Jewish thought of Matthew's day.

c. *Jeremiah Typology*

Attempting to find a typological background to this passage on the basis of thematic similarities, B.T. Dahlberg argues that the Petrine call narrative draws its imagery from the call of Jeremiah.[4] Specific points of comparison include: (1) Peter as a 'rock' against which the 'Gates of Hades will not prevail' and Jeremiah as a 'fortified city' and 'strong bronze wall' ('both the apostle and the prophet are, figuratively,

1. Cf. C.3.e, above.
2. Sparks, 'St Matthew's References', p. 155.
3. 'Jérémie', pp. 288-91.
4. 'The Typological Use of Jer. 1.4-19 in Mt. 16.13-23', *JBL* 94 (1975), pp. 73-80.

fortresses impregnable against attack'); (2) the 'delegation of divine power and authority' to each, together with their respective reticence in the face of a divine call; (3) Peter's specific authority to 'bind and loose' (as signified by the 'keys of the kingdom') and Jeremiah's commission to 'pluck up', 'break down', and 'build' (interpreted via his traditional association with the keys of the Temple [cf. *2 Bar.* 10.18; *Par. Jer.* 4.4]);[1] (4) Peter's confession that Jesus is 'Son of...God' and God's consecration of Jeremiah in the womb (Jer. 1.5); and (5) the struggle of both Jesus and Jeremiah against Jerusalem.

According to Dahlberg, 'the specific mention of Jeremiah in 16.14 may well be Matthew's signal that he is making this connection',[2] even though the ostensible purpose behind the typology is merely 'to illuminate and to articulate [Matthew's] own sober estimate of the apostolic authority delivered by Jesus to Peter and to the church'.[3] Yet not only do these parallels appear forced, the majority, as Menken notes, 'concern the comparison of the figures of Jeremiah and Peter, whereas the identification with Jeremiah in Mt. 16.14 concerns Jesus'.[4]

Other commentators also call attention to potential similarities between Jesus and the call of Jeremiah.[5] But such parallels seem to be insufficient on both textual and thematic grounds to account for Matthew's insertion of 'Jeremiah' at 16.14.

1. Similarly, T. Forberg ('Peter: The High Priest of the New Covenant', *Far East Asia Journal of Theology* 4.1 [1986], p. 115 n. 25) suggests that the mention of Jeremiah may be linked to the latter's role as high priest (so, apparently, *Par. Jer.* 4.4-5) and keeper of the Temple keys, which functions Peter is now said to inherit. On Jeremiah as high priest in *Paraleipomena Jeremiou*, see J. Riaud, 'La figure de Jérémie dans les Paralipomena Jeremiae', in A. Caquot and M. Delcor (eds.), *Mélanges bibliques et orientaux en l'honneur de M. Henri Cazelles* (AOAT, 212; Kevelaer: Butzon & Bercker; Neukirchen–Vluyn: Neukirchener Verlag, 1981), p. 378.

2. 'Typological Use', p. 78.

3. 'Typological Use', p. 80.

4. Menken, 'References', p. 17 n. 44.

5. See below. For an alternative attempt to trace parallels in Mt. 16.13-19 to Isa. 22.22; *T. Levi* 2-7, and possibly *1 En.* 12–16, see G.W.E. Nickelsburg, 'Enoch, Levi, and Peter: Recipients of Revelation in Upper Galilee', *JBL* 100 (1981), pp. 590-600.

d. *Jeremiah as a Messianic Forerunner*

The opinion of Cornelius à Lapide (1567–1637)[1] that 16.14 provides evidence for an expectation in Matthew's (and/or Jesus') day of Jeremiah's return as a messianic precursor has won over a number of recent scholars. Cited in support of this position are 2 Macc. 2.1-12, 15.11-16 and *5 Ezra* 2.18.[2] The first of these records the tradition that having instructed the exiles to take the sacred Temple fire with them into captivity, Jeremiah 'ordered that the tent and the ark should follow him, and that he went out to the mountain where Moses had gone up', there sealing away the tent, ark and altar of incense in a cave (2 Macc. 2.4-6).[3] But some of the people follow Jeremiah in order to record the way, whereupon he rebukes them, declaring: ἄγνωστος ὁ τόπος ἔσται, ἕως ἂν συναγάγῃ ὁ θεὸς ἐπισυναγωγὴν

1. *Commentar in Quatuor Evangelia*, cited by Carmignac ('Jérémie', p. 285 n. 11); cf. Jeremias' citation (*TWNT*, III, p. 220 n. 14) from Lapide's *Omnia Opera* (1686).

2. E.g., citing 2 Maccabees: Hühn, *Die alttestamentlichen Citate und Reminiscenzen*, p. 21; Smith, *Matthew*, p. 152; Staab, *Matthäus*, p. 89; O. Cullmann, *Die Christologie des Neuen Testaments* (Tübingen: Mohr [Paul Siebeck], 1957), p. 17 n. 5 [ET *The Christology of the New Testament* (London: SCM Press, 1963), p. 18 n. 2; henceforth cited in translation]; H.M. Teeple, *The Mosaic Eschatological Prophet* (Philadelphia: SBL, 1957), p. 10 (quoting Ginzberg, *Legends of the Jews*, IV, p. 341 n. 114 [cf. p. 386 n. 13]); H. Frankmölle, *Jahwebund und Kirche Christi: Studien zur Form- und Traditionsgeschichte des 'Evangeliums' nach Matthäus* (NTAbh, 10; Münster: Aschendorff, 1974), p. 234; Sand, *Gesetz und Propheten*, pp. 127-28 (with Deut. 18.15); Maier, *Matthäus*, I, p. 565; Gnilka, *Matthäusevangelium*, II, p. 58. While referring to 2 Maccabees, Schniewind (*Matthäus*, p. 187) observes: 'Man wird annehmen müssen das in der damaligen Erwartung eine Wiederkehr des Jeremia erhofft wurde...Freilich haben wir dafür keine Beleg' (similarly Schmid, *Matthäus*, p. 245).

Citing both sources: Allen, *Matthew*, p. 175; Plummer, *Matthew*, p. 225; M'Neile, *Matthew*, p. 239; Grundmann, *Matthäus*, p. 386; Albright and Mann, *Matthew*, p. 194; Klostermann, *Matthäusevangelium*, p. 138; (tentatively) Schweizer, *Matthäus*, p. 221. While affirming the explanation of Jeremiah's eschatological return, Fenton (*Matthew*, p. 268) and F. Schnider (*Jesus der Prophet* [OBO, 2; Freiburg: Universitätsverlag; Göttingen: Vandenhoeck & Ruprecht, 1973], p. 185) cite neither source.

For additional bibliographies, see Carmignac, 'Jérémie', p. 285 n. 11, as well as Jeremias, *TWNT*, III, p. 220 n. 19, and Wolff, *Jeremia*, p. 28 n. 1.

3. This tradition probably owes something to Jer. 32, since there too the prophet seals away a testimony in anticipation of the return from exile.

τοῦ λαοῦ...καὶ τότε ὁ κύριος ἀναδείξει ταῦτα (2.7-8).[1] Here it is important to note, however, that while the prophet conceals the Temple vessels, he disclaims any responsibility for retrieving them; God himself will reveal their hiding place.[2]

No more compelling is the dream of Judas Maccabaeus prior to his battle against Nicanor, in which the high priest Onias III appears, followed by a man 'of marvelous majesty and authority'. Onias interprets this 'vision within a vision' to be Jeremiah, ὁ πολλὰ προσευχόμενος περὶ τοῦ λαοῦ καὶ τῆς ἁγίας πόλεως. Thereupon the visionary prophet offers Judas Maccabaeus a golden sword as a gift from God with which he will strike down his enemies (2 Macc. 15.12-16). From this episode we learn that Jeremiah intercedes for the people and city and encourages their defense—with the message being, presumably, that if the prophet normally associated with Jerusalem's destruction is willing to vouch for the city's safety, then Maccabaeus has ample grounds for assurance! But nowhere is any association with the messiah or a messianic era indicated. Indeed, as Billerbeck asserts, 'In ancient Jewish literature, Jeremiah nowhere appears as the forerunner of the Messiah'.[3]

The last reference of importance here, *5 Ezra* 2.18, is part of an extended divine address to Jerusalem in which the Lord promises to uphold his people in their hour of tribulation: 'Do not fear, mother of the sons, for I have chosen you, says the Lord. I will send you help, my servants Jeremiah and Isaiah'. But far from providing independent attestation for a Jewish tradition of Jeremiah's (and Isaiah's) return, this passage, together with the remainder of *5* and *6 Ezra* (or 2 Esdras 1–2 and 15–16), is manifestly a Christian addition, itself likely to be dependent on Mt. 16.14![4]

1. On these and similar traditions, see Wolff, *Jeremia*, pp. 61-79.

2. Cf. Carmignac, 'Jérémie', p. 286. This obviates the suggestion of Bruce ('Synoptic Gospels', p. 222) that Mt. 16.14 records a speculation on the part of some that Jeremiah would return the vessels. Referring to 2 Maccabees, Goulder (*Midrash and Lection*, pp. 387-88) cites the association of the Temple vessels with Jeremiah, on the one hand, and with the feast of Rededication (Hannukah), on the other, in support of his thesis of a lectionary cycle underlying Matthew's Gospel.

3. Str–B, I, p. 730; cited by Carmignac ('Jérémie', p. 287).

4. So Jeremias, ''Ιερεμίας', *TWNT*, III, p. 220 and n. 16, where he suggests that this is a variation on Rev. 11.3-6 (the two witnesses) and Mk 9.4 (Moses and Elijah at the Transfiguration). See also Menken, 'References', pp. 14-15, who reports the opinion of Victorinus of Pettau (died about 304) that Jeremiah is one of

But could the mention of 'Jeremiah or one of the prophets' refer more generally to popular expectations of a prophetic return, or of a non-eschatological manifestation or reappearance by one of the prophets? In particular, is there evidence for such expectations elsewhere in Matthew? Certainly the other three opinions reported in 16.14—that Jesus bears some resemblance to John the Baptist, Elijah or the 'prophets' generally—carry such overtones. In Matthew, even more clearly than in Mark, both John the Baptist (see 11.9; 14.5 [cf. Mk 6.20, 'a righteous and holy man']; 21.26 // Mk 11.32) and Jesus (see 13.57 // Mk 6.4; 21.11, 46) are clearly identified as prophets. Matthew alone, in fact, draws a conscious parallel between the fate of the two: Herod wants to kill John, but fears the crowd, who hold him to be a prophet (14.5), much as the chief priests and the Pharisees want to arrest Jesus and put him to death, but fear the multitudes who likewise consider Jesus a prophet (21.45-46; cf. 26.3-5, 27.1).[1] And lest the parallel be overlooked, Matthew has John's disciples inform Jesus of the Baptist's fate (14.12; diff. Mk 6.29).

Nor can it escape our notice that the story of John's fate is occasioned by Herod's guilt-inspired reaction to the ministry of Jesus. Mk 6.14-16, reporting that Jesus' reputation had reached Herod, relates a series of popular opinions about him:

> Some[2] said, 'John the Baptist has been raised from the dead: that is why these powers are at work in him'. But others said, 'It is Elijah'. And others said, 'It is a prophet, like one of the prophets of old'. But when Herod heard of it he said, 'John, whom I beheaded, has been raised'.

The parallel to Mk 8.28 // Mt. 16.14 is evident.[3] Yet Matthew has deleted all but the opinion of Herod: 'He said to his servants, "This is John the Baptist, he has been raised from the dead"' (14.2). Taken

the two witnesses from Rev. 11 (text in K. Berger, *Die Auferstehung des Propheten und die Erhöhung des Menschensohnes: Traditionsgeschichtliche Untersuchungen zur Deutung des Geschickes Jesu in frühchristlichen Texten* (Göttingen: Vandenhoeck & Ruprecht, 1976), p. 257. Wolff (*Jeremia*, p. 29), on the other hand, argues that *5 Ezra* 2.18 may depend directly upon Jewish tradition, especially since the mention of Isaiah cannot derive from Mt. 16.14.

1. Cf. Menken, 'References', p. 21.

2. Following B W it^{a,b,d,ff2} Augustine; see *TCGNT in loc.*; V. Taylor, *The Gospel according to Mark: The Greek Text with Introduction, Notes, and Indexes* (London: Macmillan, 1955), p. 308, and additional sources cited there.

3. See further, Wolff, *Jeremia*, pp. 26-27.

together, Matthew's redactional emendations appear, first, to underline the similarities between John and Jesus as prophets; secondly, to stress that Herod (if no one else) believes in the possibility of John the Baptist's return; and, thirdly, to concentrate all speculation regarding further prophetic resemblances to Jesus within the Caesaraea Philippi episode.[1]

John the Baptist, of course, had already been identified in the Gospel tradition as Elijah *redivivus*, in line with the expectation expressed by Mal. 4.5-6 (cf. 3.1), Sir. 48.10, and *4 Ezra* 6.26.[2] Matthew, however, stresses this identification more strongly than does Mark (see 11.14; 27.47, 49 // Mk 15.35-36), emphasizing in particular the threefold identification of John, Elijah and Jesus as righteous sufferers. As Jesus in Matthew's Gospel explains to his disciples while they descend from the Mount of Transfiguration,

> 'I tell you that Elijah has already come, and they did not know him, but did to him whatever they pleased. So also the Son of man will suffer at their hands.' Then the disciples understood that [Jesus] was speaking to them of John the Baptist (Mt. 17.12-13; cf. Mk 9.12-13).

For not only do John and Jesus suffer martyrdom, but so did Elijah, at least according to Rev. 11.3-12 (presuming Hippolytus's and Tertullian's identification here of Elijah to be correct)[3] and *Apoc.*

1. Cf. Sand, *Gesetz und Propheten*, pp. 139-40.

2. See J. Jeremias, ''Ηλ(ε)ίας', *TWNT*, II, pp. 930-43 [= *TDNT*, pp. 928-41]. In *4 Ezra* 6 the heavenly voice declares that those who survive the messianic tribulations 'shall see the men who were taken up, who from their birth have not tasted death', a distinction accorded in Scripture only to Enoch (Gen. 5.24) and Elijah (2 Kgs 2.11), although Ezra and Baruch are said to share it as well (see the two following notes).

3. See discussion in G.B. Caird, *A Commentary on the Revelation of St John the Divine* (New York: Harper & Row, 1966), pp. 133-38. A pre-Christian origin for the tradition of Elijah's martyrdom found in Rev. 11 is proposed by Jeremias (*TWNT*, II, pp. 942-43 [= *TDNT*, pp. 939-40]) and M. Black ('The "Two Witnesses" of Rev. 11.3f. in Jewish and Christian Apocalyptic Tradition', in E. Bammel, C.K. Barrett and W.D. Davies (eds.), *Donum Gentilicium: New Testament Studies in Honour of David Daube* [Oxford: Clarendon Press, 1978], pp. 227-37, with reference to Mt. 17 par. pp. 236-37), although this view has been challenged by R.J. Bauckham, 'The Martyrdom of Enoch and Elijah: Jewish or Christian?', *JBL* 95 (1976), pp. 447-58; cf. also D.E. Aune, *Prophecy in Christianity and the Ancient Mediterranean World* (Grand Rapids: Eerdmans, 1983), p. 159.

Elij. 4.7-19. Thus whether or not we are to understand the appearance of Elijah at the Transfiguration as the realization of Herod's worst fears, Matthew's Gospel provides evidence for the expectation of the return, or at least the earthly manifestation, of both Elijah and John the Baptist.

More generally, Berger argues that Mk 6.14-16 is to be understood in terms of the widespread belief that angels and prophets (among them Elijah, Moses and Jeremiah) were able to manifest themselves in human form, although he stresses that such reappearances do not necessarily carry eschatological overtones.[1] Mt. 16.14 could therefore be seen in the same light.[2] In addition to 2 Macc. 15.14-17,[3] which gives evidence of Jeremiah's ability to appear in visionary form, and *5 Ezra* 2.18, which pairs Isaiah and Jeremiah as eschatological heralds, Berger cites Victorinus of Pettau (died about 304) in his commentary on the Apocalypse and *Carmen adv. Marcionem* 3.179-89 (= 3.6.7-17 [*PL* 2.1074C]; fourth century; 'Nulla morte virum constat, neque caede peremptum', 189) to the effect that Jeremiah did not die, but was taken up into heaven (so Origen, *Commentariorum in Evangelium Joannis* 13.57 [PG 14.509B]). In *Liv. Proph.* 2.19, as Berger points out, Jeremiah is said to remain a companion of Moses 'to this day'.[4] Nonetheless, while we do not wish to contest Berger's overall thesis regarding the 'heavenly session' of the prophets and the possibility of their individual manifestation on earth,[5] none of the passages cited provide direct evidence for a pre-Christian expectation of Jeremiah's return as a messianic precursor.

Building on the parallels in 2 Macc. 2.4-5, *Liv. Proph.* 2.3-7, 14, 17-19, *Par. Jer.* 8.4, the Syriac *Jeremiah Apocryphon*, *Pes. K.* 13.6 [112a], and so forth, between Jeremiah and Moses, Wolff argues that popular expectation of a Mosaic return was transferred in Second Temple Judaism to Jeremiah. For as in these passages Jeremiah is said

1. Berger, *Auferstehung*, pp. 17-22, cf. p. 202 and notes. Cf. Philo, *Abr.* 113-14. Menken ('References', p. 14) also cites the examples of Enoch (*1 En.* 90.31 [although the passage is very ambiguous]), Ezra (*4 Ezra* 14.9), and Baruch (*2 Bar.* 13.3; 25.1; 76.2), all of which are, by contrast, unmistakably eschatological in tone.

2. Menken, 'References', pp. 14-17; so also Schweizer, *Matthäus*, p. 221.

3. On which see Berger, *Auferstehung*, p. 202 n. 425.

4. Berger, *Auferstehung*, p. 20 n. 72; in Coptic traditions, Jeremiah is the companion of Enoch, Sybil, Michael and Gabriel.

5. Cf. Mt. 27.52-53, although here the reference is to resurrection rather than to heavenly visitation.

to have led the exiles home from Babylon after the manner of Moses, and in *4 Ezra*, *2 Baruch*, and *Par. Jer.* the comparison is drawn between the destructions of Jerusalem by Babylon and Rome, so in Mt. 16.14 Jesus is seen to be a Jeremiah *redivivus* who will return to lead an exodus from Roman oppression.[1] But again, as Menken objects, 'the parallelism of Moses and Jeremiah nowhere bears upon an eschatological return', even apart from the question of dating the sources attesting Moses' return in relation to Matthew's Gospel.[2] And even granting the possibility of Jeremiah's appearance in association with messianic redemption, the question of Matthew's redactional purpose in 16.14 would still be left unanswered. For here, as we shall see, the Evangelist's concern is not with reappearance per se, but with the light that these popular 'guesses' shed on the identity of Jesus as the Christ.

e. *Jeremiah Identified with Jesus*

Our investigtion has already indicated how the popular opinions reported in Mt. 16.14 confirm Matthew's close redactional parallels between Jesus, John and Elijah as prophets who suffer rejection and even martyrdom at the hands of their hearers.[3] The same is true of the comparison of Jesus to 'one of the prophets'. For as Menken points out,

1. *Jeremia*, pp. 28-29, 82; cf. Teeple, *Prophet*, p. 51.

2. 'References', p. 16 n. 43. On the other hand, M.E. Boismard ('Jésus, le prophète par excellence, d'après Jean 10, 24-39', in J. Gnilka (ed.), *Neues Testament und Kirche: Für R. Schnackenburg* [Freiburg: Herder, 1974], pp. 160-71) argues that Jn 10.34-36 recalls the language of Jer. 1.4-7, and that the author intends thereby not only a parallel between Jesus and Jeremiah, but a further evocation both of Moses' own call and of Deut. 18.15. Following Teeple (*Prophet*, p. 10), F. Hahn (*Christologische Hoheitstitel: Ihre Geschichte im frühen Christentum* [FRLANT, 83; Göttingen: Vandenhoeck & Ruprecht, 1964], pp. 222-23 n. 3) similarly explains the mention of Jeremiah in Mt. 16.14 as a reference to the 'prophet like Moses' of Deut. 18. Such an identification may find support in *Par. Jer.* 6.24 (cf. Riaud, 'La figure de Jérémie', pp. 375-76 [citing this passage as 6.22]); *Pes. K.* 13.6 and *Sifre Deut.* 155 (on Deut. 18.15), which also interpret Deut. 18.15 as referring to Jeremiah.

3. Cf. Menken, 'References', pp. 20-22.

> Mt differs from Mk in that in the first gospel the third popular opinion is part of a literary whole that contains repeated references to the motif of the murder of the prophets.[1]

This motif was present already both in Q (e.g. Mt. 5.12 // Lk. 6.23; Mt. 23.29-32, 34-35 // Lk. 11.47-51; Mt. 23.37 // Lk. 13.34-35) and in the parable of the wicked tenants from Mk 12.1-11 (// Mt. 21.33-44), which Matthew applies directly to Jesus by assigning him the title 'prophet' at the conclusion of the parable (21.46). Furthermore, it would appear that in Matthew's Gospel at least part of the reason why Jesus 'must go to Jerusalem [δεῖ αὐτὸν εἰς Ἱεροσόλυμα ἀπελθεῖν]' (16.21; diff. Mk 8.31) is that Jerusalem is where all prophets perish (Mt. 23.37 // Lk. 13.34; cf. Lk. 13.33).[2]

All such comparisons are entirely appropriate to the context of Jesus' first prediction of his Passion in Mt. 16.21, particularly given the vehemence of Peter's reply. That is to say, the popular opinions of Jesus' similarity to John, Elijah and 'the prophets' become, in the Matthaean redaction, not erroneous alternatives raised only for the sake of rejection, but intimations or approximations of the messiah's true identity as one who suffers.[3] Ironically, the opinions of the common people, anticipating as they do Jesus' prediction of his own death, are more accurate than that of Peter, an intimate disciple, for whom such a possibility is anathema. And this suggests that the mention of 'Jeremiah' is likewise a meaningful approximation of the messiah's true identity.[4]

Menken cites a wide range of evidence in support of this view. For in addition to numerous and obvious passages from canonical Jeremiah, Sir. 49.6-7 implics a connection between the maltreatment of Jeremiah and the destruction of the city; the historian Eupolemos has King Jehoiakim intending to burn him;[5] while both Jewish and

1. 'References', p. 22.

2. Menken, 'References', p. 22, citing Grundmann, *Matthäus*, p. 398. So Meier, *Vision,* p. 116.

3. *Contra* Carmignac, 'Jérémie', pp. 297-98.

4. Moreover, the fact that John in 3.11-12 etc., 'Elijah' in 11.14, and the prophets generally in Matthew's many scriptural quotations and allusions all 'prepare the way' for Jesus suggests that this is Jeremiah's role as well.

5. Menken argues that the king is successful (see 'References', p. 19 and n. 49), although Jeremiah's subsequent appearance in connection with the Temple furnishings makes this unlikely! Wolff (*Jeremia*, p. 16) speaks here of a 'verhindertes Martyrium'.

Christian traditions record the stoning of Jeremiah.[1] In keeping with such traditions, the ninth-century Nestorian bishop Isho'dad of Merv explains that Jeremiah is mentioned in 16.14 because, like Jesus, he was sanctified from his mother's womb, and was mistreated and persecuted for his testimony.[2]

In addition to Menken, recent commentators taking this position include Kremers, Meier, Tasker and, somewhat tentatively, Bonnard.[3] As Meier observes,

> Mt adds the suffering prophet *par excellence*, Jeremiah, who points forward to the first prediction of the passion. Jesus, like Jeremiah, will suffer rejection and martyrdom at the hands of his own people even as he predicts the fall of Jerusalem (cf. 23.37-39).[4]

This interpretation is fully in accord with both 2.17 and 27.9-10,[5] suggesting a unitary redactional purpose behind all three references to Jeremiah and inviting further investigation of the motif elsewhere in Matthew's Gospel.

Carmignac is of the opinion that the appeal to Jeremiah recognizes in him, and therefore also in Jesus, 'le prophète de malheur' *par excellence*.[6] The evidence in support of this contention is considerable.

1. *Liv. Proph.* 2.1; *Par. Jer.* 9.31; *Midrash Haggadah* on Num. 30.15 (cited, together with a wide range of patristic sources, in Wolff, *Jeremia*, pp. 90-91; see below, Chapter 2, A.1.e). Cf. Mt. 23.37 // Lk. 13.34; Heb. 11.37.

2. Cf. Carmignac, 'Jérémie', p. 293.

3. H. Kremers, *Der leidende Prophet* (diss. Göttingen, 1952; cited in Wolff, *Jeremia*, p. 29 n. 3); Tasker, *Matthew*, p. 157; Meier, *Vision*, p. 108; Bonnard, *Matthieu*, p. 243: 'Certains contemporains de Jésus avaient-ils été déjà frappés par le mélange de puissance et de souffrances qui désignaient Jésus à leur attention? Est-ce pour cela qu'ils le rapprochaient de Jérémie? Nous ne savons.' Cf. (from a sociological perspective) B.J. Malina and J.H. Neyrey, *Calling Jesus Names: The Social Value of Labels in Matthew* (Sonoma, CA: Polebridge Press, 1988), p. 115.

4. *Matthew*, p. 180.

5. This answers Wolff's contention (*Jeremia*, p. 166 n. 2) that a unitary redactional purpose is lacking because 'Matth. 27,9f beinhaltet kein Unheil'.

6. 'Jérémie', p. 292; so also Gundry, *Matthew*, p. 329; Holladay, *Jeremiah*, II, p. 93 (citing Carmignac). Holladay (*Jeremiah*, n. 245) reports the opinion of H.C. Kee (expressed in a lecture delivered June 22, 1988) that the mention of Jeremiah in Mt. 16.14 refers to the prophecy in Jer. 31.31-34 of a 'new covenant'. Since Holladay does not relate the substance of Kee's argument, a detailed response is not possible here, although, as will become evident in Chapter 3, Matthew does appear to have this prophecy in mind elsewhere in his Gospel.

Echoing his prophetic call 'to pluck up and to break down, to destroy and to overthrow' (Jer. 1.10, cf. 45.4-5), Jeremiah describes himself as 'a man of strife and contention to the whole land' (Jer. 15.10; cf. 20.8). His contemporaries evidently perceived him no differently (Jer. 36.29; 38.4). Likewise, in the eyes of the Rabbis, 'Jeremiah speaks throughout of destruction' (ירמיה כוליה חורבנא; *b. B. Bat.* 14b), which amply explains their attribution to him in the same passage of both Lamentations and the books of Kings. For both attributions highlight the prophet's obvious association with the fall of Jerusalem: not only is this the subject of Lamentations, but, as the Talmud itself explains, 'the Book of Kings ends with a record of destruction'—the destruction of Jerusalem. Thus, according to *b. Ber.* 57b, the Rabbis believed that were one to see the prophet Jeremiah—or the book of Lamentations—in a dream, it would be a warning of coming punishment, unlike Ezekiel, who signified wisdom, or Isaiah, whose appearance heralded consolation.[1] Similarly in *y. Sanh.* 11.7(5) [30b], Jeremiah sums up the character of his prophetic message with the declaration, 'I prophesy doom [אני מתנבא לרעה]', even as *b. Sanh.* 94b-95a interprets the words of Isa. 10.30, 'O poor Anathoth', as a reference to the fact that Jeremiah is destined to prophesy concerning Jerusalem from that town![2]

Among Christian exegetes who have understood 16.14 as referring to this grim reputation, Carmignac cites Origen and Erasmus, who saw in Jesus the fulfillment of Jeremiah's prophetic call.[3] Zahn, too, explained the reported similarity in subjective terms: 'that in feeling

1. In a similar vein, *Pes. R.* 29.9 relates an extended series of contrasts between the prophecies of doom and prophecies of consolation offered by Jeremiah and Isaiah, respectively.

2. The context in *y. Sanh.* is a discussion of Jeremiah's inability to provide confirmatory signs, 'for the Holy One, blessed be He, may form a plan to bring evil, but then reverse it'. See further the multiple etymologies given for 'Jeremiah' in *Pes. K.* 13.8, including one that derives the name from ἔρημος.

3. 'Jérémie', pp. 296-97; Origen: *Commentariorum in Evangelium Secundum Matthaeum* 12.9 [*PG* 13.993B] (καὶ οἱ φάσκοντες δὲ ὅτι Ἰερεμίας εἴη ὁ Ἰησοῦς, καὶ οὐχὶ τύπος τοῦ Χριστοῦ ὁ Ἰερεμίας, τάχα ἐκ τῶν εἰρημένων ἐν ταῖς ἀρχαῖς τοῦ Ἰερεμίας περὶ Χριστοῦ ἐκινήθησαν, οὐ πληρωθέντων μὲν ἐν τῷ προφήτῃ τότε ἀρξαμένων δὲ πληροῦσθαι ἐν τῷ Ἰησοῦ [Jer. 1.10]); Erasmus: *Tomus Primus Paraphraseon D. Erasmi Roterodami, in nouum Testamentum...* (Basel, 1524), p. 113.

pity for his people and lamenting over their deserved misfortune, Jesus resembles no other prophet as much as this one'.[1] Grundmann, Green and Schweizer similarly contend that Jeremiah had particular significance in the Matthaean community as a prophet of the destruction of Jerusalem;[2] while Hill suggests, whether such an insight derives from Matthew himself or preserves an earlier tradition, that the similarities lie in Jesus' and Jeremiah's difficult messages, 'each forecasting (even desiring) for his adversaries the judgment of God, and for his supporters the persecution of men'.[3] Gnilka, in fact, finds the evidence for such a view of Jeremiah precisely in the two fulfillment quotations that expressly name him. And although he takes this to be 'an inadequate notion', Gnilka concurs that the identification of Jesus with Jeremiah indicates 'that Jesus was taken to be a prophet of disaster'.[4]

2. *Conclusions*

These last two analyses of 'Jeremiah' in 16.14, far from excluding one another, are best understood as being complementary. According to Matthew, Jesus was perceived by his contemporaries as a prophet of misfortune and suffered their opprobrium as a result: the one fact explains the other. If, then, this analysis is correct, the fulfillment

1. *Matthäus*, p. 535; similarly in 2.17, 'Der Name...des Jeremia, des tränenreichen Propheten (Jer. 8,23; 9,16ff; 13,17; 14,17) und Dichters der Klagenleider, entspricht der Stimmung, in welche der teilnehmende Leser durch v. 16 versetzt ist' (Zahn, *Matthäus*, p. 109).

2. Grundmann, *Matthäus*, p. 386; Green, *Matthew*, p. 151; Schweizer, *Matthäus*, p. 221 [ET p. 340]: 'Vielleicht ist er...als Prophet des Untergangs Jerusalems der Gemeinde des Matthäus besonders wichtig geworden. Oder sollte gar einfach gemeint sein, daß viele Leute Jesus ablehnen, weil sie in ihm einen Unglückspropheten sehen...' So also Doeve, *Jewish Hermeneutics*, p. 185 n. 1; Wolff, *Jeremia*, p. 166; cf. Schlatter, *Matthäus*, p. 503; Schnackenburg, *Matthäusevangelium*, p. 151. This premise is taken further by R.E. Winkle ('The Jeremiah Model for Jesus in the Temple', *AUSS* 24 [1986], pp. 155-72), who discerns in Mt. 23.29–24.2 a series of parallels to Jer. 7 and 26 that explain the reference in 16.14.

3. D. Hill, *New Testament Prophecy* (London: Marshall, Morgan & Scott, 1979), p. 56.

4. *Matthäusevangelium*, II, p. 59, cf. p. 449 ('Jeremia für [Matt] der klassische Unheilsprophet ist', p. 548).

quotations of 2.17-18 and 27.9-10 find support for such a view in the actual text of Jeremiah, whereas 16.14 appeals more generally to the personal example of Jeremiah as a rejected prophet. A unitary redactional purpose seems to underlie all three passages.

Chapter 2

The Deuteronomistic Rejected-Prophet Motif in Matthew

Before tracing the use of Jeremiah material elsewhere in Matthew's Gospel, it is important to note the evidence for the Evangelist's depiction of Jesus and his followers as rejected prophets. So, in accordance with the suggestions of Carmignac and Menken, particular attention will be paid to Matthew's use of 'Q' traditions as the source for such a view.[1] Establishing the presence of rejected-prophet motifs in the traditions Matthew has used and in the ways he has redacted them is necessary in order to confirm that the previous conclusions regarding 2.17-18, 27.9-10 and 16.14 are redactionally consistent with the remainder of the Gospel.

A. *The Deuteronomistic View of History in Jewish and Early Christian Traditions*

1. *Jewish Literature*

O.H. Steck's foundational 1967 study, *Israel und das gewaltsame Geschick der Propheten*, like that of H.J. Schoeps and others before him, arose out of an interest in the fate of Israel's prophets as depicted in early Christian literature.[2] In an effort to explain the violent

1. Carmignac, 'Jérémie', p. 296 n. 38; Menken, 'References', p. 22. Similar traditions are also present in Mark, although less prominently so.

2. *Israel und das gewaltsame Geschick der Propheten: Untersuchungen zur Überlieferung des deuteronomistischen Geschichtsbildes im Alten Testament, Spätjudentum und Urchristentum* (WMANT, 23; Neukirchen–Vluyn: Neukirchener Verlag, 1967). See also Str–B, I, p. 943; H.J. Schoeps, *Die jüdischen Prophetenmorde* (Symbolae Biblicae Upsalienses, 2; Uppsala: Wretman, 1943) (concentrating on Mt. 23.31-32; Acts 7.52; 1 Thess. 2.15; and Heb. 11.36-37); G. Friedrich, 'προφήτης κτλ' *TWNT*, VI, pp. 835-36 [= *TDNT*, pp. 834-35];

treatment of the prophets described in such passages as the persecution beatitude (Mt. 5.11-12 // Lk. 6.22-23), the parable of the vineyard (Mt. 21.33-41 // Mk 12.1-9 // Lk. 20.9-16), the woes against the scribes and Pharisees (Mt. 23.29-36 // Lk. 11.47-51), and the lament over Jerusalem (Mt. 23.37-39 // Lk. 13.34-35), Steck traces the development of the motif of Israel's rejection of divine messengers through OT and intertestamental literature. This review of his study will concentrate only on the most obvious and significant of such passages.

a. *Hebrew Bible*

The oldest passage representing such a view, according to Steck, is Neh. 9.26-30. Ezra, confessing the sins of Israel to God at an assembly of returned exiles, laments the recalcitrance of his forebears despite the goodness of the Lord:

> They were disobedient and rebelled against thee and cast thy law behind their back and killed the prophets, who had warned them in order to turn them back to thee... Therefore thou didst give them into the hand of their enemies, who made them suffer; and in the time of their suffering they cried to thee and thou didst hear them... Many years thou didst bear with them, and didst warn them by thy Spirit through thy prophets; yet they would not give ear. Therefore thou didst give them into the hand of the peoples of the lands.

Emphasized here are the divine forbearance that motivates the sending of the prophets, the deadly obstinacy of their hearers, and the fact that this rejection of God's Law and prophets accounts for the national chastisements of 722 and 587 BCE.[1]

To Nehemiah 9 may be compared 2 Kgs 17.7-20 (which accounts primarily for the exile of the Northern Kingdom), the book of Zechariah as a whole, and 2 Chron. 36.15-16 in particular, which reads:

D.R.A. Hare, *The Theme of the Jewish Persecution of Christians in the Gospel according to St Matthew* (SNTSMS, 6; Cambridge: Cambridge University Press, 1967), pp. 61-62, 137-41; J. Dupont, *Les béatitudes*. II. *La bonne nouvelle* (Paris: Gabalda, 1969), pp. 294-318; Aune, *Prophecy*, pp. 157-59. Earlier treatments of this theme (not available to me) include A. Schlatter, *Der Märtyrer an den Anfangen der Kirche* (BFCT, 19.3; Gütersloh: Bertelsmann, 1915), pp. 18-22, and O. Michel, *Prophet und Märtyrer* (BFCT, 37.2; Gütersloh: Bertelsmann, 1932).

1. Steck, *Israel*, pp. 63-64. Ezra 9.10-11 echoes similar sentiments (Steck, *Israel*, pp. 64-65).

> The Lord, the god of their fathers, sent persistently to them by his messengers, because he had compassion on his people and on his dwelling place; but they kept mocking the messengers of God, despising his words, and scoffing at his prophets, till the wrath of the Lord rose against his people, till there was no remedy.

This latter passage, it should be noted, describes the refusal of Zedekiah and his court to heed Jeremiah (36.12), and then goes on to recount the consequences of national disobedience: that Nebuchadnezzar and his army 'burned the house of God, and broke down the wall of Jerusalem' (36.19).

In similar fashion, the book of Jeremiah (e.g. 7.25-26, 32-34; 25.3-14; 26.2-6; 29.17-20; 35.13-17; 44.4-14) explains by means of similar motifs the destruction of Jerusalem and the end of the Southern Kingdom.[1] Here the Lord declares:

> From the day that your fathers came out of Egypt to this day, I have persistently sent all my servants the prophets to them, day after day; yet they did not listen to me (7.25-26).

Likewise in the present day, says the Lord to his people, 'I have sent to you all my servants the prophets, sending them persistently...But you did not incline your ear or listen to me' (35.15; cf. 25.4-7; 44.4-5). As a result, the Lord promises to bring catastrophe upon the nation, destroying, in particular, the Temple and city: 'I will make this house like Shiloh, and this city a curse' (26.6; cf. 7.32-34; 25.8-12; 35.17; 44.2, 6; also 29.17-19). Even for the exiles in Babylon and Egypt who continue their disobedience will further punishment ensue (29.20-23; 44.8-14). Only after seventy years will God vindicate and restore his people (25.12-14; 29.10; cf. chs. 50–51).

Not all such passages, to be sure, envisage a specifically violent fate for God's messengers. Indeed, references to the actual mistreatment or murder of the prophets are relatively infrequent in the Hebrew Bible. These include 1 Kgs 18.4, 13, 19.10, 14, cf. 2 Kgs 9.7 (Jezebel kills the prophets of the Lord), 1 Kgs 22.26-27 (Ahab has Micaiah cast into prison), 2 Chron. 16.10 (Asa imprisons Hanani), 2 Chron. 24.20-22 (inspired by the 'Spirit of God', Zechariah ben Jehoiada calls the people to repentance; they stone him), Jer. 2.30 ('your own sword

1. On these passages, see Steck, *Israel*, pp. 66-77; see further pp. 110-28 on Pss. 79, 106; Neh. 1.5-11; Dan. 9.4-19; Bar. 1.15-3.8; Tob. 3.1-6; *Prayer of Azariah*; CD 20.28-30; 1QS 1.24–2.1; 4QDibHam 1.8–7.2, etc.

devoured your prophets like a ravening lion'), Jer. 26.20-23 (Jehoiakim kills the prophet Uriah), and Jer. 11.21, 20.1-2, 26.7-19, 32.2, 37.15-16, 38.6 (Jeremiah is at various times threatened with death, beaten, put on trial, imprisoned and thrown down a well).[1] By contrast, many of the prophets appear not to have been persecuted. Yet the idea that they typically met a violent end arises, apparently, from the need to demonstrate recalcitrance on the part of God's people sufficient to account for the twofold catastrophe of exile for both Israel and Judah.[2]

b. *Josephus*

Josephus,[3] in his retelling of biblical history, evidences a similar understanding of pre-exilic events. In *Ant.* 9.265-67 he expands on the mocking of Hezekiah's couriers (from 2 Chron. 30.10) by specifying that they were 'prophets' and relating that the Northerners' response was to put them to death. Similarly, he adds to the reports of 2 Kgs 21.16 and 24.4 that Manasseh 'filled Jerusalem with innocent blood' the detail that this was the blood of the prophets, whom, he says, Manasseh slaughtered 'daily [καθ' ἡμέραν]' (*Ant.* 10.38-39).[4]

c. *Intertestamental Literature*

The same interpretative framework is applied to Israel's history in a number of intertestamental works. Among these may be cited the prayer of Tobit, which explains the exile as a judgment upon Israel, calling on its 'sinners' to repent so that the Lord may restore them to

1. Cf. Lam. 2.20 and Ps. 105.15 = 1 Chron. 16.22, where mistreatment by Gentiles is in view (Steck, *Israel*, p. 60). Additional discussion in Schoeps, *Prophetenmorde*, pp. 4-5.

2. Cf. Steck, *Israel*, pp. 77-80. For such a motive with regard to the death of Zechariah in particular, see B.H. Amaru, 'The Killing of the Prophets: Unraveling a Midrash', *HUCA* 54 (1983), pp. 167-68.

3. Flavius Josephus was born 37/38 CE and died after 100. Of his works, *The Jewish War* was written following the fall of Masada in 73; *Antiquities of the Jews* (to which was appended an autobiographical *Life*), c. 93–94; thereafter, the apologetic *Against Apion*. Cf. J. Goldin, 'Josephus, Flavius', *IDB*, II, pp. 987-88.

4. Cf. Schoeps, *Prophetenmorde*, p. 7 n. 7; Steck, *Israel*, pp. 81-86; L.H. Feldman, 'Prophets and Prophecy in Josephus', *JTS* 41 (1990), p. 393; see also *Ant.* 9.281, 10.60. On rabbinic interpretation of Manasseh's crimes, see §1.e, below.

their own land (13.1-6). Likewise the lament of Baruch:[1]

> We did not heed the voice of the Lord our God in all the words of the prophets whom he sent to us, but we each followed the intent of his own wicked heart... So the Lord confirmed his word, which he spoke against us... All those calamities with which the Lord threatened us have come upon us. Yet we have not entreated the favour of the Lord by turning away, each of us, from the thoughts of his wicked heart (Bar. 1.21; 2.1, 7-8).

But this was by no means God's last word to his people. For after Baruch's lengthy prayer of confession and plea for divine mercy (1.15–3.8) and his exhortation to repentance and obedience (3.9–4.20), the work ends on a note of great triumph, in expectation of a glorious restoration (4.21–5.9):

> Take off the garment of your sorrow and affliction,
> O Jerusalem,
> and put on for ever the beauty of the glory from God...
> For God will lead Israel with joy, in the light of his glory,
> with the mercy and righteousness that come from him (Bar 5.1, 9).

Similarly, the 'Animal Apocalypse' of Book 4 (the 'Dream Visions') of *1 Enoch* describes in allegorical fashion the growing disobedience of Israel and the slaying of the prophets, which led to the destruction of Jerusalem and the exile (89.51-56). But it also relates the ultimate restoration of the nation and the eventual establishment of a messianic kingdom (89.73-90.39). Likewise, God's admonition to Moses in the

1. For texts and critical apparatus, see A.H.J. Gunneweg, 'Das Buch Baruch', in W.G. Kümmel *et al.* (eds.), *Unterweisung in lehrhafter Form* (JSHRZ, 3.2; Gütersloh: Gerd Mohn, 1975); E. Tov, *The Book of Baruch, Also called I Baruch (Greek and Hebrew): Edited, Reconstructed and Translated* (SBLTT, 8; Missoula, MT.: Scholars Press, 1975); and J. Ziegler (ed.), *Ieremias, Baruch, Threni, Epistula Ieremiae* (Göttingen: Vandenhoeck & Ruprecht, 1976). Estimates of the date of Baruch range from the early second century BCE (or as early as the fourth century BCE for selected portions of the work, according to C.A. Moore, 'Toward the Dating of the Book of Baruch', *CBQ* 36 [1974], pp. 312-20) to the period between the two Roman wars, although a pre-Christian date seems most likely. Cf. S. Tedesche, 'Baruch, Book of', *IDB*, I, pp. 362-63; Gunneweg, 'Das Buch Baruch', p. 168; Wolff, *Jeremia*, p. 117 n. 3; C.A. Moore, *Daniel, Esther, and Jeremiah: The Additions. A New Translation with Introduction and Commentary* (AB, 44; Garden City, NY: Doubleday, 1977), p. 260; G.W.E. Nickelsburg, *Jewish Literature Between the Bible and the Mishnah* (Philadelphia: Fortress Press, 1981), pp. 113-14.

book of *Jubilees*, which provides the framework for the work, contains all of these same elements:

> And I shall send to them witnesses so that I might witness to them, but they will not hear. And they will even kill the witnesses... and I shall scatter them among the nations (*Jub.* 1.12-13).

Some parts of the *Testaments of the Twelve Patriarchs*, of course, reveal the influence of Christian redaction. Nonetheless, it should be noted that the same motifs are widespread in this collection of writings. *T. Levi* 15.1, for example, declares that 'the sanctuary which the Lord chose shall become desolate through your uncleanness, and you will be captives in all the nations', and that among the sins of Israel will be their rejection of the words of the prophets and persecution of the just (16.2). Such a state of affairs will continue until the nation returns in obedience to God's commandments, whereupon the Lord will have mercy on Israel and lead them back to their own land (cf. *T. Jud.* 23.1-5; *T. Iss.* 6.1-4; *T. Zeb.* 9.5-8; *T. Dan* 5.7-9; *T. Naph.* 4.1-5; *T. Ash.* 7.2-7).[1]

Steck concludes that a 'deuteronomistic'[2] view of Israel's history was widespread, indeed pervasive, by the time the NT was written:

> This tradition is to be encountered in almost all writings that have survived from Palestinian Judaism between 200 BCE and 100 CE.[3]

Taking into account all the sources we have reviewed, the 'deuteronomistische Geschichtsbild' may be summarized as follows:

> a The whole history of Israel is pictured as one of persistent disobedience...
>
> b Therefore Yahweh again and again sent prophets to call Israel to return, to repent...
>
> c Israel always rejected these prophets, often even killing them...

1. On these passages, see further, Steck, *Israel*, pp. 147-62, with additional discussion and bibliography in M.A. Knibb, 'The Exile in the Literature of the Intertestamental Period', *HeyJ* 17 (1976), pp. 264-66.

2. So called because of its affinities with the theological outlook (as represented by 2 Kgs 17.7-20) of the 'deuteronomic' redactor(s), which stresses the relation between Israel's political fortunes and its covenantal responsibilities, particularly with respect to the events of 722 and 586 BCE (see Steck, *Israel*, p. 66 n. 3, and further, D.N. Freedman, 'The Deuteronomic History', *IDBSup*, pp. 226-28).

3. Steck, *Israel*, p. 189.

d Therefore Yahweh punished, or will punish, Israel. In the earliest Deuteronomistic tradition, the catastrophes of 722 and 587 BCE are cited. In the later tradition the *Unheilstatus* of Israel is said to continue...

e But now a new call for repentance is issued...

f1 If Israel repents, Yahweh will restore her, gathering those scattered among the nations.

f2 And He will bring judgment upon Israel's enemies...[1]

d. *The Reapplication of Deuteronomistic Motifs*

Before we can evaluate the relevance of this interpretative tradition for Matthew's Gospel, we need to note the manner in which Jewish apologists continued to apply these motifs to new historical situations. For just as this view of Israel's history first arose in an attempt to account for the Assyrian and Babylonian conquests, so it was used to interpret subsequent conquests of Israel at the hands of the Romans.

Not only does *Pss. Sol.* 9.1-3, for example, explain the Babylonian exile as a result of national sin, but *Pss. Sol.* 2.1-21, 8.1-34 and 17.1-18 apply the same explanation to Pompey's capture of Jerusalem in 63 BCE.[2] The apostasy of Jerusalem, it would seem, was complete:

> For there was no one among them
> who practiced righteousness or justice:
> From their leader to the commonest of the people,
> in every kind of sin:
> The king was a criminal
> and the judge disobedient;
> the people sinners (*Pss. Sol.* 17.19-20).

Then in a manner consistent with other examples we have seen, *Pss. Sol.* 17.21-46 goes on to pray for and to anticipate the glorious

1. This summary is provided by A.D. Jacobson, 'The Literary Unity of Q', *JBL* 101 (1982), pp. 384-85; cf. Steck, *Israel*, pp. 62-64, 122-24, and especially pp. 184-95. Not all of these elements are present in each passage that refers to the motif; rather, this is a composite summation.

2. On these passages, see Steck, *Israel*, pp. 170-71; Nickelsburg, *Jewish Literature*, pp. 204-209. The *Psalms of Solomon* date from 80–40 BCE (so A.-M. Denis, *Introduction aux pseudépigraphes grecs d'Ancien Testament* [SVTP, 1; Leiden: Brill, 1970], p. 64; cf. S. Holm-Nielsen, 'Die Psalmen Salomos', in W.G. Kümmel *et al.* (eds.), *Poetische Schrifte* [JSHRZ, 4.2; Gütersloh: Gerd Mohn, 1977], p. 58; R.B. Wright, 'Psalms of Solomon', in J.H. Charlesworth (ed.), *The Old Testament Pseudepigrapha* [Garden City, NY: Doubleday, 1985], II, pp. 640-41). The translation used here is that of Wright.

restoration of the city under the leadership of a 'righteous king' and 'Messiah'.

Likewise the *Testament* or *Assumption of Moses* juxtaposes a Deuteronomistic explanation for the fall of Jerusalem in 587 (*Ass. Mos.* 2.7–3.9) with accounts of subsequent sin and tribulation in that city (chs. 6–9). Whether these latter chapters have to do with persecutions under Antiochus IV or under Pompey—or, perhaps, with what occurred during the second Roman war[1]—does not alter the fact of the work's interpretation of national history as a repetition of the same pattern of sin, divine judgment and ultimate restoration.

Somewhat less controverted in its references and date is *4 Ezra*, which locates itself 'in the thirtieth year after the destruction of our city' (3.1), by which we are meant to understand a date of approximately 100 CE.[2] While the ultimate purpose of this work is one of apologetics and consolation,[3] it nonetheless describes Israel's situation in terms of the pattern now familiar to us. For example, there is no question in Ezra's mind that God himself destroyed Jerusalem on account of the people's sin (3.30; 5.28; cf. 8.26), for they rejected Moses, the prophets and Ezra alike (7.129-30). Ezra's final speech, in fact, recites the history of Israel in Deuteronomistic terms, and—as a new feature—locates their vindication and restoration *post-mortem* (14.28-35). More to the point, as Steck observes, for the author of this work 'the events of 70 CE demonstrate that, theologically, God's people are placed in the situation of 587 [BCE]'.[4]

Even as the author of *4 Ezra* chose a pseudonym that emphasizes restoration and new beginnings, so the author of *2 Baruch*[5] chose a

1. See J. Priest, 'Testament of Moses', in Charlesworth, *OT Pseudepigrapha*, I, pp. 920-21 (on questions of dating); p. 930 n. 8a (on this theme); cf. Nickelsburg, *Jewish Literature*, pp. 80-82, 213-14.

2. Cf. J.M. Myers, *I and II Esdras: Introduction, Translation, and Commentary* (AB, 42; Garden City, NY; Doubleday, 1974), pp. 129-31; J. Schreiner, 'Das 4. Buch Esra', in W.G. Kümmel *et al.* (eds.), *Apokalypsen* (JSHRZ, 5.4; Gütersloh: Gerd Mohn, 1981), p. 301; B.M. Metzger, 'The Fourth Book of Ezra', in Charlesworth (ed.), *OT Pseudepigrapha*, I, p. 520.

3. See E. Breech, '"These Fragments I Have Shored Against My Ruins": The Form and Function of 4 Ezra', *JBL* 92 (1973), pp. 267-74; M.P. Knowles, 'Moses, the Law, and the Unity of 4 Ezra', *NovT* 31 (1989), pp. 265-74.

4. *Israel*, p. 177; on the passages cited, see pp. 177-80.

5. *2 Baruch* (which may depend on *4 Ezra*, or a source common to both) likely

name that suggests, as might be expected of Jeremiah's scribe, a more denunciatory role. So the sin of the twelve tribes is said to have brought judgment upon the nation (1.1-5; 77.1-10) and upon Jerusalem in particular (4.1; 32.3; 44.5-6). Nonetheless, they can look forward to the restoration of Israel and to a new Jerusalem (4.2-6; 32.4-6; 44.7-15). The 'Apocalypse of Clouds' (chs. 53–74) likewise presents a moral interpretation of national history, specifically juxtaposing the judgments of God in the northern exile (ch. 62), the southern exile (64–65), and 'the disaster which has befallen Zion now' (67.1). At the conclusion of the work, Baruch's letter to the exiles reiterates similar themes (esp. 78.5–80.7; 84.5–85.9).[1]

Finally, the work known as 'The Rest of the Words of Jeremiah' (*Paraleipomena Jeremiou*) or *4 Baruch* deserves brief mention.[2] Like *4 Ezra* and *2 Baruch*, this work also addresses the circumstances of the fall of Jerusalem in the form of a reflection on its previous destruction by the Babylonians. Thus the work opens with God addressing his prophet: 'Jeremiah, my chosen one, rise up and get out of this city...because I am going to destroy it for the multitude of the sins of those who inhabit it' (1.1; so 4.7). The answer to Baruch's

dates within a decade or two of 100 CE (so A.F.J. Klijn, '2 [Syriac Apocalypse of] Baruch', in Charlesworth [ed.], *OT Pseudepigrapha*, I, pp. 616-17; cf. *idem*, 'Die syrische Baruch-Apokalypse', in W.G. Kümmel *et al.* (eds.), *Apokalypse* [JSHRZ, 5.2; Gütersloh: Gerd Mohn, 1976], pp. 111-14). Interpreting *2 Bar.* 1.1, 'And it happened in the twenty-fifth year of Jeconiah', as a cryptic reference relative to the fall of Jerusalem in 70 CE, P. Bogaert (*Apocalypse de Baruch: Introduction, traduction du syriaque et commentaire* [Paris: Cerf, 1969], I, pp. 270-95) proposes 95 or 96 as the date of composition.

1. Cf. Steck, *Israel*, pp. 180-83.

2. This work is dated (in its original Jewish form) not later than the period of the second Jewish revolt (see Denis, *Introduction*, p. 74; S.E. Robinson, '4 Baruch', in Charlesworth [ed.], *OT Pseudepigrapha*, II, p. 414) and likely related in some degree to *2 Baruch*, although it includes a Christian post-script (9.14-32); see further, Robinson, '4 Baruch', pp. 416-17; cf. Bogaert, *Apocalypse de Baruch*, II, pp. 216-20; Wolff, *Jeremia*, pp. 45-46. Bogaert (*Apocalypse de Baruch*, pp. 220-21) argues that *Paraleipomena Jeremiou* is dependent on *2 Baruch*, while G.W.E. Nickelsburg ('Narrative Traditions in the Paralipomena of Jeremiah and 2 Baruch', *CBQ* 35 [1973], pp. 60-68) proposes their mutual dependence on a common source. The Greek text and ET are available in R.A. Kraft and A.E. Purintun (eds.), *Paraleipomena Jeremiou* (SBLTT, 1; Missoula, MT: Scholars Press, 1972).

question, 'Father Jeremiah...what sort of sin have the people committed?' (2.2), would appear to be that they have failed to keep God's commandments (6.23), although this specific explanation is not stressed. Rather, the work looks forward to an imminent release from 'Babylonian' captivity (e.g. 8.1-2).

The purpose here is not to analyze each of these writings in depth, but simply to point out that in each, an interpretative framework that originally served to explain the Assyrian and Babylonian conquests is reapplied to subsequent political misfortunes. In each work, even though many other motifs and theological intentions may be present, the recent events of Jewish history are interpreted historically (and pseudonymously) as a repetition of the earlier exile(s) and theologically in terms of a recurrent pattern of national apostasy, divine judgment, and ultimate restoration.

e. *Rabbinic Literature*

H.A. Fischel, followed by Steck, describes aspects of this motif found in rabbinic literature. In his 1946 article, 'Martyr and Prophet', Fischel observes that the roles of prophet and martyr came to be identified in rabbinic tradition: that, in general, all prophets were seen to be martyrs and, conversely, all martyrs were perceived as prophets.[1] Every prophet had to reckon, therefore, with the prospect of rejection that his call entailed. This leads Jeremiah to lament in *Pes. R.* 26 (129ab; on Jer. 1.5): 'What prophet ever came forth to them whom they did not wish to slay?'[2] Other 'prophets' similarly

1. H.A. Fischel, 'Martyr and Prophet (A Study in Jewish Literature)', *JQR* 37 (1946–47), pp. 265-80, 363-86. So also W.H.C. Frend, *Martyrdom and Persecution in the Early Church: A Study of a Conflict from the Maccabees to Donatus* (Oxford: Basil Blackwell, 1965), p. 57; G.W.H. Lampe, 'Martyrdom and Inspiration', in W. Horbury and B. McNeil (eds.), *Suffering and Martyrdom in the New Testament: Studies presented to G.M. Styler by the Cambridge New Testament Seminar* (Cambridge: Cambridge University Press, 1981), pp. 123-25. It was no doubt this tendency that inspired the identification of the two Zechariahs, which Lampe goes on to discuss (pp. 125-29). The opinion of Manson ('Martyrs and Martyrdom', *BJRL* 39 [1956–57], pp. 465-66) that LXX Ἔσδρας Β′ 19.26 (Neh. 9.26: καὶ τοὺς προφήτας σου ἀπέκτειναν, οἵ διεμαρτύραντο ἐν αὐτοῖς) attests the same tendency, appears to be anachronistic in its interpretation of διαμαρτυρεῖν. Nonetheless, the wording of this passage could have encouraged the identification of the roles of martyr and prophet on the part of later interpreters.

2. איזה נביא יצא להם ולא בקשו להרוגו (cited by Steck, *Israel*, p. 90 n. 1).

treated include Abraham,[1] Moses[2] and Isaiah,[3] sometimes cited together with Amos and Micah.[4] Fischel's survey leads him to conclude that 'as early as the first century CE it had become a generally accepted teaching of Judaism that prophets had to suffer or even to undergo martyrdom'.[5]

In fact, the persecution of the prophets is sometimes cited as the reason for the destruction of Jerusalem. Accordingly, *b. Yom.* 9b asks,

According to *Midrash Haggadah* on Num. 30.15 (cited by Fischel, 'Martyr and Prophet', p. 278, and more fully by Amaru, 'The Killing of the Prophets', p. 155, with original text n. 10), Jeremiah himself was martyred by stoning at the hands of the people (cf. *Liv. Proph.* 2.1; *Par. Jer.* 9.22). This source is very late (eleventh century) and the tradition of Jeremiah's martyrdom without parallel in extant talmudic midrash. Nonetheless, Amaru ('The Killing of the Prophets', pp. 174-78) argues on form and literary-critical grounds that this account is of similar antiquity to the accounts of the deaths of Hur, Shemaiah, Ahijah, Zechariah and Isaiah (which *Midrash Haggadah* relates in the same context), all of which have second-century (or earlier) origins. On the mutual reproach of prophet and people in rabbinic literature, see J. Bowman, 'Prophets and Prophecy in Talmud and Midrash', *EvQ* 22 (1950), pp. 212-20.

1. See *Lev. R.* 27, cf. *Pes. K.* 9.3 [76a] (attributed to Jose b. Nehorai, a Palestinian Amora of the early third century, citing the persecution of Abel, Noah, Abraham, Isaac, Jacob, Joseph, Moses, David, Saul and Israel as a whole); *Gen. R.* 39.3 [on 12.1]; *Songs R.* on 8.8 (at the hands of the pagan Nimrod); cf. *4 Macc.* 9.21; 14.20; 16.18-20; 18.23; *b. Giṭ.* 57b (although these latter passages only suggest Abraham's association with the suffering of others).

2 *Pes. K.* 13.6 [112a]; *Exod. R.* 7.3 [on Exod. 6.13], cf. 31.16 [on Exod. 32.27]; *Sifre* §91 [on Num. 11.11-12]; *Num. R.* 18.4; *b. Soṭ* 35a; cf. Josephus, *Ant.* 4.22-23; *Ass. Mos.* 3.11. See further, J. Jeremias, *s.v.* 'Μωυσῆς', *TWNT*, IV, pp. 867-68, 873 [= *TDNT*, pp. 863-64, 877-78]; Bloch, 'Quelques aspects', pp. 127-38.

3. *Mart. Isa.* 5 (in which the account of Isaiah's death is dated by Knibb [Charlesworth (ed.), *Pseudepigrapha*, I, p. 149] as early as the Maccabaean period); *y. Sanh.* 10.2 [28c]; *b. Yeb.* 49b; *b. Sanh.* 103b; Josephus, *Ant.* 10.37; cf. Heb. 11.37; further, Ginzberg, *Legends*, IV, pp. 278-79; Amaru, 'The Killing of the Prophets', pp. 170-74, esp. p. 170 n. 73 on the first-century dating of this tradition according to *b. Yebamot.*

4. *Lev. R.* 10.2; *Eccl. R.* 1.1; *Pes. K.* 16.4 [125a]; *Pes. R.* 33.3 [150b] (also referring to Zechariah and Jeremiah). On all of the above-cited passages, see Fischel, 'Martyr and Prophet', pp. 274-79, 373-74; Steck, *Israel*, pp. 90-91.

5. 'Martyr and Prophet', pp. 279.

> Why was the first Sanctuary destroyed? Because of three things which prevailed there: idolatry, immorality, and bloodshed.[1]

That the third of these is true is then proven by citing 2 Kgs 21.16, which recounts that Manasseh filled Jerusalem with 'innocent blood'. In turn, *y. Sanh.* 10.2 [28c] and *b. Sanh.* 103b interpret this verse as referring to Manasseh's slaying of the prophet Isaiah (cf. *y. Sanh.* 10.2 on 2 Kgs 24.4).

At the same time, there is also a widespread tradition that draws a connection between the fall of Jerusalem and the slaying of Zechariah ben Jehoiada related by 2 Chron. 24.21-22 (so, e.g., *Targ. Lam.* 2.20; *y. Ta'an.* 4.9 [69ab]; *b. Giṭ.* 57b; *b. Sanh.* 96b; *Pes. K.* 15.7; *Lam. R.* Proem 23; 1.16.51; 2.20.23; *Eccl. R.* 3.16 [86b]; cf. *b. Yom.* 38b).[2] For as Blank points out, the prophet's dying words, 'May the Lord see, and avenge' (2 Chron. 24.22), lend themselves naturally to such an explanation. But Blank also suggests, albeit tentatively, that the popularity and frequent embellishment of the Zechariah legend in the Talmudic era may reflect apologetic concerns in response to more recent national suffering.[3]

Such an explanation for the second destruction of Jerusalem is explicitly stated elsewhere in the tradition. As evidence of specifically Deuteronomistic motifs in rabbinic thought, Steck quotes *Pes. R.* 29 (138a), in which the people of Israel, appealing for comfort, confess the sins that have brought about their downfall:

1. מקדש ראשון מפני מה חרב מפני ג׳ דברים שהיו בו ע״ז [עבודה זרה] וגלוי עריות ושפיכות דמים

2. Cf. Steck, *Israel*, p. 89 n. 1; E. Levine, *The Aramaic Version of Lamentations* (New York: Hermon, 1976), pp. 17, 120-21. These passages are cited and discussed at length by Blank, 'Death of Zechariah', pp. 336-41. Blank also draws attention (p. 339 n. 18) to the parallel explanation by Josephus (*Ant.* 11.297-301) of persecution under Artaxerxes and the Persians, including their defilement of the Temple, as resulting from the murder in the Temple of one Jeshua by his brother, the priest Johanan.

3. Blank ('Death of Zechariah', p. 340): 'Some of the details were probably derived from the experiences of the people in the first and second Christian centuries, and we may even regard the legend as an attempt to find some reason for the sufferings of the Jews at that time'. Blank has in mind not only the capture of Jerusalem, but also persecutions under Domitian and Hadrian.

> We too know that we destroyed our Temple with our evil deeds, slew our prophets, and transgressed all the commandments in the Torah.[1]

That this explanation refers to the destruction of the Second Temple is evident from the literary setting of the work as a whole.[2] Similarly, *Pes. R.* 31 (146a), expounding Isa. 49.14-15, relates the lament of Zion:

> There is no end to the evils I have done. I caused Thy Temple to be destroyed and I slew the prophets.[3]

Finally, *Exod. R.* 31.16 declares, 'The citizens of Jerusalem were...smitten because they despised the prophets',[4] citing as proof 2 Chron. 36.16 ('but they kept mocking the messengers of God, despising his words, and scoffing at his prophets...') and Jer. 5.3 ('They have made their faces harder than rock; they have refused to repent'). Although such evidence is undoubtedly late, it demonstrates that the perception of a link between the violent death of the prophets and the destruction of Jerusalem was not simply the product of Christian polemic (since the rabbis are hardly likely to have borrowed such a view from their ideological opponents), but rather constitutes one element of Israel's theological reflection upon their own historical destiny.[5]

1. שהחרבנו את ביתך בעוונותינו: הרגנו את נביאינו: ועברנו כל המצות שבתורה... (as cited by Steck, *Israel*, p. 87 n. 3). On the dating of *Pes. R.* (sixth to seventh centuries CE), see H.L. Strack, *Introduction to the Talmud and Midrash* (New York: Meridian; Philadelphia: Jewish Publication Society, 1959 [1931]), p. 213; D. Sperber, 'Pesikta Rabbati', *EncJud*, XIII, pp. 335-36.

2. Cf. Steck, *Israel*, p. 87 and n. 4; pp. 92-93 and p. 93 n. 1.

3. גרמתי לבית מקדשך שיתחרב והרגתי הנביאים (as cited in Steck, *Israel*, p. 88 n. 8).

4. וכן אנשי ירושלים לא לקו אלא על שבזו הנביאים; cf. Fischel, 'Martyr and Prophet', p. 271 n. 30. *Exod. R.* likely dates from the beginning of the seventh century; see discussion in Bowker, *Targums and Rabbinic Literature*, p. 79-80.

5. The widespread nature of the OT, apocalyptic and rabbinic evidence, as evaluated by both Jewish and Christian scholars, obviates the simplistic thesis of R.R. Ruether (*Faith and Fratricide: The Theological Roots of Anti-Semitism* [New York: Seabury, 1974], pp. 90-91) that on the basis of Isa. 53 and 'the theme of suffering in the Psalms...The Church read back into Jewish history a record of apostate Israel as rejecting and killing the prophets, in order then to read this pattern forward again to make the death of Jesus the predicted and culminating act of this history of apostasy'. This view is partly dependent on the conclusions of Schoeps

f. *Summary*

The examples cited above from rabbinic literature all date, at the earliest, from the third or fourth centuries CE, long after the NT period. Yet precisely for this reason, they seem to demonstrate the longevity of this motif and the continuity of the interpretive tradition that it represents. For the examples we have cited from both apocalyptic and rabbinic literature indicate that as early as the second century BCE and as late as the sixth century CE, if not later, Jewish tradition understood the several catastrophes visited upon Jerusalem to be the result of national sin—one element of which was the rejection of God's appointed messengers, the prophets.

To this general conclusion several important qualifications must be made. First, as Steck points out, the repeated appearance of this theological motif provides evidence not of direct literary dependence on specific OT texts (such as Neh. 9) but rather of the existence of an 'oral tradition' that formed part of a more widespread and popular theological self-understanding.[1] And, second, as Steck also insists, the emphasis of such an outlook was not on the fate of the prophets per se but rather on the present responsibility of a disobedient Israel, and therefore on the importance of their collective repentance and return.[2] Presumably it was these latter features that rendered the motif so serviceable in application to subsequent national disasters and, in turn, permitted its polemical exploitation by Christian interpreters.

(*Prophetenmorde*, p. 22), to which see the reply of Steck, *Israel*, pp. 243-44.

1. Steck, *Israel*, p. 219, cf. p. 189. Steck understands this tradition to have first arisen in Levitical circles, then to have spread more widely in a post-exilic context as 'asidäisches Gemeingut' (p. 209) that formed part of the popular proclamation of Israel's eschatological vindication. Steck names those responsible for such proclamation simply as 'Schriftgelehrter' (see further *Israel*, pp. 196-215). For critiques of this aspect of Steck's work, see P. Hoffmann, *Studien zur Theologie der Logienquelle* (Münster: Aschendorff, 1982), pp. 160-62 ('Unklar ist, von welchen Kreise in der Zeit von 150 v. Chr. bis in das 1. Jahrhundert die Tradition weitergetragen wurde'), and M. Sato, *Q und Prophetie: Studien zur Gattungs-und Traditionsgeschichte der Quelle Q* (WUNT, 2.29; Tübingen: Mohr [Paul Siebeck], 1988), pp. 343-44. Possible doubt as to the identity of the tradents does not, however, vitiate Steck's primary thesis of a 'deuteronomistic' tradition, the presence of which is widely evident.

2. *Israel*, pp. 219-21.

2. *Early Christian Literature*

The following investigation will examine relevant passages from Mark and Q, briefly tracing Matthew's adaptation of Deuteronomistic themes in his use of the latter two sources, as well as in material unique to his Gospel.[1]

a. *Mark and Matthew*

According to Edwards, the prominence given to John the Baptist in Q is due to an interest on the part of the Q community in prophecy generally. More specifically,

> When Q reports the confrontation between Jesus and the disciples of John, John is already in prison. Thus John has suffered the fate of all prophets—he has been persecuted and will soon be destroyed because of

1. While the focus of this study is limited, Deuteronomistic motifs are widespread in early Christian literature. See, e.g., Lk. 13.33; Acts 7.52; Rom. 10.16-11.5; 1 Thess. 2.14-16; *5 Ezra* 1.32; *Ign. Magn.* 8.2; *Barn.* 5.11; Justin, *Dial.* 16, 73, 95, 112, 120; Irenaeus, *Adv. Haer.* 4.33.9-10. Steck (*Israel*, p. 103) argues that 'das Urchristentum die generelle Vorstellung vom gewaltsame Geschick der Propheten als lebendige Überlieferung bereits aus spätjüdischer Tradition übernommen hat'. Furthermore, such an understanding of Israel's spiritual history was sufficiently widespread as to obviate the need for dependence by Christian authors on particular examples or texts from the pre-Christian period, since all OT prophets without distinction were perceived as having been maltreated (cf. *Israel*, pp. 243-52 and the literature cited in §1.e, above). By contrast, Matthew's particular interest in Jeremiah, as will be argued later, constitutes a subsequent development and specification of a more generalized Deuteronomistic outlook in early Christian literature.

The use of Deuteronomistic motifs on the part of Mark, Q and Matthew is consistent with Jewish or Jewish-Christian sources and interests. The relevance of this observation for Mark and Q is beyond the scope of this study. In the case of Matthew, however, the Evangelist's emphasis on Deuteronomistic themes, as demonstrated in the course of this chapter, either suggests the presence of Jewish-Christian elements in his audience or that he is in debate (whether apologetic or polemical) with the Judaism of his day. For fuller discussion of Matthew's audience and relevant bibliographies, see G. Stanton, 'The Origin and Purpose of Matthew's Gospel: Matthean Scholarship from 1945 to 1980', in H. Temporini and W. Haase (eds.), *Aufstieg und Niedergang der römischen Welt: Geschichte und Kultur Roms im Spiegel der neueren Forschung* (Berlin: De Gruyter, 1985), pp. 1910-21, 2.25.3, and the appendix below.

> the incisiveness of his message. The image of the prophet in Q is consistent in the emphasis on persecution.[1]

It is by no means certain, however, that the phrase locating John ἐν τῷ δεσμωτρίῳ (so Mt. 11.2) was originally present in Q.[2] Rather, it is entirely likely that this phrase was derived instead from Mk 6.17 (// Mt. 14.3, cf. Mk 1.14 // Mt. 4.12) and the ensuing account of John's martyrdom. At most, Q acknowledges (in enigmatic fashion) that violence was associated with John's preaching (Q 16.16) and that his message was rejected (Q 7.30, 33).[3] It is Mark who first reports the violent treatment John received, identifying him both as 'a righteous and holy man' (6.20; cf. Mt. 14.5) and as 'a real prophet' whose baptism is 'from heaven' (11.30-32 // Mt. 21.25-26). Admittedly, John plays only a minor role in Mark. Nonetheless, he appears in the Second Gospel as a rejected prophet of God in line with the precedents outlined above. As such, his martyrdom serves within that Gospel to illustrate a central premise of the parable of the 'Wicked Tenants', to which we now turn.

Related by all three Synoptic Evangelists, the parable of the Wicked Tenants appears in its earliest form in Mk 12.1b-9 (// Mt. 21.33-41 // Lk. 20.9-16). The polemical intent of the parable, which draws upon the metaphor of Israel as the Lord's vineyard (Isa. 5.1-7; 27.2-6; Jer. 12.10), is unmistakable. The owner of the vineyard sends servants to collect his due share of the produce; with ever-increasing violence the first is beaten, a second wounded in the head, a third killed, 'and so with many others, some they beat and some they killed' (vv. 3-5). Finally the owner sends his υἱὸν ἀγαπητόν...ὁ

1. R.A. Edwards, *A Theology of Q: Eschatology, Prophecy, and Wisdom* (Philadelphia: Fortress Press, 1976), p. 55. This work presents in fuller form the results of Edwards's earlier studies, 'An Approach to a Theology of Q', *JR* 51 (1971), pp. 247-69, and 'Christian Prophecy and the Q Tradition', in G. MacRae (ed.), *Society of Biblical Literature 1976 Seminar Papers* (Missoula, MT: Scholars Press, 1976), pp. 119-26.

2. So S. Schulz, *Q: Die Spruchquelle der Evangelisten* (Zürich: Theologischer Verlag, 1972), p. 191, 'Zwar könnte Lk die Angabe ausgelassen haben, da er von der Gefangennahme des Täufers schon in 3,20 berichtete, aber wahrscheinlicher ist es doch, daß Mt für diesen Zusatz verantwortlich ist'; cf. A. Polag, *Fragmenta Q: Textheft zur Logienquelle* (Neukirchen–Vluyn: Neukirchener Verlag, 1979), pp. 40-41.

3. See §2.b.2, below.

κληρονόμος, only to have the tenants kill him and cast him out of the vineyard in an attempt to seize his inheritance (vv. 6-8). So the question is asked, and then answered:

> τί [οὖν] ποιήσει ὁ κύριος τοῦ ἀμπελῶνος; ἐλεύσεται καὶ ἀπολέσει τοὺς γεωργοὺς καὶ δώσει τὸν ἀμπελῶνα ἄλλοις (v. 9).

Here can be seen most clearly the pattern of (1) the sending of the prophets, (2) their violent rejection, and (3) the ensuing divine judgment. The fate of the 'son' simply mirrors that of the 'servants' who went before him. But the prospect of ultimate restoration, so evident in other Deuteronomistic contexts, is absent, for here the judgment appears absolute and irrevocable. Indeed, the 'inheritance' of which the tenants were stewards is to be given ἄλλοις, which in its present context most naturally suggests non-Jews.[1] If this be the case, then the intent of the parable is to draw a parallel between the fate of the prophets and the fate of Jesus, which itself constitutes a significant interpretation of the latter's death.[2] Moreover, the parable provides evidence for the Christian community of continuing recalcitrance on the part of Israel, or at least the nation's leaders, and thereby serves both to explain the admission of Gentiles into the covenant promises and to account for the Jewish opposition that this proposal aroused.[3]

In his version of the parable, Matthew (21.33-46) specifies that the man who plants the vineyard is the οἰκοδεσπότης,[4] and portrays him as sending a plurality of servants (against Mark's singular) to collect his share of the produce. This permits Matthew to consolidate the

1. So J. Jeremias, *The Parables of Jesus* (London: SCM Press, 1963), p. 64; Hare, *Persecution*, p. 154. The tenants' motive (admittedly obscure) for rejecting the son (v. 7) seems to be their attempt to seize the inheritance, which might suggest a Gentile interest behind the parable. On this point, and the parable in general, see Steck, *Israel*, pp. 269-73, and the literature referred to there; esp. Taylor, *Mark*, pp. 472-76.

2. Cf. Schnider, *Jesus der Prophet*, pp. 154, 162.

3. So Steck, *Israel*, pp. 272-73; cf. 276-77, noting similar themes in 1 Thess. 2.15-16.

4. A favourite term for Matthew (Matthew 7×; Mark 1×; Luke 4×), this word can designate Jesus himself (10.25; so 13.27, interpreted in 13.37 as 'the Son of man'; cf. Lk. 13.25, κύριος), a disciple (13.52; 24.43 // Lk. 12.39), or, as here, God (20.1, 11; cf. Lk. 14.21 [// Mt. 22.7, 'king']). But all such occurrences in Matthew are in parables or metaphors; never does the Evangelist use this term literally (unlike Mk 14.14 // Lk. 14.21). Cf. Trilling, *Wahre Israel*, p. 56 n. 6.

details of Mark's several sendings ('the tenants took his servants and beat one, killed another, and stoned another', 21.35; cf. Mk 12.3-5) and to multiply their effect further by adding v. 36 ('Again he sent other servants, more than the first; and they did the same to them').[1] In addition, Matthew deletes two of Mark's designations for the son: that he is ἀγαπητός and that he is sent ἔσχατον—the first in order to lessen the distinction between the son and the servants who precede him; the second because for Matthew there are still further servants (prophets) yet to follow.[2] Finally, Matthew specifies that the distinguishing quality of the new tenants is that they will provide the householder τοὺς καρποὺς ἐν τοῖς καιροῖς αὐτῶν (v. 41; cf. v. 34), and so he renders more explicit Mark's Gentile orientation: 'Therefore I tell you, the kingdom of God will be taken away from you and given to a nation [ἔθνος] producing the fruits of it' (v. 43).

Two features here are of particular interest. First, Matthew's revised sequence seems to make stoning more serious than straightforward murder.[3] Indeed, the sequence ἀπέκτειναν... ἐλιθοβόλησαν anticipates Jesus' condemnation of Jerusalem in 23.37 as ἀποκτείνουσα τοὺς προφήτας καὶ λιθοβόλουσα τοὺς ἀπεσταλμένους πρὸς αὐτήν.[4] Since the latter passage envisages the persecution of Christian as well as Jewish prophets (so 23.34), Matthew's emendation in 21.35 subtly underscores the common treatment both Jewish and Christian prophets encounter at the hands of Israel. That is to say, a Deuteronomistic understanding is applied to both.[5] Moreover, since

1. Although Matthew multiplies the references to δούλους (21.34, 35, 36; cf. Mk 12.1, 2) so as to underscore the allusion to the prophets (see Chapter 3, §B.1, below, on 21.33-35), it is not clear that he thereby distinguishes 'former' from 'latter' prophets (cf. Trilling, *Wahre Israel*, p. 64). The key premise is that all these precede the sending of the son.

2. Both considerations, but especially the emendation of Mark's ἔσχατον, weigh decisively against the contention of Sand (*Gesetz und Propheten*, p. 142) that the sending of the son 'last' depicts him (and therefore Jesus) as the final, eschatological prophet.

3. So Lagrange, *Matthieu*, p. 415. According to Trilling (*Wahre Israel*, p. 56), both Matthew's plurality of servants and his reference to their stoning emphasize his identification of them as prophets.

4. Cf. Hare, *Persecution*, p. 120 n. 1. The verb λιθοβολεῖν occurs only in these two instances (the latter a Q passage, // Lk. 13.34) in the Synoptic Gospels.

5. So S. Pedersen, 'Zum Problem der vaticinia ex eventu. (Eine Analyse von Mt. 21, 33-46 par.; 22,1-10 par.)', *ST* 19 (1965), p. 165: the de-emphasis in

stoning is prescribed for idolaters (Deut. 13.10; 17.5, 7), sorcerers (Lev. 20.27) and soothsayers (*m. Sanh.* 7.4; cf. 11.1, *b. Sanh.* 50a), the passage may imply that the tenants 'condemned the genuine prophets, or servants, as *false* prophets'.[1]

Secondly, both implicitly in Mark and explicitly in Matthew, a Deuteronomistic interpretation of Israel's history leads to the conclusion that Israel has been rejected and the 'kingdom' transferred to the Gentiles. In Jewish literature, as we saw earlier, divine judgment on the nation typically led not to rejection but to ultimate restoration (element 'f1' of Steck's summary schema). Here, however, the judgment consequent upon the tenants' rejection of the son, as placed ironically in the mouths of 'the chief priests and the elders/Pharisees' (21.23, 45), is that κακοὺς κακῶς ἀπολέσει αὐτοὺς καὶ τὸν ἀμπελῶνα ἐκδωθήσεται ἀλλοῖς (21.41). In other words, in this parable the nation or kingdom is indeed 'restored', but not to its original subjects. Matthew's emphasis in this parable is thus twofold: (1) the culpability of Israel for their rejection of the Lord's messengers—including the 'son'—and, in consequence, (2) the transfer of the 'kingdom of God' to a more responsive people.

Matthew reinforces this rather grim outlook by two further emendations. According to Mk 12.12, Jesus' hearers perceived that the parable was directed against them, but were deterred in their attempt to arrest him by fear of the multitude. But Matthew specifies that their fear arose from the fact that the crowds 'held [Jesus] to be a *prophet*' (21.46; cf. 21.26), an ominous designation in light of the parable he has just told.

More pointedly, Matthew inserts here from Q[2] the parable of the banquet (22.2-14, cf. Lk. 14.16-24), relating it in such a way as to recall details of the previous parable. For here too the 'servants' (cf. 'servant', Lk. 14.17) are seized, mistreated and killed (οἱ δὲ λοιποὶ κρατήσαντες τοὺς δούλους αὐτοῦ ὕβρισαν καὶ ἀπέκτειναν,

Matthew of Mark's different groups shows 'dass bei Mt. das Hauptgewicht nicht darauf gelegt werden soll, dass ein Knecht nach dem anderen vergeblich geschickt wird, sondern einmal darauf, dass viele Knechte ausgeschickt werden, und zum anderen darauf, dass sie einer besonders grausamen Behandlung ausgesetzt werden'.

1. Hill, *Matthew*, p. 300, cf. 315; so also Gundry, *Matthew*, p. 426.

2. For reconstructions of the Q form, see Schulz, *Q*, pp. 391-98; Polag, *Fragmenta Q*, pp. 70-71; cf. J.S. Kloppenborg, *Q Parallels: Synopsis, Critical Notes, and Concordance* (Sonoma, CA: Polebridge Press, 1988), p. 164.

22.6, cf. 21.35). In angry response to such extreme treatment, Matthew tells us, the king 'sent his troops and destroyed those murderers[1] and burned their city' (22.7). Declaring that 'those invited were not worthy', he then reissues his invitation to others, 'both bad and good' (22.8-9). These details correspond exactly to the sentence the hearers themselves pronounced over the previous parable: 'He will put those wretches to a miserable death, and let out the vineyard to other tenants' (21.41).[2] The one difference, however, is that the nature of the punishment is now made explicit: not only they themselves, but their city as well, will be destroyed. Nor can it escape our notice that for Matthew the same audience is present to hear this affirmation of their own words (so 22.1; against Mk 12.12, 'they left him and went away').

Again, the Matthaean redaction is strongly Deuteronomistic in outlook, highlighting the murderous rejection of the 'king's envoys' and pronouncing a commensurate judgment on those responsible. More specifically, the fate of 'those murderers and...their city' suggests that the focus of Matthew's Deuteronomistic interests is the destruction of Jerusalem in 70 CE, which he explains as a consequence of the rejection of God's envoys and of his 'son' in particular.[3] In this

1. Matthew's φονεύς (unique in the Synoptic Gospels) anticipates his use of the verbal cognate φονεύειν (Matthew 5×; Mark 1×; Luke 1×) in a similarly Deuteronomistic context at 23.31, 35 (υἱοί ἐστε τῶν φονευσάντων τοὺς προφήτας).

2. According to Meyer ('The Gentile Mission in Q', *JBL* 89 [1970], p. 414), this outlook was already present in Q: 'The church of Q understood the parable to be an explanation of God's turning to the Gentiles; the incorporation of Gentiles was the result of Israel's impenitence'. Cf. D. Lührmann, *Die Redaktion der Logienquelle* (WMANT, 33; Neukirchen–Vluyn: Neukirchener Verlag, 1969), pp. 87-88; D. Zeller, *Kommentar zur Logienquelle* (Stuttgart: Katholisches Bibelwerk, 1986), p. 88; J.S. Kloppenborg, *The Formation of Q: Trajectories in Ancient Wisdom Collections* (Philadelphia: Fortress Press, 1987), p. 230. It is equally possible, however, to read the Q parable as directed not to Gentiles but to the 'sinners and tax collectors', the religiously disenfranchised within Israel itself; so Schulz, *Q*, pp. 400-402; S. Légasse, 'L'oracle contre "cette génération" (Mt 23,34-36 par. Lc 11, 49-51) et la polémique judéo-chrétienne dans la Source des Logia', in J. Delobel (ed.), *Logia: Les paroles de Jesus—The Sayings of Jesus. Mémorial Joseph Coppens* (BETL, 59; Leuven: Leuven University Press, 1982), pp. 253-54; cf. Steck, *Israel*, p. 287 n. 2 for this outlook in Q generally.

3. Cf. Trilling, *Wahre Israel*, p. 84, and literature cited at n. 63; Hummel,

respect, the juxtaposition of the two parables is highly significant. For in the first, the 'servants' must represent all the prophetic envoys who preceded the 'son', whereas in the second, the invitation to the 'wedding feast' (again, for the king's 'son') suggests the work of Christian envoys in anticipation of an eschatological consummation.[1] In other words, since Matthew's Deuteronomistic schema encompasses both Jewish and Christian prophets, as well as Jesus himself, it is the rejection of all these that results in the destruction of Jerusalem. This is the same thesis that Matthew will present once more in his reworking of Q material at 23.34-38.

b. *Q and Matthew*

Several recent studies have focused on the role of Deuteronomistic themes within the Q tradition, and a number have noted that both Q and Matthew coordinate such themes with wisdom motifs, including the depiction of Jesus as Wisdom personified. Each of these concerns will be addressed as they arise in the course of examining the relevant

Auseinandersetzung, pp. 83-85 (who refers in this context to Mt. 27.24-25, 'His blood be upon our heads, etc'). However, it has been shown by C.H. Dodd ('The Fall of Jerusalem and the Abomination of Desolation', *JRS* 37 [1947], pp. 47-54), that Synoptic language in general, and by K.H. Rengstorf ('Die Stadt der Mörder [Mt 22.7]', in W. Eltester (ed.), *Judentum, Christentum, Kirche: Festschrift für Joachim Jeremias* [BZNW, 26; Berlin: Töpelmann, 1964], pp. 106-29) that the language and substance of this passage in particular, refer to the destruction of Jerusalem in stereotypical, rather than historically specific terms: '[Die] Zuge des Gleichnisses liegt nämlich nicht eine geschichtliche Erinnerung zugrunde, sondern ein aus dem alten Orient stammender und bis in das nachbiblische palästinische Judentum erhaltener Topos' (p. 125). Nonetheless, the obvious relevance of the destruction of Jerusalem to Matthew and/or his audience suggests at the very least their temporal proximity to that event, if not their conscious retrospection upon it. For various critiques of Rengstorf's position, see Trilling, *Wahre Israel*, p. 85; Pedersen, 'Zum Problem', *passim*; Steck, *Israel*, p. 82 n. 7, p. 300 n. 5; Strecker, *Weg*, p. 35 n. 1.

1. Matthew specifies that it is a βασιλεῦς (cf. Lk. 14.16, ἄνθρωπός τις) who ἐποίησεν γάμος τῷ υἱῷ αὐτῷ (22.2), which term, as at 21.13, can for Matthew only refer to Jesus (cf. Steck, *Israel*, p. 299). Nonetheless, Jeremias (*Parables*, pp. 64, 68-69; so also Hummel, *Auseinandersetzung*, p. 85) interprets the threefold sending in 22.3, 4 and 9-10 as referring to Jewish prophets, the mission to Israel, and the Gentile mission, respectively. Cf. Hare, *Persecution*, pp. 121-22; Steck, *Israel*, p. 301. On the γάμος as eschatological celebration, see Jeremias, *Parables*, pp. 69, 117.

texts, of which there are essentially five. These include, as designated below, (1) the persecution beatitude (Mt. 5.11-12 // Lk. 6.22-23), (2) Wisdom and the children in the marketplace (Mt. 11.16-19 // Lk. 7.31-35), (3) the Sign of Jonah (Mt. 12.38-42 // Lk. 11.29-32), (4) the woes against the tomb-builders (Mt. 23.29-36 // Lk. 11.47-51), and (5) the lament over Jerusalem (Mt. 23.37-39 // Lk. 13.34-35).

1. *The Persecution Beatitude, Matthew 5.11-12 // Luke 6.22-23*[1]

Matthew	Luke
11 μακάριοί ἐστε ὅταν	22 μακάριοί ἐστε ὅταν
	μισήσωσιν ὑμᾶς οἱ ἄνθρωποι
	καὶ ὅταν ἀφορίσωσιν ὑμᾶς
ὀνειδίσωσιν ὑμᾶς καὶ διώξωσιν	καὶ ὀνειδίσωσιν
καὶ εἴπωσιν πᾶν πονηρὸν καθ' ὑμῶν	καὶ ἐκβάλωσιν τὸ ὄνομα ὑμῶν ὡς πονηρὸν
[ψευδόμενοι][2] ἕνεκεν ἐμοῦ.	ἕνεκα τοῦ υἱοῦ τοῦ ἀνθρώπου·

1. The text of Q, as reconstructed by Polag (*Fragmenta Q*, p. 32), is indicated by single underlining, with less certain readings denoted by a broken line. Cf. Steck, *Israel*, pp. 22-27; Schulz, *Q*, pp. 452-54; Kloppenborg, 'Blessing and Marginality: The "Persecution Beatitude" in Q, Thomas, and Early Christianity', *Forum* 2.3 (1986), pp. 38-44; *idem*, *Q Parallels*, p. 24.

2. Although this word is lacking only from the Western tradition (D it[b,c,d,h,k] syr[s] geo Diatessaron[var] Tertullian Origen Eusebius etc.), both UBSGNT[3] and N–A[26] include it in square brackets on the grounds that while its omission could be accounted for as an accommodation to Lk. 6.22, 'more than one scribe would have been tempted to insert the word in order to limit the wide generalization in Jesus' teaching, and to express specifically what was felt to be implied by the very nature of the case (compare 1 Pe 4.15f.)' (*TCGNT* 13). Conversely, that Matthew uses similar language elsewhere makes it more likely that he would have used it here (Matthew 8×; Mark 5×; Luke 2×; e.g. ψευδομαρτυρέω [19.18 // Mk 10.19 // Lk. 18.20], ψευδομαρτυρία [15.19; 26.59 (+ Mk 7.21; 14.55)], ψευδομαρτύς [26.60 (cf. Mk 14.56, 57, ψευδομαρτυρέω)]; cf. ψευδοπροφήτης [7.15; 24.11; 24.24 // Mk 13.22], ψευδοχρίστος [24.24 // Mk 13.22]). See further, Dupont, *Les béatitudes*. III: *Les évangélistes* (Paris: Gabalda, 1973), pp. 334-37. Moreover, Matthew's ψευδόμενοι could well derive from Lk. 6.26 (κατὰ τὰ αὐτὰ γὰρ ἐποίουν τοῖς ψευδοπροφήταις οἱ πατέρες αὐτῶν), if the latter was present in Q (cf. Polag, *Fragmenta Q*, pp. 84-85).

12 χαίρετε	23 χάρητε ἐν ἐκείνῃ τῇ ἡμέρᾳ
καὶ ἀγαλλιᾶσθε,	καὶ σκιρτήσατε,
ὅτι ὁ μισθὸς ὑμῶν	ἰδοὺ γὰρ ὁ μισθὸς ὑμῶν
πολὺς ἐν τοῖς οὐρανοῖς·	πολὺς ἐν τῷ οὐρανῷ·
οὕτως γὰρ ἐδίωξαν	κατὰ τὰ αὐτὰ γὰρ ἐποίουν
τοὺς προφήτας τοὺς πρὸ ὑμῶν.	τοῖς προφήταις οἱ πατέρες αὐτῶν.

The force of the Q beatitudes (Q 6.20b-23) hinges on the contrast between the disciples' negative experience of poverty, hunger, sorrow or rejection, and the unexpected benefits to be granted them in 'the kingdom of God' (Q 6.20c). In other words, they are 'blessed' or 'fortunate' even in the midst of suffering when they view the situation from an eschatological perspective: 'for [their] reward is great in heaven' (Q 6.23b). In this case, the envisaged situation is primarily one of verbal abuse: Q speaks of hatred (μισήσωσιν ὑμᾶς), shunning (ἀφορίσωσιν ὑμᾶς), reproach or reviling (ὀνειδίσωσιν ὑμᾶς), and generalized slander (καὶ εἴπωσιν πονηρὸν καθ' ὑμῶν). According to Hare,

> While ὀνειδίσωσιν implies the use of insulting language with or without any specific charges being made, εἴπωσιν πᾶν πονηρὸν κατά refers to specific charges involving various kinds of disapproved behaviour.[1]

While this may be so, the cause for such abuse is not so much the disciples' actions (none are related) as it is their allegiances: ἕνεκεν ἐμοῦ/τοῦ υἱοῦ τοῦ ἀνθρώπου. The disciples suffer ostracism and abuse because their adherence to Jesus (which must be public knowledge) sets them distinctively apart from their social context. Not implausibly, this is also the cause of their concomitant poverty, hunger and mourning, although the text itself does not indicate such a connection.

Whereas Q's terms all relate to non-physical abuse, Matthew's insertion of καὶ διώξωσιν (5.11b) implies a more concrete threat of violence. The basic meaning of διώκειν is 'to pursue', and so 'to harry' or 'persecute'.[2] The Evangelist uses the same term in 10.23 and 23.34 to indicate hostile actions that are sufficient to 'drive Christian missionaries out of a community', which actions seem to range from

1. *Persecution*, p. 118. On these terms, see Dupont, *Les béatitudes*, I, pp. 228-338; II, p. 286-94.
2. BAGD *s.v.*; *TWNT*, II, p. 232-33 [= *TDNT*, pp. 229-30].

legal opposition to physical violence, but do not appear to include murder or execution.[1] Furthermore, whereas in Q the prospect of social ostracism could suit either a Jewish or Gentile setting equally well,[2] within the Sermon on the Mount the context of intra-Judaic debate heightens the probability that Jewish opponents are in view.[3] And again, as Hare points out, the fact that διώκειν in 10.23 and 23.34 (and likely 5.44 as well) indicates specifically Jewish opposition favours a similar interpretation here.

Indeed, a Jewish setting is already implicit in Q, for this beatitude envisages the situation of its addressees in terms similar to that of the persecuted prophets of old. In Luke and Q the similarity is one of analogy, emphasizing the consistent attitude of generations of persecutors: even as 'their fathers did to the prophets' (Q 6.23), so the present generation will cause the Christian community to suffer.[4] But this does not necessarily imply that either Jesus or his followers are themselves prophets, for the emphasis here is on the consistent nature of the persecutors, not the identity of the persecuted.[5] It is Matthew who

1. Hare, *Persecution*, pp. 119-20; cf. Dupont, *Les béatitudes*, III, pp. 330-34.

2. As indicated by its similarity to sentiments expressed by Seneca, Epictetus and Cynic writers, on the one hand, and Jesus' address to those on the margins of society, on the other; so Kloppenborg, 'Blessing and Marginality', pp. 49-53.

3. Davies, *Setting*, pp. 289-90; Hare, *Persecution*, pp. 120-21; see, e.g., 5.17, 'the law and the prophets'; 5.20, 'the scribes and Pharisees'; 5.35, swearing by Jerusalem; 5.47, 'Gentiles'; and 5.21-48, on the reinterpretation of Torah.

4. Because our primary concern is with Matthew's use of Q as a literary source, this study will not attempt to distinguish between putative layers of Q redaction, a question of particular importance for the relation of Q 6.23c to the remainder of the persecution beatitude (6.22-23b) and its wider context in 6.20b-49 (see Steck, *Israel*, pp. 258-59; Hare, *Persecution*, pp. 116-17; A.D. Jacobson, 'Wisdom Christology in Q' [PhD dissertation, Claremont Graduate School, 1978], pp. 53-55, 95; J.S. Kloppenborg, 'The Formation of Q and Antique Instructional Genres', *JBL* 105 [1986], p. 452; *idem*, *Formation*, pp. 173, 190).

5. Cf. Schulz, *Q*, pp. 456-57; Schnider, *Jesus der Prophet*, pp. 135-36; Zeller, *Kommentar*, p. 29; *contra* Steck, *Israel*, pp. 259-60, 283; Edwards, *Theology of Q*, p. 63; I. Havener, *Q: The Sayings of Jesus* (Wilmington, DE: Michael Glazier, 1987), p. 69; cf. Kloppenborg, 'Blessing and Marginality', pp. 44-45. 'Es ist aber möglich', says Schnider (*Jesus der Prophet*, p. 136), 'daß aus der nachösterlichen Sicht heraus, die auf das Leiden Jesu zurückblickt, der Gedanke mitschwingt, auch das Schicksal des Menschensohnes selbst in eine Entsprechung zum Prophetenschicksal zu sehen'.

Our investigation, however, is not concerned with the question of whether sayings

makes this latter identification, rewording the conclusion of the beatitude so as to stress both the fact of persecution itself (οὕτως γὰρ ἐδίωξαν; cf. καὶ διώξωσιν [ὑμᾶς], 5.11b) and, by means of an attributive prepositional clause, the common identity of those persecuted, both past and present (τοὺς προφήτας τοὺς πρὸ ὑμῶν). Thus, for Matthew, the disciples whom Jesus addresses are the objects of persecution in the same way as were 'the prophets who were before [them]'—which clearly suggests not only a common fate (as in Q) but also a common prophetic identity.[1]

Finally, Matthew's version of the Q beatitude is prefaced by another beatitude that is unique to his Gospel, but closely matches the Q beatitude in substance and intent: μακάριοι οἱ δεδιωγμένοι ἕνεκεν δικαιοσύνης,[2] ὅτι αὐτῶν ἐστιν ἡ βασιλεία τῶν οὐρανῶν (5.10).[3] Because of this general similarity, and also because the (identical) apodoses of the first and seventh beatitudes (5.3b, 10b) form an *inclusio*, the persecution beatitude—eighth in Matthew's series—

such as this were the product of, or meant to address, prophets within the Q community (and therefore couched in 'prophetic' speech-forms), since these issues do not directly impinge on Matthew's use of the material. This question has been extensively explored by M. Sato (*Q und Prophetie*, *passim*, esp. pp. 298-302, 393-99, 408), who argues that prophetic forms found in Q derive both from the historical Jesus and from a circle of Christian prophets who spoke on his authority.

1. Trilling, *Wahre Israel*, p. 81; Hare, *Persecution*, p. 116, 140; M.J. Suggs, *Wisdom, Christology, and Law in Matthew's Gospel* (Cambridge, MA: Harvard University Press, 1970), p. 123; Sand, *Gesetz und Propheten*, pp. 172-73.

By comparison, there is no clear evidence that Jesus' followers were persecuted as prophets in the Gospel of Mark, although they were certainly to expect persecution (so Mk 10.30 [without Synoptic parallel]). In Mk 13.11 the disciples are promised that the Spirit will inspire them in the midst of persecution (// Mt. 10.19-20 // Lk. 12.12). But although such inspiration could possibly be construed as prophetic, the inspiration is a response to persecution, and not vice versa. Again, although Jesus promises that the deceptions of 'false prophets' will contribute to an almost unbearable eschatological tribulation (Mk 13.20-22 // Mt. 24.22-24, cf. 24.11), there is no implication in Mark's account that 'the elect' are therefore the 'true' prophets or suffer as a result.

2. On the possible meaning of this difficult phrase, see Hare, *Persecution*, pp. 130-32; Dupont, *Les béatitudes*, III, pp. 341-53.

3. The close similarity of 1 Pet. 3.14 to Mt. 5.10 makes it unlikely (unless 1 Peter knew Matthew) that the Evangelist has simply produced a doublet of the Q text, but suggests, instead, an alternative source (so Dupont, *Les béatitudes*, I, pp. 225-27; cf. Steck, *Israel*, p. 21 n. 2).

appears redundant. Moreover, the fact that Matthew has added διώκειν in 5.11 results in a threefold repetition of this verb in the consecutive vv. 10, 11 and 12, which surely indicates a concern on the part of the Evangelist to address the problem of persecution within his own community or audience. What remains to be seen, however, is whether persecution consistently implies for Matthew a prophetic identity (as in 5.12c), and vice versa.

For example, prophetic self-consciousness is present in Q's explanation of the revelation the disciples have been accorded:

> Many prophets and righteous (Matthew)/kings (Luke) desired to see what you see, and did not see it, and to hear what you hear, and did not hear it (Mt. 13.16-17 // Lk. 10.23b-24).[1]

For if the followers of Jesus have been granted a revelation that not even the ancient prophets could attain, they are not only prophets themselves, but, like John the Baptist, 'more than prophets' (cf. Q 7.26). In this passage, however, there is no mention of persecution.

Just the opposite is the case in the missionary sayings of Mt. 10.16a // Lk. 10.3 ('Behold, I send you out as lambs in the midst of wolves') and Mt. 10.14-15 // Lk. 10.10-12 ('Whenever you enter a town and they do not receive you...it shall be more tolerable on that day for Sodom than for that town').[2] Here the disciples are to expect rejection and perhaps persecution (since the metaphor of lambs among wolves implies as much; cf. *2 Clem.* 5.2-4). Yet their role is not explicitly prophetic.[3] Nonetheless, the image of 'labourers in the harvest' (Q 10.2) who heal and proclaim the nearness of the kingdom (Q 10.9) connotes eschatological ingathering for judgment, as does the concluding reference to 'that day' (Q 10.12).[4] Thus the Deuteronomistic motifs of rejection and judgment are present in Q, although trans-

1. Cf. Edwards, *Theology of Q*, p. 65; for Q reconstructions, see Schulz, *Q*, pp. 419-20; Polag, *Fragmenta Q*, p. 48.

2. See Q reconstructions in Schulz, *Q*, pp. 404-407; Polag, *Fragmenta Q*, pp. 44-47; Hoffmann, *Studien*, pp. 263-64, 268-72, 283-84.

3. *Contra* Edwards, *Theology of Q*, pp. 103-104; on the animal imagery and its background, see Hoffmann, *Studien*, pp. 294-95. Matthew omits the only possible indication of a prophetic self-consciousness, which is the interdiction on greeting (so Lk. 10.4b, on the analogy of 2 Kgs 4.29, according to Hoffmann, *Studien*, p. 298).

4. So Q 3.7, 9, 17; cf. Lührmann, *Redaktion*, pp. 59-60; Schulz, *Q*, p. 410; Jacobson, 'Literary Unity', p. 379 n. 64; Hoffmann, *Studien*, pp. 289-92; Kloppenborg, *Formation*, pp. 193.

posed into a context of eschatological rather than strictly historical reckoning.[1] Matthew expands very little on this material, beyond making more specific reference to the day of judgment (10.15) and describing in greater detail the roles of preaching (10.7) and healing in its various forms (10.8a).

Later in the same discourse, however, Matthew places the Q saying that 'a disciple is not above his teacher' (10.24 // Lk. 6.40) into a context that interprets it as a reference to the common nature of their fate.[2] For the verse immediately preceding speaks of fleeing persecution (ὅταν δὲ διώκωσιν ὑμᾶς) from one town to the next, while the verse following describes the slander both master and servant must endure ('If they have called the master of the house Beelzebul, how much more will they malign those of his household'). This emphasis on common suffering, specifically recalling the present passage, recurs in 23.34. But insofar as Matthew 10 primarily has in view the Church's mission to Israel (much more so than his sources in Mark 6 and 13, or Q 9), the latter's envisaged rejection of the disciples can be seen as one more instance of their spiritual obduracy.[3] Thus, at least

1. Cf. Schulz, *Q*, pp. 411-14; Jacobson, 'Wisdom Christology', pp. 134-35; Steck, *Israel*, pp. 287-88; Kloppenborg, *Formation*, pp. 196-97. Also note Q 10.16, although Kloppenborg (*Formation*, p. 93) does not believe this passage to be specifically Deuteronomistic in tone.

2. Cf. Hoffmann, *Studien*, pp. 255-56. Trilling (*Wahre Israel*, p. 83) observes that 'Matthäus komponiert in 10,17-25 aus disparaten Stoffen eine eindringliche "Rede" über die Verfolgung der Jünger'. That Jn 15.20 employs a variant of the saying in a similar context (οὐκ ἔστιν δοῦλος μείζων τοῦ κυρίου αὐτοῦ. εἰ ἐμὲ ἐδίωξαν, καὶ ὑμᾶς διώξουσιν) suggests that this was its original intent (so Mt. 10.23).

3. So Hare, *Persecution*, pp. 97-101, who notes that Matthew de-eschatologizes Mk 13.9-13 and applies its content instead to the immediate situation of his community. Thus Matthew's new context 'suggests that persecution arises *precisely on account of the church's mission*' (p. 100; italics original). Cf. Hoffmann, *Studien*, p. 257 and n. 80. For the emphasis on Israel, see 10.5b-6 ('Go nowhere among the Gentiles... but go rather to the lost sheep of the house of Israel'; cf. Trilling, *Wahre Israel*, pp. 99-102; Hoffmann, *Studien*, pp. 258-61), 10.17 ('They will... flog you in their synagogues'), and 10.23 ('you will not have gone through all the towns of Israel...')—notwithstanding the καὶ τοῖς ἔθνεσιν of 10.18. On the Jewish identity of the opponents in Mt. 10, see Hare, *Persecution*, pp. 101-105. In this connection, A.E. Harvey ('Forty Strokes Save One: Social Aspects of Judaizing and Apostasy', in A.E. Harvey [ed.], *Alternative Approaches to New Testament*

according to Matthew, the disciples are sent out in the full expectation that in keeping with the pattern of their past spiritual history, God's own people will refuse to hear the message that his servants bring.

Finally, Matthew draws his mission discourse to a close by coordinating four Q passages that Luke places in widely differing contexts. In the first, the exhortations not to be afraid (Q 12.2-9) clearly envisage the prospect of martyrdom for the disciples: μὴ φοβεῖσθε ἀπὸ τῶν <u>ἀποκτενόντων</u> τὸ σῶμα (Mt. 10.28). In the second, Jesus' forewarning of divided households (Mt. 10.34-36 // Lk. 12.51-53) reiterates the internecine nature of opposition to the disciples' message and recalls the earlier statement that this too will have mortal consequences (i.e. παραδώσει δὲ ἀδελφὸς ἀδελφὸν εἰς θάνατον, 10.21 // Mk 13.12). In the third and fourth, which are the most dramatic, the declarations of Q 14.26-27 and 17.33 (on the simplest reading) make martyrdom a virtual precondition for discipleship: 'he who does not take his cross and follow me is not worthy of me'; 'he who loses his life for my sake will find it' (Mt. 10.38-39).[1] Taken together within the context of the mission discourse, these sayings clearly indicate not only that the disciples will face death in response to their preaching of the kingdom (cf. 10.6), but that such mortal opposition will arise from the mission to Israel in particular.

It is in this context that we are to understand the final paragraph of Matthew's mission discourse (10.40-42). In contrast to the general expectation of rejection (10.14), persecution (vv. 16-17, 23), slander (v. 25), hatred (v. 22), internecine strife and betrayal (vv. 21, 34-36), and even death (vv. 21d, 28, 38-39), Jesus promises great rewards to those who 'receive' his emissaries. This passage consists of three parallel clauses: ὁ δεχόμενος ὑμᾶς...ὁ δεχόμενος προφήτην...ὁ δεχόμενος δίκαιον. The parallelism makes it clear that these references to the 'prophet' and 'righteous one' are, in fact, descriptions of the disciples whom Jesus is addressing.

In this passage, then, Jesus first reiterates the common identity of master and disciple ('He who receives you receives me' [10.40]). This affirmation of a common welcome counterbalances the previous

Study [London: SPCK, 1985], pp. 90-93) argues convincingly that the prospect of flogging in the synagogue indicates that the missionaries remained under Jewish religious jurisdiction, and therefore considered themselves as within Israel.

1. Cf. Hare, *Persecution*, p. 101 and n. 2.

warning of a common rejection (10.24-25). Secondly, and most significantly, he envisages that some will welcome the missionary disciples εἰς ὄνομα προφήτου (10.41a)—that is, as prophets and precisely because they are prophets. This counterbalances the previous warning that the disciples will be rejected because they are prophets (5.12c; cf. 23.34, 37). Thirdly, Jesus foresees that some will welcome the disciples εἰς ὄνομα δικαίου (10.41c), which title, in tandem with that of 'prophet', is associated with persecution elsewhere in Matthew's Gospel (23.29, 35). Here, by contrast, the opposite is in view. Then in conclusion, confirming that he has been addressing the situation of the disciples, the Evangelist adds the saying regarding 'a cup of cold water' given εἰς ὄνομα μαθητοῦ (10.42; from Mk 9.41).

Clearly, this encouraging conclusion to Matthew's Mission Discourse is in dialogue, as it were, with the dire prospects that the foregoing material has envisaged: that although many will reject them, some will welcome them. More specifically, the mention of 'prophets' (and 'righteous ones') who share the fate of their Lord reveals, albeit by negation, that here too Matthew's use of material is governed by Deuteronomistic interests.

2. *Wisdom and the Children in the Marketplace, Matthew 16-19 // Luke 7.31-35*[1]

Matthew	Luke
16 Τίνι δὲ ὁμοιώσω τὴν γενεὰν ταύτην;	Τίνι οὖν ὁμοιώσω τοὺς ἀνθρώπους τῆς γενεᾶς ταύτης καὶ τίνι εἰσὶν ὅμοιοι;
ὁμοία ἐστὶν παιδίοις καθημένοις ἐν ταῖς ἀγοραῖς ἃ προσφωνοῦντα τοῖς ἑτέροις	32 ὅμοιοί εἰσιν παιδίοις τοῖς ἐν ἀγορᾷ καθημένοις καὶ προσφωνοῦσιν ἀλλήλοις ἃ
17 λέγουσιν· ηὐλήσαμεν ὑμῖν καὶ οὐκ ὠρχήσασθε,	λέγει· ηὐλήσαμεν ὑμῖν καὶ οὐκ ὠρχήσασθε,
ἐθρηνήσαμεν[2] καὶ οὐκ ἐκόψασθε.	ἐθρηνήσαμεν καὶ οὐκ ἐκλαύσατε.

1. Reconstructions in Schulz, *Q*, pp. 379-80; Polag, *Fragmenta Q*, p. 42; Hoffmann, *Studien*, pp. 196-98; cf. Kloppenborg, *Q Parallels*, p. 60.

2. ἐθρηνήσαμεν ℵ B D Z f^{1} 892 it$^{(pt)}$ vg cop^{sa,bo}| ἐθρηνήσαμεν ὑμῖν C L W θ f^{13} 𝔐 it$^{(pt)}$ syr (likely an expansion reflecting the previous strophe, with the *lectio brevior* exhibiting broad textual support [*TCGNT* 30]; a similar insertion is present in A f^{1} 𝔐 at // Lk. 7.32).

18 ἦλθεν γὰρ Ἰωάννης	33 ἐλήλυθεν γὰρ Ἰωάννης ὁ βαπτιστὴς
μήτε ἐσθίων μήτε πίνων,	μὴ ἐσθίων ἄρτον μήτε πίνων οἶνον,
καὶ λέγουσιν· δαιμόνιον ἔχει.	καὶ λέγετε· δαιμόνιον ἔχει.
19 ἦλθεν ὁ υἱὸς τοῦ ἀνθρώπου	34 ἐλήλυθεν ὁ υἱὸς τοῦ ἀνθρώπου
ἐσθίων καὶ πίνων, καὶ λέγουσιν· ἰδοὺ	ἐσθίων καὶ πίνων, καὶ λέγετε· ἰδοὺ
ἄνθρωπος φάγος καὶ οἰνοπότης,	ἄνθρωπος φάγος καὶ οἰνοπότης,
τελωνῶν φίλος καὶ ἁμαρτωλῶν.	φίλος τελωνῶν καὶ ἁμαρτωλῶν.
καὶ ἐδικαιώθη ἡ σοφία	35 καὶ ἐδικαιώθη ἡ σοφία
ἀπὸ τῶν ἔργων[1] αὐτῆς.	ἀπὸ πάντων τῶν τέκνων αὐτῆς.

In Q this passage is part of a larger discussion about John the Baptist. Here in Matthew it connects John's ministry with violence and violent entry into the kingdom. According to Lk. 16.16, 'the law and the prophets were until John; since then the good news of the kingdom of God is preached, and every one enters it violently [εἰς αὐτὴν βιάζεται]'.[2] In Matthew, however, the element of violence is accentuated:

> From the days of John the Baptist until now the kingdom of heaven has suffered violence [βιάζεται] and men of violence take it by force [βιασταὶ ἁρπάζουσιν αὐτήν] (Mt. 11.12).

So in its Matthaean context this saying (however enigmatic) provides an ominous introduction to the simile of the children in the marketplace.

Q's ironic address to them in the words of the childrens' song ('We piped to you, and you did not dance; we wailed, and you did not mourn') condemns 'this generation'[3] for having rejected both the

1. That this is Matthew's original is likely, given the evidence of B* ℵ W syr^{pt} cop$^{sa(pt),bo}$ as against τέκνων in B^2 C D L Θ f^1 f^{13} 𝔐 syr^{pt} cop$^{sa(pt)}$ (which represents an assimilation to the Lukan parallel).

2. Reconstructions in Polag, *Fragmenta Q*, p. 74; Schulz, *Q*, pp. 261-62; Hoffmann, *Studien*, pp. 51-52 (with the latter two favouring the Matthaean wording, βιάζεται καὶ βιασταὶ ἁρπάζουσιν αὐτήν); for a summary of the critical discussion concerning this passage, see Kloppenborg, *Formation*, pp. 113-15; concerning its placement, see *idem*, *Q Parallels*, p. 56; and concerning the meaning of βιάζεται in particular, see G. Schrenk, *s.v.* 'βιάζομαι', *TWNT*, I, pp. 608-12 [= *TDNT*, pp. 609-13]; Jacobson, 'Wisdom Christology', pp. 79-80; Hoffmann, *Studien*, pp. 68-69.

3. On this motif see Lührmann, *Redaktion*, pp. 24-48; A. Polag, *Die*

ascetic John and the indulgent Jesus (Q 7.31-32). But the connection between this pronouncement of judgment and the earlier reference to violence (if Matthew has preserved the Q order) seems not to have been immediately evident. Hence Matthew clarifies the link by specifying, first, that John is rejected as a prophet, and secondly, that Jesus is rejected as a representative, if not a personification of Wisdom.

Accordingly, between Q's association of 'the days of John the Baptist' with violence in the kingdom of heaven (Mt. 11.12) and this acknowledgment that the people have rejected him (11.18), Matthew identifies John as Elijah *redivivus* (11.14). Already in Q, John is 'a prophet...and more than a prophet' (Q 7.26 // Mt. 11.9), so that the idea of prophetic rejection is implicitly present.[1] But lest the point be overlooked, Matthew specifies here that John suffered rejection as a prophet, after the manner of Elijah (cf. Mt. 14.5; 17.12).[2] This hints at his imminent fate, for John is about to become a further example of the violence that attends the kingdom's advent.

No less pregnant, though with a focus on Jesus, is the pericope's conclusion: καὶ ἐδικαιώθη ἡ σοφία ἀπὸ τῶν ἔργων [Matthew]/ πάντων τῶν τέκνων [Luke] αὐτῆς. This is one of the few places where Q refers unmistakably to Σοφία or heavenly Wisdom. Behind this reference can be discerned the influence of a more widespread concept of personified Wisdom, who commissions wise men and prophets to send her message to Israel, only to have them suffer rejection and so cause her to withdraw in judgment.

The rejection of Wisdom and her emissaries. According to *1 En.* 42.1-2 (cf. also Sir. 24.7; Bar. 3.9-14), Wisdom withdraws to her heavenly abode because she is rejected by men:

> Wisdom could not find a place in which she could dwell;
> but a place was found (for her) in the heavens.

Christologie der Logienquelle (WMANT, 45; Neukirchen–Vluyn: Neukirchener Verlag, 1977), pp. 89-91; Jacobson, 'Wisdom Christology', p. 85 n. 181; Légasse, 'L'oracle contre "cette génération"', pp. 245-48.

1. Indeed, insofar as John's call to repentance and his announcement of judgment in Q 3.7-9, 16-17 are themselves Deuteronomistic in tone (cf. Kloppenborg, *Formation*, pp. 105-106), Q likely anticipates the rejection not only of his message but of the messenger as well.

2. The identification of John with Elijah is already implicitly present in Q 7.27 (cf. Kloppenborg, *Formation*, pp. 109-10; Hoffmann, *Studien*, pp. 63).

Then Wisdom went out to dwell with the children of the people,
but she found no dwelling place.
(So) Wisdom returned to her place
and she settled permanently among the angels.

The permanence of Wisdom's withdrawal is a sign of judgment:

Because I have called and you refused to listen...
and you have ignored all my counsel...
I also will laugh at your calamity...
When distress and anguish come upon you.
Then they will call upon me, but I will not answer...
Therefore they shall eat the fruit of their way...
(Prov. 1.24-31; cf. *4 Ezra* 5.9-10).

In addition to judgment, the feature here that most closely approximates the Deuteronomistic tradition is Wisdom's inspiration of 'prophets' (κατὰ γενεὰς εἰς ψυχὰς ὁσίας μεταβαίνουσα φίλους θεοῦ καὶ προφήτας κατασκευάζει, 'in every generation she passes into holy souls and makes them friends of God, and prophets', Wis. 7.27; cf. 10.16; 11.1), who are presumably among her emissaries (שלחה נערתיה תקרא על־גפי מרמי קרת, 'She has sent out her maids to call from the highest places in the town', Prov. 9.3). For, like her, they too are rejected. According to Bonnard, Wisdom herself acts like a prophet by proclaiming divine truth at the crossroads and in the temple courts (e.g. Prov. 1.20-21, 8.1-3).[1] In such a reconstruction a passage such as Q 11.49 itself becomes part of the evidence in favour of seeing Wisdom as the sender of prophets.[2]

1. *La sagesse en personne annoncée et venue: Jesus Christ* (LD, 44; Paris: Cerf, 1966), pp. 24-28, 116-17.

2. On the activities of personified Wisdom, see U. Wilckens, 'Σοφία κτλ.', *TWNT*, VII, pp. 508-10, 516 [= *TDNT*, pp. 508-509, 515]; Bonnard, *Sagesse*, *passim*; F. Christ, *Jesus Sophia: Die Sophia-Christologie bei den Synoptikern* (ATANT, 57; Zürich: Zwingli Verlag, 1970), pp. 127-28; Suggs, *Wisdom, Christology, and Law*, pp. 39-44; Schulz, *Q*, p. 344 (with further references n. 162 regarding Wisdom's sending of prophets); J.M. Robinson, 'Jesus as Sophos and Sophia: Wisdom Tradition and the Gospels', in R.L. Wilken (ed.), *Aspects of Wisdom in Judaism and Early Christianity* (Notre Dame: Notre Dame University Press, 1975), pp. 1-15; F.W. Burnett, *The Testament of Jesus-Sophia: A Redactional Critical Study of the Eschatological Discourse in Matthew* (Lanham, MD: University Press of America, 1981), pp. 94-98; R.A. Piper, *Wisdom in the Q-tradition: The Aphoristic Teaching of Jesus* (SNTSMS, 61; Cambridge: Cambridge

Accordingly, Q 7.35 may be interpreted in one of two ways: either Wisdom—identified with and rejected in the persons of John and Jesus— is 'justified' by the 'sinners and tax gatherers' (her 'children') who come to Jesus,[1] or Jesus and John are themselves the 'children' in question, whose ministries constitute the vindication of Wisdom. In either case, Q depicts both John and Jesus as the rejected emissaries of Wisdom.[2]

Matthew, however, makes more careful distinctions. For having already identified John with Elijah, he links Jesus to Wisdom more directly by emending Q's τέκνων to ἔργων: 'Wisdom is justified by

University Press, 1989), pp. 162-70.

Although certain features of this reconstruction have been challenged (see M.D. Johnson, 'Reflections on a Wisdom Approach to Matthew's Theology', *CBQ* 36 [1974], pp. 44-64, for a critique both of the reconstructed 'Sophia-myth' and of Suggs' interpretation of wisdom traditions in Matthew), its emphasis on the rejection of divine emissaries closely resembles the Deuteronomistic framework we have been discussing. Steck (*Israel*, pp. 205-208; 224-25; cf. Christ, *Jesus Sophia*, pp. 124-26; Jacobson, 'Literary Unity', p. 387 and n. 104) argues that wisdom and prophetic/Deuteronomistic motifs had begun to be assimilated into one another prior to their incorporation into the Q tradition; Schulz (*Q*, p. 344) and Hoffmann (*Studien*, pp. 161-62; 182-84), on the other hand, attribute the combination of Deuteronomistic and sapiential motifs to Q redaction.

The association of Jesus with wisdom in Q, however, does not depend solely on thematic appeals to a reconstructed Sophia-myth. Rather, form-critical and generic considerations place Q—and Jesus—firmly within the orbit of the wisdom tradition; see R. Bultmann, *Die Geschichte der synoptischen Tradition* (FRLANT, 12.29; Göttingen: Vandenhoeck & Ruprecht, 1958), pp. 73-113 [ET *History of the Synoptic Tradition* (London: Basil Blackwell, 1963), pp. 69-108]; J.M. Robinson, 'Logoi Sophon: On the Gattung of Q', in H. Koester and J.M. Robinson (eds.), *Trajectories Through Early Christianity* (Philadelphia: Fortress Press, 1971), pp. 71-113; Polag, *Christologie*, pp. 137-38 (very tentatively); J.S. Kloppenborg, 'Antique Instructional Genres', pp. 443-62; *idem*, *Formation*, *passim*, esp. pp. 171-245, 263-328; Piper, *Wisdom in the Q-tradition*, *passim*.

1. So Christ, *Jesus Sophia*, pp. 66-67, 71-73; Hoffmann, *Studien*, p. 229; Sato, *Prophetie*, p. 180; cf. Lührmann, *Redaktion*, pp. 29-31; Zeller, *Kommentar*, pp. 44: 'Die Ausdeutung des Gleichnisses stammt wohl erst von jüdischen Christen. Sie haben sich in den "Kindern der Weisheit" selbst dargestellt.'

2. Cf. U. Wilckens, 'Σοφία κτλ.', *TWNT*, VII, p. 516; Bonnard, *Sagesse*, p. 128; Suggs, *Wisdom, Christology, and Law*, pp. 35-44; Schulz, *Q*, p. 386; Robinson, 'Jesus as Sophos', pp. 5-6; Edwards, *Theology of Q*, p. 99; Jacobson, 'Wisdom Christology', pp. 87-91; J.S. Kloppenborg, 'Wisdom Christology in Q', *LTP* 34 (1978), p. 130; *idem*, *Formation*, p. 111; Burnett, *Testament*, p. 88.

her works' (11.19). This recalls the statement in 11.2 that John in prison had heard about τὰ ἔργα τοῦ Χριστοῦ (cf. Lk. 7.18, πάντων τούτων). The resulting juxtaposition, therefore, explicitly identifies Christ and his works with those of Wisdom. Moreover, the two references now frame 11.2-19 as a redactional unit.[1] Thus the reference here to 'Sophia' further underscores Matthew's understanding of Jesus as a rejected divine emissary—no less so than John the Baptist.

This interpretation is confirmed by Matthew's transfer of the woes against Chorazin and Bethsaida from their original context (Q 10.2-16) to their place here in 11.20-24. For these woes, which unfavourably contrast Israel's response to Jesus (and the nation's consequent judgment) with that of the Gentiles, belong 'to the orbit of the Deuteronomistic preaching of repentance'.[2] Matthew, in fact, highlights this theme (and the rejection it implies) by means of an editorial 'seam'— 'Then [Jesus] began to upbraid the cities where most of his mighty works had been done, because they did not repent' (11.20). And this same contrast between unrepentant Israel and faithful Gentiles is evident as well in Matthew's treatment of the 'Sign of Jonah', to which we must now turn.

3. *The Sign of Jonah, Matthew 12.39-41 // Luke 11.29-32*[3]

Matthew	Luke
39 ὁ δὲ ἀποκριθεὶς εἶπεν αὐτοῖς· γενεὰ πονηρὰ καὶ μοιχαλὶς σημεῖον ἐπιζητεῖ,	29 Τῶν δὲ ὄχλων ἐπαθροιζομένων ἤρξατο λέγειν· ἡ γενεὰ αὕτη γενεὰ πονηρά ἐστιν· σημεῖον ζητεῖ,

1. Christ, *Jesus Sophia*, pp. 76-77; Suggs, *Wisdom, Christology, and Law*, p. 37 (cf. pp. 56-58, where Suggs takes this to indicate that Jesus is no longer simply an envoy of Wisdom, but now 'Sophia incarnate'); Burnett, *Testament*, pp. 55, 89-91. According to Suggs (*Wisdom, Christology and Law*, pp. 19, 28, 96) and Lührmann (*Redaktion*, p. 99), the full identification of Jesus with Wisdom first takes place in Matthew, rather than in Q; so Robinson ('Jesus as Sophos', pp. 9-10), who distinguishes between different layers of Q redaction, the latest of which is taken further by Matthew; similarly Burnett, *Testament*, pp. 51-54.

2. Kloppenborg, 'Antique Instructional Genres', pp. 452-53; cf. Suggs, *Wisdom, Christology, and Law*, pp. 56-57.

3. Reconstructions in Schulz, *Q*, pp. 250-52; Polag, *Fragmenta Q*, pp. 52-54; cf. Kloppenborg, *Q Parallels*, p. 98.

καὶ σημεῖον οὐ δοθήσεται αὐτῇ	καὶ σημεῖον οὐ δοθήσεται αὐτῇ
εἰ μὴ τὸ σημεῖον Ἰωνᾶ τοῦ	εἰ μὴ τὸ σημεῖον Ἰωνᾶ.
προφήτου.	
40 ὥσπερ γὰρ ἦν Ἰωνᾶς	30 καθὼς γὰρ ἐγένετο Ἰωνᾶς
ἐν τῇ κοιλίᾳ τοῦ κήτους	τοῖς Νινευίταις σημεῖον,
τρεῖς ἡμέρας καὶ τρεῖς νύκτας,	
οὕτως ἔσται ὁ υἱὸς τοῦ ἀνθρώπου	οὕτως ἔσται καὶ ὁ υἱὸς τοῦ ἀνθρώπου
ἐν τῇ καρδίᾳ τῆς γῆς	τῇ γενεᾷ ταύτῃ.
τρεῖς ἡμέρας καὶ τρεῖς νύκτας.	...[31]...

41/32 ἄνδρες Νινευῖται ἀναστήσονται ἐν τῇ κρίσει
μετὰ τῆς γενεᾶς ταύτης καὶ κατακρινοῦσιν αὐτήν,
ὅτι μετενόησαν εἰς τὸ κήρυγμα Ἰωνᾶ, καὶ ἰδοὺ πλεῖον Ἰωνᾶ ὧδε.

According to Edwards, the theme of this Q unit is the declaration of judgment against 'this generation', in concert with the larger context of which it is a part (Q 11.14-23, the Beelzebul accusation; 11.24-26, the return of the evil spirit; 11.29-32, the sign of Jonah).[1] As a judgment directed against their lack of faith, Jesus refuses to grant 'this generation' the sign they seek. Yet the 'sign of Jonah' is an exception: 'no sign shall be given...except the sign of Jonah' (Q 11.29). In Q this is a self-reference on the part of Jesus by which he compares himself to Jonah as a vindicated messenger of God:

> The figure of Jonah has meaning primarily because he is a preacher of repentance, prior to a great judgment (as the Q community thought Jesus was also). Secondly, Jonah is also one who has overcome death, as Jesus has. Both are vindicated preachers.[2]

1. R. A. Edwards, *The Sign of Jonah in the Theology of the Evangelists and Q* (London: SCM Press, 1971), pp. 88-89.

2. Edwards, *The Sign of Jonah*, p. 86, cf. p. 83. Edwards claims that 'both Jonah and Solomon are great men of Israel to whom certain Gentiles responded with greater certainty and forthrightness than any Israelite' (p. 56). Such an interpretation, however, reads the element of rejection back into the earlier situation(s) from the circumstances of Jesus and 'this generation'. The point is that if even Gentiles were attentive to τὸ κήρυγμα Ἰωνᾶ and τὴν σοφίαν Σολομῶνος (which juxtaposition closely equates the wisdom and prophetic traditions), how much more so should Israel hear Jesus, who is greater than they (cf. Schulz, *Q*, pp. 255-57; *contra* Lührmann, *Redaktion*, pp. 40-41, who understands Q to compare Jonah with the coming Son of man).

Moreover, as with the parable of the banquet, the analogy of Jonah has specific relevance to the Gentile mission: 'The men of Nineveh will arise at the judgment with this generation and condemn it, for they repented at the preaching of Jonah, and something greater than Jonah is here' (Q 11.32).

In 'this generation', therefore, as much as in the days of Jonah, Gentiles repent at the message of the kingdom while Israel remains impenitent, thereby bringing judgment on itself.[1] Although Jonah (unlike Jesus) is not depicted as a 'rejected prophet', this contrast between 'faithful' Gentiles and 'faithless' Israel is nonetheless implicitly Deuteronomistic in tone.[2] But Jesus is 'something greater than Jonah' insofar as the judgment he portends is more final and absolute.

In a manner that we now recognize to be typical, Matthew stresses the prophetic identity of both Jonah and Jesus (who is πλεῖον Ἰωνᾶ) and their common suffering. Thus, according to 12.39, no sign will be given except τὸ σημεῖον Ἰωνᾶ τοῦ προφήτου (cf. Lk. 11.29 τὸ σημεῖον Ἰωνᾶ). This becomes significant in conjunction with Matthew's emphasis on Jonah's sojourn in the belly of the whale—which the rabbis understood as 'an experience of death, or at least near death', and which the Evangelist explicitly compares to Jesus' three days in the tomb (12.40). For, as Edwards observes:

> The mention of the fact that Jonah was a prophet in that pericope where Matthew stresses the suffering of Jonah and Jesus [points] to the passion of Jesus as the significant element in the Jonah comparison. Both Jonah and Jesus suffer for the good of God's work, on behalf of Israel and for the Gentiles. Judgment upon this generation is still evident, but now it is focused to relate to the specific fact of the passion of Christ.[3]

1. Cf. Meyer, 'Gentile Mission', pp. 405-408. In this connection, Jeremias (*TWNT*, III, pp. 411 n. 17 [= *TDNT*, p. 408]), followed by Schnider (*Jesus der Prophet*, pp. 175-76) and Kloppenborg (*Formation*, pp. 133), cite a passage from *Lam. R.* Proem 31 attributed to the second-century Tanna Simeon b.Yoḥai: 'One prophet I sent to Nineveh and she turned in penitence, but to Israel in Jerusalem I sent many prophets... Yet she hearkened not'. Similar in its use of the 'prophetic correlative' as a proclamation of eschatological judgment is the 'Logia Apocalypse' of Q 17.23-35 (so Kloppenborg, *Formation*, pp. 160-64).

2. Hoffmann (*Studien*, p. 181): 'Jesus wird... in einer der deuteronomistischen Tradition verwandten Art als Weisheits- und Umkehrprediger dargestellt, der von diesem Geschlecht abgelehnt wird'. Cf. Jacobson, 'Wisdom Christology', pp. 170-71.

3. Edwards, *Sign of Jonah*, pp. 97-98. Edwards's use of the term 'passion'

So by specifically identifying Jonah as a prophet and Jesus as 'more than a prophet' (12.41c; cf. 11.9), Matthew demonstrates that the latter's ministry and Passion bear all the hallmarks of the Deuteronomistic vision of a prophet's destiny.

Furthermore, Matthew reiterates this interpretation by appending to Mark's version of the request for a sign (Mk 8.11-12) an additional reference to the 'sign of Jonah' (Mt. 16.1-2a, 4).[1] In Mark this refusal of a sign is the first of several incidents that build towards the Caesaraea Philippi confession (i.e., the request for a sign, 8.11-13; the disciples' failure to understand the two multiplications of bread, 8.14-21; and the healing of the blind man, 8.22-26). Matthew, too, interprets the request for a sign in relation to the ensuing confession and passion prediction (Mt. 16.13-23 // Mk 8.27-33). Yet he lays greater stress than does Mark on Jesus' suffering. So having first interpreted the 'sign of Jonah' as a reference to Jesus' death and vindication in 12.39-40, he recalls this fact in 16.4 as part of his own preparation for the imminent announcement of Jesus' suffering messiahship.[2]

should not be taken to mean that Q includes a 'theology of the cross' in the Markan or Pauline sense; it refers rather to the fact of Jesus' rejection. Accordingly, Edwards compares this to other Matthaean passages that correlate the common fate of Jesus and the prophets, and that stress the culpability of Israel (e.g. 5.12; 23.30, 31, 37). Sand (*Gesetz und Propheten*, pp. 161-62 and n. 189) objects that the designation of Jesus as 'more than Jonah' removes him altogether from the category of prophet. On the contrary, it would suggest that if Jonah is a prophet, so, *a fortiori*, is Jesus. But Sand is correct insofar as Jesus' identity is by no means limited to the category of 'prophet'.

1. Cf. Edwards, *Sign of Jonah*, p. 81.
2. Edwards, *Sign of Jonah*, pp. 100, 105.

4. *The Woes Against the Tomb Builders, Matthew 23.29-36 // Luke 11.47-51*[1]

Matthew	Luke
29 Οὐαὶ ὑμῖν,	47 Οὐαὶ ὑμῖν,
γραμματεῖς καὶ Φαρισαῖοι	
ὑποκριταί,	
ὅτι οἰκοδομεῖτε τοὺς τάφους	ὅτι οἰκοδομεῖτε τὰ μνημεῖα
τῶν προφητῶν	τῶν προφητῶν,
καὶ κοσμεῖτε τὰ μνημεῖα τῶν	
δικαίων,	
30 καὶ λέγετε· εἰ ἤμεθα	
ἐν ταῖς ἡμέραις τῶν πατέρων ἡμῶν,	οἱ δὲ πατέρες ὑμῶν
οὐκ ἂν ἤμεθα αὐτῶν κοινωνοὶ	
ἐν τῷ αἵματι τῶν προφητῶν.	ἀπέκτειναν αὐτούς.
31 ὥστε μαρτυρεῖτε ἑαυτοῖς	48 ἄρα μάρτυρές ἐστε καὶ
	συνευδοκεῖτε
ὅτι υἱοί ἐστε	τοῖς ἔργοις τῶν πατέρων ὑμῶν,
τῶν φονευσάντων τοὺς προφήτας.	ὅτι αὐτοὶ μὲν ἀπέκτειναν αὐτούς,
32 καὶ ὑμεῖς πληρώσατε	ὑμεῖς δὲ οἰκοδομεῖτε.[2]
τὸ μέτρον τῶν πατέρων ὑμῶν.	
33 ὄφεις, γεννήματα ἐχιδνῶν, πῶς	
φύγητε ἀπὸ τῆς κρίσεως τῆς γεέννης;	
34 Διὰ τοῦτο ἰδοὺ	49 διὰ τοῦτο καὶ
	ἡ σοφία τοῦ θεοῦ εἶπεν·
ἐγὼ ἀποστέλλω πρὸς ὑμᾶς	ἀποστελῶ εἰς αὐτοὺς
προφήτας καὶ σοφοὺς καὶ	προφήτας καὶ ἀποστόλους,
γραμματεῖς	
ἐξ αὐτῶν ἀποκτενεῖτε καὶ	καὶ ἐξ αὐτῶν ἀποκτενοῦσιν
σταυρώσετε	
καὶ ἐξ αὐτῶν μαστιγώσετε	

1. Reconstructions in Steck, *Israel*, pp. 28-34; Schulz, *Q*, pp. 108-109, 336-38; Polag, *Fragmenta Q*, pp. 56; cf. Hoffmann, *Studien*, pp. 162-66. According to Steck (*Israel*, pp. 28-29; 281) and Schulz (*Q*, pp. 108-109), Mt. 23.30 was also present in Q; see further Kloppenborg, *Formation*, pp. 141-42; *idem*, *Q Parallels*, pp. 108-110.

2. οἰκοδομεῖτε Π^{75} ℵ B D L 1241 it$^{(pt)}$ syr cop$^{sa,bo(pt)}$ (with the broadest and earliest support) | οἰκοδομεῖτε αὐτῶν τὰ μνημεῖα A C W Θ Ψ 33 892 𝔐 it$^{(pt)}$ vg cop$^{bo(pt)}$ (supplying an object for οἰκοδομεῖτε from the previous strophe [*TCGNT*

ἐν ταῖς συναγωγαῖς ὑμῶν	
καὶ διώξετε ἀπὸ πόλεως εἰς πόλιν·	καὶ διώξουσιν,
35 ὅπως ἔλθῃ ἐφ' ὑμᾶς	50 ἵνα ἐκζητηθῇ
πᾶν αἷμα δίκαιον	τὸ αἷμα πάντων τῶν προφητῶν
ἐκχυννόμενον	τὸ ἐκκεχυμένον
ἐπὶ τῆς γῆς	ἀπὸ καταβολῆς κόσμου
	ἀπὸ τῆς γενεᾶς ταύτης,
ἀπὸ τοῦ αἵματος Ἅβελ τοῦ δικαίου	51 ἀπὸ αἵματος Ἅβελ
ἕως τοῦ αἵματος Ζαχαρίου	ἕως αἵματος Ζαχαρίου
υἱοῦ Βαραχίου,	
ὃν ἐφονεύσατε μεταξὺ	τοῦ ἀπολομένου μεταξὺ
τοῦ ναοῦ καὶ τοῦ θυσιαστηρίου·	τοῦ θυσιαστηρίου καὶ τοῦ οἴκου·
36 ἀμὴν λέγω ὑμῖν,	ναὶ λέγω ὑμῖν,
ἥξει ταῦτα πάντα	ἐκζητηθήσεται
ἐπὶ τὴν γενεὰν ταύτην.	ἀπὸ τῆς γενεᾶς ταύτης.

The premise of Q, according to R.J. Miller, is that by building tombs for the prophets—even out of a desire to honour them and so to disavow responsibility for their deaths—the lawyers themselves demonstrate complicity in vaticide. That is to say, the building of such tombs reveals a felt need on their part to atone for the misdeeds of their ancestors, lest their ancestors' culpability be seen to accrue to them. But why ought the present generation feel any such responsibility, and what evidence is there that the accusation is true? As Miller sees it:

> *The missing premise is that 'this generation' [Q 11.50] is persecuting the bearers of the Q tradition...* Only in this way does tomb-building become an act of hypocrisy: they honor the prophets whom their fathers killed (attempting to dissociate themselves from their ancestors), while themselves persecuting the prophets of the present (showing that they truly are the sons of those who murdered the prophets).[1]

159]) | οἰκοδομεῖτε τοὺς τάφους αὐτῶν $f^{1(13)}$ (indicating the influence of Mt. 23.29).

1. R.J. Miller, 'The Rejection of the Prophets in Q', *JBL* 107 (1988), p. 230 (emphasis original). Alternatively, Steck (*Israel*, p. 281) argues that the lawyers' attempt at distancing themselves from the deeds of their ancestors reflects a refusal to repent, thereby revealing the same spiritual intransigence that led their 'fathers' to reject the prophets.

Such an appeal to psychology, however, is unnecessary, for according to the imprecatory logic of Q the building of tombs implies consent and thereby itself indicates complicity. This is the nuance brought out by Lk. 11.48: 'So you are witnesses and consent to the deeds of your fathers; for they killed them, and you build'. It is Matthew, not Q, who appeals to the psychological motivation of distancing themselves from their forebears:

> [You say] 'If we had lived in the days of our fathers, we would not have taken part with them in shedding the blood of the prophets'. Thus you witness against yourselves, that you are sons of those who murdered the prophets (23.30-31).

Yet even here, the force of the accusation hinges solely on the admission of 'sonship' (with its implication of inherited nature), both consciously ('If we had lived in the days of our fathers') and unconsciously (the building of tombs).

In this sense, the killing of 'prophets and apostles' in the present generation, which Wisdom foretells from her vantage in the past, is a separate issue. It does not explain tomb-building itself, but merely demonstrates further—and in irrefutably bloody fashion—the true nature of the 'sons' (hence διὰ τοῦτο, v. 49; ἵνα, v. 50[1]). Certainly this implies the persecution and martyrdom of Christians, as Miller rightly observes. The reference to προφήτας καὶ ἀποστόλους (if this phrase was present in Q 11.49; cf. Mk 6.30, Mt. 10.1 // Lk. 6.13, etc.), as well as the reiterated judgment of 'this generation' (Q 11.50-51), requires as much. [2]

Matthew, in fact, reinforces this link between the vaticide ancestors and their present descendants by inserting v. 32: 'Fill up, then, the

1. On the significance of these terms, see Miller, 'Rejection', pp. 227-28, 232.

2. Against Steck (*Israel*, pp. 222-24), the initial reference in this passage is—at least in its present context—to Christian rather than OT prophets; cf. E. Haenchen, 'Matthäus 23', *ZTK* 48 (1951), p. 53. Although Steck (*Israel*, pp. 282-83, followed by Christ, *Jesus Sophia*, p. 129) argues that 'this generation' is made responsible only for the crimes of their forebears (without implying similar misdeeds of their own), Hoffmann (*Studien*, pp. 166-71) and Légasse ('L'oracle contre "cette génération"', pp. 249-50) rightly draw attention to the emphasis on the rejection and persecution of Christian emissaries elsewhere in Q (cf. 6.22-23; 10.3, 10-11, 16; 13.34). Even more to the point is the fact that 'this generation' has already rejected the (prophetic) testimony of John and Jesus (Q 7.31-34; cf. Schnider, *Jesus der Prophet*, pp. 139)!

measure of your fathers', implying that they will or have already done so.[1] This is followed by the rhetorical denunciation, 'Serpents, brood of vipers, how can you escape the judgment of Gehenna?' (v. 33), which borrows from Q 3.7 the language of John the Baptist's vilification of the multitudes (cf. Mt. 3.7; 12.34). This radically alters the force of Q's διὰ τοῦτο in Mt. 23.34. For whereas in Q διὰ τοῦτο explained a past statement of 'Wisdom' ('Therefore the Wisdom of God said...'), in Matthew it explains the present action of Jesus ('Therefore I send...'). So Matthew makes Jesus, rather than Wisdom, the sender of προφήτας καὶ σοφοὺς καὶ γραμματεῖς, thereby transferring to him a significant sapiential/Deuteronomistic function.[2] The force of Matthew's logic is, in fact, that Jesus will send his envoys to Israel in order that they might, by rejecting them, 'fill up the measure of their fathers' and so bring to bear the 'judgment of Gehenna'.

The intent of Matthew's reference to Jesus is further revealed in his description of the envoys' common fate, for he expands Q's simple καὶ ἐξ αὐτῶν ἀποκτενοῦσιν καὶ διώξουσιν to read ἐξ αὐτῶν ἀποκτενεῖτε καὶ σταυρώσετε καὶ ἐξ αὐτῶν μαστιγώσετε ἐν ταῖς συναγωγαῖς ὑμῶν καὶ διώξετε ἀπὸ πόλεως εἰς πόλιν (23.34). Matthew seems to have chosen this language to reflect both the promises of persecution in 10.17 and 23 (καὶ ἐν ταῖς συναγωγαῖς αὐτῶν μαστιγώσουσιν ὑμᾶς...ὅταν δὲ διώκωσιν ὑμᾶς ἐν τῇ πόλει ταύτῃ, φεύγετε εἰς τὴν ἑτέραν)[3] and the third and final prophecy of Jesus' own fate in Jerusalem (20.19, καὶ μαστιγῶσαι καὶ σταυρῶσαι

1. On this phrase as an 'editorial connective' between the 'woes' and the announcement of persecution and coming judgment, see Haenchen, 'Matthäus 23', p. 52; Garland, *Intention*, p. 166; Burnett, *Testament*, pp. 58-62.

2. Cf. Hare, *Persecution*, pp. 87-88; 291; Christ, *Jesus Sophia*, pp. 129-31. On the originality of ἡ σοφία τοῦ θεοῦ εἶπεν, see Haenchen, 'Matthäus 23', p. 53; Hare, *Persecution*, pp. 86, 92; Steck, *Israel*, p. 29 n. 3; Lührmann, *Redaktion*, p. 46; Suggs, *Wisdom, Christology, and Law*, pp. 14, 59; Schulz, *Q*, p. 336; Miller, 'Rejection', pp. 228-29. On the Deuteronomistic character of this Q passage, see pp. 222-27; Schulz, *Q*, pp. 342-345.

3. Cf. Haenchen, 'Matthäus 23', p. 54; Trilling, *Wahre Israel*, p. 82; Hare, *Persecution*, pp. 91-92; Christ, *Jesus Sophia*, p. 133; Garland, *Intention*, pp. 176-77; Légasse, 'L'oracle contre "cette génération"', p. 242. Matthew consistently employs διώκειν (Matthew 6×; Mark 0×; Luke 3×) to describe the treatment accorded the disciples (5.10; 5.11, 12 [+ Q 6.22-23]; 5.44 [+ Q 6.28]; 10.23; 23.34 [= Q 11.49]) and is the only Evangelist to apply μαστιγοῦν to their circumstances (10.17, 23.34).

// Mk 10.34, καὶ μαστιγώσουσιν αὐτὸν καὶ ἀποκτενοῦσιν).[1] Thus it is clear that for Matthew both the one who sends the prophets and the prophets themselves suffer the same treatment at the hands of their persecutors, who thereby demonstrate that they are the 'sons' and inheritors of those who treated the ancient prophets in the same manner.[2]

This same redactional motive is evident throughout the remainder of the passage. Thus Matthew changes a series of third person descriptions found in Q into direct address, as, for example, in v. 34, 'I send you...some of whom you will kill' (cf. Lk. 11.49, 'I will send them...some of whom they will kill'). The most extreme example, however, is in v. 35, where Matthew makes 'this generation' responsible for the death of Zechariah, whom, he declares, '*you* murdered between the sanctuary and the altar' (cf. Lk. 11.50, 'Zechariah, who perished...').[3] And even his simple inversion of the Q order in this last verse (from μεταξὺ τοῦ θυσιαστηρίου καὶ τοῦ οἴκου to

1. The reference to the crucifixion of the disciples is not to be evaluated from the perspective of historical probability (i.e., could Jewish authorities have crucified the followers of Jesus?) but as a literary and theological motif intended to demonstrate continuity between master and disciple, in fulfillment of Jesus' own teaching (see §A.2.b.1, above, on Mt. 10.24-39; cf. Steck, *Israel*, pp. 294-95).

2. *Contra* Hare (*Persecution*, p. 91), who proposes (unnecessarily) that the reference to crucifixion was 'clumsily added to the completed gospel by an early glossator'. The same premise of a common fate is emphasized in the missionary discourse itself, as implied by the Evangelist's use of similar vocabulary; see Mt. 10.24 (Q 6.40) and especially 10.25. The comment of Légasse, ('L'oracle contre "cette génération"', p. 251) applies equally well in both contexts: 'Si l'on s'interroge sur les circonstances de cette polémique, son rapport avec l'échec de la mission juive est évident'; cf. Schnider, *Jesus der Prophet*, pp. 159-60.

3. Hare, *Persecution*, pp. 93-94: 'Apostate Israel is here seen as a corporate personality whose individual members in the present (i.e. those who reject Jesus and his messengers) must bear full responsibility for the murderous rejection of God's messengers in the past'. This contemporizing or 'actualization' of past history may account for Matthew's use of the present participle ἐκχυννόμενον to describe the shedding of righteous blood in place of Q's perfect participle ἐκκεχυμένον (cf. Steck, *Israel*, p. 31 n. 8; Schulz, *Q*, p. 338; Garland, *Intention*, p. 176; for an alternative explanation, see Chapter 3, §B.3, below, on 26.28). But already in Q, as was the case with the sending of the disciples (Q 10.2) and the 'Sign of Jonah' (Q 11.39-42), this passage combines Deuteronomistic and eschatological motifs, pronouncing judgment on 'this generation' as the climactic response to a history of recalcitrance (cf. Schulz, *Q*, pp. 342-43).

μεταξὺ τοῦ ναοῦ καὶ τοῦ θυσιαστηρίου) indicates how Matthew emphasizes the sanctity of the location and therefore the gravity of the crime.[1]

Furthermore, although the identity of his Ζαχαρίου υἱοῦ Βαραχίου has occasioned considerable debate, the most likely possibility is that the Evangelist does not confuse, but rather purposefully conflates the Zechariah of 2 Chronicles 24 with the prophet for whom the canonical book is named.[2] For not only does ben Jehoiada the priest suffer death by stoning for having rebuked the unfaithful nation in a prophetic manner,[3] so too ben Berechiah begins his testimony by inveighing against Israel's rejection of the former prophets and their message (Zech 1.4-6). It appears, therefore, since the examples of ben Berechiah the writer and ben Jehoiada the martyr-priest would both amply support his Deuteronomistic interests, that Matthew has conflated them into one by appending the disputed patronym to his Q-*Vorlage*.[4]

1. So Steck, *Israel*, p. 31 n. 8 [32]; Hoffmann, *Studien*, p. 165; Légasse, 'L'oracle contre "cette génération"', p. 244.

2. Cf. Chapter 1, §C.3.f and Chapter 2, §A.1.e (on Zechariah), above. The Q text refers to the first and last martyrs of the Hebrew canon, assuming that 2 Chronicles was placed at or near the end of the canonical order. Blank ('Death of Zechariah', pp. 327-46) has shown that the two Zechariahs were often confused in rabbinic exegesis. Cf. Ginzberg, *Legends*, IV, pp. 259, 304; VI, p. 396; Schoeps, *Prophetenmorde*, pp. 17-21; with fuller discussion of 23.35 in Steck, *Israel*, pp. 33-40; Garland, *Intention*, p. 182 n. 69. The personal address of this polemic would be more intelligible if Matthew also intended an allusion to the death of Zechariah ben Bariscaeus (Josephus, *War*, 4.334-44), as some have argued (e.g. Steck, *Israel*, pp. 33-40; Christ, *Jesus Sophia*, p. 133). Although this is a rather remote possibility, it would constitute a further reference to the events of 70 CE, to which Matthew alludes in 22.7 and 23.38. But an allusion to this figure does not obviate a primary reference to the scriptural Zechariah(s), since Matthew's 'Zechariah ben Berechiah' is a composite figure already.

3. So 2 Chron. 24.20: ורוח אלהים לבשה את־זכריה/καὶ πνεῦμα θεοῦ ἐνέδυσεν τὸν Αζαριαν; cf. 24.19, 'he sent prophets among them...'). Ben Jehoiada is designated as a prophet by rabbinic tradition, for example, *y. Ta'an.* 4.9 [69ab]; *b. Giṭ.* 57b; *b. Sanh.* 96b (which implies that the cause of his death was that he 'foretold the destruction of Jerusalem to the Israelites').

4. Purposeful conflation (as well as confusion) also underlies the rabbinic references to the biblical Zechariahs; so Amaru, 'The Killing of the Prophets', p. 168. Moreover, according to Amaru (p. 167): 'The most common Zechariah legend in rabbinic literature is one that relates [his] call for vengeance [in 2 Chron. 24.22] to

In addition, M. McNamara has pointed out that *Targ. Lam.* 2.20 refers to the Zechariah of 2 Chronicles 24 as 'bar Iddo'[1]—and since this patronym is that of the grandfather of the writing prophet ('Zechariah ben Berechiah ben Iddo', Zech. 1.1), it is evident that *Targum Lamentations* combines the two identities in precisely the same manner as does Matthew.[2] Thus, in that *Targum Lamentations* cites the death of Zechariah as one of the causes for the destruction of Jerusalem while at the same time telescoping the circumstances of the Babylonian and Roman wars into one (cf. *Targ. Lam.* 1.19; 5.11, 13), its outlook has substantial affinities to that of the Evangelist.

One feature of Matthaean redaction, however, appears to reflect an opposite tendency. According to Q 11.50-51a, Christian emissaries meet with a murderous response ἵνα ἐκζητηθῇ τὸ αἷμα πάντων τῶν προφητῶν τὸ ἐκκεχυμένον ἀπὸ καταβολῆς κόσμου (ἀπὸ τῆς γενεᾶς ταύτης), ἀπὸ αἵματος Ἅβελ ἕως αἵματος Ζαχαρίου. But rather than refer to the fate of the prophets, Matthew specifies instead πᾶν αἷμα δίκαιον ἐκχυννόμενον ἐπὶ τῆς γῆς ἀπὸ τοῦ αἵματος Ἅβελ τοῦ δικαίου ἕως τοῦ αἵματος Ζαχαρίου (23.35). Perhaps Matthew did not consider Abel among the prophets (which Q seems to imply). In any event, his wording recognizes that the persecution of the just is not limited to those with a specifically prophetic role. This is consistent, first, with Matthew's repeated emphasis on αἷμα

the Babylonian slaughter of innocents at the time of the destruction of the First Temple. The midrash is an old one, attributed in [*Giṭ.* 57b] to a second-century Tanna who claimed to have heard it from an old man in Jerusalem.' In this case, the cry for vengeance results in Nebuzaradan's slaughter of members of the Sanhedrin, young men and women, school children, and young priests, details which may well have been derived from Jewish experiences under Titus, Domitian and Hadrian (so Blank, 'Death of Zechariah', pp. 340-41). This account of the 'slaughter of innocents' in relation to the persecution/martyrdom of the prophet, particularly in the larger context of the fall of Jerusalem, bears some resemblance to Matthew's account of Herod's slaughter in 2.16-18. But it is no longer possible to determine whether any such interest underlay Matthew's reference to 'Zechariah'.

1. *Targ. Lam.* 2.20 laments the murder (which it locates on the day of Atonement!) 'of Zechariah son of Iddo, the High Priest and faithful prophet [לזכריה בר עדוא כהנא רבא תביא מהימן]'.

2. *The New Testament and the Palestinian Targum to the Pentateuch* (AnBib, 27; Rome: Pontifical Biblical Institute, 1966), pp. 162-63.

δίκαιον (or ἀθῷον),[1] and, secondly, with the fact that προφῆται καὶ δικαίοι are already closely linked in the Evangelist's mind (e.g., 10.41; 13.17; 23.29), suggesting that the fate of one implies the fate of the other. So here, once again, we see the juxtaposition of the suffering of the martyrs of old with that of Jesus himself, and possibly with that of his followers as well.

Thus both in Q and (even more so) in Matthew, the pronouncements of judgment and rejection reflect a situation of profound alienation between Jewish and Christian communities. The fact that this alienation is described in specifically Deuteronomistic terms provides a significant insight into its nature. For it does not represent alienation from Judaism per se. As Miller rightly observes:

> It is rather the alienation of a Jeremiah or an Isaiah, the alienation of rejected prophets... [which] reinforces [the community's] self-understanding as faithful Jews living among an unfaithful people.[2]

This is, in fact, the essence of the Deuteronomistic perspective: the faithful community reflects on the sins of its forebears in order to explain its own origin out of the midst of tribulation, and so justifies its continuing existence on theological grounds. This same apologetic concern is even more strongly present in Matthew's version of the 'Lament over Jerusalem', which we must consider next.

1. The theme of innocent suffering, of course, is already present in Q (cf. Kloppenborg, *Formation*, p. 145-46), but Matthew makes it explicit by inserting the necessary adjective, which is 'intended to invite comparison with the crucifixion of Jesus' (Lindars, *NT Apologetic*, p. 20). According to Blank ('Death of Zechariah', pp. 336-38), the connection between Abel and Zechariah is that the innocent blood of both cried out to the Lord for vengeance. See Garland, *Intention*, p. 181 n. 68, p. 184 n. 70; also Heb. 12.24.

2. Miller, 'Rejection', p. 232.

5. *The Lament over Jerusalem, Matthew 23.37-39 // Luke 13.34-35*[1]

Matthew	Luke
Ἰερουσαλὴμ Ἰερουσαλήμ, ἡ ἀποκτείνουσα τοὺς προφήτας καὶ λιθοβολοῦσα τοὺς ἀπεσταλμένους πρὸς αὐτήν, ποσάκις ἠθέλησα	
ἐπισυναγαγεῖν	ἐπισυνάξαι
τὰ τέκνα σου, ὃν τρόπον ὄρνις	
ἐπισυνάγει	
τὰ νοσσία αὐτῆς	τὴν ἑαυτῆς νοσσιὰν
ὑπὸ τὰς πτέρυγας, καὶ οὐκ ἠθελήσατε. ἰδοὺ ἀφίεται ὑμῖν ὁ οἶκος ὑμῶν	
ἔρημος.[2]	
λέγω γὰρ ὑμῖν,	λέγω [δὲ] ὑμῖν,
οὐ μή με ἴδητε	οὐ μὴ ἴδητε με
ἀπ' ἄρτι ἕως ἂν εἴπητε·	ἕως [ἥξει ὅτε][3] εἴπητε·
εὐλογημένος ὁ ἐρχόμενος ἐν ὀνόματι κυρίου.	

This passage represents Q's 'Deuteronomistic' outlook more clearly than any other.[4] For here Jerusalem, no doubt representing all Israel, is denounced for 'killing the prophets and stoning those who are sent' to her.[5] Q's parallel between τοὺς προφήτας and τοὺς ἀπεσταλμένους equates the two groups of divine messengers and their common fate.[6] Thus, according to Haenchen,

1. As the alternative layout indicates, both Matthew and Luke follow Q closely; reconstructions in Steck, *Israel*, pp. 48-50; Schulz, *Q*, pp. 346-47; Polag, *Fragmenta Q*, p. 66; Hoffmann, *Studien*, pp. 171-73; cf. Kloppenborg, *Q Parallels*, p. 158.

2. The textual evidence in favour of this reading is discussed below, Chapter 3, §B.1.

3. The difficult textual question in this verse (see *TCGNT*, p. 163) is not directly relevant to our discussion of Matthew's use of Q.

4. Cf. Steck, *Israel*, pp. 227-32; Schulz, *Q*, pp. 352-54, 358-60; Kloppenborg, *Formation*, pp. 228-29; Miller, 'Rejection', pp. 234-35.

5. Cf. Steck, *Israel*, p. 227; although the central role of Jerusalem is apparently without precedent (see *Israel*, n. 8). The use of the present participles ἀποκτείνουσα and λιθοβολοῦσα implies that such activities are ongoing and present (so Schulz, *Q*, p. 354 n. 219).

6. This understands the phrase προφήτας καὶ... ἀπεσταλμένους as a synthetic parallelism that progresses towards greater specificity. On the function of parallelism as representing semantic or conceptual progression, see J.L. Kugel, *The Idea*

> the ἀπεσταλμένοι do not indicate a second, different group. . . they are merely another expression for 'prophets', in keeping with the requirements of *parallismus membrorum.*[1]

That the fate envisaged for these emissaries is stoning suggests that they were viewed as false prophets (as at 21.35).[2] Their rejection is juxtaposed to the rejection of the speaker: 'How often I would have gathered you...and you would not'. By implication, then, Jesus will be repudiated as violently as the rest.[3]

In Jerusalem's rejection of the prophets and their message, she has also rejected the protection that their presence would have afforded.[4] As a result, her 'house' is declared forsaken. This may refer either to the Temple or to the city and nation as a whole, from which the divine glory (cf. 23.21) is seen to depart. As F. Christ observes:

> Most likely, the Temple and with it also the city (and all the people) are meant: along with the Temple, God simultaneously abandons Israel in general.[5]

For according to Q, 'Jerusalem has rejected YHWH's help by persecuting the prophets and rejecting his protection'.[6] And, most ominous

of Biblical Poetry: Parallelism and its History (New Haven: Yale University Press, 1981).

1. 'Matthäus 23', p. 57.
2. Cf. p. 114, above.
3. Cf. Hoffmann, *Studien*, pp. 174, 188.
4. Cf. *2 Bar.* 2.1; *Par. Jer.* 1.1-3 (according to which Jerusalem cannot be destroyed until the prophet Jeremiah and his circle have departed from the city); Steck, *Israel*, p. 229 n. 1.
5. Christ, *Jesus Sophia*, p. 140; cf. p. 149; similarly O. Michel, *s.v.* 'οἶκος', *TWNT*, V, p. 127 and n. 27 [= *TDNT*, p. 125]; Hummel, *Auseinandersetzung*, p. 88; Schulz, *Q*, p. 256 n. 230; Garland, *Intention*, pp. 198-200. An inclusive reading is more appropriate to the context than a reference to either the city/ nation (so Str–B, I, pp. 943-44; Trilling, *Wahre Israel*, p. 86; Hare, *Persecution*, p. 154; Steck, *Israel*, p. 228 n. 3; cf. Strecker, *Weg*, p. 113) or the Temple alone (so Haenchen, 'Matthäus 23', pp. 55-56; Davies, *Setting*, p. 298).

For the identification of Wisdom (and therefore, in this context, Jesus) with the Shekinah, cf. Sir. 24.10; 11QPs 18.20 (Christ, *Jesus Sophia*, pp. 142 n. 572, 145 n. 582; for further references and discussion see Burnett, *Testament*, pp. 64-66, with the suggestion that the protective 'wings' in Q 13.34c may themselves allude to the Shekinah [cf. Str–B, I, p. 943]).

6. Edwards, *Theology of Q*, p. 133; cf. Wilckens, 'Σοφία κτλ.' *TWNT*, VII, p. 516 [= *TDNT*, p. 515]; Robinson, 'Jesus as Sophos', p. 13; Meyer, 'Gentile

of all, no opportunity for repentance is envisaged; rather, the sentence of divine abandonment appears absolute.

But while judgment falls on the city as a direct result of such rejection, it is less certain that, as Steck and Miller argue, 'the saying interprets the destruction of the city' in particular.[1] For, strictly speaking, ἀφίεται ὑμῖν ὁ οἶκος ὑμῶν simply describes departure, not destruction, and other Q references to such an eventuality are lacking. Nonetheless, if the tradition that the departure of the divine presence from the Temple is the prelude to the city's destruction can be taken as a guide (so Josephus, *War* 5.412-13; 6.295-300; Tacitus, *Histories* 5.13; *2 Bar.* 8.2; 64.6-7; *Par. Jer.* 4.1), this could refer implicitly to the threatened fall of Jerusalem.[2]

It is not certain that either Matthew or Luke preserves the original order of Q with respect to this passage, since its present location is governed in both Gospels by redactional considerations.[3] In Matthew Q's oft-repeated denunciations of 'this generation' in general and the diatribe against the 'scribes and Pharisees' of ch. 23 in particular come to a climax as the Evangelist coordinates in sequence (1) Q's demonstration of the tomb-builders' murderous lineage (23.29-31), (2) the declaration to them, 'Fill up...the measure of your fathers'

Mission', p. 416. But Edwards (*Theology of Q*, pp. 67, 132-33) goes too far in suggesting that Mt. 23.39 // Lk. 13.35b represents the Q community's recognition of the legitimacy of those prophets who come to them 'in the name of the Lord'. It refers rather to the coming Son of man.

1. Miller, 'Rejection', p. 234; cf. Steck, *Israel*, pp. 227-30.

2. This is not to say, however, that it need originally have referred to the events of 70 CE (i.e. as a *vaticinium ex eventu*), since the threat of coming judgment is a feature of apocalyptic pronouncement that pervades Q as a whole. See Steck, *Israel*, pp. 237-39; Schulz, *Q*, 357; Garland, *Intention*, pp. 201 n. 121; Hoffmann, *Studien*, p. 175; Burnett, *Testament*, pp. 70-72.

3. So Haenchen, 'Matthäus 23', pp. 56-57; Steck, *Israel*, pp. 40-48; Schulz, *Q*, pp. 347-48; Schnider, *Jesus der Prophet*, pp. 142-43; Jacobson, 'Wisdom Christology', pp. 210-11; Miller, 'Rejection', p. 236. Cf. Bultmann, *History of the Synoptic Tradition*, pp. 114-15; Wilckens, 'Σοφία κτλ.', *TWNT*, VII, p. 515; Lührmann, *Redaktion*, pp. 44, 48; Christ, *Jesus Sophia*, pp. 136-37; Meyer, 'Gentile Mission', p. 415; Suggs, *Wisdom, Christology, and Law*, pp. 64-66; Hoffmann, *Studien*, p. 40; Légasse, 'L'oracle contre "cette génération"', pp. 238-39 (all favouring the Matthaean order); also Hare, *Persecution*, pp. 94-95; Garland, *Intention*, pp. 188-97 (for the Lukan order). See the summary in Kloppenborg, *Formation*, pp. 227-28 and n. 230; *idem*, *Q Parallels*, p. 158.

(v. 32), (3) the prophecy that they will 'kill and crucify' the prophetic envoys whom Jesus sends (vv. 34-35), and finally, (4) the pronouncement of judgment upon Jerusalem (23.37-39). The implication of this climactic juxtaposition is that Jerusalem rejects not only the prophets of old but also the prophets of every generation, the present one included. This brings into greater prominence the implicit premise of Q 13.34 that Jesus stands in a direct line with previous prophets and emissaries, and so will suffer a similar fate.

Indeed, it is the rejection of Jesus (ποσάκις ἠθέλησα...καὶ οὐκ ἠθελήσατε) that, in Matthew's Gospel, finally brings judgment to bear. So for Matthew it is Jesus himself who both pronounces and acts out the sentence of divine abandonment, for the Evangelist interprets 23.38 as referring to the final departure of Jesus (whom he has already identified with the Shekinah, Mt. 18.20; cf. *m. Ab.* 3.2) from the Temple.[1]

1. Cf. F.D. Weinert, 'Luke, the Temple, and Jesus' Saying about Jerusalem's Abandoned House (Luke 13.34-35)', *CBQ* 44 (1982), pp. 68-71; so also Hummel, *Auseinandersetzung*, p. 141; Garland, *Intention*, pp. 202-203. On Jesus in the role of Shekinah, cf. Haenchen, 'Matthäus 23', pp. 55-56; Strecker, *Weg*, p. 113. Matthew's infrequent οἶκος (Matthew 10×; Mark 13×; Luke 33×) is not uniform in meaning (cf. οἰκία [26×; 18×; 24×], although 'für Mt sind...beide Ausdrucke keineswegs synonym', [Schenk, *Sprache*, p. 371]). He retains it only four times from Mark (Mt. 9.6; 12.4; 21.13[2×]; with eight deletions from Mk 2.1; 3.20; 5.19; 7.17, 30; 8.3, 26; 9.28; cf. Mt. 9.23 οἰκία for Mk 5.38 οἶκος) and possibly twice from Q (21.44; 23.38 [also 11.8 from Q 7.25?]; cf. Lk. 7.36; 10.5; 12.39, 52; 14.23; 15.6 and parallels). In Mt. 9.6 (// Mk 2.11), 9.7 (// Lk. 5.25), 11.8 (cf. Lk. 7.25), and 12.44 (// Lk. 11.24), οἶκος refers literally or metaphorically to a dwelling place; 10.6 and 15.24 refer to the nation of Israel; while 12.4 (// Mk 2.26, τοῦ οἶκου τοῦ θεοῦ) and 21.3 [2×] (// Mk 11.17 = LXX Isa. 56.7) refer specifically to the Temple. In any event, οἶκος is frequently used for the Temple in the LXX (e.g. 3 Kgdms 5.19b; 6.1-22, etc.; cf. Steck, *Israel*, p. 35 n. 2; Schulz, *Q*, p. 344 n. 164).

In the present context, Matthew's emendation of Q 11.51 ([τοῦ ἀπολομένου μεταξὺ τοῦ θυσιαστηρίου καὶ] τού οἴκου) to τοῦ ναοῦ (23.35) reflects, first, an avoidance of οἴκος in a sense limited to the Temple building (so Steck, *Israel*, p. 31 n. 8) and, secondly, a preference for ἱερόν (11×; 9×; 14×) for the Temple precincts and ναός (9×; 3×; 4×) for the sanctuary (although the two are not strongly differentiated). Thus it would appear that in Matthew, as in Q, the designation ὁ οἶκος ὑμῶν includes, but is not limited to the Temple, for judgment on the Temple strongly symbolizes judgment on the nation as a whole. For further discussion,

Such an interpretation is indicated, first, by Matthew's causal rendering of 23.39a, λέγω γάρ ὑμῖν (cf. Lk. 13.35, λέγω δὲ ὑμῖν): the Temple is forsaken, says Jesus, for 'you will not see me, etc'.[1] Secondly, Jesus' pronouncement in 23.39, citing Ps. 118.26 (οὐ μή με ἴδητε ἀπ' ἄρτι ἕως ἂν εἴπητε· εὐλογημένος etc.), must here refer to the future return of the Son of man. Where Luke has placed the saying (in 13.35), it anticipates the acclamation of the crowds—who also quote Ps. 118.26—at Jesus' 'triumphal entry' into Jerusalem (Lk. 19.28 // Mk 11.9). But Matthew's placement of Q 13.35 after the triumphal entry (21.9) means that in his Gospel it cannot have the same meaning as in Luke, but must convey a future reference instead.[2] In other words, so absolute is his departure that Jesus will not return to the Temple until he returns in glory. Thirdly, Matthew eliminates the intervening episode of the 'widow's mite' (Mk 12.41-44 // Lk. 21.1-4), with the result that the definitive statement of Jesus' departure from the Temple (Mt. 24.1 from Mk 13.1) follows immediately upon the words of rebuke and renunciation in 23.37-39.[3] Jesus then goes on to predict the utter downfall of the Temple itself: 'Truly, I say to you, there will not be left here one stone upon another' (24.2).

Thus Matthew's direct juxtaposition of 23.29-36 (Q 11.47-51), 23.37-39 (Q 13.34-35) and 24.1-2 (// Mk 13.1-2 // Lk. 21.5-6) suggests a causal link between (1) Israel's persecution of the prophets (and Jesus in particular), (2) the announcement of judgment upon 'this generation' (with Jerusalem and the Temple as its focus), (3) Jesus' departure from the Temple precincts, and (4) the anticipated destruction of the Temple itself.[4] Most ominously, this passage is

representing an apparent consensus of scholarly opinion, see Burnett, *Testament*, pp. 122-29.

1. Cf. Schweizer, *Matthäus*, p. 290 [ET p. 445]; Burnett, *Testament*, pp. 73-74.

2. Cf. Burnett, *Testament*, pp. 114-15.

3. Cf. Hummel, *Auseinandersetzung*, p. 85; Schweizer, *Matthäus*, p. 292 [ET p. 448]; Garland, *Intention*, pp. 26-27. On the wording of Mt. 24.1, see Burnett, *Testament*, pp. 116-19.

4. Although neither Israel's rejection of Jesus (which awaits the crucifixion) nor Jesus' symbolic departure (which anticipates Jerusalem's destruction) are yet complete, both would have been comprehensible to the Matthaean community as proleptic depictions of later events. As F. Christ (*Jesus Sophia*, p. 146; cf. Zeller, *Kommentar*, p. 86) says, 'Jesus... verläßt Israel schon jetzt: bei seinem *Tod*. Jesu Tod als der Prophetenmorde bildet die Ursache der Tempelzerstörung: So wahr ihr

Jesus' last address to Jerusalem and to the nation (τὰ τέκνα σου) in Matthew's Gospel, making his final declaration to them one of definitive judgment.[1]

In the Matthaean redaction, then, Israel's 'house' is declared 'forsaken and desolate' as a judgment on the nation's rejection of the prophets—those of old, Jesus and the Christian prophets alike. So it is difficult to escape the conclusion that here, as in 22.7 (and possibly 23.35), Matthew makes reference to the fall of Jerusalem in 70 CE as a divine response to Israel's rejection of the prophets, both past and present. What may in Q have originally been a device to shame Israel into the kingdom via the inclusion of the Gentiles[2] (analogous to that of Paul in Rom. 11.11, 14) has become in Matthew not only a final sentence but also an explanation of Israel's historical experience. And it is such an understanding, as we saw earlier, that lies at the heart of the Deuteronomistic outlook.

c. *Summary*

Jacobson has argued not only that 'Q stands within a prophetic tradition' but that 'the deuteronomistic tradition provides the theological framework for Q', or at least a significant portion of it.[3] Certainly

Jesus gekreuzigt habt, wird Gott euch verlassen.' Thus it is not necessary to choose between the death of Jesus and the rejection of Christian envoys (so Hummel, *Auseinandersetzung*, p. 88) as the final cause for judgment, since both, according to Matthew, demonstrate the same obduracy on the part of Israel. As Hummel (p. 90) himself observes, 'Die Kreuzigung Jesu und die Verfolgung der "Gerechten" durch die "Väter" und durch "diese Generation" werden beide unter dem Geschichtspunkt der göttlichen Vergeltung für vergossenes Blut gesehen. Beide stehen bei Matthäus nebeneinander.' Also of relevance for Matthaean redaction are the rabbinic references (esp. *t. Yom.* 1.2; *Targ. Isa.* 1.15; 59.2-3; cf. 4.4-5; 26.21; 30.20; 32.14; 57.17) to the shedding of innocent blood as causing the departure of the Shekinah (cf. Kosmala, 'His Blood on us', p. 110; Garland, *Intention*, p. 201 n. 121). On the antipathy between sin and the Shekinah in rabbinic thought, see J. Abelson, *The Immanence of God in Rabbinic Literature* (rpr. New York: Hermon, 1969), pp. 135-40.

1. Cf. Steck, *Israel*, pp. 292-93.

2. So Meyer, 'Gentile Mission', p. 417; cf. Lührmann, *Redaktion*, p. 86 (citing T.W. Manson, *The Teaching of Jesus: Studies in its Form and Content* [Cambridge: Cambridge University Press, 1948], p. 31).

3. 'Literary Unity', pp. 383, 386-87; cf. *idem*, 'Wisdom Christology', pp. 226-29, 233-34.

the Q passages that have to do with the preaching of judgment can be characterized in this way (especially Q 3.7-9, 16-17; 6.22-23; 7.24-35; 11.29-32, 39-52), as can some of Q's sapiential material (e.g. 13.34-35; 14.16-24).[1] Thus Q understands John, Jesus and the Christian missionaries as rejected prophets rebuffed by a habitually impenitent Israel.

The Deuteronomistic perspective of Q provides a means to understand the common fate of persecution and even death that these individuals encounter, for, 'by implication, Jesus is the prophet par excellence, and his followers' suffering is not in imitation of his death, but a tragic repetition of the lot of the prophets'.[2] Accordingly, as the tradents of Q come to terms with the failure of the mission to Israel in contrast to the growing success of Gentile outreach, the suffering of Christian missionaries, on the one hand, and declarations of impending judgment against Israel, on the other, both take their place within the theological and apologetic framework of a Deuteronomistic outlook. And such an outlook likely provides, in turn, a potent resource for shaping the self-definition of the Q community.

The motives underlying Mark's inclusion of Deuteronomistic material, however, are more difficult to discern, since he places no great emphasis either on the prophetic identity of John and Jesus—at least in regard to their respective rejections—or on a Deuteronomistic view of Israel's spiritual history. That the parable of the 'Wicked Tenants' alone represents such an outlook highlights the fact that Deuteronomistic motifs are not a significant feature of Markan theology and redaction.

Matthew, on the other hand, stresses a number of Deuteronomistic features in redacting his source material. He affirms that, as prophetic emissaries to an unreceptive Israel, Jesus' followers will be rejected (5.10-12; 10.14-15) and have to endure persecution, suffering and even death (10.16a, 21, 23, 28, 34-36, 38-39; cf. 11.12). Their fate will be like that of the prophets of ancient Israel (5.12c; 21.35 // 23.37) and that of John the Baptist, whom Matthew portrays as a rejected prophet in his own right (11.9, 14, 18; 17.12).

1. So Kloppenborg, *Formation*, pp. 166-70, 323; cf. Polag, *Christologie*, pp. 86-97.

2. W.H. Kelber, *The Oral and the Written Gospel* (Philadelphia: Fortress Press, 1983), pp. 201-202; cf. Edwards, *Theology of Q*, p. 47.

But Matthew's Deuteronomistic outlook focuses, above all, on the fate of Jesus and its relation to the fall of Jerusalem. In Matthew's Gospel Jesus is a suffering and rejected prophet (either as an emissary of Wisdom, 11.19, or after the manner of Jonah, 12.39-41), so that whatever his disciples suffer simply follows the pattern of Jesus' own rejection (10.24-25; 23.34). For Matthew, it is the consequences of the nation's rejection of Jesus and his emissaries that are of the greatest significance. The present investigation tends to confirm Steck's thesis that Matthew took over from both Mark and Q a theological construct that applied a 'Deuteronomistic' interpretation to the events of 70 CE.[1] Matthew's distinctive contribution, however, was to clarify and intensify the link between the nation's sin and spiritual obduracy—as evidenced climactically in its rejection of Jesus and his followers—and the fall of Jerusalem.

This redactional tendency is especially evident in Matthew's juxtaposition of the parables of the vineyard and the marriage feast (21.28–22.14), together with his additions to the latter (e.g. 22.7). It is also evident in his coordination in 23.29–24.2 of the condemnation of the scribes and Pharisees, the lament over the city, and the announcement of the Temple's destruction.[2] Moreover, Matthew's emphasis on blood guilt in connection with crucifixion (23.34-35, cf. 27.3-8, 24-25) provides us with a key to unlocking how he understands the rejection of Israel and the transfer of the kingdom to 'others' or 'Gentiles' (21.41, 43; cf. 11.20-24, 12.41), who, as members of the Christian community, constitute the 'new' Israel.[3]

B. *Matthew's Portrayal of Jesus as a Rejected Prophet*

The relevance of the Deuteronomistic motif for Matthew's depiction of Jesus hinges on the Evangelist's portrayal of him as a prophet, and,

1. Cf. Steck, *Israel*, pp. 292-304.

2. Steck (*Israel*, pp. 302-304) sees in these two sequences a conscious redactional parallel on Matthew's part. The presence of similar themes does not, however, necessitate compositional parallelism.

3. So Steck, *Israel*, pp. 290-304 (without, however, subscribing to Steck's contention [pp. 305-16] that Matthew is responsible for combining distinct Palestinian Jewish and Hellenistic Christian formulations of the Deuteronomistic outlook). Cf. Hare, *Persecution*, pp. 149-62; Garland, *Intention*, pp. 204-205.

more precisely, as a suffering or rejected prophet.[1] The discussion of 'Jesus-as-prophet', which attracted considerable critical attention earlier in the century, has recently been the focus of renewed study, with scholars attempting to define the traits that marked Jesus and his ministry as specifically prophetic. Among the features thought to identify Jesus as a prophet have been cited, for example, (1) his endowment with the divine Spirit (Mt. 3.16)[2] as the source of his miraculous power and authority (7.29), (2) his ecstatic experiences (e.g. at his baptism, temptation and transfiguration), (3) his insight into inner thoughts and motivations (9.4; 12.25; 22.18), (4) his prophetic predictions (e.g. regarding his own fate [16.21; 17.22-23; 20.18-19] or that of Jerusalem [23.38; 24.2]), and (5) his 'prophetic' symbolic actions (e.g. the temple-cleansing [21.12-13]; the fig tree [21.19], or the bread and cup [26.26-29]). Likewise, the content of his teaching is said to be similar to that of the prophets in its rhetorical forms, its polemic against cultic formalism, its ethical emphasis and call to repentance in the face of eschatological judgment (4.17; 11.20-24), and its declaration of the reign of God. Finally, Jesus' personal piety and intimacy with God, together with his inner consciousness of a calling to be an instrument of the divine will shaping the national destiny of God's people, are all thought to mark him as 'one of the prophets'.[3]

1. Matthew's interest in prophecy and prophetic precedents generally is indicated by his frequent use of this word-group (προφήτης [37×; 6×; 29×]; προφητεύω [4×; 2×; 2×]; προφητεία [1×; 0×; 0×]; ψευδοπροφήτης [3×; 1×; 1×]; cf. προφῆτις [0×; 0×; 1×]), which terms he employs some 44 times out of a total of 87 in the Synoptic Gospels (or 51% when Matthew constitutes only 37.4% of Synoptic material) and 206 in the NT as a whole (or 21% for 13.3% of total NT material). A number of these, of course, occur in Matthew's fulfillment-citations.

2. References to Matthew are cited only by way of illustration, without implying that the scholarly debate has focused in each instance on the particular evidence of this Gospel.

3. So, *inter alia*, H.J. Cadbury, 'Jesus and the Prophets', *JR* 5 (1925), pp. 607-22 (drawing particular attention [p. 610] to the motif from Jeremiah of the shedding of innocent blood); G. Kittel, C.H. Dodd and N. Micklem, ''ΙΗΣΟΥΣ 'Ο ΔΙΔΑΣΚΑΛΟΣ ΚΑΙ ΠΡΟΦΗΤΗΣ', *Theology* 17 (1928), pp. 202-11; C.H. Dodd, 'Jesus as Teacher and Prophet', in G.K.A. Bell and A. Deissmann (eds.), *Mysterium Christi: Christological Studies by British and German Theologians* (London: Longmans, 1930), pp. 57-65; L. Goppelt, *Typos: Die typologische Deutung des Alten Testaments im Neuen* (repr.; Darmstadt: Wissenschaftliche

Some commentators have emphasized that Jesus, like the prophets before him, was persecuted on account of his message.[1] And a few have seen in Jesus' specifically prophetic martyrdom the seeds for an interpretation of his death as having atoning value.[2]

Buchgesellschaft, 1969), pp. 70-97 [ET *Typos: The Typological Interpretation of the Old Testament in the New* (Grand Rapids: Eerdmans, 1982), pp. 61-82]; A.J.B. Higgins, 'Jesus as Prophet', *ExpTim* 57 (1945–46), p. 292; V. Taylor, *The Names of Jesus* (London: Macmillan, 1953), pp. 15-17; H. Duesburg, *Jésus, prophète et docteur de la loi* (Paris: Castermann, 1955), pp. 27-28; F. Gils, *Jésus, prophète d'après les évangiles synoptiques* (OBL, 2; Louvain: Publications Universitaires, 1957), pp. 49-88; 155-62; G. Friedrich, 'προφήτης κτλ', *TWNT*, VI, pp. 842-49 [= *TDNT*, pp. 841-48]; R.H. Fuller, *The Foundations of New Testament Christology* (London: Lutterworth, 1965), pp. 125-31; J. Jeremias, *Neutestamentliche Theologie*. I. *Die Verkündigung Jesu* (Gütersloh: Gerd Mohn, 1971) [ET *New Testament Theology*. I. *The Proclamation of Jesus* (London: SCM Press, 1971), pp. 77-80; cited henceforth in English translation]; Schnider, *Jesus der Prophet, passim* (with review of previous literature 11-20); Sand, *Gesetz und Propheten*, pp. 138-67; Hill, *NT Prophecy*, pp. 58-69; Aune, *Prophecy*, pp. 153-57, 160-88; Sato, *Prophetie*, p. 301, 373-75. For a comparison between Jesus and contemporary (messianic) prophetic figures, see D. Hill, 'Jesus and Josephus' "Messianic Prophets"', in Best and Wilson (eds.), *Text and Interpretation*, pp. 143-54; R.A. Horsley, 'Popular Prophetic Movements at the Time of Jesus: Their Principal Features and Social Origins', *JSNT* 26 (1986), pp. 3-27 (esp. pp. 20-24).

On the subject generally, see Cullmann, *Christology*, pp. 14-50; J. Knox, 'The Prophet in New Testament Christology', in R.A. Norris (ed.), *Lux in Lumine: Essays to Honor W. Norman Pittenger* (New York: Seabury, 1966), pp. 23-34; G. Vermes, *Jesus the Jew: A Historian's Reading of the Gospels* (London: SCM Press, 1973), pp. 86-99.

1. E.g. Goppelt, *Typos*, pp. 93-94 [ET pp. 79-80]; P.E. Davies, 'Jesus and the Role of the Prophet', *JBL* 64 (1945), p. 252; taken further in his more recent study, 'Did Jesus Die as a Martyr-Prophet?', *BR* 19 (1974), pp. 37-47; J. Daniélou, 'Le Christ Prophète', *VSpir* 78 (1948), pp. 168-69 (on Mt. 23.32, 36); Cullmann, *Christology*, p. 25; J. Jeremias, 'παῖς θεοῦ', *TDNT*, V, pp. 713-14 (with the ET [1967; see p. ix] reflecting the author's revisions for the second edition of *The Servant of God* [SBT, 20; London: SCM Press, 1965]); Hill, *NT Prophecy*, p. 62 ('as a prophet he foresaw his death in terms of prophetic martyrdom').

2. E.g. J. Downing, 'Jesus and Martyrdom', *JTS* 14 (1963), pp. 286-91; Jeremias, 'παὶς θεοῦ', *TDNT*, V, pp. 715-17. Opposed to such an interpretation is Strecker (*Weg*, pp. 182-84) on the grounds that Matthew does not stress the element of suffering as do the Jewish martyrologies. As Steck (*Israel*, pp. 252-54, 261-64) points out, the Deuteronomistic view of history, while including a focus on the death of the prophets, is distinct from martyr theology. For the former stresses, above all,

The designation of Jesus as a 'prophet' is often thought to have carried with it profound eschatological implications.[1] This view is based on an apparent consensus in first-century Judaism that the prophetic spirit had departed from Israel, only to return at the end of the age,[2] particularly in the person of Elijah[3] or the 'prophet-like-Moses' of Deut. 18.15-18.[4] On such a view, any manifestation of a prophetic ministry would have been understood to signal the 'end-time' and messianic era. Certainly the Greek term προφήτης was not widely applied to contemporary figures.[5]

Aune, however, has argued persuasively that this predominantly rabbinic position was not universally held and may have been influenced by a variety of apologetic (i.e. anti-enthusiast or anti-sectarian) motives.[6] And R.A. Horsley demonstrates that in the first century there were a number of popularly-based prophetic figures active outside the realm of 'official' Judaism.[7] Indeed, even within

the fate of the nation and its corporate destiny, whereas the latter concentrates in the first instance on the fate of the individual. Cf. Löhse, *Martyrer und Gottesknecht*, *passim* (esp. pp. 66-78; 94-110 [in connection with Isa. 53]). According to Löhse (*Martyrer und Gottesknecht*, pp. 203-10; cf. Manson, 'Martyrs and Martyrdom', pp. 479-84), the post-NT church developed an understanding of the atoning value of Christian martyrdom by combining elements of Jewish martyr-theology with reflection on the sufferings of Christ.

1. Cf. Cullmann, *Christology*, pp. 13-14, 31-38; Hill, *NT Prophecy*, pp. 33-37.

2. Cf. Ps 74.9; LXX Dan. 3.38; 1 Macc. 4.46; 9.27; 14.41; *2 Bar.* 85.3; *T. Benj.* 9.2; 1QS 9.10-11 (*Manual of Discipline*); *b. Sanh.* 11a; *b. Yom.* 9b; *b. Soṭ.* 48b; *t. Soṭ.* 13.2; *S. 'Ol. R.* 30; cf. Joel 2.28-29 [MT 3.1-2]; *Sib. Or.* 3.781; Josephus, *War*, 1.35.

3. Cf. Mal. 4.5-6 [MT 3.23-24]; Sir. 48.10; *Gen. R.* 71.9; 99.11.

4. Cf. 4Q Testim 5-8. On the significance of these two figures in Matthew's Gospel, see Chapter 4, §§B.1 and 4, below.

5. 'Ordinarily... the designation "prophet"... was reserved for ancient Israelite prophets or for eschatological prophets who were expected to appear just prior to the end' (Aune, *Prophecy*, p. 81; cf. p. 138 [for Josephus], pp. 195-96).

6. Aune, *Prophecy*, pp. 103-106; cf. R. Meyer, 'προφήτης', *TWNT*, VI, pp. 813-20 [= *TDNT*, p. 812-19]. On the cessation of prophecy according to Josephus, see Feldman, 'Prophets and Prophecy in Josephus', pp. 400-407.

7. R.A. Horsley, '"Like One of the Prophets of Old": Two Types of Popular Prophets at the Time of Jesus', *CBQ* 47 (1985), pp. 435-63. Cf. L. Gaston, *No Stone Upon Another: Studies in the Significance of the Fall of Jerusalem in the Synoptic Gospels* (Leiden: Brill, 1970), p. 462, on Josephus, *War*, 6.285-86.

rabbinic circles there was some acknowledgment that the 'Holy Spirit'—the spirit of prophecy—could still be imparted to especially pious individuals, without this implying the arrival of the eschaton![1]

On the other hand, the claim to prophetic inspiration on the part of various Jewish splinter-groups[2] supports, if only indirectly, the later rabbinic view, since such claims were typically eschatological in nature. In any event, Christian texts speak of Jesus' prophetic identity in such a way as to imply a validation of his ministry (e.g. Lk. 7.16; 24.19; Acts 3.22; Jn 4.19; 6.14, etc.). But the question of what specific overtones such an identification conveyed for Matthew requires further investigation on its own.

Examination of the Synoptic texts reveals that both Matthew and (to a lesser extent) Luke explicitly refer to Jesus as a prophet in such a way as to highlight his suffering and rejection, although they do so quite independently.[3] Both take their cue from Mk 6.4 (// Mt. 13.57 // Lk. 4.24; cf. Jn 4.4) where Jesus responds to the disbelief of the Nazarenes by declaring, 'A prophet is not without honour except in his own country, and among his own kin, and in his own house'. Thus, although the alternative versions of the saying are shorter than Mark's, all four Gospels concur in presenting Jesus' own estimation of himself as a rejected prophet. As Fuller aptly concludes:

> Without using 'prophet' as a direct self-designation, Jesus clearly indicates that he understood his role in prophetic terms in so far as it involved rejection and martyrdom.[4]

1. Cf. E. Sjöberg, 'πνεῦμα', *TWNT*, VI, p. 384 [= *TDNT*, p. 386].
2. See references cited by Aune, *Prophecy*, p. 104 and n. 16.
3. Luke's unique material stresses Jesus' prophetic identity: in 7.16 the onlookers cry, 'A great prophet has arisen among us' in response to Jesus' raising of the widow's son, even as the travellers on the road to Emmaus describe him as 'a prophet mighty in deed and word before God and all the people' (24.19). Likewise, the comment of the Pharisee in 7.39, 'If this man were a prophet, he would have known who and what sort of woman this is who is touching him', anticipates a prophetic prescience, which, in fact, Jesus demonstrates by discerning his thoughts. But only Jesus' retort to Herod's messengers in 13.33, 'it cannot be that a prophet should perish away from Jerusalem', emphasizes the element of prophetic suffering (although for an interpretation that plays down even this element, see R.H. Fuller, *The Mission and Achievement of Jesus* [SBT, 12; London: SCM Press, 1954], pp. 62-64). Thus Luke presents Jesus' rejection as only one feature among several that collectively mark him as a prophet.
4. Fuller, *Foundations*, p. 127; echoed by Hill, *NT Prophecy*, p. 57. So also

Although the phrase οὐκ ἔστιν προφήτης ἄτιμος derives from Mark, the description of Jesus as ἄτιμος takes on particularly ominous overtones within the context of Matthew's Gospel. For although Matthew rarely uses this word-group,[1] the one other instance in which he applies such language to Jesus is in 27.9: τὴν τιμὴν τοῦ τετιμημένου ὃν ἐτιμήσαντο ἀπὸ υἱῶν Ἰσραήλ (cf. 27.6). For Matthew, then, it would appear that these two responses are of a piece: the devaluation and rejection of the prophet Jesus by his own family and townspeople foreshadows his yet more momentous rejection by the people as a whole.[2]

In light of this emphasis, it seems curious that Matthew should omit from his version of Herod's discussion about the identity of Jesus (Mt. 14.2) the comment of Mk 6.15 // Lk. 9.8 that Jesus is 'like one of the prophets of old'.[3] But, as we have seen, Matthew does so only in order to strengthen the parallel between Jesus and John, whose martyrdom he goes on to recount, and so to concentrate all further discussion of Jesus' prophetic identity in 16.13-14. For in that passage, John the Baptist, Elijah and Jeremiah all represent approximations of Jesus' identity: they are all prophetic and suffering prototypes of the messiah, who is about to announce his own impending fate.

Davies, 'Jesus', p. 242; Higgins, 'Jesus', p. 292; Dupont, *Les béatitudes*, II, pp. 296-97; cf. Friedrich, *TWNT*, VI, pp. 842-43 [= *TDNT*, p. 841]; Gils, *Jésus*, p. 47; Sand, *Gesetz und Propheten*, pp. 142-43 ('Während...Jesus sich selbst nicht als Prophet bezeichnet, handelt und redet er doch in einer den Propheten gleichbaren Art'). The proverbial nature of the saying, with its emphasis on rejection, does not vitiate, but rather supports a self-reference by Jesus to his prophetic role; *contra* Aune, *Prophecy*, p. 156. Cf. Schnider, *Jesus der Prophet*, pp. 149-51, 161, who sees here a simple refusal to believe in Jesus, but without it implying either violent rejection or a specifically prophetic identity.

1. E.g. τιμή only at 27.6, 9 (and nowhere else in the Synoptics); τιμάω in 15.4, 19.19 (= Exod. 20.12), cf. 15.6; 15.8 (= Isa. 29.13). Note especially the deletion of ἀτιμάζω (so Mk 12.4 // Lk. 20.11) from 21.36.

2. As a further detail, Matthew modifies Mark's version of the townspeople's question (Mk 6.3; οὐχ οὗτός ἐστιν ὁ τέκτων, ὁ υἱὸς τῆς Μαρίας?) to read οὐχ οὗτός ἐστιν ὁ τοῦ τέκτονος υἱός? (Mt. 13.55), behind which we may discern either hints of a controversy surrounding Jesus' birth (so Schnider, *Jesus der Prophet*, pp. 160) or, more likely, the implied rejection of Jesus' messianic sonship (i.e. as echoing 3.17 and 17.5, οὗτός ἐστιν ὁ υἱός μου).

3. Discussed in detail by Cullmann, *Christology*, pp. 31-35; Schnider, *Jesus der Prophet*, pp. 182-83.

The foregoing review of Matthew's appropriation of the Deuteronomistic rejected-prophet motif reinforces the likelihood that a similar interpretation must be applied to the fourth opinion Matthew reports, that Jesus is popularly seen as 'one of the prophets'. For to be a prophet, at least in Matthew's Gospel, is to suffer and be rejected. Thus in the Transfiguration narrative (17.12-13 // Mk 9.13), Matthew's comparison of Jesus to John specifically underscores their common fate as suffering prophets, for Matthew adds the observation 'So also the Son of man will suffer at their hands'.[1]

Matthew's insertion of the designation 'prophet' for Jesus in 21.11 introduces a new element. When Jesus enters Jerusalem to the acclamation of those who accompany him, Matthew tells us, ἐσείσθη πᾶσα ἡ πόλις λέγουσα· τίς ἐστιν οὗτος? The crowds reply, οὗτος ἐστιν ὁ προφήτης Ἰησοῦς ὁ ἀπὸ Ναζαρὲθ τῆς Γαλιλαίας (21.10-11). The only other occasion on which 'all the city' reacts like this is in response to the news of Jesus' first advent (2.3, ὁ δὲ Βασιλεὺς Ἡρῴδης ἐταράχθη καὶ πᾶσα Ἱεροσόλυμα μετ' αὐτοῦ). So here, Matthew's addition injects an ominous note into the narrative.[2]

More significant, however, is the fact that with Jesus having already been designated as 'Lord' (21.3), 'King' (21.5) and 'Son of David' (21.9) in the verses immediately preceding, the title 'prophet' here in 21.11 provides a final definition of his messianic identity.[3] Specifically, the term effects the transition to the ensuing account of the Temple 'cleansing'. For following Jesus' 'triumphal' entry into the city, Matthew draws attention to the specifically 'prophetic' nature of his actions in the Temple courts, even as Jesus himself quotes from the words of the prophets to explain his actions (Mt. 21.13 // Mk 11.17).

1. This is the motive behind Matthew's consistent drawing of parallels between the two: so 3.2 // 4.17; 3.7 // 12.34, 23.33; 3.10 // 7.19, 12.33, and the Matthaean redaction of Q 7.33-34; cf. Schnider, *Jesus der Prophet,* pp. 44-45, 53.

2. Cf. also the reaction of πᾶς ὁ λαός in 27.25, as well as the other two uses of σείω in 27.51 and 28.4. Although here the reference is to the inhabitants of Jerusalem, even Gentile cities react the same way in the Matthaean redaction: see 8.34, πᾶσα ἡ πόλις (+ Mk 5.14).

3. Cf. Schnider, *Jesus der Prophet,* pp. 104-105, 236-37. Sand (*Gesetz und Propheten*, pp. 140-41; citing Schlatter, *Matthäus*, p. 611; cf. Cullmann, *Christology*, p. 35) reads too much into the passage when he takes the definitive article (ὁ προφήτης Ἰησοῦς) to indicate that in the opinion of the crowd, Jesus is *the* (i.e. the final, eschatological) prophet.

We have already discussed how in 21.33–22.14 Matthew brings together the parables of the vineyard and the marriage feast in order to sharpen his polemic against the Jerusalem authorities. This is also, it appears, the purpose of the parable of the 'Two Sons' in 20.28-32. In Matthew's narrative this polemic is further juxtaposed (albeit subtly) with the suggestion that Jesus himself is a rejected prophet. For the above-mentioned parables simply extend Jesus' debate with the 'chief priests and elders of the people' regarding the authority of John—and, ultimately, of Jesus himself (Mt. 21.23-27 // Mk 11.27-33). In the course of their exchange, the authorities refuse to acknowledge that John's authority was either 'from heaven' or 'from men', the latter because 'men' themselves consider him a prophet (Mt. 21.26 // Mk 11.32). Here John is clearly portrayed as a rejected prophet. But the issue of the Baptist's authority only serves to shed light on the earlier question of Jesus' own authority. According to both Mark and Matthew, if the authorities were unwilling to acknowledge the prophetic authority of John, so they will refuse to acknowledge the (implicitly prophetic) authority of Jesus. For the implication of Jesus' reply, 'Neither will I tell you by what authority I do these things' (Mt. 21.27 // Mk 11.33), is that their authority is one and the same.

At the conclusion of the Parable of the Vineyard, Mark observes that 'they tried to arrest him, but feared the multitude, for they perceived that he had told this parable against them' (Mk 12.12). Matthew, however, rewords the passage, making the authorities fear the multitude because the latter 'held [Jesus] to be a prophet' (εἰς προφήτην αὐτὸν εἶχον, 21.46). The change is, indeed, a subtle one. Nonetheless, it once more places Jesus in opposition to the authorities as a prophet, pointedly recalling the opposition of the tenant-farmers to the landlord's servants in the preceding parable. Moreover, Matthew has modelled this passage after 21.26, where the authorities similarly fear the multitude, there because they hold *John* to be a prophet (πάντες γὰρ ὡς προφήτην ἔχουσιν τὸν Ἰωάννην, // Mk 11.32, εἶχον).[1] Thus the implication of Jesus' enigmatic reply on

1. Cf. Gils, *Jésus prophète*, p. 25. Matthew's insertion of a similar phrase in 14.5 (diff. Mk 6.20) is of similar significance insofar as it connects John's identity as a prophet with the account of his martyrdom (cf. Sand, *Gesetz und Propheten*, p. 127).

that occasion is clear: even as John and Jesus both derive their authority from the same source, so the people hold both to be prophets and so both are rejected. The example of John and the warning of the parable, in fact, both portend a violent fate for Jesus once the attempt to arrest him finally succeeds.

When at his arrest Jesus' disciples attempt to defend him, Jesus insists that 'all this has taken place that the Scriptures of the prophets might be fulfilled' (26.56; cf. Mk 14.49, 'But let the Scriptures be fulfilled'). Whereas Mark's reference is to Scripture in general, Matthew would have us notice that the suffering of the messiah is in particular accord with the words 'of the prophets'. For it is the experience of the prophets that most closely anticipates Jesus' own fate.

In a similar vein, Mt. 26.68 draws from Mk 14.65 (// Lk. 22.64) the cruel command of the high priest's attendants that their prisoner (who in Mark and Luke is blindfolded) prophesy and reveal the identity of those who have struck him. But Matthew inserts a significant reminder of Jesus' messianic identity, rendering the command, 'Prophesy to us, you Christ! Who is it that struck you?'[1] So in a manner reminiscent of the earlier debate about Jesus' true identity (16.13-28), Matthew not only presents him as a mistreated prophet (the words of the guards being closer to the truth than they know) but also makes his 'prophetic suffering' an integral part of his

1. While the text of Mt. 26.68 is firmly established, that of Mk 14.65 suffers considerable confusion. The simplest, and most likely original reading is προφήτευσον (so ℵ A B C D K L Π 067 1241 it$^{(pt)}$ vg syr^{p} cop$^{bo(pt)}$), to which various elaborations have been added: νῦν or ἡμῖν or both (G Ψ f^{1} it$^{(mss)}$ cop$^{sa(mss)}$ syr^{s}); with one or the other of these followed by Χριστέ (1242 it^{aur}), as well as τίς ἐστιν ὁ παίσας σε [from Mt. 26.68 = Lk. 22.64] (N W X Θ f^{13} 33 700 892 1071 1424 cop$^{sa(mss)}$ etc.). Cf. *TCGNT*, 115. Thus the addition of Χριστέ is due, in fact, to Matthew rather than to Mark. From another perspective, S. McLoughlin ('Les accords mineurs Mt-Lc contre Mc et le problème synoptique. Vers la théorie des deux sources', *ETL* 43 [1967], pp. 31-35 [= I. de la Potterie (ed.), *De Jésus aux évangiles. Tradition et rédaction dans les évangiles synoptiques* (BETL, 25; Gembloux: Duculot; Paris: Lethielleux, 1967) (same pagination)] proposes—albeit without textual support—that the phrase τίς ἐστιν ὁ παίσας σε represents a subsequent assimilation to Luke, in which case it could not be taken as evidence of Matthaean redactional intent. But even were this the case, Matthew has still embellished Mark's προφήτευσον with ἡμῖν Χριστέ, thus significantly juxtaposing the concept of prophecy with the office of messiah.

messiahship.[1] Once again, Jesus-the-messiah is treated like 'one of the prophets', and, as such, is rejected.

The parallel to Matthew 16 is all the more forceful if Hill is correct in his assertion that,

> the demand for a sign made by the Pharisees (Mark 8.11 par. [i.e. Mt. 16.1-4, cf. 12.38-40]) in all probability carries with it the assumption that Jesus is a prophet who ought to authenticate his claim.[2]

For if this is the case, then both in that context and the present one the question of Jesus' messianic identity is set against a backdrop of testing and, ultimately, rejection of him as a false prophet. This would explain the appropriateness of the death sentence (26.66), for according to Deut. 18.20, a false prophet must die.[3] Even more appropriate is the fact that the only 'sign' indicating Jesus' authenticity will be the sign of the prophet Jonah, which focuses—whether explicitly, as in 12.38-40, or implicitly, as in 16.1-4—on Jesus' suffering and death, followed by his vindication.[4]

Finally, the attribution to Jesus of a prophetic identity may shed some light on the bystanders' strange misinterpretation of Jesus' cry from the cross, ηλι ηλι λεμα σαβαχθανι (27.46 // Mk 15.35). The report by Mark and Matthew of the crowd's comment, 'This man is calling Elijah', makes little sense when both have already related that their respective transliterations, in fact, refer to LXX Ps. 21.2 [MT 22.2]. But the purpose of the comment, at least for Matthew, is to reiterate the parallel between the suffering Jesus and the rejected Elijah. For in Mark and Matthew alike, mention of Elijah has hitherto referred primarily to John the Baptist, and in particular to his suffering and rejection. It is appropriate, therefore, that the bystanders

1. Cf. Gils, *Jésus*, pp. 23-24; see also P. Benoit, 'Les Outrages à Jésus Prophète', in W.C. van Unnik *et al.* (eds.), *Neotestamentica et Patristica* [*Freundesgabe Oscar Cullmann*] (NovTSup, 6; Leiden: Brill, 1962), pp. 94-107; Schnider, *Jesus der Prophet*, pp. 156-58.

2. *NT Prophecy*, p. 51. Cf. Lk. 7.39. Statements that Jesus was in league with or possessed by Beelzebul (which Matthew emphasizes in 9.34; 10.25; 12.24 // Mk 3.22) are clearly accusations that Jesus is a false prophet (cf. Dodd, 'Jesus as Teacher and Prophet', p. 57).

3. So *m. Sanh.* 11.1; cf. Jeremias, *NT Theology*, pp. 77-78; Hill, *NT Prophecy*, p. 52.

4. Cf. §A.2.b.3, above.

should not only call attention to this similarity, but should comment, 'Let us see whether Elijah will come to take him down' (Mk 15.36). In other words, they want to see whether Elijah will rescue Jesus from his suffering, or, as Matthew puts it, 'come to save him' (27.47). Matthew's independent transliteration of the cry itself (ηλι for Mark's ελωι, if this is indeed the correct reading[1]), therefore, seems intended to underscore the reference not only to Psalm 22, but to the name of Elijah ('Ηλίας) as well.[2]

Jesus as the Eschatological Mosaic Prophet

The sentence against a false prophet alluded to earlier, follows immediately on Moses' declaration that 'The LORD your God will raise up for you a prophet like me from among you...him you shall heed' (Deut. 18.15-18). There has been considerable debate, both in the NT and in modern scholarship, as to whether Jesus fulfills these expectations.[3] The anticipation of the eschatological Mosaic prophet is already evident at Qumran (4QTestim 5-8), as well as in Samaritan theology and possibly Philo.[4] Of particular significance in the NT are the apostolic preaching of Peter (Acts 3.22) and the defense of Stephen (Acts 7.37), both of which explicitly identify Jesus as the fulfillment of Deut. 18.15, as well as Jn 5.46, according to which Jesus declares: 'If you believed Moses, you would believe me, for he wrote of me' (cf. Jn 7.40). The Synoptic Gospels make the same

1. ηλι ηλι (for אלי [from MT Ps. 22.2]) A D (L) W Θ 090 $f^{1.13}$ 𝔐 | ελωι ελωι (for Aramaic אלהי) א B 33 cop (which, despite strong external support, is apparently an assimilation to Mk 15.34 [*TCGNT*, p. 70]).

2. Cf. M'Neile, *Matthew*, p. 421.

3. See representative discussions in J. Jeremias, *s.v.* 'Μωυσῆς', *TWNT*, IV, pp. 871-78 [= *TDNT*, pp. 867-73]; Gils, *Jésus*, p. 30-42 (Gils [pp. 38-39] also sees 'one of the prophets' in Mt. 16.14 par. as a reference to Deut. 18.15); Friedrich, *s.v.* 'προφήτης κτλ.', *TWNT*, VI, pp. 848-49 [= *TDNT*, pp. 846-48]; Teeple, *Prophet*, pp. 74-97; Davies, *Setting*, p. 189 n. 2; Hahn, *Christologische Hoheitstitel*, pp. 380-404; Longenecker, *Christology*, pp. 32-38; cf. Taylor, *Names*, p. 16; Knox, 'Prophet', pp. 28-29; Hill, *NT Prophecy*, p. 54; for negative estimations, see, e.g., Lindars, *NT Apologetic*, pp. 204-10; Kingsbury, *Structure, Christology, Kingdom*, pp. 88-92; Aune, *Prophecy*, pp. 154-55.

4. *Spec. Leg.* 1.64-65, cited in Longenecker, *Christology*, pp. 34 n. 33. Further discussion in J. Jeremias, *s.v.* 'Μωυσῆς', *TWNT*, IV, pp. 862-68 [= *TDNT*, VIII, pp. 857-64]; Teeple, *Prophet*, pp. 29-68; Schnider, *Jesus der Prophet*, pp. 89-100.

identification, for the *bat qol* at Jesus' Transfiguration—to which Moses and Elijah are themselves witnesses— commands the disciples ἀκούετε αὐτοῦ (Mt. 17.5 // Mk 9.7; cf. Lk. 9.35) in terms that echo the similar αὐτοῦ ἀκούσεσθε of LXX Deut. 18.15.[1] Moreover, we have already observed in Chapter 1 elements of a Moses typology underlying Matthew's depiction of Jesus.[2]

For our purposes, however, possible Matthaean references to Jesus as the prophet-like-Moses are not directly relevant, for this concept 'differs sharply' from the Deuteronomistic interpretation of Israel's history.[3] Specifically, the latter outlook is fundamentally historical and retrospective in focus, rather than eschatological and future oriented. Likewise, it is concerned more with understanding the reversals and calamities experienced by God's people than with anticipating the appearance of a legislator, deliverer and national leader like Moses. Yet while Matthew's depiction of Jesus as a 'prophet-like-Moses' does not specifically serve Deuteronomistic concerns, it is not inconsistent with this motif. For, as we have seen, Moses too is understood to be a suffering and rejected prophet.[4] Certainly this is true of Moses' depiction elsewhere in the NT (Acts 7.38-40; Heb. 11.24-26; Rev. 11.3[?]; cf. Lk. 9.31; 24.26-27, 44-46; Acts 26.22-23, where Moses is said to have prophesied the suffering of the messiah).[5] Again, Matthew's own comparison of Moses' and Jesus' infancies stresses their respective persecution. Thus the links between these two 'prophets' in Matthew's Gospel underscore, however indirectly, Jesus' identity as a suffering and rejected prophet.[6]

1. Schnider, *Jesus der Prophet*, pp. 100-101.

2. See also Chapter 4, §B.4 and Chapter 5, §B.2, below.

3. Jacobson, 'Literary Unity', p. 385 n. 99, so Steck, *Israel*, pp. 240-43; Polag, *Christologie*, p. 122.

4. Cf. p 106 n. 2, above. So Jeremias (*TDNT*, IV, p. 863 [= *TWNT*, p. 867]): 'it is plain that in Rabb[inic] writings elements of suffering are constantly linked with this figure'.

5. Jeremias, *TWNT*, IV, p. 877 [= *TDNT*, p. 873].

6. As noted earlier, the tradition that Jeremiah fulfills the expectation of Deut. 18.15 (*Par. Jer.* 6.24; *Pes. K.* 13.6 [112a]; *Sifre Deut.* 155 [on Deut. 18.15]), while most suggestive in the context of our study, is difficult to evaluate. For although Boismard argues for such an association in the Gospel of John, Matthew betrays no similar awareness, unless Mt. 16.14 be read in this manner (so Teeple, Hahn; see p. 90 n. 2, above, for references).

As this review of the relevant passages demonstrates, a series of significant parallels emerge in Matthew's description of John, Jesus and the Christian disciples alike as suffering prophets. First, John the Baptist is depicted as a prophet in his own right, both in the opinion of Jesus (11.9) and that of the people (14.5; 21.26; cf. 3.4). But he is also compared to the prophet Elijah (11.14; 17.12), both times in connection with his rejection and violent death. Furthermore, both passages compare him in this regard to Jesus. Finally, Matthew records the comment of Jesus that John is not just a prophet, but 'more than a prophet' (11.9).[1]

Similarly, Jesus is reported to be a prophet, both in the popular mind (21.11, 46) and, albeit implicitly, by his own admission (13.57). This latter comment, moreover, implies the prospect of rejection. This is consistent with Matthew's comparison of Jesus to previous prophets, whether Jonah (12.40-41, cf. 16.4), or the triumvirate of John the Baptist, Elijah and Jeremiah (16.14), or other unnamed emissaries (21.34-39; cf. 23.37)—all of whom suffered by virtue of their divinely appointed roles. In a similar vein, we have seen how Matthew's repeated comparisons of Jesus and John consistently stress their common rejection (see also 11.16-19; 21.26 // 21.46). Furthermore, Matthew's Gospel repeatedly suggests that Jesus was accused and rejected as a false prophet (9.34; 10.25; 12.24; 16.1; 26.68). But Jesus also transcends the category of 'prophet', for he is 'greater than Jonah' (12.41), even as his question to the disciples in 16.15, 'But who do *you* say that I am?', implies his superiority to the prophetic antecedents they have just named.

For their part, the followers of Jesus are also designated as 'prophets' (10.41; 23.34; cf. 23.37), in which role they too are compared to the prophets of old—particularly as regards the fate of rejection that the disciples will share with their predecessors (5.12c; 21.35 // 22.6; 23.34-37). Their suffering, like that of John the Baptist, is also repeatedly compared to that of Jesus (10.23-25, 38-39; 23.34). Specifically, the reference in 23.37 to stoning may suggest that they, like their OT counterparts in 21.35 and like Jesus himself, are rejected as false prophets. Finally, Matthew relates that, like Jesus and John

1. On the meaning of this qualification (i.e. designating John as the eschatological prophet), see Cullmann, *Christology*, p. 24; Sand, *Gesetz und Propheten*, p. 137.

before them, the disciples too are greater than the prophets of Israel, insofar as the revelation they have received is more excellent (13.16-17).

There is a broad consensus of scholarship that the category of 'prophet', although belonging to the earliest sphere of christological reflection, was ultimately abandoned in favour of other titles and concepts that accounted more adequately for the full scope of Jesus' life and ministry.[1] If this was so, it renders all the more significant those elements of Jesus' prophetic identity that Matthew has chosen to retain—or, rather, to re-integrate into his narrative. He has done so, it appears, in order to account for Israel's rejection of Jesus and his message on the grounds that he is a prophet, and that he therefore suffered the fate common to all prophets. For Matthew's interest in designating Jesus as a 'prophet' is not primarily christological, but rather apologetic, even polemical, in keeping with the interests of a Deuteronomistic outlook.

Thus Matthew employs and accentuates the Deuteronomistic motifs of his source materials in order to underscore the spiritual obduracy and consequent responsibility of Israel with regard to the rejection of Jesus, on the one hand, and the destruction of Jerusalem, on the other. By depicting John, Jesus and the disciples as rejected prophets, and by comparing these both to one another and to the prophets of old, Matthew seeks to demonstrate that the fate of Jesus and those associated with him is consistent with that of all God's messengers. Such an explanation would likely constitute a powerful apologetic both to Jewish Christians and to the Jewish community from which they found themselves increasingly estranged in the aftermath of the war against Rome.

At the same time, however, Matthew is careful to include material pointing out that Jesus, John, and the disciples alike all transcend the category of 'prophet'. Perhaps this is because Matthew makes use of a prophetic identity primarily to draw attention to its Deuteronomistic implications, but without deriving from it specifically christological conclusions.

1. See Cullmann, *Christology*, pp. 44-49.

Chapter 3

TEXTUAL ALLUSIONS IN MATTHEW TO JEREMIAH TRADITIONS

Two questions concerning Matthew's use of biblical and associated exegetical traditions must be addressed before we turn to the texts themselves. The first has to do with Matthew's allusions to Scripture in places where an obvious fulfillment formula or quotation does not appear. In other words, what degree of verbal or thematic similarity are we to demand between Matthew's text and that of his putative source(s) in order to postulate a literary relationship? The second concerns the appropriateness of adducing evidence from Jewish exegetical procedures and themes as a means of clarifying a Christian document.

A. *Method*

With regard to identifying Matthaean allusions, it is not possible to designate a minimum number of words or forms of words that must be in agreement between an allusion and its source in order to establish a definite relationship. This is because an allusion may rely on a Hebrew text at variance with the MT or employ translation variants that differ from the LXX in any of its known forms. Rendering an OT text even more difficult to trace may be an exegete's midrashic adaptation of it to its present context. We saw this to be the case in Chapter 1 with respect to Matthew's use of both Jer. 31.15 and Zech. 11.13. Indeed, the fact that (as in Qumran literature) scriptural phraseology is woven into the fabric of the narrative, simply because the author customarily thinks in such terms, results in some distortion of wording and grammatical forms.[1]

1. Cf. Gundry: '*an allusive quotation... reflects the language and phrase-forms with which the writer is most familiar and in which he habitually thinks*—all the more so in the case of Jewish authors, whose education from childhood was steeped in OT

The procedure followed by R.H. Gundry in his study of Matthew's use of the OT was, rather than establishing formal criteria for comparison, simply 'to require that a recognizable thought-connection exist between the OT and NT passages'.[1] But Gundry's textual analysis is frequently vitiated by a lack of control, as the examination of particular examples will demonstrate.

Nolan suggests a somewhat more precise method:

> A scriptural allusion may be defined as a conscious evocation of an OT personage, event, institution, passage, or literary technique, made by the writer in order to communicate through the medium of received religious tradition. No clearly defined set of rules can be given for gauging the precise influence of an OT theme, passage, or reality, or an apparent parallel in Matthew. But two criteria are certainly valid. For that influence to be highly significant, there must be both a series of verbal similarities between the texts, and a theological motive giving them some coherence and direction.[2]

Nolan's second criterion, however, must be qualified in light of Matthew's atomistic and non-contextual method of citation (as with Jer. 31.15 in 2.18), for 'coherence and direction' often consist solely in the use Matthew makes of an OT text, and not necessarily in its relation to the passage's original, contextual meaning.

There are, nonetheless, precedents for Matthew's reappropriation of Scripture elsewhere in Jewish tradition (e.g. *Targum Jonathan* in the case of Jer. 31.15), precedents that contribute to the evocative power of the text in question. For this reason, investigation into the NT's use of OT material must—even at the level of establishing valid allusions— respect the history of interpretation that would likely have influenced a Christian writer's use of scriptural tradition.

R.B. Hays provides a full examination of this question in his discussion of 'intertextuality'.[3] Drawing on similar studies in the field of literary criticism, Hays proposes a set of seven criteria to provide a

lore' (*Use of the OT*, p. 3; emphasis his); also van Dodewaard, 'La force évocatrice', p. 486: for the authors of the NT, 'le climat littéraire était tel, que celui qui écrivait sur la religion écrivait par là-même en style biblique'. See also (with reference to Mark) Kee, 'Function of Scriptural Quotations', p. 166.

1. *Use of the OT*, p. 5.
2. *Royal Son*, p. 23.
3. R.B. Hays, *Echoes of Scripture in the Letters of Paul* (New Haven: Yale University Press, 1989), pp. 14-33.

measure of control in verifying the presence of scriptural allusions within a NT (or, for his study, Pauline) text.[1] These are (1) availability,[2] (2) volume (prominence or degree of explicitness), (3) recurrence,[3] (4) thematic coherence (i.e. with the line of reasoning or argument to which the allusion allegedly contributes), (5) historical plausibility, (6) history of interpretation, and (7) satisfaction (i.e. whether the allusion 'makes sense').[4]

Although all these criteria may not be applicable in any one instance, they would appear to be helpful in demonstrating that a specific allusion is not only present in a text, but also was intended by the writer to be operative.[5] Hays, of course, is conscious of the limitations imposed on NT exegetes by the scarcity of historical sources that might serve as a control for such an investigation. Nonetheless, his description of similar approaches to Renaissance poetry, when applied to Matthew, aptly describes the intent of both the present chapter and this study as a whole:

> to hear and understand the poet's allusions we need to know not only the tradition to which the allusion points but also the way in which that tradition was understood in the poet's time and the contemporary historical experience or situation with which the poet links the tradition.[6]

1. Hays, *Echoes of Scripture*, pp. 29-32.
2. In this respect, Hay's comment (*Echoes of Scripture*, p. 30) on Paul's use of the OT applies with even greater force to Matthew: 'His practice of citation shows that he was acquainted with virtually the whole body of texts that were later acknowledged as canonical within Judaism, and that he expected his readers to share his acknowledgement of these texts as Scripture'.
3. 'Where...evidence exists that [the author] considered a passage of particular importance, proposed echoes from the same context should be given additional credence' (*Echoes of Scripture*, p. 30).
4. This is similar to the criterion of 'elegance' required of hypotheses in the natural sciences.
5. In relation to his discussion of hermeneutical principles (*Echoes of Scripture*, pp. 25-29), Hays distinguishes between 'allusion' and 'echo', of which the latter transcends conscious authorial intention: 'To limit our interpretation of Paul's scriptural echoes to what he intended by them is to impose a severe and arbitrary hermeneutical restriction' (*Echoes of Scripture*, p. 33; cf., pp. 20, 29). By contrast, this study is limited to what can plausibly be posited, via the application of such criteria, to have formed part of Matthew's redactional intent.
6. *Echoes of Scripture*, p. 18.

For it is precisely this significant interplay between text, tradition and historical context that the present investigation into Matthew's use of Jeremiah traditions seeks to explore.

The procedure in attempting to identify textual allusions to Jeremiah traditions in Matthew's Gospel will be to focus on the degree of probability that the Evangelist intended the postulated reference. In keeping with the criteria outlined above, the greater the concurrence between the OT and Matthaean texts of common vocabulary, translation variants and grammatical features, the more frequent the recurrence in Matthew's Gospel of a given theme or exegetical tradition, and the more coherent such an interpretation appears in light of historically relevant literary analogues, the higher such a probability will be.

Specifically, this study will focus on features that are unique to or found predominantly within the literature associated with Jeremiah. The availability of alternative sources for a particular phrase or expression will, of course, reduce the likelihood of dependence on Jeremiah literature. But it may not eliminate such a possibility altogether, since (as in the case of Matthew's notorious 'He shall be called a Nazarene' [2.23]; or even 27.9-10, as we saw in Chapter 1) allusions can be intentionally composite and complex. Where this is the case, further corroborative (e.g. thematic) evidence will be required to substantiate the allusion. That is to say, where Matthew's wording seems to evoke more than one source, it must be shown either that an allusion to Jeremiah is primary or that Jeremiah material makes a substantial contribution to the larger whole, both verbally and conceptually. Only if the contribution of Jeremiah is distinctive can an allusion be substantiated. This will likewise be the case for allusions derived from Mark or Q of which Matthew does not otherwise indicate any awareness.[1]

The Matthaean references to be investigated are derived, for the most part, from the 'Loci citate vel allegati' of the 26th edition of the Nestle–Aland Novum Testamentum Graece and the lists provided by

1. Cf. Gundry: the balance of probability weighs in favor of Matthew making use of allusions derived from his source-material, since 'wc can hardly think that a writer who introduces such out-of-the-way citations as, e.g., Hos 11.1 (2.6) would not have known the OT well enough to have recognized allusive quotations in the tradition upon which he worked' (*Use of the OT*, p. 4).

W. Dittmar.[1] These include allusions not only to the canonical book of Jeremiah, but also to related works that either were considered to have come from the hand of the prophet or were closely associated with him in some way. This investigation will therefore include the book of Lamentations, which tradition had assigned to the prophet,[2] and the pseudepigraphical book of Baruch (or '1 Baruch').[3]

One of the most crucial questions regarding sources for Matthew's exegetical traditions has to do with the value of rabbinic materials—specifically, the Talmud (Mishnah and Gemara), Tosefta, Midrashim, Targumim and related materials—that were codified after the NT era.[4] Ascription of ideas or opinions to a specific rabbi can (to the

1. *Vetus Testamentum in Novo*, henceforth cited as 'Dittmar'. Page references to this source will not be cited as all entries are arranged in canonical order by chapter and verse. Dittmar quotes MT and LXX entries in full. Comparative reference will also be made to Hühn, *Die alttestamentlichen Citate und Reminiscenzen* (cited as Hühn, without page references), whose work represents a maximal approach to the study of OT allusions, as well as to the UBSGNT (3rd edn) 'Index of Quotations' and 'Index of Allusions and Verbal Parallels'.

2. This is clearly indicated by the order of the books in the LXX, by the LXX title, 'ΘΡΗΝΟΙ ΙΕΡΕΜΙΟΥ', and by the preface it inserts: 'And it came to pass after Israel had gone into captivity, and Jerusalem was laid waste, that Jeremiah sat weeping and composed this lament [ἐθρήνησε τὸν θρῆνον τοῦτον] over Jerusalem and said...' (cf. Wolff, *Jeremia*, p. 4). This appears to be based on the statement of 2 Chron. 35.25 that Jeremiah wrote laments, although here the occasion is the death of King Josiah. It is later recorded by rabbinic tradition (*b. B. Bat.* 15a) that 'Jeremiah wrote the book which bears his name, the book of Kings and Lamentations'. *Targum Lamentations*, in its own explanation of Jeremiah's authorship, combines both occasions for writing (*Targ. Lam.* 1.1, 18; 4.20; cf. Levine, *Aramaic Lamentations*, p. 77). For further discussion of the question of authorship, see D.R. Hillers, *Lamentations: Introduction, Translation, and Notes* (AB, 7A; Garden City, NY: Doubleday, 1972), pp. xix-xxiii, from which the translation of the LXX cited above is taken.

3. Brief discussion of the authorship of Baruch is found in Moore, *Daniel, Esther, and Jeremiah*, pp. 255-56, 260. Since no allusions are claimed for the so-called *Epistle of Jeremiah*, it is not included in this investigation.

4. For an introduction to the Mishnah, Gemaras, Tosefta and various Midrashim, see Bowker, *Targums and Rabbinic Literature*, pp. 53-92, and literature cited there. The traditional dates for the principal works are: Mishnah and Tosefta, c. 200 CE; *Talmud Yerushalmi*, fifth century; *Talmud Babli*, fifth to sixth century. For a historical review and introductory discussion of NT exegesis in light of Jewish sources, see G. Vermes, 'Jewish Studies and New Testament Interpretation', *JJS 31* (1980), *passim*, and for a succinct review of approaches to Jewish material in recent

extent that such an ascription may be deemed reliable) help to establish a *terminus a quo* for an individual tradition, although even then the material cited is rarely early enough to be contemporary with the NT. Yet many talmudic and midrashic traditions (e.g. *Baraitot*) lack ascriptions, as do all the periphrastic translations of the Targumim.

Despite the fact that Christianity first arose as a Jewish sect out of a Jewish milieu, an appeal to Jewish sources encounters difficulties not only of relative dating, but also, more critically, of widely differing, even contradictory theological outlooks.[1] For whereas the purpose of Jewish exegesis is, whether proximately or ultimately, the elucidation of Scripture itself in relation to the many concerns of Jewish life, the purpose of Christian exegesis is rather, whether proximately or ultimately, the elucidation of the life and ministry of Jesus in relation to the many concerns of the Christian community. Christian exegesis—above all that of Matthew—is fundamentally messianic in character, whereas Jewish exegesis (although Qumran may be cited as an exception) is not. This is not to deny that messianic exegesis can be found in Jewish sources and non-messianic exegesis in Christian sources. There remains, however, a fundamental distinction in theological orientation between the two as to whether the exegete looks to Moses or to the messiah for primary inspiration.[2]

Nonetheless, where there is a thematic or exegetical parallel between Jewish and Christian documents, three possibilities exist as to derivation: (1) that the Christian writer copied from rabbinic codifications; (2) that the Jewish compilers drew from a Christian source; or (3) that both drew independently from common traditions.[3]

NT scholarship, see A.J. Saldarini, 'Judaism and the New Testament', in E.J. Epp and G.W. MacRae (eds.), *The New Testament and its Modern Interpreters* (Philadelphia: Fortress Press; Atlanta: Scholars Press, 1989), pp. 25-54.

1. Although Vermes ('Jewish Studies', p. 13) goes so far in stressing the 'Jewishness' of NT literature as to suggest that 'for a historical understanding, the age-old distinction between the New Testament and its Jewish background should be abolished and the former looked at deliberately as part of a larger whole', the theological distinctiveness of the respective traditions, developing as they did in quite different directions, cannot be overlooked.

2. So R.T. France, 'Jewish Historiography, Midrash, and the Gospels', in France and Wenham (eds.), *Gospel Perspectives*, p. 123. The implications of such an approach to Scripture with regard to the fulfillment formulae has already been discussed in Chapter 1, §A.1, above.

3. The likelihood of a fourth eventuality, that the apparent parallel is the result of

The first is ruled out by the lateness of the rabbinic writings in their completed forms;[1] the second is rendered highly unlikely by polemical considerations. For Jewish sources (particularly the Talmud, which represents the triumph of Pharisaic orthodoxy over the available alternatives) are hardly likely to have lent conscious support to sectarian interpretative traditions.[2] The opposite (as in the case of the interpretation of Isa. 53) is more likely to have been the case.

Hence the most likely explanation for thematic and exegetical parallels between Jewish and Christian documents is that both have drawn independently from common traditions.[3] This is especially to be expected in documents that derive from Christian communities containing Jewish-Christian elements, as seems to be the case with the Gospel of Matthew. Here the negative consideration of relative dating does not carry its customary force, since the appearance of particular Jewish motifs or interpretative traditions in an earlier Christian source may itself be taken as presumptive evidence for the relative antiquity of a given feature. For the longer and more irrevocable the estrangement between early Jewish and Christian communities, the less likely either community would have been to make use of the exegetical traditions of the other.[4] Hence any 'Jewish' feature in question need not simply be considered contemporary with the Christian document in which it may be found, but probably dates back

pure coincidence, may be reduced by appeal to formal or verbal similarities. See further, G. Vermes, 'Jewish Literature and New Testament Exegesis: Reflections on Methodology', *JJS* 33 (1982), pp. 372-73.

1. This consideration does not, of course, apply to Qumran literature.

2. Buchanan ('Use of Rabbinic Literature', p. 112) urges investigation into the NT influence on rabbinic literature, but fails to explain why he considers such influence plausible. As Vermes observes, 'to render such a conjecture viable it must be demonstrable that the rabbis of the Tannaitic and Amoraic age were not only aware of the New Testament teachings but actually willing to learn from them: which is asking a lot' ('Methodology', p. 372).

3. See Buchanan, 'Use of Rabbinic Literature', pp. 115-20, for numerous examples of this phenomenon, both conceptual and philological, together with a review (pp. 110-12) of previous approaches to the question.

4. This observation undergirds Sandmel's criticism of Strack–Billerbeck ('Parallelomania', *JBL* 81 [1962], p. 9) for adducing 'rabbinic parallels' to a Gentile-oriented work such as the Gospel of Luke.

to a time when there existed a freer exchange of ideas between the two groups.[1]

Such an approach to thematic and exegetical parallels, however, needs to be worked out with caution, simply because talmudic, midrashic and targumic materials are voluminous, and comprise a specialized literature on their own.[2] Nonetheless, as Buchanan argues, such an approach can expect a measure of success when the exegete: (1) uses only written source materials, rather than attempting to reconstruct oral tradition; (2) employs all available parallels, rather than a tendentious few; (3) uses the parallels in their proper contexts;[3] (4) does not attempt to force ambiguous or partial evidence; (5) uses rabbinic materials in conjunction with evidence from Josephus, Philo, Qumran and the Samaritan literature; and (6) rejects 'that which is historically anachronistic or impossible'.[4]

Yet since early Christianity, as a sect of Jewish origin, would be expected to demonstrate broad areas of conceptual agreement with its community of origin, such comparative studies of parallels must focus primarily on elements that are dissimilar and distinctive. For it is not the presence of common features as such that is noteworthy, but the distinctive uses to which these features are put and the distinctive contexts in which they are found.[5]

1. Two relevant qualifications are, first, that a Christian author of Jewish origin (such as Paul) is likely to employ such interpretative methods and traditions simply out of habit or training; and, second, that it is within the nature of polemic to employ the arguments of the 'opponent' to one's own advantage. But to have force, the latter consideration requires the demonstration of polemical intent (whether explicit or implicit) in the particular passage.

2. S.T. Lachs ('Rabbinic Sources for New Testament Studies: Use and Misuse', *JQR* 74 [1983], pp. 159-73) rightly urges caution in this regard, adducing a catalogue of embarrassing errors by NT scholars. He does not, however, propose a suitable methodology of his own.

3. Cf. Sandmel ('Parallelomania', p. 2): 'The issue for the student is not the abstraction but the specific. Detailed study is the criterion, and the detailed study ought to respect the context and not be limited to juxtaposing mere excerpts' (although Sandmel refers primarily to apparent conceptual similarities, rather than exegetical parallels, as in our own study).

4. 'Use of Rabbinic Literature', p. 112. By this last criterion Buchanan means the tendentious reading back into an earlier period of a development that is demonstrably later.

5. So Sandmel ('Parallelomania', pp. 3-5), who notes that 'only by a supposition of such distinctiveness can I account to myself for the origin and growth

In Matthew's Gospel, of course, the distinctive features have to do with the messianic orientation of the narrative as a whole. This is not to say that Matthew employs scriptural allusions in the same manner as he does his fulfillment citations, that is, as messianic proof-texts. Nonetheless, as I will argue, even Matthew's allusions serve to illustrate and support a minor, yet significant feature of his portrayal of Jesus' messianic identity, namely, that Jesus is a rejected prophet after the manner of Jeremiah.

The working hypotheses throughout this study are (1) that having expressly signaled his interest in Jeremiah—both the prophet and his words—Matthew wants his audience to be alert to the evocative force of further, incidental allusions within the text of his Gospel, and (2) that Matthew's audience, sharing with him a common religious and cultural background (particularly so with regard to Scripture and certain traditions as to its interpretation) would have been alert to language that is evocative of scriptural precedents.[1] For the language with which Matthew portrays Jesus has at certain points a semantic multivalency that is intended to enrich his depiction of 'messianic history' via subtle resonances with the words and figures of Scripture, including Jeremiah.[2]

Before embarking on our investigation, however, we do well to observe the warning of Tasker:

of Christianity and its ultimate separation from Judaism'. The insistence on highlighting distinctive elements is of particular relevance to Matthew's use of Deuteronomistic motifs, and therefore also to this study as a whole. The weakness of the otherwise excellent proposal by Vermes ('Methodology', pp. 373-75) that the NT evidence be treated as but one stage in the development of concepts and traditions recorded in earlier or later form by Apocrypha and Pseudepigrapha, Philo, Josephus, Mishnah, Targum, Talmud, and so on, is that it fails to respect this consideration. For the differing ideologies of, for example, Qumran, Jewish apocalyptic expectation, early Christian messianism, the Zealots, Pharisees and Sadducees, or even the schools of Shammai and Hillel, while overlapping in many areas, do not represent the separable elements of a single developmental continuum.

1. Cf. L. Hartman, 'Scriptural Exegesis in the Gospel of Matthew and the Problem of Communication', in Didier (ed.), *L'évangile selon Matthieu*, pp. 133-37.

2. Although not focusing specifically on Jeremiah, Hartman adduces numerous examples of how this insight may be applied to Matthew's text ('Scriptural Exegesis', pp. 137-51, esp. pp. 147-48).

> Gospel criticism ought not to become a test of ingenuity in discovering the maximum number of possible Old Testament passages which may have some bearing as explanations for the order of incidents, or the manner in which they are described in the Gospels.[1]

It is best, therefore, to err on the side of restraint. For even if Matthew had numerous scriptural antecedents in mind for retelling the gospel story, references to Jeremiah form only a small proportion of these and are likely to have been comparatively few in number.

B. *Texts*

The purpose of this section is to identify a number of passages in Matthew's Gospel where allusions to Jeremiah appear to be operative. Where various scholars have perceived allusions to Jeremiah, I wish to set out the evidence for such claims and to evaluate the data anew. Where such allusions can be established, I wish to see whether and to what extent they cohere with or support the redactional interest that is evident in Matthew's Deuteronomistic outlook in general and in 2.17-18, 16.14 and 27.9-10 in particular.

In addition to the evidence of these three explicit references to Jeremiah, Matthew seems to anticipate a significant role for the prophet from the outset of his Gospel. He opens his account with the words, Βίβλος γενέσεως Ἰησοῦ Χριστοῦ υἱοῦ Δαυὶδ υἱοῦ Ἀβραάμ, substantiating these genealogical claims in the verses that follow. His carefully contrived pattern of three sets of fourteen generations is intended, as Johnson observes, to be 'an interpretation of the structure and goal of history' that underscores 'the predetermined character of the coming of Jesus, the Messiah'.[2] But while it is clear that Matthew draws significant links between Jesus and his forebears Abraham and David (cf. 1.1), the genealogical table has three turning points and not simply two. For so Matthew indicates in his conclusion to this section:

1. *The Old Testament in the New Testament* (London: SCM Press, 1946), p. 43.

2. M.D. Johnson, *The Purpose of the Biblical Genealogies, with Special Reference to the Setting of the Genealogies of Jesus* (SNTSMS, 8; Cambridge: Cambridge University Press, 1988), pp. 209, 214, cf. p. 254.

> Πᾶσαι οὖν αἱ γενεαὶ ἀπὸ 'Αβραὰμ ἕως Δανὶδ γενεαὶ δεκατέσσαρες, καὶ ἀπὸ Δανὶδ ἕως τῆς μετοικεσίας Βαβυλῶνος γενεαὶ δεκατέσσαρες, καὶ ἀπὸ τῆς μετοικεσίας Βαβυλῶνος ἕως τοῦ Χριστοῦ γενεαὶ δεκατέσσαρες (1.17).[1]

In other words, while the exile may simply have provided a convenient turning-point 'midway' between David and the birth of the messiah, one must reckon with the possibility that the Evangelist wished to suggest as much of a theological resonance or relationship between Jesus and the Babylonian exile as with David or Abraham.

Goulder suggests that each cycle of fourteen names foreshadows an aspect of Jesus' mission, so that, for example, Matthew's concern with 'the fulfilling of the μετοικεσία Βαβυλῶνος, which dominates the end of the Gospel', leads him to emphasize Jeremiah, Daniel and Zechariah, who were in turn 'the prophet of the Fall of Jerusalem. . . the prophet in Babylon [and] the prophet of the return'.[2] Indeed, as Schnackenburg suggests, it is precisely in his departure into exile that the messiah recapitulates the historical experience of Israel.[3] Granted, Jesus' departure is to Egypt, but the

1. μετοικεσίας does not occur in the NT outside Matthew 1; but compare μετοικίζω at Acts 7.4, 43, the latter citing LXX Amos 5.27 with reference to Babylon. Cf. H.C. Waetjen, 'The Genealogy as the Key to the Gospel According to Matthew', *JBL* 95 (1976), p. 209.

2. *Midrash and Lection*, p. 233. As a further, albeit very tentative possibility, it is frequently observed that Matthew includes four women in his genealogical list, possibly in order to demonstrate that irregular marital unions provide no bar to the messianic lineage (see discussions in Johnson, *Purpose*, pp. 164-65; Brown, *Birth*, pp. 71-74; Davies and Allison, *Matthew*, pp. 171-72). Of these four, Matthew designates Rahab as the mother of Boaz (Mt. 1.5), apparently following a Palestinian tradition that made her the progenitress of a distinguished lineage in return for her alliance with Israel (so Schlatter, *Matthäus*, p. 3; see, e.g., *t. Meg.* 14b; *Sifre Deut.* 3, §§338, 357; *Pes. R.* §40 [167b]; *Midrash Haggadah* on Num. 30.11; intertestamental and rabbinic discussion of Rahab is summarized by Johnson, *Purpose*, pp. 162-65). Perhaps significant as well is the fact that in *Sifre Num.* 378 (quoted in full by Johnson, *Purpose*, pp. 163-64, who suggests that insofar as it seems to be attributed to 'R. Eliezer' [i.e., Eleazar, a Tanna who flourished *ca.* 80-120 CE], the tradition may be of first century origin); *Num. R.* 8.9; *Ruth R.* 2.1 (on Ruth 1.2); *b. Meg.* 14b; and *Pes. K.* 13.5, 12, these distinguished descendents include the priestly line of which Jeremiah was a member. While Matthew provides no direct indication of his reason for mentioning Rahab here in 1.5, her traditional association with the prophet would make Jeremiah a direct ancestor of Jesus.

3. *Matthäusevangelium*, I, p. 27.

quotation of Jer. 31.15 in Mt. 2.17-18 clearly identifies this experience with the Babylonian exile. Accordingly, the juxtaposition in the opening chapters of Matthew's Gospel of an emphasis on the Babylonian exile (or the generation of Jerusalem's first destruction) with an explicit reference to Jeremiah's own words concerning exile encourages us to seek further instances in which Deuteronomistic and Jeremiah motifs have been combined.

1. *Allusions to Jeremiah as a Prophet of Judgment*

For example, our study thus far has indicated that a Deuteronomistic interest in the Hebrew prophets, Jesus and his disciples as the rejected emissaries of God is prominent in chs. 21 through 23 of Matthew's Gospel. This concentration of Deuteronomistic motifs must now be summarized and restated, taking into account possible allusions to Jeremiah.

When Jesus enters Jerusalem on a donkey, the crowds acclaim him not only as 'Son of David' but also as a prophet (21.11). His first action upon entering the city is to drive the merchants and money-changers from the Temple precincts (21.12-13); on his return the following day, Jesus curses the fig tree (21.12-13, 18-19). In Jesus' response to the ensuing challenge by the Temple authorities, Matthew subtly underscores the prophetic identity of both Jesus and John the Baptist (21.23-27). In the Matthaean redaction, the parables and dialogue that follow this initial exchange pronounce judgment on those who reject the 'servants' and 'son' of the householder (21.33-43), again identify Jesus as a prophet (21.46), acknowledge that Jesus is speaking against 'the chief priests and Pharisees' (22.46), and predict the destruction of 'their city' for those who refuse an invitation to the wedding banquet of the king's son (22.1-10). Even more explicit is the juxtaposition of Jesus' condemnation of the scribes and Pharisees, his prediction that 'all the righteous blood shed on earth'—including that of Jesus' own emissaries—'will come upon this generation', his lament over Jerusalem, and his prediction of the Temple's destruction (23.1–24.2). In this context Matthew includes a number of allusions to Jeremiah, which may be set out as follows.

Matthew 21.13 (// Mark 11.17). By way of explanation for his extraordinary actions against the Temple merchants, Jesus declares: γέγραπται· ὁ οἶκός μου οἶκος προσευχῆς κληθήσεται, ὑμεῖς δὲ αὐτὸν ποιεῖτε σπήλαιον λῃστῶν.[1] Here Mt. 21.13 has taken over from Mk 11.17 a combined quotation of LXX Isa. 56.7 and Jer. 7.11.[2] A reference to Jeremiah is unmistakable insofar as the expression 'den of robbers' is found only in LXX Jer. 7.11 (μὴ σπήλαιον λῃστῶν ὁ οἶκός μου = MT המערת פרצים היה הבית הזה) and 12.9 (μὴ σπήλαιον [LXX^A λῃστῶν[3]/LXX^B,S ὑαίνης] ἡ κληρονομία μου ἐμοί).[4] Moreover, only in Jer. 7.11 does λῃστής translate MT פריץ ('man of violence'), as opposed to *Targum Jonathan*, for example, which renders the expression כנישת רשיעין ('synagogue of the wicked').

Maier and Beare see here a contextual reference to the manifold sins of Israel recounted in Jer. 7.5-9, so that Jesus' quotation amounts to an accusation of similar offenses.[5] According to Zahn and Lane, on the other hand, the citation of Jer. 7.11 recalls the context of Jer. 7.12-14 in which the Lord promises to destroy the Temple for the unresponsiveness of his people, thus anticipating Jesus' words of doom in 23.38 ('Your house is forsaken...') and 24.2 ('There will not be left here one stone upon another').[6] For as Goppelt observes, Jesus'

1. ποιεῖτε ℵ B L Θ 892 1010 cop^bo; Cyr | ἐποιήσατε C 𝔐 D W f^{13} | πεποιήκατε f^1; Or [the latter two variants represent assimilations to Luke and Mark, respectively].

2. With the exception of Wolff (*Jeremia*, p. 157; cf. p. 165 n. 7), for whom the Markan origin of this quotation apparently obviates any relevance for Matthew, recognition of this reference appears to be universal. See especially Haenchen, *Weg*, pp. 384-85 (to Mk 11.17); Lohmeyer and Schmauch, *Matthäus*, pp. 298-99.

3. According to Ziegler (*Ieremias, in loc.*), this reading is based on 7.11.

4. Indeed, of the ten LXX occurrences of λῃστής, six are in Jeremiah literature (Jer. 7.11, 12.9 [A], 18.22; Ep. Jer. 13, 17, 57), although the word is frequent in Josephus (77×) and in the NT (Mt. 26.55 // Mk 14.48 // Lk. 22.52; Mt. 27.38 // Mk 15.27; Mt. 27.44; Lk. 10.30, 36; Jn 10.1, 8; 18.40; 2 Cor. 11.26) and is found as a loan-word in rabbinic literature. See K.H. Rengstorf, *s.v.* 'λῃστής', *TWNT*, IV, pp. 262-67 [= *TDNT*, pp. 257-62]. The connection between Jeremiah and the Gospels is in no way lessened by the fact that similar expressions occur in Josephus, for in these instances they are not used metaphorically but as literal descriptions of bandit retreats (ἐπὶ τοὺς ἐν τοῖς σπηλαίοις ὥρμητο λῃστάς, *War*, 1.304; λῃστῶν τινῶν ἐν σπηλαίοις κατοικούντων, *Ant.* 14.415; τοὺς ἐν τοῖς σπηλαίοις λῃστάς, *Ant.* 14.421).

5. Maier, *Matthäus*, II, p. 162; Beare, *Matthew*, p. 417.

6. Zahn (*Matthäus*, p. 624, stressing Jeremiah's polemic against impious confidence in the inviolability of the Temple; cf. p. 660 n. 89); W.L. Lane, *The Gospel according to Mark: The English Text with Introduction, Exposition, and Notes* (Grand Rapids: Eerdmans, 1974), p. 452. Similarly C.K. Barrett, 'The

ultimate intention as portrayed in Matthew's Gospel was not simply to 'cleanse' or restore the Temple to its proper use, but to replace it with something 'greater than the temple' (12.6; cf. 26.61).[1]

Doeve concurs as to the relevance of the context in Jeremiah:

> in what follows, the prophet speaks of the destruction of the Temple, of the city, and of the people, because Israel had refused to hear God when he spoke to them (Jer. 7.12-15).[2]

Doeve then goes on to argue that Jeremiah 7 provided a mnemonic and pedagogical link for the preservation and ordering of traditions about Jesus, and so sees a consistent pattern linking, in turn, Jer. 7.11 with Mt. 21.10-17 (the Temple cleansing), Jer. 7.20 ('Behold, my anger and my wrath will be poured out on this place...upon the trees of the field and the fruit of the ground') with 21.18-22 (the fig tree and subsequent teaching), Jer. 7.25 ('I have persistently sent all my servants the prophets to them') with 21.28-32 (the question of authority), and Jer. 7.26 ('yet they did not listen to me, or incline their ear') with 21.33-46 (the parable of the vineyard).[3] The thematic links are not, however, as strong in every case as Doeve suggests. Furthermore, as noted by W.R. Telford, since the Synoptic material in question

House of Prayer and the Den of Thieves', in E.E. Ellis and E. Gräßer (eds.), *Jesus und Paulus: Festschrift für Werner Georg Kümmel zum 70. Geburtstag* (Göttingen: Vandenhoeck & Ruprecht, 1975), pp. 15, 18 (although Barrett [pp. 19-20] is not certain that this composite quotation originally belonged with the Temple cleansing pericope), and Gnilka, *Matthäusevangelium*, II, p. 208: 'Das Jeremiawort kündet die Zerstörung des Tempels an. In unserer Perikope zeichnet das [Jesaiawort] die göttliche Absicht, das [Jeremiawort] deren Vernichtung durch menschliche Schuld. Die Funktion des Tempels ist an ihr Ende gekommen'. According to Schlatter (*Matthäus*, pp. 613-14), the quotation serves to explain the opposition of the Jerusalem priesthood to Jesus' claims and implies a prophetic criticism of the Temple cultus. Gaechter (*Matthäus*, pp. 663-64) sees the entire context of 7.1-15 to be in view here; so also, apparently, Dodd, *According to the Scriptures*, p. 86; Fenton, *Matthew*, p. 333.

1. Goppelt, *Typos*, p. 76, cf. pp. 102; 138 [ET pp. 66, 86, 115].
2. J.W. Doeve, 'Purification du Temple et desséchement du figuier: Sur la structure du 21 chapitre de Matthieu et parallèles', *NTS* 1 (1954–55), p. 300.
3. Doeve, 'Purification', pp. 300-306.

> contains echoes of so many Old Testament passages other than those cited by Doeve, it would appear arbitrary to give significance to the specific complex of passages from which [Doeve] wishes to draw a pattern.[1]

Yet even without an appeal to the context of Jer. 7.11, the Temple 'cleansing' by itself constitutes a solemn declaration of judgment, so that the cleansing and the citation together cast a pall of judgment over Jesus' otherwise triumphal entry into the city (21.8-11, 14-17). Indeed, whereas he enters Jerusalem as βασιλεύς (21.4 = Zech 9.9), Jesus enters the Temple as προφήτης, for so the crowds identify him in 21.11. For this reason, Matthew makes Jesus' citation of Isaiah and Jeremiah more emphatic than does Mark, giving it the character of a prophetic pronouncement in its own right. In 21.13 Matthew deletes the interrogative particle from Mk 11.17, with the result that Jesus' introduction to the combined citation is no longer οὐ γέγραπται ὅτι, but, far more simply and emphatically, γέγραπται. The citation of Jeremiah, then, serves to make more explicit the exact nature of Jesus' specifically 'prophetic' role. As Lindars observes, it 'puts onto Jesus the character of the most persecuted prophet of the Old Testament'.[2]

Matthew 21.18-21(// Mark 11.12-14, 20-23). No less remarkable than Jesus' expulsion of the Temple merchants is his symbolic cursing of the fig tree upon his return to Jerusalem the following morning. The symbolic nature of this episode is suggested by the fact that figs and fig trees often served in the OT as symbols of fruitfulness and prosperity. Figs were among the prodigious fruits that the spies brought back from Canaan (Num. 13.23); they symbolized the spoils of war, destruction and divine judgment (Isa. 28.4; 34.4; Jer. 5.17; Hos. 2.12; Joel 1.7, 12; Nah. 3.12); and their reappearance signalled the return of prosperity and peace (Joel 2.22; Hag. 2.19; cf. 1 Kgs

1. W.R. Telford, *The Barren Temple and the Withered Tree: A Redaction-Critical Analysis of the Cursing of the Fig-Tree Pericope in Mark's Gospel and its Relation to the Cleansing of the Temple Tradition* (JSNTSup, 1; Sheffield: JSOT Press, 1980), p. 22. Cf. the critique of J.D.M. Derrett, 'Fig Trees in the New Testament', *HeyJ* 14 (1973), p. 250 n. 2. In the case of Mt. 21.18-22, it is more likely that Jer. 8.13 is in view, as we will see shortly.

2. *NT Apologetic*, p. 107. On Matthew's further deletion from Mk 11.17 of the concluding phrase from Isa. 56.7, 'My house shall be called a house of prayer for all nations', see Meier, *Matthew*, p. 235.

4.25 // 2 Kgs 18.31 // Isa. 36.16 // Mic. 4.4 // Zech. 3.10).[1] Even more relevant in this context, however, is the fact that the fig tree was frequently taken to symbolize the nation itself or individuals within it, although by no means exclusively so (e.g. Judg. 9.7-15; Isa. 28.4; Jer. 24; 29.17; Mic. 7.1; Hos. 9.10, 16).[2]

But such a general symbolic link is not sufficient to explain Jesus' purpose: some more specific background or precedent seems necessary. W.R. Telford examines a series of passages that have been thought to underlie the fig tree episode in Matthew and Mark, principal among them being Isa. 28.3-4, Jer. 8.13, Hos. 9.10, 16, Joel 1.7, 12 and Mic. 7.1. While his analysis shows that all five passages and their contexts share common themes relating to judgment upon Israel,[3] the closest parallels are to be found in Jeremiah, Hosea and Micah.

In Jer. 8.13, God laments the people's indifference to his will:

> When I would gather them, says the LORD,
> there are no grapes on the vine,
> nor figs on the fig tree;
> even the leaves are withered.

All the basic themes of Jer. 8.13 are echoed in the Gospel story: 'the search for figs, the lack of fruit, the withered tree'.[4] In both contexts, moreover, these features serve to illustrate a sentence of divine judgment on God's people. Furthermore, the words of Jeremiah are cited elsewhere in the immediate context (Jer. 7.11 in Mk 11.17), and with the same general intent. This is all the more significant in Mt. 21.13,

1. Cf. Telford, *Barren Temple*, pp. 134-35.

2. Telford, *Barren Temple*, pp. 136-37. Evidence from intertestamental and rabbinic sources is consistent with and expands on these themes (*Barren Temple*, pp. 176-96).

3. Telford, *Barren Temple*, pp. 155, 161-63.

4. Telford, *Barren Temple*, p. 144. Cautious affirmations of a primary allusion (in Mark) to Jer. 8.13 are made by E. Schweizer, *Das Evangelium nach Markus* (NTD, 1; Göttingen: Vandenhoeck & Ruprecht, 1967), p. 131 [ET *The Good News According to Mark* (Richmond, VA: John Knox, 1970), p. 230; R.H. Hiers, 'Not the Season for Figs', *JBL* 87 (1968), p. 394 n. 3; and especially, H. Giesen, 'Der verdorrte Fiegenbaum—Eine symbolische Aussage? Zu Mk 11,12-14,20f.', *BZ* 20 (1976), p. 104 (stressing the symbolic nature of Jesus' 'hunger'; cf. Mt. 5.6), all cited by Telford, *Barren Temple*, p. 144 nn. 81, 82.

where Matthew has repositioned the explicit citation just prior to the fig tree incident.[1]

On the other hand, LXX Jer. 8.13 translates נבל ('droop, wither, fall') by the perfect of καταρρεῖν ('flow down', hence 'drop off'), rather than by ξηραίνειν,[2] which is central to the Gospel accounts. Since, according to Telford, the LXX of Jeremiah 'does not refer to God's search for figs' but refers more generally to the gathering of fruits (i.e. καὶ συνάξουσι τὰ γενήματα αὐτῶν, λέγει κύριος), 'there is no evidence...of any direct verbal influence upon our story, via the LXX, on the part of Jer. 8.13'.[3] But Telford's assertion is surely an overstatement, since, like Mk 11.13 and Mt. 21.19 (καὶ ἰδὼν συκῆν...οὐδὲν εὗρεν...εἰ μὴ φύλλα μόνον), LXX Jer. 8.13 refers explicitly to figs and fig trees alike (καὶ οὐκ ἔστι σῦκα ἐν ταῖς συκαῖς, καὶ τὰ φύλλα κατερρύηκεν).

At the same time, however, an alternative approach is possible. The difficult opening phrase of MT Jer. 8.13 (אסף אסיפם) can be understood either as deriving from the root סוף, 'come to an end' (*hiphil* 'destroy'; so *Targum Jeremiah*, Aquila, Peshitta, *b. Meg.* 31b, *Pes. R.* 33.13[?], Rashi, Kimchi) or from the verb אסף, 'gather, harvest' (LXX 8.13 συνάξουσι; Vulg. *congregans congregabo eos*).[4] The fact that

1. It may be relevant that rabbinic tradition (*b. Meg.* 31b) assigned a passage beginning at Jer. 8.13 to be read on the ninth of Ab, the traditional date of the Temple's destruction, although here the Gemara itself indicates that the tradition is late (cf. Hayward, *Targum of Jeremiah*, pp. 1-2). In addition, it is interesting to note that the 'praise of babes and sucklings' motif from Ps. 8.2 occurs immediately prior to the fig tree incident both in Mt. 21.16 and in *Targ. Songs* 2.13, where the people of Israel, likened to 'unripe figs', sing praises to the Lord (Telford, *Barren Temple*, p. 182). But the significance of this concurrence is difficult to assess.

2. As in Isa. 64.5, Ps. 1.3. LXX never renders נבל by ξηραίνειν (although it appears as a parallel term in Isa. 40.7-8; cf. Isa. 1.30, 24.4, 34.4; Ezek. 47.12), contrary to Telford's suggestion (*Barren Temple*, p. 144).

3. Telford, *Barren Temple*, p. 144-45.

4. On this latter option, see GKC §68.2; cf. Zeph. 1.2. This confusion is reflected in modern translations, with Luther, RSV, NEB, JB, Bright (AB), Carroll (OTL), Holladay (Hermeneia), and Thompson (NICOT) opting for 'harvest', while the NJB, RV, AV, Segond, and McKane (ICC) select the alternative meaning favoured by the rabbis. See further Hayward, *Targum of Jeremiah*, p. 75 n. 13; Holladay, *Jeremiah*, I, pp. 283-84; McKane, *Jeremiah*, pp. 188-89. Hayward (*Targum of Jeremiah*) notes, however, that despite interpreting 8.13 as 'I will surely destroy them, says the Lord,and they shall come to an end [שיצאה אשיצינון אמר יוי ויסופון]', 'the similar word in v. 14 [Hebrew האספו]...is rendered as "gathered

both readings correspond—if only at a thematic level—to the focus of the episode on 'gathering' versus destructive judgment heightens the possibility that an allusive reference to Jer. 8.13 undergirds this passage.[1]

Moreover, some of the features relevant to Hos. 9.16 and Mic. 7.1 are less prominent in Matthew's adaptation of the Markan material. Common to Mk 11.20 and Hos. 9.16, for example, is the sentence of judgment in the form of 'withering from the roots', whereas for Matthew the fig tree simply 'withered at once' (Mt. 21.19d). And the suggestion of an 'untimely' or unseasonable search (linking Mk 11.13d, 'it was not the season for figs', with Mic. 7.1, where God searches in vain for a righteous man under the symbol of a 'first-ripe fig'),[2] while remaining implicit in the Matthaean account, is rendered less obvious by the deletion of Mk 11.13d, 'it was not the season for figs'.[3] Nonetheless, at least two possible verbal links to Hosea remain: the verb ξηραίνειν and the curse of never bearing fruit again (LXX Hos. 9.16, καρπὸν οὐκέτι μὴ ἐνέγκῃ, with 21.19, μηκέτι ἐκ σοῦ καρπὸς γένηται εἰς τὸν αἰῶνα).[4] Thus while a reference to Jer. 8.13 may have been intended by Matthew, if not Mark, it cannot be the only passage he had in mind, since echoes of at least one other prophetic word are equally present.

Finally, insofar as Matthew, like Mark, relates that Jesus turned his own word of judgment into a teaching on faith in prayer, the polemical aspects of the incident, and therefore the appropriateness of an allusion to Jeremiah, appear to have been played down. But our

together" [Aramaic אתכנש, from כנש]'!

1. In 27.6-7 Matthew similarly exploits variant readings of Zech. 11.13, although here verbal evidence of his method is present in the text (i.e. 'potter', 'treasury'). Cf. 1QpHab 4.10-13; 8.3-13; 9.8-12; 11.2-9; 11.17–12.10 (on which see further, Stendahl, *School of St Matthew*, pp. 124-25, 188-98; Patte, *Early Jewish Hermeneutic*, p. 305). *Targum Jonathan*, incidentally, assimilates Jer. 8.13 to the enacted parable of Jer. 24 by narrowing the reference to 'poor figs', and has the Lord explain that he threatens destruction 'because I gave them my law from Sinai, and they have transgressed it'. Either or both considerations, had Matthew known them, would have made Jer. 8.13 an attractive backdrop for the fig tree episode.

2. So Telford, *Barren Temple*, pp. 150-52; Derrett, 'Figtrees', p. 253 n. 3.

3. See W.J. Cotter, 'For It Was Not the Season for Figs', *CBQ* 48 (1986), pp. 62-66.

4. Cf. Telford, *Barren Temple*, p. 150.

estimation of the teaching on prayer will in turn be affected by whether or not we are willing to see in the 'mountain cast into the sea' a reference to the Temple mount and all that it represents.[1]

Matthew 21.33-35(// Mark 12.1-3). As noted earlier in discussing Deuteronomistic motifs,[2] the use of common themes and vocabulary links the parable of the 'Wicked Tenants' with the parable of the Vineyard in Isaiah 5 (e.g. φραγμὸν περιέθηκα; ἐφύτευσα ἄμπελον; ᾠκοδόμησα πύργον; προλήνιον ὤρυξα ἐν αὐτῷ: LXX Isa. 5.2).[3] Yet Mt. 21.33-34 may also be linked with Jer. 12.10-11, where the Lord complains:

> Many shepherds have destroyed my vineyard [LXX τὸν ἀμπελῶνά μου], they have trampled down my portion, they have made my pleasant portion a desolate wilderness [εἰς ἔρημον ἄβατον].

Jer. 12.10-11 is, however, only one of a number of metaphoric references in the OT to Israel as the Lord's vine or vineyard. Others include Ps. 80.8-14 (MT 80.9-14), Jer. 2.21 ('I planted you a choice vine...how then have you...become a wild vine?'), Ezek. 15.1-8, 19.10-14, Hos. 9.10 and 10.1.

Although the allusion to Isaiah 5 is dominant in Matthew, the context and vocabulary of Isaiah's parable of the Vineyard are similar to those of Jeremiah 12. Furthermore, Mt. 23.38 may allude to God's word of judgment in Jer. 12.7.[4] Likewise, the language of Mt. 9.36, 10.6 and 15.24, like that of Jer. 12.10-11, implicitly refers to Israel's leaders as unfaithful 'shepherds'. Therefore, although the connection between Jer. 12.10 and Mt. 21.33 is admittedly tenuous, these considerations could have recalled for Matthew the text in Jeremiah, thereby reinforcing the appropriateness of the parable of the Vineyard in the mind of the Evangelist.

The key to understanding the parable of the 'Wicked Tenants' is that the 'servants' represent God's rejected prophets. This has led some to

1. See further Telford, *Barren Temple*, pp. 78-84. Such an interpretation would include a reference to Zech. 14.4 (Plummer, *Matthew*, p. 292).

2. Cf. Chapter 2, §A.2.a, above.

3. These elements were present already in Mk 12.1. Although he emends Mark's ἀπολήνιον, Matthew adds ἐν αὐτῷ to conform his text more closely to LXX Isa. 5.2. Cf. Gundry, *Use of the OT*, pp. 43-44.

4. See the following.

suggest an allusion here to Jer. 7.25.[1] But since the expression 'my servants the prophets' occurs throughout Jeremiah, others propose that Jesus may have had this phrase in mind as it appears in such passages as Jer. 7.25, 25.4, 29.19, 35.15 and 44.4.[2] Pedersen even detects in these passages (and 26.5) a consistent formula (including the designation of the prophets as 'servants') used in conjunction with prophetic threats or warnings of judgment.[3] It is possible, in fact, that the wording of Mt. 21.34, ἀπέστειλεν τοὺς δούλους αὐτοῦ πρὸς τοὺς γεωργούς (cf. Mk 12.2, καὶ ἀπέστειλεν πρὸς τοὺς γεωργοὺς τῷ καιρῷ δοῦλον) contains an echo of the LXX version of this formula (i.e. καὶ [ἐξ]ἀπέστειλα πρὸς ὑμᾶς [πάντας] τοὺς δούλους/παῖδάς μου τοὺς προφήτας [ἡμέρας καὶ] ὄρθρου καὶ ἀπέστειλα καὶ οὐκ [εἰσ]ηκούσατε [μου]). Certainly the emphases here in Matthew's parable on prophetic rejection and divine judgment are consistent with the formula as it is used in Jeremiah.

Descriptions of the prophets as 'servants', however, are widespread in the OT (e.g. Ezek. 38.17; Dan. 9.6, 10; Amos 3.7; Zech. 1.6). And in several of these passages the Deuteronomistic motifs of prophetic rejection and subsequent judgment are equally present. Pedersen is undecided as to whether the parable of the 'Wicked Tenants' (and similar NT passages) reveals a link with Jeremiah in particular or the influence of prophetic tradition in general, even though he notes Matthew's special interest in Jeremiah.[4] The general nature of Matthew's language here, however, favours the latter explanation.

In discussing the reference to 'beating' in Mt. 21.35 (καὶ λαβόντες οἱ γεωργοὶ τοὺς δούλους αὐτοῦ ὃν μὲν ἔδειραν, ὃν δὲ ἀπέκτειναν ὃν δὲ ἐλιθοβόλησαν) that is derived from Mk 12.3, N-A[26] suggests also an allusion to Jer. 20.2. LXX Jer. 20.2, of course, uses a different verb (καὶ ἐπάταξεν αὐτόν for MT ויכה [נכה]). Yet it may be significant that Jeremiah is the only OT prophet who was actually beaten (see also Jer. 37[44].15 [ἐπάταξαν]; cf. 2 Chron. 25.16; Isa. 50.6).

The major influence on Mt. 21.35, however, is certainly Mt. 23.37

1. So Green, *Matthew*, p. 179; N-A[26]; cf. Trilling, *Wahre Israel*, p. 64; Schweizer, *Matthäus*, p. 270.

2. So Zahn, *Matthäus*, p. 629 n. 30.

3. 'Zum Problem', p. 180-86. Cf. also *Targ. Jer.* 7.13; 22.21; 32.33.

4. Pedersen, 'Zum Problem', p. 187 n. 45; cf. p. 188.

(Ἰερουσαλήμ, Ἰερουσαλήμ, ἡ ἀποκτείνουσα τοὺς προφήτας καὶ λιθοβολοῦσα τοὺς ἀπεσταλμένους πρὸς αὐτήν), since here Matthew has reformulated Mk 12.3 (καὶ λαβόντες αὐτὸν ἔδειραν καὶ ἀπέστειλαν κένον) in accordance with that later passage by adding references to 'killing' (cf. Mk 12.5) and 'stoning'. The significance of Matthew's mention of 'stoning' will be examined in our discussion of 23.37. Here we simply note Drury's summary analysis:

> As in Mark, the fate of Jeremiah who was beaten (Jeremiah 20.2) is in the parable. The messenger who is killed is perhaps the prophet Uriah from Jeremiah 26.20-3. Matthew adds a messenger who is stoned at 21.35. He seems to be the Zechariah of 2 Chronicles 24.20 who was stoned for rebuking the people.[1]

It is not certain that the fates of these individual prophets can be distinguished so clearly. Still, it is worth noting once again that according to a first-century tradition, Jeremiah suffered death by stoning (*Par. Jer.* 9.21-32; *Liv. Proph.* 2.1).[2]

Matthew 23.37 (// Luke 13.34). In Mt. 23.37, as the climax of his long diatribe against the religious leadership of his day, Jesus laments that Jerusalem is a killer of prophets: Ἰερουσαλὴμ Ἰερουσαλήμ, ἡ ἀποκτείνουσα τοὺς προφήτας καὶ λιθοβολοῦσα τοὺς ἀπεσταλμένους πρὸς αὐτήν. Vouga views this designation as alluding to Jeremiah since the city is so described only in Jer. 2.30, 26.20, Lam. 2.20 and Neh. 9.26.[3] On closer examination, however, it

1. *The Parables in the Gospels: History and Allegory* (New York: Crossroad, 1985), pp. 96-97. Similarly, Hühn; Schmid, *Matthäus*, p. 305; Maier, *Matthäus*, II, pp. 188-89; Gnilka, *Matthäusevangelium*, II, p. 228. N-A^{26} compares Jer. 20.2 with Mt. 21.34 and Jer. 26.21-33 with Mt. 21.36.

2. *Vitae Prophetarum* ('The Lives of the Prophets'), while difficult to date, is likely of first-century origin, perhaps from the first quarter; so D.R.A. Hare, 'The Lives of the Prophets', in Charlesworth (ed.), *OT Pseudepigrapha*, II, pp. 380-81. Wolff (*Jeremia*, p. 36 n. 4), however, proposes a date following 70 CE, and Denis (*Introduction*, pp. 89-90) a date near the end of the first or beginning of the second century CE. On *Paraleipomena Jeremiou* (not later than 136 CE), see p. 104 n. 2, above.

3. 'Seconde Passion', p. 80; similarly, Holladay, *Jeremiah*, II, p. 110. Schweizer (*Matthäus*, p. 290) compares 23.37 to Jer. 7.23-25 ('Israel tötet Gottes Boten... So ist Jesu Tod zu erwarten'), while Sand (*Gesetz und Propheten*, p. 94) compares 23.37 to Jer. 13.22, 26-27 ('Woe to you, O Jerusalem! How long will it be before you are made clean?', v. 27).

may be observed that Jer. 2.30 is addressed not only to Jerusalem (2.1-2; 4.3-4), but also to Judah (2.28) and the בית ישׂראל (2.26; cf. 2.31; 3.12).[1] Jer. 26.20 mentions Jerusalem only as the object of Uriah's prophetic imprecations. While blame for their actions could be laid, synecdochically, on the city as a whole, only King Jehoiakim and those led by Elnathan b. Achbor are held directly responsible for the murder of the prophet Uriah. Lam. 2.20 most clearly refers to the city (cf. 2.18) and its sanctuary, whereas Neh. 9.26 just as clearly blames the nation as a whole for killing the Lord's prophets. Given other OT examples (e.g. 1 Kgs 19.10; 2 Kgs 21.16; 25.4) of Jerusalemite vaticide, the reference in 23.37 appears to be generally Deuteronomistic in tone, rather than alluding more specifically to the words of Jeremiah.[2]

As well as referring to Jer. 7.23-25, Schweizer compares Mt. 23.37-39 to Jerusalem's lament in Bar. 4.12: ἠρημώθην διὰ τὰς ἁμαρτίας τῶν τέκνων μου, διότι ἐξέκλιναν ἐκ νόμου θεοῦ.[3] For in Bar. 4.1, the rejected 'law' is identified with 'wisdom', which Jerusalem in Matthew's Gospel has likewise rejected in the person of Jesus and his envoys (23.34), resulting in her desolation (23.38). Yet insofar as Matthew plays down the sapiential overtones of the Q passage (cf. Lk. 11.49), such an allusion would seem less obvious in his Gospel. In addition, the motif of 'desolation' is usually traced to alternative sources (see below).

Dittmar also suggests a link here between Matthew and Jeremiah traditions, comparing Mt. 23.37 with the address to Jerusalem in Bar. 5.5, although the similarity appears limited to the single phrase καὶ ἴδε σου συνηγμένα τὰ τέκνα. But Bar. 5.5 is altogether contrary to the Matthaean passage in tone and intent.

Yet it is not without significance that Mt. 23.37 describes the victims of 'Jerusalem' in the plural, for, as Jeremias observes,

1. On the difficulties involved in the structure and unity of 2.1–4.4, and with 2.30 in particular, see Holladay, *Jeremiah*, I, pp. 62-63, 79, 106-107.

2. This criticism applies equally to the attempts of Winkle ('Jeremiah Model', pp. 164-68) to establish parallels, especially in Mt. 23.34-37, to Jer. 7 and 26. Winkle fails to acknowledge the widespread incidence of Jeremiah's Deuteronomistic motifs.

3. *Matthäus*, pp. 284-85.

> For in Mt. 23.37, the plural makes it likely that there is reference to the legendary stoning of Jeremiah as well as to Zechariah the son of Jehoiada (2 Chron. 24.20-22).[1]

If this be the case, then a reference to one or both of these martyrs is likely in 21.35 (ὅν δὲ ἐλιθοβόλησαν) as well. According to Haenchen, Steck and Wolff, Matthew has only Christian prophets in mind here (as in v. 34).[2] Matthew's Gospel, however, views the fate of Jewish and Christian 'prophets and emissaries' as being identical, and therefore, from a literary point of view, indistinguishable.

Since no other prophet apart from Zechariah is known to have suffered stoning, the plural ἀπεσταλμένους might have been meant originally to contain a reference to Jeremiah. Wolff, however, points out that Jeremiah was customarily thought to have died in Egypt rather than Jerusalem—in particular, *Liv. Proph.* 2.1 places Jeremiah's stoning 'in Taphnai of Egypt' (cf. Jer. 43.8), while the Midrash to Num. 30.15 refers simply to 'Egypt'.[3] Yet, as Wolff himself notes, the Christian conclusion to *Paraleipomena Jeremiou* locates Jeremiah's lapidation in Jerusalem (*Par. Jer.* 8.6; 9.22).[4]

In the Matthaean redaction the apostrophe to a vaticide Jerusalem stands together with the reference to the death of Zechariah. And since Matthew has conflated the identities of ben Berechiah the prophet and ben Jehoiada, who suffered stoning for having spoken as a prophet, the primary reference here may well be to the fate of this composite figure. The plural object does not, however, rule out an allusion to Jeremiah, for Matthew's interest in Jeremiah elsewhere in this Gospel favours an allusion to his death even here in 23.37.

1. *TWNT*, III, p. 220 (= *TDNT*, pp. 219-20); so also Menken, 'References', p. 19; Davies and Allison, *Matthew*, p. 266. Cf. Heb. 11.37 and Schoeps, *Prophetenmorde*, p. 20-22.

2. Haenchen, 'Matthäus 23', p. 55; Steck, *Israel*, pp. 291-92; Wolff, *Jeremia*, p. 95 n. 1.

3. Wolff, *Jeremia*, p. 89-90.

4. *Jeremia*, p. 95. Bogaert (*Apocalypse de Baruch*, I, pp. 198-200) sees Jeremiah's stoning in *Par. Jer.* 9 as the application to Jeremiah of an earlier, Jewish tradition associated with Honi the Circle-Drawer. But so clear are the doctrinal references (Jeremiah is revived three days after his death, giving thanks to 'Jesus Christ, the light of all the aeons' [9.13-14]; he refers to twelve apostles, and to the return of Christ on the Mount of Olives [9.20]) that 9.11-32 'n'a pu être composée que par un chrétien' (p. 213).

Matthew 23.38 (// Luke 13.35). The question as to whether Mt. 23.38 (ἰδοὺ ἀφίεται ὑμῖν ὁ οἶκος ὑμῶν ἔρημος) refers either to Jer. 12.7 alone or to both Jer. 12.7 and 22.5 involves a considerable number of difficulties, not least of which is the textual issue.[1] Despite the frequently-stated opinion that ἔρημος is a scribal interpolation,[2] evidence for its inclusion 'is both geographically widespread and early',[3] with strong attestation from the Alexandrian tradition. Conversely, the word should probably be omitted from Lk. 13.35, which mirrors Mt. 23.38 in every other respect, on solid textual grounds.[4] This permits us to observe that ℵ K W Π f^1 565 and 1010, representing Alexandrian, Byzantine and Caesaraean text-types, concur in omitting ἔρημος from Luke while including it in Matthew, whereas, at most, only part of the Syriac tradition (p, h; Irenaeus and

1. External witnesses for ἔρημος include: 𝔓^{77vid} ℵ C D K W X Δ Θ Π Σ 0138 f^1 f^{13} 28 33 565 700 892 1009 1010 1241 etc., Byz Lect it (*pm*) vg syr^{p,h,pal} cop$^{bo(pt)mae}$ arm eth geo Irenaeus^{lat} Clement Origen Cyprian Eusebius Chrysostom Basil Cyril^{pt} Cosmas. To this *UBSGNT*/N-A^{26} list may be added *5 Ezra* 1.33 (third century); Didascalia Apostolorum 23 = Apostolic Constitutions 6.5; 'Expository Treatise Against the Jews' 7 (attributed with some uncertainty to the third century Hippolytus); and 'Oration Concerning Simeon and Anna', p. 12 (possibly fifth century, attributed with even less certainty to Methodius). On the other hand, ἔρημος is omitted by B L ℓ^{184} it^{ff2} syr^{s} cop$^{sa,bo(pt)}$ Irenaeus Origen and Cyril^{pt}.

2. Plummer, *Matthew*, p. 325; Gaechter, *Matthäus*, p. 755; Trilling, *Wahre Israel*, p. 68 n. 72; Hummel, *Auseinandersetzung*, p. 89; Steck, *Israel*, p. 50 n. 5; Christ, *Jesus Sophia*, p. 137; Klostermann, *Matthäus*, p. 191; Schulz, *Q*, p. 346; Hoffmann, *Studien*, p. 172.

3. D.E. Garland, *The Intention of Matthew 23* (NovTSup, 52; Leiden: Brill, 1979), p. 200 n. 120 (taking it to be a Matthaean insertion). As Metzger observes, 'on the one hand it can be argued that copyists added ἔρημος in order to conform the quotation to the text of Jer. 22.5. On the other hand, however, in view of what was taken to be the preponderant weight of external evidence a majority of the [UBS] committee preferred to include ἔρημος, explaining its absence in some witnesses as the result of deletion by copyists who thought the word superfluous after ἀφίεται' (*TCGNT*, *in loc.*).

4. 𝔓^{45vid} 𝔓^{75} ℵ A B K L R S V W Γ Π f^1 565 1010 *pm* cop$^{sa,bo(pt)}$; with D E G H M N X Δ Θ f^{13} 33 syr^{p} cop$^{bo(pt)}$ Irenaeus Origen Eusebius (predominantly Byzantine witnesses) including ἔρημος. It is not possible to cite the Latin witnesses since N-A^{26} lists 'it' (the majority of Latin witnesses) and 'vg^{cl}' (Clementine Vulgate, 1592) for inclusion and 'lat' (part of Old Latin in agreement with the Vulgate) for omission of ἔρημος, while Aland's *Synopsis* does just the opposite, citing 'lat' for inclusion and 'it vg^{codd}' for omission.

Origen are divided on this point) demonstrates inclusion in Luke with omission from Matthew—though, admittedly, Vaticanus omits the word from both! On balance, then, external evidence favours inclusion of ἔρημος in 23.38.

The question of whether Matthew added ἔρημος in order to evoke Jer. 12.7 and/or 22.5 is itself part of the internal evidence to be weighed.[1] Against this proposal, Garland objects that neither Jer. 12.7 nor 22.5 actually include the crucial adjective.[2] LXX^{S} Jer. 22.5 comes closest with ἐρήμωσις for MT חרבה (cf. Jer. 7.34; 32 [25].18; 51[44].6, 22). It could be that Matthew inserted the adjectival equivalent ἔρημος as an alternative rendering of חרבה, for which there is ample precedent (e.g. LXX^{S} Jer. 7.34 [LXX^{A,B} ἐρήμωσιν]; 30.7 [MT 49.13]; Isa. 5.17; 44.26; 48.21; Ezek. 5.14; 13.4; 25.13, etc.). The fact that the same Hebrew noun can be rendered by the cognate verb ἐρημοῦν (e.g. Jer. 33.24, 27; 36.10; 38.10) demonstrates its flexibility. Furthermore, it may be observed that ἔρημος is found in LXX Jer. 22.6 (ὅτι τάδε λέγει κύριος κατὰ τοῦ οἴκου βασιλέως Ιουδα... ἐὰν μὴ θῶ σε εἰς ἔρημον), so that an allusion

1. Referring to Jer. 12.7 and/or 22.5 with various degrees of affirmation are Hühn; Dittmar; *UBSGNT* (3rd edn); Allen, *Matthew*, p. 251; M'Neile, *Matthew*, p. 342; Zahn, *Matthäus*, p. 660 n. 89; Lagrange, *Matthieu*, p. 453; Montefiore, *Synoptic Gospels*, II, p. 306; Smith, *Matthew*, p. 182 ('Jer. xx.5' [*sic*]); Robinson, *Matthew*, p. 194; Goppelt, *Typos*, p. 94 [ET p. 80]; Staab, *Matthäus*, p. 127; Tasker, *The OT in the NT* (1954), p. 36; Argyle, *Matthew*, p. 178; Schmid, *Matthäus* 333; Schniewind, *Matthäus*, p. 236 (with Ezek. 11.23); Trilling, *Wahre Israel*, p. 86 n. 72; Rothfuchs, *Erfüllungszitate*, p. 95 n. 25; Albright and Mann, *Matthew*, p. 284 (Jer. 12.7; 26.6); Fenton, *Matthew*, p. 249; Klostermann, *Matthäusevangelium*, p. 191; France, *Jesus and the OT*, pp. 71-72; Schweizer, *Matthäus*, p. 290; Green, *Matthew*, p. 195; Edwards, *Theology of Q*, p. 132 (as present in *Q*; similarly Polag, *Fragmenta Q*, p. 102); Maier, *Matthäus*, II, p. 263-64; Meier, *Matthew*, p. 274 (citing 1 Kgs 9.7-8; Jer. 12.7; 22.5; Tob. 14.4); Beare, *Matthew*, p. 460 (referring to all of Jer. 22.1-9); Bonnard, *Matthieu*, p. 344; Gundry, *Matthew*, p. 473. Gaechter (*Matthäus*, p. 756) sees here the continuing influence of Jer. 7.4-15.

2. *Intention*, p. 200 n. 120. Jer. 12.7: עזבתי את־ביתי נטשתי את־נחלתי = Ἐγκαταλέλοιπα τὸν οἶκόν μου, ἀφῆκα τὴν κληρονομίαν μου; Jer. 22.5: נאם־יהוה כי־לחרבה יהיה הבית הזה = λέγει κύριος, ὅτι εἰς ἐρήμωσιν ἔσται ὁ οἶκος οὗτος. Cf. Jer. 12.10-11: 'Many shepherds have destroyed my vineyard... they have made my pleasant portion a desolate wilderness [LXX εἰς ἔρημον ἄβατον]; they have made it a desolation; desolate, it mourns to me'.

to this passage could refer to the prospect of desolation announced in both 22.5 and 22.6.

We cannot, however, overlook the fact that in addition to descriptions of cities generally (LXX Lev. 26.31, 33; Job 15.28; Isa. 24.12; 61.4; Ezek. 36.35, 38) and Jerusalem in particular as ἔρημος (LXX Neh. 2.17; Isa. 64.10, cf. 52.9; Bar. 4.12), there is a significant parallel between Mt. 23.38 and the Lord's complaint in LXX Hag. 1.9, ὁ οἶκός μού ἐστιν ἔρημος (cf. 1.4). Even more striking is the following passage from Tobit's advice to his son, which combines similar descriptions of city and Temple alike:

> καὶ Ἰεροσόλυμα ἔσται ἔρημος, καὶ ὁ οἶκος τοῦ θεοῦ ἐν αὐτῇ κατακαήσεται καὶ ἔρημος ἔσται μέχρι χρόνου.[1]

So it cannot be maintained that Jer. 22.5-6 provides the closest parallel to 23.38. While it is not impossible that Matthew adapted and combined the ἐρήμωσιν/ἔρημον of 22.5-6 with the ἀφῆκα of Jer. 12.7, with ὁ οἶκος μου as the common term, this is not the simplest explanation. Rather, both ἔρημος and ἐρήμωσις seem to be stereotyped OT designations for desolation.[2]

As for the possibility that Q 13.35 intended an allusion to Jer. 12.7 alone via an independent rendering of עזב,[3] we may observe that the LXX translates this verb by Q's ἀφίειν at Exod. 9.21, Ruth 2.16, 2 Kgdms 15.16, 2 Chron. 28.14, Job 39.14, and Isa. 32.14. Moreover, ἀφίειν is present in the second clause of Jer. 12.7, suggesting that Matthew conflated the two clauses, combining the subject of the first clause (τὸν οἶκόν μου) with the verb (ἀφῆκα) from the second.[4] Just such a confusion, involving the same Greek and Hebrew verb pairs as in Jeremiah, appears to have taken place in Isa. 32.14.[5] But only in Jeremiah 12 do we find the specific

1. LXX^{A,B} Tob. 14.4; LXX differs in a number of respects, and omits the second ἔρημος in reference to the house of God. Cf. LXX Dan. 9.17, τὸ ἁγίασμά σου τὸ ἔρημον.

2. Cf. *T. Levi* 15.1; *Targ. Jer.* 2.12 (which specifies the sanctuary as 'desolate'); 15.9; 25.37-38; 29.18. See further, Garland, 'Intention', p. 200 n. 120; regarding ἐρήμωσις, see Dodd, 'Fall of Jerusalem', p. 49, 53-54.

3. Gundry (*Use of the OT*, p. 88), ignoring Luke, ascribes such a possibility to Matthew rather than to Q.

4. Gundry, *Use of the OT.*

5. That is, whereas Jer. 12.7 translates עזב by ἐγκαταλείπειν and נטש by ἀφίειν, Isa. 32.14 does just the opposite, rendering נטש by ἐγκαταλείπειν and עזב

combination of ἀφίειν with the meaning 'to forsake', ὁ οἶκος in reference to the Lord's 'house' and 'heritage', and the personal pronoun. It would therefore appear that in 23.38 Matthew uses stereotyped OT language of desolation (ἔρημος) as an intensification of language derived from Q that is reminiscent of Jer. 12.7 (ἰδοὺ ἀφίεται ὑμῖν ὁ οἶκος ὑμῶν).

Matthew 24.2 (// Mark 13.2). Smith, Maier and Gnilka draw parallels between Mt. 24.2, where Jesus foretells the destruction of the Jerusalem Temple, and similar promises of destruction in Jer. 7.14, 9.10-11, 26.6, 18, Ezek. 24.21 and Mic. 3.12.[1] While one need not look far in Scripture to find dire imprecations against the land (e.g. Jer. 4.27; 5.10; 9.11; 25.11; Ezek. 7; 33.28-29; Mic. 1.6) or the city of Jerusalem (e.g. Isa. 25.2; 27.10; Jer. 9.11; 25.18; Ezek. 9; 16.35-42), predictions of the destruction of the Temple itself are more infrequent (cf. Jer. 7.14; 26.6, 9; Jer. 26.18 [= Mic. 3.12]; Ezek. 24.21; cf. 21.2). Of the four prophets cited above, however, Jeremiah is the prophet par excellence of the destruction of the city. And a key feature of his preaching is his inveighing against impious trust in the Temple's sanctity and inviolability (7.4).

The clear citation of Jer. 7.11 in Mt. 21.13 favours a further allusion to Jeremiah here at 24.2.[2] Yet such an allusion would be thematic rather than literary, since no specific verbal influences are evident.

Not all of the allusions suggested above can be established with equal certainty. Most certain among them, however, is the citation of Jer. 7.11 (with Isa. 56.7) in Mt. 21.13, which suggests for Jesus a role like that of Jeremiah in pronouncing words of judgment against misuse of the Temple. This lends weight to the possibility of further

by ἀφίειν (οἶκοι ἐγκαταλελειμμένοι...καὶ οἴκους ἐπιθυμητοὺς ἀφήσουσιν = כי־ארמון נטש המון עיר עזב).

1. Smith, *Matthew*, p. 183; Maier, *Matthäus*, II, 270; Gnilka, *Matthäusevangelium*, II, p. 312. So also N-A[26]; cf. Beare, *Matthew*, p. 462. Focusing on 23.29–24.2, Winkle ('Jeremiah Model', pp. 168-72) explains Matthew's interest in Jeremiah, and the reference in 16.14 in particular, on the grounds that 'Jesus' judgment on the temple while in the temple complex paralleled Jeremiah's judgment on the temple while that prophet was in the temple complex'.

2. Perhaps relevant in this context is Matthew's redactional interest in the replacement of the Jerusalem Temple by the 'temple' of Jesus' body (26.61; 27.40); see below on 26.59-66.

allusions for which the evidence is less precise: to Jer. 8.13 (with Hos. 9.16) in Jesus' cursing of the fig tree (Mt. 21.18-21); to the beating and stoning of Jeremiah, in Mt. 21.35 and 23.37; and especially to Jeremiah's predictions of the destruction of the Temple, recalled in Mt. 23.38 (specifically, Jer. 12.7) and 24.2. Less certain, however, are the allusions some scholars have perceived in the parable of the 'Wicked Tenants' to Jer. 12.10-11, and to Jeremiah's description of prophets as 'servants'.

In Mt. 21.11–22.10 and 23.1–24.2, then, Matthew has coordinated a Deuteronomistic depiction of Jesus, his predecessors and his followers, as prophets rejected by Israel, and of Jerusalem's destruction as the consequence of such rejection, with a series of allusions to Jeremiah. That several of these allusions were already present in Mark or Q does not diminish their force in this Gospel. Rather, such allusions are highlighted by the redactional context into which Matthew has placed them.

I also wish to draw attention to a series of possible allusions to Jeremiah, which, while scattered more widely throughout Matthew's text, are consistent with the image of Jeremiah as a figure associated with the judgment of God's people.

Matthew 15.13. From Mk 7.1-23 Matthew derives an account of the controversy that arises when 'Pharisees and scribes. . . from Jerusalem' take Jesus to task for the apparent transgressions of his disciples regarding ritual cleanliness. Jesus responds to the charges by accusing his challengers of hypocrisy, quoting against them Isa. 29.13 and declaring to the crowds his own understanding of true defilement. At this point Matthew inserts into his Markan material the disciples' report that the Pharisees were offended by this reply, eliciting Jesus' blunt rejoinder in 15.13: πᾶσα φυτεία ἣν οὐκ ἐφύτευσεν ὁ πατήρ μου ὁ οὐράνιος ἐκριζωθήσεται.[1]

In its description of the Pharisees and scribes as a φυτεία, this saying likely reflects a widely-used metaphor for Israel, or the faithful within Israel. The metaphor appears to derive in the first instance from the 'Song of the Sea', according to which God will 'plant'

1. Apart from the vocabulary of 'planting' and 'uprooting', the phrase ὁ πατήρ [μου/ὑμῶν] ὁ οὐράνιος is distinctively Matthaean (Matthew 7×; Mark 0×; Luke 0×; cf. Mt. 5.48; 6.14, 26, 32; 18.35; 23.9; with οὐράνιος elsewhere in the NT only at Lk. 2.13, Acts 26.19), clearly indicating the Evangelist's redactional interest in this passage.

his people on his mountain (καταφύτευσεν αὐτοὺς εἰς ὄρος κληρονομίας σου = ותטעמו בהר נחלתך). Similar language is widespread throughout the OT, but takes on special meaning in the Second Temple period as a designation for the faithful remnant within the nation:

> it is frequently used as a self-designation for Israel (Isa. 60.21, also 5.1ff.; Jer. 45.4; Ps. 1.3) or for particular groups that see themselves as true Israel (*Pss. Sol.* 14.3-4; *Jub.* 1.16; 7.34; 1QS 8.5; 11.8; 1QH 6.15-17; 7.10, 18-19; 8.4ff.; 10.[25-]31; CD 1.7; *1 En.* 10.16).[1]

Among passages such as these, Matthew's specific term φυτεία (a NT *hapax*) is found in Ezek. 17.7 and *Pss. Sol.* 14.4 (ἡ φυτεία αὐτῶν ἐρριζωμένη εἰς τὸν αἰῶνα), as well as appearing in its literal sense at 4 Kgdms 9.29 and Mic. 1.6 (cf. φύτευμα: Isa. 17.10; 60.21; 61.3).[2] None of these passages, however, fully explains Jesus' use of the metaphor, for according to Mt. 15.13 this is a φυτεία that—in contrast to all the precedents cited above—has *not* been planted by God. The primary focus of this passage is therefore not on the actual identification of Jesus' opponents as a φυτεία, but rather on the prospect that, having been illegitimately planted, they will be 'uprooted'.

Matthew's use of the contrasting verbs φυτεύειν and ἐκριζοῦν recalls the Lord's charge to Jeremiah: ἰδοῦ κατέστακα σε σήμερον... ἐκριζοῦν καὶ κατασκάπτειν καὶ ἀπολλύειν καὶ ἀνοικοδομεῖν καὶ καταφυτεύειν (Jer. 1.10).[3] The terms of the prophet's call are frequently repeated throughout the remainder of the book. The MT either repeats the verbal infinitives from Jer. 1.10 (so 18.7, 9; 31.28) or selects an appropriate finite form (12.17; 24.6; 31.40; 32.41; 42.10; 45.4). What is remarkable, however, is that while the LXX consistently translates נטע ('to plant') either by the root form φυτεύειν (2.21; 12.2; 39[32].41; 49[42].10; 51.34 [MT 45.4]) or by the compound καταφυτεύειν (1.10; 11.17; 18.9; 24.6; 38[31].28), not once after Jer. 1.10 is נתש ('to uproot') again translated by

1. Schweizer, *Matthäus*, p. 213; cf. Bonnard, *Matthieu*, p. 229; Gnilka, *Matthäusevangelium*, II, p. 25.

2. Josephus uses both φυτεία (*Ant.* 3.281; 12.151) and φύτευμα (*Apion* 1.199) in their literal senses.

3. The MT reveals a homophonic word-play between several of the Hebrew verbs, of which the first and last are significant for this study: לנתוש ולנתוץ ולהאביר ולהרוס לבנות ולנטוע.

ἐκριζοῦν. Rather, it is rendered by ἐκλείπειν (Jer. 38[31].40 [// καθαιρεῖν]), ἐκτίλλειν (Jer. 24.6; 49[42].10; 51.34 [MT 45.4]; so 3 Kgdms 14.15; Θ Dan. 11.4; cf. *Pss. Sol.* 14.4b), ἐξαίρειν (Jer. 12.17; 18.7; so 2 Chron. 7.20), or καθαιρεῖν (Jer. 38[31].28; so Ps. 9.6).

Outside the Book of Jeremiah, נטע and נתש are again paired in the final verse of Amos (9.15), but here the corresponding LXX verbs are καταφυτεύειν and ἐκσπᾶν.[1] Several of the same verbs from LXX Jer. 1.10 do, however, reappear in Sir. 49.7 (ἐκριζοῦν καὶ κακοῦν καὶ ἀπολλύειν, ὡσαύτως οἰκοδομεῖν καὶ καταφυτεύειν)—precisely because the passage summarizes Jeremiah's ministry! Thus the concurrence of φυτεύειν and ἐκριζοῦν is limited in the LXX to the two passages that explicitly treat the call of Jeremiah.[2]

Of course, the meaning of these verbs makes them a natural pair, as in Jesus' suggestion of how to address a sycamine tree: ἐκριζώθητι καὶ φυτεύθητι ἐν τῇ θαλάσσῃ (Lk. 17.6). Even so, these verbs are not frequent in the NT and, apart from these two instances, are not elsewhere found together (φυτεύειν: Mt. 21.33 // Mk 12.1 // Lk. 20.9 [from LXX Isa. 5.2]; Lk. 13.6; 17.28; 1 Cor. 3.6, 7, 8; 9.7; ἐκριζοῦν: Mt. 13.29;[3] Jude 1.12).

Because this particular word pair is so closely linked with the account of Jeremiah's call (notwithstanding the example of Jesus and

1. In addition to the parallel translation variants already noted, the renderings of נתש by ἐκλείπειν (Jer. 38[31].40) and ἐκσπᾶν (Amos 9.15) are unique in the LXX.

2. ἐκριζοῦν occurs elsewhere in the LXX only at Judg. 5.14 [B]; Wis. 4.4; Sir. 3.9; S Dan. 4.14, 26; Θ Dan. 7.8; Zech. 2.4; 1 Macc. 5.51; and 2 Macc. 12.7.

3. The similarity of 15.13 to Matthew's parable of the Weeds and Wheat (13.24-30, 36-43) is frequently noted (e.g. Plummer, *Matthew*, p. 213 n. 1; Schniewind, *Matthäus*, p. 182; Fenton, *Matthew*, p. 253; Lohmeyer and Schmauch, *Matthäus*, p. 249), although there are also significant dissimilarities (so Gnilka, *Matthäusevangelium*, II, p. 25). Both parables employ the agricultural metaphor of 'good' and 'bad' plants, anticipating judgment on those that are illegitimately planted. Yet 15.13 concerns the scribes and Pharisees in particular, whereas 13.24-30, 36-43 is eschatological in focus, describing 'the kingdom of heaven' and those within it. More to the point, the language of Mt. 13.24-41 (σπείραντι...ἐπέσπειρεν... ἔσπειρας... σπείρων... σπείρας, contrasting συλλέξωμεν... ἐκριζώσητε... συλλέξατε... συλλέγεται... συλλέξουσιν) reflects that of 15.13 only minimally. That Mt. 13 does not employ the same contrasting terms makes the language of 15.13 even more prominent.

the sycamine tree), Matthew's choice of the verbs φυτεύειν and ἐκριζοῦν is strongly reminiscent of LXX Jer. 1.10.[1] An allusion to that passage is rendered even more appropriate by the context in which Matthew has placed it: that of controversy with the leaders of Israel. What God had accomplished through the ministry of Jeremiah in his own day, suggests the Evangelist, will likewise be accomplished in the ministry of Jesus, whose words recall the prophetic mandate to 'plant' and to 'uproot'.

Matthew 3.12(// Luke 3.17). Hayward notes that 'the separation of straw from grain compared with the separation of wicked from righteous [found in *Targ. Jer.* 23.28] is very similar to the thought expressed in Mt. 3.12',[2] in which John the Baptist declares concerning Jesus:

> His winnowing fork is in his hand, and he will clear his threshing floor, and gather his wheat into the granary, but the chaff he will burn with unquenchable fire.

The Hebrew of Jer. 23.28b reads מה־לתבן את־הבר נאם־יהוה ('What is the grain compared with the straw, word of the Lord?'), which the Targum paraphrases as 'Behold, just as a man separates the straw from the grain, so one separates the wicked from the righteous, says the Lord'.[3] An extended metaphor comparing straw and grain is also found in *Gen. R.* 83.5, *Songs R.* 7.3.3, and *Midr. Pss.* 2.13-14, but in these instances the intended comparison is between Israel and the Gentile nations.[4]

1. Matthew's use of φυτεία is also consistent with such an allusion, since φυτεία serves as a translation variant for נטע (so 4 Kgdms 19.29) or its cognate מטע (so Ezek. 17.7; Mic. 1.6), as does also the related φύτευμα (for נטע in Isa. 17.10; for מטע in Isa. 60.21; 61.3), these being the only occurrences of φυτεία and φύτευμα in the LXX.

2. Hayward, *Targum of Jeremiah*, p. 27. Holladay (*Jeremiah*, I, p. 644) draws a similar comparison for MT Jer. 23.28.

3. הא כמא דפריש בין תבנא לעבורא כין פריש בין רשיעיא לצדיקיא אמר יוי. To this may be compared the altogether different interpretation of 23.28 in *b. Ber.* 55a, ascribed to Simeon b. Yoḥai (cf. *b. Ned.* 8a,b).

4. So in *Gen. R.* 83.5, for example, an argument between wheat, straw and stubble as to which of them is the cause for the field having been sown is referred for judgment to the hour of winnowing. The wheat will be gathered with praise, whereas the straw will be burnt and the stubble scattered. Even so, declares Israel, 'the hour will come in the messianic future' when the true worth of each nation will emerge, as

Although the Baptist's words here in 3.12 have clear eschatological overtones (cf. 3.10b), his point is to distinguish the righteous from the unrighteous within Israel, with his immediate audience, the 'Pharisees and Sadducees', clearly falling into the latter category.[1] In its original context, moreover, Jer. 23.28b has to do with the need to distinguish false prophecy from true (23.9-40), a concern which Matthew demonstrates elsewhere in his Gospel.

But Jer. 23.28 is not the most likely precedent for the Baptist's language in Mt. 3.12. The comparison of the wicked to chaff (either מץ; Job 21.18 [// תבן]; Pss. 1.4; 35.5; Hos. 13.30; or קש; Ps. 83.14; Isa. 40.24; 41.2; Jer. 13.24; Obad. 18; Mal. 3.19) was proverbial. *Targ. Jer.* 23.28 may, in fact, have been based on the image of winnowing as 'a metaphor for judgment and defeat' found in Jer. 4.11, and especially in 15.7 (cf. also 51.2, 33).[2] For while זרה is frequent in its wider sense of 'to scatter, disperse [in judgment]' (e.g. Lev. 26.33; Jer. 49.32; Ezek. 6.8, 36.19; Zech. 1.19), the image of God with a winnowing fork (מזרה) occurs in the OT only at Jer. 15.7:

> Who will have pity on you, O Jerusalem?...
> I have stretched out my hand against you and destroyed you...
> I have winnowed them with a winnowing fork [ואזרם במזרה] in the gates
> of the land... I have destroyed my people;
> They did not turn from their ways (15.5-7).[3]

it is written, 'Thou shalt fan them, and the wind shall carry them away' (Isa. 41.16).

1. Cf. Hoffmann, *Studien*, p. 31. This is typical of a Deuteronomistic outlook: 'In Israel selbst (nicht mehr zwischen Israel und den heidnischen Feinden) kommt es nun zur Scheidung in Fromme und Sünder; auf sie wird die Heils-bzw. Unheilsaussage bezogen' (*Studien*, p. 160). Hoffmann's own opinion (p. 292 n. 13) is that 'Das Bildwort [vom Mann mit der Worfschaufel] scheint Jer. 51,33 aufzunehmen und umzudeuten'. But this passage speaks only of Babylon as a threshing-floor (MT כגרן; LXX ὡς ἅλων) whose harvest-time is imminent.

2. Cf. Holladay, *Jeremiah*, I, p. 441. The phrase κατακαύσει πυρί ἀσβέστῳ in 3.12 carries similar overtones: 'Das Feuer ist die Begleiterscheinung des göttlichen Gerichts' (Gnilka, *Matthäusevangelium*, I, p. 63, citing as background Amos 7.4; Zeph. 3.8; Jer. 21.12; Ezek. 22.31; Ps. 89.37, etc.); cf. Schlatter, *Matthäus*, p. 83, citing Isa. 34.10 and Jer. 7.20.

3. Cf. Montefiore, *Synoptic Gospels*, II, p. 15; Hill, *NT Prophecy*, p. 45; Sato, *Prophetie*, p. 129.

Indeed, Isa. 27.12—'in that day the Lord will thresh [יחבט]'—might be seen as an alternative source of such imagery (cf. *4 Ezra* 4.28-32; *2 Bar.* 70.2; Rev. 14.14-16) were it not for the fact that this passage speaks positively of ingathering and restoration,[1] whereas Jer. 15.7, like *Targ. Jer.* 23.28 and Mt. 3.12, calls down judgment upon Israel. For this latter focus on the judgment of Jerusalem would more probably have commended itself to the Evangelist. Thus whether or not Matthew was aware of the additional exegetical traditions associated with Jer. 23.28 in *Targum Jeremiah*, he could have seen in Jer. 15.7 a striking and significant parallel to the language of John the Baptist.[2]

Matthew 4.19(// Mark 1.17). A number of interpreters have proposed that Jesus' call to Simon and Andrew to leave their nets and become 'fishers of men' in Mt. 4.19 contains an allusion to Jer. 16.16.[3] This passage is one of several in the OT in which the metaphors of fishing and hunting convey a sense of divine judgment:

1. Cf. H. Wildberger, *Jesaja* (BKAT, 10; Neukirchen–Vluyn: Neukirchener Verlag, 1972–82), p. 1023. On winnowing generally, see *Jesaja*, p. 1202. Some indication of the overtones such an image would likely convey to its NT hearers is provided by the ascription of similar activity to Satan in Lk. 22.31.

2. Possibly related is the uniquely Matthaean parable of the wheat and the weeds (13.24-30), since these similarly refer to the 'sons of the kingdom' and the 'sons of the evil one' respectively (13.38). But while the same conceptual parallels are present, Mt. 13.25-27, 29-30 refer to τὰ ζιζάνια, whereas Mt. 3.12 // Lk. 3.17 (and LXX Jer. 23.28!) specify τὸν σῖτον and τὸ ἄχυρον.

3. E.g. (in addition to Dittmar and N-A[26]), Hühn (with Ezek. 47.10); M'Neile, *Matthew*, p. 46; Albright and Mann, *Matthew*, p. 40; Lane, *Mark*, pp. 67-69; H. Anderson, *The Gospel of Mark* (London: Marshall, Morgan & Scott; Grand Rapids: Eerdmans, 1976), p. 88; Maier, *Matthäus*, I, p. 84; J.A. Fitzmyer, *The Gospel According to Luke (I-IX): Introduction, Translation, and Notes* (Garden City, NY: Doubleday, 1981), pp. 568-69; and, more tentatively, Hill, *Matthew*, p. 106; Green, *Matthew*, p. 74; Davies and Allison, *Matthew*, p. 398; cf. Holladay, *Jeremiah*, I, p. 479. Opposed are Haenchen, *Weg*, p. 81 n. 10; Schweizer, *Markus*, p. 25 [ET p. 48]; and Bonnard, *Matthieu*, p. 50; while Fenton (*Matthew*, p. 73) discerns an allusion to Ezek. 47.10 (on which proposal see further, J.D.M. Derrett, ''ΗΣΑΝ ΓΑΡ 'ΑΛΙΕΙΣ [Mk 1.16]: Jesus's Fishermen and the Parable of the Net', *NovT* 22 [1980], pp. 108-37, with particular reference [pp. 125-31] to Mt. 13.47-49). Gundry (*Matthew*, p. 62) sees here an implied restoration (i.e. in the context of Jer. 16.14-15) rather than judgment (in the context of Jer. 16.17-18); similarly, but without reference to context, Johnson, 'Matthew', *IB*, VII, p. 276; Gnilka, *Matthäusevangelium*, I, p. 101.

> Behold, I am sending for many fishers, says the Lord, and they shall catch them; and afterwards I will send for many hunters, and they shall hunt them...[1]

According to J. Mánek, these images are rooted in the cosmological myth of God's victory over the powers of chaos.[2] But if so, no trace of it remains here. Rather, as in Ezek. 12.13 and 17.20—or even more clearly, Amos 4.2 and Hab. 1.14-17—the images depict God's use of foreign powers to entrap and thereby chastise his own people (cf. Ezek. 29.4-5, 32.3 and 38.4, where the same dire prospect is addressed to the enemies of Israel; in a more general sense, see Eccl. 9.12).

If Mark—and Matthew—intend an allusion in 4.19 to Jer. 16.16, then Jesus is calling those who follow him to an eschatological mission of ingathering whereby the disciples will serve as his agents in proclaiming the imminent kingdom and preparing for the divine judgment that it brings.[3] The use of the fishing metaphor for messianic and eschatological judgment in the literature of Qumran (which Betz and others see as based directly on Jer. 16.16) confirms the currency of such an interpretation at the time of Jesus and John.[4]

On the basis of an exhaustive review of fishing and hunting metaphors in ancient Near Eastern mythology, Jewish tradition, and Graeco-Roman thought, W. Wuellner concludes that these images uniformly represent 'man's varied experiences of retributive supreme justice, of

1. The terms for 'fishers' or 'fishermen' are extremely rare in the OT: דיגים in Isa. 19.8, דוגים in Jer. 16.16 and Ezek. 47.10. The LXX translates all three by ἁλεεῖς (an alternative form); '[ἐν πλοίοις] ἁλιέων' also occurs at LXX Job 40.31 (ET 41.7), but without a comparable term appearing in the MT. However, only in the Jeremiah passage does the word comport a metaphoric, rather than a literal sense.

2. 'Fishers of Men', *NovT* 2 (1958), p. 138.

3. C.W.F. Smith, 'Fishers of Men: Footnotes on a Gospel Figure', *HTR* 52 (1959), pp. 190-95.

4. Cf. O. Betz, 'Donnersöhne, Menschenfischer, und der Davidische Messias', *RevQ* 3 (1961–62), p. 53, citing 1QH 2.8, 3.26, 5.7-8, 1QpHab 1.14-15; W. Wuellner, *The Meaning of 'Fishers of Men'* (Philadelphia: Westminster Press, 1967), pp. 126-31. So also (for 1QH 5.7-8) M. Mansoor, *The Thanksgiving Hymns: Translated and Annotated with an Introduction* (STDJ, 3; Leiden: Brill, 1961), p. 132 n. 14; E. Lohse, *Die Texte aus Qumran, hebräisch und deutsch: Mit masoretischer Punktation, Übersetzung, Einführung, und Anmerkungen* (Munich: Kösel, 1971), p. 131 n. 21; Wolff, *Jeremia*, p. 128.

ultimately transforming renewal, and of irresistible commitments to saying or doing something that transcends everything else'.[1] More specifically, according to Wuellner, the meaning of the 'fishers of men' metaphor in the ministry of Jesus and his disciples is that

> men were fished by yielding to the call to repentance, issued by the fishers of men who proclaimed the nearness of the Kingdom of God for which there were empirical 'signs' that testified to or proved the reality of the divine imminence, or the dynamic of the divine revelation.[2]

According to his analysis, however, the widespread currency of the fishing metaphor renders improbable any direct reference to Jer. 16.16 (or any other OT passage) on the part of Matthew or Mark.[3] Admittedly, the only evidence for an allusion on Matthew's part is the common term ἁλιεῖς.[4] Yet an interpretation of the call to be made 'fishers of men' that sees an allusion to Jer. 16.16 accords well both with the programmatic proclamation of Jesus immediately preceding ('Repent, for the kingdom of heaven is at hand', 4.17) and with the

1. Wuellner, *Meaning*, pp. 64-65.

2. *Meaning*, p. 141. This answers the objection of Lachs ('Rabbinic Sources', pp. 162-63; *Rabbinic Commentary*, pp. 58-59) that the punitive overtones of the verb דוג in Jer. 16.16 and Ezek. 47.10 are not appropriate to the Matthaean context. Lachs proposes instead that the broader associations of the verb צוד [Aramaic צדי] (i.e. as referring solely to persuasive argumentation) underly the Evangelists' metaphor. Yet this root is equally present, and with no less imprecatory overtones, in Jer. 16.16 (צידים, 'hunters').

3. Wuellner, *Meaning*, pp. 140, 170; on where, in Wuellner's view, the 'fishers of men' metaphor fits into the theology of Matthew, see *Meaning*, pp. 214-16.

4. Referring to ἦσαν γὰρ ἁλιεῖς in Mk 1.16 and elsewhere, C.H. Bird ('Some γαρ Clauses in St Mark's Gospel', *JTS* NS 4 [1953], p. 173) argues that 'a clause introduced by *gar* indicates that a biblical passage, or word, or idea is being recalled by the immediate situation', even though there is no direct or explicit quotation present. In the case of Mark 1.16 // Mt. 5.18, this '"assertive-allusive" use of *gar*' suggests that ἦσαν γὰρ ἁλιεῖς 'might be designating St Peter and St Andrew as the fishermen of Ezekiel 47, to catch a very great multitude of men made alive by the healing water that was to flow from the temple' (pp. 174, 176). Bird also draws attention to the verb which Jer. 16.16 (ἰδοὺ ἐγὼ ἀποστέλλω τοὺς ἁλεεῖς) and the apostolic commissioning passages (e.g. Mk 3.14 ἵνα ἀποστέλλῃ αὐτοὺς) have in common. After an extensive review of the Markan evidence, however, M.E. Thrall (*The Greek Particles in the New Testament* [NTTS, 3; Grand Rapids: Eerdmans,1962], pp. 42-50) denies 'on linguistic grounds' that γάρ can have such a function; cf. Wuellner, *Meaning*, p. 170.

parable of the net in 13.47-50 (cf. 3.12 with 13.24-30). For both carry unmistakable overtones of eschatological judgment, which suggests a common purpose in the mind of the redactor—one that is altogether in keeping with the OT texts cited. And of these texts, Jer. 16.16 is the only one that specifically refers to 'fishermen' in their task of gathering people for judgment, rather than simply to 'nets', 'hooks', or other tools of the trade. Thus a reference to Jer. 16.16 in Mt. 4.19, although by no means certain, is not improbable.

Matthew 13.7, 22(// Mark 4.7, 18). Schlatter notes a similarity between Mt. 13.22 and Jer. 4.3, 'Break up your fallow ground, and sow not among thorns (καὶ μὴ σπείρητε ἐπ' ἀκάνθαις)'.[1] The OT frequently uses the image of thorns to denote agricultural or spiritual barrenness (e.g. 2 Sam. 23.6; 2 Kgs 14.9 = 2 Chron. 25.18; Isa. 7.23-25; 55.13; Jer. 12.13; Hos. 10.8), to which may be related Jesus' saying about gathering grapes from thorns (Mt. 7.16; cf. Lk. 6.44). Jer. 4.3 is the only OT passage, however, to speak of sowing good seed among thorns (ἐπὶ ἀκάνθας, so Mt. 13.7; against Mk 4.7 εἰς, Lk. 8.7 ἐν μέσῳ; but cf. 13.22 // Mk 4.18 // Lk. 8.14 εἰς τὰς ἀκάνθας). Yet both Jeremiah and Matthew are more likely to have derived their imagery from the general agricultural conditions of Palestine.

In fact, the agricultural and economic situation of Palestine might be thought sufficient to account for each of the metaphors we have examined. Yet in every instance except that of the seed sown among thorns, some further consideration suggests that local conditions are not the only factors at work in Matthew's use of the particular image. In Mt. 15.13 Jesus employs—with ironic force—a common scriptural metaphor for God's people with distinctive Septuagintal language describing the call of Jeremiah (Jer. 1.10, Sir. 49.7). In Mt. 3.12, John the Baptist's image of Jesus coming to judge with winnowing fork in hand recalls God's similar role in Jer. 15.7. Particularly suggestive in a Matthaean context is the focus of Jeremiah 15 on the judgment of Jerusalem, since that city will ultimately become the object of Jesus' judgment in this Gospel. Finally, the currency of Jer. 16.16 as a metaphor for eschatological judgment in the literature of Qumran favours a similar use of that passage in Jesus' description of his disciples' new mission of eschatological ingathering (Mt. 4.19).

1. *Matthäus*, p. 436 (although Schlatter expressly forswears etiological speculation [*Matthäus*, p. ix]); so also Hühn; cf. Holladay, *Jeremiah*, I, p. 129.

2. *Allusions to Jeremiah as a Rejected Prophet*

In the passages that we have reviewed to this point, allusions to Jeremiah in the words and actions of Jesus (and, in one instance, John the Baptist) have depicted the messiah and his emissaries as agents of God's judgment against his own people, city and Temple. In addition, references to the stoning and killing of God's prophets—whether or not they refer specifically to the fate of Jeremiah—vividly portray a further, significant aspect of the Deuteronomistic schema: that the prophets not only announce divine judgment, but are themselves judged and rejected by God's people. In this respect too, a number of Matthaean passages describe Jesus in a manner that recalls the ministry and words of Jeremiah.

Matthew 13.57 (// Mark 6.4). In Mt. 13.57, as we saw earlier,[1] Jesus laments the fact that the people of his own town and family refuse to believe him (cf. 10.36). Gnilka observes that, despite the expression of similar sentiments by Dio Chrysostom, Diogenes and Epictetus, 'the fate of the prophet Jeremiah comes closer'. Specifically, Gnilka quotes the threat of the Anathothites: 'Do not prophesy in the name of the Lord, or you will die by our hand' (Jer. 11.21).[2] For although opposition to the prophetic word is a Deuteronomistic motif, it appears particularly pronounced— indeed, deadly—in the case of Jeremiah (cf. Jer. 12.6, οἱ ἀδελφοί σου καὶ ὁ οἶκος τοῦ πατρός σου . . . ἠθέτησάν σε; also 20.10; 26.8-9; 38.4).

Admittedly, parallels between these Jeremiah passages and Mt. 13.57 are not sufficient to indicate a direct influence. Nonetheless, the situations of Jeremiah and Jesus are sufficiently similar as to encourage us to seek further parallels in Matthew's depiction of Jesus as a rejected prophet.

Matthew 26.59-66(// Mark 14.55-64). We noted at the outset of this study the surprising lack of fulfillment quotations in Matthew's Passion narrative, and suggested that his rendering of Jesus' words in 26.56 ('all this has taken place that the Scriptures of the prophets might be fulfilled'; cf. Mk 14.49, 'But let the Scriptures be fulfilled') takes the place of more specific fulfillment quotations by designating

1. Cf. Chapter 2, §B, above.

2. *Matthäusevangelium*, I, p. 514; so also Hühn (with Jer. 12.6); Sand, *Gesetz und Propheten*, pp. 142-43.

Jesus' betrayal and arrest as typical of the fate of the prophets. To this general rule, of course, Mt. 27.9-10 provides a significant exception, but it is not the only instance in which Jesus' fate 'fulfills' the prophecies of Jeremiah.

J.W. Doeve draws attention to the traditions in Mt. 26.59-63, 66 and Mk 14.55-61 of false witnesses at Jesus' trial, in contrast to their omission from the otherwise similar trial narratives of Luke and John. Although Doeve maintains that these elements of tradition circulated orally by virtue of midrashic and mnemonic connections to Jer. 26.5-11,[1] reservations about such techniques should not impede a closer examination of Jeremiah 26 as a possible literary 'type' that the Markan and Matthaean trial scenes were intended to recall.

The trial scene in Matthew opens with an express declaration that 'the chief priests and the whole council sought ψευδομαρτυρίαν κατὰ τοῦ 'Ιησοῦ ὅπως αὐτὸν θανατώσωσιν' (26.59; cf. Mk 14.55, ἐζήτουν... μαρτυρίαν εἰς τὸ θανατῶσαι αὐτόν). Having identified their testimony as false, Matthew then emphasizes the false character of the witnesses themselves: πολλῶν προσελθόντων ψευδομαρτύρων (26.60; cf. Mk 15.57, πολλοὶ γὰρ ἐψευδομαρτύρουν κατ' αὐτοῦ). Matthew omits Mark's assertion that the false witnesses could not agree (Mk 14.56, 59); he permits their testimony, however false, to stand.

Jesus was widely understood to have prophesied against the Jerusalem Temple (cf. Mt. 23.38 // Lk. 13.35; 24.2 // Mk 13.2; 27.40 // Mk 15.29; cf. Mt. 12.6; Acts 6.14). Such a perception forms the substance of the false witnesses' accusations. Mark's periphrastic ἡμεῖς ἠκούσαμεν αὐτοῦ λέγοντος ὅτι ἐγὼ καταλύσω τὸν ναὸν τοῦτον τὸν χειροποίητον καὶ διὰ τριῶν ἡμερῶν ἄλλον ἀχειροποίητον οἰκοδομήσω (14.58) becomes in Mt. 26.61 the more focused οὗτος ἔφη· δύναμαι καταλῦσαι τὸν ναὸν τοῦ θεοῦ καὶ διὰ τριῶν ἡμερῶν οἰκοδομῆσαι. Here Matthew makes the reference to the Jerusalem Temple more explicit by inserting τοῦ θεοῦ, a designation unique in the Synoptic Gospels (cf. Lk. 1.9). And since elsewhere in his Gospel Matthew emphasizes the three-day period of Jesus' death, διὰ τριῶν ἡυερῶν probably contains an oblique reference to the

1. *Jewish Hermeneutics*, pp. 182-88; followed by Hartman, 'Problem of Communication', p. 148. The connection to Jer. 26 is also noted by Hühn and by Smith, *Matthew*, p. 201, and explored in detail by Kosmala, 'His Blood on us', pp. 103-104.

resurrection.[1] The combination of these two factors may imply that Jesus' own body is that 'temple' which he is able to destroy and build.[2]

The similarity between this scene in which the 'chief priests and the Sanhedrin', assisted by ψευδομαρτύροι, find in Jesus' apparent declaration against the Temple a basis for condemning him to death, and that of Jeremiah 26, is altogether striking. For in Jeremiah 26, Jeremiah is accused of having prophesied against the city and the house of the Lord, that they shall be made desolate (ἐρημωθήσεται; LXX 33.9). On these grounds the priests and ψευδοπροφῆται (LXX 33.7, 8, 11, 16), pronounce judgment against him:

> This man deserves the sentence of death, because he has prophesied against this city, as you have heard (LXX ἠκούσατε) with your own ears (Jer. 26.12).[3]

1. See, e.g., Mt. 12.40 (+ Q 11.30), which quotes, then reinterprets LXX Jon. 1.17; Mt. 27.63 (M); cf. Mt. 27.40 // Mk 15.29. A reference to the resurrection is all the more likely because the temporal specificity of διὰ τριῶν ἡμερῶν ('*within* three days'; BDF §223), although taken over unchanged from Mark, is consistent with Matthew's repeated emendation of Mark's expression μετὰ τρεῖς ἡμέρας, '*after* three days' (Mk 8.31; 9.31; 10.34) to τῇ τρίτῃ ἡμέρᾳ, '*on* the third day' (Mt. 16.21; 17.23; 20.19; BDF §200).

2. While Aune (*Prophecy*, pp. 174-75, following B. Gärtner, *The Temple and the Community in Qumran and the New Testament: A Comparative Study in the Temple Symbolism of the Qumran Texts and the New Testament* [Cambridge: Cambridge University Press, 1965], pp. 105-22) argues that the saying refers to the creation of an eschatological community, this interpretation renders inexplicable the mention of 'three days'. But emphasis on Jesus' resurrection does not rule out the possibility of an implicit reference to the messianic rebuilding of the Temple, on which see the summary discussion of J.B. Green, *The Death of Jesus: Tradition and Interpretation in the Passion Narrative* (WUNT, 2.33; Tübingen: Mohr [Paul Siebeck], 1988), pp. 277-81 (cf. Senior, *Passion Narrative*, pp. 170-71).

As a separate issue, although Matthew's contrasting pair of infinitives καταλῦσαι...οἰκοδομῆσαι (as opposed to the finite καταλύσω... οἰκοδομήσω of Mark) bears a tantalizing resemblance to the terms of Jeremiah's call in both Jer. 1.10 (ἀπολλύειν καὶ ἀνοικοδομεῖν) and Sir. 49.7 (ἀπολλύειν ὡσαύτως οἰκοδομεῖν), to which Mt. 15.13 makes reference, there is no evidence that Matthew recognized such a link here, since he does not emend Mark's choice of verbs, and his use of the infinitive is required in any case by the modal δύναμαι.

3. In Jer. 26 the false prophets accurately relate Jeremiah's words (v. 6) against the Temple, while in Mt. 26 the false witnesses relate (albeit in confused form) Jesus' anti-Temple polemic (cf. 12.6, τοῦ ἱεροῦ μεῖζόν ἐστιν ὧδε). Both, then, are condemned for anti-Temple utterances that ultimately prove true. In Matthew the logical confusion generated by having 'false' witnesses agree in

Nor should it escape our notice that according to Josephus's version of this episode, Jeremiah is himself accused of false prophecy[1] (λαμβάνοντες τὰ λεγόμενα ὡς οἰωνιζομένου κατὰ τοῦ βασιλέως τοῦ προφήτου τὸν Ἰερεμίαν ᾐτιῶντο; *Ant.* 10.90) in language that recalls Jeremiah's own denunciations of the false prophets (so LXX 14.14, 34[27].7). For Josephus highlights the fact that the objections against Jeremiah—as also those against Jesus—amount to accusations of false prophecy, even though neither the OT nor Matthew make this explicit.[2]

In Matthew and Mark the condemnation to death (note Mt. 26.65, 'Why do we still need witnesses? You have heard [ἠκούσατε] the blasphemy') comes only after Jesus' declaration concerning his messiahship (26.64). But Matthew's opening statement in 26.59 that ἐζήτουν ψευδομαρτυρίαν κατὰ τοῦ Ἰησοῦ ὅπως αὐτὸν θανατώσωσιν is sufficient, even without the subsequent words of judgment, to connect the false testimony with Jesus' ultimate fate, and so establish a clear parallel to Jeremiah.

Doeve goes so far as to suggest that Matthew alone mentions the death sentence a second time in 27.1 because there are two such condemnations in Jeremiah 26 (i.e. vv. 8, 11).[3] More solid evidence that Matthew was conscious of an allusion to Jeremiah is provided by his several mentions of 'innocent blood'. For, as Doeve notes:

> In Jeremiah xxvi 15 the prophet says that if they kill him, they will bring innocent blood upon themselves, upon the city and upon the inhabitants. This text is twice echoed in the story of the passion as Matthew gives it. In Matt. xxvii 4 Judas says that he has betrayed innocent blood; in xxvii 24 and 25 Pilate is represented as saying that he is innocent of the blood of Jesus, while the people cry, 'His blood be upon us and on our children'.[4]

testimony that is validated in one form by Jesus' resurrection, and in another by the destruction of Jerusalem, strongly suggests that the narrative is intended to invoke a conscious literary and theological motif.

1. Cf. Feldman, 'Prophets and Prophecy in Josephus', p. 413.
2. Cf. Hare, *Jewish Persecution*, p. 27 n. 4.
3. Doeve, *Jewish* , pp. 187-88.
4. Doeve, *Jewish Hermeneutics*, p. 185; cf. Kosmala, 'His Blood on us', p. 104. Winkle ('Jeremiah Model', p. 168; cf. Gundry, *Matthew*, p. 470) similarly understands the phrase ἔλθῃ ἐφ' ὑμᾶς πᾶν αἷμα δίκαιον of 23.35 to allude to LXX Jer. 33.15, αἷμα ἀθῷον... ἐφ' ὑμᾶς (cf. Jon. 1.14), a possibility rendered more likely by the influence of Jer. 26 here in Matthew's trial narrative.

To this we may add Kosmala's observation that in LXX Jer. 33 [26].9 (cf. vv. 7, 8, 12; also LXX 19.14) πᾶς ὁ λαός gather against the prophet, making this the likely source of Matthew's language in 27.25 where, again, πᾶς ὁ λαός call down 'innocent blood' upon themselves.[1] This is the only place in the Passion account where Matthew uses λαός to refer to the crowds who attend Jesus' trial and crucifixion, and it is the only occurrence in his entire Gospel of the expression πᾶς ὁ λαός.[2] This suggests the likelihood of an allusion to Jeremiah not only here in Matthew 26, but at 27.25 as well.

Matthew 27.25. According to Bonnard and Schlatter, the emphatic ellipsis of Mt. 27.25, τὸ αἷμα αὐτοῦ ἐφ' ἡμᾶς, probably reflects the phrasing of LXX Jer. 28[51].35, τὸ αἷμα μου ἐπὶ τοὺς Χαλδαίους,[3] since both depict the inhabitants of Jerusalem as identifying where blame for the shedding of innocent blood should be laid. Indeed, as the blood of Jesus was 'innocent/righteous' (so Pilate says in the verse immediately preceding), so too *Targ. Jer.* 51.35 expands MT ודמי אל־ישׁבי כשׂדים ('My blood be upon the inhabitants of Chaldea') to read:

> and the debt of innocent blood which was shed in me shall be upon the inhabitants of the land of the Chaldeans.[4]

An allusion to Jer. 51.35, then, would be ironic in tone: no longer must foreign invaders answer for the innocent blood of Jerusalem, but now the Jerusalemites themselves answer—and that willingly—for the innocent blood of Jesus.

But it is doubtful that Matthew's emphasis lies here. Assignations of

1. Kosmala, 'His Blood on us', pp. 96-98, 105.

2. Apart from Matthew's use of τοῦ λαοῦ to qualify the title 'scribe' (2.4) or 'elder' (21.13; 26.3, 47; 27.1), or its appearance in a quotation (2.6 [Mic. 5.2?]; 4.16 [LXX Isa. 6.10]; 15.8 // Mk 7.6 [LXX Isa. 29.13]), λαός (Matthew 14×; Mark 2×; Luke 36×) refers to the 'people' of Israel at 1.21, 4.23, 26.5 (// Mk 14.2) and 27.64. But in the Passion narrative, Matthew customarily follows Mark in employing ὄχλος (50×; 38×; 41×; e.g. Mt. 26.47; 27.15, 20 [// Mk 14.43; 15.11; cf. 15.8]; and further, Mt. 26.55 [+ Mk 14.48]; 27.24). Accordingly, 'Πᾶς ὁ λαός bezeichnet hier sicher nicht nur die zufällig zusammengeströmte Menge, sondern das jüdisches Volk als solches und ganzes' (Steck, *Israel*, p. 295; so also Trilling, *Wahre Israel*, pp. 72-73, 75).

3. Bonnard, *Matthieu*, p. 398 (with 2 Sam. 1.13-16, 3.29); Schlatter, *Matthäus*, p. 776 (with Lev. 20.9; Ezek. 18.13); cf. Hühn; N-A[26].

4. וחובת דם זכי דאתאשיד בי על יתבי ארע כסדאי.

guilt using αἷμα εἰς/ἐπί [κεφαλήν] = דם ב/על־[ראש] are sufficiently commonplace that alternative parallels can be found for each of the features found in 27.25, including the elliptical syntax (LXX 2 Kgdms 1.16, cf. Acts 18.6), the overtones of 'innocent' blood (3 Kgdms 2.32), and even the curse on succeeding generations (3 Kgdms 2.33; cf. 3 Kgdms 2.37; Ezek. 33.4; Acts 5.28). The frequency of the expression, in fact, could easily obviate any individual source.

Nonetheless, since Matthew has already been shown to have Jer. 26.15 in mind, it seems reasonable to explain his emphasis on the consequences of shedding Jesus' blood in 27.25 by assuming that the Evangelist now expands that reference by portraying the Jerusalemites as bringing upon themselves Jeremiah's hitherto unfulfilled curse.[1] More precisely, as Green explains, the mention of 'our children' may refer to the war with Rome:

> Mt seems to have regarded the destruction of Jerusalem as the execution of judgment on Israel for its rejection of Christ. Those who suffered then were the children of Jesus' contemporaries.[2]

Matthew 27.39 (// Mark 15.29). As seems fitting for such a sorrowful event, the account of Jesus' crucifixion contains at least one, and possibly two allusions to the book of Lamentations. We will examine the more likely of these first.

Commenting on Mk 15.29, Taylor observes that 'one would expect a phrase like τινες τῶν παρεστῶτων ([Mark] xv.35)' in place of the more unusual καὶ οἱ παραπορευόμενοι (so Mt. 27.39: οἱ δὲ παραπορευόμενοι ἐβλασφήμουν αὐτὸν κινοῦντες τὰς κεφαλὰς αὐτῶν). The explanation for the latter phrase, Taylor argues, 'can only be that Mark is influenced by Lam. ii. 15':

1. Cf. Trilling, *Wahre Israel*, pp. 70-71; Green, *Matthew*, p. 221. Zahn (*Matthäus*, p. 658 n. 83) links 27.25 with Jer. 26.15 (also Deut. 21.7-8; 2 Sam. 1.16) in his discussion of 23.35.

2. Green, *Matthew*, p. 221. So also Fitzmyer, 'Anti-Semitism', pp. 670-71. '[Matthew's] perspective is that of the period roughly AD 80-85, after the great crisis of the destruction of Jerusalem and its Temple'. Fitzmyer makes the important observation that the intent of this verse is not condemnatory or anti-Semitic per se, but reflects Matthew's apologetic purpose in explaining the failure of Jesus' own people to accept him as the messiah, the destruction of Jerusalem, and the emergence of the Christian community as an entity in its own right.

> πάντες οἱ παραπορευόμενοι ὁδὸν ἐσύρισαν καὶ ἐκίνησαν τὴν κεφαλὴν αὐτῶν ἐπὶ τὴν θυγατέρα Ἰερουσαλήμ.[1]

Were it not for the substantival participle παραπορευόμενοι, one might account for the remainder of the verse—in particular κινοῦντες τὰς κεφαλὰς αὐτῶν—simply on the basis of LXX Ps. 21.8 (ἐκίνησαν κεφαλήν),[2] the influence of which is substantiated by Luke's expansion (Lk. 23.35) of Mk 15.31.

Neither παραπορεύεσθαι and its present participle nor κινέω are uncommon in the LXX, where the latter indicates a derisive shaking of the head.[3] But the unusual combination of the two strongly favors an allusion to Lam. 2.15, with κινέω providing the link to Ps. 22[21].8. Moreover, παραπορέυεσθαι is found elsewhere in the NT only at Mk 2.23, 9.30 and 15.29, all of which Matthew emends. The fact that it did not suffer the same editorial fate in 27.39 suggests that Matthew recognized here a larger significance that he wished to retain.[4] Thus it appears that just as Lam. 2.15 announced the mocking of 'the daughter of Jerusalem' because of the ruin wrought by false prophets in her midst (Lam. 2.14), so by means of this allusion Matthew highlights the mocking of Jesus—itself based on an accusation of false prophecy (27.40)—as having ironic reference to the impending fate of the vaticide Jerusalem.[5]

1. Taylor, *Mark*, p. 591 (echoed by Gundry, *Use of the OT*, pp. 62-63); so Hühn; N-A^{26}; Plummer, *Matthew*, p. 397 (with Lam. 1.12); Haenchen, *Weg*, p. 538; Lohmeyer and Schmauch, *Matthäus*, p. 391 n. 2; Gnilka, *Matthäusevangelium*, II, p. 473; cf. Allen, *Matthew*, p. 294; Albright and Mann, *Matthew*, p. 348. Schlatter (*Matthäus* 781) cites Jer. 19.8, while according to Benoit (*Matthieu*, p. 160) this passage evokes Lam. 2.15, Jer. 18.16, and Ps. 21.8.

2. So Dittmar; M'Neile, *Matthew*, p. 419; Bonnard, *Matthieu*, p. 402.

3. So LXX 4 Kgdms 19.21 = Isa. 37.22; Job 16.4; Pss. 21[22].8; 108 [109].25; Lam. 2.15; Zeph. 2.15; Sir. 12.18; 13.7 (for נוע); also Jer. 18.16, 48.17 (for נוד). Jer. 18.16; in fact, forms a further parallel insofar as it refers to the imminent destruction of the land: οἱ παραπορευόμενοι [LXX^{A}; LXX^{B,S} διαπορευόμενοι]... κινήσουσι τὴν κεφαλὴν αὐτῶν.

4. Indirect support for this position can be found in the Western Codex Bezae Cantabrigiensis (D), which employs the singular τὴν κεφαλὴν αὐτῶν for τὰς κεφαλάς—thereby conforming Mt. 27.39 more closely to LXX Lam. 2.15, despite offering a non-conformist text for Mk 15.29 whence the allusion originated!

5. That the language of taunt or mockery employed by Matthew and Lamentations is as frequently directed in the OT towards a corporate object—whether Jerusalem (2 Kgs 19.21 = Isa. 37.22; Jer. 19.8), the land (Jer. 18.16, 48.27), or a foreign

Matthew 27.34 (// Mark 15.23). Against Mark's ἐσμυρνισμένον οἶνον, Mt. 27.34 has the soldiers offer Jesus οἶνον μετὰ χολῆς μεμιγμένον. Zahn sees the Hebrew ראש or רוש as underlying this Greek phrase (i.e. χολή, 'gall, bile', as in LXX Deut. 29.17; 32.32; Ps. 68[69].22; Jer. 8.14; Lam. 3.19).[1] So Matthew's expression may reflect, in condensed form, LXX Ps. 68.22:

> καὶ ἔδωκαν εἰς τὸ βρῶμα μου χολὴν
> καὶ εἰς τὴν δίψαν μου ἐπότισάν με ὄξος.[2]

It is curious, however, that Matthew introduces 'gall' here, since Jesus is later offered 'vinegar [ὄξους]' to drink at 27.48. For the latter more naturally recalls the wording of LXX Ps. 68 (i.e. ἐπότισάν με ὄξος rather than τὸ βρῶμα μου χολὴν). But can we demand precision of the Evangelist? Or did he simply intend the mention of 'gall' in 27.34 to be an expansion of an allusion to Psalm 68/69 in 27.48 that he derived from Mk 15.36?[3]

Alternatively, the likelihood of an allusion to Lam. 2.15 in 27.39 introduces the probability of a further reference to Lamentations a few verses later in Mt. 27.34. For Lam. 3.15 uses the drinking of gall as a metaphor for bitter judgment (ἐχόρτασέ με πικρίας, ἐμέθυσέ με χολῆς), which is subsequently echoed in 3.19 ('Εμνήσθην . . . ἐκ διωγμοῦ μου, πικρίας καὶ χολῆς). And because it is a personal lament (cf. Lam. 3.1, ἐγω ἀνὴρ ὁ βλέπων πτωχείαν...), these verses are even more readily applicable to the suffering Jesus than the words of Lam. 2.15, which are uttered in the person of Jerusalem.

Furthermore, similar images of judgment occur in LXX Jer. 8.14 (ὁ θεὸς...ἐπότισεν ἡμᾶς ὕδωρ χολῆς, ὅτι ἡμάρτομεν ἐναντίον

16.4; 27.23; Ps. 22.8; 64.9; 109.25; S Dan. 4.19; Sir. 12.18; 13.7) would facilitate such a reading.

1. *Matthäus*, p. 712 n. 81.

2. So M'Neile, *Matthew*, p. 417 (with Lam. 3.15); Gaechter, *Matthäus*, p. 921; Schmid, *Matthäus*, p. 372 (with Prov. 5.4; Lam. 3.15); Gundry, *Use of the OT*, p. 144-45; Lohmeyer and Schmauch, *Matthäus*, p. 389; Hill, *Matthew*, p. 353; Schweizer, *Matthäus*, p. 335; Senior, *Passion Narrative*, p. 272 (with further references n. 2); Bonnard, *Matthieu*, p. 403; Gnilka, *Matthäusevangelium*, II, p. 472. Such an allusion would account for the variant ὄξος [μετὰ χολῆς] to 27.34 in A W Γ Δ Φ 0250 𝔐 700 892 1241, etc., although this may simply represent an assimilation to 27.48.

3. So Lindars, *NT Apologetic*, pp. 101-102.

αὐτοῦ)[1] and 9.14 [MT v. 15] (ποτιῶ αὐτοὺς ὕδωρ χολῶς), making such language typical of the prophet Jeremiah. This impression is strengthened by the observation that of the sixteen occurrences of χολή, only the five cited from Psalm 68, Jeremiah and Lamentations use it as a figure for judgment. On the other hand, the case for an allusion to Lam. 3.15 may be somewhat weakened by the fact that according to Matthew, Jesus merely tastes but does not drink the proffered mixture.[2]

The rejection of Jesus by those of his own village and family (Mt. 13.57) suggested an analogy to the situation of Jeremiah. But further investigation has shown that Matthew's allusions to Jeremiah focus rather on the rejection of Jesus by the leaders and, ultimately, the people of Jerusalem. In keeping with Jesus' declaration that his arrest takes place in fulfillment of 'the Scriptures of the prophets' (26.56), the immediately ensuing account of his trial appears to have been modeled after the similar trial of Jeremiah. We recall also that in the course of his trial, Jesus is mocked, struck and commanded to prophesy (27.67-68), a reminder that Jesus is here a rejected prophet. Following the intervening episode of Peter's denials, Matthew next recounts the episode of Judas's silver, with its climactic reference to 'what had been spoken by the prophet Jeremiah' (27.3-10). Jesus is subsequently sent before Pilate, where Matthew uses the words of the governor's wife to remind us that Jesus is a 'righteous (δίκαιος) man' (27.19). Pilate having declared his own innocence, 'all the people' then unwittingly invoke Jeremiah's prophecy of innocent blood coming upon the city (Mt. 27.24-25). Finally, as the climax and triumph of the opposition against him, Jesus is crucified. Here Matthew reminds us, ironically, of the mocking of Jerusalem in Lam. 2.15 (Mt. 27.39) and emphasizes the bitter cup of judgment that Jesus is made to drink, via an allusion to LXX Ps. 68.22 and, possibly, Lam. 3.15 (Mt. 27.34). In the account of Jesus' betrayal, trial and death, it is once more evident that Matthew has combined

1. This verse follows the image of the fruitless fig tree in Jer. 8.13, to which Matthew may have intended a reference in 21.18-21.

2. Alternatively, Matthew's assertion that Jesus actually tasted the mingled wine and gall, rather than refusing it altogether, could be seen as an emendation that conforms the narrative more closely to Ps. 68.22 (and Lam. 3.15) while at the same time remaining faithful to Mark's account, where we are told, simply, ὅς δὲ οὐκ ἔλαβεν (Mk 15.23).

generally Deuteronomistic motifs with specific allusions to the words of Jeremiah.

3. *Allusions to Jeremiah's Prophecy of a 'New Covenant'*

Allusions to the words and circumstances of Jeremiah as a prophet of judgment and rejection do not, however, exhaust Matthew's interest in him. Rather, Matthew incorporates into his text at least two allusions to the 'new covenant' of Jer. 31.31-34, once again coordinating these references with Deuteronomistic motifs.

Matthew 26.28 (// Mark 14.24). As has already been pointed out, Matthew's reference to the 'shed blood' of Jesus in the words over the cup (Mt. 26.28) makes a significant contribution to the redactional motifs of 'innocent blood' and prophetic rejection. For by harmonizing Jesus' invocation of 'all the righteous blood shed on earth' in 23.35 (ἐκχυννόμενον; against ἐκκεχυμένον of Lk. 11.50), with that of 26.28 (τὸ αἷμά μου... ἐκχυννόμενον), Matthew heightens the Deuteronomistic tone of both passages.[1] In other words, 23.35 and 26.28 now interpret one another, so that the 'shed blood' of Jesus is seen to be both 'innocent' and 'righteous', in line with that of the prophets of the OT and those of Matthew's community. Thus the concept of αἷμά... ἐκχυννόμενον refers to the violent nature of Jesus' death by recalling for us the similarly violent fate of the 'prophets, wise men and scribes'.

But it is no less significant that Jesus' words over the cup refer to the institution of a 'covenant' in his blood, leading a number of interpreters to suggest that Matthew alludes here to the prophecy of Jeremiah.[2] Apparently early copyists felt such an allusion to be

1. Cf. J. Behm, 'ἐκχέω, ἐκξύν(ν)ω', *TWNT*, II, pp. 465-66 [= *TDNT*, p. 468]; Garland, *Intention*, pp. 177-78; J. Jeremias, *Die Abendmahlsworte Jesu* (Göttingen: Vandenhoeck & Ruprecht, 1960), p. 216 [ET *The Eucharistic Words of Jesus* (London: SCM Press, 1966), p. 225].

2. Referring to Jer. 31.31-34 are Hühn; Dittmar; Benoit, *Matthieu*, p. 150; Staab, *Matthäus*, p. 144 (with Exod. 24.8 and Zech. 9.11); Argyle, *Matthew*, pp. 200-201; Rothfuchs, *Erfüllungszitate*, p. 95 n. 25; Albright and Mann, *Matthew*, pp. 322-23; Schweizer, *Matthäus*, p. 320; Green, *Matthew*, p. 213; Maier, *Matthäus*, II, p. 369; Meier, *Matthew*, p. 320; Bonnard, *Matthieu*, p. 379 ('allusion probable'); Gnilka, *Matthäusevangelium*, II, p. 401 ('Wenn auch vom neuen Bund nicht explizit gesprochen wird, so ist der Gedanke doch vorhanden'); cf. J. Behm, *s.v.* 'διαθήκη', *TWNT*, II, p. 136 [= *TDNT*, p. 133]; Haenchen, *Weg*,

operative, and indicated this by inserting καινῆς from LXX Jer. 38.31.[1] But the absence of the adjective from the earliest texts of Matthew, together with the likelihood that the words over the cup reflect the formula of Exod. 24.8[2] or (perhaps) Zech. 9.11,[3] do not exhaust the possible allusions to Jeremiah.

Apart from the addition of γάρ and the substitution of περί for ὑπέρ, the one substantive Matthaean addition to the Markan *Vorlage* is the phrase εἰς ἄφεσιν ἁμαρτιῶν. As Gundry observes, 'εἰς ἄφεσιν ἁμαρτιῶν (Mt) is an allusion to Jer. 31.34, ἄφεσιν exactly corresponding to the meaning of סלח ("to forgive") against the free ἵλεως ἔσομαι of the LXX'.[4] In fact, although סלח is not once translated by ἄφεσις in the LXX, the verbal cognate ἀφεῖναι frequently serves this purpose (Lev. 4.20; 5.10, 13, 16, 18; 6.6; 19.22; Num. 14.19; 15.25, 26, 28; Isa. 55.7). And although the

pp. 483-84, and, to the contrary, Wolff, *Jeremia*, p. 165 n. 7. In addition to discerning a reference to Jer. 31 (*Matthäus*, p. 43), Schlatter further proposes (p. 741) that despite Matthew's paschal interpretation, the primary function of the bread and cup (26.26-27) is to console the sorrowing disciples, on the analogy of Jer. 16.7; so also Zahn (*Matthäus*, p. 697), citing in addition Lam. 4.4.

1. τοῦτο γάρ ἐστιν τὸ αἷμά μου τῆς ^{T}διαθήκης τὸ περὶ πολλῶν ἐκχυννόμενον εἰς ἄφεσιν ἁμαρτιῶν: so $\mathfrak{P}^{37}$ $\mathfrak{P}^{45vid}$ ℵ B L Z Θ 33 *pc* cop^{mae} cop$^{bo(pt)}$; ^{T}καινῆς 𝔐 A C D W Γ Δ Φ 074 f^{1} f^{13} lat syr^{s,p} cop^{sa} cop$^{bo(pt)}$ (inserted via Synoptic conflation and/or harmonization with LXX Jer. 38.31). Such an addition, which Jeremias believes to be pre-Pauline, is already present as a result of 'emerging theological reflection' in the alternative version of the formula in 1 Cor. 11.25b and Lk. 22.20 (*Abendmahlsworte*, pp. 163-64, 180 [ET, pp. 171-72, 187]). Cf. Löhse, *Märtyrer und Gottesknecht*, p. 126.

2. So Behm, 'διαθήκη'; Dittmar; Gundry, *Use of the OT*, p. 57; McConnell, *Law and Prophecy*, pp. 188-89; Filson, *Matthew*, p. 274.

3. So Grundmann, *Matthäus*, p. 536; Lindars (*NT Apologetic*, pp. 132-33) argues for a primary reference to Zech. 9.11 on the grounds that the redemptive and eschatological interests of that passage correspond most closely to the intent of the early church.

4. *Use of the OT*, p. 58; so also Grundmann, *s.v.* 'ἁμαρτάνω κτλ.', *TWNT*, I, p. 307 [= *TDNT*, p. 304] (with Isa. 53.12); Goppelt, *Typos*, p. 134 [ET, p. 112]; Dodd, *Scriptures*, p. 45; Tasker, *Matthew*, p. 246; Davies, *Setting*, pp. 83-84; Fenton, *Matthew*, p. 418; Hill, *Matthew*, p. 339; Meier, *Vision*, p. 184 n. 220; France, *Jesus and the OT*, p. 94; cf. Schweizer, *Matthäus*, p. 321. Schniewind (*Matthäus*, p. 257) not only sees the influence of Jer. 31.34 in this passage, but finds the hope of a new covenant expressed both generally throughout Mt. 5 and in 11.27-30, and specifically in the provision of forgiveness according to Mt. 6.12; 7.11; 9.1-8; 11.19; 12.31-32; 16.19 = 18.18; 18.23-35, etc.

combination of ἀφεῖναι with ἁμαρτία is by no means infrequent (see, in addition, Exod. 32.32; Lev. 5.6; Ps. 24.18; Isa. 22.14; 33.24; 55.7; Sir. 2.1), reference to such forgiveness in relation to what is here (even without the addition of καινή) a 'new' or renewed covenant is found only in Jer. 31.31-34.

At the same time, it is significant that Matthew deletes the identical phrase from Mark's description of the ministry of John: βαπτίζων ἐν τῇ ἐρήμῳ καὶ κηρύσσων βάπτισμα μετανοίας εἰς ἄφεσιν ἁμαρτιῶν (Mk 1.4; cf. Mt. 3.1-2: κηρύσσων ἐν τῇ ἐρήμῳ Ἰουδαίας). For Matthew, only 'the Son of man has authority on earth to forgive sins' (9.6); such a function is inappropriate to his vision of John the Baptist.[1] While it appears that Matthew has simply transferred the phrase from Mk 1.4 to Mt. 26.28, the explicit covenantal significance of Mt. 26.28 indicates that the allusion to Jeremiah is not thereby obviated.[2]

One may conclude, therefore, that 26.28 alludes both to the provisions of the 'new covenant' in Jer. 31[38].34 and to the violent nature of Jesus' death, in keeping with his identity as a rejected prophet.[3] That Jeremiah is prominent elsewhere in this Gospel as a rejected and suffering prophet suggests the further relevance of Matthew's reference to him in the words over the cup.

Matthew 23.8-10. If Matthew alludes to the 'new covenant' of Jer. 31.31-34 in Mt. 26.28, the likelihood of a further such allusion in Mt. 23.8-10 is considerably enhanced. J.D.M. Derrett expands on a

1. Cf. Sand, *Gesetz und Propheten*, p. 129; Senior, *Passion Narrative*, p. 83.

2. Thus while the actual phrase εἰς ἄφεσιν ἁμαρτιῶν likely derives from Mark, it nonetheless reflects the wording of both LXX and MT Jer. 31[38].34: [ἵλεως ἔσομαι] ταῖς ἀδικίαις αὐτῶν καὶ τῶν ἁμαρτιῶν αὐτῶν = אסלח לעונם ולחטאתם.

3. The proposed complementarity of the themes of prophetic rejection and covenantal redemption—by virtue of the common motif of 'innocent blood'—finds further support in the provocative suggestion of T.B. Cargal ('"His Blood be upon us and upon our Children": A Matthean Double Entendre?', *NTS* 37 [1991], pp. 101-12, esp. pp. 109-11) that by alluding to the prayer of Deut. 21.8 (that Israel be forgiven 'the guilt of innocent blood') and by recalling the promise of Mt. 1.21 (that Jesus will 'save τὸν λαὸν αὐτοῦ from their sins'), the cry of the people in Mt. 27.25 represents not only their acceptance of responsibility for Jesus' innocent death, but also, at a more subtle level, an invocation upon them and their children of the atoning efficacy of Jesus' shed blood.

suggestion by Theodore Beza to argue that Mt. 23.8-10 embodies a midrashic expansion of Isa. 54.13 and Jer. 31.33-34.[1] On such a view, the apodosis of Isa. 54.13b, ורב שלום בניך ('and great shall be the prosperity of your sons'), is taken as an expansion of its protasis, וכל־בניך למודי יהוה ('and all your sons shall be taught of the LORD')—with ורב in particular being exploited to yield a variety of interpretative possibilities. For the term רב can mean 'teacher' or 'rabbi' (hence 23.8, ὑμεῖς δὲ μὴ κληθῆτε ῥαββί· εἷς γάρ ἐστιν ὑμῶν ὁ διδάσκαλος), 'patron' or 'father of the synagogue' (hence 23.9, καὶ πατέρα μὴ καλέσητε... εἷς γάρ ἐστιν ὑμῶν ὁ πατὴρ ὁ οὐράνιος), or something like 'schoolmaster' or 'instructor' (so yielding 23.10, μηδὲ κληθῆτε καθηγηταί, ὅτι καθηγητὴς ὑμῶν ἐστιν εἷς ὁ Χριστός).[2] At an initial, 'presumably dominical', stage, according to Derrett, br would have identified God—whereas Matthew has placed Jesus in this role (cf. 11.27), so that Isa. 54.13 is understood to mean that direct knowledge of God comes from the messiah.[3]

The connection between Isaiah 54 and Jer. 31.33-34—and therefore the relevance of both to Matthew—is obvious, insofar as Jer. 31.33-34 also stresses direct communication with God in the messianic age, without need of didactic intermediaries:

1. J.D.M. Derrett, 'Matt. 23:8-10 a Midrash on Isa. 54:13 and Jer. 31:33-34', *Bib* 62 (1981), pp. 377-81. Zahn (*Matthäus*, p. 652) links Isa. 54.13 and Jer. 31.34 to this passage, as does Schniewind (*Matthäus*, p. 226), while N-A[26] and Schweizer (*Matthäus*, p. 281) explain 23.8 by reference to Jer. 31.34 alone. Haenchen (*Weg*, p. 423) reports the comment of Joachim Jeremias on this verse, 'Gott selbst der Lehrer—das ist Jer. 31,31-34! Das ist die Gemeinde der Heilszeit, des "allgemeinen Priestertums."' Cf. Jeremias, *NT Theology*, p. 169 n. 1; Garland, *Intention*, p. 61 n. 102. For further proponents of a reference to Jer. 31, see the footnotes following. On the intention of Jer. 31.31-34, see the summaries of Davies, *Setting*, pp. 122-30; B.W. Anderson, 'The New Covenant and the Old', in B.W. Anderson (ed.), *The Old Testament and Christian Faith: A Theological Discussion* (New York: Harper & Row, 1963), pp. 225-42; W.L. Holladay, 'New Covenant, The', *IDBSup*, pp. 623-25 (cf. *idem*, *Jeremiah*, II, p. 94); Carroll, *Jeremiah*, pp. 610-14; with full bibliography in Holladay, *Jeremiah*, II, p. 149-50.

2. Lachs (*Rabbinic Commentary*, p. 373 n. 28) notes a similar word-play on the teacher (רב) as 'father' (אב) in *Sifre Deut.* §34. A play on the root meaning of 'rabbi' is indicated already by the discussion of 'greatness' in 23.8 (so Fenton, *Matthew*, pp. 367-68).

3. Derrett, 'Midrash', pp. 372, 382; Jn 6.42-47 apparently takes the idea further, asserting that God himself teaches *about* Jesus.

> I will put my law within them, and I will write it upon their hearts... and no longer shall each man teach his neighbour and each his brother, saying, 'Know the Lord', for they shall all know me... says the Lord.[1]

Derrett's proposal, then, is that Isa. 54.13 has provided Matthew with the interpretative key to the provisions of the new covenant in Jeremiah 31. For in their original contexts both passages deal with issues of covenant, ἡ διαθήκη τῆς εἰρήνης in LXX Isa. 54.10 being brought into association with the διαθήκην καινήν of LXX Jer. 38.31-33.[2]

But we need not follow all the details of Derrett's complex reconstruction in order to establish a valid allusion to the texts of Isaiah and Jeremiah. As it stands, Jesus' explanation for proscribing the title of rabbi is enigmatic: εἷς γάρ ἐστιν ὑμῶν ὁ ⸀διδάσκαλος,⸆ πάντες δὲ ὑμεῖς ἀδελφοί ἐστε.[3] Whereas the relationship between having one teacher and being all brothers is by no means clear in Matthew, the logic of such a connection emerges if this saying is understood to be a simple conflation of Isa. 54.13 and Jer. 31.34. Among the promises of God's covenant in Isaiah is the explicit prospect of the 'sons' (who are therefore, implicitly, brothers) being διδακτοῦς θεοῦ. Among the promises of the covenant in Jeremiah just the opposite is the case: those who are explicitly brothers will no longer teach one another, 'for they shall all know me...says the Lord', the implicit premise being that God himself will teach them (so 31.33: 'I will put my law within them, and I will write it upon their hearts, and I will be their God').

Jesus' words in Mt. 23.8 stress both premises: the disciples, as

1. So Grundmann, *Matthäus*, p. 487 ('Die Ablehnung des christlichen Rabbinats...dürfte irhen Ursprung haben in pneumatischen Kreisen des Urchristentums, die in der Gemeinde Jer. 31, 33f verwirklicht sehen und sich dabei auf Jesus berufen'); Schweizer, *Matthäus*, p. 281; Sand, *Gesetz und Propheten*, p. 83; Maier, *Matthäus*, II, p. 241 ('bezieht sich die Bezeichnung "Brüder" auf Jer. 31,34. Danach wird es in der Endzeit nur noch "Brüder" geben, von denen keiner den anderen lehren muß, weil sie alle Gotteserkenntnis haben [vgl. Jes 54,13]).' Of such a connection, Gnilka (*Matthäusevangelium*, II, p. 276 n. 24), however, is doubtful.

2. Derrett, 'Midrash', p. 375.

3. ⸀καθηγητής ℵ*;2 D (W) Δ Θ 0107 0138 $f^{1,13}$ 𝔐 *pm* (likely by assimilation to v. 10) | *text* ℵ1 B U 33 1010 *pc* | ⸆ὁ Χριστός K Γ Δ 0138 f^{13} 𝔐 (again an assimilation to v. 10).

beneficiaries of the new covenant, have one teacher, and are all brothers. It is on this basis that they must eschew honorific titles. Nor is the link here between Mt. 23.8-10 and Jeremiah 31 merely thematic, for the likelihood of such an allusion is heightened by the concurrence of significant features of vocabulary (LXX Jer. 38.34: οὐ μὴ διδάξωσιν...ἕκαστος τὸν ἀδελφόν; cf. Mt. 23.8: εἷς γάρ ἐστιν ὑμῶν ὁ διδάσκαλος, πάντες δὲ ὑμεῖς ἀδελφοί ἐστε).

Here, as in Mt. 26.28, the allusion to Jeremiah occurs in connection with Deuteronomistic motifs, for the discussion of honorific forms of address contributes to Jesus' excoriation of the 'scribes and Pharisees' as 'hypocrites' and 'blind guides' for Israel. But the allusion to the prophecy of a 'new covenant' indicates, once again, that Matthew's use of Jeremiah traditions does not focus solely on Deuteronomistic themes. Rather, it suggests that the Evangelist is in contact with the wider stream of early Christian thought which saw in Jeremiah 31 a prophetic anticipation of its own conclusions regarding the significance of Jesus as the messiah.[1]

But it is not immediately clear from 23.8 alone, as Derrett seems to suggest, that according to Matthew Jesus himself is now the 'teacher' in question (the variant reading ὁ Χριστός notwithstanding). For the subsequent clauses of Jesus' argument refer both to the 'Father' and to the 'Christ' in parallel terms (23.9-10), suggesting that διδάσκαλος in 23.8 could refer to either one. By contrast, Jesus is indeed depicted as the sole arbiter of divine knowledge in Mt. 11.27, leading some interpreters to detect there also an allusion to Jeremiah 31.

1. Derrett, 'Midrash', p. 375-76, and n. 18; with particular reference to Dodd, *According to the Scriptures*, pp. 44-46. See especially 1 Cor. 11.25; 2 Cor. 3.2-3, 6; Heb. 8.8-12; 10.16-17; cf. 1 Jn 2.12-14. Elsewhere in Matthew, compare 13.17 (// Lk. 10.24); 20.26-27 (// Mk 10.43-44). According to Jeremias (*Abendmahlsworte*, p. 188 n. 2 [ET, p. 195 n. 2]), Jer. 31 was already current in non-Christian circles. For a full review of the question, albeit resulting in a negative estimation, see Wolff, *Jeremia*, pp. 116-47. Cf. Bar 2.35; *Jub.* 1.23-25; CD 6.19; 8.21; 19.33-34; 20.12; *1 En.* 1.8; (on which see Chapter 5, §B.3, below); and for synagogue use of this chapter, see Chapter 1, §B.3, above.

It is interesting to note that Hebrews focuses on the same two elements of the Jeremiah passage (quoted in full by Heb. 8.8-12) to which this study of Matthew draws attention: direct teaching by God (Jer. 31.33 = Mt. 23.8-10; Heb. 9.16) and forgiveness of sins (Jer. 31.34 = Mt. 26.28; Heb. 9.17), perhaps suggesting a common interpretative tradition underlying both. Cf. the use of Exod. 24.8 and Jer. 31.31-34 both in Mt. 26.28 and in Heb. 9.20, 10.16-17.

Matthew 11.27 (// Luke 10.22). A key premise of the declaration in Mt. 11.27 is that Jesus is the source and arbiter of divine knowledge: 'no one knows the Father except the Son and anyone to whom the Son chooses to reveal him'. In other words, Jesus receives his knowledge of God without need of human tradition or intermediaries, and through Jesus his disciples can ultimately make the same claim. Such personal knowledge of God was originally the prerogative of Moses (Exod. 33.13), the prophets (Num. 24.16; 1 Sam. 3.7), and God's anointed one (Isa. 11.2) or servant (Isa. 53.11). But hope is expressed that one day all will know the name of the Lord (1 Kgs 8.43; Isa. 52.6; cf. Ezek. 38.16) and that 'the earth shall be full of the knowledge of the Lord' (Isa. 11.9).[1]

Among the passages Schniewind appeals to in this regard is Jer. 31.33-34, which combines the prospect of universal and unmediated divine knowledge with the promise of a ברית חדשה (31.31) that will bring about the forgiveness of sins. While Jesus' words in Mt. 11.27 probably echo a whole range of OT passages and the hopes they express, the currency of Jer. 31.31-34 in both Christian and non-Christian circles suggests its relevance for the present passage as well. As R.H. Fuller comments on the third clause of 11.27, 'No one knows the Father except the Son':

> It is significant that the OT repeatedly complains that Israel did *not* know God, for it constantly disobeyed his will (Isa. 1.3; Jer. 2.8; cf. 8.7). Hence the knowledge of God is eventually relegated to the eschatological hope (Jer. 31.34). It is this eschatological knowledge which Jesus, as the Son, enjoys, and which he is... revealing to other men, as the fourth clause of the verse asserts [i.e. 'and anyone to whom the Son chooses to reveal him'].[2]

But unless Matthew's ἐπιγινώσκει represents the verb ידע from MT

1. Schniewind, *Matthäus*, pp. 150-52; and further, Kloppenborg, 'Wisdom Christology in Q', pp. 142-44; Hoffmann, *Studien*, pp. 122-33 on the meaning of 'knowledge' in this *Q* passage.

2. *Mission and Achievement of Jesus*, p. 93; so also Zahn, *Matthäus*, p. 442 n. 48 (with 1 Kgs 8.43, 60; Hos. 2.22; 4.1; 6.3, 6); Hahn, *Christologische Hoheitstitel*, p. 325 n. 1. Dodd ('Jesus as Teacher and Prophet', p. 63) appeals rather to Jer. 1.5, 9.24 and Amos 2.7. Alternatively, Schulz (*Q*, pp. 224-25) and Robinson ('Jesus as Sophos', pp. 9-10) see here a wisdom-motif, with Jesus equated with Sophia as the exclusive mediator of divine knowledge.

Jer. 31.34—a common LXX equivalence—the influence of Jeremiah 31 here is at most thematic. Moreover, the focus of Mt. 11.27 is not on a widely available and unmediated divine knowledge like that of Jer. 31.34, but rather on a restricted and strictly mediated knowledge: 'no one knows the Father *except* the Son and anyone *to whom the Son chooses* to reveal him'.

This raises an important question regarding Matthew's use and interpretation of Jer. 31.33-34 in Mt. 23.8. Unless the Evangelist is simply inconsistent, a comparison of 11.27-30 with 23.8-10 suggests that in the latter passage, Matthew interprets Jer. 31.33-34 in a particularly christocentric manner. Jeremiah 31 promises the universal availability of knowledge about God, whereas Mt. 11.27 restricts that availability to Jesus as a revelational mediator. Interpreting the allusion to Jer. 31.34 in Mt. 23.8 by reference to 11.27 suggests that, for Matthew, Jesus is indeed the διδάσκαλος in question (a premise the variant reading has sought to clarify). Whether Mt. 11.27 itself refers to the promises of Jeremiah's covenant, however, is not thereby clarified.

Matthew 11.29. More probable is the possibility that underlying Mt. 11.29 (ἄρατε τὸν ζυγόν μου ἐφ' ὑμᾶς καὶ μάθετε ἀπ' ἐμοῦ...καὶ εὑρήσετε ἀνάπαυσιν ταῖς ψυχαῖς ὑμῶν) is the promise of 'rest' found in Jer. 6.16:

> Thus says the Lord: 'Stand by the roads, and look,
> and ask for the ancient paths,
> where the good way is; and walk in it,
> and find rest for your souls (ומצאו מרגוע לנפשכם/καὶ εὑρήσετε
> [ἁγνισμὸν/ἁγιασμὸν] ταῖς ψυχαῖς ὑμῶν)
> But they said, "We will not walk in it"'.

An allusion to Jeremiah can be established here on the grounds that 'Mt's ἀνάπαυσιν ("rest") correctly renders מרגוע against both readings in the LXX (ἁγνισμὸν, "purification" [LXX^{B}]; ἁγιασμὸν, "sanctification" [LXX^{A}])'.[1] This is not to contradict the scholarly

1. Gundry, *Use of the OT*, p. 136; cf. *idem*, *Matthew*, p. 219; likewise Hühn; Dittmar; N-A^{26}; *UBSGNT* (3rd edn) (p. 908); Zahn, *Matthäus*, p. 444 n. 52; Lagrange, *Matthieu*, p. 229; Montefiore, *Synoptic Gospels*, II, pp. 176, 186; Smith, *Matthew*, p. 130; Torrey, *Documents*, p. 64; Benoit, *Matthieu*, p. 81; Stendahl, *School of St Matthew*, p. 141-42; Fenton, *Matthew*, p. 187; Gaechter, *Matthäus*, p. 386; Schniewind, *Matthäus*, pp. 153-54 (with Jer. 31.25); Rothfuchs,

consensus that sees Sir. 51.23-30 underlying Mt. 11.28-30 as a whole.[1] For not only are the image of the yoke and the motif of Wisdom's invitation derived from Sirach 51, but so also is the key term ἀνάπαυσιν (εὗρον ἐμαυτῷ πολλὴν ἀνάπαυσιν, Sir. 51.27). This might obviate the reference to Jer. 6.16 were it not for the fact that apart from ἀνάπαυσιν, the correspondence between Matthew and LXX Jeremiah is exact. In the mind of the Evangelist, then, Sir. 51.27 has suggested not only a verbal link to Jer. 6.16, but also the proper rendering of that verse. Thus it appears that in 11.29 Matthew resumes the earlier theme of Jesus as the source of divine knowledge (11.27-28, 29a: 'shoulder my yoke and learn from me') and glosses it with a more specific reference to Jeremiah.[2]

According to Vouga, insofar as the central concern of 11.28-30 is the proper interpretation of Torah, the citations from Jeremiah (which he understands to include both 31.23-25 and 6.16) serve to

Erfüllungszitate, p. 95 n. 25; Christ, *Jesus-Sophia*, p. 106 ('Reminiszenz'); Albright and Mann, *Matthew*, p. 146; Filson, *Matthew*, p. 144; France, *Jesus and the OT*, p. 243; Jeremias, *NT Theology*, p. 206 n. 1; Strecker, *Weg*, p. 172 n. 4 ('vormatthäischer Abfassung'); Hill, *Matthew*, p. 208; Schweizer, *Matthäus*, p. 177; Goulder, *Midrash and Lection*, p. 362 n. 103; Sand, *Gesetz und Propheten*, p. 154 n. 123; Green, *Matthew*, p. 122; Maier, *Matthäus*, I, p. 400 (with Isa. 28.12); Meier, *Matthew*, p. 128; Bonnard, *Matthieu*, p. 170; Schnackenburg, *Matthäus*, I, p. 106; cf. Holladay, *Jeremiah*, I, p. 221, II, p. 95; etc.; contrary, Wolff, *Jeremia*, p. 165 n. 7 ['nicht wahrscheinlich']; for the image of the yoke, Schlatter (*Matthäus*, p. 388) refers to Lam. 3.27. The objection by C. Deutsch (*Hidden Wisdom and the Easy Yoke: Wisdom, Torah and Discipleship in Matthew 11.25-30* [JSNTSup, 18; Sheffield: JSOT Press, 1987], p. 136 n. 89) that Jer. 6.16 lacks the image of the yoke (although it is present in Jer. 5.5, as emphasized in the Targum [*Hidden Wisdom*, p. 115 n. 18]) or any reference to wisdom, overlooks Matthew's composite method of quotation (see following note).

1. Cf. Klostermann, *Matthäusevangelium*, p. 103-104; L. Cerfaux, 'Les sources scripturaires de Mt., XI, 25-30', *ETL* 31 (1955), p. 340; Lührmann, *Redaktion*, pp. 66-67; Suggs, *Wisdom, Christology, Law*, pp. 101-106; Gundry, *Matthew*, p. 220; and, most comprehensively, Deutsch, *Hidden Wisdom*, pp. 113-39.

2. D.C. Allison ('Two Notes on a Key Text: Matthew 11.25-30', *JTS* 39 [1988], pp. 477-85) has drawn attention to a strikingly similar passage in *Par. Jer.* 5.32. He suggests that, unless this verbal agreement is the product of mere coincidence or *Par. Jer.* 5.32 was itself influenced by Mt. 11.29, both represent adaptations of Jer. 6.16, even if by means of some intermediate source: '*Paraleipomena Jeremiou* is filled from beginning to end with allusions to the book of Jeremiah. Is it therefore not easier to presume that the source of *Par. Jer.* v. 32 was Jer. 6.16, not Mt. 11.25-30?' ('Two Notes', pp. 483-84).

buttress the claims of both the Matthaean Christ and the Matthaean community to be the authoritative interpreters of Scripture, as over against the synagogue.[1] The relevance of citing Jeremiah, he suggests, lies in that prophet's concern for true prophecy and his concomitant opposition to false prophecy, particularly as they relate to the ultimate fate of Jerusalem.[2]

For Hill, 11.29 offers a spiritual rest that 'comes from returning to God and faithfulness to the will of God', as Jeremiah 6 admonishes.[3] According to Green, Matthew's citation from Jer. 6.16c implies that even as Jeremiah's hearers rejected the way of rest ('But they said, "We will not walk in it"', 6.16d), so too the message of Jesus will be rejected.[4] This latter suggestion is especially appealing insofar as the rejection of the divine messenger is a specifically Deuteronomistic theme that pervades Jeremiah and Matthew alike. It could even be that Matthew was prompted to allude to Jer. 6.16 by an interpretative tradition of the kind reflected in *Targ. Jer.* 6.17 (cf. 6.19, 29; 22.21), which takes this passage to refer to the rejected admonitions of godly teachers (מלפין) and prophets (נביייא). The primary difficulty with such an interpretation, however, is the fact that the context of Mt. 11.25-30 provides no hint of rejection. In other words, the allusion to Jer. 6.16 in Mt. 11.29 appears not to take account of its original context.

Thus the possibility of an allusion to Jer. 6.16 raises a larger difficulty: that of its relation to the remainder of Matthew's references to Jeremiah. In this section of the study we have seen that Matthew alludes to two key promises contained in Jeremiah's prophecy of a 'new covenant': forgiveness of sins (Mt. 26.28) and universal knowledge of God (Mt. 23.8; with Isa. 54.13). There was insufficient evidence to indicate the influence of Jer. 31.34 in Mt. 11.27, although that verse provided the key to understanding Matthew's interpretation

1. Vouga, 'Seconde Passion', p. 78; citing G. Bornkamm, G. Barth and H.J. Held, *Überlieferung und Auslegung im Matthäusevangelium* (Neukirchen-Vluyn: Neukirchener Verlag, 1970), pp. 122; 139 n. 1; 148 [ET *Tradition and Interpretation in Matthew* (London: SCM Press, 1982), pp. 131; 148 n. 2; 158-59]; see also p. 96 n. 1 [ET p. 103 n. 1]. Cf. K.H. Rengstorf, 'Ζυγός', *TWNT*, II, p. 902-903 [= *TDNT*, pp. 899-90); and *2 Bar.* 41.3; *m. Ab.* 3.5; *b. Sanh.* 94b.

2. 'Seconde Passion', p. 81.

3. Hill, *Matthew*, p. 208.

4. Green, *Matthew*, p. 122.

of Jer. 31.34 in Mt. 23.8. And although the revelational theme of Mt. 11.27-30 in general, together with the positive tone of Mt. 11.29 in particular, suggests that it too may be related to the provisions of the new covenant, Jer. 6.16 speaks rather of returning to 'ancient paths' and walking in them. Unlike 23.8 and 26.28, Mt. 11.29 does not refer to Jer. 31.33-34.

To restate the difficulty, then, neither the immediate context of the phrase from Jer. 6.16 (rest for the soul as a consequence of returning to 'ancient paths') nor the larger context of that verse (Israel's rebelliousness in Jer. 6.1-30) seem to match Matthew's use of the allusion. On the contrary, the assertion in Mt. 11.27-30 of a christocentric revelation—particularly in contrast to the 'yoke' of Torah[1] —suggests that Matthew has purposely wrested this phrase from its original context in order to declare that true spiritual rest comes not from returning to the 'ancient ways', but rather from the new 'yoke', which is the wisdom and teaching of the messiah.

C. *Summary and Conclusions*

In Chapters 1 and 3 we have examined some 22 passages from Matthew's Gospel, investigating possible allusions to 20 different verses or passages in the book of Jeremiah, four in Lamentations and two in Baruch. The intention has been to discover allusions to Jeremiah material that either are primary or make a substantial and significant contribution in cases of multiple reference. In so doing, this study has attempted to weigh the degree of literary similarity and conceptual continuity between particular passages from Jeremiah and Matthew, and so to determine whether an allusion is operative. In six of the Matthaean passages, moreover, a thematic reference to Jeremiah (and his generation) appeared relevant, even though no specific text or series of textual antecedents seemed to be in view.[2]

In evaluating literary parallels it is not enough merely to establish their presence. Rather, it is essential to demonstrate their significance both in relation to one another and within the context of Matthew's redactional concerns. The redactional interests relevant to our study

1. Cf. Mt. 23.5.

2. E.g., 1.11-12 (the Babylonian exile); 13.57 (cf. Jer. 11.21, Jeremiah's rejection by his neighbours); 16.14 ('Jeremiah'); 21.35; 23.37 (cf. Jer. 20.2; 37.15, etc.; beating and stoning); and 24.2 (cf. Jer. 7.14; 26.6, 9; prophecies against the Temple).

are evident in two areas. It has been argued, first, that Matthew takes over and accentuates from his source materials a Deuteronomistic understanding of Israel's rejection of the prophets. According to Matthew, even as Israel refused to hear the prophets of old, so they refuse to hear John the Baptist, Jesus and those whom Jesus sends. All these are seen in Matthew's Gospel as persecuted, rejected, even killed. It is this rejection, in fact, that accounts both for the fall of Jerusalem and for the rise of the (Matthaean) Christian community as a 'new' Israel.

Secondly, we have observed that this Deuteronomistic outlook accords well with at least two of Matthew's three explicit references to the prophet Jeremiah. For 2.17-18 and 27.9-10 envisage deadly opposition to the messiah both from the political realm (Herod and his court) and from Jesus' own circle of disciples (Judas). And both envisage dire consequences as a result: in the first instance, for the slaughtered children of Bethlehem; in the second, for those on whom the wages of 'innocent blood' are to fall. The fact that Matthew's appeal to the words of 'Jeremiah the prophet' is in 2.17-18 contrary to the contextual meaning of the cited passage, and in 27.9-10 altogether contrived and obscure, only serves to highlight the importance of the prophet Jeremiah for Matthew.

Matthew does not make explicit his reasons for referring to Jeremiah in 16.14. Nonetheless, it would appear that insofar as this reference represents an approximation of Jesus' identity—with Jeremiah being the paradigmatic 'suffering prophet'—the reference to Jeremiah here is entirely in keeping with (1) Matthew's Deuteronomistic depiction of Jesus as a suffering prophet, (2) his similar portrayal of John the Baptist, on the analogy of Elijah (since both are also mentioned in 16.14), and (3) the two fulfillment citations that likewise cite Jeremiah. And it is our contention that the majority of the remaining textual and thematic allusions to Jeremiah in Matthew's Gospel are also consistent, in whole or in part, with these redactional interests.

This study has endeavoured to demonstrate that Matthew's explicitly stated interest in the prophet Jeremiah, coupled with his sensitivity to OT themes and scriptural precedents, heightened his awareness of allusions to Jeremiah in his source materials (Mark and Q) and led him to incorporate further such allusions into his text. And it is the recognition of this heightened awareness that increases the likelihood, first, that Matthew saw allusions in his sources that he does not otherwise acknowledge and, secondly, that he has included in his narrative thematic allusions for which the textual basis is less precise.

Since the evidence in the different passages is of varying weight, it is appropriate to review the evidence for Matthew's allusions to Jeremiah in order of probability, beginning with those instances where such an allusion is most likely. From his reading of Mark, Matthew develops four clear citations or allusions to Jeremiah: (1) Jesus' denunciation of Temple misuse, 'you make it a den of thieves' (21.13 // Mk 11.17 = Jer. 7.11); (2) Jesus' interpretation of the Passover cup, 'this is my blood of the covenant, which is poured out for many for the forgiveness of sins' (26.28 [cf. Mk 14.24] = Jer. 31.34); (3) the traditions of the false witnesses and Jesus' condemnation to death, together with the motif of 'innocent blood' (26.59-66 [cf. Mk 14.55-61] = Jer. 26.5-16); and (4) the derision and wagging of heads by the passers-by at Jesus' crucifixion (27.39 // Mk 15.29 = Lam. 2.15). While Matthew simply takes over the allusions in 21.13 and 27.39 in their Markan form, in 26.28 and 26.59 he develops the relevant themes more fully than does Mark, indicating that he both recognized and exploited the allusions in question.

A number of further possible allusions already present in Matthew's sources focus on Deuteronomistic themes of judgment and prophetic rejection. For example, the preaching of John the Baptist includes the image of God's eschatological representative coming with winnowing fork in hand (3.12 // Lk. 3.17), which sets up an allusion to Jer. 15.7. Similarly, Jesus' call for the disciples to be 'fishers of men' (4.19 // Mk 1.17) recalls the words of judgment in Jer. 16.16.

Less distinct, but still consistent with themes of judgment and rejection, is the possible link to Jer. 8.13 (as well as Hos. 9.16, if not also Mic. 7.1) in the account of the cursing of the fruitless fig tree as a symbol of God's people (21.18-21; cf. Mk 11.12-14, 20-23). There is also the possibility, although difficult to verify, of an allusion to Jer. 12.7, derived from Q, which Matthew expands in Jesus' words against the Temple and people: 'Behold, your house is forsaken and desolate' (23.38 // Lk. 13.35). The difficulty here, of course, is that Matthew's addition to the Q text (in which the allusion to Jeremiah is already present) uses stereotyped language, rather than referring specifically to any one passage from the OT.

Of a slightly different nature is the possible allusion to Lam. 3.15 in the expression 'wine mingled with gall' of 27.34 (// Mk 15.23). For if such an allusion is what Matthew intends, it again highlights the theme of judgment, although here applied to Jesus himself. Furthermore, as noted earlier, it coheres well with the allusion in 27.39 to Lam. 2.15, which refers not only to the judgment that Jesus bears, but also (probably) to the judgment that will come upon Jerusalem.

In unique Matthaean material, at least three of the four most likely allusions are consistent with the thematic interests present in the allusions based on Mark and Q. In Mt. 15.13 Jesus' response to the complaints of his opponents suggests that his ministry resembles the terms of Jeremiah's call to be a prophet (Jer. 1.10). Like that of Mt. 26.28, the allusion in 23.8 to Jer. 31.33-34 (in combination with Isa. 54.13) spells out the implications of the 'new covenant' established by Jesus: not only is there 'forgiveness of sins', but also universal knowledge of God. And 27.25 appears to be a further expansion of Matthew's extended allusion to Jeremiah 26, with the Evangelist depicting 'all the people' of Jerusalem as bringing down on themselves the 'innocent blood' of Jesus. For whereas Jeremiah foretold that dire consequences would follow should his own blood be shed, Matthew sees that prediction as now having been fulfilled as a result of Jerusalem's rejection of Jesus, who is a rejected prophet after the manner of Jeremiah.

A fourth allusion not accounted for by Mark or Q is in Jesus' invitation to discipleship: 'Take my yoke and learn from me...and you will find rest for your souls' (11.29 = Jer. 6.16), which may also be related to the provisions of the new covenant. But whereas both Mt. 23.8-10 and 26.28 refer to Jer. 31.33-34, Mt. 11.29 seems to intend a contrast with the original meaning of Jer. 6.16: no longer will the disciples walk in the 'ancient paths', but rather in the new way of Jesus' teaching.

This study has acknowledged from the outset that the reference in Mt. 16.14 is thematic rather than textually specific. The same would appear to be the case for several other uniquely Matthaean passages. At the beginning of his Gospel, Matthew indicates that the Babylonian exile—the setting and focus of Jeremiah's ministry—provides one of three major turning points in the genealogical schematization of history which sets the stage for the messiah's advent (1.11-12, 17). Further analogies between Jeremiah and Jesus are suggested by the facts that both are rejected by their own townspeople (13.51) and that, like Jeremiah, the disciples of Jesus are persecuted, beaten and stoned (21.35; 23.37). Even more to the point is the similarity between Jesus' words against the Temple (24.2) and those of Jeremiah, particularly so in light of the references to the Temple—and to Jeremiah—in Matthew's trial scene.

We may conclude, therefore, that the most probable Matthaean allusions to Jeremiah, both those derived from Mark and Q, and those that occur in uniquely Matthaean material, focus on two separate but ultimately related themes.[1] The first is the Deuteronomistic theme that we have found to be prominent throughout Matthew's Gospel. Allusions to Jeremiah highlight Jesus' words of judgment against the leaders of Israel and those who misuse the Temple, and his condemnation by false witnesses for having spoken against the Temple itself, so that his betrayal and death bring 'innocent blood' on those who reject him. The second theme underlying Matthew's allusions to Jeremiah is that of the new covenant. Furthermore, these two themes are related, for allusions to the provisions of the new covenant contribute not only to Jesus' polemic against the scribes and Pharisees (23.8-10), but also to his words over the cup (26.28), wherein the reference to Jesus' death as a consequence of his rejection is made more obvious by Matthew's verbal parallel with the 'shed blood' of the prophets (23.35).[2]

It is an integral feature of the Deuteronomistic view of history that, having judged his people, God will restore them, reaffirming his relationship with them. It may well be that such an understanding undergirds Matthew's interest in the new covenant, so that he sees the Christian community as the new object of divine restoration following, or in the context of, the fall of Jerusalem. Here the theme of 'innocent blood' may play a key role, providing, as it does, the common factor between the death of the prophet Jesus, which Matthew sees as having caused the fall of Jerusalem, and the restoration of God's people in the 'new covenant' of Jesus' shed blood. For these two features appear to represent the judgmental and restorative features, respectively, of Matthew's Deuteronomistic schema.

Matthew's fulfillment citations and allusions do not, however, carry

1. Thus satisfying Hays's criterion of 'thematic coherence' with respect not only to the individual passages that contain such references, but also to the larger interests of the Gospel as a whole.

2. So also, albeit from a devotional rather than a scholarly perspective, the comments of P. Hinnebusch, *St Matthew's Earthquake: Judgment and Discipleship in the Gospel of Matthew* (Ann Arbor, MI: Servant, 1980), pp. 143-50.

the burden of his Deuteronomistic schema by themselves. Rather, Matthew uses various allusions to Jeremiah as a means of further specifying and sharpening the broad Deuteronomistic outlook that he has taken over from Mark and Q, and which he then adapts to his own redactional ends.

Not all of the allusions set out above can be established with complete certainty. Some are generally Deuteronomistic in tone, and so recall in stereotyped fashion the fate of all the prophets, without distinction, whom Jewish tradition saw as being rejected by the people of Israel, and even suffering martyrdom at their hands. Other allusions employ general OT language and imagery derived only in part from Jeremiah, and so may not have in view a specific reference to that prophet. Nonetheless, the strong thematic cohesion that exists among these various allusions is striking, suggesting that Matthew was conscious of many of them as having reference to Jeremiah and his circumstances—whether taken over from his source materials or inserted as part of his own redactional emendations.

Our study so far thus confirms that a unitary redactional interest underlies not only the two formula quotations that explicitly refer to Jeremiah, but also, to some extent, a series of less obvious allusions to Jeremiah within the body of Matthew's narrative. Matthew, it appears, has cast Jesus in the role of Jeremiah as a rejected prophet of doom who speaks words against the Temple (and the city), who suffers reproach and judgment as a result, and yet whose prophecies of doom ultimately come to pass. In fact, the words of prophecy that remained unfulfilled in Jeremiah's day (i.e. the consequences of innocent blood falling on Jerusalem) now come to pass in connection with the person and generation of Jesus. Matthew may even have seen further similarities between the words of John the Baptist and the role of Jesus' disciples, on the one hand, and the prophecies and circumstances of Jeremiah, on the other.

At the same time, Jeremiah is also significant for Matthew as the prophet of the 'new covenant'. For as Jeremiah prophesied the coming of the new covenant, so Jesus accomplishes it. Although this is a factor unaccounted for by the Matthaean formula quotations, it serves to illuminate further the central reference to 'Jeremiah' as an approximation of Jesus' identity in 16.14.

Chapter 4

TYPOLOGICAL REFERENCES IN MATTHEW TO JEREMIAH TRADITIONS

Having focused earlier on the prominence, availability, recurrence and thematic interrelatedness of Matthew's references and allusions to Jeremiah, this chapter will explore additional features of the Evangelist's method. To the extent that Matthew's references to Jeremiah have in view not only individual texts or themes but also the prophet himself, we may speak of a Jeremiah 'typology': a cumulative image of the prophet and his ministry to which the Evangelist appeals so as to highlight particular aspects of Jesus' ministry, if not also that of his disciples. In order to verify this approach we will now examine Matthew's typological use of other OT figures—specifically, Noah, Abraham, Moses, Elijah, David and Jonah—in order to shed light on the identity of Jesus (and John the Baptist).

A. *Typology as an Exegesis of History*

By 'typology', at least as it refers to the NT's use of the OT, is meant the perception of significant correspondences between the characteristics and circumstances of two different historical individuals, institutions, or events, such that each is understood either as an anticipation or as a fulfillment of the other. In this sense, a 'type' or τύπος (meaning in classical Greek a matrix or archetype that forms a pattern to be copied, or else the image or copy thereby produced) provides a model or historical pattern, the characteristics of which anticipate and thereby illuminate the features of a corresponding 'antitype' or ἀντίτυπος.[1]

1. For a thorough investigation of the etymological derivation and semantic range of τύπος, see R.M. Davidson, *Typology in Scripture: A Study of Hermeneutical*

So the apostle Paul, for example, sees in Adam a τύπος τοῦ μέλλοντος (Rom. 5.14), insofar as the lives of both Adam and Christ entail universal consequences for all humanity: 'as in Adam all die, so in Christ shall all be made alive' (1 Cor. 15.22). Yet the two are not equals. The former merely anticipates the latter, who supersedes his antecedent: 'Thus it is written, "The first man Adam became a living being"; the last Adam became a life-giving spirit' (1 Cor. 15.45).[1] The spiritual significance of this relationship is to be evident in the lives of Paul's readers: 'just as we have borne the image of the man of dust, we shall [or: let us] bear the image of the man of heaven' (1 Cor. 15.49).[2] In this passage Adam and Christ are not significant independent of one another. Only insofar as this typological relation-

ΤΥΠΟΣ *Structures* (Berrien Springs, MI: Andrews University Press, 1981), pp. 116-40 (in classical and later Greek literature) and pp. 141-84 (in the NT); also Goppelt, *Typos*, pp. 59-62 [ET, pp. 50-53], and K.J. Woollcombe, 'The Biblical Origins and Patristic Development of Typology', in G.W.H. Lampe and K.J. Woollcombe, *Essays on Typology* (SBT; London: SCM Press, 1957), pp. 60-69 (both including discussions of Platonic idealism and Philo). As G.W. Buchanan (*Typology and the Gospel* [Lanham, MD: University Press of America, 1987], p. 3) observes, the terms 'type' and 'antitype' usually refer to correspondences on the plane of history, whereas the term 'prototype' or 'archetype' refers to an ideal, transcendent model in relation to its mundane counterpart (the latter also designated an 'antitype').

For a review of typology as a hermeneutical method from the Church Fathers onward, providing also a comprehensive account of the debate in twentieth century scholarship, see Davidson, *Typology in Scripture*, pp. 17-93, with a summary of principal issues, pp. 93-114; cf. Buchanan, *Typology*, pp. 14-22.

1. On Paul's Adam/Christ typology in these passages, cf. Goppelt, *Typos*, pp. 155-56; 160-63 [ET, pp. 129-30; 133-36]; Davidson, *Typology in Scripture*, pp. 297-316. Paul's treatment of the relationship between Adam and Christ reveals both equivalent typology (whereby the conditions that apply to one apply equally—or, as in this case, with greater force—to the other; that is 'as in Adam all...so in Christ all' [1 Cor. 15.22]) and antithetical typology (whereby the antitype reverses the situation or circumstances of the type; that is 'in Adam all die... in Christ shall all be made alive' [1 Cor. 15.22]; 'because of one man's trespass, death reigned... much more will those who receive... grace... reign in life through the one man Jesus Christ' [Rom. 5.17]).

2. NT typology frequently uses τύπος (e.g. Phil. 3.17; 1 Thess. 1.7; 2 Thess. 3.9; 1 Tim. 4.12; Tit. 2.7; 1 Pet. 5.3) or its cognate ὑποτύπωσις (1 Tim. 1.16; 2 Tim. 1.13) in an ethical and paraenetic sense (cf. Davidson, *Typology in Scripture*, pp. 153-81).

that obtains in one (death in Adam) is now taken up into the universal condition pertaining to the other (life in Christ).

By way of illustration, typology can be distinguished from allegory by virtue of its primarily historical orientation, for the intent of allegory is not to establish intra-historical correspondences but to derive transcendent or supra-historical significances from the features of text or history. To state the matter another way, biblical typology derives spiritual meaning from its discernment of patterns and resonances within the divinely-guided course of history itself, whereas allegory seeks to discover a direct relationship between individual words or events and their spiritual significance(s).[1]

Thus in Galatians 4, for example, Paul does not first establish a historical relationship between Hagar or Sarah and those who presently follow the pattern of their respective lives. Rather, he says ἅτινά ἐστιν ἀλληγορούμενα· αὗται γάρ εἰσιν δύο διαθῆκαι (Gal. 4.24). Only once the individual significance of Hagar and Sarah as being 'two covenants' is established can they be related to their spiritual heirs of a later day and a later dispensation. This is in contrast to the cases of 'Adam' and 'Christ', whose anticipation and fulfillment of one another across the bounds of history was itself primary.

In this sense, typology is similar—although not identical—to scriptural fulfillment of the sort indicated by Matthew's fulfillment citations. For type is related to antitype as a scriptural text or prophetic promise is related to its fulfillment in the life of Christ. Matthew himself makes this explicit. In ch. 2 Joseph and his family must flee to Egypt to escape the wrath of Herod, and must remain there until the King's death. As to the meaning of this episode,

1. Cf. Woollcombe, 'Biblical Origins', p. 40: 'Typological exegesis is the search for linkages between events, persons or things *within the historical framework of revelation*, whereas allegorism is the search for a secondary and hidden meaning underlying the primary and obvious meaning of a narrative' (emphasis original). See also the literature cited by Davidson, *Typology in Scripture*, pp. 100-101.

As a qualification of the distinction set out above, Heb. 8–9 uses a 'vertical' or idealist typology in describing the heavenly sanctuary (see discussion and review of the scholarly debate by Davidson, *Typology in Scripture*, pp. 99-100, 336-67). But even here, insofar as Heb. 8.5 appeals to the scriptural precedent of Exod. 25.40, where Moses is shown a heavenly תבנית (LXX τύπος) of the sanctuary, the historical or 'horizontal' emphasis remains primary (cf. *Typology in Scripture*, pp. 357, 367-88).

there until the King's death. As to the meaning of this episode, Matthew concludes by citing Hos. 11.1: 'This was to fulfill what the Lord had spoken by the prophet, "Out of Egypt have I called my son"' (2.15). On the face of it, this is simply another fulfillment citation, a verse quoted (entirely out of context) in order to demonstrate the messiah's fulfillment of Scripture. Yet the 'prophecy' itself points to a larger correspondence: as God called Israel, his 'son', out of Egypt, so he calls Jesus from the same land.[1] There is thus for Matthew not only a textual, but also a typological correspondence—however tenuous and whatever the widely differing circumstances of their respective situations—between these two 'sons' of God.[2]

In this instance, moreover, scriptural fulfillment establishes a typological relationship, with this conjunction of methods clearly illustrating the similarity of their respective approaches. For whereas scriptural fulfillment looks for a relationship of promise and fulfillment between the words of the sacred text and the life of the messiah, typology delineates a similar relationship between the events described in Scripture and those of the messiah's life—that is, sacred history past and present. The one relies on textual exegesis, while the other constitutes an exegesis of history. And both, by so doing, are predicated on a perception of the unity of a providentially-ordered historical experience, whereby the words and deeds of God in the past correspond meaningfully to his words and deeds in the present.[3]

1. Less likely is the proposal of Teeple (*Prophet*, p. 75) that this passage refers to a Jesus/Moses typology. While there is no indication that Moses was customarily designated a 'son of God', this title was frequently applied to Israel, even by Moses himself (Exod. 4.22-23).

2. In a pair of brief articles ('Typology—the Key to Understanding Matthew's Formula Quotations?', *Colloquium* 15 [1982], pp. 43-51; 'Second Thoughts on Matthew's Formula Quotations', *Colloquium* 16 [1983], pp. 45-47), V. Eldridge goes so far as to propose that typology, suggested in several instances by significant terms or phrases in the OT text at hand, provides the hermeneutical key to understanding Matthew's noncontextual use of Scripture in the majority of his formula citations. But it must be emphasized that neither typology nor fulfillment exegesis provides the 'key' to the other; rather, both are mutually illuminating since they are parallel phenomena.

3. France (*Jesus and the OT*, pp. 39-40, 83) argues that typology and fulfillment exegesis are essentially dissimilar: whereas fulfillment exegesis sees the OT as self-consciously prophetic and in need of later fulfillment, typology is merely retrospective, discerning OT types in a way that does not depreciate their historical

Or, to be more exact, the central conviction of specifically christological typology is that history—above all the history of God's people—finds its unity and coherence precisely in relation to the present manifestation of the Messiah. As Lampe puts it:

> The saving work of Christ, inaugurating the New Covenant between God and man, was thus seen as the moment which gave significance to the whole course of covenant-history that had preceded it... The Old Testament had therefore to be read anew, with fresh presuppositions, in order to be understood as Christians believed that God meant it to be understood, namely as a book which pointed forward to the climax of Christ's life and work.[1]

One of the tasks of critical OT study has been to disentangle the Hebrew Scriptures from the expectations placed upon them by the NT. A typological reading of the OT is understood to be a fundamental falsification, insofar as these documents are self-sufficient, semantically independent, and internally coherent literary artifacts. But an early Christian would hardly have been troubled by such considerations. For since the appearance of the messiah constituted the supreme and definitive revelation of God's salvific providence, all previous revelation was seen as secondary and so open to being co-opted as

independence or suggest that they are mere anticipations of a future antitype. But even a cursory examination of Matthew's use of the OT shows that such a distinction cannot be maintained, for the Evangelist's OT texts are only rarely cited from overtly 'prophetic' passages. Rather, NT typology and fulfillment exegesis are both retrospective, reinterpreting features of the OT text and history from a christological and eschatological perspective.

1. G.W.H. Lampe, 'The Reasonableness of Typology', in Lampe and Woollcombe, *Essays on Typology*, pp. 25-26. By contrast, 'the Jew looked back to the mighty acts of God in ancient history to find the reality which gave coherence and unity to all subsequent development. The Christian, in some measure, reversed this position. The great acts of God in Israelite history acquired significance because of their character as foretastes of what was later accomplished in Christ' (*Essays on Typology*, 28). At the same time, Goppelt (*Typos*, pp. 34-47 [ET, pp. 32-41]) observes in intertestamental literature an eschatological typology similar in many respects to that of the early Christians, anticipating the conditions of the messianic era on the model of primordial creation or the exodus and Mosaic period, or with specific reference to Adam, Moses and David. A further contemporary example is Josephus's bold typological comparison of himself to Joseph, Jeremiah, Daniel, and Esther and Mordecai (cf. D. Daube, 'Typology in Josephus', *JJS* 31 [1980], pp. 26-33; I am grateful to Dr John Kloppenborg for drawing this article to my attention).

testimony to this greater light. Indeed, the fact that significant correspondences—both textual and typological—could be found between the old dispensation and the new itself constituted proof, in the minds of early Christians, of the messiahship of Jesus of Nazareth.

Yet this does not, at least in the NT (though *Barnabas* and the early Church Fathers are another matter altogether), constitute as great a depreciation of the OT as has sometimes been suggested. For typology is a recognition of the consistency of salvation history, and so respects OT figures and events as testifying in their own right to God's relationship with his people.[1] That is to say, the relationship of type to antitype is not inherent in the events or individuals themselves, but exists only insofar as both reflect the larger working of a divine economy of salvation.[2] Thus NT typology does not, for the most part, attempt to reinterpret the OT, but simply views the OT as provisional in light of a greater revelation.[3]

According to Buchanan, biblical typology is closely related to a cyclical understanding of time and history common in predominantly agricultural societies.[4] In other words, under the hand of God history 'repeats' itself. Now there is no doubt that ancient Jews and early Christians conceived of history in such terms. The clearest examples of this are the schematizations of history found in the Jewish apocalyptic writings (e.g. the 'Apocalypse of Weeks', *1 En.* 91.12-17; 93.1-10; or the 'Apocalypse of Clouds', *2 Bar.* 53.1-74.4).

Still, distinctions, however subtle, need to be drawn between

1. Cf. Goppelt, *Typos*, p. 244 [ET, p. 202].

2. Cf. E.E. Ellis, *Paul's Use of the Old Testament* (Edinburgh: Oliver & Boyd, 1957), p. 128.

3. Davidson, basing his conclusions primarily on Paul (*Typology in Scripture*, pp. 401-402; cf. 284-85, 296 [on 1 Cor. 10.1-13]; pp. 308-11 [on Rom. 5.12-21]), argues that NT typology understands OT types as intentionally prophetic and anticipatory of their NT fulfillment. But even this is an obviously retrospective view, arrived at only from the perspective of a greater, and subsequent, messianic revelation. The debate between prophetic and retrospective views of typology forms a major crux in modern scholarly discussion: 'The older conception (mostly represented by authors before the 1950s) views typology in terms of divinely preordained and predictive *prefigurations*. The more recent consensus describes typology in terms of historical *correspondences* retrospectively recognized within the consistent redemptive activity of God' (*Typology in Scripture*, p. 94; emphasis original).

4. *Typology and the Gospel*, pp. 27-33. This view apparently originated with Bultmann; cf. Davidson, *Typology in Scripture*, pp. 17, 59.

(1) a cyclical or schematized view of history (which is understood to reflect providential guidance and control), (2) a perception of the archetypal correspondence between *Urzeit* and *Endzeit* (reflecting the cataclysmic nature of the eschaton), and (3) the NT vision of Christ's typological fulfillment of covenant history. For while early Christians certainly understood the revelation of Christ in terms that reflected historical antecedents, and so recognized in that christocentric revelation correspondences to primeval history (e.g. Adam/Christ or Noah/Christ typologies), they were nonetheless convinced that Jesus of Nazareth represented the culmination and unrepeatable fulfillment of all historical precedents. Their Christology, in other words, was fundamentally eschatological: history had reached its climax and conclusion in the advent of the messiah.

In what follows, we will have repeated opportunity to observe that in the Gospel of Matthew Christ not only corresponds to, but also consistently supersedes the historical types to whom he is compared. In fact, these two features of correspondence and fulfillment are the distinguishing marks of all christological typology in the NT.[1] For this reason, NT typology does not depend on a cyclical view of time or history. Rather, as Gundry observes, typology interprets history in a manner that is at once telic (Jesus Christ being the τέλος in question) and eschatological (in that Christ's advent inaugurates the final drama of the history of salvation).[2]

B. *Typology in Matthew*

Matthew's use of Jeremiah traditions relates to two features of his redactional method. First, as we have seen, the Evangelist uses scriptural quotations and allusions to demonstrate their 'fulfillment' in the events of his own day. Secondly, he appeals to the analogies of such individuals as Abraham, David, Moses, Jonah and Noah in order to shed light on the person and theological significance of Christ. My concern here is with the second of these features: Matthew's use of

1. Here I understand 'fulfillment' to include Goppelt's concept of 'Steigerung' ('heightening' or 'escalation'): 'Jede Typologie wird durch typologische Entsprechung und Steigerung konstituiert' (*Typos*, p. 244 [ET p. 202]; cf. Davidson, *Typology in Scripture*, pp. 281, 398-99).

2. Gundry, *Use of the OT*, p. 209 n. 3.

'typology'—though it will be sufficient simply to point out the presence of typological correspondences, since definitive conclusions as to the significance of each (particularly in the case of Davidic and Mosaic typologies) is beyond the scope of this study.[1] Against this background, an attempt will be made to determine whether Matthew's exegetical and typological references to Jeremiah also reflect particular aspects of his Christology.

1. *Elijah*

Although the primary emphasis of Matthew's typology, like that of his fulfillment exegesis, is on demonstrating how the life of Jesus conforms to the expectations of Scripture, he also takes over from both Mark and Q a typological link between Elijah and John the Baptist. Mark's Gospel opens with a combined citation of Mal. 3.1 and Isa. 40.3 that identifies John as the returning Elijah of eschatological expectation (Mk 1.2-3). Matthew separates out the reference to Malachi (Mt. 3.3), preferring to quote it later in its Q form (11.10 = Q 7.27)[2] and so to underscore the typological significance of John by means of Jesus' affirmation that 'he is the Elijah who is to come' (11.14; cf. Mk 6.15).

But John the Baptist is not presented as simply an Elijah *redivivus*. He is certainly this. Yet he is even greater than Elijah, as Jesus himself affirms: 'Truly, I say to you, among those born of women there has risen no one greater than John the Baptist' (11.11a // Lk. 7.28a).[3] For although Elijah, the greatest of Israel's prophets, is compared to John, the latter is 'more than a prophet' (11.9b // Lk. 7.26b). As Elijah's antitype, therefore, John the Baptist does not simply reflect the biblical antecedent, but fulfills and surpasses it.

1. In this respect the present approach is to be distinguished from that of Buchanan (*Typology and the Gospel*, pp. 45-58), who attempts (with very limited success) to find thematic and structural correspondences (in sequence) between each book of the Hexateuch and various features of Matthew's 28 chapters. The figures named in this study do not constitute an exhaustive list of possible typological resonances, but are simply examples of the most prominent and obvious possibilities.

2. Woollcombe ('Biblical Origins', p. 41) apparently overlooks this passage in claiming that 'in Matthew's view, John did not literally fulfill the prophecy of Malachi'.

3. Cf. Goppelt, *Typos*, p. 74 [ET, p. 64].

As Elijah's antitype, John the Baptist is not only the forerunner of the messiah, but also one who suffers (11.12-13). This aspect of the Elijah/Baptist typology is subsequently reiterated in Jesus' words on the Mount of Transfiguration: 'I tell you that Elijah has already come, and they...did to him whatever they pleased' (17.12a // Mk 9.13). Furthermore, this typological identification of John with Elijah reflects significantly on the person of the messiah himself. For in Matthew's portrayal Jesus adds the comment, 'So also the Son of man will suffer at their hands' (17.12b), and then later on the cross seems to call upon Elijah to relieve his suffering (27.47, 49).[1] This emphasis on suffering also likely explains how Matthew would have understood the popular suggestions, reported in 16.13, that 'the Son of man' bore some resemblance to John the Baptist and to Elijah.

This is not to suggest that Matthew depicts Jesus himself as an antitype of Elijah. Rather, it is to observe that the Evangelist coopts and strengthens the Elijah/Baptist typology of his sources in the service of his Christology. He does this, it seems, for both positive and negative reasons: positively, to heighten the association of the messiah with suffering generally; negatively, by identifying John with Elijah to refute any suggestion that Jesus was himself an 'Elijah-messiah'.[2]

2. *Abraham*

Matthew opens his Gospel with the announcement that Jesus is 'the son of David, the son of Abraham' (1.1). The fact that Matthew first refers to Jesus as the 'son of David', and only then refers to him as the 'son of Abraham' (against the chronological order of the genealogy) seems to suggest that a greater significance is given to the former title in his Gospel. In fact, Matthew's three references to Abraham in his introduction and genealogy (1.1, 2, 17; cf. Lk. 3.34) are the only places in his Gospel where the name Abraham (Matthew 7×; Mark 1×;

1. On these passages, see Chapter 1, §D.1.d and 2.b, above. For an alternative suggestion regarding Jesus' call to 'Elijah' (that is that, together with the rending of the Temple veil immediately following [27.51], which recalls Elisha's rending of his garments in 2 Kgs 2.12, it designates Jesus as 'Elijah himself, or one that is greater'), see Daube, *NT and Rabbinic Judaism*, pp. 23-25.

2. For Elijah as a messianic figure, cf. Jeremias, *s.v.* ''Ηλ(ε)ίας', *TWNT*, II, p. 933 [*TDNT*, p. 931]; Teeple, *Prophet*, pp. 4-8, 48; N.M. Cohen, *Jewish Bible Personages in the New Testament* (Lanham, MD: University Press of America, 1989), pp. 85, 87-88. Note esp. Sir. 48.10-11.

Luke 15×) does not derive from either Mark or Q.[1]

The most obvious explanations of the title 'son of Abraham' in Mt. 1.1 are, first, that Matthew thereby anticipates the schematic divisions of his genealogy,[2] and, secondly, that he declares the messiah's physical descent from the first patriarch in order to show that Jesus is a true Israelite according to the flesh. But there may also be an implicit appeal here to God's promise that by Abraham (and his seed) 'all the nations of the earth shall bless themselves' (Gen. 18.18; 22.18; 26.4; cf. 12.3; 27.29; 28.14).[3] For this was already a significant feature of pre-Matthaean Christology (cf. Rom. 4.1-25, esp. v. 17; Gal. 3.6-18, esp. v. 8).[4]

Matthew may also be alluding to this promise in his portrayal of the risen Jesus' final charge to his followers to make disciples of πάντα τὰ ἔθνη (28.19; cf. LXX Gen. 22.18; 26.4: καὶ ἐνευλογηθήσονται ἐν τῷ σπέρματί σου πάντα τὰ ἔθνη τῆς γῆς; also LXX Gen. 18.18).[5] In line with this it is interesting to note that the Gentile

1. Cf. Mt. 3.9(2×) // Lk. 3.8 (the preaching of John the Baptist disparages physical descent from Abraham); Mt. 8.11 // Lk. 13.28 (a similar, although more subtle disparagement, since here the 'sons of the kingdom' are excluded from eschatological table fellowship with the patriarchs); Mt. 22.32 // Mk 12.26 (citing Exod. 3.6 in reference to 'Abraham, Isaac, and Jacob' as emblematic of those to whom God demonstrates his faithfulness).

2. Johnson (*Purpose*, pp. 149-51) adduces examples of rabbinic genealogies in which both Abraham and David serve as pivots, and concludes that 'υἱοῦ Δαυίδ υἱοῦ 'Αβραάμ represents the mainstream of Jewish messianism in both intertestamental and rabbinic literature as well as Christian messianism'. Cf. Lk. 1.69, 73; 3.31, 34.

3. So Albright and Mann, *Matthew*, p. 3; Brown, *Birth*, p. 68; Beare, *Matthew*, p. 65; Gnilka, *Matthäusevangelium*, I, p. 7; Davies and Allison, *Matthew*, pp. 158-59.

4. In addition, *T. Levi* 8.14-15 reads: 'A king will arise and shall found a new priesthood in accord with the Gentile model and *for all nations*. His presence is beloved, as a prophet of the Most High, a descendant of Abraham, our father' (emphasis added). But the provenance of such a sentiment in *Testament of Levi* (i.e., whether Jewish or Christian) is hotly debated.

5. References to Abraham in 1.1-2, 17 and 28.19 would thus provide a further instance of Matthew's use of parallel themes at the opening and close of his Gospel (cf. Chapter 1, §C.4, above). On the other hand, Matthew's wording may simply be a continuation of the allusion to Dan. 7.14 (καὶ ἐδόθη αὐτῷ ἐξουσία, καὶ πάντα τὰ ἔθνη τῆς γῆς... αὐτῷ λατρεύουσα) in 28.18 (cf. Gnilka, *Matthäusevangelium*, II, pp. 507-508).

Magi are the first in Matthew's Gospel to do homage to Jesus (2.1-12). Likewise, 3.9 can be understood to stress the potential universality of Abrahamic sonship, while 8.11-12 is significant as Jesus' response to the faith of the Gentile centurion. So, as Green points out:

> Abraham, the father of Israel, is shown to be the father of the representative figure of the new Israel, and through him of all its members, whether or not literally descended from him.[1]

Such a comparison between Abraham and Jesus lends itself well to typological interpretation. But if this is what Matthew intended, it remains only latent and a comparatively undeveloped feature of his Christology.[2]

3. *David*

Just the opposite, however, is the case with Matthew's title 'son of David'. David, of course, was the greatest of Israel's kings. So it is only natural that popular messianic expectation would have been strongly influenced by Davidic typology and have expressed its hopes in terms of a 'son of David'.[3]

1. Green, *Matthew*, p. 52; Green also suggests an analogy between the miraculous births of Abraham's first son, Isaac, and that of Jesus. Cf. Kingsbury, *Structure, Christology, Kingdom*, pp. 85-86.

2. Cohen (*Jewish Bible Personages*, p. 96) suggests a series of typological parallels between Isaac (Abraham's 'only son') and Jesus, although the similarities are general and specific evidence for such a link (at least in Matthew) is lacking.

3. Among the OT texts that demonstrate this interest are Isa. 11.1, 10, Jer. 23.6, 33.15 and Zech. 3.8, 6.12. Both messianic speculation and Davidic hagiography are widely evident in Second Temple writings, e.g., Sir. 47.1-22; 51.13h (on which see Patte, *Early Jewish Hermeneutic*, p. 84; P.W. Skehan and A.A. Di Lella, *The Wisdom of Ben Sira* [New York: Doubleday, 1987], p. 570; for text, I. Levi (ed.), *The Hebrew Text of the Book of Ecclesiasticus: Edited with Brief Notes and a Selected Glossary* [Leiden: Brill, 1904], p. 740); *Pss. Sol.* 17; 18.5; Wis. 7-9; *Bib. Ant.* 59-63; Josephus, *Ant.* 6.156-57, 394; 4QpIsa frag. 7-10, 11-17; 4Q174 (4QFlor 1.2; צמח דוד) and 4QPatrBless 3-4 (משיח הצדק צמח דויד; cf. Kee, 'Function of Scriptural Quotations', p. 181; for texts, J.M. Allegro, 'Further Messianic References in Qumran Literature', *JBL* 75 [1956], pp. 174-87; *idem*, 'Fragments of a Qumran Scroll of Eschatological Midrashim', *JBL* 77 [1958], pp. 350-54); *4 Ezra* 12.32; *b. Sanh.* 97a-98b. See J.L. MacKenzie, 'Royal Messianism', *CBQ* 19 (1957), pp. 25-52; Nolan, *Royal Son*, pp. 158-69; Johnson, *Purpose*, pp. 116-20. Cf. also *Targ. Jer.* 23.5; 30.9, 21; 33.13, 15; these texts are set out in full by J.J. Brierre-Marbonne, *Exégèse targumique des prophéties*

Indeed, Matthew gives David (Matthew 17×; Mark 7×; Luke 13×) a key role in his messianic genealogy. Not only does David provide a schematic turning-point between Matthew's first and second series of fourteen generations (1.6, 17), but the numerical value of the Hebrew name דוד (i.e. 4 + 6 + 4 = 14) may also have inspired Matthew's division of the genealogy into three sets of fourteen. On such a view (which, of course, assumes a bilingual author and audience, with the latter sensitive to the technique of *gematria*), the genealogy would show Jesus to be 'the thrice-Davidic son of David'.[1] Furthermore, immediately following the genealogy Matthew affirms that Joseph is a 'son of David' (1.20), in which case—notwithstanding the break in physical lineage necessitated by the virgin birth—Jesus too is of Davidic lineage.[2]

In keeping with the messianic honour that the title implies, Jesus is often addressed by individual suppliants as 'son of David' (9.27; 15.22 [+ Mk 7.25]; 20.30-31 [// Mk 10.47-48].[3] Indeed, such is his healing ability that, according to Matthew, the amazed crowds wonder, with obvious messianic intent, 'Can this be the Son of David?' (12.23). The same crowds—and later the children in the Temple—then go on to answer their own question, as Jesus rides into Jerusalem, with the bold acclamation drawn from Psalm 118, 'Hosanna to the Son of David!' (21.9, 15) —with the title again conveying unmistakable messianic overtones.[4]

messianiques (Paris: Geuthner, 1936), pp. 50-55, citing (p. 50 n. 2) similar interpretations of Jer. 23.6 in *b. B. Bat.* 75b; *Lam. R.* 1.16 [58b; Soncino §51]; *Midr. Ps.* 21.1-2; and *Midr. Prov.* on 19.21; to which may be added *y. Ber.* 2.5a (cited by Lachs, *Rabbinic Commentary*, p. 14).

1. Johnson, *Purpose*, p. 192; cf. Davies, *Setting*, pp. 74-77; McConnell, *Law and Prophecy*, pp. 154-55; Davies and Allison, *Matthew*, pp. 163-65.

2. According to Kingsbury ('The Title "Son of David" in Matthew's Gospel', *JBL* 95 [1976], pp. 597-98), 'since in Jewish circles it was the acknowledgment of a male child by a man that made that child his son, and not the physical act of procreation as such, the fact that Matthew depicts Jesus as being adopted into the line of David (1.20, 25) does not mean that his Davidic lineage is therefore in any sense questionable'.

3. On this theme, see D.C. Duling, 'The Therapeutic Son of David: An Element in Matthew's Christological Apologetic', *NTS* 24 (1978), pp. 392-410.

4. Daube (*NT and Rabbinic Judaism*, pp. 20-21) notes the rabbinic tradition, albeit late, that Ps. 118 'was composed when David became king, and will be recited when the Messiah appears'—and, in particular, the detail that some parts of the

Matthew's attention to the title 'son of David' in the mouths of the blind men in 9.27 and 20.30-31, at the healing of the blind and dumb demoniac in 12.22-23, as well as of other outcasts (e.g. the Gentile woman, 15.22)—and especially in connection with the healing of the τυφλοὶ καὶ χωλοί in 21.14 (i.e. between the acclamations of 21.9 and 15)—may be intended as a pointed rejoinder to the historical David's cursing of the τυφλοὶ καὶ χωλοί in LXX 2 Kgdms 5.8.[1] This would provide an instance of antithetical typology: whereas David forbade the blind and lame from entering 'into the house [אל־הבית/εἰς οἶκον κυρίου]', Jesus heals the blind and lame in the Temple, thereby reversing the curse and demonstrating by his compassion that he is greater than David.[2]

A similar motive may explain why the title 'son of David' is never placed on the lips of the disciples in Matthew's Gospel. This omission doubtless anticipates the outcome of the controversy in which Jesus, having invited the Pharisees to acknowledge that the messiah will be David's son, interprets Psalm 110 to show that the messiah, while of Davidic lineage, is also David's 'Lord' (22.41-45 // Mk 12.35-37).[3] For Matthew, Jesus both fulfills and supersedes the messianic expectations of the title 'son of David', with both functions being appropriate to a typological relationship.[4] As Nolan aptly puts it:

psalm are placed in the mouths of the crowd welcoming David or the messiah.

1. Cf. Gundry, *Use of the OT*, p. 140, 210; Cohen, *Jewish Bible Personages*, p. 80.

2. Other commentators, however, emphasizing the fact that Jesus is addressed as a 'son of David', see here an association with the popular renown of Solomon as a powerful healer and exorcist. See B. Chilton, 'Jesus *ben David*: Reflections on the *Davidssohnfrage*', *JSNT* 14 [1982], pp. 92-99.

3. So Goppelt, *Typos*, pp. 98-99 [ET pp. 83-84]. On the use of Ps. 110 in Christian tradition, see D. Hay, *Glory at the Right Hand: Psalm. 110 in Early Christianity* (SBLMS, 18; Nashville: Abingdon Press, 1973), esp. 110-18 on the present passage. According to Chilton ('Jesus *ben David*', pp. 100-105), the debate in 22.41-45 reflects an attempt (obscured to some extent in the Matthaean redaction) to differentiate between the therapeutic and messianic overtones of the title 'son of David' (see following note). Cf. McConnell, *Law and Prophecy*, pp. 156-57.

4. See discussion of this title, with particular attention to its supersession, in Kingsbury, *Structure, Christology, Kingdom*, pp. 99-103; *idem*, 'Son of David', *passim*. While the Q text regarding the 'queen of the South' and her visit to Solomon (12.42 // Lk. 11.31) is principally concerned with wisdom motifs, Goppelt (*Typos*, p. 99 [ET, p. 84]) sees in 'something greater than Solomon is here' a further

> The evangelist so dissociates the Christ from the Son of David in 22.42-45 that he can hint at the transcendence of the former without depreciating the descent from David.[1]

Further evidence of Davidic typology is found in Matthew's specification that Jesus' ancestor is Δαυὶδ τὸν βασιλέα (1.6), with βασιλεύς continuing to be applied to Jesus with messianic import elsewhere in the Gospel (2.2; 21.5; 27.11, 29, 37, 42). The citation of Mic. 5.1 and 2 Sam. 5.2 in Mt. 2.6 provides a specific scriptural basis for such a typology by establishing the reason for Jesus' birth in Bethlehem, as stated in 2.1: it is the city of David's birth (1 Sam. 16.1; 17.12, etc.) from which the ideal king is prophesied to come.[2]

Nolan sees Jesus' Davidic (hence kingly) identity as a key to understanding Herod's murderous opposition in Matthew 2.[3] More subtle is Jesus' appeal to the precedent of David eating the bread of the Presence to justify the conduct of his own disciples (12.3-6 // Mk 2.25-26). For since David, a type of the righteous king, took sacred bread from the Temple (according to tradition, on a Sabbath) and permitted his followers to share it, without this implying profanation or sacrilege, how much more so in the case of the one who is both 'greater than the Temple' and 'Lord of the Sabbath' (12.6, 8).[4]

Taken together, the preceding examples provide clear evidence that for Matthew Jesus does not simply repeat the patterns of David's life,

indication that Jesus is 'mehr als der erste Davidssohn, über welchem das für die messianische Erwartung grundlegende Verheißungswort an Davids Haus (2 Sam 7,11ff.) steht'. Cf. Gundry, *Use of the OT*, p. 210.

1. Nolan, *Royal Son*, p. 149. According to Goppelt (*Typos*, p. 100 [ET, pp. 48-85]), the texts cited thus far delineate a separate typological relationship between Jesus and the 'son of David', although Matthew's use of 'son of David' may simply be intended as one feature of a broader David/ Jesus typology.

2. On this citation, see Gundry, *Use of the OT*, pp. 91-93; Brown, *Birth*, pp. 184-86.

3. Nolan, *Royal Son*, pp. 154-58.

4. Cf. Goppelt, *Typology*, pp. 100-102 [ET, pp. 85-86]; Gärtner, *Temple and Community*, p. 116; France, *Jesus and the OT*, pp. 46-47. Nolan (*Royal Son*, pp. 170-200) sees Davidic overtones in a wide variety of incidents from Mt. 3–28, including Jesus' baptism and transfiguration, temptation, choice of twelve apostles, and feeding of the multitudes—as well as his depiction as a shepherd, teacher, healer, 'Davidic master of the temple', son and heir, foundation stone, bridegroom and suffering king—although it is difficult to see how all of these are specifically Davidic in intent.

or even fulfill the popular expectations to which they had given rise. Rather, the messiah's fulfillment of Davidic typology goes well beyond the parameters of such a model. While Jesus is a 'king' of Davidic lineage, to whom honour is due and in whom God's power is manifest, he is, for Matthew, much more than a national or political messiah. His reign will extend far beyond that of David, his earthly type.

4. *Moses*

The earlier discussion of Moses typology in Matthew's infancy narrative provides a starting point for the discussion of Moses' place within the Gospel as a whole.[1] Even the language of Matthew's infancy narrative seems intended to recall the biblical story of Moses' birth and providential protection (e.g. 2.14, 16, ἀνεχώρησεν εἰς Αἴγυπτον . . . τότε Ἡρῴδης ἀνεῖλεν πάντας τοὺς παῖδας; cf. LXX Exod. 2.15, Φαραω . . . ἐζήτει ἀνελεῖν Μωυσῆν· ἀνεχώρησεν δὲ Μωυσῆν). Furthermore, as Brown observes, 'the puzzling plural verb in Matthew [2.20, τεθνήκασιν γὰρ οἱ ζητοῦντες τὴν ψυχὴν τοῦ παιδίου] (when only Herod has died) may represent a direct quotation from the LXX of

1. See above, Chapter 1, §B.5, where the relevant literature is cited. On the widespread Moses/Messiah typology in rabbinic and Qumran literature, see H.J. Schoeps, *Theologie und Geschichte des Judenchristentums* (Tübingen: Mohr [Paul Siebeck], 1949), pp. 87-98; J. Jeremias, 'Μωυσῆς', *TWNT*, IV, pp. 862-68 [*TDNT*, pp. 857-64]; R. Bloch, 'Quelques aspects', pp. 149-66; R. Schnackenburg, 'Die Erwartung des "Propheten" nach dem Neuen Testament und den Qumran-Texten', *SE*, I, pp. 631-36. Cf. the rabbinic adage, כגואל ראשון—כגואל אחרון ('As the first redeemer [i.e. Moses], so the last redeemer [i.e. the Messiah]'; so *Midr. Qoh.* 1.28 on 1.9, etc.). Also note the several examples from Josephus (cited by Jeremias, *TWNT*, IV, p. 866 [*TDNT*, p. 862]; Horsley, '"Like One of the Prophets of Old"', pp. 455-61; *idem*, 'Popular Prophetic Movements', pp. 8-10; Feldman, 'Prophets and Prophecy in Josephus', p. 410) of messianic leaders who consciously acted out a Moses typology, calling for an exodus into the wilderness with promises of confirmatory signs and wonders.

Material regarding the life of Moses is collected by G. Vermes, 'La figure de Moïse au tournant des deux testaments', in *Moise, l'homme de l'alliance* (Paris: Desclée, 1955), pp. 63-92; R. Bloch, 'Quelques aspects', pp. 93-167; C. Perrot, 'Les récits d'enfance dans la haggada antérieure au IIe siècle de notre ère', *RSR* 55 (1967), pp. 497-504; and, most exhaustively, W.A. Meeks, *The Prophet-King: Moses Traditions and the Johannine Christology* (NovTSup, 14; Leiden: Brill, 1967), pp. 100-281.

Exod 4.19 [τεθνήκασιν γὰρ πάντες οἱ ζητοῦντές σου τὴν ψυχήν]'.[1]

It has also been suggested that the account of Jesus' forty days of temptation in the wilderness (4.1-11) owes something to Israel's forty years in the wilderness, when the people put Moses—and God—to the test.[2] If, however, this were so, it would seem more appropriate to a depiction of Jesus as the new Israel than as a new Moses.

More relevant to a Moses typology is the proposal that, in order to recall Moses' fasting on Mount Sinai, Matthew combined Mark's notice that Jesus was in the wilderness 'forty days' (Mk 1.13) with Q's observation that he fasted for the entire time (cf. Lk. 4.2). Thus Matthew specifies Jesus' having νηστεύσας ἡμέρας τεσσεράκοντα καὶ νύκτας τεσσεράκοντα (4.2), with the only purpose of the latter detail being that it echoes the language of LXX Exod. 34.28 and Deut. 9.9.[3] Admittedly, the connection of Moses' fasting and receipt of the Law with Jesus' fasting and temptation is not immediately evident. It becomes a possibility only when Jesus' forty days and nights in the wilderness are seen as a preparation for his teaching of the Law, which Matthew places in the chapter immediately following.

Of central importance to a Moses typology is the much-controverted question of whether Matthew's division of Jesus' teaching into five discourses (5.1–7.27; 9.36–10.42; 13.1-52; 18.1-35; 23.1–[or 24.1–]25.46) is intended to reflect the fivefold division of the Mosaic Torah.[4] Against this proposal is the fact that Matthew's five sections

1. Brown, *Birth*, p. 113 n. 38; cf. Davies, *Setting*, p. 78; Gundry, *Use of the OT*, pp.130-31.

2. So, e.g., Teeple, *Prophet*, pp. 75-76.

3. So Teeple, *Prophet*, pp. 77; W. Wilkens, 'Die Versuchung Jesus nach Matthäus', *NTS* 28 (1982), pp. 485-86. The same language is also used of Elijah in LXX 3 Kgdms 19.8; although note the negative estimation of Davies, *Setting*, pp. 45-48. Teeple and Wilkens also suggest that the detail of Jesus surveying 'from a very high mountain... all the kingdoms of the world' (4.8) recalls Moses' view of the promised land from Mount Nebo (Deut. 34.1-2). Cf. the fuller discussion and cautious conclusions of T.L. Donaldson, *Jesus on the Mountain: A Study in Matthean Theology* (JSNTSup, 8; Sheffield: JSOT Press, 1985), pp. 92-94 ('though the Moses/Nebo parallel has had some influence on the external details of the scene of temptation, it does not have any bearing on the content of the temptation'), with further bibliography, p. 247 n. 48.

4. This is not to say that Matthew's Gospel as a whole must necessarily exhibit a fivefold structure, for such a proposal leaves out of account the Infancy and Passion narratives and also depreciates the intervening narrative sections. Cf.

bear no resemblance to the five books of the Pentateuch. Nonetheless, several considerations weigh in favor of such a correspondence. First, the formula by which Jesus introduces his teaching, 'You have heard that it was said...ἐγὼ δὲ λέγω ὑμῖν' (5.21-22, 27-28, 31-32, 33-34, 38-39, 43-44), assumes by its use of the emphatic personal pronoun an authority corresponding to or greater than that of Moses.[1] Secondly, it is surely not coincidental that, like Moses on Sinai, having prepared by forty days and nights of fasting, Jesus delivers this first discourse from a mountain (5.1).[2] Not only the structure, therefore, but to some extent also the content and manner of Jesus' teaching recall that of Moses.

Thirdly, the formulae with which Matthew concludes the first four teaching sections (καὶ ἐγένετο ὅτε ἐτέλεσεν ὁ Ἰησοῦς [τοὺς λόγους

discussions of the structure of Matthew's Gospel (and bibliographic surveys) in Kingsbury, *Structure, Christology, Kingdom*, pp. 1-7; D.R. Bauer, *The Structure of Matthew's Gospel: A Study in Literary Design* (JSNTSup, 31; Sheffield: Almond Press, 1988), pp. 21-55; Davies and Allison, *Matthew*, pp. 58-72.

1. Teeple (*Prophet*, pp. 78-81) rightly insists that Jesus does not thereby overthrow, but rather authoritatively reinterprets the Mosaic Law (on Jesus' affirmation of Torah, cf. 5.17-20; 22.40; on the issue of his authority, cf. 7.29; 8.8-9; 9.6-8; 21.23-27; 28.18). See also Goppelt, *Typos*, p. 78 [ET, pp. 67-68]; G. Friedrich, 'προφήτης κτλ.', *TWNT*, VI, p. 848 [= *TDNT*, p. 847]. With respect to possible allusions to the Pentateuch in Mt. 9 and 17, van Dodewaard ('La force évocatrice', pp. 489-90) and Hartman ('Scriptural Exegesis', p. 147) make the attractive suggestion that by citing Moses, Jesus establishes his own position as a second Moses. Such an observation would be even more applicable to Mt. 5. A Mosaic typology cannot, however, be established on this basis alone, since it would require a similar Mosaic role for every rabbi who ever quoted Moses, a Davidic typology behind every citation of the Psalms, an Isaiah or Daniel typology in every citation of Isaiah or Daniel, and so on. Nonetheless, Matthew often sets out the parameters of a typological relationship via scriptural quotations—although such quotations do not provide the sole grounds for the typology—and includes an explicit naming of the type in question.

2. Proposing an allusion here to Sinai are Kilpatrick, *Origins*, p. 108; Teeple, *Prophet*, p. 77; Fenton, *Matthew*, p. 77; Lohmeyer and Schmauch, *Matthäus*, pp. 75-76; Klostermann, *Matthäusevangelium*, p. 33; Green, *Matthew*, pp. 74-75; G. Bornkamm, 'Enderwartung und Kirche in Matthäus', in *Überlieferung und Auslegung*, p. 32 [ET, p. 35]; Gundry, *Matthew*, p. 66; Luz, *Matthäus*, I, pp. 197-98. Cf. summary discussion by Donaldson, *Jesus on the Mountain*, pp. 111-12, following the cautious affirmation of Davies, *Setting*, p. 108, but arguing for a Mount Zion rather than a Mount Sinai typology.

τούτους/τὰς παραβολὰς ταύτας, etc.]; 7.28; 11.1; 13.53; 19.1), and especially that of 26.1 (καὶ ἐγένετο ὅτε ἐτέλεσεν ὁ Ἰησοῦς πάντας τοὺς λόγους τούτους), appear to reflect a similar phrase at the conclusion of the Pentateuch. So in LXX Deut. 31.24 Moses completes the writing of the book of the Law: Ἡνίκα δὲ συνετέλεσεν Μωυσῆς γράφων πάντας τοὺς λόγους τοῦ νόμου τούτου (cf. 32.44-45).[1] The striking similarity of Matthew's wording suggests that he intended 26.1 to be seen as an allusion to Moses and the Pentateuch, and then, as a structural anticipation of this conclusion, formed the first four formulae on the same basis.

Further evidence for a Moses typology in Matthew has been discerned in the narrative section (chs. 8–9) that follows the Sermon on the Mount. For there Matthew coordinates in sequence ten of Jesus' miracles from Mark, Q and his unique material, possibly recalling the ten miracles of Moses in Egypt that were celebrated by rabbinic tradition (*m. Ab.* 5.4) and were expected to have their counterpart in the last days (Mic. 7.15).[2]

In addition, Matthew may have emended his account of the Transfiguration in order to recall Moses' experience on Mount Sinai. Already present in Mk 9.2 is the otherwise inexplicable detail that Jesus and his three disciples ascended the mountain 'after six days' (17.1), probably in imitation of Exod. 24.16: 'The glory of the Lord settled on Mount Sinai, and the cloud covered it six days, and on the seventh day he called to Moses out of the midst of the cloud'. Here too a νεφέλη φωτεινή[3] represents the divine presence, out of the midst of which a voice testifies to the Son's identity (17.5 // Mk 9.7) in terms

1. As in Deut. 31.24, so in Matthew the formula is not simply conclusive, but rather is a transitional statement that is prefaced by a temporal particle and introduces a subsequent action. Matthew has merely substituted the equivalent ὅτε (Matthew 12×; Mark 12×; Luke 12×; cf. Schenk, *Sprache*, p. 447) for the less common ἡνίκα of the LXX (in the NT only at 2 Cor. 3.15, 16). Cf. Lagrange, *Matthieu*, p. lxxxv. Similarly, Teeple (*Prophet*, p. 83) sees a primary reference to Deut. 32.45, but only via an independent rendering of the MT.

2. So Schoeps, *Theologie und Geschichte*, p. 93; cf. G. Friedrich, 'προφήτης κτλ.', *TWNT*, I, p. 848 [= *TDNT*, p. 847]; Schnackenburg, 'Erwartung', p. 637; Teeple, *Prophet*, pp. 82-83; but see the critiques by Davies, *Setting*, pp. 86-92, and Gundry, *Matthew*, p. 138.

3. Presumably this is Matthew's attempt, inspired by the account in Exodus, to convey simultaneously the notions of cloud and glory; cf. Mk 9.7, νεφέλη.

strongly reminiscent of Deut. 18.15 (ἀκούετε αὐτοῦ).[1] Even more significant is Matthew's statement, which is not found in Mark, regarding the transformation of Jesus' face: καὶ ἔλαμψεν τὸ πρόσωπον αὐτοῦ ὡς ὁ ἥλιος (17.2; cf. Lk. 9.29). For in Exod. 34.29 Moses' face shone with divine glory, a feature made much of elsewhere in early Christian tradition (2 Cor. 3.7-18; cf. 2 Pet. 1.17-18).[2]

Finally, it is important to observe that in this same episode Moses and Elijah appear, speaking with Jesus (17.3 // Mk 9.4). Peter's offer to construct three booths (or 'tabernacles', recalling the festal commemoration of Israel's desert experience, and possibly also the command to build a tabernacle in Exod. 26, etc.) seems to imply equality among Moses, Elijah and Jesus. But both the command from the cloud ('This is my beloved Son. . . listen to *him*', 17.5) and the disappearance of the other two (with the emphatic οὐδένα εἶδον εἰ μὴ αὐτὸν Ἰησοῦν μόνον, 17.8) emphasize Jesus' superiority.[3] So here also Matthew sets out a Moses/Jesus typology, although, as always in his Gospel, with a stress on Jesus' supersession of this typological antecedent.[4]

5. *Jonah*

We have already explored in some detail Matthew's use of Q's references to Jonah (12.39-41 // Lk. 11.29-32),[5] and so need only summarize our findings here. Like Jonah, Jesus is for Matthew a

1. Cf. Schnackenburg, 'Erwartung', p. 637; Teeple, *Prophet*, pp. 84-86, 120; Davies, *Setting*, pp. 50-52. As Donaldson (*Jesus on the Mountain*, p. 143) observes, 'Especially noteworthy is the fact that the verb ἐπισκιάζω, used of the cloud in Mk 9.7 [// Mt. 17.5], also appears with reference to the cloud over the Tent of Meeting in Ex 40.35—one of the few occurrences of this word in the LXX'.

2. So Davies, *Setting*, pp. 50-52. Cf. Schlatter, *Matthäus*, p. 527 (followed by Gundry, *Use of the OT*, pp. 82-83), who sees in Jesus' face shining 'like the sun' a point of contact with the similar rabbinic tradition regarding Moses (*Sifre Num.* §140; פני משה כפני חמה). The two details of Jesus fasting 'forty days and forty nights' (4.2) and of Jesus' face reflecting the divine glory reinforce one another as allusions to Moses on Sinai, for the analogous incidents are juxtaposed in Exod. 34.28-29.

3. Cf. Davies, *Setting*, pp. 53-54.

4. On Jesus' transcendence of Mosaic categories in Matthew, see Davies, *Setting*, pp. 93-108; regarding the widespread acknowledgment in early Christian tradition of Jesus' superiority to Moses, see Teeple, *Prophet*, pp. 94-97.

5. See Chapter 2, §A.2.b.3, above.

preacher of repentance whose ministry portends a great judgment.[1] Moreover, like Jonah, Jesus suffers as a result of his ministry, enduring a three-day encounter with death: 'For as Jonah was three days and three nights in the belly of the whale, so will the Son of man be three days and three nights in the heart of the earth' (12.40). But neither Jonah nor the 'Son of man' remain in the domain of death: both return to life, which return is understood—at least in the case of Jesus—as a sign of vindication.[2]

In his expansion of Q in 12.40a, Matthew specifically quotes LXX Jon. 2.1 (ἦν Ιωνας ἐν τῇ κοιλίᾳ τοῦ κήτους τρεῖς ἡμέρας καὶ τρεῖς νύκτας),[3] once more adducing a specific scriptural warrant in support of his typology. For Matthew the typological relationship sheds light on the meaning of Jesus' ministry in terms of Jesus' and Jonah's respective identities as prophets, their ministries as preachers of repentance, their personal destinies of suffering and death, and their experiences of resurrection.[4]

So in this typological juxtaposition we again find both continuity and discontinuity. The point of the Q comparison, which Matthew retains, is in the double contrast that it entails:

> The men of Nineveh will arise at the judgment with this generation and condemn it; for they repented at the preaching of Jonah, and behold, something greater than Jonah is here (12.41).

The first contrast is between the repentance of the Gentiles and the implied impenitence of Israel, who are God's people. But even more

1. In his discussion of this Q passage, Edwards (*Sign of Jonah*, pp. 85-86) proposes that 'the phrase, "the sign of Jonah", is the result of Q's tendency to correlate OT figures with the Son of Man in the context of judgment'. He designates this feature of Q 'the eschatological correlative', which 'is a formal way of bringing together the past, present, and future by correlating an OT figure, or a present phenomenon, with the imminent appearance of the Son of Man'. In the context of the present discussion it would seem appropriate, however, to view this tendency to juxtapose analogous past, present and future phenomena simply as a further species of typology, particularly insofar as the 'eschatological [or, more properly, prophetic] correlative' is widely present in the OT, as well as in Qumran literature. Cf. the critique of Kloppenborg, *Formation*, pp. 129-30; see also further examples at Mt. 24.27 // Lk. 17.24; Mt. 24.37-39 // Lk. 17.26-27; Lk. 17.28-30.

2. Cf. France, *Jesus in the OT*, pp. 43-45; Strecker, *Weg*, pp. 104-105.

3. Cf. Gundry, *Use of the OT*, pp. 136-37.

4. Cf. Cohen, *Jewish Bible Personages*, pp. 104-105.

striking is the contrast between 'Jonah the prophet' and Jesus himself, who is 'greater than Jonah' and yet remains unrecognized. On both grounds, then, shall the people of Nineveh 'arise at the judgment with this generation and condemn it'.[1] Thus will the Ninevites themselves testify from their eschatological vantage point to Jesus' fulfillment of the type of Jonah.

6. *Noah*

In his supplement to the Olivet Discourse Matthew includes a Q passage very similar to that which concerned Jonah, except that here the focus is on Noah:

> For as were the days of Noah, so will be the coming of the Son of man. For as in those days before the flood they were eating and drinking, marrying and giving in marriage, until the day when Noah entered the ark, and they did not know until the flood came and swept them all away, so will be the coming of the Son of man (24.37-39).[2]

The effect of the Matthaean redaction in this passage is to emphasize Noah by deleting the parallel reference to Lot (Lk. 17.28-29; cf. v. 32; also 2 Pet. 2.5-8). Both Noah and the coming Son of man are (not unlike Jonah and Jesus) figures who represent the promise of salvation in the midst of a great and sudden judgment.

As J.C. VanderKam points out, Noah figures prominently in a wide range of Second Temple and NT literature, most frequently in association with righteousness (e.g. Sir. 44.17; *Jub.* 5.19; 7.34; 10.17; Wis. 10.4; *1 En.* 65.6; 67.1; 84.6; Heb. 11.7; 2 Pet. 2.5; Josephus, *Ant.* 1.75; *4 Ezra* 3.11, etc.)[3] Especially significant for this study, however, are the literary and theological functions of Noah's righteousness. For particularly in the case of *Jubilees* and *1 Enoch*, as VanderKam observes:

1. Cf. Goppelt, *Typos*, p. 75 [ET, p. 65].
2. Cf. Lk. 17.26-30; Q reconstructions in Schulz, *Q*, pp. 277-81; Polag, *Fragmenta Q*, pp. 76-78.
3. J.C. VanderKam, 'The Righteousness of Noah', in J.J. Collins and G.W.E. Nickelsburg (eds.), *Ideal Figures in Ancient Judaism: Profiles and Paradigms* (SBLSCS, 12; Chico, CA: Scholars, 1980), pp. 15-23. To this list may be added 1 Pet. 5.18-22, where a reference to the Christ as δίκαιος may well have suggested the ensuing comparison of baptism to the waters of the flood 'in the days of Noah'.

> the theologians who composed these books employed and edited the stories about Noah and his times because of their intense concern with the eschatological judgment and the righteousness that would guarantee salvation on that day. That is to say, Noah's flood was for them a type of the last judgment, and his righteousness... serves as a model of that obedience to the divine will which will enable one to endure the Lord's universal assize.[1]

From this analysis it is evident that the typological function of Noah in both Q and Matthew is altogether consistent with his role in other contemporary literature. The novel feature in Christian literature, of course, is the addition—whether explicit, as in Q and Matthew, or implicit, as in 2 Pet. 2.9; cf. 1 Pet. 3.20-22—of the eschatological messiah as the focus of the comparison and antitype to Noah.

Strictly speaking, Q's original comparison was between the 'days' of Noah and those of the 'Son of man', respectively (Q 17.26), whereas Matthew makes a somewhat more confusing comparison between the 'days of Noah', when people were preoccupied with other things, and the παρουσία τοῦ υἱοῦ τοῦ ἀνθρώπου (24.37). Nonetheless, to the extent that the relationship between Noah and the Son of man provides a focus for the contrast between proffered salvation and cataclysmic judgment—that is, a typological comparison between God's judgments past and future—we may also speak of that relationship as being typological. And since Matthew clearly understands 'Son of man' as a title for the messiah, he intends in his use of this passage a typological comparison between Noah and Christ. From this is derived the moral force of Jesus' concluding exhortation: 'Watch therefore, for you do not know on what day your Lord is coming' (24.42).

1. 'Righteousness', p. 25. Also relevant in comparison to Christian Noah typology is the observation of Patte (*Early Jewish Hermeneutic*, p. 163) that in *Jubilees* 5–6, 'Noah appeared as the type of those who would be saved from the "eschatological flood". He was therefore the moral type to be imitated. Yet he was also the type of the eschatological Israel with which God would renew the Covenant: the eschatological Israel would be a "new Noah"'. Further texts (in addition to those listed above) citing Noah (and Lot) and their respective generations in the context of divine judgement include Philo, *Vit. Mos.* 2.58-64; *T. Naph.* 3.4-5; *Gen. R.* §27 (on Gen. 6.5); and *m. Sanh.* 10.3 (on all of which see Lührmann, *Redaktion*, pp. 75-83); also *m. Ab.* 10.2.

C. *Typological Comparisons with Jeremiah*

All of the preceding examples serve as precedents for seeing in Matthew's use of traditions about Jeremiah a further typological comparison with Jesus.[1] For as we have seen with regard to Elijah and John the Baptist, to Moses and Jonah as types of Christ, and to Jesus as the exiled 'son' (2.15), Matthew cites specific passages of Scripture in support of a typology he wishes to establish, even when that typology is already present in his sources. So also Matthew establishes typological correspondences between Jeremiah and Jesus on the basis both of specific textual references and allusions and of more general thematic comparisons between the two.

The parameters of this typology are already evident from our study in Chapter 1 of Matthew's three explicit references to Jeremiah and in Chapter 3 of his several allusions to the literature of Jeremiah. In brief, Matthew employs these several references to Jeremiah—both to the prophet himself and to his writings—to depict Jesus as a suffering prophet who was opposed politically from birth, rejected by his own townspeople and nation, betrayed from within his own circle of disciples, denounced by false witnesses for having cited the words of Jeremiah against the Temple, and mocked at the hour of his death by a scornful populace. The account of the trial of the prophet in Jeremiah 26 seems especially to be in view. For Matthew depicts the fulfillment of Jeremiah's prophecy that in his undeserved death—or, as Matthew understands it, the death of one like him—'innocent blood' would come upon the city.

An altogether different thrust, however, is apparent in Matthew's references to the 'new covenant' of Jeremiah 31—in particular, its provisions of 'forgiveness of sins' and universal knowledge of God. Here Matthew sees in Jeremiah not only a figure of judgment, but also one who has to do with the restoration and reconstituting of the community of faith. Thus just as Jeremiah prophesied a new beginning, Jesus brings it to fulfillment.

Additional features that may support a Jeremiah typology include the prominence of the Babylonian exile in Matthew's genealogy and

1. This approach is in contrast to that of Dahlberg (which we discussed in relation to 16.14 [Chapter 1, §D.1.c, above]), in that it is based more broadly on a wide range of allusions throughout Matthew's Gospel.

Jesus' use of metaphors for divine judgment that seem to be taken from or are typical of Jeremiah (e.g. 'fishers of men', 'planting' and 'uprooting', the fig tree, and the forsaken Temple; cf. John the Baptist's 'winnowing fork' as a description of Jesus' ministry). In some of these instances, however, literary dependence on Jeremiah cannot be firmly established.

In Chapter 2 we saw that Matthew depicts John the Baptist, Jesus and Jesus' disciples not only as prophets, but as more than prophets. John and Jesus consistently transcend their typological antecedents. The same is true with respect to the comparisons between Jeremiah and Jesus. Others may compare him to any number of predecessors. 'But who', demands Jesus of his disciples, 'do you say that I am?' His superiority is evident in Peter's reply: 'You are the messiah' (16.14-16). More specifically, whereas Jeremiah only prophesied the dire consequences of his 'innocent blood' coming upon the city, or, conversely, the eschatological blessing of a 'new covenant', Matthew demonstrates that Jesus has, in fact, brought both to pass.

Were it not for the explicit reference to 'Jeremiah' in 16.14, it might be possible to account for most of Matthew's allusive references to the prophet simply as instances of scriptural rather than specifically typological fulfillment. But this passage represents a significant approximation of the messiah's identity that is confirmed, first, by the two fulfillment texts of 2.17-18 and 27.9-10, with their common focus on rejection, and, secondly, by the allusions that have been highlighted here.

Taken together, these explicit and implicit references suggest that here, as elsewhere, Matthew's use of scriptural fulfillment is not random, but rather focuses on and is intended to buttress a specific Jeremiah typology.

Chapter 5

THE JEREMIAH OF MATTHEW'S DAY

The thesis that Matthew makes use of Jeremiah typology in order to draw attention to the Deuteronomistic emphasis derived from his literary sources is strengthened immeasurably if it can be shown that Jeremiah was already seen within Second Temple Judaism as a prominent exemplar of Deuteronomistic themes. To this end, and building largely on Christian Wolff's *Jeremia im Frühjudentum und Urchristentum*, this chapter will survey relevant features of the various images and traditions associated with Jeremiah in biblical and post-biblical Judaism. Among the sources and authors examined will be Sirach, 2 Maccabees, the Epistle of Jeremiah, *Eupolemus*, the literature of Qumran, Philo, Josephus, Pseudo-Philo (Biblical Antiquities), *2 Baruch*, *Paraleipomena Jeremiou*, *Lives of the Prophets*, the Syriac Jeremiah Apocryphon, and, to some extent, rabbinic materials. The purpose here, however, will not be to investigate possible lines of literary or theological dependence, but rather to demonstrate how the literary and theological context of Second Temple Judaism illuminates Matthew's own use of Jeremiah traditions.

A. *Traditions of Destruction and Desolation*

Jeremiah's primary association with the fall of Jerusalem and the defeat and exile of Judah derives in the first instance, of course, from the canonical books of Jeremiah and Lamentations, and requires little elaboration. The ascription of the latter work to Jeremiah,[1] first attested by the LXX, indicates, in fact, that as early as the second, if not the third century BCE, this prophet was already characterized as a figure of woe and desolation. No less significant is the treatment of

1. Cf. p. 165 n. 2, above.

Jeremiah in the closing chapter of 2 Chronicles. For there we note not only a typically Deuteronomistic summary of Judah's last days ('The Lord, the God of their fathers, sent persistently to them by his messengers...but they kept mocking the messengers of God, despising his words, and scoffing at his prophets, till the wrath of the Lord rose against his people, and there was no remedy', 36.15-16 [// LXX 1 Esd. 1.48-49]), but also the fact that Jeremiah is the only prophet actually mentioned in the immediate context. So in 2 Chron. 36.12 (// 1 Esd. 1.45) we learn of Zedekiah's refusal to 'humble himself before Jeremiah the prophet, who spoke from the mouth of the Lord', while in 36.21 (// 1 Esd. 1.54) the destruction and exile are said to take place 'to fulfill the word of the Lord by the mouth of Jeremiah'. We have already had more than one occasion to observe Jeremiah's role as a suffering prophet par excellence. To recapitulate briefly, Jeremiah is mocked and cursed (Jer. 15.10; 20.7-8), persecuted and plotted against (Jer. 17.18; 18.18; 20.10), beaten and put into stocks (Jer. 20.2; 37.15), imprisoned (Jer. 32.2-3; 33.1; 37.15-16), cast into a cistern (Jer. 38.6), threatened with burning (*Eupolemus*, Fragment 4, in Eusebius, *Praeparatio Evangelica* 9.39.3)[1] or some less specific means of death (Jer. 11.19, 21; 26.8, 11), and, ultimately, martyred by stoning (*Liv. Proph.* 2.1; *Par. Jer.* 9.31-32; *Midrash Haggadah* on Num. 30.15).[2]

1. *Pharisaic/Rabbinic Judaism*

According to the rabbis, Jeremiah was the prophet of doom and destruction (*y. Sanh.* 11.7 [30b]; *b. Sanh.* 94b-95a; *b. B. Bat.* 14b), lamenting the necessity of his own persecution (*Pes. R.* 26).[3] It is

1. Greek text (with ET) in C.L. Holladay, *Fragments from Jewish Hellenistic Authors.* I. *Historians* (Chico, CA: Scholars Press, 1983), pp. 132-35. The work of Eupolemos likely dates from the mid-second century BCE; cf. N. Walter, 'Fragmente jüdisch-hellenistischer Historiker', in *Historische und legendarische Erzählungen* (JSHRZ, 1.2; Gütersloh: Gerd Mohn, 1976), pp. 95-96; Wolff, *Jeremia*, pp. 16-17; Holladay, *Fragments*, p. 93; F. Fallon, 'Eupolemos', in Charlesworth, *OT Pseudepigrapha*, II, pp. 862-63, 871.

2. Cf. Wolff, *Jeremia*, pp. 90-93; Menken, 'References', pp. 18-19. We must keep in mind, however, that there was also a tradition that Jeremiah died a natural death (e.g. *2 Bar.* 85.3[?]; *S. 'Ol. R.* 26; Jerome, *Comm. in Isa.* 30.6 [*PL* 24.342]), and that his demise was variously located in Egypt, Babylon or Judah (cf. Amaru, 'The Killing of the Prophets', pp. 175-76).

3. Cf. Chapter 1, §D.1.e and Chapter 2, §A.1.e, above.

therefore not surprising that *Gen. R.* 64.5 makes Jeremiah the son of a persecuted and fleeing prophet, interpreting the double curse of Jer. 20.14 ('Cursed be the day on which I was born, the day when my mother bore me') as referring not only to Jeremiah's birth but also to the day of his conception. Persecution, in other words, characterized his lineage and creation, as well as his personal experience. And in a similar vein *Exod. R.* 24.1 applies the description of Deut. 32.5, 'a perverse and crooked generation [דור עקש ופתלתל]', to those of Jeremiah's day,[1] explaining their 'foolishness' or 'perversity' by reference to Ps. 79.2: 'They have given the bodies of thy servants to the birds of the air for food'.[2] Thus not only persecution but also vaticide were said to be among the crimes of Jeremiah's generation.

2. *Sirach*

In Sir. 49.7 the fall of Jerusalem is said to have been caused by the people's mistreatment of Jeremiah.[3] In his praise of 'famous men and our fathers' (Sir. 44.1–50.21), Jesus ben Sirach interrupts the generally laudatory tone of his recitation to describe how the sins of the kings of Judah led to the sack of Jerusalem at the hands of a foreign nation:

1. These two references are cited by Schoeps, *Prophetenmorde*, p. 15. The latter text (cf. LXX γενεὰ σκολιὰ καὶ διεστραμμένη) is similar to the epithet γενεὰ ἄπιστος καὶ διεστραμμένη of Mt. 17.17 // Lk. 9.41 (cf. Mk 9.19 γενεὰ ἄπιστος), as well as the address of Mt. 12.39 and 16.4, γενεὰ πονηρὰ καὶ μοιχαλίς (// Lk. 11.29, γενεὰ πονηρά; cf. Mt. 12.45; Mk 8.38; Acts 2.40). The tradition recorded in *Exod. R.* 24.1, had Matthew known it, together with this form of address (which he emphasizes), would accord well with his use of Jeremiah typology. Cf. *Lam. R.* Proem 15, which also records the rejection and scorn of Jeremiah's generation.

2. Here the expression 'thy servants [עבדיך]' is apparently intended to recall the frequent equivalence 'my servants the prophets [עבדי הנביאים]' in Jer. 7.25, 25.4, 26.5, 29.19, 35.15, 44.4, Ezek. 38.17, Dan. 9.6, 10, Amos 3.7, Zech. 1.6, etc. (cf. Chapter 3, §B.1, above, on Mt. 21.33-34), thus referring implicitly to the fate of the prophet Jeremiah in particular. Cf. H. Freedman and M. Simon's suggestion (*Midrash Rabbah* [London: Soncino, 1939], III, p. 295 n. 2) of an allusion here to Jer. 7.33.

3. Similar, albeit more general sentiments are expressed by *b. Yom.* 9b; *Pes. R.* 29 (138a), 31 (146a); *Exod. R.* 31.16.

who set fire to the chosen city of the sanctuary, and made her streets
desolate by the hand of Jeremiah, for they had afflicted him
(ἐν χειρὶ Ιερεμιου· ἐκάκωσαν γὰρ αὐτόν/ביד ירמיהו כי עינוהו[1])
yet he had been consecrated...
to pluck up and afflict and destroy,
and likewise to build and to plant (49.6-7)

The LXX particle γάρ establishes, even more firmly than the Hebrew כי, a causal relationship between persecution and destruction, while the awkward rendering of the Hebrew idiom ביד ירמיהו by ἐν χειρὶ Ιερεμιου permits the impression that the prophet is himself a direct agent—presumably via his prophetic word—of the city's downfall.[2] Then, in conclusion, the responsibilities of Jeremiah's commissioning from Jer. 1.10 are rearranged so as to contrast more clearly their positive and negative aspects. Thus, as Wolff observes,

> Here, Jeremiah is the suffering prophet, whose mistreatment causes the destruction of Jerusalem and whose preaching is intended for the downfall and restoration of the nations.[3]

In a similar vein are the repeated references to the fact that Jerusalem could not be destroyed until Jeremiah (and his circle) had left the city (*2 Bar.* 2.1; *Par. Jer.* 1.1-3, 8; *Pes. K.* 13; *Pes. R.* 26.16; *Targ. Esth.* II to Est. 1.3), which makes the prophet's departure (not unlike that of Jesus according to Mt. 23.37–24.2) the immediate cause of its downfall.[4] But this fact is typically related to Jeremiah's more positive role as a mighty intercessor for the people and city (Jer. 15.11; 18.20; 37.3; 42.2-4; 2 Macc. 15.14; *Par. Jer.* 2.3; 9.3-6; cf. *2 Bar.* 85.2; *Liv. Proph.* 2.3; Syriac Jeremiah Apocryphon 160, 170, 176[5]). So his

1. Syriac = בימי ('in the days of').

2. Levi (*L'Ecclésiastique, ou la sagesse de Jésus, fils de Sira: Texte original hébreu édité, traduit, et commenté* [Paris: Leroux, 1898], I, p. 146) translates this line as 'à cause de Jérémie, qui avait été persecuté', noting that 'ביד signifie encore "à cause de", c'est à dire, comme l'avait prédit Jérémie, ou comme punition de ce qu'ils lui avait fait'. The LXX, however, interprets the כי, rather than ביד, as indicating causality.

3. Wolff, *Jeremia*, p. 15; cf. Menken, 'References', p. 18.

4. The departure of Jeremiah (along with Baruch and others) in *2 Bar.* 5.5 coincides with the departure of the Shekinah from the temple (*2 Bar.* 8.1-2).

5. This is a third or fourth century Christian redaction of an earlier Jewish work, possibly in Greek (cf. Wolff, *Jeremia*, pp. 53-54). For text and introduction, see A. Mingana, 'A Jeremiah Apocryphon', in *Woodbrooke Studies: Christian Documents in Syriac, Arabic, and Garshūni, Edited and Translated with a Critical Apparatus,*

prayers are said to be 'like an unbreachable wall' for Jerusalem (*Par. Jer.* 1.2; cf. *2 Bar.* 2.1).[1]

3. *Josephus*

Like the sources already cited, Josephus too recounts the sufferings of Jeremiah (e.g. *Ant.* 10.90-95, 114-115, 119-125). In addition, he makes the highly significant observation that Jeremiah prophesied not only the destruction of Jerusalem in his own day (*Ant.* 10.89, 93, 112, 117-118) and its subsequent restoration (10.113; 11.1), but also its destruction under Titus:[2]

> This prophet also announced the misfortunes that were to come upon the city, and left behind writings concerning the recent capture of our city, as well as the capture of Babylon (*Ant.* 10.79).[3]

Even more striking is the fact that Josephus sees himself not only as a 'second Jeremiah' in his warnings to the citizens of the doomed city, but also as being mistreated for his efforts more severely than the prophet after whom he modeled himself![4] Having gone over to the

with Introductions by R. Harris (Cambridge: Heffer, 1927), I, pp. 125-38, 148-233 [= *BJRL* 11 (1927), pp. 329-42, 352-437]. The late and uncertain date of this work obviates any direct relevance for Matthew. Nonetheless, it demonstrates the longevity and ongoing significance of key themes also illustrated in earlier Jeremiah literature. Related to the Syriac version is the *Coptic Jeremiah Apocryphon* edited by K.H. Kuhn ('A Coptic Jeremiah Apocryphon', *Le Muséon* 83 [1970], pp. 95-135, 291-350), which, like the Syriac, is dependent on *Paraleipomena Jeremiou*, and therefore must be dated after that work ('Apocryphon', pp. 101, 104).

1. According to *Paraleipomena Jeremiou* Jeremiah's prayers are like a 'pillar' and 'wall', whereas according to *2 Baruch* those of Baruch serve such a function. This would appear to be a further instance of the way in which, as Nickelsburg has argued ('Narrative Traditions', pp. 65-66), *2 Baruch* reverses the roles of the prophet and his scribe found in his source material, to which *Paraleipomena Jeremiou* bears independent witness. On the several texts cited above, and Jeremiah's role in general as an intercessor, cf. Wolff, *Jeremia*, pp. 83-89.

2. As did also, according to *Ant.* 10.79-80, 106, 276, both Ezekiel and Daniel.

3. οὗτος ὁ προφήτης καὶ τὰ μέλλοντα τῇ πόλει δεινὰ προεκήρυξεν, ἐν γράμμασι καταλιπὼν καὶ τὴν νῦν ἐφ' ἡμῶν γεγομένην ἅλωσιν τήν τε Βαβυλῶνος αἵρεσιν.

4. Cf. Daube, 'Typology in Josephus', p. 20; and further, Feldman, 'Prophets and Prophecy in Josephus', pp. 388, 406, 421-22; S.J.D. Cohen, 'Josephus, Jeremiah, and Polybius', *History and Theory* 21 (1982), pp. 367-68, 370-77 (with bibliographical survey, p. 366 n. 2); T. Rajak, *Josephus: The Historian and his Society* (London: Gerald Duckworth, 1983), p. 170.

Roman side, Josephus appeals for the zealot defenders of Jerusalem to surrender (*War* 5.362, 376-420), urging them to spare themselves further suffering much as Jeremiah had urged King Zedekiah and his subjects in the face of the Babylonian threat (*Ant.* 10.117, 125, 128; cf. Jer. 38.2-3, 17-18). The defenders, however, revile and attack him (*War* 5.362, 375), whereupon Josephus responds that his fate is worse than that of Jeremiah:

> For, though Jeremiah loudly proclaimed that they were hateful to God for their transgressions against Him, and would be taken captive unless they surrendered the city, neither the king nor the people put him to death. But you... assail with abuse and missiles me who exhort you to save yourselves, exasperated at being reminded of your sins (*War* 5.392-93).[1]

Nor was this Josephus's only similarity to Jeremiah, for they were also both of priestly descent (*Life* 1.1; *Ant.* 10.80). Furthermore, where similarities did not (at least according to the biblical record) already exist, Josephus, as Daube observes, simply invented them:

> According to the Bible, Jeremiah, when he exhorted Zedekiah to give in to the Babylonians and thus save the city, did not single out the Temple; according to Josephus, he did [*Ant.* 10.126, 128; cf. Jer. 38.17-23]—as did Josephus himself in that appeal to his compatriots where he likened himself to Jeremiah. Nothing in the Bible warrants Josephus' notice that as the Babylonian general was granting freedom to Jeremiah, the latter induced him to do the same for his disciple Baruch [*Ant.* 10.156, 158; cf. Jer. 40.1-6]; Josephus himself did obtain from Titus the release of his brother and many friends [*Life* 419-21].[2]

Josephus's gratuitous reformulation of biblical history for the purposes of his narrative self-portrait demonstrates the importance for him of Jeremiah as a typological model. In fact, it is this interest

1. βοῶντα γοῦν τὸν Ἰερεμίαν, ὡς ἀπέχθοιντο μὲν τῷ θεῷ διὰ τὰς εἰς αὐτὸν πλημμελείας, ἁλώσοιντο δ'εἰ μὴ παραδοῖεν τὴν πόλιν, οὔθ' ὁ βασιλεὺς οὔθ' ὁ δῆμος ἀνεῖλεν. ἀλλ' ὑμεῖς...ἐμὲ τὸν παρακαλοῦντα πρὸς σωτηρίαν ὑμᾶς βλασφημεῖτε καὶ βάλλετε, παροξυνόμενοι πρὸς τὰς ὑπομνήσεις τῶν ἁμαρτημάτων...

J. Neusner (*A Life of Yohanan ben Zakkai, Ca. 1-80 CE* [SPB, 6; Leiden: Brill, 1970], pp. 157-59; similarly in *First-Century Judaism in Crisis: Yohanan ben Zakkai and the Renaissance of Torah* [Nashville: Abingdon Press, 1975], pp. 146-47), in noting Josephus's appeal to the example of Jeremiah, suggests that the same model influenced the depiction of Yohanan ben Zakkai's warning to his fellow-citizens, and later encounter with Vespasian, in the days of the Roman war (Cf. *ARN* 4.6).

2. Daube, 'Typology in Josephus', pp. 26-27.

in Jeremiah, according to Daube, that accounts for Josephus ascribing to him a prophecy of the second fall of Jerusalem.[1]

Nor does Josephus compare himself alone to Jeremiah. In *War* 6.300-309 he describes the unfortunate prophet Jeshua ben Ananias in similar terms. For Jeshua began more than seven years of lamentation against the Holy City, characterized simply by the unchanging cry 'Woe to Jerusalem', by standing in the Temple and shouting:

> A voice from the east, a voice from the west, a voice from the four winds; a voice against Jerusalem and the sanctuary, a voice against the bridegroom and the bride, a voice against all the people (6.301).[2]

Jeshua's message of woe against the city and the fact that he was beaten and tortured for his pains are themselves reminiscent of Jeremiah.[3] But in his notes to the translation, Thackeray[4] also points out that the phrase φωνὴ ἐπὶ νυμφίους καὶ νύμφας specifically recalls Jer. 7.34, where the Lord declares,

> I will make to cease... from the streets of Jerusalem the voice of mirth and the voice of gladness, the voice of the bridegroom and the voice of the bride; for the land shall become a waste.

This same lamentation over 'bridegrooms and brides' is also found in Jer. 16.9, 25.10 and 33.11, but only once elsewhere in the prophetic corpus (Joel 2.16) is there anything similar, which makes this motif characteristic of the prophet Jeremiah.[5] So Josephus appeals once

1. 'Typology in Josephus', p. 27.

2. φωνὴ ἀπ' ἀνατολῆς, φωνὴ ἀπὸ δύσεως, φωνὴ ἀπὸ τῶν τεσσάρων ἀνέμων, φωνὴ ἐπὶ Ἱεροσόλυμα καὶ τὸν ναόν, φωνὴ ἐπὶ νυμφίους καὶ νύμφας, φωνὴ ἐπὶ τὸν λαὸν πάντα.

3. Cf. Horsley, 'Like One of the Prophets of Old', p. 450-51. Vermes (*Jesus and the World of Judaism* [London: SCM Press, 1983], pp. viii-ix) suggests a further parallel between ben Ananias and the treatment of Jesus in the Synoptic Gospels; cf. the Slavonic addition at 5.199.

4. *Josephus*, III, pp. 464-65; cf. Gaston, *No Stone*, pp. 117, 442; Garland, *Intention*, p. 78 n. 51.

5. Joel 2.16: 'Let the bridegroom leave his room, and the bride her chamber'. The similarity to Jeremiah is particularly evident in the vocabulary of the LXX (φωνὴν νυμφίου καὶ φωνὴν νύμφης) and in the repeated reference by both Jeremiah and Josephus to the 'voice' as the subject of each imprecation. In its declaration against Babylon, the angel of Rev. 18.23 makes similar use of Jer. 7.34, etc.: 'the voice of the bridegroom and bride shall be heard in you no more'.

again to the typological precedent of Jeremiah in his depiction of Jeshua ben Ananias as a prophet of woe.

4. *Pseudo-Philo*

Josephus is not alone in applying the model of Jeremiah to various other national reversals. Pseudo-Philo's *Biblical Antiquities* 56[1] also uses Jeremiah typology in its portrayal of Saul. For when Samuel announces the Lord's selection of him as a ruler for Israel, Saul replies,

> Who am I and what is the house of my father that my lord should say to me this word? For I do not understand what you are saying, because I am young [*Non enim intelligo quem dicis, quoniam iuvenis sum*].

Here Saul's choice of words anticipates the similar objection by Jeremiah ('Behold, I do not know how to speak, for I am only a youth', Jer. 1.6), as Samuel, with remarkable prophetic prescience, immediately perceives:

> Who will grant that your word be accomplished?... Nonetheless, consider this, that your words will be compared to the words of the prophet whose name will be Jeremiah [*Tamen intende, quia assimilabuntur verba tua verbis prophete cui nomen erit Hieremias*].[2]

So Saul's first words as monarch-designate foreshadow the troubled nature of his reign. As Wolff concludes, 'when Saul answers with the words of Jeremiah, the prophet of misfortune, he is already to be characterized, with regard to his calling, as a king of misfortune'.[3]

1. The *Liber Antiquitatum Biblicarum* of Pseudo-Philo dates from the mid- to late first century CE; so Denis, *Introduction*, p. 162; Wolff, *Jeremia*, p. 9 n. 1; Nickelsburg, *Jewish Literature*, pp. 267-68; D.J. Harrington, 'Pseudo-Philo', in Charlesworth (ed.), *OT Pseudepigrapha*, II, p. 299; although C. Dietzfelbinger ('Pseudo-Philo: Antiquitates Biblicae [Liber Antiquitatum Biblicarum]', in W.G. Kümmel *et al.* (eds.), *Unterweisung in erzählender Form* [JSHRZ, I.2; Gütersloh: Gerd Mohn, 1975], pp. 95-96) proposes a *terminus ad quem* of 132 CE.

2. *Bib. Ant.* 56.6. The Latin text is cited by Wolff, *Jeremia*, p. 9; the ET is that of Harrington (see previous note).

3. *Jeremia*, p. 10; cf. p. 15: 'Jeremia ist für ihn der Prophet des Unglücks, mit dem deshalb Saul, der gescheiterte erste König Israels, parallelisiert wird'; similarly, Holladay, *Jeremiah*, II, p. 92.

5. *Qumran*

More personal in their appeal to Jeremiah as a figure of strife are the laments of 1QH:

> To them that preach misguidance,
> I am but a man of strife (2.14)
> ...
> So, for mine own part,
> to them that were once my [familiars]
> I am become [a reproach],
> an object of strife and discord unto my friends (5.22-23).[1]

Wolff suggests that these passages are modeled after Jer. 15.10, where the prophet cries out, 'Woe is me, my mother, that you bore me, a man of strife and contention to the whole land!'[2] Similarly, 1QH 8.30-31 ('There bursts forth, as it were, a blazing fire held in my [bones]...exhausting my strength every moment')[3] recalls Jeremiah's lament over his prophetic ministry, 'there is in my heart, as it were, a burning fire shut up in my bones, and I am weary with holding it in' (Jer. 20.9).[4] These are by no means the only citations of Jeremiah (and Lamentations) in the literature of Qumran.[5] But those cited

1. ואהיה איש ריב למליצי תעות...ואני הייתי על ע[ ]דני לריב ומדנים לרעי. The Hebrew text is from Lohse, *Texte aus Qumran*, *in loc.*; the ET is that of T.H. Gaster, *The Dead Sea Scriptures: In English Translation with Introduction and Notes* (Garden City, NY: Doubleday, 1976), pp. 149, 165 (who sees allusions to Judg. 12.2 [*sic*], Jer. 15.10 in 1QH 2.14, and to Prov. 6.19, 10.12 in 1QH 5.22-23).

2. אוי־לי אמי כי ילדתני איש ריב ואיש מדון לכל־הארץ. Cf. *Jeremia*, pp. 127-28; so Holladay, *Jeremiah*, II, p. 93. Philo (*Conf. Ling.* 44) also cites Jer. 15.10, but alters the text to mean the exact opposite of the original, which reinterpretation presumably constitutes a back-handed acknowledgment of the power of this biographical detail (cf. Holladay, *Jeremiah*, II, pp. 153-54).

3. ויפרח כאש בוער עצור בע[צמי]...להתם כוח לקצים.

4. והיה בלבי כאש בערת עצר בעצמתי ונלאיתי כלכל. The parallel is noted by S. Holm-Nielsen, *Hodayot: Psalms from Qumran* (Acta Theologica Danica, 2; Aarhus: Universitetsforlaget, 1960), pp. 157 n. 64, 167-68; J. Maier, *Die Texte vom Toten Meer* (Munich: Reinhardt, 1960), II, p. 101; Mansoor, *Thanksgiving Hymns*, p. 157 n. 3; Wolff, *Jeremia*, p. 128; Gaster, *Dead Sea Scriptures*, p. 178 n. 34.

5. See, e.g., the multiple allusions to canonical Jeremiah and Lamentations (highlighted by M.P. Horgan, 'A Lament over Jerusalem ["4Q179"]', *JSS* 18 [1973], pp. 222-34) in the lament over the desolation of Jerusalem, 4QapLam/4Q179 (brought to my attention by Dr Eileen Schuler; text in DJD, V, pp. 75-77; cf. 4Q385b col. ii.b.4-5); or those in CD, 1QH, 1QS and 4QDibHam

above are representative, indicating how at Qumran the experiences of Jeremiah were seen as paradigmatic for the sufferings of God's faithful.

The examples cited above lead to the conclusion that Matthew's use of Jeremiah typology is consistent both with the general view of him in Second Temple Judaism as a suffering and rejected prophet of misfortune (associated in particular with the fall of Jerusalem) and with the contemporary use of Jeremiah typology in the works of Josephus, Pseudo-Philo and the Qumran community.[1]

B. *Traditions of Restoration and Return*

We must not, however, overlook the fact that Jeremiah was also seen as the prophet of Israel's restoration and return—in particular, the

pointed out by Holladay (*Jeremiah*, II, pp. 92-93; with additional bibliography); as well as the reference to Jer 45.1, 4-5 in CD 8.20 (cf. §B.3, below).

In addition, Dr Devorah Dimant of the University of Haifa is editing a series of pseudo-Jeremiah fragments from the fourth Qumran cave (e.g., 4Q383, 4Q384, 4Q385^{b}, 4Q387^{b} and 4Q389a), publication of which will further illuminate the significance of Jeremiah at Qumran. They are part of a larger collection that also includes pseudo-Ezekiel and pseudo-Moses fragments, although Dimant notes that the pseudo-Jeremiah material is the briefest and most fragmentary in the collection. In a preliminary investigation, Dimant makes the significant observation that since 4Q385b and 4Q389a 'do not attest to any of the terminology or style distinctive of the Qumran community, and therefore do not form part of the literature authored by the community', their presence, like that of Greek fragments of *Epistle of Jeremiah* in 7Q, points to an interest in Jeremiah traditions on the part of the community that requires further study (communications with the author, 13 June 1992, 22 October 1992).

1. Cf. Wolff, *Jeremia*, p. 189: 'Jeremia erschien zumeist als Unheilsprophet und war mit der Zerstörung Jerusalems eng verbunden'. Matthew's depiction of Jesus as a type of Jeremiah can also be compared to the contemporary popular prophetic figures described by Horsley ('Like One of the Prophets of Old', pp. 450-61): either 'individual figures who delivered oracles of judgment or deliverance [or] leaders of sizable movements eager to participate in some new divine act of liberation' in fulfillment of an obvious typological precedent (p. 461). Yet Matthew's Jeremiah typology is closer to the first category of individuals who 'undertook to interpret the deeper or broader significance of their own socio-political situation' (p. 453), of whom Horsley cites Jeshua ben Ananias and John the Baptist, as well as the several lesser figures described by Josephus (*War* 6.285-88), as examples.

restoration of the Temple. So the book of Ezra begins, echoing 2 Chron. 36.22-23:

> In the first year of Cyrus king of Persia, that the word of the Lord by the mouth of Jeremiah might be accomplished, the Lord stirred up the spirit of Cyrus king of Persia so that he made a proclamation... 'Thus says Cyrus king of Persia: The Lord, the God of heaven, has given me all the kingdoms of the earth, and he has charged me to build him a house at Jerusalem, which is in Judah...' (Ezra 1.1).

The particular 'word' in question, of course, is Jeremiah's prophecy, 'Thus says the Lord: When seventy years are completed for Babylon, I will visit you, and I will fulfill to you my promise and bring you back to this place' (Jer. 29.10; cf. 25.12; 2 Chron. 36.21; Zech. 1.12, 7.5). It is this same 'seventy years' that the book of Daniel, addressing a subsequent crisis of national faith, later reinterprets to mean 'seventy weeks of years' (Dan. 9.2, 24–27), and that Ep. Jer. 3, *Sib. Or.* 3.280-81, *1 En.* 85-90, *T. Levi* 16.1–17.1 and *Ass. Mos.* 3.13-14 each make use of to exhort their respective audiences.[1] The longevity and versatility of this motif in subsequent writings serve to highlight the continuing relevance of Jeremiah's prophecy as an assurance of restoration in the midst of tribulation, even if thereby extending Israel's consciousness of being in exile.

1. *The Temple Furnishings*

Jeremiah's prophetic assurance of an eventual restoration is further reflected in the legends that came to be associated with him. There is, for example, a widespread tradition, extant in a variety of forms, that makes Jeremiah responsible for hiding the various sacred vessels and accoutrements from the sanctuary.[2] The earliest form of the legend is that of Eupolemus (in Eusebius, *Praeparatio Evangelica* 9.39.5), who simply reports that the only parts of the Temple furnishings that Nebuchadnezzar was not able to despoil were the ark and the tablets it contained, since these Jeremiah had preserved. A more elaborate version, likely from the first century BCE, appears in 2 Macc. 2.1-8[3]

1. On these passages, see Wolff, *Jeremia*, pp. 113-16; Knibb, 'Exile', pp. 253-61.

2. For discussion of this theme, see Wolff, *Jeremia*, pp. 61-79, on which the present review is largely dependent. Cf. Nickelsburg, 'Narrative Traditions', pp. 63-65, 67-68.

3. Cf. C. Habicht, '2. Makkabäerbuch', in W.G. Kümmel *et al.* (eds.).,

where Jeremiah instructs the deportees to take with them some of the sacred fire and then orders 'that the tent and the ark should follow with him [τὴν σκηνὴν καὶ τὴν κιβωτὸν εκέλευσεν ὁ προφήτης... συνακολουθεῖν]', whereupon he seals up the tent, ark, and altar of incense in a cave (2.4-5). This story is eschatological in focus, for when the people ask for details of the hiding-place, Jeremiah replies,

> The place shall be unknown until God gathers his people together again and shows his mercy. And then the Lord will disclose those things, and the glory of the Lord and the cloud will appear (2.7-8).

Later versions of this legend are found in *Liv. Proph.* 2.11, 14-18, *Par. Jer.* 3.9-11, 18-19, and Syriac Jeremiah Apocryphon 169, 173, 188 (cf. also, though without mention of Jeremiah, *Biblical Antiquities* 26.12-15; *2 Bar.* 6.7-9; *Liv. Proph.* 12.12-13)—to which may be compared accounts of Jeremiah saving the priestly vestments (Syriac Jeremiah Apocryphon 189; cf. *2 Bar.* 10.19) and committing the keys of the Temple to heaven for safekeeping (*2 Bar.* 10.18; *Par. Jer.* 4.4; Syriac Jeremiah Apocryphon 173; cf. *y. Šeq.* 6.2 [24a]; *b. Ta'an.* 29a; *Lev. R.* 19.16; *ARN* 4.6; *Pes. R.* 26.16).[1]

Jeremiah's dealings with the Temple furnishings envisage the prospect of ultimate restoration, for they cast him in the role of a caretaker and safekeeper. At the same time, however positive its outlook, this legend reinforces all the more strongly Jeremiah's primary association with destruction. For all of his actions, while gestures of hope, are nonetheless necessitated by the national catastrophe that he himself has foretold.

2. *Moses Typology*

Also relevant in this connection is the depiction of Jeremiah as a second Moses.[2] Like Moses (LXX Ps. 105.23), Jeremiah is ὁ

Historische und legendarische Erzählungen (JSHRZ, 1.3; Gütersloh: Gerd Mohn, 1975), pp. 169-77; Wolff, *Jeremia*, p. 20 n. 2. Here we note that 2 Macc. 2.1, 4 'claims to have have taken the story of Jeremiah and the temple furnishings from an extant written source' (Nickelsburg, 'Narrative Traditions', p. 68). Holladay (*Jeremiah*, I, p. 121, II, p. 91) understands this tradition to derive from Jer. 3.16-17; J.A. Goldstein (*II Maccabees: A New Translation with Introduction and Commentary* [AB, 41A; Garden City, NY: Doubleday, 1983], pp. 182-183) suggests possible parallels from classical literature.

1. On this latter theme, see Bogaert, *Apocalypse de Baruch*, I, pp. 234-41.
2. Cf. Wolff, *Jeremia*, pp. 79-83.

ἐκλεκτὸς τοῦ θεοῦ (*Par. Jer.* 1.1, 5; 3.5, 7; 7.16) and speaks with God face to face (*Par. Jer.* 1.4-5, 12; 3.6-7, 17; cf. Num. 12.8).[1] As Moses saved the exiles from poisonous serpents, so Jeremiah, according to *Liv. Proph.* 2.3-4, saved Egyptian Jews and Gentiles from asps' bites. With regard to the Temple furnishings in particular, just as Moses saw 'the inheritance of God' from Mount Nebo, that is where Jeremiah buried the Ark, which was also first shown to Moses, in anticipation that God's 'inheritance' would be restored (2 Macc. 2.4, 8). Furthermore, *Liv. Proph.* 2.14-18 informs us that only Aaron and Moses will be able to retrieve the Ark and tablets that Jeremiah hid, that Jeremiah carved the name of God in a rock at their hiding-place, and that 'a cloud like fire' guards the place until the last day, concluding:

> God bestowed this favour upon Jeremiah, that he might himself perform the completion of his mystery, so that he might become a partner of Moses, and they are together to this day (2.19).

Finally, *Paraleipomena Jeremiou* has Jeremiah leading the exiles home from Babylon and across the Jordan after the manner of Moses' entry into the promised land (8.1-4; cf. 6.23; 7.20; Syriac Jeremiah Apocryphon 184).[2]

Moses/Jeremiah typology in the apocalyptic writings of Second Temple Judaism is consistent with the comparison between these two figures both in canonical Jeremiah[3] and in rabbinic literature.[4] Its

1. Cf. Riaud, 'La figure de Jérémie', pp. 375, 379-81. In this sense, Jeremiah's role as a mighty intercessor is reminiscent of Moses ('La figure de Jérémie', p. 381).

2. Cf. Wolff, *Jeremia*, p. 50; Riaud, 'La figure de Jérémie', pp. 382-83. Jeremiah's role in exile is similarly consolatory, for God commands, 'You, Jeremiah, go with your people into Babylon and stay with them, preaching to them (εὐαγγελιζόμενος αὐτοῖς) until I return them to the city' (*Par. Jer.* 3.15; see also 5.21; cf. Riaud, 'La figure de Jérémie', pp. 375, 381-82).

3. See P.E. Broughton, 'The Call of Jeremiah: The Relation of Deut. 18.9-22 to the Call and Life of Jeremiah', *AusBR* 6 (1958), pp. 41-46; W.L. Holladay, 'The Background of Jeremiah's Self-Understanding', *JBL* 83 (1964), pp. 153-64; *idem*, 'Jeremiah and Moses: Further Observations', *JBL* 85 (1966), pp. 17-27.

4. So *Pes. K.* 13.6 and *Sifre Deut.* 155. See also *Pes. K.* 13.13; *Num. R.* 9.49 (on Num. 5.30); *Midr. Pss.* 1.3 ('וכן תמצא בירמיה מה שכתוב בזה כתב בזה [So, too, you find of (Moses and) Jeremiah, that what is said of the one is also said of the other]' [ET Braude]; so Meeks, *Prophet-King*, pp. 189, 200; but cf. Wolff, *Jeremia*, p. 82 n. 4), cf. 4Q385b col. i.

significance for the purpose of our study is the extent to which Moses typology may have contributed to Matthew's interest in Jeremiah. We have already seen that Matthew's depictions of Jesus as a Mosaic antitype (which includes Jesus' fulfillment of Deut. 18.15, whereby he, rather than Jeremiah, is the 'prophet-like-Moses') and as a Deuteronomistic 'prophet-like-Jeremiah' are different in focus and intent.[1] But while the dominant emphasis of Matthew's Jeremiah typology is that of rejection and suffering, Jeremiah is also significant in Matthew's Gospel, at least implicitly, as the prophet of the 'new covenant'.

So Matthew's depiction of Jesus as a 'second Moses', which theme implies covenantal renewal, is not inconsistent with an interest in the covenantal aspects of a Jeremiah typology.[2] Admittedly, Moses/Jeremiah typologies in apocalyptic and rabbinic literature focus on the Ark, the Exodus or the respective roles of these two prophets as mighty intercessors. Nonetheless, had Matthew been aware of this prior association of Jeremiah with Moses, his own interest in Mosaic typology would probably have suggested the further relevance for his depiction of Jesus of an independently developed Jeremiah typology.

3. *The 'New Covenant'*

As indicated earlier in discussing Mt. 23.8-10, Jeremiah's prophecy of a ברית חדשה (Jer. 31.31; LXX 38.31 διαθήκην καινήν) did not go unnoticed in Second Temple Judaism. Such a consciousness has been proposed, for example, in Baruch's summary of Moses' address from Bar 2.35: καὶ στήσω αὐτοῖς διαθήκν αἰώνιον τοῦ εἶναί με αὐτοῖς εἰς θεὸν καὶ αὐτοὶ ἔσονταί μοι εἰς λαόν.[3] Wolff demonstrates, however, that the recitation of Moses' words in Bar. 2.29-35 is closer to the language of Deuteronomy than to Jer. 31.31. Moreover, the concept of an 'everlasting covenant', rather than a 'new covenant' was widespread (Ps. 105.10; Isa. 55.3; 61.8; Jer. 32.40; 50.5; Ezek. 16.60; 37.26), as was the covenantal formula 'I will be their God, and they

1. See pp. 158-61, above.

2. Holladay ('Background', pp. 163-64) suggests that such a comparison of Moses and Jeremiah as covenantal mediators is already implicit in the Moses typology of canonical Jeremiah.

3. So J. Behm, *s.v.* 'διαθήκη', *TWNT*, II, pp. 130-31 [= *TDNT*, p. 128]; Jeremias, *Abendmahlsworte*, p. 188 n. 2 [ET, p. 195 n. 2]; Gunneweg, 'Das Buch Baruch', p. 175 n. IIp (with Jer. 32.38-40); Holladay, 'New Covenant', *IDBSup*, p. 625.

will be my people' (e.g. Lev. 26.12; Jer. 7.23; 11.4; 24.7; 30.22; 31.1; 32.38; Ezek. 11.20; 36.28; 37.27).[1] Yet while such evidence is weighty, some consideration should be given to the fact that Baruch, the scribe of Jeremiah, is the speaker in this instance, and that of the passages cited only Jer. 31.31-33, 32.38-40 and Ezek. 37.23, 26-27 combine the reference to a future covenant with the particular formula found in Bar. 2.35. Hence the contribution of Jeremiah to a renewed covenant—or, in this instance, to an 'eternal' covenant—may yet be in view.

Wolff is sceptical that any reference to Jeremiah 31 underlies *Jub.* 1.17 ('And I shall be their God, and they will be my people truly and rightly'),[2] since there is no mention here of a 'new covenant'. He admits that the renewal of God's covenant is in view, but argues that the language of *Jub.* 1.15-18 and 22-25 more readily recalls the promises of Israel's first covenant than those of Jer. 31.31-34.[3] Yet in *Jub.* 1.23-24 God promises:

> I shall create for them a holy spirit, and I shall purify
> them so that they will not turn away from following me...
> and their souls will cleave to me and to all my commandments.
> And they will do my commandments.

Thus this passage envisages not only repentance and spiritual faithfulness, but also a radical internalization of Torah that will enable obedience—which is precisely what both Jer. 31.33 and Ezek. 36.26 propose.

In contrast to *Jubilees*, the Damascus Document explicitly refers to the adherents of the community as entering into 'the new covenant (הברית החדשה) in the land of Damascus' (CD 6.19; 8.21 [= 19.33-34]; 20.12). The language is that of Jer. 31.31, as is most obvious from the wording of CD 20.12: [ה] ברית ואמנה אשר קימו בארץ דמשק והוא ברית החדשה ('the covenant and compact which they established in the land of Damascus, that is, the "new covenant"').[4] Moreover, CD 8.18

1. Wolff, *Jeremia*, pp. 117-19.
2. As proposed by Behm, Jeremias and Holladay.
3. Wolff, *Jeremia*, pp. 122-23.
4. Proponents of allusions to Jer. 31 in these passages include Behm, *s.v.* 'διαθήκη', *TWNT*, II, p. 131 [= *TDNT*, p. 128]; C. Rabin, *The Zadokite Documents*. I. *The Admonition*. II. *The Laws. Edited with a Translation and Notes* (Oxford: Clarendon Press, 1958), p. 25 (p. 19 n. 4), p. 36 (p. 21 n. 2), p. 39 (p. 12 n. 3); Maier, *Texte*, I, p. 55 n. a; II, p. 54; M. Black, *The Scrolls and*

distinguishes between the 'new covenant' and 'the covenant of the fathers' that will avail for 'those in Israel who in those latter days show repentance and eschew the way of the rabble'.[1]

In addition, CD 8.18-21 invokes divine wrath against the 'builders of the rickety wall' (an allusion to Ezek. 13.10-16 describing Israel's false prophets and unfaithful leaders), adding, 'It is to this that Jeremiah was referring when he spoke to Baruch the son of Neriah, and Elisha when he spoke to his servant Gehazi'. The latter references are apparently to Jer. 45.1, 4-5 (Jeremiah promises to break down what he has built, and pluck up what he has planted) and to 2 Kgs

Christian Origins: Studies in the Jewish Background of the New Testament (London: Nelson, 1961), pp. 91-92; F.M. Cross, *The Ancient Library of Qumran and Modern Biblical Studies* (Garden City, NY: Doubleday, 1961), p. 219; H. Braun, *Qumran und das Neue Testament* (Tübingen: Mohr [Paul Siebeck], 1966), II, p. 318 (as well as in the reconstructed text of 1QpHab 2.3; cf. I, p. 212; so, apparently, Lohse, *Texte aus Qumran*, pp. 229, 296 n. 2); Holladay, 'New Covenant', *IDBSup*, pp. 624-25; *idem*, *Jeremiah*, II, p. 93; cf. Wolff, *Jeremia*, p. 124 n. 3. The Hebrew text is from the edition of Rabin.

Because, according to Wolff, the Qumran covenant was seen as simply a renewal and more faithful following of the ancient covenant, 'der Bund von Qumran kein neuer Bund im Sinne von Jer 31,31ff ist' (*Jeremia*, pp. 126-27). But this is to apply too narrow an interpretation (from the perspective of Christian exegesis) to Jer. 31, which can itself be read as a reiteration of Israel's first covenant (cf. discussions cited above, p. 210 n. 1).

The influence of Jer. 31.34 may also be indicated by the language of CD 20.4, which describes members of the community as those 'taught of God [למודי אל]', wherein Rabin (*Zadokite Documents*, p. 38 [p. 4 n. 3]) discerns an allusion to Isa. 54.13, 'all your sons shall be taught by the Lord [למודי יהוה]'.

But immediately following is the parallel expression 'men of knowledge [אנשי דעות]', possibly also recalling the vocabulary of Jer. 31.34: 'No longer shall each man teach [ילמדו] his neighbour... saying, "Know [דעו] the Lord," for they shall all know [ידעו] me'.

1. Following the sense of Gaster's translation (*Dead Sea Scriptures*, p. 77): 'the same love which God showed to the men of old who pledged themselves to follow Him will he show also to their successors. The Ancestral Covenant shall stand good for them [כי להם ברית האבות].' While such passages might seem to imply two separate, yet concurrently valid covenants, this is not the case, for according to Cross (*Ancient Library of Qumran*, p. 219.), the sectarians 'understood this "New Covenant" to be at once the "renewed (old) covenant" and the "eternal covenant" to be established at the end of days'.

5.26-27 (Elisha curses Gehazi for his dishonesty), respectively.[1] But it is striking that this condemnation of those who proved unfaithful to the previous covenant ('all who reject his commandments and forsake them, and go on walking in the stubbornness of their own hearts', 8.19) should be followed immediately by the further condemnation of 'all those who entered into the new covenant in "the land of Damascus" but subsequently relapsed and played false and turned away from the well of living waters' (MS B 19.33-34).[2] In other words, the relevance of Jeremiah to the one group of apostates apparently suggests his relevance also to the other, if only in the mention of the ברית החדשה itself.

It cannot, therefore, be said that Jer. 31.31-34 is the only scriptural text that contributed to the expectation of a renewal or reaffirmation of God's covenant with Israel. Other passages, especially Jer. 32.40-41 and Ezek. 37.24-28, are no less significant. Nonetheless, the prophecy of a ברית חדשה or διαθήκην καινήν of Jer. 31.31-34 makes a distinctive contribution to the larger concept of covenantal renewal in the literature of Second Temple Judaism.

C. *Summary and Conclusions*

Both the minatory and the consolatory aspects of Jeremiah's prophetic ministry, as evidenced in the different sources we have reviewed, are in keeping with his first calling 'to pluck up and to break down; to destroy and to overthrow; to build and to plant' (Jer. 1.10). 2 Chron. 36.21-22, in fact, as perhaps the earliest commentary on his career, summarizes Jeremiah's ministry by emphasizing both aspects in parallel phrases: even as Nebuchadnezzar destroyed Jerusalem and exiled Judah 'to fulfill the word of the Lord by the mouth of Jeremiah [למלאות דבר־יהוה בפי ירמיהו]', so Cyrus repatriates the exiles to rebuild

1. So Rabin, *Zadokite Documents*, p. 36 (p. 20 n. 1); also Gaster, *Dead Sea Scriptures*), p. 77 nn. 36, 37; whence the ET is taken. But according to Wolff (*Jeremia*, p. 126, following Lohse, *Texte*, p. 289 n. 53), 'Man kann die Erwähnung Jeremias und Elisas kaum anders denn als Randglosse verstehen, die womöglich auf pseudepigraphische jüdische Schriften anspielt'.

2. This juxtaposition depends on the conflation of MS A, which includes the reference to Jeremiah and Elisha, but concludes at 8.21 = B 19.33, part way through the description of those who 'entered the new covenant in the land of Damascus', with MS B, which continues with the condemnation of the apostates.

the Temple, 'that the word of the Lord by the mouth of Jeremiah might be accomplished [לכלות דבר־יהוה בפי ירמיהו]'. And it is significant that even here the Temple is perceived to be the focus of Jeremiah's prophecies of restoration, just as the Temple and the city of Jerusalem had earlier formed the consistent focus of his prophecies of doom.

Matthew, it would appear, also saw both aspects of Jeremiah's career as significant. For in his Gospel the prophet is associated both with persecution, threats against the Temple and the destruction of Jerusalem, and, to a lesser extent, with the promised restoration of God's people by means of a 'new covenant'. In addition to these dominant emphases, two further possibilities have emerged: first, that the significance for Matthew of Jesus leaving the Temple and Holy City as a necessary prelude to its destruction may owe something to the similar departure of Jeremiah and his circle; and, secondly, that Moses/Jeremiah typology in Jewish tradition is consistent with the covenantal implications of Matthew's Moses and Jeremiah typologies, notwithstanding an emphasis in the latter instance on Deuteronomistic themes.

So, as we have seen, Matthew's Jeremiah typology coheres, on the one hand, with the Deuteronomistic emphasis that the Evangelist took over from his sources—including his depiction of Jesus as a rejected prophet—and, on the other, with the soteriological understanding of Jesus' death that was basic to early Christian theology (i.e. emphasizing the 'new covenant'). It likewise found a ready place within the context of the destruction (whether imminent or recent) of Jerusalem.[1] Jeremiah was for Matthew's contemporaries not only the archetypal suffering prophet, but also the prophet par excellence of the destruction of the city. And both of these considerations were eminently suited to Matthew's understanding and purposes: first, in explaining Jesus' death (he is rejected and killed because all prophets, without exception, suffer the same fate), and, secondly, in explaining the fall of Jerusalem (it is destroyed as an act of divine retribution for the peoples' rejection of John, the Christian disciples, and above all, Jesus).

1. Wolff (*Jeremia*, p. 96) draws a similar conclusion regarding the widespread use of traditions about Jeremiah in Jewish literature of the period: 'Daraus ist zu schließen, daß sich frühjüdische Kreise vor allem nach 70 n. Chr. lebhafter mit der Gestalt dieses Propheten beschäftigten. Dafür sprechen aber nicht nur die zahlreichen verschiedenen Überlieferungen, die sich an Jeremia hefteten, sondern auch die Bestrebungen, den Propheten immer mehr in den Vordergrund zu rücken.'

Chapter 6

MATTHEW'S VISION OF JEREMIAH

The results of this study thus far suggest that Matthew's interest in Jeremiah, whether textual or typological, was not primarily christological, but rather, apologetic, covenantal and ecclesiological. That is to say, because Matthew's references to Jeremiah represent a distillation and re-focusing of Deuteronomistic interests, they appear to have been motivated by the circumstances and interests of his own community: the need both to explain the fall of Jerusalem (hence 'apologetic', in the sense of enunciating a specific theodicy to account for that event) and to justify the establishment of the Christian community as a 'new Israel' in place of that which had suffered such a disastrous reversal (hence 'covenantal' and 'ecclesiological').[1] Accordingly, Matthew's depiction of Jesus as a suffering and rejected 'prophet-like-Jeremiah' must be examined, first, within the context of other contemporary responses to the fall of Jerusalem in 70 CE, and, secondly, with an eye to the needs of the community for which he wrote.

A. *Reactions to the Fall of Jerusalem in Second Temple Judaism*

Because Matthew's Deuteronomistic outlook links the rejection of John, Jesus and the Christian prophets to the destruction of the Temple and the city of Jerusalem, Matthew's Gospel must also be viewed

1. Taken by themselves, Matthew's fulfillment quotations are primarily christological in purpose, providing a basic outline of the life of the messiah in order to demonstrate its providential character. So, likewise, is Matthew's typology primarily christological in focus, indicating the messiah's 'fulfillment' of historical antecedents in the divine economy of salvation (above). But the example of Jeremiah (interpreted Deuteronomistically) provides a bridge between Christology and ecclesiology, whereby the Evangelist articulates the relevance of Jesus' experience to the experience of his community.

within the context of other contemporary Jewish responses to the fall of Jerusalem and the theological questions it raised. A theological imperative for consoling the people of God following the disaster of 70 CE (as well as that of 135 CE) can be seen in such works as Pseudo-Philo's *Biblical Antiquities* and the *Apocalypse of Abraham*—as well as, of course, in the later rabbinic literature. More specifically, such works as *4 Ezra*, *2 Baruch* and *Paraleipomena Jeremiou* draw on the analogy of the sixth-century BCE destruction, exile and later return, in order to console the post-70 CE Jewish community. The narrative analogy in these works between the destructions past and present becomes a means of reconstituting the community by providing a theological justification for its continued existence. Most significant for our purposes, however, is the fact that *2 Baruch* and *Paraleipomena Jeremiou* appeal directly to Jeremiah and his circle as figures who, on the basis of their association with the earlier destruction of Jerusalem, are able to address a similar situation in the reader's own day.

If, therefore, other writings contemporary with Matthew's Gospel have drawn on the analogy of Jeremiah in a positive sense, might not Matthew have done likewise, although with an opposite intent? Matthew's purpose, after all, was not to console the synagogue, but rather to explain its demise and replacement by the fledgling church. To this end Matthew's appeal to Jeremiah serves to focus and concretize the Deuteronomistic 'theodicy' already present in his sources.

1. *The Significance of the Temple*

The enormous impact on the religious psyche of first-century Judaism of the destruction of Jerusalem and its Temple can only be appreciated when one understands the significance of the city and the Temple as symbols of covenantal security.[1] Originally, the Temple had been the resting place for the Ark of the Covenant, whence it derived its sanctity and significance.[2] That God had caused his 'name' and 'glory'

1. It is unnecessary to distinguish here between the religious significance of the city of Jerusalem and that of the Temple proper, since the two are intimately connected. As W.D. Davies (*The Gospel and the Land: Early Christianity and Jewish Territorial Doctrine* [Berkeley: University of California Press, 1974], pp. 150-51; cf. pp. 152-54) observes, 'the pertinent texts move without warning from the Temple to Jerusalem and vice versa, so that these two entities, in their earthly and heavenly forms, are in constant association'.

2. Cf. R.E. Clements, *God and Temple* (Oxford: Basil Blackwell, 1965),

to dwell in the midst of his people affirmed his election and sanctification of Israel, as well as his protection of the city of Jerusalem.[1]

Yet the prophetic critiques of the Temple, and even more its actual destruction in 587 BCE, highlight the fact that the covenantal sanction afforded by God's 'presence' was not inviolable. The postexilic prophets acknowledged that God's presence and power were not limited to the Temple, or even to the land of Israel.[2] In *b. Yom.* 21b rabbinic tradition even asserts that the Shekinah—as well as a number of other significant features such as the Ark and the Holy Spirit—had never actually been present in the Second Temple (cf. *Num. R.* 15.10),[3] although according to that same passage 'they were present, but they

pp. 63-78; Davies, *Gospel and Land*, pp. 131-32.

1. Cf. Clements, *God and Temple*, pp. 71, 83; citing esp. Isa. 31.4-5. On the concepts of God's 'name' and 'glory' as designating the divine presence, see pp. 94-96, 113-18.

2. See, e.g., Mic. 3.12; Jer. 7.3-4, 12-15 (cited in Clements, *God and Temple*, pp. 84-85); Ezek. 1.1, 9.7, 11.15-16, 22-23 (*God and Temple*, pp. 103-105; with further discussion by Gaston, *No Stone*, pp. 105-110). As a result of such teaching, 'the people had come to experience that the divine presence could be with them even when no temple existed', since, after all, God's true dwelling place was in the heavens (Clements, *God and Temple*, pp. 130-31; cf. Isa. 66.1-2). Clements argues that, for the repatriated exiles, the absence of divine blessing from the return of God's presence to a rebuilt Temple occasioned the transfer of such hopes to the realm of the transcendent and eschatological (*God and Temple*, pp. 123-27; similarly, R.G. Hamerton-Kelly, 'The Temple and the Origins of Jewish Apocalyptic', *VT* 20 [1970], pp. 1-15). On the heavenly Jerusalem in intertestamental Judaism, see N.W. Porteous, 'Jerusalem-Zion: The Growth of a Symbol', in A. Kuschke (ed.), *Verbannung und Heimkehr* (Tübingen: Mohr [Paul Siebeck], 1961); rpr. *Living the Mystery: Collected Essays* (Oxford: Basil Blackwell, 1967), pp. 109-10. At the same time, however, the hope for restoration and glorification of the earthly Jerusalem was never altogether replaced; see Davies, *Gospel and Land*, pp. 134-50.

3. Cited by Clements, *God and Temple*, p. 126 n. 2; Gaston, *No Stone*, p. 109 n. 3; cf. Abelson, *Immanence of God*, pp. 261, 267; R.J. McKelvey, *The New Temple: The Church in the New Testament* (London: Oxford University Press, 1969), p. 23; and, more generally, *Lev. R.* 21.9 (on Lev. 16.3). Gaston (*No Stone*, pp. 114-17) finds other assertions of the comparative inadequacy of the Second Temple in *1 En.* 89.73; *Ass. Mos.* 4.8; 5.3-4; 6.1; *T. Levi* 16.1; *Jub.* 23.21, and *Pss. Sol.* 1.8; 2.3; 8.13; as does F.J. Murphy (*The Structure and Meaning of Second Baruch* [SBLDS, 78; Atlanta; Scholars Press, 1985], pp. 113-16). In addition, see Tob. 14.5 and *2 Bar.* 68 (as well as *2 Baruch* as a whole).

were not as helpful [as before].'[1] In Joel 2.27 and 4[3].16-17 ('I am the Lord your God, who dwells in Zion, my holy mountain, and Jerusalem shall be holy'), however, as well as in several depictions from post-70 CE literature that speak of the departure of the Shekinah from the Herodian Temple, there is the conviction of the Shekinah having always been present in the rebuilt sanctuary.[2]

Second Temple Judaism understood God's presence to imbue not only the Temple, but also the whole of Jerusalem and its people.[3] Nonetheless, the destruction of the city and its Temple would not for that reason have seemed any less devastating. On the contrary, the security of both the city and the Temple constituted a sign of divine favor and covenant faithfulness, while a corresponding zeal to preserve their sanctity, particularly in the aftermath of the Maccabaean crisis, had become a means of demonstrating 'political and religious loyalty' on the part of God's people.[4] In short, the fall of Jerusalem constituted a

1. אין מידוה הוה סיועי לא מסייעא. So also, in almost identical language, *2 Bar.* 68.5-6: 'Zion will be rebuilt again, and the offerings will be restored, and the priests will again return to their ministry. And the nations will come again to honor it. *But not as fully as before*' (emphasis added).

2. For references, see p. 143, above. The rabbinic tradition may have been motivated by apologetic concerns, that is, by an attempt to minimize the theological implications of the destruction. According to Abelson (*Immanence of God*, p. 267 n. 2), *Num. R.* 15.10 envisages the future restoration of the Shekinah and the other features missing from the Second Temple. Cf. 2 Chron. 2.4; 5.14; 6.6, 10, 20; 7.1, 2, 16, etc., where (from a postexilic perspective) the 'name' and 'glory' are again said to fill the Temple (Clements, *God and Temple*, pp. 128-29); also Mt. 23.21: 'he who swears by the temple swears by it *and by him who dwells in it*' (emphasis added).

3. So Jer. 3.16-17: 'And when you have multiplied and increased in the land... says the Lord, they shall no more say, "The ark of the covenant of the Lord." It shall not come to mind, or be remembered, or missed; it shall not be made again. At that time Jerusalem shall be called the throne of the Lord.' Cf. Gaston, *No Stone*, pp. 108-109: 'The temple can no longer simply be assumed as the location of the presence of God with his people, for this function is often taken over by the city as a whole... The building of the second temple was significant not so much because of the temple itself, but because the rebuilding became an expression of trust in God's promises concerning Jerusalem and the people in the Zion tradition.'

4. Cf. Gaston, *No Stone*, pp. 110-11. By way of illustration, one can cite the popular reaction to Caligula's attempt in 40 CE to set up a statue of himself in the Jerusalem Temple (Josephus, *Ant.* 18.261-309; *War* 2.184-203; Philo, *Leg. Gai.* 29-43; Tacitus, *History* 5.9; cf. Mk 13.14 par.); also Pilate's introduction into the Holy City of Roman military standards, which were symbols of pagan religion

religious catastrophe of the first order.[1] Comparisons to the impact of the Holocaust in our own times are not inappropriate.[2] Hence the need to account for the fall of Jerusalem was both obvious and paramount. Various segments of the Jewish community took up this challenge in different ways.

2. *Literary Responses*

a. *Qumran.* The secession of the Qumran sectarians from mainstream Judaism, and their condemnation of the Jerusalem cultus as corrupt and profaned, anticipated in some important respects later responses to the actual destruction of the Temple. This community largely acted—for ideological, rather than historical reasons—as if the Jerusalem Temple were not in existence. Or, at least, for those at Qumran the focus of their religious life had shifted. As Gärtner points out:

(Josephus, *Ant.* 18.261-309; *War* 2.169-74, cf. 6.316).

1. The perceived social—indeed, even cosmic—dimensions of the disaster are well expressed in the Mishnah:

> Rabban Simeon b. Gamaliel says in the name of R. Joshua: Since the day that the Temple was destroyed there has been no day without its curse; and the dew has not fallen in blessing and the fruits have lost their fatness... (*m. Soṭ* 9.12).
>
> R. Phineas b. Jair says: When the [Second] Temple was destroyed, scholars and noblemen were put to shame and walked with covered head, and the men of good works were disregarded, and men of violence and men of loud tongue [i.e. demagogues] prevailed... R. Eliezer the Great says: Since the day that the Temple was destroyed, the Sages began to be like school-teachers, and the school-teachers like synagogue-attendants, and synagogue-attendants like the people of the land, and the people of the land became more and more debased (*m. Soṭ* 9.16; cf. *b. Soṭ* 49a).

Of similar import are the discussions of Akiba and his contemporaries regarding the ruin of Jerusalem (e.g. *b. B. Bat.* 60b; *Sifre Deut.* §43; *Pes. R.* §34; quoted by Bogaert, *Apocalypse de Baruch*, I, pp. 134-42; in addition to the reactions recorded in early Christian literature, *Apocalypse de Baruch*, I, pp. 142-44). Jerome expressed a comparable reaction to the sack of Rome in 410: 'Quid salvum est, si Roma perit?' (*Ep.* 123.17; quoted by R. Kirschner, 'Apocalyptic and Rabbinic Responses to the Destruction of 70', *HTR* 78 [1985], p. 29 n. 10). For analyses of the Temple's significance from a sociological perspective, see Malina and Neyrey, *Calling Jesus Names*, pp. 79-80; R.A. Horsley, *Sociology and the Jesus Movement* (New York: Crossroad, 1989), pp. 72-75.

2. So J. Neusner, 'Judaism in a Time of Crisis: Four Responses to the Destruction of the Second Temple', *Judaism* 21 (1972), pp. 326-27.

> Once the focus of holiness in Israel had ceased to be the Temple, it was necessary to provide a new focus. This focus was the community, which called itself 'the Holy place' and 'the holy of holies'.[1]

Prayer and obedience to Torah took the place of Temple sacrifices, and thus effected atonement on the sectarians' behalf (e.g. 1QS 9.3-6).[2]

A similar view of the community as a 'spiritual temple', also originating prior to the destruction of Jerusalem, was present among early Christians, as indicated by such passages as 1 Cor. 3.16-17, 6.19, 2 Cor. 6.16, Eph. 2.19-22, and 1 Pet. 2.9.[3] Here, however, the impetus for such a view did not derive from dissatisfaction with the Jerusalem cultus. Rather, it arose from the conviction that a greater and more effective atonement had been accomplished through the cross of Christ (e.g. Rom. 3.21-26; Heb. 8.1–10.25).

One feature that these two bodies of writings share is their interest in defining the limits of their respective communities in terms of, and thereby in relation to, the concerns of mainstream Judaism. The fact that they describe their respective communities in Temple imagery indicates how that institution continued to be of significance for them. Certainly they would not have bothered to redefine something religiously irrelevant.[4] Moreover, for both the Qumran and the early Christian communities, issues of covenant and covenant adherence were critical.

b. *Pharisaic Judaism*. One of the features of pre-70 CE Pharisaism, according to Neusner, was an expanded emphasis on the sanctification

1. Gärtner, *Temple and Community*, p. 15 (cited by Neusner, 'Four Responses', p. 318), cf. pp. 22-43; and Gaston, *No Stone*, pp. 163-76. See, e.g., 1QS 8.4-10; 9.3-6. On the opposition to the Jerusalem Temple at Qumran, see Gaston, *No Stone*, pp. 119-28.

2. Cf. Gärtner, *Temple and Community*, pp. 20-21; 44-46; Neusner, 'Four Responses', pp. 318-19. As Gaston (*No Stone*, pp. 135-37) demonstrates, ritual lustration, when coupled with a proper inner disposition, was likewise of expiatory value at Qumran.

3. On the congregation of the faithful as the dwelling place of God in Qumran tradition and the NT, see Gärtner, *Temple and Community*, *passim*; Gaston, *No Stone*, pp. 128, 163-241.

4. The precise meaning of Temple imagery for non-Jewish audiences (e.g. in the Corinthian correspondence) is of secondary importance. The point is simply that because of his own Jewish background, Paul's language and theological agenda are dictated, at least in part, by the significance of the Jerusalem Temple.

of daily life, whereby the obligations of ritual purity normally incumbent only on the Temple priesthood were expanded to include all faithful members of the community.[1] Two particular areas where this applied—as attested also in the Christian Gospels—were in matters of food and of tithing, of '*how and what one [might] eat*'.[2] Just as the presence of God was not limited to the Temple, so the obligation to honor the holiness of that presence extended beyond the Temple itself.

Of particular relevance for this discussion is the fact that such an interpretation provided one means of resolving the religious crisis brought about by the Temple's destruction. That is to say, a pious awareness of the obligation to holiness that had once extended outward from the Temple created the means whereby the faithful might continue to honor God's presence in their midst even in the absence of the Temple.[3] Accordingly, it was decreed that in the absence of Temple sacrifice, the prayers meant to accompany sacrifice—or even the study of sacrifice— might now suffice, and that acts of loving-kindness in accordance with Hos. 6.6 might now atone for the sins of God's people.[4]

Neusner goes so far as to suggest that the codification of Pharisaic teaching in the form of the Mishnah was occasioned by the two principal disasters of the day: the destruction of Jerusalem and its Temple in 70 CE and the failed messianic revolt of 132–135 CE.[5] Specifically,

1. Neusner, 'Four Responses', pp. 321-24. For a summary of Neusner's position, and a comparison of the rabbinic agenda to that of the Gospels, including Matthew, see H.C. Kee, 'The Transformation of the Synagogue after 70 CE: Its Import for Early Christianity', *NTS* 36 (1990), pp. 14-19; similarly, J.A. Overman, *Matthew's Gospel and Formative Judaism: The Social World of the Matthean Community* (Minneapolis: Augsburg–Fortress, 1990), pp. 35-71.

2. Neusner, 'Four Responses', p. 322 (emphasis original).

3. 'Four Responses', pp. 324-25.

4. See Neusner, *A Life of Yohanan ben Zakkai*, pp. 188-91. Cf. *m. Ab.* 3.3: 'If three have eaten at one table and have spoken over it words of the Law, it is as if they had eaten from the table of God' (cited by Gaston, *No Stone*, p. 132); *b. Ber.* 55a: 'As long as the Temple stood, the altar atoned for Israel. But now a man's table atones for him'; *b. Men.* 110a, according to which whoever studies the laws of the Temple sacrifices is reckoned as having offered the sacrifice itself.

5. J. Neusner, *Ancient Israel After Catastrophe: The Religious World View of the Mishnah* (Charlottesville: University Press of Virginia, 1983) *passim*; *idem*, *Wrong Ways and Right Ways in the Study of Formative Judaism: Critical Method and Literature, History, and the History of Religion* (BJS, p. 145; Atlanta: Scholars Press, 1988), pp. 218-35. Neusner argues that a similar historical process of

the exposition and compilation of a 'rule of life' for exiled Judaism was a conscious attempt to find meaning and impose order on the religious community it addressed. Thus the Mishnah reiterated the community's prime responsibility for sanctification of life—lack of attention to which, so it was thought, had precipitated the calamities that had befallen them.

c. *Pseudo-Philo*. Similar concerns and alternative solutions come to the fore in other Jewish responses to the fall of Jerusalem. Pseudo-Philo, for example, appeals to the positive examples of faithful leaders, as well as the negative examples of unfaithful or wicked leaders, as a means of demonstrating God's providential guidance throughout the history of Israel. The underlying message, addressed to a nation once more in crisis under Roman oppression, is that the repeated pattern of Israel's sin, punishment, repentance and deliverance reveals a conscious providential direction. A repentant nation will survive, as it has many times before, because God remains faithful to his covenant,[1] and so will continue to raise up good leaders for his people. As G.W.E. Nickelsburg says of Pseudo-Philo.

> In the midst of oppression, disillusion, dissolution, and despair spawned by the events of 70, this author preaches a message of hope, appealing to God's promises to Abraham and Israel's status—even now—as God's chosen people.[2]

messianic hope (aroused by the Emperor Julian's permission in 361 to rebuild the Temple) followed by post-messianic disillusionment with the failure of the plan (accompanied by the Christianization of the Roman Empire and outbursts of anti-Semitic violence) was repeated in the fourth to fifth centuries, and gave rise to further codifications as represented in one form by the first Gemara (the Jerusalem Talmud) and in another by the various midrashic traditions represented by *Genesis* and *Leviticus Rabbah*, *Sifra* (on Leviticus), and *Sifre* (on Numbers and Deuteronomy); see *idem*, *Midrash in Context: Exegesis in Formative Judaism* (Philadelphia: Fortress Press, 1983), pp. 14-119; *Wrong Ways and Right Ways*, pp. 238-46.

1. Cf. G.W.E. Nickelsburg: 'Israel's election and covenantal status are fundamental to Pseudo-Philo's exposition... At many points when Israel is brought low, their status as the covenantal people is reaffirmed... most often in narratives that depict the nation suffering because of its disobedience to the covenantal laws' ('Good and Bad Leaders in Pseudo-Philo's Liber Antiquitatum Biblicarum', in Collins and Nickelsburg (eds.), *Ideal Figures*, p. 59).

2. 'Good and Bad Leaders', p. 63. Cf. G.B. Sayler, *Have the Promises Failed? A Literary Analysis of 2 Baruch* (SBLDS, 72; Chico, CA: Scholars

d. *Apocalypse of Abraham*. Using the first patriarch as an exemplum is the *Apocalypse of Abraham*, which relates the visions revealed to Abraham following his conversion from idolatry.[1] Among these revelations is the description of a glittering 'idol of jealousy' (25.1) in the Jerusalem Temple, together with an account of how the idolatry of Abraham's descendants will lead to the burning of the Temple and the oppression of the nation (25.5-6; 27.1-5). This causes Abraham to question the efficacy of God's covenant with him and his descendants (cf. 20.1-5; 28.2-3; 29.1). God's response, which is typical of apocalyptic literature, is to recount a periodized schema of history that culminates in the vindication of Israel and the eschatological punishment of their heathen oppressors (chs. 28–32). Only at the conclusion of the final age, and the dawning of the 'Age of Justice', will the Temple and its sacrifices be restored (29.17-18). Yet here, once again, is a message of post-destruction consolation that focuses on the assurance of God's covenantal faithfulness.[2]

e. *4 Ezra*. Most pertinent for our purposes are those responses, both apocalyptic and rabbinic, that appeal to the precedent of the fall of Jerusalem in 587 BCE, together with the literature that it occasioned.[3]

Press, 1984), pp. 120-23.

1. This apocalypse, extant only in Old Slavonic, dates from the decades following 70 CE; cf. R. Rubinkiewicz, 'Apocalypse of Abraham', in Charlesworth (ed.), *OT Pseudepigrapha*, I, p. 683 and nn. 15, 16; Sayler, *Promises*, p. 135.

2. Cf. Sayler, *Promises*, pp. 134-39; Rubinkiewicz, 'Apocalypse of Abraham', p. 685; J.R. Mueller, 'The Apocalypse of Abraham and the Destruction of the Second Jewish Temple', in K.H. Richards (ed.), *Society of Biblical Literature 1982 Seminar Papers* (Chico, CA: Scholars Press, 1982), pp. 343-48.

3. Knibb ('Exile', *passim*) argues that in a number of intertestamental works, the writers thought of their situation—whether before or after the events of 70 CE—as a continuation of the Babylonian exile. This is evident either in their reapplication of Jeremiah's seventy-year prophecy (Jer. 25.11-12; 29.10-14; so esp. Dan. 9.24-27; *1 En.* 85–90) or the 390 days of Ezek. 4.4-8 (esp. CD 1.5-11; 3.10-14); or on the basis of a Deuteronomistic outlook (so *Testaments of the Twelve Patriarchs*; *Jub.* 1.9-18; Tob. 14.4-7; and the books of Baruch [cf. Bar. 3.8]; *4 Ezra*; and *2 Baruch*, which are 'based entirely on the assumption that Israel was in a state of exile' [p. 268]). In the case of *4 Ezra* and *2 Baruch*, Knibb suggests that 'the sense of having been in a more or less permanent state of exile since 587' may have influenced the respective authors' choice of pseudonym (p. 271)—though here it seems more likely that both the sense of exile and the choice of pseudonym are retrospective, resulting from reflection on the impact of the Roman conquest.

First among these is *4 Ezra*, which purports to describe the revelations accorded to Ezra, exiled in Babylon, 'in the thirtieth year after the destruction of our city' (3.1). Ezra's primary concern is one of theodicy: he bitterly questions the justice of God in having punished his people for their sins while leaving the much greater transgressions of the pagan nations unanswered, all the more so since God has apparently failed to engender in his people an obedience of which they are otherwise incapable.[1] For Ezra, who is depicted as a second Moses (esp. 14.1-9), this is a betrayal of God's covenant with the nation that he himself has chosen (cf. 3.13-19, 28-36; 4.23; 5.28-30).

The sharp conflict between Ezra and his angelic interlocutor Uriel has occasioned much scholarly debate.[2] For after having firmly rejected Uriel's rigid orthodoxy, which insists on the absolute and inscrutable justice of God's dealings with his people, Ezra eventually acquiesces, even to the point of himself becoming a spokesman for God. In so doing, *4 Ezra* calls into question any simplistic explanation for the fall of Jerusalem as a divine punishment for the sins of Israel. Indeed, the consolation offered by this work is not primarily intellectual (Ezra's deepest doubts and most difficult questions are never really answered), but rather, mystical (in keeping with the genre of apocalyptic) and experiential.[3]

1. So M.E. Stone, 'Reactions to Destructions of the Second Temple: Theology, Perception, and Conversion', *JSJ* 12 (1981), pp. 200-201. In expounding its theodicy, *4 Ezra* employs a tradition of the evil *yetzer* (cf. A.L. Thompson, *Responsibility for Evil in the Theodicy of IV Ezra: A Study Illustrating the Significance of Form and Structure for the Meaning of the Book* [SBLDS, 29; Missoula, MT: Scholars Press, 1977], pp. 49-63): 'Yet thou didst not take away from them their evil heart, so that thy law might bring forth fruit in them. For the first Adam, burdened with an evil heart, transgressed and was overcome, as were also all who were descended from him. Thus the disease became permanent; the law was in the people's hearts along with the evil root, but what was good departed, and the evil remained' (3.20-22); 'For a grain of evil seed was sown in Adam's heart from the beginning, and how much ungodliness it has produced until now' (4.30).

2. Cf. summaries in A.P. Hayman, 'The Problem of Pseudonymity in the Ezra Apocalypse', *JSJ* 6 (1975), pp. 45-50; Thompson, *Responsibility for Evil*, pp. 85-107; Knowles, 'Unity of 4 Ezra', pp. 258-60.

3. So Thompson (*Responsibility for Evil*, pp. 340-41): 'There is no effective rational theodicy in IV Ezra... IV Ezra [belongs] to that theodicy tradition in Israel and the Ancient Near East which finds consolation in experience even when neat, rational solutions to the problem of evil are not forthcoming'; Stone ('Reactions to Destructions', p. 203): 'The problems and concerns that have beset Ezra and the

The turning-point of *4 Ezra* is Ezra's vision of the heavenly Jerusalem, indestructible and enduring (9.38–10.59).[1] This assures him that God's purpose for his people (as symbolized by the Holy City) cannot be thwarted. Furthermore, it introduces a series of visions that depict God's providential control over the pagan nations (notably the Roman Empire, 11.1–12.30) and the ultimate victory of the messiah (12.31-35; 13.1-53). Corresponding to these revelations is a concomitant change in Ezra himself as he comes to a new awareness of the relevance and efficacy of the Torah.[2] So he asks at the close of the work for the privilege of restoring to the people the 24 canonical books, together with 70 additional works reserved for the 'wise' (14.22, 26, 44-46).

f. *2 Baruch*. *2 Baruch* likewise challenges important features of orthodox Jewish opinion concerning the Jerusalem Temple, once again in response to popular reactions that its destruction aroused. Here the pseudepigraphical spokesman is Baruch, the scribe of Jeremiah,[3] to whom God foretells the destruction of the Holy City, explaining the city's fall as a consequence of Israel's apostasy and describing in a series of visions the imminent, eschatological culmination of the entire course of world history.

The primary purpose and function of *2 Baruch* is one of consolation, with its concomitant assurance of eschatological reward. In the

questions that he has asked... are not solved merely by the knowledge of eschatological reward of which he has been repeatedly assured... They are resolved by an experience of overpowering strength'; cf. Breech, 'Fragments', pp. 273-74.

1. Cf. Stone, 'Reactions to Destructions', p. 203.

2. Cf. Knowles, 'Unity of 4 Ezra', pp. 268-73.

3. Throughout this work Jeremiah is portrayed as subordinate to Baruch. Here we may recall Nickelsburg's argument that both *2 Baruch* and *Paraleipomena Jeremiou*, which contain similar material, are based on a common set of Jeremiah traditions, and that the latter work preserves these in a form more closely allied to the original ('Narrative Traditions', *passim*). Nickelsburg's thesis is significant for our purposes insofar as it posits the existence of Jeremiah traditions that predate both works, which both authors found relevant and applicable to the post-70 situation.

In discussing the author's choice of Baruch, Bogaert (*Apocalypse de Baruch*, I, pp. 110-19) notes the rabbinic tradition that made Baruch a disciple of Ezra in Babylon (e.g. *b. Meg.* 16b; *Songs R.* 5.5), which he explains as arising from a rabbinic recognition of similarities between *4 Ezra* and *2 Baruch*.

words of Bogaert, 'the *Apocalypse of Baruch* is a cry of hope.'[1] Whereas *4 Ezra* protests (at least initially) the injustice of God's ways, *2 Baruch* defends them. The grounds for its theodicy are, first, that God himself has permitted the destruction of the sanctuary, a fact that vindicates rather than vitiates his power and justice, for he has intended this for the chastening of his people (13.9-10).[2] Secondly, any present suffering endured by the faithful will be more than amply compensated by their future reward (15.8; 43.1; 48.48-50; 83.4-5) and by the condemnation of their oppressors (13.11-12; 40.1-4; 72.2-6). Indeed, according to Bogaert, suffering itself is not without meaning, for it has 'a certain expiatory value' (so 13.9; 78.5-6; cf. 13.10: 'they were once punished, that they might be forgiven').[3] And, thirdly, *2 Baruch* offers a radical re-evaluation of the significance of the Temple, directing attention away from the earthly sanctuary as a dwelling-place for God and toward the heavenly realm instead.[4]

2 Baruch appears to have been addressed to the 'few' who comprise 'a faithful minority within the broader Jewish community', of whom 'many' have turned from the covenant and adopted Gentile ways (e.g. 18.1-2; 41.3; 42.4; 48.22-24).[5] For this minority, obedience to Torah is the characteristic of faithful 'Israel' as they await the eschatological

1. *Apocalypse de Baruch*, I, p. 386.

2. Cf. Sayler, *Promises*, p. 52.

3. *Apocalypse de Baruch*, I, pp. 386-88; cf. Sayler, *Promises*, p. 46 and n. 9. Bogaert is mistaken, however, in his insistence on the 'pessimisme radical' of *4 Ezra*, for this view ignores the equally radical consolation to which Ezra ultimately attains.

4. Cf. Murphy, *Structure and Meaning*, pp. 71-116: 'The author of 2B wanted to direct the attention of Israel away from the destruction of the Temple and Zion as a cause for mourning [and] towards the real place of God's dwelling, heaven... It is perhaps the author's greatest achievement that he gets the people to turn away from the destruction of the Temple precisely by making them look at it in a different light. It becomes for them an example of the corruptibility of this world, and of the inevitability of punishment due to sin. It is no longer the *sine qua non* of contact with the presence of God' (pp. 114-15). Murphy compares this relativization of the Temple to that accomplished at Qumran (pp. 114-15), while contrasting the expectation of a rebuilt Temple in the *Apocalypse of Abraham* (p. 137; following the suggestion of Mueller, 'Apocalypse of Abraham', pp. 348-49). The same argument is set out in Murphy's subsequent article, 'The Temple in the Syriac *Apocalypse of Baruch*', *JBL* 106 (1987), pp. 671-83.

5. Sayler, *Promises*, p. 115; cf. pp. 49, 62-64.

fulfillment of God's covenant promises.[1] Torah, in other words, serves as a temporal substitute for the ruined Temple. As Baruch laments, 'we have left our land, and Zion has been taken away from us, and we have nothing now apart from the Mighty One and his Law' (85.3; cf. 84.8).[2]

g. *Paraleipomena Jeremiou*. Because *2 Baruch* and *Paraleipomena Jeremiou* reflect many of the same traditions, the differences between the two works likely indicate the slightly different interests of their respective authors. The most significant difference is that *Paraleipomena Jeremiou* does not direct its full attention to the heavenly consolation, as does *2 Baruch*, but rather anticipates an imminent return of exiles to the Holy City (4.9; 6.21-25; 8.1-6).[3] This author, however, agrees that God, not the Gentiles, is ultimately responsible for the city's destruction (1.6-11; cf. 3.2; 4.2). And like the author of *2 Baruch*, this writer stresses the importance of covenantal obedience as the basis for the community's renewed existence—although it is an obedience not in terms of Torah per se, but rather having to do with the question of mixed marriages. The exiles who have married Babylonian wives—that is, who have embraced 'the pollutions of the Gentiles of Babylon' (7.37)—are not permitted to cross the Jordan or to re-enter Jerusalem (8.1-9).[4] Despite such differences, however, it should be noted that here again questions

1. Cf. Sayler, *Promises*, pp. 61, 73-74.

2. So Bogaert, *Apocalypse de Baruch*, I, pp. 390-91: 'la substitution de la Loi au Temple est la transformation clé qui command la survivance du judaïsme après 70'. This renewed emphasis on Torah obedience suggests an important affinity between *2 Baruch* and the outlook of the compilers of the Mishnah.

3. Cf. Sayler, *Promises*, pp. 113, 41. As Robinson ('4 Baruch', p. 416) points out, 'the conclusion to be drawn by the original audience was that if the Jews would conform sufficiently to the will of God, as interpreted by the scribe, they could bring about a restoration of the Temple cultus in an invincible Jewish state'. Robinson draws attention to Jeremiah's instructions to the people: 'Everything that you have heard from the letter observe, and the Lord will lead us into our city' (7.23). This hope of return and rebuilding seems appropriate to the period of the second revolt, a chronology supported by Abimilech's 66-year sleep (5.2, 29; i.e. 70 CE + 66 = 136 CE); cf. Nickelsburg, *Jewish Literature*, p. 315; Robinson, '4 Baruch', p. 414.

4. Here *Paraleipomena Jeremiou* accounts for the Samaritans as those who intermingled with the Babylonians, only to be rejected by them (8.9-11).

regarding the community's identity and regarding the separation of the faithful from the unfaithful within it are important features of the writer's apologetic.[1]

h. *Lamentations Rabbah*. In contrast to the Mishnah and the Gemaras of Jerusalem and Babylon, *Lamentations Rabbah*—like *4 Ezra*, *2 Baruch* and *Paraleipomena Jeremiou*—draws directly on the analogy of the Babylonian destruction by its use of the canonical book of Lamentations.[2] While *Lamentations Rabbah* is considerably later than any of the other writings we have examined,[3] the practice of reading Lamentations with reference to the fall of Jerusalem in 70 CE seems to go back at least to the second century.[4] This practice is associated in

1. Brief mention may also be made of the Greek Apocalypse of Baruch (or *3 Baruch*), extant in Greek and Slavonic versions. It is either a Christian work that makes use of Jewish traditions or a Jewish work that has been modified by a Christian redactor, which may be dated in the first two centuries CE (cf. H.E. Gaylord, '3 [Greek Apocalypse of] Baruch', in Charlesworth (ed.), *OT Pseudepigrapha*, I, pp. 655-57). This work is perhaps closer in sentiment to *2 Baruch* insofar as the consolation it proposes for the destruction of Jerusalem (1.1-2) is an assurance of the divine ordering of the celestial realms, Baruch being given a guided tour of the first five heavens. Here he learns how God not only controls the cosmos but also reigns justly over human history (in particular, the generations of Noah and the Tower of Babel). He is assured that, even in the absence of the Temple and the holy of holies, the angels—especially the archangel Michael—are able to bring the prayers and good deeds of the faithful before the throne of God, whence also they convey divine blessings and judgments. Like *2 Baruch*, this theodicy concentrates on issues of divine justice and heavenly consolation. See Nickelsburg, *Jewish Literature*, pp. 299-303.

2. Cf. Kirschner, 'Apocalyptic and Rabbinic Responses', pp. 28-29. A further feature linking a number of these works, according to Bogaert (*Apocalypse de Baruch*, I, pp. 129-32, 144-56), is their formal adherence to the genre of lamentation. Bogaert cites Josephus, *War* 5.19; *Apoc. Abr.* 27; *4 Ezra* 10.21-23; *2 Bar.* 35.2-5; 10.6–12.4; *Par. Jer.* 4.6-9; *3 Bar.* 1.1-2; *Sib. Or.* 5.397-413; as well as *Lam. R.*; *Pes. K.*; and *Pes. R.*; cf. also 4QapLam/4Q179. The use of this genre was itself most likely inspired, at least originally, by canonical Lamentations.

3. Kirschner ('Responses') suggests that since the work mentions no sage later than the fourth century, while citing *Gen. R.* (c. 400) and serving as a source for *Pes. K.* (c. 600), '*Lam. Rab.*'s redaction may be reliably if imprecisely fixed somewhere between the two'. Cf. Bogaert, *Apocalypse de Baruch*, I, p. 152.

4. In a related observation that anticipates the more broadly based conclusions presented here, Wolff (*Jeremia*, p. 166; cf. pp. 186-87) suggests that the synagogue's interpretation of Jer. 30–33—attested in *Lam. R.* (cited in *Jeremia*, p. 157

particular with Judah ha-Naṣi (b. 135) and his associates, who, we are told, set out to expound the entire work on the evening of the ninth of Ab (*y. Šab.* 16.1; *Lam. R.* 4.20 §23; cf. *y. Ta'an.* 4.5; *b. Ḥag.* 5b). This confirms, incidentally, the anonymous Tannaitic dictum that whereas the reading of all other Scripture or teaching is forbidden on the ninth of Ab, one is permitted to read from 'Lamentations, Job, and the sad parts of Jeremiah' (*b. Ta'an.* 30a).

The date of the ninth of Ab is significant, for, according to the Mishnah,

> On the ninth of Ab it was decreed against our fathers that they should not enter the land, the Temple was destroyed the first and the second time, and Beth-Tor [Bethar] was captured and the City was ploughed up.[1]

This correlation of dates, particularly in association with the book of Lamentations, contributes further to a larger program of theodicy and consolation for the surviving community. For in the context of worship and liturgy on the ninth of Ab, as the people recall not just one but two destructions of Jerusalem (and a number of other reversals besides), they are reminded in the words of Lamentations that, despite judgment, 'the steadfast love of the Lord never ceases, his mercies never come to an end' (Lam. 3.22).[2]

n. 6)—accounts for the use of Jer. 31 in Mt. 2.17 and (apparently) Jer. 32 in Mt. 27.9-10: 'Diese Kapitel [aus Jer. 31–32] stehen in einem Komplex von Heilsworten, der Jer. 30–33 umfaßt und Trost für das unter Fremdherrschaft leidende Israel enthält. Nach den Ereignissen des Jahres 70 n. Chr. werden diese Weissagungen für das jüdische Volk Bedeutung gehabt haben, stammen sie doch von dem Propheten, der eine ähnliche Katastrophe erlebt hatte. Die christliche Gemeinde um Matth. wird dadurch zur Beschäftigung mit jenen Jeremiakapiteln angeregt worden sein und hier die für sie wichtigen Stellen gefunden haben.'

1. *M. Ta'an.* 4.6. On the concurrence of dates for the first and second destruction of the Temple, see Josephus, *War* 6.249-50, 268; *m. Ta'an.* 2.10; *y. Ta'an.* 4.5; *y. Suk.* 5.1 [55b]; *b. Ta'an.* 29a; *b. 'Arak.* 11b; also Bogaert, *Apocalypse de Baruch*, pp. 169-76; Wolff, *Jeremia*, p. 34.

2. In related fashion *Pesiqta deRab Kahana*, which is later still, follows the liturgical readings for the Sabbaths surrounding the 9th of Ab, as does Piska 26 of *Pesiqta Rabbati* (cf. Bogaert, *Apocalypse de Baruch*, pp. 52-153, 223). Following the suggestion of *2 Bar.* 86.1 ('When you, therefore, receive the letter, read it in your assemblies. And think about it in particular...on the days of your fasts'), Bogaert (*Apocalypse de Baruch*, pp. 157-62) argues that at an early period this work also formed part of the synagogue lections, indeed that it serves as a source for some of the material in *Pes. R.* 26 (*Apocalypse de Baruch*, pp. 222-41; cf. Kirschner,

The outlook of *Lamentations Rabbah* is not apocalyptic but exegetical, deriving its inspiration from the actual text of Scripture.[1] So the consolation it offers is not transcendent or eschatological. Rather, it emphasizes divine empathy, as God enters into and shares the suffering of his people.[2]

3. *Common Themes in the Literature*

The purpose in the foregoing section has been, first, to demonstrate the currency and breadth of Jewish responses to the Roman destruction(s) of Jerusalem that are (with the exception of *Lamentations Rabbah*) roughly contemporary with Matthew's Gospel; and, secondly, to note a number of common themes among them as Jews came to terms with a religious catastrophe of enormous but not unprecedented magnitude. While these themes may be obvious, highlighting them here provides a context for the response to destruction that Matthew also articulates.

a. *Covenant*. The first such theme is that of the covenant, which is prominent in all the works we have reviewed. This may be so obvious as hardly to require mentioning, since it is the fact of God's covenant with Israel that raises the problem of theodicy in the first place.[3] The question is, in other words, how God could have allowed his chosen

'Apocalyptic and Rabbinic Responses', p. 31).

1. Cf. Kirschner, 'Apocalyptic and Rabbinic Responses', pp. 31-32.

2. 'Apocalyptic and Rabbinic Responses', pp. 39-44. As Kirschner points out, this doubtless reflects the waning of apocalyptic expectation in the course of centuries under Roman subjection: 'The emphasis of *Lam. Rab.* on divine identification signifies a rabbinic recognition that Zion would not soon be restored' (p. 46). For alternative reactions recorded elsewhere in Jewish tradition, see A.J. Saldarini, 'Varieties of Rabbinic Response to the Destruction of the Temple', in K.H. Richards (ed.), *Society of Biblical Literature 1982 Seminar Papers* (Chico, CA: Scholars Press, 1982), pp. 437-58. Amongst these may be mentioned *Mekilta* on Exod. 18.27 (cited by E.P. Sanders, *Paul and Palestinian Judaism: A Comparison of Patterns of Religion* [Philadelphia: Fortress Press, 1977], pp. 94-95), which distinguishes between conditional and unconditional covenants, specifying that whereas the Torah and the Aaronic covenant were given to Israel unconditionally, the land of Israel, the Temple and the Davidic kingdom were given only on condition of obedience (cf. Sanders, *Paul*, pp. 95-97).

3. Overman (*Matthew's Gospel and Formative Judaism*, pp. 23-34) explores the centrality of the covenant in many of the same works that we have reviewed, but focuses on the issue of faithfulness (or unfaithfulness) in Torah observance.

people, his chosen city and his chosen sanctuary to suffer defeat and destruction.

b. *Sin*. A second significant theme in these writings is the Deuteronomistic explanation for Jerusalem's destruction: that it was caused by the sins of Israel. In blaming Israel and upholding divine justice, this explanation affirms God's covenant faithfulness. Among the specific causes adduced are such matters as (1) profanation of the cultus (*Pss. Sol.* 2.3; 8.11-13 [with reference to the capture by Pompey]; *Ass. Mos.* 6.1-2), (2) sexual impropriety, either by itself (*Pss. Sol.* 2.11-13; 8.8-10) or in association with the cultus (*T. Levi* 14.1–15.3), (3) adoption of Gentile practices (*Pss. Sol.* 17.5), including idolatry (*T. Jud.* 23; *Apoc. Abr.* 25-27), (4) greed, avarice and violence on the part of Israel's rulers (*Ass. Mos.* 6.4–7.10), (5) violating the commandments of God (*2 Bar.* 77.4; 79.2; *Par. Jer.* 6.23; *Pes. R.* 29), and simply (6) 'sin' in general (*4 Ezra* 3.28-30; 8.26, 31; *2 Bar.* 1.2-3; *Par. Jer.* 1.1; 4.7-8).[1]

B. Šab. 119b lists a wide range of causes for the destruction of Jerusalem, including desecration of the Sabbath, neglect of prayer, failure to educate children and lack of respect for elders and scholars.[2] Similarly varied are the reasons proposed by *Targum Lamentations*:

> interrupting the Daily Sacrifice (II,19), not obeying the Sinai covenant (II,9,17), desecrating the temple (I,19), not frequenting the temple (I,4), sinning against God's *Memra* (I,20; II,17), not repenting or praying in Jerusalem (IV,6), etc.[3]

1. Cf. the prayer from the Additional Service for Festivals: 'On account of our sins we were exiled from our land and removed far from our country, and we are unable to go up... to fulfill our obligations in thy chosen house, that great and holy temple which was called by thy name, because of the hand that hath been stretched out against thy sanctuary' (quoted by Neusner, *First-Century Judaism*, p. 25; Stone, 'Reactions to Destructions', p. 197 n. 10).

2. Cf. the similar listing of Yohanan b. Torta in *y. Yom.* 1.1 (38c), cited by Stone, 'Reactions to Destructions', p. 200 n. 21.

3. Levine, *Aramaic Lamentations*, p. 17. Cf. *Targ. Lam.* 1.1: 'The Attribute of Justice reported [Jerusalem's] great sinfulness, and she was evicted. Because of her many sins within her, she will dwell alone.' On this verse Levine comments that the midrashic elaborations of Israel's sins 'are attempts to make the popular mind convinced that there was justification for the national catastrophe. It was neither a function of historical "accident", nor Divine caprice; it was also not a function of their

Our investigation has already highlighted the opinion that the Second Temple was destroyed because of Jerusalem's rejection of the prophets (*Exod. R.* 31.16)—even its slaying of them (*Pes. R.* 29, 31).[1] To those passages cited earlier may be added *Targ. Lam.* 4.13, which explains the fall of the city as follows:

> All this transpired only because of the sins of her prophets who prophesied a false prophecy to her, and the iniquity of the priests who burned incense to idols. For they themselves caused innocent blood to be shed in her.[2]

Here Jerusalem's fall is not attributed to vaticide per se, but, in keeping with Lam. 4.13, to false prophecy[3] and the shedding of innocent blood. In its immediate context this explanation refers to the slaughter wrought by 'Nebuchadnezzar the wicked and Nebuzaraddan the enemy' (*Targ. Lam.* 4.12). Yet since the Targum understands Lamentations as having in mind the destructions of both the First and the Second Temples,[4] the explanation is not necessarily limited to the former occasion.

From a strictly historical perspective, of course, the logic of attributing the fall of the Herodian temple to Israel's rejection of the prophets is less than obvious, particularly in rabbinic writings where there is a demurral regarding the presence of prophecy in the Second

having been rejected or abandoned. Rather, the catastrophe was the inevitable result of massive sins...In other words, theodicy required elaboration of the transgressions' (*Aramaic Lamentations*, p. 80).

1. See above, Chapter 2, §A.1.c.

2. לא הוות כל דא אלהן מחובת נביאהא דמנבאן לה נבואה שקרא ומעוויית כהנתא דאסיקו קטורת בוסמין לטעותא ואנון גרמו לאתשד בגווה דם זכאין

3. So also *Targ. Lam.* 2.13: 'The false prophets within you: they have prophesied falsehood to you, and there is no substance to their prophecy. Nor did they make known the punishment destined to overtake you because of your sins, to turn you in repentance. Rather, they prophesied to you groundless prophecy and erring words.' This is in contrast to the rejected ministry of Jeremiah: 'And when it was prophetically told to Jeremiah the High Priest that Jerusalem would be destroyed by the hands of the wicked Nebuchadnezzar if they would not repent, he immediately entered, to rebuke the people of the House of Israel. But they would not listen. Consequently, the wicked Nebuchadnezzar entered, and destroyed Jerusalem and razed the Temple with fire, on the ninth day of the month of Ab' (*Targ. Lam.* 1.2).

4. See esp. *Targ. Lam.* 1.19: 'these are the Romans who came up with Titus and Vespasian the wicked' (also 4.17, 22; 5.11, 13); cf. Levine, *Aramaic Lamentations*, p. 104.

Temple period. Even more problematic are references to actual persecution and/or vaticide. In all likelihood, therefore, the attribution of catastrophe to Israel's rejection of the prophets is probably to be understood primarily as a literary or apologetic motif that serves to associate the destructions of the First and Second Temples more closely with one another, and so articulates a consistent theodicy for both.[1]

c. *Re-evaluation of the Temple.* A third theme frequently found in these writings, although not always so, is that of the re-evaluation of the significance of the Temple as the locus of God's presence. That the Shekinah departs prior to Jerusalem's destruction, thereby withdrawing divine protection from the city and its Temple, is an affirmation of divine sovereignty (so *2 Baruch*). No less significant, however, is the theological diminution of the Temple's significance, either by transferring its significance to the community (so Qumran and rabbinic literature) or by de-emphasizing Jerusalem in favor of the heavenly city (so *4 Ezra* and *2 Baruch*; cf. also *3 Baruch*). Of the Jewish works surveyed, only *Paraleipomena Jeremiou* seems to anticipate an imminent rebuilding of the earthly sanctuary.

d. *Re-definition of the Community.* A fourth theme of note has to do with the extensive attention given to community in these Jewish materials—not only the consolation of the community, but also its re-definition. If Israel's sin has led to divine judgment, the only course

1. So Amaru ('The Killing of the Prophets', pp. 178-79): 'The "killing of the prophets" legends which developed in Jewish tradition served a different purpose than those developed in the Church Fathers. The Rabbis were not interested in propheticide for its own sake, or for purposes of justifying Judaism over against another theological tradition... [Such legends] reflect an attempt to deal in code language with the disasters that befell the Jewish people in the first century... On the one hand, the martyr legends affirm the rabbinic belief that the destruction of the Second Commonwealth, like the First, was ultimately caused by Israel's sinfulness. On the other hand, they offer assurance that the martyred rabbis who had taken the place of the priest and prophet as Israel's religious leaders would not go unavenged.' Here we may once more recall the similar suggestion by Blank ('Death of Zechariah', pp. 340-41) that the elaboration in rabbinic literature of traditions about the death of Zechariah as having contributed to the destruction of the First Temple may be due, in part, to the need to explain the destruction of the second, together with the suffering of subsequent generations. A similar explanation could also account for interest in Manasseh's slaying of Isaiah.

open to the people is that of repentance and a renewed attention to the demands of holiness. The community must redefine and reconstitute itself in obedience to the covenant, with that obedience being prerequisite to ensuring its own survival. Such a motive undergirds, at least in part, the Mishnah's attention to the sanctification of life. The issues of faithfulness and community identity likewise come to the fore and are addressed directly in *4 Ezra* (as Ezra first despairs of the possibility of obedience, but later becomes an advocate for Torah), *2 Baruch* (which distinguishes the 'few' from the apostate 'many,' while Baruch attempts to console the remnant of Israel), *Paraleipomena Jeremiou* (where Jeremiah insists on separating the Israelites from Gentile 'pollutions'), Pseudo-Philo (who anticipates the advent of a new deliverer for God's people) and the *Apocalypse of Abraham* (with its polemic against idolatry).

B. *Matthew and the Fall of Jerusalem*

Each of the themes set out above, which are found in Jewish writings as part of their response to the fall of Jerusalem, is also present in Matthew's Gospel. Covenant and covenant identity are issues implicit throughout Matthew that come to expression in at least three ways. First, the existence of the early Christian community (Matthew's ἐκκλησία) is predicated on an understanding of Jesus' life and ministry as having instituted a new covenant, and therefore a new people for God. Secondly, the question of covenant identity underlies the polemic against the leaders of Israel and the promise as to the opening of the kingdom to Gentiles.[1] And, thirdly, as noted in Chapter 3, Matthew specifically alludes in 23.8-10 and 26.28 to the 'new covenant' of Jer. 31.33-34.

The issue of God's covenant with his people—and, more specifically, the question of their faithfulness to that covenant—was, of course, already implicit within a Deuteronomistic view of Israel's history. For such an interpretation explained Israel's national reversals as God's response to his people's unfaithfulness: a paradoxical manifestation of divine faithfulness in the form of judgment, a call to repentance and the promise of restoration. According to the Christian

1. On the relevance of covenant to Matthew's view of his community, see H.C. Kee, *Knowing the Truth: A Sociological Approach to New Testament Interpretation* (Minneapolis: Fortress Press, 1989), pp. 95-98.

tradition to which Matthew was heir, Israel's unfaithfulness was understood to be manifest in its rejection of the prophets—above all its rejection of Jesus, but also the rejection of John the Baptist and the Christian emissaries generally—which had resulted in the shedding of 'innocent blood'.

This motif, as we have seen, was operative in material drawn both from Mark (the rejection of John, 14.1-12, and the parable of the Wicked Tenants, 21.33-46) and from Q (the persecution beatitudes, 5.11-12; cf. 5.10; the Mission Discourse, 10.14-16, 23-25, 28, 34-39; the rejection of Jesus and John as Wisdom's emissaries, 11.16-19; the sign of Jonah, 12.39-41; the parable of the Banquet, 22.2-14; the woes against the Tomb Builders, 23.29-36; and the lament over Jerusalem, 23.37-39).[1] It is also present, however, in uniquely Matthaean material, of which the two fulfillment formulae of 2.17-18 and 27.9-10 are, for our purposes, the most notable instances. For these two passages focus attention on the persecution and rejection of Jesus, even from an early age, and on the motif of the shedding of innocent blood (cf. 23.30, 35 [with 26.28]; 27.4-6, 24-25).

Of particular significance among these latter Matthaean passages is the declaration of the crowd in 27.25, 'His blood be on us, and on our children', which, taken in context, assigns the consequences of Jesus' death specifically to the generation of the fall of Jerusalem.[2] The cumulative effect of Matthew's Deuteronomistic interest is, therefore, to explain from a Christian perspective both Israel's rejection of the messiah and the suffering of the Christian community, and thereby to account for the fall of Jerusalem in the community's own day.

Here we recognize strong lines of continuity between Matthew's explanation for the fall of Jerusalem and certain features of Jewish

1. Davies (*Setting*, pp. 298-99) demonstrates in a similar series of texts (e.g. 16.21 [δεῖ αὐτὸν εἰς Ἱεροσόλυμα ἀπελθεῖν καὶ πολλὰ παθεῖν]; 21.10; 22.1-10; 23.37-38; 24.1-3) Matthew's consistent 'emphasis on the Holy City as the guilty city' in contrast to 'Galilee as the scene of redemption', which reveals on the part of the Evangelist 'a marked awareness of Jerusalem and its fate'.

2. So Gaston, *No Stone*, p. 486; Neusner, 'Four Responses', p. 326; Green, *Matthew*, p. 221; Cope, *Matthew*, pp. 128-29; cf. V. Mora, *Le refus d'Israel: Matthieu 27,25* (LD, 124; Paris: Cerf, 1986), pp. 68-81; and, more generally, Fitzmyer, 'Anti-Semitism and the Cry of "All the People"', p. 671.

apologetic as set out above.[1] The issue on which these two communities differed was not the reason for the fall. Jewish and Christian writings are in full accord that Jerusalem's fate was the direct result of Israel's sin, with both arriving at this conclusion retrospectively.[2] Jewish writings list a wide variety of particular sins. That of Israel's rejection of the prophets, however, is included among them, as it is also in Christian writings generally and Matthew in particular. Also noteworthy in both Jewish and Christian writings are the concurrent motifs of prophetic rejection, vaticide, the shedding of innocent blood and false prophecy. Where Jewish and Christian writings differ, of course, is in regard to Jesus as the specific prophet whose rejection accounts for the fate of the city.

Also present in Matthew's Gospel is a re-evaluation of the Jerusalem Temple as the locus of God's presence. Negatively, notwithstanding Jesus' affirmation that Jerusalem is 'the city of the great king' (5.35) and the Temple the dwelling place of God (23.22), the parable of the Banquet foresees the destruction of the Holy City (22.7). Likewise, Jesus' prophetic apostrophe to Jerusalem (23.37-38) and subsequent address to his disciples (24.1-2) envisages the abandonment and fall of the Temple itself. Moreover, Jesus' use of Hos. 6.6 (Mt. 12.7; cf. 9.13) relativizes the demands of Temple sanctity (λέγω δὲ ὑμῖν ὅτι τοῦ ἱεροῦ μεῖζόν ἐστιν ὧδε, 12.6),[3] while his discussion of the half-shekel Temple tax suggests that 'the sons are free' from its obligations and that they submit only so as not to give offense (17.24-27). On the other hand, Jesus' actions and citation of Scripture in 'cleansing' the Temple (21.12-14) are strongly critical of commercial activity in the Temple precincts as an affront to the sanctity of the place.[4]

1. Cf. Nickelsburg, *Jewish Literature*, pp. 303-304; Sayler, *Promises*, pp. 243-46.

2. So Neusner (*First-Century Judaism*, p. 25): 'Whether the sins were those specified by Christians or by Talmudic rabbis hardly matters. This was supposed to be a sinning generation.' But because such a conclusion appears to have been arrived at retrospectively, Neusner insists that its only value is apologetic, not historical.

3. On Yohanan ben Zakkai's similar use of Hos. 6.6, see Neusner, *Life of Yohanan ben Zakkai*, pp. 188-91.

4. Such a critique is all the more pointed if, as G.W. Buchanan ('Mark 11.15-19: Brigands in the Temple', *HUCA* 30 [1959], pp. 169-77; *idem*, 'An Additional Note to "Mark 11.15-19: Brigands in the Temple"', *HUCA* 31 [1960], pp. 103-105) and C. Roth ('The Cleansing of the Temple and Zechariah 14.21', *NovT* 4 [1960], pp. 174-81) have argued, the Evangelists saw in Jesus' citation of Jer. 7.11

Positively, there are tentative suggestions in Matthew's Gospel as to how the Temple has been or will be replaced. The reference in 26.61 to Jesus' ability to destroy and rebuild the Temple 'in three days,' for example, although placed in the mouths of 'false witnesses', suggests the possibility of the Temple's replacement, perhaps by means of Jesus' resurrection.[1] Similarly, Jesus' role in departing from the Temple prior to its destruction is, as we have seen, reminiscent of the departure of the Shekinah. When correlated with Jesus' promise to be present with his disciples when they gather in his name (18.20), this suggests that Jesus is equated with the Shekinah, with the result that the gathered disciples, the church, can be seen as the new temple. Further support for such a view may perhaps be derived from 5.14 ('You are the light of the world; a city set on a hill cannot be hid'), where the disciples are described in language potentially reminiscent of Jerusalem;[2] or from 16.18, if the reference to a 'rock' of foundation for the new community involves an allusion to the foundation of the Temple Mount.[3] But these latter suggestions are only tentative. Jesus' relativization of the Temple and prophecy of its destruction would alone have been sufficient to foster a significant re-evaluation of its religious significance for the Matthaean community.

Yet here it should be observed that neither the question of the Temple's significance nor that of Israel's obedience—nor even the

a polemic against Zealot activity in the Temple precincts.

1. Cf. Senior, *Passion Narrative*, pp. 168-71: 'Jesus' claim to authority over the very existence of the temple as reported by Matthew echoes a theme already evoked in his gospel—the Son of Man has power and authority over both the Sabbath and the temple' [p. 169].

2. So K.M. Campbell, 'The New Jerusalem in Matthew 5.14', *SJT* 31 (1978), pp. 335-63. Campbell concludes that Jesus 'is designating his disciples as the new community of Zion' (p. 363) on the basis of, *inter alia*, the similarity of the description in 5.14 to apocalyptic expectations of a new and glorious Jerusalem (e.g. Tob. 3.9-11; *Sib. Or.* 5.420) and because 'the phrase "city on a hill" would call to mind in Palestine not just any city, but the city of God on Mt. Zion' ('The New Jerusalem', p. 363).

3. So Gaston, *No Stone*, pp. 195, 225-27. The image of the rock as a foundation for the community is also present in Qumran literature (Overman, *Matthew's Gospel and Formative Judaism*, pp. 137-38), although without obvious reference to Jerusalem. *Odes* 22.12, which Overman also cites, is likely dependent on Matthew, since the *Odes of Solomon* are Christian in origin (so Charlesworth, 'Odes of Solomon', in *OT Pseudepigrapha*, II, pp. 725-27).

issue of Christian self-definition—first arose in response to the fall of Jerusalem. Such issues were already implicit to some degree in the acclamation of Jesus as Israel's messiah, on the one hand, and in the problem of his rejection by the majority of his people and subsequent crucifixion, on the other. In fact, the Deuteronomistic motifs that Matthew emphasizes, whether in relation to issues of covenant, sin, the significance of the Temple, or community identity, were already present in his sources. Matthew's contribution was simply to reiterate the relevance of these themes to the concerns of his community in the aftermath of Jerusalem's fall in 70 CE, precisely because the destruction of the city and its Temple had posed anew this series of theological concerns.

As we have seen, Matthew's Deuteronomistic outlook can be accounted for largely on the basis of his source materials. But if that be so, what assurance have we that the Evangelist, for all his reiteration of the motif, has the fall of Jerusalem in mind? Similar emphases on issues of sin, covenant, Temple and community in contemporary Jewish writings have suggested an analogy. But the key to Matthew's redactional and theological purpose lies in his references to Jeremiah. For Jeremiah, as the review of this prophetic figure in the literature of Second Temple Judaism has shown, was for the Evangelist's Jewish contemporaries both the suffering prophet par excellence and the prophet par excellence of the fall of Jerusalem. The association of Jeremiah with the fall of the city and the destruction of its Temple in 70 CE, as variously indicated by Josephus, Pseudo-Philo, *2 Baruch* and *Paraleipomena Jeremiou* (also later by *Targum Lamentations* and *Lamentations Rabbah*), was therefore natural. And this association coheres with (1) Matthew's references to Jeremiah in 2.17-18 and 27.9-10 as having relevance to Jesus as a figure of suffering, one rejected by his own people, (2) Matthew's comparison of Jesus to Jeremiah and other rejected prophets in 16.14, and (3) Matthew's allusions to Jeremiah in the course of his narrative, even though the Evangelist may not have drawn immediate attention to their source or significance.

When compared to the portrayals of Jeremiah in contemporary Jewish literature, Matthew's references to Jeremiah, both explicit and implicit, indicate that his emphasis on Deuteronomistic motifs is not to be taken as simply general in nature, but that he specifically had in view the fall of Jerusalem and the destruction of the Herodian Temple.

In other words, the similarity of Matthew's Gospel to other contemporary responses to destruction is not merely thematic (i.e. concentrating only on questions of sin, covenant, Temple and community identity), but must also be seen as highlighting and providing a rationale for the events of the recent past. And this was so because, as with the other Jewish writings cited, the appeal to Jeremiah established a specific analogy to the previous destruction of Jerusalem.[1]

This comparison of Matthew's Gospel to other contemporary Jewish responses to the fall of Jerusalem thus confirms the earlier contention of this study that the Evangelist's redactional motive was not primarily christological, but rather apologetic, covenantal and ecclesiological. At a time of religious crisis for Judaism, Matthew took the opportunity to reiterate the theological justification for his own community's existence. In order to substantiate this thesis more fully, it will be helpful to describe in greater detail the social setting of Matthew's Gospel.

C. *The Social Setting of Matthew's Gospel*

In attempting to explain the function and purpose of NT polemic, or polemical apologetic, a number of scholars have appealed to the work of sociologist Lewis Coser. According to Coser, who reformulates proposals from earlier studies by Georg Simmel, social conflict presupposes and defines relationships both within and between competing social groups.[2] In fact, says Coser, 'the closer the relationship, the more intense the conflict'.[3] This applies in particular to religious

1. *Contra* Sayler (*Promises*, p. 145), who contrasts Matthew and 2 *Baruch* in this regard: 'Unlike 2 Baruch, Matthew does not use the destruction of 587 BCE as a model for the destruction of 70 CE. Instead, he elaborates Israel's past rejection of the prophets into an historical pattern of rejection which culminates in the death of Jesus, the last of God's messengers to Israel.'

2. L.A. Coser: 'Conflict sets boundaries between groups within a social system by strengthening group consciousness and awareness of separateness, thus establishing the identity of groups within the system' (*The Functions of Social Conflict* [New York: Free Press, 1956], p. 34; cf. pp. 36, 59). Similarly L. Kriesberg, *Social Conflicts* (Englewood Cliffs, NJ: Prentice-Hall, 1982), pp. 94-95 (cf. Overman, *Matthew's Gospel and Formative Judaism*, p. 146).

3. *Functions*, p. 67. Cf. Kriesberg (*Social Conflicts*, p. 66): 'For social conflicts to become manifest, three components are needed. First, the groups or parties to the conflict must be conscious of themselves as collective entities, separate

associations, although here Coser distinguishes between external conflict (including apostasy, whereby a group member adopts the values of the opposition) and internal conflict, or heresy, which threatens to split the group from within by means of a heterodox interpretation of the group's central values and aims.[1]

According to this analysis, external conflict can serve a positive social value by strengthening a group's internal cohesion:

> If a sect is defined as a body of 'elect' which through conflict sets itself off from the main body of the larger religious group, we may expect that such separation will carry in its wake a high degree of internal cohesion... Exclusion is attained through conflict with the outside and the maintenance of this exclusive standing requires the sect to be an internally cohesive conflict group.[2]

The corollary of this premise is that, because it is engaged in conflict with an outside group, a sect will be all the more vigilant to guard against internal dissent or heresy, for 'groups engaged in continued struggle with the outside tend to be intolerant within'.[3] In other words, internal and external conflict are to some degree commensurate, since both are aimed at defining or maintaining group identity. In fact, says Coser, groups may seek out enemies—either from within or without, whether real or perceived—in order to maintain a cohesive structure and identity.[4]

These principles have been applied both to the social world of early Christianity in general[5] and to Matthew's Gospel in particular.[6]

from others. Second, one or more groups must be aggrieved with their position relative to other groups. Finally, they must think that they can reduce their dissatisfaction by another group's acting or being different'.

1. *Functions*, pp. 69-71. For a more nuanced discussion of internal dissent, see *idem*, *Continuities in the Study of Social Conflict* (New York: Free Press; London: Collier-Macmillan, 1967), pp. 115-20.

2. *Functions*, p. 91; cf. p. 95; also, more generally, *Continuities*, pp. 33-35.

3. *Functions*, p. 103; cf. pp. 95-102.

4. *Functions*, p. 104; cf. p. 110.

5. So, with reference to Pauline literature, W.A. Meeks, *The First Urban Christians: The Social World of the Apostle Paul* (New Haven: Yale University Press, 1983), p. 96; for the Q community, Kloppenborg, *Formation*, pp. 167-68; for the Evangelists, in continuity with Jesus, J.D.G. Dunn, 'Pharisees, Sinners, and Jesus', in J. Neusner *et al.* (eds.), *The Social World of Formative Christianity and Judaism: Essays in Tribute to Howard Clark Kee* (Philadelphia: Fortress Press, 1988), pp. 275-76; and referring primarily to doctrinal disputes in the first three

Thus Przybylski concludes:

> On the basis of sociological conflict theory it is not surprising that the Matthean conflict is quite intense. After all, the conflict is between Jews who at one time belonged to a homogeneous group, and even after separation the two groups hold much in common. There was one primary point of disagreement—the messianic role of Jesus in Judaism.[1]

Accordingly, Matthew's polemic, which functions as an index of intracommunal conflict, serves to demarcate the boundaries between 'Christian Jews' and 'non-Christian Jews', establishing the identity of the Christian community in contradistinction to that of the 'scribes and Pharisees'. Vilification of the latter, in other words, is at least partly self-justificatory, thereby serving to define and to maintain a cohesive identity for the Matthaean community.

More nuanced is the proposal of J.A. Overman, according to whom Matthew's community experiences conflict on two separate fronts. On the one hand, says Overman, the Evangelist's attention to questions of Torah interpretation, internal discipline, institutionalization, leadership roles and authority in the Christian community is partly polemical in nature, and corresponds to similar developments in the world of Pharisaic Judaism following the destruction of the Jerusalem Temple.[2] In direct response to consolidation and institutionalization taking place within formative Judaism, Matthew's community feels the need, as a distinct minority, to close ranks and define its own religious and social

centuries of the church's existence, J.G. Gager, *Kingdom and Community: The Social World of Early Christianity* (Englewood Cliffs, NJ: Prentice-Hall, 1975), pp. 79-88 (Gager refers in turn to 'the conflict with Judaism over the claim to represent the true Israel; the conflict with paganism over the claim to possess true wisdom; and the conflict among Christian groups over the claim to embody the authentic faith of Jesus and the apostles' [p. 82]).

6. So B. Przybylski, 'The Setting of Matthean Anti-Judaism', in P. Richardson and D. Granskou (eds.), *Anti-Judaism in Early Christianity*. I. *Paul and the Gospels* (Waterloo: Wilfred Laurier University, 1986), pp. 198-99 (citing Coser and Simmel); Overman, *Matthew's Gospel and Formative Judaism*, pp. 146-47 (citing Coser and Kriesberg). Malina and Neyrey (*Calling Jesus Names*, *passim*) also employ models from sociology and cultural anthropology to describe the various social conflicts operating in Matthew's Gospel, although they do not make detailed reference to Coser (despite the citation, *Calling Jesus Names*, p. 159).

1. Przybylski, 'Matthaean Anti-Judaism', p. 199.

2. Overman, *Matthew's Gospel and Formative Judaism*, pp. 72-149; summarized pp. 152-54.

identity. On the other hand, the social imperative of internal cohesiveness, and in particular the concern expressed about civil courts and proceedings (e.g. 5.25-26, 40) seems to reflect a similar withdrawal from secular society.[1] On both fronts, then, not only does conflict with 'outsiders' lead to internal consolidation for this 'sectarian' minority, but the details and issues of that conflict determine the direction and structure of the latter's social development.

C.S. Rodd, however, in response to Gager, has challenged the application of Coser's analysis to a social milieu for which we have no independent access. Even apart from criticisms and refinements offered by other sociologists, Coser's analysis, argues Rodd, 'is adumbrated at a fairly high level of generalization and abstraction', and hence difficult to apply to such a narrow and specific situation as that of the early Christian world.[2] Moreover, says Rodd,

> there is a world of difference between sociology applied to contemporary society, where the researcher can test his theories against evidence which he collects, and historical sociology where he has only fossilized evidence that has been preserved by chance or for purposes very different from that of the sociologist.[3]

1. Overman, *Matthew's Gospel*, pp. 106-13; cf. pp. 154-56.

2. C. S. Rodd, 'On Applying a Sociological Theory to Biblical Studies', *JSOT* 19 (1981), pp. 100, 104; cf. B. Holmberg, *Sociology and the New Testament: An Appraisal* (Minneapolis: Fortress Press, 1990), pp. 8, 86 n. 25.

3. Rodd, 'Sociological Theory', p. 105. For a further critique of conflict theory, see Horsley, *Sociology and the Jesus Movement*, pp. 156-62; with an attempt to apply a refined model to the earliest followers of Jesus, pp. 162-65. Horsley (*Sociology and the Jesus Movement*, pp. 37, 153) criticizes, as a fundamental assumption of Coser's theory, the functionalist premise that conflict has an integrative social function; that it tends towards stabilization and equilibrium in inter-group relationships. We cannot make this assumption for Matthew's community, and even less for the subsequent history of the church. In fact, just the opposite appears to have been the case, as conflict between the followers of Jesus and the rest of Judaism eventually gave rise to a separate religious movement, but without diminution of serious conflict. Yet Coser's analysis may also accommodate such an eventuality, since for him conflict serves as a mechanism not only for social change within social systems, but also for the transformation of the social systems themselves (*Continuities*, pp. 19-33). Thus, according to Coser's analysis, there is a 'dialectical relationship between conflict and order, between stability and change' (*Continuities*, p. 111).

The problem at hand is illustrated by the difficulties inherent in the distinction, as maintained throughout Coser's study, between 'church' and 'sect'. For such a categorization, originating in the work of Weber and Troeltsch, is itself largely based on an analysis of mediaeval Christendom, which leads to the logical contradiction of 'using Christian sects of later ages to analyze and explain that very movement that they all wanted to imitate to the best of their capacity: New Testament Christianity!'[1] Nor is it possible, in keeping with the same social model, to contrast Matthew's community with a larger, 'homogeneous' Judaism, as both Przybylski and Overman suggest.[2] For by the time of the Gospel's composition, homogeneity was only just beginning to emerge from the welter of differing legal, cultic, pietistic and apocalyptic, nationalist and political interests that characterized Judaism prior to the fall of Jerusalem, and no doubt for some time afterward.[3] Rather, as Dunn's analysis of 1 Maccabees, *Jubilees*, *1 Enoch*, Qumran literature, the *Psalms of Solomon* and the *Assumption of Moses* shows (in the last three instances possibly referring, like Matthew, to the Pharisaic party), negative labelling and vilification were characteristic of inter-factional conflict within Judaism of that day.[4]

1. So Holmberg, *Sociology and the NT*, p. 110; cf. pp. 86-88. On the other hand, as Kee (*Knowing the Truth*, p. 38; cf. pp. 103-104) points out, Weber was extremely cautious regarding the applicability of such 'ideal types' to specific historical situations.

2. Przbylski, 'Matthean Anti-Judaism', p. 199 (cited above); Overman, *Matthew's Gospel*, pp. 9-23.

3. Cf. Holmberg, *Sociology and the NT*, pp. 91, 98-99. Moreover, self-definition is not only accomplished in the context of conflict or polemic. For a discussion of how the Matthean parable of the labourers in the vineyard (20.1-16) may have served the Evangelist's definition of his community, see J. Riches, 'Parables and the Search for a New Community', in Neusner *et al.* (eds.), *Social World*, pp. 247-51, 254-57.

4. Dunn, 'Pharisees, Sinners, and Jesus', pp. 276-80; cf. Malina and Neyrey, *Calling Jesus Names*, pp. 66-67. The rebuttal by Horsley (*Sociology and the Jesus Movement*, p. 136) that 'the conflict between the Jesus movement and the Pharisees appears not as a conflict between two religious reform movements but as one between local Galilean communities and representatives of the central governing authorities', however relevant for the historical origins of Christianity, does not apply to Matthew. The widespread evidence cited by Overman (*Matthew's Gospel*, pp. 9-23) is consistent with that presented by Dunn, and, in fact, supports Dunn's interpretation.

It is clear, nonetheless, that one significant feature of Matthew's redaction is his interpretation of conflict as it relates to the concerns of his community. Here, as we have seen, Matthew's Gospel mediates between and therefore reflects both the 'interests' of traditions about Jesus and those of the Christian community for which the Evangelist writes. Matthew is, therefore, both the recipient of Jesus traditions that shape his own religious outlook and the shaper of those traditions into forms that correspond to the needs and interests of his immediate audience.[1] And Coser's analysis offers a new way of looking at this data.[2]

This study has concentrated on Matthew's interpretation of conflict on three different but related levels: (1) the conflict between Jesus and the Jewish leaders, (2) the conflict between Israel and Rome, and (3) the conflict between Christian prophets or missionaries from the Matthaean community and the non-Christian Jewish community. Each of these conflicts, as interpreted according to a Deuteronomistic model, was constitutive for the community's identity and self-understanding. For a Deuteronomistic outlook provided the interpretative framework for the reciprocal definition of such competing, even conflicting, religious groups.[3]

1. Of course, the correlation between tradition and community may be either positive or negative, either affirming or challenging the latter's understanding of Jesus and his teaching (cf. Holmberg, *Sociology and the NT*, pp. 123-25), so that the presence of any particular element of tradition is no guarantee that the community was in agreement with it.

Furthermore, the interests of the community can only be inferred (with no assurance of accuracy) from those of the Evangelist. Yet if one is to talk about the 'Matthaean community' at all, one is forced to assume a positive correlation between Matthaean redactional emphases and the interests or needs of the community for which he wrote. For of all such redactional emphases, the Evangelist's depiction of Jesus' disciples is the most likely to reflect the situation of his own community.

2. Cf. Holmberg (*Sociology and the NT*, pp. 12-15) on the unavoidable use of models, even imperfect ones: 'Models... should be used heuristically, i.e., as a help to frame new questions and look for evidence nobody cared about before ...theoretical concepts do not impose a rule, but hasten and facilitate the interrogation of evidence' (p. 15).

3. Concentrating on Mt. 23–25, and comparing it to *4 Ezra* and *2 Baruch*, G.N. Stanton ('The Gospel of Matthew and Judaism', *BJRL* 66 [1984], pp. 280-84) provides a similar analysis of the social function of Matthew's apocalypticism, suggesting that the prospect of apocalyptic vindication provides 'a final note of consolation and encouragement' for a minority Christian community, as they respond to

With regard to the first level of conflict, those who professed allegiance to Jesus of Nazareth identified themselves with a rejected and vindicated prophet/messiah.[1] It was not their allegiance to Jesus per se that was distinctive, but the Christian allegiance to Jesus as rejected by his own people that set this community apart. They were those, in other words, who did *not* reject Jesus. With regard to the conflict between Israel and Rome, Matthew's Gospel, as we have seen, is similar to other contemporary Jewish writings in its Deuteronomistic explanation for the fall of Jerusalem in terms of sin, covenant, Temple symbolism and the subsequent redefinition or reconstitution of the faithful community. And with respect to the third level of conflict, Matthew understands the persecuted and rejected prophets of his own community to be, in this respect, like the prophets of old. Here, once again, the identity of these emissaries derives, at least in part, from their experience of conflict.

All three levels of conflict can, however, also be subsumed under a fourth category that is especially germane to a Deuteronomistic outlook: that of conflict between true and false prophecy.[2] Using this model, we are able to see with particular clarity how Matthew's Deuteronomistic concerns function not only theologically (i.e. as theodicy, with respect both to the rejection of Jesus and to the fall of Jerusalem) but also with regard to community definition and self-

'the trauma of the parting of the ways from Judaism, to the perceived hostility of both Jewish and Gentile society at large and to serious internal dissension within the community'. In this respect, Deuteronomistic and apocalyptic outlooks apparently served similar functions.

1. In terms of conflict theory, a Deuteronomistic interpretation of history can account for the reintegration of a previously vilified, yet subsequently vindicated community leader, as Coser himself points out: 'The Jewish prophets... were feared, despised, and outcast by the religious and secular powers of their day. Yet, as Max Weber has noted, [because of the oracles of the prophets] "... the belief of the people was not only unbroken by the fearful political fate, but in a unique and quite unheard of historical paradox was definitely confirmed"' (Coser, *Continuities*, pp. 132-33, citing Weber, *Ancient Judaism*). For Matthew, of course, the vindicated prophet is Jesus.

2. On false prophecy in the NT generally, cf. Schnider, *Jesus der Prophet*, pp. 63-67. As Patte observes in his study of *Sib. Or.* 3.62-91 (*Early Jewish Hermeneutic*, pp. 188-89, 201), and as does J. Reiling in his survey of Philo and Josephus ('The Use of ΨΕΥΔΟΠΡΦΗΤΗΣ in the Septuagint, Philo and Josephus', *NovT* 13 [1971], pp. 151-55), the problem of false prophecy is also dealt with in other contemporary Jewish works.

understanding. For the distinction between true and false prophecy provides the Matthaean community with an explanation, at a single stroke, of (1) its origins (referring to Jesus, like John the Baptist, as a true prophet, with themselves as his followers), (2) its religious distinctiveness and *raison d'être* (referring to the fall of Jerusalem as a judgment on those who have rejected true prophecy), and (3) its present experience (either actual suffering or simply the apprehension of persecution, with the concomitant need to define community boundaries in the face of such a danger).

Matthew provides clear evidence that 'false prophets' were of concern to his community. For in the conclusion to the Sermon on the Mount, Matthew records Jesus' warning.

> Beware of false prophets [ἀπο τῶν ψευδοπροφητῶν], who come to you in sheep's clothing but inwardly are ravenous wolves. You will know them by their fruits... (7.15-16).
>
> Not every one who says to me, 'Lord, Lord', shall enter the kingdom of heaven, but he who does the will of my Father who is in heaven. On that day many will say to me, 'Lord, Lord, did we not prophesy in your name [τῷ σῷ ὀνόματι ἐπροφητεῦσαν], and cast out demons in your name, and do many mighty works in your name?' And then I will declare to them, 'I never knew you; depart from me, you evildoers' (7.21-23).

In these two instances Matthew has added references to false prophecy to Q material, the meaning of which is thereby altogether transformed (cf. Lk. 6.43-46; 13.25-27). As a result of these emendations, the second mention of false prophecy in 7.22 reiterates the reference in 7.15, indicating that the entire section from 7.15 to 7.23 has one rather than two groups of heretics in view.[1]

It is characteristic of this group of heretics that they practise

1. So Davies, *Setting*, p. 200; E. Schweizer, 'Observance of the Law and Charismatic Activity in Matthew', *NTS* 16 (1969–70), pp. 224-25; H. Geist, 'Die Warnung vor den falschen Propheten—eine ernste Mahnung an die heutige Kirche: Zu Mt 7,15-23; 24,11f.24', in H. Merklein and J. Lange (eds.), *Biblische Randbemerkungen: Schülerfestschrift für Rudolf Schnackenburg zum 60. Geburtstag* (Würzburg: Echter Verlag, 1974), p. 140; P.S. Minear, 'False Prophecy and Hypocrisy in the Gospel of Matthew', in J. Gnilka (ed.), *Neues Testament und Kirche. [Festschrift] Für Rudolf Schnackenburg* (Freiburg: Herder, 1974), p. 80; Davies and Allison, *Matthew*, pp. 693-94, 710-11; *contra* Bonnard, *Matthieu*, p. 105; D. Hill, 'False Prophets and Charismatics: Structure and Interpretation in Matthew 7,15-23', *Bib* 57 (1976), pp. 339-41.

deception ('wolves in sheep's clothing'), but are betrayed by their actions ('you will know them by their fruits'). Specifically, they call on the Lord and the power of his name by prophesying, casting out demons and performing δυνάμεις πολλάς, yet in so doing they fail either to produce 'good fruit' or to do 'the will of my Father who is in heaven'. This combination of deceptive practices and Christian proclamation suggests that these false prophets represent an internal rather than an external threat to the community; that they are those who claim to be followers of Jesus by assuming the appearance of discipleship while in reality remaining something altogether different.[1]

Whereas in the first instance the (disguised) identity of the false prophets is apparently clearly discernible ('bad fruit' versus 'good'), in the second it only becomes evident in the context of final judgment. The Lord's judgment will be to expel them, declaring them to be ἐργαζόμενοι τὴν ἀνομίαν. In fact, says Jesus, the advent of false prophets will be 'a sign of [his] coming and of the close of the age' (24.3):

> And many false prophets [ψευδοπροφῆται] will arise and lead many astray... (24.11).

1. So Davies, *Setting*, pp. 199-200; Schweizer, 'Observance of the Law', pp. 216-17; E. Cothenet, 'Les prophètes chrétiens dans l'évangile selon Saint Matthieu', in Didier (ed.), *L'évangile selon Matthieu*, p. 300; Geist, 'Warnung', pp. 141-42; Aune, *Prophecy*, pp. 223-24. Barth ('Gesetzesverständnis', in *Überlieferung und Auslegung*, p. 68 n. 2 [ET, p. 73 n. 2]) notes that in Matthew the figure of the sheep consistently refers to the faithful, either actual (10.16; 18.12; 25.32-33; 26.31) or potential followers of Jesus (9.36; 10.6; 15.24; 18.12). A. Sand ('Propheten, Weise, und Schriftkundige in der Gemeinde des Matthäusevangeliums', in J. Haine [ed.], *Kirche im Werden: Studien zum Thema Amt und Gemeinde im Neuen Testament* [Munich: Schöningh, 1976], pp. 174-75; presumably following Zahn, *Matthäus*, p. 314) suggests that 'sheep's clothing' refers to the dress of an OT prophet.

Matthew's Gospel demonstrates a consistent interest in the need to distinguish true from false elements within the Christian community; so, e.g., 5.13 (tasteless salt), and the parables of the houses built on sand and rock (7.24-27), the wheat and tares (13.24-30, 37-43, referring, like 7.23, to ἀνομία [13.41]), the net (13.47-50), wedding garment (22.11-14), ten bridesmaids (25.1-13), talents (25.14-30), and sheep and goats (25.31-46). This concern may also account for Matthew's deletion of the episode of the non-adherent exorcist (Mk 9.39; cf. Cothenet, 'Les prophètes chrétiens', pp. 301-302).

> For false Christs and false prophets [ψευδόχριστοι καὶ ψευδοπροφῆται] will arise and show great signs and wonders, so as to lead astray, if possible, the elect (24.24).

Here, too, there are signs of Matthew's redactional activity: 24.11 is an addition to Markan material (cf. Mk 13.13). Mt. 24.24, on the other hand, derives from Mk 13.22.[1] But the similar description of the false prophets' activities indicates that the same group is in view here as in the Sermon on the Mount.[2] Jesus begins his account of the last days with a warning that adversaries will come 'in [his] name' (24.4), as previously in 7.22. Their attempt to lead the disciples astray (24.4-5, 24c) will include σημεῖα μεγάλα καὶ τέρατα[3] (24.24b), a description that recalls the δυνάμεις πολλάς of 7.22.[4] In both passages the work of the false prophets is characterized as ἀνομία.[5] Here, moreover, the threat of deception and apostasy occurs in the context of further internal and external dangers to the Christian

1. Although D omits ψευδόχριστοι from Mk 13.22.

2. So Davies: 'That [Matthew] is thinking of false prophets within the Church would seem to be substantiated by xxiv.24 not only by the fact that it is the elect who are led astray by them... but also by the juxtaposition of false prophets with false Christs: false Christs, unlike Antichrist, could only arise within the Church' (*Setting*, p. 201; cf. Burnett, *Testament*, p. 248, and on the situation envisaged in 24.10-28 generally, *Testament*, pp. 247-73). The distinction proposed by Barth ('Gesetzesverständnis', p. 70; cf. Geist, 'Warnung', p. 143) of a separate group of opponents in 24.24 is unnecessary.

3. Or καὶ τέρατα μεγάλα in 28 1241 1424; καὶ τέρατα (= Mk 13.22) ℵ W* *pc*.

4. *Contra* Geist, 'Warnung', p. 143.

5. This term does not designate 'moral laxity' (Kilpatrick, *Origins*, p. 127), 'libertinism' (Hummel, *Auseinandersetzung*, p. 27), 'antinomianism' (Barth, 'Gesetzesverständnis', pp. 152-53), or 'moral conduct' (Schweizer, 'Observance of the Law', p. 225) per se. Rather, as the contexts of 7.15-20 (cf. 7.23), 13.41 and 23.28 indicate, it refers to the failure of an inward obedience despite the outward appearance of piety, a situation described in 24.12 as 'love growing cold' (so Davies, *Setting*, pp. 202-206; Cothenet, 'Prophètes chrétiens', p. 300, cf. p. 306; Burnett, *Testament*, pp. 253-56). In this connection, Hill ('False Prophets and Charismatics', pp. 342-47; cf. Minear, 'False Prophecy and Hypocrisy', pp. 88-93) points out the similarity between the false prophets and the Pharisees of ch. 23, although this does not necessitate an identification of the two groups. For a review of proposed identifications of the false prophets in question (albeit referring to 7.15-23), see Hill, 'False Prophets and Charismatics', pp. 327-38; Davies and Allison, *Matthew*, pp. 701-702.

community: tribulation, death and universal hatred 'by all nations' on the one hand (24.9); 'stumbling' (σκανδαλισθήσονται),[1] betrayal and more hatred, on the other (24.10).

The polemic against false prophets stands in contrast to the depiction, as we saw earlier, of at least some members of the Christian community as true prophets.[2] The latter are characterized by their having been sent (together with σοφοί and γραμματεῖς) by Jesus himself (23.34a).[3] The same passage implies that these Christian prophets were involved in a mission to Israel (ἐγὼ ἀποστέλλω πρὸς ὑμᾶς προφήτας), as were the disciples generally (10.16-23). And it was in this context, as emissaries to Israel, that these prophets experienced rejection (23.34b; 23.37 // 21.35; cf. 5.12).[4] Matthew's references to

1. Cf. Bornkamm, 'Enderwartung und Kirche', in *Überlieferung und Auslegung*, p. 44 n. 2; Burnett, *Testament*, pp. 249-50.

2. Cf. summaries above, Chapter 2, §A.2.c. Minear proposes that even as Matthew's disciples/prophets serve as positive models for congregational leadership, so the warnings against false prophets are directed to Christian leaders: 'Each Christian prophet faced the danger of becoming, quite unaware, a false prophet' ('False Prophecy and Hypocrisy', p. 85). His analysis is vitiated, however, by its dependence on a hypothetical reconstruction of Matthew's community situation.

3. On the one hand, the distinction between 'prophets', 'righteous', 'wise' and 'scribes' seems to imply a series of distinct identities, if not separate ministerial offices within the community (so Kilpatrick, *Origins*, pp. 111, 126-127; Haenchen, 'Matthäus 23', p. 43; D. Hill, 'Dikaioi as a Quasi-technical Term', *NTS* 11 [1964–65], pp. 296-302; Hummel, *Auseinandersetzung*, pp. 27-28; Strecker, *Weg*, pp. 37-38; Sand, 'Propheten, Weise, und Schriftkundige', pp. 173-84; Burnett, *Testament*, pp. 172-78; Overman, *Matthew's Gospel and Formative Judaism*, pp. 113-24; *contra* Steck, *Israel*, p. 313 n. 2). Yet as we saw earlier, 5.11-12 identifies disciples with the prophets and their fate; 10.40-42 identifies disciples with prophets and righteous (cf. Schweizer, 'Observance of the Law', p. 223); the 'wise and scribes' of 23.34 are apparently Matthew's substitute for Q's more general 'apostles' (cf. Lk. 11.49); and 23.37 places prophets and 'emissaries' in parallel. All of this suggests a general identification of disciples as 'prophets', whatever more particular role specific members of this latter group may have played within the community.

4. This is not to deny that the Matthaean community was also engaged in a mission to Gentiles (10.18; 24.14; 26.13; 28.19), among whom they likewise experienced persecution (24.9). Nonetheless, the terms of Jesus' address in 23.34 seem to suggest that the Jewish mission was still active. Here we recall once more Harvey's observation ('Forty Strokes Save One', pp. 90-93) that the prospect of judicial flogging (Mt. 10.17) anticipates the Christian emissaries remaining within the sphere of Jewish religious jurisprudence—in other words, within Israel.

'stoning' (21.35-36; 23.37) may, in fact, imply that they were rejected as false prophets, as may also Jesus' warning that 'if they have called the master of the house Beelzebul, how much more will they malign those of his household' (10.25).

Matthew's references to Jeremiah may be of further relevance in this regard. Such references focus in the first instance on Jesus, contributing to the depiction of him as a rejected prophet, and, for the most part, address the situation of the community only indirectly. Yet the internal struggle against false prophets and prophecy could have provided an additional dimension to Matthew's example of Jeremiah. For Jeremiah's own ministry was characterized by opposition to and from false prophets. Jeremiah himself, of course, was accused of false prophecy (Jer. 26.9-11)—as was, apparently, Jesus also (Mt. 26.61-68).

This dynamic is rendered especially prominent by the innovative language of LXX Jeremiah. Gundry, for example, argues that Mt. 7.22 in particular intentionally alludes to LXX Jer. 14.14 and 34.12 [MT 27.15].

> Both passages in Jer concern false prophets, as does Mt 7.22. Throughout Mt and the rest of the NT the expression '(in) the name of...' regularly takes a preposition. Here the Hebrew has בְּ. Therefore, Mt's simple dative shows slavish dependence on the LXX of Jer 34.12.[1]

In LXX Jer. 34.12 προφητεύουσιν [LXX^{A} + ἐπί] τῷ ὀνόματι μου renders MT נבאים בשמי, with God as the speaker. To this may be compared similar renderings of נבא בשם יהוה by an instrumental dative at 26[33].9 [LXX^{S} + ἐπί] and 26[33].20 [LXX^{A} + ἐπί] and by ἐπί at

1. *Use of the OT*, p. 135 (cf. *idem*, *Matthew*, p. 122); the discrepancy in verse (as well as chapter) numbering for the LXX of MT Jer. 27.15 follows the Ziegler (*Septuaginta Gottingensis*) edition, whereas the Rahlfs *Septuaginta* follows the versification of the MT. One or both of Jer. 14.14 and 34.12/27.15 is also cited by Hühn; Dittmar; N-A^{26}; *UBSGNT* (3rd edn), p. 908; Zahn, *Matthäus*, p. 319; Klostermann, *Matthäus*, p. 71; Smith, *Matthew*, p. 110; Fenton, *Matthew*, p. 114; Rothfuchs, *Erfüllungszitate*, p. 95 n. 25; Schweizer, *Matthäus*, pp. 113-14; Shires, *Finding the OT*, p. 194; Maier, *Matthäus*, I, p. 249; Schlatter, *Matthäus*, p. 259; Vouga, 'Seconde Passion', p. 79; Gnilka, *Matthäusevangelium*, I, p. 273; Davies and Allison, *Matthew*, pp. 693, 715; Holladay, *Jeremiah*, II, p. 95 (who draws attention [pp. 92-93] to a similar use of Jer. 14.14 at Qumran, in CD 6.1); to the contrary, Wolff, *Jeremia*, p. 165 n. 7.

Jer. 11.21, 14.14, 15, 23.25 and 29[36].9.[1] All but 11.21 and 26[33].9, 20 refer directly to false prophecy, as is the case in Matthew's text. But even these, while describing the ministry of Jeremiah, do so in the context of opposition, in the latter case that of false prophets.

Yet even though the specific combination of the verb נבא with בשם יהוה is found only in Jeremiah, all three of the LXX uses of the instrumental dative for this combination are textually ambiguous. And even if we ignore the textual ambiguities, it is not clear why Matthew would have wanted here to recall LXX Jer. 34.12. Granted, this is the only passage that both refers to false prophecy and employs the simple dative. Otherwise, however, it is theologically indistinguishable from the other passages cited. Gundry's appeal to Jer. 14.14, which uses the preposition ἐπί, altogether undermines Matthew's alleged reference to the dative of 34.12. For if 14.14 forms a valid parallel, so also must LXX Jer. 14.15, 23.25, 29[36].9 and even MT 29.21. Furthermore, Deut. 18.19-22, which likewise addresses the problem of false prophets and prophecy, offers close parallels to both Jeremiah and Matthew (LXX [λαλήσῃ ὁ προφήτης] ἐπὶ τῷ ὀνόματί μου/κυρίου/θεῶν ἑτερῶν [*quater*]).[2]

Recognition of the distinctive LXX term ψευδοπροφήτης, however,

1. Except when he deletes the ὄνομα formula altogether from his source material, Matthew rarely alters the preceding preposition. The only exception is at 10.42 (εἰς from Mark 9.41 ἐν). Compare the following:

	Matthew	=	Mark	=	Luke
διά	24.9		13.13		21.17
ἐν	21.9		11.9		19.38
	23.39		[citing LXX Ps. 117.26]		13.35
ἐπί	18.5		9.37		9.48
	24.5		13.6		24.8

2. Two additional considerations suggest that Matthew need not have derived this grammatical construction from Jeremiah. First, Matthew appears at 12.21 to have deleted the preposition ἐπί from his quotation of LXX Isa. 42.4 to yield a similar instrumental dative with ἐλπίζειν. Unless Matthew is following an early textual variant (so Gundry, *Use of the OT*, p. 115), these uses of the dative suggest a stylistic tendency on his part, notwithstanding his clear preference for the preposition εἰς with ὄνομα (10.41 [2×]; 10.42; 18.40; 28.19). Second, as BDF §206(2) observes, the τῷ σῷ ὀνόματι in 7.22 'is good Greek' (cf. Mk 9.38 A X; Jas 5.10 A K L), to which can be compared 'τῷ τῆς πόλεως ὀνόματι in an inscription from Asia Minor of 37 AD'.

offers an alternative solution, since ψευδοπροφῆται are of special concern to Matthew. For this word is, with only one exception, unique to Jeremiah within the LXX,[1] and in three passages coincides, as in Mt. 7.15-22, with mention of prophecy in the name of the Lord.[2] In these passages, moreover, Jeremiah's concern to distinguish between true and false prophets in Jerusalem, especially as emphasized by the innovative language of the LXX, is altogether consistent with Matthew's redactional emphasis on a similar need within his own community. For a significant feature of Matthew's ψευδοπροφῆται, as in Jeremiah, is their claim to prophesy τῷ...ὀνόματι [κυρίου] (whatever grammatical variations this formula may exhibit). On the other hand, Philo, Josephus and the *Testament of Judah* also refer to ψευδοπροφῆται, indicating the currency of this designation in the intertestamental period.[3] And at least in 24.24, which apparently refers to the same group of opponents, Matthew derives the term ψευδοπροφῆτης not from Jeremiah, but from his Markan source. On balance, then, the language of 7.22 recalls that of several passages in LXX Jeremiah 33, 34 and 36, although the evidence does not indicate a more specific derivation, much less 'slavish dependence'.[4]

The theme of opposition between true and false prophecy is already inherent to some extent within a Deuteronomistic view of history, according to which the people heed those who speak falsely and reject

1. On ψευδοφήτης in the LXX as an interpretative rendering of נביא in Jer. 6.13; 33[26].7, 8, 11, 16; 34[27].9; 35[28].1; 36[29].1, 8; and Zech. 13.2, see Reiling, 'Use of ΨΕΥΔΟΠΡΟΦΗΤΗΣ', pp. 147-56. As Reiling demonstrates, this designation attempts to differentiate false prophets from true: the Hebrew text refers without distinction to הנביאים.

2. So ψευδοπροφήτης in LXX Jer. 33[26].7, 8, 11, 16 with 'prophecy in the name of the Lord' at vv. 9, 20; in 34.7 [MT 27.9] with v. 12 [MT v. 15]; and in 36[29].1, 8 with v. 9.

3. E.g., Philo, *Spec. Leg.* 4.8; Josephus, *Ant.* 8.236, 318, 402, 409; 9.133-37; 10.66, 104, 111; *War* 2.261; 6.286: Reiling, 'The Use of ΨΕΥΔΟΠΡΟΦΗΤΗΣ', pp. 151, 155. Also *T. Jud.* 21.9 (cf. BAGD s.v. ψευδοπροφήτης) and CD 6.1.

4. At the same time, we noted in Chapter 3 Matthew's possible linking of the false witnesses at Jesus' trial (Mt. 26) with the testimony of the false prophets who testified against Jeremiah (Jer. 26), whereby the fate of Jesus is linked to that of Jerusalem, and the citation of Lam. 2.15 in 27.39 with reference to the mocking of Jesus and, potentially, the downfall of Jerusalem as the consequence of false prophecy within her. Both allusions suggest the wider relevance of 'false prophecy' to Matthew's redactional programme.

the true prophets of God. But since the danger posed by false prophets was undoubtedly a concern within Matthew's own community, a Deuteronomistic understanding of Israel's historical experience seems to have encouraged Matthew to draw literary and thematic analogies to the situation of Jeremiah.

The foregoing analysis suggests, therefore, a scenario similar in several respects to that proposed by Coser, albeit in more general terms. For the Deuteronomistic outlook was itself an interpretation of conflict that served the need for community self-definition. More specifically, it now appears that in Matthew's Gospel both external and internal conflicts were formulated in parallel terms. With regard to external conflict, Jesus had been rejected by Israel as a false prophet, although Matthew affirms him to be a true prophet.[1] In turn, the Christian disciples and emissaries to Israel were likewise persecuted and rejected as false prophets. But as was the case with Jesus, so for the Matthaean disciples: from a Deuteronomistic perspective, such rejection only served to validate their respective ministries.

A similar affirmation of the faithful disciples as true prophets was implicit, at least, in the community's simultaneous internal struggle against false prophets. For just as the disciples had to distance themselves and their rejected leader from accusations of false prophecy, so they had to distinguish between true and false prophets in their own midst.[2]

1. There is, moreover, some slight indication that the accusations of false prophecy may have been reciprocal, that is that the leaders of Israel were themselves understood to be false prophets. The Q text in 12.27 (// Lk. 11.19) could imply as much: 'And if I cast out demons by Beelzebul, by whom do your sons cast them out? Therefore they shall be your judges.' But if this represents the view of earlier Christian tradition, Matthew does not emphasize it; see Davies, *Setting*, pp. 199-200.

2. This analysis bears some resemblance to, and therefore may serve to qualify the conclusions of, Vouga ('Seconde Passion', pp. 76-77, 81-82), who suggests that the figure of Jeremiah 'sert de cadre interprétatif de la narration matthéenne de la destinée de Jésus'. According to Vouga, there is in Matthew's references to the prophet a triple parallelism coordinating:

1. Jeremiah's opposition to false prophets in view of Jerusalem's destruction, whereby he is 'pris entre la parole de sa vocation et l'appartenance à son peuple';
2. Jesus' opposition to 'false prophets' (in the persons of scribes and Pharisees), which will lead to his death and the destruction of Jerusalem,

Charges and counter-charges of false prophecy within Matthew's Gospel indicate, first, the social and theological proximity of the conflicting groups. So close were they, in fact, and so difficult the problem of accurate discernment, that for some a final revelation of their true nature had to await the last judgment (7.23). Secondly, the gravity of the charges (in some instances, reciprocal) demonstrates the intensity of the conflict, since the accusation of false prophecy attacks the very heart of the opposing group's religious identity, most clearly so where there are allegations of demon-possession. Thirdly, the consistent nature of the charges reveals a direct analogy between internal and external conflicts, since both were formulated in the same terms. Of course, similar conclusions could be drawn simply from an analysis of Matthew's Deuteronomistic perspective, without any reference to conflict theory. But if Coser's thesis has any relevance to a social situation so far removed from its own context, it is in drawing our attention to the function and to the inter-relatedness of the various levels of conflict in which Matthew's community was involved.

It now appears that the conflicts portrayed in Matthew's Gospel were fourfold: (1) between Jesus and the Jewish leaders; (2) between Israel and Rome; (3) between Christian prophets and those of the Jewish community who rejected their testimony; and (4) between faithful and unfaithful adherents ('true' versus 'false' prophets) within the Christian community itself. This study has attempted to demonstrate ways in which these conflicts may be coordinated within a generally Deuteronomistic outlook. The more specific contention here is that Matthew uses the name, example and testimony of Jeremiah to draw attention to at least some, if not all of these conflicts.

whereby he is 'pris entre la proclamation du Royaume des cieux et la fidélité à Israël'; and

3. The community's opposition to 'false prophets' (in the persons of 'charismatic enthusiasts'), once more in view of Jerusalem's destruction, whereby the community is 'prise entre son *status confessionis* christologique et son appartenance à la Synagogue'. While affirming the relevance of Matthew's Jeremiah references to questions of community identity, however, the present study has not found christological interests to be in view, as Vouga proposes. Nor does Vouga address the issue of how Matthew's Deuteronomistic outlook (and with it the references to Jeremiah) serve to redefine the community of God's people.

D. *Theodicy and Apologetics in Matthew's References to Jeremiah*

The attempt in this chapter to set Matthew's Gospel within the context of contemporary Jewish efforts to come to terms with the enormous impact of the fall of Jerusalem now permits a reformulation of the original thesis. In composing his Gospel, Matthew was heir to a variety of traditions about Jesus and his earliest followers, some of which depicted them as rejected prophets and accounted for the increasing failure of the mission to Israel—in contrast to the growing success of the Gentile mission—on these grounds. For Matthew, the fate of Jerusalem provides a critical stimulus for further sharpening this Deuteronomistic outlook. And to this end the Evangelist, first, reiterates the prophetic identities of John the Baptist, Jesus and the Christian disciples, and then, secondly, links the deaths of John and (above all) Jesus with the destruction of Jerusalem as cause and effect within a divine economy of covenantal accountability.

Similarly, the persecution experienced or anticipated by the later disciples—presumably including those of Matthew's own community—is understood to be typical of the fate encountered by all prophets sent to Israel, with Jesus not least among them. Jesus' own teaching indicates as much, for 'a disciple is not above his teacher, nor a servant above his master' (10.24). Thus the rejection experienced by Christian prophets serves to reinforce the validity of the Evangelist's Deuteronomistic outlook. For when the situations of the Christian prophets, Jesus and his Jewish predecessors are juxtaposed, they prove to be mutually illuminating.

The central contention here is that Matthew draws attention to his own sharpening of Deuteronomistic concern by referring to the prophet Jeremiah. Such references are both textual and typological in nature, explicit and implicit. The formula quotations of 2.17-18 and 27.9-10 both refer explicitly to the text of Jeremiah. And both describe rejection and mortal opposition to the messiah: at the beginning of his life by the Jewish authorities; at the end of his life by one of his own followers, and leading directly to his death. In coming to this conclusion we observed Matthew's creative use of the relevant scriptural texts. In 2.17-18 he cites Jer. 31[38].15 without regard to its original meaning or context, so that Rachel is made to lament for all those who have departed from Ramah/Bethlehem: the exiles of old, the exiled infant messiah, and the slaughtered innocents whose fate anticipates that of the nation as a whole. In 27.9-10 the Evangelist ascribes to Jeremiah a quotation from Zech. 11.13, taking advantage of significant textual variants in the Zechariah passage to suggest a link to Jer. 19.1-13, as well as to Jeremiah 32 and, just possibly, Lam. 4.2. Thus while Zechariah supplies the literal text of the quotation, Jeremiah, as the unexpected ascription indicates, provides its thematic substance: the betrayal of 'innocent blood' and the purchase of a burial plot that is emblematic of such a misdeed.

It has been argued that there are also a number of implicit textual allusions to Jeremiah, although not all of them can be established with equal certainty. Such allusions appear to coalesce around two related themes. The first is that of judgment, whether with reference to the ministries of John (3.12) and the disciples (4.19), or the judgment of Jesus against misuse of the Temple (21.13; 23.38; cf. 21.18-21; 24.2), for which he in turn is judged (26.59-66; 27.34, 39). The second theme is that of the new covenant established by the blood of Jesus (26.28), together with its particular features from Jer. 31.31-34 (11.27, 29; 23.8-10). The general tenor of these references is clear even if the evidence for some may be subject to debate.

In addition to textual quotations and allusions, there are also typological references to Jeremiah in Matthew's Gospel—although it is important to recall that textual and typological references are closely related, even interdependent. The most obvious typological reference is in 16.14 where the comparison of Jeremiah to Jesus suggests that the latter was characterized by suffering and rejection. The fact that Matthew inserted the name of Jeremiah into such a significant context provides a clear indication of its relevance for the Evangelist. Moreover, a number of additional features that appear in Matthew recall the life of Jeremiah, among them Matthew's genealogical reference to the generation of the Babylonian exile (1.11-12, 17), the rejection of Jesus by his own townspeople (13.51), the tradition of Jeremiah's death by stoning (21.35, 23.37, although here with reference to the disciples rather than to Jesus), and the fact that Jesus' departure from the Temple (23.37-24.2), like that of Jeremiah and his circle in an earlier day, anticipates and even causes its destruction.

Of particular significance in this connection is the motif of innocent blood. Both 2.17-18 and 27.9-10 describe the consequences of rejecting the messiah in terms of the shedding of innocent blood—in the first instance, that of the Bethlehemite children (although Jesus is the intended target of the slaughter); in the second, that of Jesus himself. Just as in the infancy narrative, so later in the Gospel the consequences of such opposition are seen to fall on the nation of Israel: whether the innocent children, Judas, or those who call down on themselves and their own 'children'—that is the generation of the Temple's destruction—responsibility for the shedding of Jesus' blood (27.25).

Reiterating this theme, Jesus' warning that 'all the innocent blood shed on earth' would come upon the present generation (23.35-36) anticipates, in all probability, a further reference to the prophecies of Jeremiah in the scene of Jesus' trial before Caiaphas (26.59-66). For according to Matthew's depiction of the trial and ensuing condemnation of Jesus, Jeremiah's prediction of 'innocent blood' falling upon the inhabitants of Jerusalem should they slay him, although unfulfilled in his own day, came to pass in the crucifixion of Jesus because the blood of one like Jeremiah was shed.

At the same time, Matthew's verbal parallel between the 'shed blood' of the prophets (23.35) and that of Jesus in the words over the cup (26.28) suggests that the theme of 'innocent blood' explains not only the reason for the judgment of God's people, but also the grounds for their restoration. Thus the death of the prophet Jesus, interpreted from a Deuteronomistic perspective, provides the theological turning point between the original covenant community of Israel and that which was established by the 'new covenant' of Jesus' blood.

The relevance of Jeremiah for Matthew, therefore, was twofold. Most obviously, Matthew understood Jesus to be a prophet-like-Jeremiah: a figure of doom and suffering rejected by his own people for uttering words of judgment against Jerusalem and its Temple that ultimately proved to be true. Yet Jeremiah was also the prophet of the 'new covenant', so that reference to him and his words demonstrated for Matthew the complementarity of rejection and renewal, judgment and restoration, within the covenant purposes of God. Matthew found in Jeremiah the key to explaining both the demise of Israel and the establishment of the Christian community. Precisely because Jesus was like Jeremiah—with the rejection of the one by God's people being like the rejection of the other, and the corollary being that the fate of Jerusalem in the present day was like the fate of Jerusalem of old—Matthew saw his ἐκκλησία as a redefined 'Israel', a reconstituted people of God whose identity was at once bound up with and yet also separate from the rest of contemporary Judaism.

The foregoing study has attempted to establish the validity of this interpretation in several different ways. We have seen that in order to adumbrate his portrait of Jesus Matthew appeals, in greater or lesser degree, to other significant figures from Israel's past, among them Abraham, David, Moses, Jonah and Noah.[1] Each of these typologies provides a precedent for positing a similar use of traditions about Jeremiah. And except in the case of Noah, Matthew's references to these figures are both explicit and implicit, referring to the individual by name in the narrative while incorporating into the text specific OT phrases either by or about the figure in question.

With respect to Jeremiah himself, we have seen that perceptions regarding the prophet remain consistent throughout a considerable range of Jewish writings that were roughly contemporary with Matthew's Gospel. For in keeping with his call (Jer. 1.10), Jeremiah was constantly associated with both the downfall and ultimate restoration of Jerusalem. He was a figure of woe, persecution and desolation in Pseudo-Philo, Qumran and later rabbinic literature, the actual cause of Jerusalem's destruction according to Jesus ben Sirach, and the prophetic example to which Josephus compares himself when recounting his own unheeded warnings that Jerusalem would be overthrown. In addition, his career provided the pseudepigraphical point of departure for several apocalyptic responses to the events of 70 and 135 CE, among them *2 Baruch*, *3 Baruch* and *Paraleipomena Jeremiou*.[2]

Conversely, Jeremiah's prophecy of a seventy-year exile, traditions connecting him with the sacred Temple vessels (including the Temple keys), and typological comparisons with Moses all associate this prophet with restoration and return.[3] Of similar import, particularly within the Qumran community, is Jeremiah's prophecy of a 'new covenant' between God and his people.

Furthermore, this study has compared Matthew's use of Jeremiah traditions and his Deuteronomistic interpretation of the Roman war with other contemporary Jewish responses to the same events. We saw

1. In similar fashion, Elijah serves for Matthew as a 'type' of John the Baptist.

2. Or, as in the case of *2 Baruch* and *Paraleipomena Jeremiou*, the common Jeremiah traditions that underlie them both.

3. While none of these traditions are present in Matthew, I suggest, albeit tentatively, that because apocalyptic and rabbinic literature link Moses and Jeremiah typologically, the focus of Matthew's Moses typology on issues of covenant identity is at least consistent with this aspect of his Jeremiah typology.

how an explanation for the fall of Jerusalem in Deuteronomistic terms was able to account for that event both historically (i.e., as a repetition of the city's fate at the hands of previous conquerors) and theologically (i.e., as one more instance of divine judgment in response to covenantal unfaithfulness on the part of God's people). Indeed, the fact that the destructions of Jerusalem in 70 CE, and more thoroughly in 135 CE, could be seen as part of a larger pattern in the divine economy, rather than as isolated incidents, provided grounds for the hope of restoration, and so permitted the articulation of a meaningful theodicy in the face of overwhelming disaster.

In articulating their respective theodicies, Matthew's Gospel and the contemporary Jewish writings cited share a number of significant thematic features. For they focus in common on an examination of the relevance of the covenant, exploring the implications of such a disaster in terms of both God's and Israel's covenant faithfulness. Significant features of this examination include (1) a prophetic critique of the Temple and its cultus, re-evaluating the Temple's significance as the locus of the divine presence, (2) an explanation of national disaster as having been caused by national sin and apostasy, and, by way of response, (3) an attempt to redefine or reformulate the community of God's faithful.

In all such responses, Jewish and Christian alike, the ultimate focus is on the last of these issues. Jewish writers asked how the community could explain the destruction of Jerusalem, survive its impact, and reconstitute itself so that a similar disaster would not be repeated. For the followers of Jesus, critiques of the Temple and of Israel's faithlessness, on the one hand, and the parameters of Christian self-definition, on the other, had already been articulated prior to the crisis of the war with Rome. Yet these issues assumed a new relevance for Matthew and his community in the context of the debate between church and synagogue as to which constituted the true and faithful people of God, the 'sons of the kingdom.'

The fall of the Temple, it would seem, provided the final proof that God's first people had been judged, and that God's favor now rested on the followers of Jesus. Matthew's references to Jeremiah serve to call attention to such an interpretation of events. In short, even as God foretold the fall of Jerusalem through Jeremiah—thereby judging his people for their rejection of the prophetic message, yet with a view to their ultimate restoration—so, according to Matthew, God warned of imminent judgment on Jerusalem and its Temple in the person of Jesus, only to bring a new covenant community into existence in anticipation of its destruction.

One further matter which would have lent additional relevance to Matthew's use of Jeremiah traditions is that of the opposition within the Evangelist's community between true and false prophecy. It is not my contention that such a characterization is directly dependent on Jeremiah typology, since the opposition between true and false prophecy was already inherent within a Deuteronomistic outlook. Matthew, in fact, depicts the followers of Jesus as true prophets apart from any allusions to Jeremiah. Nonetheless, since (1) Jeremiah's ministry was characterized by opposition both to and from false prophets, (2) Jesus' ministry is compared to that of Jeremiah, and (3) their own ministry reflected that of Jesus, members of the Matthaean community may well have found additional relevance for their own experience in the Gospel's references to Jeremiah. Although indirect, the connection is not implausible.

It must again be stressed, however, that Matthew's references to Jeremiah do not of themselves bear the full weight of the Evangelist's Deuteronomistic interests, although they obviously play a contributory role. Rather, they serve primarily as pointers and sign-posts in the direction of a larger redactional emphasis. Nonetheless, the example of Jeremiah sums up for Matthew a whole range of Deuteronomistic motifs. These include (1) prophetic suffering and rejection, (2) the struggle between true and false prophets (or more generally between covenantal fidelity and infidelity), (3) divine judgment and theodicy in the history of God's people, and (4) restoration following disaster.

In terms of Matthew's adaptation of his source material, the example of Jeremiah provides a focus for more general Deuteronomistic concerns. From a theological perspective, however, just the opposite is the case, for the Evangelist interprets the example of Jeremiah according to a Deuteronomistic understanding of Israel's history. From either point of view, Matthew uses Jeremiah traditions as a bridge between Christology and ecclesiology, linking the experience of Jesus and his first disciples with the experience of his own community. In this way Jeremiah serves for Matthew (although by no means exclusively so) as a hermeneutical pivot on which turns not only the link between Israel in the past and Israel in the present—or between the covenant communities old and new—but also between

Jesus past and present—that is between tradition and discipleship in the kingdom of Christ.

Taken by themselves, Matthew's appeals to the words and example of Ἰερεμίου τοῦ προφήτου—whether the explicit references at 2.17, 16.14 and 27.9, or the less obvious allusions that the Evangelist has placed strategically throughout his Gospel narrative—do not represent a major feature of Matthew's redactional endeavour. Rather they are, as in the exchange between Jesus and his disciples at Caesarea Philippi, ultimately overshadowed by the more momentous proclamation of Jesus' messianic identity. Nonetheless, as this study has attempted to demonstrate, Matthew's references to Jeremiah highlight one important feature of that identity—a feature that was of importance to members of the Evangelist's community as they attempted to come to terms, like so many other Jews of that time, with the fate of Jerusalem, and as they sought as Christians to forge a new identity for themselves out of the crucible of religious and political turmoil which characterized their day.

Appendix

A Deuteronomistic Outlook and the Provenance of Matthew's Gospel

The relationship between church and synagogue, Jew and Gentile, in Matthew's Gospel has been extensively debated in recent years.[1] The view of the early Church Fathers (Papias, Irenaeus, Origen, *et al.*) that Matthew wrote in Hebrew for Jewish-Christian believers[2] is now almost universally rejected, although it is still maintained in modified form by some scholars.[3] Since, however, a variety of Jewish features are undoubtedly present in Matthew, the modern debate focuses on whether the Evangelist wrote from within a Jewish-Christian community—and, further, what degree of Jewish identity that community retained.

In 1930 B.W. Bacon argued that Matthew consciously organized his Gospel to parallel the five books of Moses, and so set Matthew's Gospel within the context of post-70 CE Judaism. Concurring with E. von Dobschütz that the Evangelist was a converted rabbi whose catechetical skills had been placed in the service of the gospel,[4] Bacon understood Matthew to be a 'Greek-speaking Jewish convert'.[5]

1. The present overview, in particular its schematization of the various critical positions, is indebted to Stanton, 'Origin and Purpose', pp. 1910-21.

2. For a discussion of these traditions, see Nepper-Christensen, *Matthäusevangelium*, pp. 37-75.

3. According to Schlatter, 'der Verfasser ist. . . ein Palästiner. . . [wer] sein Denken und Reden gleichzeitig aus zwei Sprachen schöpfte, aus dem Semitismus und aus dem Griechischen', although he adds that 'die Frage, ob eine Formel ursprünglich hebräisch oder ursprünglich griechisch oder in beiden Sprachgebieten ursprünglich gewesen sei, hat für die Deutung des Mat. keine Bedeutung' (*Matthäus*, pp. viii-ix). Cf. Gaechter, *Matthäus*, pp. 19-20 ('Matthäus nicht im mehr plebejischen Aramäisch schrieb, sondern in Hebräisch, der Sprache der Gebildeten' [p. 19]). This position has received renewed stimulus from the publication by G. Howard (*The Gospel of Matthew According to a Primitive Hebrew Text* [Macon, GA: Mercer University Press, 1987]) of a medieval Jewish version of Matthew in Hebrew, although Howard (p. 225) proposes that the Hebrew text is an independent composition rather than being the source for or a translation of Greek Matthew.

4. E. von Dobschütz, 'Matthäus als Rabbi und Katechet', *ZNW* 27 (1928), pp. 338-48 [ET 'Matthew as Rabbi and Catechist', in Stanton (ed.), *Interpretation*, pp. 19-29.

5. B.W. Bacon, *Studies in Matthew* (London: Constable; New York: Henry Holt, 1930), p. 29, cf. pp. 40-41, 81-82 ('unmistakably he is of Jewish origin and training, with unbounded reverence for the Law'). In his earlier article ('The "Five Books" of Matthew against the Jews', *The*

G.D. Kilpatrick, building on the work of both von Dobschütz and Bacon, related the attention given by Matthew to Torah, moral teaching and Jewish customs, on the one hand, together with the vilification of Pharisaic practices and reflections of Jewish persecution, on the other, to the rabbinic attempt following 70 CE to exclude all heretical and heterodox Jews from 'normative' Judaism. Nonetheless, for Kilpatrick, 'the opposition between Christian and Pharisee is for the evangelist an opposition within Judaism... We have, in fact, not an elimination of Judaism, but a reorientation', a subordination of Judaism 'to the central doctrine of Christ'.[1]

Acknowledging his debt to Kilpatrick, G. Bornkamm, in an essay that set the agenda for most of the subsequent debate, concurred that Matthew's Gospel reflects the interests of a Jewish-Christian congregation:

> The controversy within the Judaism led by the Pharisees is in full swing (sharp controversies, persecution), but the union is not yet torn apart and is tenaciously defended by the congregation itself, which regards itself as the true Judaism.[2]

For this reason, says Bornkamm, 'the struggle with Israel is still a struggle within its own walls', with Matthew emphasizing that both Jesus and his disciples are sent 'to the lost sheep of the house of Israel' (10.6; 15.24).[3]

R. Hummel carried Bornkamm's argument further, although in a distinctive fashion. According to Hummel, the continuity between Jews and those of Matthew's church consists in their common focus on Torah. For Christians, however, Jesus' interpretation of Torah vis-à-vis that of Judaism is definitive, and therefore constitutive of the community's identity.[4] Moreover, Matthew believes any separation between church and synagogue, should it occur, to be yet in the future (so 8.12, ἐκβληθήσονται;[5] 21.43, ἀρθήσεται...δοθήσεται), even though the rejection of the messiah by many Jews has opened the way for the Gentiles.[6] Hence

Expositor 8.15 [1918], pp. 56-66), Bacon notes only that Matthew is addressed to a Jewish audience, but does not imply that it was written from within Judaism.

1. Kilpatrick, *Origins*, pp. 122-23.

2. Bornkamm, 'Enderwartung und Kirche', p. 19 n. 2 [ET p. 22 n. 2]. According to Bornkamm, 'Daß hier das Bild der judenchristlichen Gemeinde ersteht, die am Gesetz festhält und sich vom Verbande des Judentums noch nicht gelöst hat, vielmehr im scharfen Gegensatz zu einer gesetzesfreien Lehre und Mission steht, ist völlig deutlich' (p. 19). Cf. the conclusion of P. Richardson (*Israel in the Apostolic Church* [SNTSMS, 10; Cambridge: Cambridge University Press, 1969], p. 194): 'In so far as he works towards a theory of the Church as "true Israel", [Matthew] does it as a Jewish Christian for a Jewish Christian community, as part of a dispute with a pharisaic Synagogue which is also claiming to be "true Israel"'.

3. Bornkamm, 'Enderwartung und Kirche', pp. 36-37 [ET pp. 39-40]. Bornkamm appears to have modified his position in subsequent studies, now understanding there to be a definite separation between Judaism and the Matthaean community; cf. J.P. Meier, *Law and History in Matthew's Gospel: A Redactional Study of Mt. 5.17-48* (AnBib, 71; Rome: Biblical Institute, 1976), pp. 9-10; Stanton, 'Origin and Purpose', pp. 1913-14.

4. Cf. Hummel, *Auseinandersetzung*, pp. 36-64, 157-59.

5. Supported by $\aleph^{a}$ B C K L W X Δ Θ Π f^{1} f^{13} 33 892 vg $cop^{sa,bo}$ etc.; the alternative reading ἐξελεύσονται ($\aleph^{*}$ 0250 it^{k} syr^{mss}) is also in the future tense.

6. Hummel, *Auseinandersetzung*, pp. 31-33 (Matthew's church 'befindet sich im Stadium der

Matthew's church incorporates both Jews and Gentiles alike.

There have been several attempts to locate Matthew's Gospel more precisely in relation to contemporary developments within post-destruction Judaism, either before the council(s) of Jamnia and the *Birkat ha-Minim* (e.g. Hummel, Goulder, Brown)[1] or shortly after them (so Kilpatrick, Davies).[2] But the incompleteness of our knowledge of the period renders such conclusions necessarily tentative. After examining the evidence, Davies, for example, postulates that Matthew's Sermon on the Mount may have been a Christian response to Jamnia, perhaps corresponding both in structure and in content to features of emerging Pharisaic legislation; that is, that

> It was the desire and necessity to present a formulation of the way of the New Israel at a time when the rabbis were engaged in a parallel task for the Old Israel that provided the outside stimulus for the Evangelist.[3]

So while Davies views Matthew's debate with Pharisaic Judaism as being '*intra muros*, that is, as a dialogue... within Judaism', he is cautious in his conclusions, observing that the juxtaposition of Matthew with Jamnia, while not entirely 'a leap into the dark', is, nonetheless, an adventure 'into the twilight of available sources'.[4]

While cautioning that rabbinic traditions about Jamnia may reflect a much longer process of social reconstruction, J.A. Overman attempts to carry forward the results of Davies's study.[5] He proposes that such social and institutional developments within formative (post-destruction) Judaism as the office of rabbi, the *Birkat ha-Minim*, and the local synagogue, together with the Pharisaic attempt to legitimate their religious programme by asserting the antiquity of the oral tradition and emphasizing their own role as the most accurate interpreters of Torah, prompted similar developments in the Matthaean Christian community. There is thus, for example, a commensurate emphasis in Matthew's Gospel on the appropriateness of institution-

Konsolidierung eines ausgeprägten Eigenlebens, ohne sich jedoch vom jüdischen Verband zu lösen' [p. 33]); pp. 146-53, 159-61 ('weil die Kirche nicht als die heilsgeschichtliche Ablösung Israels, als das wahre bzw. neue Israel gedacht ist, brauchte sie sich nicht vom Judentum zu trennen... Sie verstand sich als eschatologische Gemeinde, die zur Überbietung des pharisäischen Judentums gerufen war' [p. 160]).

1. Hummel, *Auseinandersetzung*, pp. 29-33; Goulder, *Midrash and Lection*, pp. 151-52 (Goulder posits a post-war, Jewish Matthew as a foundation for his thesis that Matthew 'wrote his Gospel to follow annual Festal cycle' of Torah readings [p. 227]); S. Brown, 'The Matthaean Community and the Gentile Mission', *NovT* 22 (1980), pp. 213-21. Brown understands Matthew's community to be in the process of turning to a Gentile mission as a result of sharp opposition from orthodox Judaism following the war with Rome (pp. 217-18). Yet 'the absence in the gospel of any explicit reference to excommunication... suggests a date before the decision at Jamnia... Furthermore, it is difficult to believe that Matthew would have allowed a recommendation of Pharisaic teaching (Mt xxiii 2f.) to stand in his gospel if his community had definitively separated from Judaism' (p. 216).

2. Kilpatrick, *Origins*, pp. 111-14; Davies, *Setting*, pp. 256-315.

3. *Setting*, p. 315; cf. Davies and Allison, *Matthew*, p. 58: 'the signs point in one direction: the author of the First Gospel was a member of the Jewish people'.

4. *Setting*, pp. 290, 315.

5. Overman, *Matthew's Gospel and Formative Judaism*, pp. 38-43.

alized roles (scribe, prophet, missionary and rabbi), on community standards and discipline, and on the proper interpretation of Torah (as opposed to that of the 'scribes and Pharisees').[1] In this way, 'Matthew and his community claim the same tradition, the same authority—even, at points, the same roles—as formative Judaism', leading Overman to conclude that 'Matthew takes his stand within contemporary Judaism'.[2] Nonetheless, the intensity of this conflict is leading the community into a new openness to the Gentile world.[3]

Indeed, a number of scholars see a predominantly Gentile interest in Matthew, and so argue that a complete break with Judaism has already taken place—even, as some propose, that the Gospel is no longer concerned with issues of Jewish polemic. K.W. Clark, for example, whose 1947 article on 'The Gentile Bias in Matthew' initiated this turn in the modern debate, lays stress on such passages as 8.12 ('the children of the kingdom will be cast out'), 21.43 ('the kingdom of God will be taken away from you, and given to a people producing the fruit of the kingdom'), and 28.19 ('Go and make disciples of all the Gentile peoples'). Furthermore, he argues that the parables of 21.28–22.14 and 25.1-46, as well as such features as 'kingdom of heaven', φυλακτήρια, genealogical interest, and scriptural proof-texting—which are usually ascribed to a Semitic cast of mind—can as easily reflect a Gentile bias as a Jewish one. In fact, according to Clark, Matthew envisages a Judaism now excluded from the possibility of salvation:

> Judaism as such has definitely rejected Jesus as God's messiah, and God has finally rejected Judaism. This gentile bias is the primary thesis in Matthew, and such a message would be natural only from the bias of a gentile author.[4]

P. Nepper-Christensen, G. Strecker and W. Trilling, whose writings appeared at almost the same time, have each taken up this line of reasoning. Nepper-Christensen contends that the Gospel's alleged Semitisms, its use of scriptural quotations, and its typology are not indicative of a Jewish or Jewish-Christian audience. Rather, passages such as 10.5 and 15.24 reflect the situation of the earliest Christian mission and not that of Matthew's community.[5] Thus, in short, Nepper-Christensen's reply to the question he raises regarding the provenance of Matthew's Gospel (*Ein judenchristliches Evangelium?*) is strongly negative.

In similar fashion, Strecker distinguishes between pre-Matthaean and Matthaean levels of tradition. Thus while the Gospel reflects both Jewish and Gentile interests, the former are neither dominant nor characteristic of the Evangelist, but belong to an

1. *Matthew's Gospel and Formative Judaism*, pp. 43-149.

2. *Matthew's Gospel and Formative Judaism*, pp. 153, 157 (emphasis added); cf. pp. 148-49.

3. *Matthew's Gospel and Formative Judaism*, p. 158: 'We would characterize the Matthaean community, then, as mostly, if not thoroughly, Jewish but in the process of turning to the wider Gentile world'.

4. K.W. Clark, 'The Gentile Bias in Matthew', *JBL* 66 (1947), pp. 165-72; rpr. *The Gentile Bias and Other Essays* (NovTSup, 54; Leiden: Brill, 1980), p. 4. For a detailed reply to Clark, see Davies and Allison, *Matthew*, pp. 17-31.

5. *Matthäusevangelium*, pp. 180-85, 193-96; cf. pp. 185-89 on 10.23.

earlier stage in the life of the community. By contrast, 'the non-Jewish, Hellenistic features of the redaction suggest that the author is to be classified as a Gentile Christian'. So while some Jewish-Christian elements may remain in the Matthaean church, 'a new, Gentile Christian generation is superseding Jewish Christianity'.[1]

Trilling's position is somewhat more nuanced. In concert with Clark, Nepper-Christensen, Strecker, *et al.*, he takes passages such as 21.33-45, 23.34-37 and 27.15-26 to indicate that for Matthew 'church and synagogue have separated'.[2] Matthew sees Israel's rejection of Jesus and the destruction of Jerusalem as grounds for the church's separation from 'old' and 'false' Israel, which he characterizes by the phrase 'scribes and Pharisees'. Conversely, he understands his own community not as a new Israel but as '*the original, true* Israel, as God intended it to be from the beginning',[3] which is constituted by the fundamental conviction that Jesus is the messiah of Israel.

Yet Trilling also argues that Jewish-Christianity's ongoing controversy with rabbinic Judaism has influenced both the form and the content of Matthew's Gospel,[4] so that 'the theology of the Gospel of Matthew is not only the result of controversy, but also of the internal unfolding of faith within the context of the church'.[5] And this factor accounts for the universalism of Matthew's outlook, which is reflected in such passages as 10.18, 12.18-21, 13.38, 15.21-28, 24.14 and, above all, in 28.19.[6] So Trilling concludes that Matthew's Gospel reveals a community in flux, with material of Jewish-Christian interest being adapted to the needs of a Gentile readership. For this reason, 'the readership and final author testify to an attitude that can be designated neither as typically Gentile Christian nor as typically Jewish Christian'.[7]

Following much of Trilling's reasoning, although taking issue with some of his

1. Strecker, *Weg*, pp. 34-35.
2. *Wahre Israel*, p. 79.
3. *Wahre Israel*, p. 96; emphasis original.
4. This influence is both positive (e.g. the use of the OT and emphasis on Torah) and negative (i.e. polemical) in nature, but 'beide Seiten, die positive und die negative, am leichtesten als Erscheinungsformen eines und desselben Prozesses verstanden können, nämlich der langjährigen, zähen und erbitterten Auseinandersetzung mit dem Judentum in einem jüdischen Milieu' (*Wahre Israel*, p. 221). Cf. Cope, *Matthew*, pp. 125-30 ('Matthew must be placed in the context of the painful time of separation of the church from Judaism which is also reflected in John's gospel' [pp. 126-27]; 'Matthew was written by a Jewish-Christian who belonged to a church which was already separated from Pharisaic Judaism and in sharp conflict with Pharisaism' [p. 130]).
5. Trilling, *Wahre Israel*, p. 222.
6. Cf. *Wahre Israel*, pp. 124-42.
7. *Wahre Israel*, p. 224. Trilling's conclusions are similar in many respects to those of S.H. Brooks (*Matthew's Community: The Evidence of his Special Sayings Material* [JSNTSup, 16; Sheffield: JSOT Press, 1987], pp. 115-22), who sees in Matthew's unique ('M') material, especially chs. 10 and 23, a historical process wherein former adherents of the synagogue ('Christian Jews') come into conflict with the synagogue leadership over the teaching authority of Jesus, resulting in overt persecution and, ultimately, complete separation from Judaism/Israel. The break with Israel on the part of what are now 'Jewish Christians' and the failure of the Jewish mission opens the way for the mission to the Gentiles.

conclusions, D.R.A. Hare sees Israel's rejection of the gospel as a precondition rather than as a result of Jesus' mission (so 13.13; cf. Mk 4.12), and so interprets Matthew to be saying that God has completely and permanently rejected Israel (so 21.43; 22.7-8; 23.27-39).[1] Thus Matthew's community is neither the 'New' nor the 'True Israel', since these terms would suggest degrees of continuity and continuity is entirely absent from Matthew's thought:

> The Church is in no sense a continuation of Israel but a different ἔθνος, non-Israel, which replaces Israel in *Heilsgeschichte* (21.43). This new People of the Kingdom is neither Jewish nor Gentile, but, although Matthew does not use the term, a 'third race'.[2]

Taking a somewhat different approach is S. van Tilborg, whose study of how Matthew depicts the Jewish leaders highlights such pejorative terms as ὁδηγοὶ τυφλοί, μωροί, πλανοί, ὑποκριταί, πονηροί, φονεῖς and υἱοὶ τῶν φονευσάντων. So negative is Matthew's presentation of the Jewish leaders—in fact, so anti-Jewish in van Tilborg's view—that Matthew could not himself have been Jewish. Rather, since the Evangelist has lost sight of his actual opponents, his Gospel must be located 'in a world in which Judaism was no longer a serious competitor'.[3]

Of critical importance in this debate is the question of whether 28.19 (μαθητεύσατε πάντα τὰ ἔθνη) includes or excludes Israel. After examining the semantic range of גוים/ἔθνη, Hare and Harrington conclude that the phrase must be

1. Hare, *Jewish Persecution*, pp. 149-56. It should be noted that the Matthaean phrase τὰς συναγωγὰς αὐτῶν (4.23; 9.35; 10.17; 12.9; 13.54; cf. 23.34; so 7.29, 'their scribes'), which is frequently cited as evidence in this debate (e.g. Hare, *Jewish Persecution*, pp. 104-105), cannot be determinative, since it is susceptible of quite opposite interpretations: either as 'their synagogues' in contrast to 'our synagogues', or as 'their synagogues' in contrast to 'our churches/congregations'. The phrase can be appealed to for support by those on either side of the question.

2. Hare, *Jewish Persecution*, p. 157, see also Hare's response to Trilling (and Hummel), pp. 157-61. Cf. Frankemölle (*Jahwebund und Kirche Christi*, p. 225): 'Die christliche Gemeinde und die jüdische Synagoge gehören für Mt zwei verschiedenen Welten an. . . Der Bruch zwischen beiden ist endgültig'. Also persuaded by Hare's arguments in favor of a separation between church and synagogue, and explaining Matthew's theology in *heilsgeschichtlich* terms, is Meier (*Law and History*, p. 163): 'the *Sitz* of the gospel is a church in transition... from a narrow Jewish-Christian past to a predominantly Gentile future'. For a summary of the debate concerning 'true Israel' in the early Church Fathers, including the idea of Christianity as a *tertium genus*, see Richardson, *Israel*, pp. 9-32.

3. Van Tilborg, *Jewish Leaders*, p. 171. M.J. Cook ('Interpreting Pro-Jewish Passages in Matthew', *HUCA* 54 [1983], pp. 135-46) concurs with van Tilborg's assessment that Matthew is consistently anti-Jewish, arguing that the key passages usually appealed to in order to demonstrate the Evangelist's 'pro-Jewish' sympathies reveal the opposite intent: 5.17-20 and 23.2 affirm the validity neither of Torah nor of scribal authority, but rather serve to introduce their supersession; 10.5-6 and 15.24 'are merely a literary device by which Matthew is setting up the Jews for eventual vilification' (p. 142). But unlike van Tilborg and others, Cook is not thereby convinced that Matthew was himself a Gentile.

translated 'all the Gentiles', and so excludes Israel.[1] Meier points out, however, that in such key passages as 21.43, 24.7, 24.14 and 25.32 ἔθνος includes both Jews and Gentiles, so that the same could be true of 28.19.[2] Furthermore, as W.G. Kümmel observes, 23.39 anticipates Jesus' acclamation by Jewish believers at his parousia.[3]

Kümmel's treatment of the data relevant to either a Jewish or a Gentile orientation on Matthew's part likely represents the best resolution of this debate. For Kümmel concludes that, taken alone, neither set of considerations is determinative; yet the evidence of the Gospel, taken as a whole, suggests that Matthew presents the teaching of Jesus (which includes the offer of salvation 'for all nations') to a community with strong Jewish roots—though a community separated from and in sharp conflict with mainstream (especially Pharisaic) Judaism.[4] Moreover, the universalizing features of Jesus' teaching make an ongoing missionary outreach to Gentiles and the presence of Gentile Christians in Matthew's church no less certain, although it may well be that within the community 'the distinction between Jew and Gentile is no longer significant'.[5]

1. D.R.A. Hare and D.J. Harrington, '"Make Disciples of all the Gentiles" (Mt. 28.19)', *CBQ* 37 (1975), pp. 359-69.

2. J.P. Meier, 'Nations or Gentiles in Matthew 28.19?', *CBQ* 39 (1977), pp. 94-102. Cf. Trilling, *Wahre Israel*, pp. 26-28.

3. W.G. Kümmel, *Introduction to the New Testament* (Nashville: Abingdon Press, 1975), p. 116. No less relevant—and controverted—is the meaning of the angel's declaration in 1.21, '[Jesus] will save τὸν λαὸν αὐτοῦ from their sins'.

4. *Introduction*, pp. 112-18.

5. *Introduction*, p. 116. Other scholars advocating various 'mediating' positions between 'Jewish' or 'Jewish-Christian' and 'Gentile-Christian' extremes include Stendahl, *School of St Matthew*, pp. xi-xiv; K. Tagawa, 'People and Community in the Gospel of Matthew', *NTS* 16 (1969–70), pp. 149-62 (regarding many of the statements directed against 'Israel' as warnings to Matthew's own community; similarly S. Légasse, 'L'anti-judaisme dans l'évangile selon Matthieu', in Didier (ed.), *L'évangile selon Matthieu*, p. 426); Stanton, 'Matthew and Judaism', p. 271 ('Matthew's community has recently parted company with Judaism after a period of prolonged hostility' [p. 273]); Mora, *Le refus d'Israel*, pp. 92-94, pp. 121-22 ('une synagogue chrétienne' [p. 92]); Przybylski, 'Matthean Anti-Judaism', pp. 181-200 ('the immediate context of the final redaction of the Gospel of Matthew is the concern of Jewish Christians to define themselves in opposition to the Judaism practised in their immediate environment. While engaged in this activity, the Matthean community is at the same time aware of a larger context, namely, its relationship with Gentile Christianity' [p. 192]); Gnilka, *Matthäusevangelium*, II, p. 534 ('Die Gemeinde strebt aus der Synagoge hinaus. Doch ist die Verbindung zu ihr noch nicht vollständig abgerissen. Die juristische Autorität der Synagoge war für die Gemeinde oder für zahlreiche Gemeindemitglieder noch ein Faktum'); A.-J. Levine, *The Social and Ethnic Dimensions of Matthaean Social History: 'Go Nowhere Among the Gentiles. . . '* (*Matt. 10.5b*) (Studies in the Bible and Early Christianity, 14; Lewiston, NY: Edwin Mellen, 1988) (attempting to undercut the racial polarization of Jewish versus Gentile orientations by proposing that Matthew 'presents a program of salvation history constructed along two axes: a temporal axis that incorporates ethnic categories and a social axis that transcends the division between Jew and Gentile' [p. 273], so that the Matthaean emphasis on salvation for the socially marginalized allows for the historical expansion of the missionary mandate to include Gentiles, while not thereby depriving Jews of the same opportunity); and Kee, 'The Transformation

Kümmel's final words on this issue well deserve to be heard and heeded:

> Obviously the real interest of Mt lies not in his relationship to Judaism or to Jewish Christianity or to Gentile Christianity, but on the one hand in the proof that Jesus is the 'messiah' long promised by God. . . and on the other hand in his ever-repeated stress on the fact that. . . salvation is to be gained only in the ἐκκλησία of Christ and as a member of the people that bring forth the fruits of the Kingdom of God (21.43).[1]

In other words, the debate about provenance must not lose sight of the fact that Matthew's primary intent is not that of arbitrating ethnic conflicts within his community, but rather that of presenting the religious significance of Jesus of Nazareth as the messiah of Israel and eschatological Saviour of 'all the nations'. The categories of 'Israel' and 'all nations' are for Matthew not so much contradictory as complementary.

All this being true, it yet remains that a consideration of the Gospel's Deuteronomistic features provides a helpful and alternative perspective from which to understand both Matthew's attitude towards contemporary Judaism and his concept of his own community. As noted in Chapter 2, Matthew understands the destruction of Jerusalem to be a sign of divine judgment caused by Israel's rejection of Jesus' prophetic mission. That the people—or, more precisely, the leaders of Israel —were continuing their contumacy, as viewed by the Evangelist, is confirmed by their persecution of the Church's Christian prophets and messengers, in keeping with the nation's rejection of the prophets of old.[2]

Such an insight illuminates Matthew's understanding of relations between church and synagogue in his own day. For the purpose of the Deuteronomistic outlook is, on the one hand, to explain the historical reversals suffered by God's people as manifestations of divine judgment, while, on the other, to provide a rationale for the restoration and continuation of the covenant community in the period following judgment. The judgment envisaged by the Deuteronomistic schema is never absolute

of the Synagogue', p. 22 (Matthew 'reflect[s] the mounting mutual antagonism between the two divergent movements' of συναγωγῇ and ἐκκλησία).

1. *Introduction*, pp. 117-18.

2. Steck (*Israel*, pp. 304-12) sees an inconsistency between the rejection of Jesus as having led to the destruction of Jerusalem and supersession of Israel (e.g. in 23.29–24.2) and the rejection of the Christian emissaries as having done the same (e.g. in 22.4-9 and 23.34-35). He explains the former as characteristic of Hellenistic (Jewish) Christianity and the latter as characteristic of Palestinian Jewish-Christians who have themselves been active in the mission to Israel. According to Steck, Matthew combines the two views, placing them in historical sequence with the destruction of Jerusalem as an intermediary turning point. Thus, for Matthew, the mission to Israel *as Israel* would have continued only until 70, with the fall of Jerusalem representing a definitive rejection of the nation. But it is not clear that the interpretations of the fate of Jesus and that of his messengers, respectively, can be assigned separate provenances, since reflection on either could have encouraged a Deuteronomistic interpretation of the other. At least for Matthew, the destruction of Jerusalem, with all that it implies, is the *cumulative consequence* of πᾶν αἷμα δίκαιον ἐκχυννόμενον ἐπὶ τῆς γῆς (23.35), including that of Jesus (τὸ αἷμα. . . τὸ περὶ πολλῶν ἐκχυννόμενον, 26.28), so that ἥξει ταῦτα πάντα ἐπὶ τὴν γενεὰν ταύτην (23.36).

or without the possibility of resolution. Rather, God's judgment of unfaithful Israel provides an opportunity for repentance and restoration: the reconstituting of faithful Israel.

The presence of Deuteronomistic motifs in Matthew, which focus on the rejection of Jesus and his envoys as well as on the destruction of Jerusalem, suggests that the most appropriate setting for the Gospel is one in which the Matthaean community was attempting to redefine its existence in the context of, or in the period immediately following the national catastrophe of 67-70 CE. Matthew's Deuteronomistic outlook is most appropriate in the social and theological context of the debate over which community now constitutes the 'true' Israel—whether that of the synagogue and Pharisaic Judaism, or that of the ἐκκλησία that is founded on the confession of Jesus as Israel's messiah (16.18).

Matthew considered his own community to be a kind of reconstituted Israel. His community was clearly separate from the Israel of Pharisaic Judaism, which by persecuting the church's prophets and missionaries identified itself with the generation that rejected Jesus. Matthew has, in fact, abandoned the name 'Israel' for his church, since for him the nationalist and racial overtones of this title were too narrow for his understanding of Jesus' universal appeal.[1] Yet many features of 'Jewish' interest in his Gospel indicate that his community still defined itself in terms of and in relation to the Israel of old.

These apparently contradictory premises seem to be reconcilable when viewed from the perspective of a Christianized Deuteronomistic outlook: God has judged and 'rejected' Israel, as demonstrated by the destruction of Jerusalem; but now, following disaster, he calls into being a reconstituted community of the faithful, the Church. This self-understanding permits Matthew and his community to employ elements of the tradition that are manifestly 'Jewish' in focus, while at the same time fiercely opposing Pharisaic Judaism and stressing the universalistic or 'Gentile' features of Jesus' message. Matthew's Deuteronomistic outlook, in other words, accounts for features that speak of both continuity and discontinuity, however radical, between Second Temple Judaism and nascent Christianity. Matthew probably did not think of his Christian community as *extra muros*, since, in his view, it was the synagogue that was *extra muros*. From his perspective, the kingdom had now been, or would shortly be, transferred to a nation/people producing the fruits thereof. Therefore, Matthew takes the Christian definitions of 'kingdom' and 'people of God' now to be normative, no matter how the understanding of the synagogue differed on these matters.

It is in this sense that we must speak of Matthew's Christianized Deuteronomistic perspective. For the Christian conviction that the messiah had instituted a new covenant community, or at least that the messiah's advent provided a new focus and

1. Cf. Richardson: 'Matthew uses "Israel" in a completely literal way to apply always to the nation; there are no marginal cases where it might apply to the Church' (*Israel*, p. 189); see 2.6, 20, 21; 8.10; 9.33; 10.6, 23; 15.24, 31; 19.28; 27.9, 42. Matthew prefers the broader concept of the 'kingdom of heaven' (see esp. 4.17; 8.11-12; 13.24-30, 37-42, 47-50, 52; 21.31; 22.2-10; 24.14), or else that of ἐκκλησία (16.18; 18.17).

identity for the community of God's people, introduces a new factor into the Deuteronomistic schema. Within a Jewish context, the Deuteronomistic call to repentance envisages a return to Torah obedience and to an identity defined in terms of the covenants with Abraham and Moses. But the Christian introduction of 'realized messianism' to the formulation of that covenant identity necessarily alters such a Deuteronomistic outlook. Recognizing the impact of Christology and christocentric soteriology on Matthew's thinking helps to resolve certain inconsistencies that scholars have seen in his use of the Deuteronomistic framework.

While van Tilborg, for example, acknowledges the relevance for Matthew of the Deuteronomistic schema—as well as that 'in the traditional concept about Israel's guilt in the murdering of the prophets the possibility of conversion was always left open'—he also argues that the Evangelist envisaged no further possibility of Israel's conversion.[1] In the narrowest of senses, of course, this is true. The 'kingdom of heaven' can no longer be defined in national or racial terms. At the same time, however, Matthew's emphasis on the Jewish character of Jesus' teaching and ministry indicates a strong sense of continuity between his own and the Jewish community. For Israel is not excluded altogether from the eschatological invitation, as van Tilborg claims.[2] The invitation is simply broadened to incorporate Gentiles.

More nuanced is the suggestion of Steck that, for Matthew, the mission to Israel as a call for the spiritual awakening of the entire nation came to an end with the Roman war, since Israel as a nation has forfeited its special status and the nature of the mission to Judaism has been transformed. But Israel has not been cut off altogether:

> Despite this abrogation, Matthew has not fully turned away from Judaism. He and his community seek to win over Judaism as well. But from now on this activity is based on the concept of the mission to the nations, and is to be described as a mission *to Judaism*, rather than as the 'awakening of Israel'.[3]

Thus 'Israel' is rejected only insofar as that title implies an exclusive claim to divine favor. Garland's insistence that 'the community of believers in Jesus now [stands] in the former place of Israel',[4] while true in onc sense, overlooks the fact that 'Israel' itself has been redefined. For now not just one nation, but 'all the nations' are the objects of divine favor.

Steck also argues, however, that because the nation of Israel has ceased to be 'Israel' in a theological sense (i.e. the exclusive object of divine favor and the locus of salvation)—and because, in effect, a Deuteronomistic interpretation of history can only be applied to Israel as a theological entity—the Deuteronomistic outlook is itself

1. *Jewish Leaders*, p. 71. Cf. Garland, *Intention*, pp. 210-15; Hare, *Jewish Persecution*, pp. 148-49: 'The pessimism of Matthew is not limited in a temporal way, as is the pessimism of Hosea, Jeremiah and Paul. There is no suggestion that after the full number of the Gentiles have been admitted to the Kingdom the resistance of Israel will be supernaturally overcome, as in Romans 11.25f. For Israel the future holds only Judgment.'

2. *Jewish Leaders*, p. 72.

3. Steck, *Israel*, pp. 313-14 (emphasis original); cf. also pp. 315-16.

4. Garland, *Intention*, p. 212; following Steck, *Israel*, pp. 304-305.

superseded as a meaningful interpretative framework for Matthew's community:

> Since Israel has ceased to be Israel, there can be for Matthew after 70 no preachers to Israel, and consequently no actual application of the Deuteronomistic prophet testimony.[1]

According to Steck, the Deuteronomistic motif continues to be operative for Matthew only in the sense that the judgment on the nation of Israel in the destruction of Jerusalem is to be understood, not as a divine punishment that anticipates repentance and restoration, but as a final judgment on the enemies of true Israel.[2] In this respect, he contrasts Matthew's Gospel with the responses to the destruction of 70 CE recorded in the *Biblical Antiquities* of Pseudo-Philo, in *4 Ezra* and in *2 Baruch*, where the possibility of repentance and return remains open.[3]

But such a conclusion is unnecessarily harsh. With respect to the mission to Israel, Steck himself acknowledges that Matthew does not apply a Deuteronomistic interpretation only to the experiences of those who preached to Israel prior to 70 CE, but also to Christian prophets in general and to missionaries of the Evangelist's own community. Opposition from Judaism was clearly ongoing in Matthew's day, and his use of the Deuteronomistic model to interpret this opposition surely indicates its continuing relevance for his community.

But Steck's argument does point to a logical inconsistency in Matthew's presentation. For while Matthew applies the Deuteronomistic model quite stringently in his interpretation of Israel's national sin, he transcends that model in not focusing exclusively on Israel with respect to salvation. This inconsistency, however, may be explained by the exigencies of Matthew's own theological convictions, for from a Christian perspective it is no longer to the Mosaic covenant that one turns in penitence—as anticipated in the Deuteronomistic schema—but rather to the new covenant and to confession of Jesus as messiah (16.18). So the Evangelist's outlook is, as we noted earlier, that of a christianized or christocentric Deuteronomistic perspective.

The inconsistency of Matthew's application may also be explained by a logical tension inherent within the Deuteronomistic framework itself. For according to this interpretative model, the people of God come to terms with historical reversals through a retrospective confession of past unfaithfulness and a present reaffirmation of obedience. The Deuteronomistic outlook is the outlook of those who see themselves as 'faithful' in the present, but only penitentially so. Thus they identify in their repentance with those who formerly rejected and persecuted the prophets, but, paradoxically, identify also in their reaffirmation of obedience with the persecuted prophets whose views they now affirm—with Matthew and his community identifying with Jesus and his prophetic emissaries.

1. Steck, *Israel*, p. 315.

2. Steck: 'Mit der Abrogation der Konzeption der Erweckung Israels durch das Verwerfungsgericht von 70 ist auch die sie umgreifende Konzeption des [deuteronomistische Geschichtsbild] an ihr dunkles Ende (F2) gekommen, das für Israel als solches bereits Faktum ist' (*Israel*, p. 312).

3. *Israel*, p. 312 n. 7.

Matthew's report of Jesus' words to his disciples on the eve of his arrest, πάντες ὑμεῖς σκανδαλισθήσεσθε ἐν ἐμοὶ ἐν τῇ νυκτὶ ταύτῃ (26.31 // Mk 14.27), may reflect such an outlook, both on Matthew's own part and within his community. Three features suggest the possible relevance of 'falling away' for Matthew's community: (1) the prominence of Peter in his Gospel, since Peter responds by protesting that he will never fall away or deny Jesus (26.33, 35a), only to do so three times (cf. 26.34, 69-75); (2) the fact that Matthew appends to Peter's protest the comment ὁμοίως καὶ πάντες οἱ μαθηταὶ εἶπαν (26.35b; cf. Mk 14.31, ὡσαύτως δὲ καὶ πάντες ἔλεγον), only to have them all do the same, since μαθητής is for Matthew a special designation for followers of Jesus;[1] and (3) the fact that 'scandal' or 'falling away' represents an ongoing danger to the community elsewhere in Matthew.[2] With his emphasis on the ever-present danger of apostasy and the salutary examples of Peter and the Twelve, Matthew seems to suggest that his own community cannot be entirely dissociated from those who presently reject Jesus. Despite the fierceness of his polemic against those who do reject the messiah, the Evangelist seems to recognize that members of his own community could do the same.

But more to the point in explanation of Matthew's inconsistent application of the Deuteronomistic model is the fierce antagonism that existed in his day between church and synagogue, which antagonism prevented the Evangelist from adopting an entirely retrospective view. He could not speak simply of Israel's past opposition to the prophetic message, as would be typical of a Deuteronomistic outlook, since such opposition was presently ongoing. Thus he was forced to adopt the perspective of the rejected prophets not just retrospectively, but also with regard to the Church's present experience, and so to distinguish the Christian community from unfaithful Israel.

For Matthew, therefore, the clearest indication that 'all the nations' of the Christian church now stood in continuity with the true 'Israel' of old, and not just over against it, was provided by the fact of persecution itself. The fact the Christian prophets were persecuted testified, first, to the validity of their message and, secondly, to their common identity with those who had been rejected before them. From Matthew's perspective, rejection constituted a species of vindication, confirming that the Christian message was as valid as that of the ancient prophets—indeed, that Christian prophets, in direct line with the prophets of Israel, represented the faithful people of God, or faithful 'Israel', sent to an unfaithful and recalcitrant nation.

1. On the use of μαθητής (Matthew 72×; Mark 46×; Luke 37×) and μαθητεύειν (3×; 0×; 0×) and the depiction of the disciples as referring to Matthew's church, see U. Luz, 'Die Junger im Matthäusevangelium', *ZNW* 62 (1971), pp. 141-171 [ET 'The Disciples in the Gospel according to Matthew', in Stanton (ed.), *Interpretation of Matthew*, pp. 98-128]; M.J. Wilkins, *The Concept of Disciple in Matthew's Gospel (as Reflected in the Use of the Term* μαθητής*)* (NovTSup, 59; Leiden: Brill, 1988), pp. 126-172, 221-22.

2. So Bornkamm ('Enderwartung und Kirche', p. 44 n. 2): 'σκάνδαλον, σκανδαλίζεσθαι sind wieder von Matth. am häufigsten gebrauchte termini, wiederholt verwendet für Verführung und Abfall *in der Gemeinde* als endzeitliche Erscheinungen (so 13.21, 41; 17.7 [*sic:* read 17.27]; 24.10)' (emphasis original).

Bibliography

Texts, Translations and Reference Sources

Aland, K. (ed.), *Synopsis Quattuor Evangeliorum. Locis parallelis evangeliorum apocryphorum et patrum adhibitis* (Stuttgart: Deutsche Bibelstiftung, 1976).

—*Vollständige Konkordanz zum griechischen Neuen Testament*. II. *Spezialübersichten* (ANTF 5.2; Berlin, New York: de Gruyter, 1978).

—*Synopsis of the Four Gospels: Greek-English Edition of the Synopsis Quattuor Evangeliorum* (N.p.: United Bible Societies, 1982).

Aland, K., *et al.* (eds.), *Novum Testamentum Graece* (Stuttgart: Deutsche Bibelgesellschaft, 26th edn, 1979).

—*The Greek New Testament* (N.p.: United Bible Societies, 3rd corrected edn, 1983).

Bauer, W., *A Greek-English Lexicon of the New Testament and Other Early Christian Literature* (trans. W.F. Arndt and F.W. Gingrich; rev. F.W. Gingrich and F.W. Danker; Chicago: University of Chicago Press, 2nd edn, 1979).

Blass, F., and A. DeBrunner, *A Greek Grammar of the New Testament and Other Early Christian Literature* (trans. R.W. Funk; Cambridge: Cambridge University Press; Chicago: University of Chicago Press, 1961).

Braude, W.G. (trans.), *The Midrash on Psalms* (2 vols.; Yale Judaica Series, 12; New Haven: Yale University Press, 1959).

—*Pesikta Rabbati: Discourses for Feasts, Fasts, and Special Sabbaths* (2 vols.; Yale Judaica Series, 18; New Haven: Yale University Press, 1968).

Braude, W.G. and I.J. Kapstein (trans.), *Pesikta de-Rab Kahana: R. Kahana's Compilation of Discourses for Sabbath and Festal Days* (Philadelphia: Jewish Publication Society, 1975).

Brown, F., S.R. Driver and C.A. Briggs, *A Hebrew-English Lexicon of the Old Testament, with an Appendix containing the Biblical Aramaic* (Oxford: Clarendon Press, n.d.).

Buttrick, G.A. (ed.), *The Interpreter's Dictionary of the Bible* (4 vols. with supplementary volume, ed. K. Crim; Nashville: Abingdon Press, 1962, 1976).

Charlesworth, J.H. (ed.), *The Old Testament Pseudepigrapha* (2 vols.; Garden City, NY: Doubleday, 1983, 1985).

Computer Concordance to the Novum Testamentum Graece of Nestle-Aland, 26th Edition, and to the Greek New Testament (ed. The Institute for New Testament Textual Research and the Computer Center of Münster University with the collaboration of H. Bachmann and W.A. Slaby; Berlin: de Gruyter, 3rd edn, 1985).

Danby, H., *The Mishnah: Translated from the Hebrew with Introduction and Brief Explanatory Notes* (London: Oxford University Press, 1933).

Dietzfelbinger, C., 'Pseudo-Philo: Antiquitates Biblicae (Liber Antiquitatum Biblicarum)', in W.G. Kümmel *et al.* (eds.), *Unterweisung in erzählender Form* (JSHRZ, 1.2; Gütersloh: Gerd Mohn, 1975), pp. 89-271.

Edwards, R.A., *A Concordance to Q* (SBLSBS, 7; Missoula, MT: SBL, 1975).

Epstein, I. (ed.), *The Babylonian Talmud* (18 vols.; London: Soncino, 1961).

Fitzmyer, J.A., *The Dead Sea Scrolls: Major Publications and Tools for Study* (SBLSBS, 8; Missoula, MT: Scholars Press, 1977).

Forestell, J.T., *Targumic Traditions and the New Testament: An Annotated Bibliography with a New Testament Index* (SBL Aramaic Studies, 4; Chico, CA: Scholars Press, 1979).

Freedman, H., and M. Simon (eds.), *Midrash Rabbah* (10 vols.; London: Soncino, 1939).

Gaster, T.H., *The Dead Sea Scriptures: An English Translation with Introduction and Notes* (Garden City, NY: Anchor/Doubleday, 1976).

Ginzberg, L., *The Legends of the Jews* (7 vols.; Philadelphia: Jewish Publication Society, 1909–38).

Gunneweg, A.H.J., 'Das Buch Baruch', in W.G. Kümmel *et al.* (eds.), *Unterweisung in lehrhafter Form* (JSHRZ, 3.2; Gütersloh: Gerd Mohn, 1975), pp. 165-81.

Habicht, C., '2. Makkabäerbuch', in W.G. Kümmel *et al.* (eds.), *Historische und legendarische Erzählungen* (JSHRZ, 1.3; Gütersloh: Gerd Mohn, 1975), pp. 165-285.

Hammer, R., *Sifre: A Tannaitic Commentary on the Book of Deuteronomy. Translated from the Hebrew with Introduction and Notes* (Yale Judaica Series, 24; New Haven: Yale University Press, 1986).

Hatch, G., and H.A. Redpath, *A Concordance to the Septuagint and the Other Greek Versions of the Old Testament (including the Apocryphal Books)* (2 vols.; Oxford: Clarendon Press, 1897).

Hayward, R. (trans.), *The Targum of Jeremiah: Translated, with a Critical Introduction, Apparatus, and Notes* (Aramaic Bible, 12; Wilmington, DE: Michael Glazier, 1987).

Holladay, C.L., *Fragments from Hellenistic Jewish Authors*. I. *Historians* (Chico, CA: Scholars Press, 1983).

Holm-Nielsen, S., *Hodayot: Psalms from Qumran* (Acta Theologica Danica, 2; Aarhus: Universitetsforlaget, 1960).

—'Die Psalmen Salomos', in W.G. Kümmel *et al.* (eds.), *Poetische Schrifte* (JSHRZ, 4.2; Gütersloh: Gerd Mohn, 1977), pp. 49-112.

Jastrow, M., *A Dictionary of the Targumim, the Talmud Babli and Yerushalmi, and the Midrashic Literature* (2 vols.; New York: Pardes Publishing House, 1950).

Kautzsch, E. (ed.), *Gesenius' Hebrew Grammar* (rev. A.E. Cowley; Oxford: Clarendon Press, 1988 [1910]).

Kittel, G., and G. Friedrich (eds.), *Theologisches Wörterbuch zum Neuen Testament* (10 vols.; Stuttgart: Kohlhammer, 1933–73).

Kittel, R., *et al.* (eds.), *Biblia Hebraica Stuttgartensia* (Stuttgart: Deutsche Bibelgesellschaft, 1984).

Klijn, A.F.J., 'Die syrische Baruch-Apokalypse', in W.G. Kümmel *et al.* (eds.), *Apokalypsen* (JSHRZ, 5.2; Gütersloh: Gerd Mohn, 1976), pp. 103-91.

Kraft, R.A., and A.E. Purintun (eds.), *Paraleipomena Jeremiou* (SBLTT, 1; Missoula, MT: Scholars Press, 1972).

Kuhn, K.H., 'A Coptic Jeremiah Apocryphon', *Le Muséon* 83 (1970), pp. 95-135, 291-350.

Levi, I., *L'Ecclésiastique ou la sagesse de Jésus, fils de Sira: Texte original hébreu édité, traduit, et commenté* (2 vols.; Paris: Leroux, 1898).

—*The Hebrew Text of the Book of Ecclesiasticus: Edited with Brief Notes and a Selected Glossary* (SSS 3; Leiden: Brill, 1904).

Levine, E., *The Aramaic Version of Lamentations* (New York: Hermon, 1976).

Liddell, H.G., and R. Scott, *A Greek-English Lexicon* (rev. H.S. Jones; Oxford: Clarendon Press, 1940).

Lisowsky, G., *Konkordanz zum hebräischen Alten Testament* (Stuttgart: Deutsche Bibelgesellschaft, 2nd edn, 1981).

Lohse, E., *Die Texte aus Qumran, hebräisch und deutsch: Mit masoretischer Punktation, Übersetzung, Einführung, und Anmerkungen* (Munich: Kösel, 1971).

Maier, J., *Die Texte vom Toten Meer* (2 vols.; Munich: Reinhardt, 1960).

Mansoor, M., *The Thanksgiving Hymns: Translated and Annotated with an Introduction* (STDJ, 3; Leiden: Brill, 1961).

Metzger, B.M., *A Textual Commentary on the Greek New Testament: A Companion Volume to the United Bible Societies' Greek New Testament (Third Edition)* (London: United Bible Societies, 1975).

Migne, J.P., *Patrologia Cursus Completus: Series Latina* (221 vols.; Paris, 1844–64).

—*Patrologia Cursus Completus: Series Graece* (162 vols.; Paris, 1857–66).

Mingana, A., 'A Jeremiah Apocryphon', in *Woodbrooke Studies: Christian Documents in Syriac, Arabic, and Garshūni, Edited and Translated with a Critical Apparatus, with Introductions by R. Harris* (Cambridge: Heffer, 1927), I, pp. 125-38, 148-233 (= *BJRL* 11 (1927), pp. 329-42, 352-437).

Morgenthaler, R., *Statistik des neutestamentliches Wortschatzes* (Zürich: Gotthelf, 1958, 1973).

Moulton, J.H., and G. Milligan, *The Vocabulary of the Greek New Testament, Illustrated from the Papyri and other Non-literary Sources* (London: Hodder & Stoughton, 1930).

Neusner, J. (ed.), *The Tosefta* (New York: Ktav, 1977–).

Neusner, J. (trans.), *The Talmud of the Land of Israel: A Preliminary Translation and Explanation* (London and Chicago: University of Chicago, 1982–).

—*Sifre to Numbers: An American Translation and Explanation* (2 vols.; BJS, 118-19; Atlanta: Scholars Press, 1986).

—*Pesiqta deRab Kahana: An Analytical Translation* (2 vols.; BJS, 122-23; Atlanta: Scholars Press, 1987).

—*Lamentations Rabbah: An Analytical Translation* (BJS, 193; Atlanta: Scholars Press, 1989).

—*Song of Songs Rabbah: An Analytical Translation* (2 vols.; BJS, 197-98; Atlanta: Scholars Press, 1989).

Rabin, C., *The Zadokite Documents*. I. *The Admonition*. II. *The Laws, Edited with a Translation and Notes* (Oxford: Clarendon Press, 1958).

Rahlfs, A. (ed.), *Septuaginta* (2 vols.; Stuttgart: Deutsche Bibelgesellschaft, 1935, 1979).

Rengstorf, K.H., *A Complete Concordance to Flavius Josephus* (4 vols.; Leiden: Brill, 1973–83).

Schreiner, J., 'Das 4. Buch Esra', in W.G. Kümmel *et al.* (eds.), *Apokalypsen* (JSHRZ, 5.4.; Gütersloh: Gerd Mohn, 1981), pp. 289-412.

Skehan, P., and A.A. Di Lella, *The Wisdom of Ben Sira: A New Translation with Notes, Introduction, and Commentary* (AB, 39; New York: Doubleday, 1987).

Sperber, A., *The Bible in Aramaic* (4 vols.; Leiden: Brill, 1959–73).

Strack, H.L., and P. Billerbeck, *Kommentar zum Neuen Testament aus Talmud und Midrasch* (3 vols.; Munich: Beck, 1926).

Thackeray, H.St.J., and R. Marcus, *Josephus* (9 vols.; London: Heinemann; Cambridge, MA: Harvard University Press, 1926–65).

Tov, E., *The Book of Baruch, Also called I Baruch (Greek and Hebrew): Edited, Reconstructed and Translated* (SBLTT, 8; Missoula, MT: Scholars Press, 1975).

Walter, N., 'Fragmente jüdisch-hellenistischer Historiker', in W.G. Kümmel *et al.* (eds.), *Historische und legendarische Erzählungen* (JSHRZ, 1.2; Gütersloh: Gerd Mohn, 1976), pp. 89-163.

Ziegler, J. (ed.), *Ieremias, Baruch, Threni, Epistula Ieremiae* (Göttingen: Vandenhoeck & Ruprecht, 1976).

Secondary Literature

Abelson, J., *The Immanence of God in Rabbinic Literature* (repr. New York: Hermon, 1969).

Albright, W.F., and C.S. Mann, *Matthew: Introduction, Translation, and Notes* (AB, 26; Garden City, NY: Doubleday, 1971).

Allegro, J.M., 'Further Messianic References in Qumran Literature', *JBL* 75 (1956), pp. 174-187.

—'Fragments of a Qumran Scroll of Eschatological *Midrāšîm*', *JBL* 77 (1958), pp. 350-54.

Allen, W.C., *A Critical and Exegetical Commentary on the Gospel according to Saint Matthew* (ICC; Edinburgh: T. & T. Clark, 1907).

Allison, D. C., 'The Son of God as Israel: A Note on Matthean Christology', *IBS* 9 (1987), pp. 74-81.

—'Two Notes on a Key Text: Matthew 11.25-30', *JTS* 39 (1988), pp. 477-85.

Amaru, B.H., 'The Killing of the Prophets: Unravelling a Midrash', *HUCA* 54 (1983), pp. 153-80.

Anderson, B.W. 'The New Covenant and the Old', in B.W. Anderson (ed.), *The Old Testament and Christian Faith: A Theological Discussion* (New York: Harper & Row), pp. 225-42.

Anderson, H., *The Gospel of Mark* (NCB; London: Marshall, Morgan & Scott; Grand Rapids: Eerdmans, 1976).

Argyle, A.W., *The Gospel according to Matthew: Commentary* (CBC; Cambridge: Cambridge University Press, 1963).

Atkinson, B.F.C., *The Christian's Use of the Old Testament* (London: Inter-Varsity Press, 1952).

Audet, J.P., 'A Hebrew-Aramaic List of Books of the Old Testament in Greek Transcription', *JTS* NS 1 (1950), pp. 135-54.

Aune, D.E., *Prophecy in Early Christianity and the Ancient Mediterranean World* (Grand Rapids: Eerdmans, 1983).

Bacon, B. W. 'The "Five Books" of Matthew against the Jews', *The Expositor* 8.15 (1918), pp. 56-66.

—*Studies in Matthew* (London: Constable; New York: Henry Holt, 1930).

Barr, J., *Old and New in Interpretation: A Study of the Two Testaments* (London: SCM Press, 1966).

Barrett, C.K., 'The House of Prayer and the Den of Thieves', in E.E. Ellis and E. Grässer (eds.), *Jesus und Paulus: Festschrift für Werner Georg Kümmel zum 70. Geburtstag* (Göttingen: Vandenhoeck & Ruprecht, 1975), pp. 13-20.

Bauckham, R.J., 'The Martyrdom of Enoch and Elijah: Jewish or Christian?', *JBL* 95 (1976), pp. 447-58.

Bauer, D.R., *The Structure of Matthew's Gospel.: A Study in Literary Design* (JSNTSup, 31; Sheffield: Almond Press, 1988).

Baumstark, A., 'Die Zitate des Mt.-Evangeliums aus dem Zwölfprophetenbuch', *Bib* 37 (1956), pp. 296-313.

Beare, F.W., *The Gospel According to Matthew* (New York: Harper & Row, 1981).

Benoit, P., *L'évangile selon Saint Matthieu* (Paris: Cerf, 1950).

—'La mort de Judas', in *Exégèse et théologie* (Paris: Cerf, 1961), I, pp. 341-59.

—'Les outrages à Jésus prophète (Mc xiv 65 par.)', in W.C. van Unnik *et al.* (eds.), *Neotestamentica et Patristica* (*Freundesgabe Oscar Cullmann*) (NovTSup, 6; Leiden: Brill, 1962), pp. 92-110.

Berger, K., *Die Auferstehung des Propheten und die Erhöhung des Menschensohnes: Traditionsgeschichtliche Untersuchungen zur Deutung des Geschickes Jesu in frühchristlichen Texten* (SUNT, 13; Göttingen: Vandenhoeck & Ruprecht, 1976).

Betz, O., 'Donnersöhne, Menschenfischer, und der Davidische Messias', *RevQ* 3 (1961–62), pp. 41-70.

Bird, C.H., 'Some γαρ clauses in St Mark's Gospel', *JTS* NS 4 (1953), pp. 171-87.

Black, M., *The Scrolls and Christian Origins: Studies in the Jewish Background of the New Testament* (London: Nelson, 1961).

—'The "Two Witnesses" of Rev. 11.3f. in Jewish and Christian Apocalyptic Tradition', in E. Bammel, C.K. Barrett and W.D. Davies (ed.), *Donum Gentilicium: New Testament Studies in Honour of David Daube* (Oxford: Clarendon Press, 1978), pp. 227-37.

—'The Theological Appropriation of the Old Testament by the New Testament', *SJT* 39 (1986), pp. 1-17.

Blair, E.P., *Jesus in the Gospel of Matthew* (New York: Abingdon Press, 1960).

Blank, S.H., 'The Death of Zachariah in Rabbinic Literature', *HUCA* 12-13 (1937–38), pp. 327-46.

Bloch, R., 'Quelques aspects de la figure de Moïse dans la tradition rabbinique', in *Moïse, l'homme de l'alliance* (Paris: Desclée, 1955), pp. 93-167.

—'Midrash', *DBSup* V, col. 1263-1281.

Bogaert, P., *Apocalypse de Baruch: Introduction, traduction du syriaque et commentaire* (2 vols.; SC, 144, 145; Paris: Cerf, 1969).

Boismard, M.E., 'Jésus, le prophète par excellence, d'après Jean 10,24-39', in J. Gnilka (ed.), *Neues Testament und Kirche: Für R. Schnackenburg* (Freiburg: Herder, 1974), pp. 160-71.

Bonnard, P., *La sagesse en personne annoncée et venue: Jesus Christ* (LD, 44; Paris: Cerf, 1966).

—*L'évangile selon Saint Matthieu* (CNT, 1; Geneva: Labor et Fides, 1982).

Bornkamm, G., G. Barth and H.J. Held, *Überlieferung und Auslegung im Matthäusevangelium* (Neukirchen–Vluyn: Neukirchener Verlag, 1970).

Bourke, M.M., 'The Literary Genus of Matthew 1-2', *CBQ* 22 (1960), pp. 160-75.

Bowker, J., *The Targums and Rabbinic Literature: An Introduction to Jewish Interpretations of Scripture* (Cambridge: Cambridge University Press, 1969).

Bowman, J., 'Prophets and Prophecy in Talmud and Midrash', *EvQ* 22 (1950), pp. 107-14, 205-20, 255-75.

Braun, H., *Qumran und das Neue Testament* (2 vols.; Tübingen: Mohr [Paul Siebeck], 1966).

Breech, E., 'These Fragments I Have Shored against my Ruins: The Form and Function of 4 Ezra', *JBL* 92 (1973), pp. 267-74.

Brierre-Marbonne, J.J., *Exégèse targumique des prophéties messianiques* (Paris: Geuthner, 1936).

Bright, J., *Jeremiah: Introduction, Translation, and Notes* (AB, 21; Garden City, NY: Doubleday, 1965).

Brooke, G.J., 'The Biblical Texts in the Qumran Commentaries: Scribal Errors or Exegetical Variants?', in C.A. Evans and W.F. Stinespring (eds.), *Early Jewish and Christian Exegesis: Studies in Memory of William Hugh Brownlee* (Atlanta: Scholars Press, 1987), pp. 85-100.

Brooks, S.H., *Matthew's Community: The Evidence of his Special Sayings Material* (JSNTSup, 16; Sheffield: JSOT Press, 1987).

Broughton, P.E., 'The Call of Jeremiah: The Relation of Deut 18.9-22 to the Call and Life of Jeremiah', *AusBR* 6 (1958), pp. 41-46.

Brown, R., *The Birth of the Messiah: A Commentary on the Infancy Narratives in Matthew and Luke* (New York: Doubleday, 1977).

Brown, S., 'The Matthean Community and the Gentile Mission', *NovT* 22 (1980), pp. 193-221.

Brownlee, W.H., *The Midrash Pesher of Habakkuk* (SBLMS, 24; Missoula, MT: Scholars Press, 1979).

Bruce, A.B., 'The Synoptic Gospels', in W.R. Nicholl (ed.), *Expositor's Greek Testament*. I (London: Hodder & Stoughton, 1901).

Bruce, F.F., 'The Book of Zechariah and the Passion Narrative', *BJRL* 43 (1961), pp. 336-53.

Buchanan, G.W., 'Mark 11.15-19: Brigands in the Temple', *HUCA* 30 (1959), pp. 169-77.

—'An Additional Note to "Mark 11.15-19: Brigands in the Temple".' *HUCA* 31 (1960), pp. 103-105.

—'The Use of Rabbinic Literature for New Testament Research', *BTB* 7 (1977), pp. 110-22.

—*Typology and the Gospel* (Lanham, MD: University Press of America, 1987).

Bultmann, R., *Die Geschichte der synoptischen Tradition* (FRLANT, 12.29; Göttingen: Vandenhoeck & Ruprecht, 1958).

Burnett, F.W., *The Testament of Jesus-Sophia: A Redactional-Critical Study of the*

Eschatological Discourse in Matthew (Lanham, MD: University Press of America: 1981).

Cadbury, H.J., 'Jesus and the Prophets', *JR* 5 (1925), pp. 607-22.

Caird, G.B., *A Commentary on the Revelation of St John the Divine* (New York: Harper & Row, 1966).

Campbell, K.M., 'The New Jerusalem in Matthew 5:14', *SJT* 31 (1978), pp. 335-63.

Cangh, J.M. van, 'La Bible de Matthieu: Les citations de l'accomplissement', *RTL* 6 (1975), pp. 205-11.

Cargal, T.B., '"His Blood Be upon us and upon our Children": A Matthean Double Entendre?', *NTS* 37 (1991), pp. 101-12.

Carmignac, J., 'Pourquoi Jérémie est-il mentionné en Matthieu 16,14?', in G. Jeremias (ed.), *Tradition und Glaube: Das frühe Christentum in seiner Umwelt (Festgabe K.G. Kuhn)* (Göttingen: Vandenhoeck & Ruprecht, 1971), pp. 283-98.

Carroll, R.P., *Jeremiah: A Commentary* (OTL; Philadelphia: Westminster, 1986).

Carson, D.A., and H.G.M. Williamson (eds.), *It Is Written: Scripture Citing Scripture: Essays in Honour of Barnabas Lindars* (Cambridge: Cambridge University Press, 1988).

Cave, C.H., 'St Matthew's Infancy Narratives', *NTS* 9 (1962–63), pp. 382-90.

Cerfaux, L., 'Les sources scripturaires de Mt XI,25-30', *ETL* 31 (1955), pp. 331-42.

Charlesworth, J.H., *The Pseudepigrapha and Modern Research: With a Supplement* (SBLSCS, 7S; Missoula, MT: Scholars Press, 1981).

—*The Old Testament Pseudepigrapha and the New Testament* (Cambridge: Cambridge University Press, 1985).

—'The Pseudepigrapha as Biblical Exegesis', in C.A. Evans and W.F. Stinespring (eds.), *Early Jewish and Christian Exegesis: Studies in Memory of William Hugh Brownlee* (Atlanta: Scholars Press, 1987), pp. 139-52.

Chilton, B., 'Jesus *ben David*: Reflections on the *Davidssohnfrage*', *JSNT* 14 (1982), pp. 88-112.

—*Targumic Approaches to the Gospels: Essays in the Mutual Definition of Judaism and Christianity* (Studies in Judaism; Lanham, MD: University Press of America, 1986).

Christ, F., *Jesus-Sophia: Die Sophia-Christologie bei den Synoptikern* (ATANT, 57; Zürich: Zwingli-Verlag, 1970).

Clark, K.W., 'The Gentile Bias in Matthew', *JBL* 66 (1947), pp. 165-72.

Clements, R.E., *God and Temple* (Oxford: Basil Blackwell, 1965).

Cohen, N.M., *Jewish Bible Personages in the New Testament* (Lanham, MD: University Press of America, 1989).

Cohen, S.J.D., 'Josephus, Jeremiah, and Polybius', *History and Theory* 21 (1982), pp. 366-81.

Collins, J.J., and G.W.E. Nickelsburg (eds.), *Ideal Figures in Ancient Judaism: Profiles and Paradigms* (SBLSCS 12; Chico, CA: Scholars Press, 1980).

Cook, M.J., 'Interpreting Pro-Jewish Passages in Matthew', *HUCA* 54 (1983), pp. 135-46.

Cope, O.L., *Matthew: A Scribe Trained for the Kingdom of Heaven* (CBQMS, 5; Washington: Catholic Biblical Association, 1976).

Coser, L.A., *The Functions of Social Conflict* (New York: Free Press, 1956).

—*Continuities in the Study of Social Conflict* (New York: Free Press; London: Collier-Macmillan, 1967).

Cothenet, E., 'Les prophètes chrétiens dans l'évangile selon Saint Matthieu', in M. Didier (ed.), *L'évangile selon Matthieu: Rédaction et théologie* (BETL, 29; Gembloux: Duculot, 1972), pp. 281-308.

Cotter, W.J., 'For it Was not the Season for Figs', *CBQ* 48 (1986), pp. 62-66.

Cross, F.M., *The Ancient Library of Qumran and Modern Biblical Studies* (Garden City, NY: Doubleday, 1961).

Cullmann, O., *Die Christologie des Neuen Testaments* (Tübingen: Mohr [Paul Siebeck], 1957).

Dahlberg, B.T., 'The Typological Use of Jer. 1:4-19 in Mt. 16:13-23', *JBL* 94 (1975), pp. 73-80.

Daniélou, J., 'Le Christe Prophète', *VSpir* 78 (1948), pp. 154-70.

Daube, D., *The New Testament and Rabbinic Judaism* (London: Athlone Press, 1956).

—'The Earliest Structure of the Gospels', *NTS* 5 (1958–59), pp. 174-87.

—'Typology in Josephus', *JJS* 31 (1980), pp. 18-36.

Davidson, R.M., *Typology in Scripture: A Study of Hermeneutical ΤΥΠΟΣ Structures* (Andrews University Seminary Doctoral Dissertation Series, 2; Berrien Springs, MI: Andrews University Press, 1981).

Davies, P.E., 'Jesus and the Role of the Prophet', *JBL* 64 (1945), pp. 241-54.

—'Did Jesus Die as a Martyr-Prophet?', *BR* 19 (1974), pp. 37-47.

Davies, W.D., *The Setting of the Sermon on the Mount* (Cambridge: Cambridge University Press, 1963).

—*The Gospel and the Land: Early Christianity and Jewish Territorial Doctrine* (Berkeley: University of California Press, 1974).

Davies, W.D., and D.C. Allison, *The Gospel according to Saint Matthew. I. Introduction and Commentary on Matthew I-VII* (ICC; Edinburgh: T. & T. Clark, 1988).

Denis, A.-M., *Introduction aux pseudépigraphes grecs d'Ancien Testament* (SVTP, 1; Leiden: Brill, 1970).

Derrett, J.D.M., 'Figtrees in the New Testament', *HeyJ* 14 (1973), pp. 249-65.

—''ΗΣΑΝ ΓΑΡ 'ΑΛΙΕΙΣ (Mk 1.16): Jesus's Fishermen and the Parable of the Net', *NovT* 22 (1980), pp. 108-37.

—'Matt. 23:8-10 a Midrash on Isa. 54:13 and Jer. 31:33-34', *Bib* 62 (1981), pp. 372-86.

Deutsch, C., *Hidden Wisdom and the Easy Yoke: Wisdom, Torah, and Discipleship in Matthew 11.25-30* (JSNTSup, 18; Sheffield: JSOT Press, 1987).

Didier, M. (ed.), *L'évangile selon Matthieu: Rédaction et théologie*.(BETL, 29; Gembloux: Duculot, 1972).

Dittmar, W., *Vetus Testamentum in Novo: Die alttestamentlichen Parallelen des Neuen Testament im Wortlaut der Urtexte und der Septuaginta. 1. Hälfte: Evangelien und Apostelgeschichte* (Göttingen: Vandenhoeck & Ruprecht, 1899).

Dobschütz, E. von, 'Matthäus als Rabbi und Katechet', *ZNW* 27 (1928), pp. 338-48.

Dodd, C.H., ''ΙΗΣΟΥΣ Ο ΔΙΔΑΣΚΑΛΟΣ ΚΑΙ ΠΡΟΦΗΤΗΣ', *Theology* 17 (1928), pp. 205-208.

—'Jesus as Teacher and Prophet', in G.K.A. Bell and A. Deissmann (eds.), *Mysterium Christi: Christological Studies by British and German Theologians* (London: Longmans, 1930), pp. 53-66.

—'The Fall of Jerusalem and the Abomination of Desolation', *JRS* 37 (1947), pp. 47-54.

—*According to the Scriptures: The Substructure of New Testament Theology* (London: Nisbet, 1952).

—*The Old Testament in the New* (Philadelphia: Fortress Press, 1963).

Dodewaard, J.A.E. van, 'La force évocatrice de la citation, mise en lumière en prenant pour base l'évangile de S. Matthieu', *Bib* 36 (1955), pp. 482-91.

Doeve, J.W., *Jewish Hermeneutics in the Synoptic Gospels and Acts* (Assen: Van Gorcum, 1954).

—'Purification du Temple et desséchement du figuier: Sur la structure du 21 chapitre de Matthieu et parallèles (Marc xi.1-xii.12, Luc xix.28-xx.19)', *NTS* 1 (1954–55), pp. 297-308.

Donaldson, T.L., *Jesus on the Mountain: A Study in Matthean Theology* (JSNTSup, 8; Sheffield: JSOT Press, 1985).

Downing, J., 'Jesus and Martyrdom', *JTS* 14 (1963), pp. 279-93.

Drury, J., *The Parables in the Gospels: History and Allegory* (New York: Crossroad, 1985).

Duesburg, H., *Jésus, prophète et docteur de la loi* (Paris: Castermann, 1955).

Duling, D.C., 'The Therapeutic Son of David: An Element in Matthew's Christological Apologetic', *NTS* 24 (1977–78), pp. 392-410.

Dunn, J.D.G., *Unity and Diversity in the New Testament: An Enquiry into the Character of Earliest Christianity* (London: SCM Press; Philadelphia: Westminster Press, 1977).

—'Pharisees, Sinners, and Jesus', in J. Neusner *et al.* (eds.), *The Social World of Formative Christianity and Judaism: Essays in Tribute to Howard Clark Kee* (Philadelphia: Fortress Press, 1988), pp. 264-89.

Dupont, J., *Les béatitudes* (3 vols.; EBib; Paris: Gabalda, 1969–73).

Edersheim, A., *The Life and Times of Jesus the Messiah* (2 vols.; London: Longmans, Green, 1883).

Edgar, S.L., 'New Testament and Rabbinic Messianic Interpretation', *NTS* 5 (1958–59), pp. 47-54

—'Respect for Context in Quotations from the Old Testament', *NTS* 9 (1962–63), pp. 55-62.

Edwards, R.A., 'An Approach to a Theology of Q', *JR* 51 (1971), pp. 247-69.

—*The Sign of Jonah in the Theology of the Evangelists and Q* (SBT, 2.18; London: SCM Press, 1971).

—'Christian Prophecy and the Q Tradition', in G. MacRae (ed.), *Society of Biblical Literature 1976 Seminar Papers* (Missoula, MT: Scholars Press, 1976), pp. 119-26.

—*A Theology of Q: Eschatology, Prophecy, and Wisdom* (Philadelphia: Fortress Press, 1976).

—*Matthew's Story of Jesus* (Philadelphia: Fortress Press, 1985).

Eldridge, V.J., 'Typology—the Key to Understanding Matthew's Formula Quotations?', *Colloquium* 15 (1982), pp. 43-51.

—'Second Thoughts on Matthew's Formula Quotations', *Colloquium* 16 (1983), pp. 45-47.

Ellis, E.E., *Paul's Use of the Old Testament* (Edinburgh: Oliver & Boyd, 1957).

Fawcett, S.V., 'Rachel's Tomb', *IDB*, IV, p. 5.

Feldman, L.H., 'Prophets and Prophecy in Josephus', *JTS* 41 (1990), pp. 386-422.

Fenton, J.C., *The Gospel of St Matthew* (Harmondsworth: Penguin Books, 1963).

Filson, F.V., *A Commentary on the Gospel according to St Matthew* (BNTC; London: A. & C. Black, 1971).

Findlay, J.A., *Jesus in the First Gospel* (London: Hodder & Stoughton, 1925).

—'The First Gospel and the Book of Testimonies', in H.G. Wood (ed.), *Amicitia Corolla: A Volume of Essays Presented to James Rendel Harris, D. Litt., on the Occasion of his Eightieth Birthday* (London: University of London, 1933), pp. 57-71.

Finegan, J., *Die Überlieferung der Leidens- und Auferstehungsgeschichte Jesu* (BZNW, 15; Giessen: Töpelmann, 1934).

Fischel, H.A., 'Martyr and Prophet (A Study in Jewish Literature)', *JQR* 37 (1946–47), pp. 265-80, 363-86.

Fishbane, M., 'Use, Authority, and Interpretation of Mikra at Qumran', in M.J. Mulder (ed.), *Mikra: Text, Translation, Reading and Interpretation of the Hebrew Bible in Ancient Judaism and Early Christianity* (CRINT, 2.1; Assen: Van Gorcum; Philadelphia: Fortress Press, 1988), pp. 339-77.

Fitzmyer, J.A., 'The Use of Explicit Old Testament Quotations in Qumran Literature and in the New Testament', *NTS* 7 (1960–61), pp. 297-333.

—'Anti-Semitism and the Cry of "All the People" (Mt. 27,25)', *TS* 26 (1965), pp. 667-71.

—*The Gospel According to Luke: Introduction, Translation, and Notes* (2 vols.; AB, 28-28A; Garden City, NY: Doubleday, 1981, 1985).

Forberg, T. 'Peter: The High Priest of the New Covenant', *Far East Asia Journal of Theology* 4.1 (1986), pp. 113-21.

France, R.T., 'Herod and the Children of Bethlehem', *NovT* 21 (1979), pp. 98-120.

—'The Formula Quotations of Matthew 2 and the Problem of Communication', *NTS* 27 (1980–81), pp. 233-51.

—*Jesus and the Old Testament: His Application of Old Testament Passages to himself and his Mission* (Grand Rapids: Baker, 1982).

France, R.T., and D. Wenham (eds.), *Gospel Perspectives*. III. *Studies in Midrash and Historiography* (Sheffield: JSOT Press, 1983).

Frankmölle, H., *Jahwebund und Kirche Christi: Studien zur Form- und Traditionsgeschichte des 'Evangeliums' nach Matthäus* (NTAbh, NS 10; Münster: Aschendorff, 1974).

Freedman, D.N., 'The Deuteronomic History', *IBSup*, pp. 226-28.

Frend, W.H.C., *Martyrdom and Persecution in the Early Church: A Study of Conflict from the Maccabees to Donatus* (Oxford: Basil Blackwell, 1965).

Fuller, R.H., *The Mission and Achievement of Jesus: An Examination of the Presuppositions of New Testament Theology* (SBT, 12; London: SCM Press, 1954).

—*The Foundations of New Testament Christology* (London: Lutterworth, 1965).

Gaechter, P., *Das Matthäus Evangelium* (Innsbruck: Tyrolia, 1963).

Gager, J.G., *Kingdom and Community: The Social World of Early Christianity* (Englewood Cliffs, NJ: Prentice-Hall, 1975).

Gärtner, B., *The Temple and the Community in Qumran and the New Testament: A Comparative Study in the Temple Symbolism of the Qumran Texts and the New Testament* (Cambridge: Cambridge University Press, 1965).

Garland, D.E., *The Intention of Matthew 23* (NovTSup, 52; Leiden: Brill, 1979).

Gaster, M., *Studies and Texts in Folklore, Magic, Medieval Romance, Hebrew Apocrypha, and Samaritan Archaeology* (3 vols.; London: Maggs, 1925–28).

Gaston, L., *No Stone Upon Another: Studies in the Significance of the Fall of Jerusalem in the Synoptic Gospels* (Leiden: Brill, 1970).

Geist, H., 'Die Warnung vor den falschen Propheten: Eine ernste Mahnung an die heutige Kirche: zu Mt 7,15-23; 24,11f.24', in H. Merklein and J. Lange (eds.), *Biblische Randbemerkungen: Schülerfestschrift für Rudolf Schnackenburg zum 60. Geburtstag* (Würzburg: Echter Verlag, 1974), pp. 139-49.

Giesen, H., 'Der verdorrte Fiegenbaum—Eine symbolische Aussage? Zu Mk 11,12-14,20f.', *BZ* 20 (1976), pp. 95-111.

Gils, F., *Jésus, prophète d'après les évangiles synoptiques* (Louvain: Publications Universitaires, 1957).

Gnilka, J., *Das Matthäusevangelium* (2 vols.; HTKNT, 1; Freiburg: Herder, 1986, 1988).

Goldin, J., 'Josephus, Flavius', *IDB*, II, pp. 987-88.

Goldstein, J.A., *II Maccabees: A New Translation with Introduction and Commentary* (AB, 41A; Garden City, NY: Doubleday, 1983).

Goppelt, L., *Typos: Die typologische Deutung des Alten Testaments im Neuen* (repr. Darmstadt: Wissenschaftliche Buchgesellschaft, 1969).

Goulder, M.D., *Midrash and Lection in Matthew* (London: SPCK, 1974).

Green, H.B., 'The Structure of St Matthew's Gospel', *SE*, IV, pp. 47-59.

—*The Gospel according to Matthew in the Revised Standard Version* (New Clarendon Bible; Oxford: Oxford University Press, 1975).

Green, J.B., *The Death of Jesus: Tradition and Interpretation in the Passion Narrative* (WUNT, 2.33; Tübingen: Mohr [Paul Siebeck], 1988).

Grundmann, W., *Das Evangelium nach Matthäus* (THKNT, 1; Berlin: Evangelische Verlagsanstalt, 1971).

Gundry, R.H., *The Use of the Old Testament in St Matthew's Gospel with Specific Reference to the Messianic Hope* (NovTSup, 18; Leiden: Brill, 1967).

—*Matthew: A Commentary on his Literary and Theological Art* (Grand Rapids: Eerdmans, 1982).

Haenchen, E., 'Matthäus 23', *ZTK* 48 (1951), pp. 38-63.

—*Der Weg Jesu: Eine Erklärung des Markus-Evangeliums und der kanonischen Parallelen* (Berlin: Töpelmann, 1966).

Hahn, F., *Christologische Hoheitstitel: Ihre Geschichte im früher Christentum* (FRLANT, 83; Göttingen: Vandenhoeck & Ruprecht, 1964.

Hamerton-Kelly, R.G., 'The Temple and the Origins of Jewish Apocalyptic', *VT* 20 (1970), pp. 1-15.

Hare, D.R.A., *The Theme of Jewish Persecution of Christians in the Gospel according to Saint Matthew* (SNTSMS, 6; Cambridge: Cambridge University Press, 1967).

Hare, D.R.A., and D.J. Harrington, '"Make Disciples of all the Gentiles" (Mt. 28:19)', *CBQ* 37 (1975), pp. 359-69.

Harris, R.J., *Testimonies* (2 vols.; Cambridge: Cambridge University Press, 1916, 1920).

Hartman, L., 'Scriptural Exegesis in the Gospel of Matthew and the Problem of Communication', in M. Didier (ed.), *L'évangile selon Matthieu: Rédaction et Théologie* (BETL, 29; Gembloux: Duculot, 1972), pp. 132-52.

Harvey, A.E., 'Forty Strokes Save One: Social Aspects of Judaizing and Apostasy', in A.E. Harvey (ed.), *Alternative Approaches to New Testament Study* (London: SPCK, 1985), pp. 79-96.

Havener, I., *Q: The Sayings of Jesus* (Good News Studies, 19; Wilmington, DE: Michael Glazier, 1987).

Hay, D., *Glory at the Right Hand: Psalm 110 in Early Christianity* (SBLMS, 18; Nashville: Abingdon Press, 1973).

Hayman, A.P., 'The Problem of Pseudonymity in the Ezra Apocalypse', *JSJ* 6 (1975), pp. 45-56.

Hays, R.B., *Echoes of Scripture in the Letters of Paul* (New Haven: Yale University Press, 1989).

Hengel, M., and H. Merkel, 'Die Magier aus dem Osten und die Flucht nach Ägypten (Mt 2) im Rahmen der Antiken Religionsgeschichte und der Theologie des Matthäus', in P. Hoffmann (ed.), *Orientierung an Jesus: Zur Theologie der Synoptiker. Für Josef Schmid* (Freiburg: Herder, 1973), pp. 139-69.

Hiers, R.H., 'Not the Season for Figs', *JBL* 87 (1968), pp. 394-400.

Higgins, A.J.B., 'Jesus as Prophet', *ExpTim* 57 (1945–46), pp. 292-94.

Hill, D., '*Dikaioi* as a Quasi-Technical Term', *NTS* 11 (1964–65), pp. 296-302.

—*The Gospel of Matthew* (NCB; London: Marshall, Morgan & Scott, 1972).

—'False Prophets and Charismatics: Structure and Interpretation in Matthew 7:15-23', *Bib* 57 (1976), pp. 327-48.

—'Jesus and Josephus' "Messianic Prophets"', in E. Best and R.McL. Wilson (eds.), *Text and Interpretation: Studies in the New Testament Presented to Matthew Black* (Cambridge: Cambridge University Press, 1979).

—*New Testament Prophecy* (London: Marshall, Morgan & Scott; Atlanta: John Knox, 1979).

Hillers, D.R., *Lamentations: Introduction, Translation, and Notes* (AB, 7A; Garden City, NY: Doubleday, 1972).

Hillyer, N., 'Matthew's Use of the Old Testament', *EvQ* 36 (1964), pp. 12-26.

Hinnebusch, P., *St Matthew's Earthquake: Judgement and Discipleship in the Gospel of Matthew* (Ann Arbor, MI.: Servant, 1980).

Hoffmann, P., *Studien zur Theologie der Logienquelle* (Münster: Aschendorff, 1982).

Holladay, W.L., 'The Background of Jeremiah's Self-Understanding', *JBL* 83 (1964), pp. 153-64.

—'Jeremiah and Moses: Further Observations', *JBL* 85 (1966), pp. 17-27.

—'New Covenant, The', *IDBSup*, pp. 623-25.

—*A Commentary on the Book of the Prophet Jeremiah* (ed. P.D. Hanson; 2 vols.; Minneapolis: Augsburg–Fortress, 1986, 1989).

Holmberg, B., *Sociology and the New Testament: An Appraisal* (Minneapolis: Fortress Press, 1990).

Horgan, M.P., 'A Lament over Jerusalem ("4Q179")', *JSS* 18 (1973), pp. 222-34.

Horsley, R.A., '"Like One of the Prophets of Old": Two Types of Popular Prophets at the Time of Jesus', *CBQ* 47 (1985), pp. 435-63.

—'Popular Prophetic Movements at the Time of Jesus: Their Principal Features and Social Origins', *JSNT* 26 (1986), pp. 3-27.

—*Sociology and the Jesus Movement* (New York: Crossroad, 1989).

Howard, G., *The Gospel of Matthew According to a Primitive Hebrew Text* (Macon, GA: Mercer University Press, 1987).

Hühn, E., *Die alttestamentlichen Citate und Reminiscenzen im Neuen Testament* [= *Die messianischen Weissagungen des israelitischjudischen Volkes bis zu den Targumim, II*] (Tübingen: Mohr [Paul Siebeck], 1900).

Hummel, R., *Die Auseinandersetzung zwischen Kirche und Judentum im Matthäusevangelium* (BEvT, 33; Munich: Chr. Kaiser Verlag, 1966).

Jackson, F.J.F., and K. Lake (eds.), *The Beginnings of Christianity. Part I: The Acts of the Apostles* (5 vols.; London: Macmillan, 1920–33).

Jacobson, A.D., 'Wisdom Christology in Q' (PhD dissertation, Claremont Graduate School, 1978).

—'The Literary Unity of Q', *JBL* 101 (1982), pp. 365-89.

Jeremias, J., *Die Abendmahlsworte Jesu* (Göttingen: Vandenhoeck & Ruprecht, 1960).

—*The Parables of Jesus* (London: SCM Press, 1963).

—''Ιερεμίας', *TWNT*, III, pp. 218-21 [= *TDNT*, pp. 218-21].

—*Jerusalem in the Time of Jesus: An Investigation into Economic and Social Conditions during the New Testament Period* (Philadelphia: Fortress Press, 1969).

—*Neutestamentliche Theologie*. I. *Die Verkündigung Jesu* (Gütersloh: Gerd Mohn, 1971). [ET *New Testament Theology*. I. *The Proclamation of Jesus*; London: SCM Press, 1971]).

Johnson, M.D., *The Purpose of the Biblical Genealogies with Special Reference to the Setting of the Genealogies of Jesus* (SNTSMS, 8; Cambridge: Cambridge University Press, 1988).

—'Reflections on a Wisdom Approach to Matthew's Christology', *CBQ* 36 (1974), pp. 44-64.

Johnson, S.E., 'The Gospel According to Matthew', *IB*, VII, pp. 229-625.

Juel, D., *Messianic Exegesis: Christological Exegesis of the Old Testament in Early Christianity* (Philadelphia: Fortress Press, 1988).

Kee, H.C., 'The Function of Scriptural Quotations and Allusions in Mark 11–16', in E.E. Ellis and E. Grässer (eds.), *Jesus und Paulus: Festschrift für Werner Georg Kümmel zum 70. Geburtstag* (Göttingen: Vandenhoeck & Ruprecht, 1975), pp. 165-88.

—*Knowing the Truth: A Sociological Approach to New Testament Interpretation* (Minneapolis: Fortress Press, 1989).

—'The Transformation of the Synagogue after 70 C.E.: Its Import for Early Christianity'. *NTS* 36 (1989–90), pp. 1-24.

Kelber, W.H., *The Oral and the Written Gospel* (Philadelphia: Fortress Press, 1983).

Kilpatrick, G.D., *The Origins of the Gospel according to Saint Matthew* (Oxford: Clarendon Press, 1946).

Kingsbury, J.D., *Matthew: Structure, Christology, Kingdom* (Philadelphia: Fortress Press, 1975).

—'The Title "Son of David" in Matthew's Gospel', *JBL* 95 (1976), pp. 591-602.

Kirschner, R., 'Apocalyptic and Rabbinic Responses to the Destruction of 70', *HTR* 78 (1985), pp. 27-46.

Kittel, G., ''ΙΗΣΟΥΣ Ο ΔΙΔΑΣΚΑΛΟΣ ΚΑΙ ΠΡΟΦΗΤΗΣ', *Theology* 17 (1928), pp. 202-205.

Kloppenborg, J.S., 'Wisdom Christology in Q', *LTP* 34 (1978), pp. 129-47.

—'Blessing and Marginality: The "Persecution Beatitude" in Q, Thomas, and Early Christianity', *Forum* 2.3 (1986), pp. 36-56.

—'The Formation of Q and Antique Instructional Genres', *JBL* 105 (1986), pp. 443-62.

—*The Formation of Q: Trajectories in Ancient Wisdom Collections* (Studies in Antiquity and Christianity; Philadelphia: Fortress Press, 1987).

—*Q Parallels: Synopsis, Critical Notes, and Concordance* (Sonoma, CA: Polebridge Press, 1988).

Klostermann, E., *Das Matthäusevangelium* (HNT, 4, Tübingen: Mohr [Paul Siebeck], 1971).

Knibb, M.A., 'The Exile in the Literature of the Intertestamental Period', *HeyJ* 17 (1976), pp. 253-72.

Knowles, M.P., 'Moses, the Law, and the Unity of 4 Ezra', *NovT* 31 (1989), pp. 257-74.

Knox, J., 'The Prophet in New Testament Christology', in R.A. Norris (ed.), *Lux in Lumine: Essays to Honor W. Norman Pittenger* (New York: Seabury, 1966), pp. 23-34.

Kosmala, H., '"His Blood on us and on our Children" (The Background of Mat. 27,24-25)', *ASTI* 7 (1968–69), pp. 94-126.

Kriesberg, L., *Social Conflicts* (Englewood Cliffs, NJ: Prentice-Hall, 1982).

Kugel, J.L., *The Idea of Biblical Poetry: Parallelism and its History* (New Haven: Yale University Press, 1981).

Kugel, J.L., and R.A. Greer, *Early Biblical Interpretation* (Library of Early Christianity; Philadelphia: Westminster Press, 1986).

Kümmel, W.G., *Introduction to the New Testament* (Nashville: Abingdon Press, 1975).

Lachs, S.T., 'Rabbinic Sources for New Testament Studies: Use and Misuse', *JQR* 74 (1983), pp. 159-73.

—*A Rabbinic Commentary on the New Testament: The Gospels of Matthew, Mark, and Luke* (Hoboken, NJ: Ktav; New York: Anti-Defamation League of B'nai B'rith, 1987).

Lagrange, M.-J., *Evangile selon Saint Matthieu* (Paris: Lecoffre, 1927).

Lampe, G.W.H., 'The Reasonableness of Typology', in G.W.H. Lampe and K.J. Woollcombe, *Essays on Typology* (SBT; London: SCM Press, 1957), pp. 9-38.

—'Martyrdom and Inspiration', in W. Horbury and B. McNeil (eds.), *Suffering and Martyrdom in the New Testament: Studies Presented to G.M. Styler by the Cambridge New Testament Seminar* (Cambridge: Cambridge University Press, 1981), pp. 118-35.

Lane, W.L., *The Gospel according to Mark: The English Text with Introduction, Exposition, and Notes* (NICNT; Grand Rapids: Eerdmans, 1974).

LeDéaut, R., 'La tradition juive ancienne et l'exégèse chrétienne primitive', *RHPR* 51 (1971), pp. 31-50.

Légasse, S., 'L'"anti-judaisme" dans l'évangile selon Matthieu', in M. Didier (ed.),

L'évangile selon Matthieu: Rédaction et théologie (BETL, 29; Gembloux: Duculot, 1972), pp. 417-28.

—'L'oracle contre "cette génération" (Mt 23,34-36, par. Lc 11,49-51) et la polémique judéo-chrétienne dans la Source des Logia', in J. Delobel (ed.), *Logia: Les paroles de Jésus—The Sayings of Jesus. Mémorial Joseph Coppens* (BETL, 59; Leuven: Leuven University Press, 1982), pp. 237-56.

Levey, S.H., 'The Date of Targum Jonathan to the Prophets', *VT* 21 (1971), pp. 186-96.

Levine, A.-J., *The Social and Ethnic Dimensions of Matthean Social History: 'Go Nowhere Among the Gentiles' (Matt. 10:5b)* (Studies in the Bible and Early Christianity, 14; Lewiston, NY: Edwin Mellen, 1988).

Lindars, B., *New Testament Apologetic: The Doctrinal Significance of the Old Testament Quotations* (London: SCM Press, 1961).

—'"Rachel Weeping for her Children"—Jeremiah 31.15-22', *JSOT* 12 (1979), pp. 47-62.

Lohmeyer, E., *Das Evangelium nach Matthäus* (Kritisch-exegetischer Kommentar über das NT; ed. W. Schmauch; Göttingen: Vandenhoeck & Ruprecht, 1967).

Löhse, B., *Märtyrer und Gottesknecht: Untersuchungen zur urchristlichen Verkündigung vom Sühntod Jesu Christi* (FRLANT, NS 46; Göttingen: Vandenhoeck & Ruprecht, 1963).

Longenecker, R.N., *Biblical Exegesis in the Apostolic Period* (Grand Rapids: Eerdmans, 1975).

Lührmann, D., *Die Redaktion der Logienquelle* (WMANT, 33; Neukirchen–Vluyn: Neukirchener Verlag, 1969).

Luz, U., 'Die Jünger im Matthäusevangelium', *ZNW* 62 (1971), pp. 141-71.

—*Das Evangelium nach Matthäus.* I. *Mt 1-7* (EKKNT, 1.1; Zürich: Benzinger Verlag; Neukirchen–Vluyn: Neukirchener Verlag, 1985).

McConnell, R.S., *Law and Prophecy in Matthew's Gospel: The Authority and Use of the Old Testament in the Gospel of Saint Matthew* (Basel: Friedrich Reinhardt, 1969).

McKane, W., *A Critical and Exegetical Commentary on Jeremiah.* I. *Introduction and Commentary on Jeremiah I-XXV* (ICC; Edinburgh: T. & T. Clark, 1986).

McKelvey, R.J., *The New Temple: The Church in the New Testament* (London: Oxford University Press, 1969).

MacKenzie, J.L., 'Royal Messianism', *CBQ* 19 (1957), pp. 25-52.

McLoughlin, S., 'Les accords mineurs Mt-Lc contre Mc et le problème synoptique: Vers la théorie des deux sources', *ETL* 43 (1967), pp. 17-40 (= I. de la Potterie [ed.], *De Jésus aux évangiles: Tradition et rédaction dans les évangiles synoptiques* [BETL, 25; Gembloux: Duculot; Paris: Lethielleux, 1967], pp. 17-40).

McNamara, M., *The New Testament and the Palestinian Targum to the Pentateuch* (AnBib, 27; Rome: Pontifical Biblical Institute, 1966).

Maier, G., *Matthäus-Evangelium* (2 vols.; Neuhausen: Hänssler, 1979, 1980).

Malina, B., and J.H. Neyrey, *Calling Jesus Names: The Social Value of Labels in Matthew* (Sonoma, CA: Polebridge Press, 1988).

Mandelbaum, B., 'Pesikta de-Rav Kahana', *EncJud*, XIII, pp. 333-34.

Mánek, J., 'Fishers of Men', *NovT* 2 (1958), pp. 138-41.

Manns, F., 'Un midrash chrétien: le récit de la mort de Judas', *RevScRel* 54 (1980), pp. 197-203.

Manson, T.W., 'The Argument from Prophecy', *JTS* 46 (1945), pp. 129-36.

—*The Teaching of Jesus: Studies in its Form and Content* (Cambridge: Cambridge University Press, 1948).

—'Martyrs and Martyrdom', *BJRL* 39 (1956–57), pp. 463-84.

Mead, R.T., 'A Dissenting Opinion about Respect for Context in Old Testament Quotations', *NTS* 10 (1963–64), pp. 279–89.

Meeks, W.A., *The Prophet-King: Moses Traditions and the Johannine Christology* (Leiden: Brill, 1967).

—*The First Urban Christians: The Social World of the Apostle Paul* (New Haven: Yale University Press, 1983).

Meier, J.P., *Law and History in Matthew's Gospel: A Redactional Study of Mt. 5:17-48* (AnBib, 71; Rome: Biblical Institute Press, 1976).

—'Nations or Gentiles in Matthew 28:19?', *CBQ* 39 (1977), pp. 94-102.

—*The Vision of Matthew: Christ, Church, and Morality in the First Gospel* (New York: Paulist Press, 1979).

—*Matthew* (New Testament Message, 3; Wilmington, DE: Michael Glazier, 1980).

Menken, M.J.J., 'The References to Jeremiah in the Gospel according to Matthew' (Mt. 2.17; 16.14; 27, 9), *ETL* 60 (1984), pp. 5-24.

Metzger, B.M., 'The Formulas introducing Quotations of Scripture in the New Testament and in the Mishnah', *JBL* 70 (1951), pp. 297-307.

Meyer, P.D., 'The Gentile Mission in Q', *JBL* 89 (1970), pp. 405-17.

Michel, O., *Prophet und Märtyrer* (BFCT, 37.2; Gütersloh: Bertelsmann, 1932).

Micklem, N., ''ΙΗΣΟΥΣ Ο ΔΙΔΑΣΚΑΛΟΣ ΚΑΙ ΠΡΟΦΗΤΗΣ', *Theology* 17 (1928), pp. 208-211.

Miller, R.J., 'The Rejection of the Prophets in Q', *JBL* 107 (1988), pp. 225-40.

Miller, M.P., 'Targum, Midrash, and the Use of the Old Testament in the New Testament', *JSJ* 2 (1971), pp. 29-82.

Milton, H., 'The Structure of the Prologue to St Matthew's Gospel', *JBL* 81 (1962), pp. 175-81.

Minear, P.S., 'False Prophecy and Hypocrisy in the Gospel of Matthew', in J. Gnilka (ed.), *Neues Testament und Kirche: [Festschrift] Für R. Schnackenburg* (Freiburg: Herder, 1974), pp. 76-93.

M'Neile, A.H., *The Gospel according to St Matthew: The Greek Text with Introduction, Notes, and Indices* (London: Macmillan, 1915).

Montefiore, C.G., *The Synoptic Gospels* (2 vols.; London: Macmillan, 1927).

Moo, D.J., *The Old Testament in the Gospel Passion Narratives* (Sheffield: Almond Press, 1983).

—'Tradition and Old Testament in Matt. 27:3-10', in R.T. France and D. Wenham (eds.), *Gospel Perspectives: Studies in Midrash and Historiography* (Sheffield: JSOT Press, 1983), III, pp. 157-75.

Moore, C.A., 'Toward the Dating of the Book of Baruch', *CBQ* 36 (1974), pp. 312-20.

—*Daniel, Esther, and Jeremiah: The Additions. A New Translation with Introduction and Commentary* (AB, 44; Garden City, NY: Doubleday, 1977).

Mora, V., *Le refus d'Israel: Matthieu 27,25* (LD, 124; Paris: Cerf, 1986).

Moule, C.F.D., 'Fulfilment-Words in the New Testament: Use and Abuse', *NTS* 14 (1967–68), pp. 293-320.

Mueller, J.R., 'The Apocalypse of Abraham and the Destruction of the Second Jewish Temple', in K.H. Richards (ed.), *Society of Biblical Literature 1982 Seminar Papers* (Chico, CA: Scholars Press, 1982), pp. 341-49.

Mulder, J.M. (ed.), *Mikra: Text, Translation, Reading and Interpretation of the Hebrew Bible in Ancient Judaism and Early Christianity* (CRINT, 2.1; Assen: Van Gorcum; Philadelphia: Fortress Press, 1988).

Murphy, F.J., *The Structure and Meaning of Second Baruch* (SBLDS, 78; Atlanta: Scholars Press, 1985).

—'The Temple in the Syriac *Apocalypse of Baruch*', *JBL* 106 (1987), pp. 671-83.

Myers, J.M., *I and II Esdras: Introduction, Translation, and Commentary* (AB, 42; Garden City, NY: Doubleday, 1974).

Nellesen, E., *Das Kind und seine Mutter: Struktur und Verkündigung des 2. Kapitels im Matthäusevangelium* (SBS, 39; Stuttgart: Katholisches Bibelwerk, 1969).

Nepper-Christensen, P., *Das Matthäusevangelium: Ein jüdenchristliches Evangelium?* (Acta Theologica Danica, 1; Aarhus: Universitetsforlaget, 1958).

Neusner, J., *A Life of Yohanan ben Zakkai, Ca. 1–80 C.E.* (SPB, 6; Leiden: Brill, 1970).

—'Judaism in a Time of Crisis: Four Responses to the Destruction of the Second Temple', *Judaism* 21 (1972), pp. 313-27.

—*First-Century Judaism in Crisis* (Nashville: Abingdon Press, 1975).

—*Midrash in Context: Exegesis in Formative Judaism* (Philadelphia: Fortress Press, 1983).

—*Ancient Israel After Catastrophe: The Religious World View of the Mishnah* (Charlottesville: University Press of Virginia, 1983).

—*What is Midrash?* (Guides to Biblical Scholarship, New Testament Series; Philadelphia: Fortress Press, 1987).

—*Wrong Ways and Right Ways in the Study of Formative Judaism: Critical Method and Literature, History, and the History of Religion* (BJS 145; Atlanta: Scholars Press, 1988).

Neusner, J., *et al.* (eds.), *The Social World of Formative Christianity and Judaism: Essays in Tribute to Howard Clark Kee* (Philadelphia: Fortress Press, 1988).

Nickelsburg, G.W.E., 'Narrative Traditions in the Paraleipomena of Jeremiah and 2 Baruch', *CBQ* 35 (1973), pp. 60-68.

—'Good and Bad Leaders in Pseudo-Philo's *Liber Antiquitatum Biblicarum*', in J.J. Collins and G.W.E. Nickelsburg (eds.), *Ideal Figures in Ancient Judaism: Profiles and Paradigms* (SBLSCS, 12; Chico, CA: Scholars Press, 1980), pp. 49-65.

—'Enoch, Levi, and Peter: Recipients of Revelation in Upper Galilee', *JBL* 100 (1981), pp. 575-600.

—*Jewish Literature between the Bible and the Mishnah: A Historical and Literary Introduction* (Philadelphia: Fortress Press, 1981).

Nolan, B.M., *The Royal Son of God: The Christology of Matthew 1–2 in the Setting of the Gospel* (OBO, 23; Fribourg: Editions Universitaires; Göttingen: Vandenhoeck & Ruprecht, 1979).

Oberweis, M., 'Beobachtungen zum AT-Gebrauch in der Matthäischen Kindheitsgeschichte', *NTS* 35 (1988–89), pp. 131-49.

O'Rourke, J.J., 'The Fulfillment Texts in Matthew', *CBQ* 24 (1962), pp. 394-403.

Overman, J.A., *Matthew's Gospel and Formative Judaism: The Social World of the Matthean Community* (Minneapolis: Augsburg–Fortress, 1990).

Patte, D., *Early Jewish Hermeneutic in Palestine* (SBLDS, 22; Missoula, MT: Scholars Press, 1975).

Pedersen, S., 'Zum Problem der vaticinia ex eventu. (Eine Analyse von Mt. 21,33-46 par.; 22,1-10 par.)', *ST* 19 (1965), pp. 167-88.

Perrot, C., 'Les récits d'enfance dans la haggada antérieure au IIe siècle de notre ère', *RSR* 55 (1967), pp. 481-518.

Pesch, R., 'Der Gottessohn im matthäischen Evangelienprolog (Mt. 1-2): Beobachtungen zu den Zitationsformeln der Reflexionzitate', *Bib* 48 (1967), pp. 395-420.

Piper, R.A., *Wisdom in the Q-tradition: The Aphoristic Teaching of Jesus* (SNTSMS, 61; Cambridge: Cambridge University Press, 1989).

Plummer, A., *An Exegetical Commentary on the Gospel according to St Matthew* (London: Stock, 1910).

Polag, A., *Die Christologie der Logienquelle* (WMANT, 45. Neukirchen–Vluyn: Neukirchener Verlag, 1977).

—*Fragmenta Q: Textheft zur Logienquelle* (Neukirchen–Vluyn: Neukirchener Verlag, 1979).

Porteous, N.W., 'Jerusalem-Zion: The Growth of a Symbol', in A. Kuschke (ed.), *Verbannung und Heimkehr* (Tübingen: Mohr [Paul Siebeck], 1961), pp. 235-52.

Przybylski, B., 'The Setting of Matthean Anti-Judaism', in P. Richardson and D. Granskou (eds.), *Anti-Judaism in Early Christianity*. I. *Paul and the Gospels* (Studies in Christianity and Judaism, 2; Waterloo: Wilfred Laurier University, 1986), pp. 181-200.

Rajak, T., *Josephus: The Historian and his Society* (London: Gerald Duckworth, 1983).

Reiling, J., 'The Use of ΨΕΥΔΟΠΡΟΦΗΤΗΣ in the Septuagint, Philo, and Josephus', *NovT* 13 (1971), pp. 147-56.

Rengstorf, K.H., 'Die Stadt der Mörder (Mt 22:7)', in W. Eltester (ed.), *Judentum, Urchristentum, Kirche: Festschrift J. Jeremias* (Berlin: Töpelman, 1960), pp. 106-29.

Resch, A., *Agrapha: Aussercanonische Schrift-Fragmenta* (TU, 15; Leipzig: Hinrichs, 1906).

Riaud, J., 'La figure de Jérémie dans les *Paralipomena Jeremiae*', in A. Caquot and M. Delcor (eds.), *Mélanges bibliques et orientaux en l'honneur de M. Henri Cazelles* (AOAT, 212; Kevelaer: Butzon & Bercker; Neukirchen–Vluyn: Neukirchener Verlag, 1981), pp. 373-85.

Richardson, P., *Israel in the Apostolic Church* (SNTSMS, 10; Cambridge: Cambridge University Press, 1969).

Riches, J., 'Parables and the Search for a New Community', in J. Neusner *et al.* (eds.), *The Social World of Formative Christianity and Judaism: Essays in Tribute to Howard Clark Kee* (Philadelphia: Fortress Press, 1988), pp. 235-63.

Roberts, B.J., *The Old Testament Text and Versions: The Hebrew Text in Transmission and the History of the Ancient Versions* (Cardiff: University of Wales Press, 1951).

Robinson, J.M., 'Logoi Sophon: On the Gattung of Q', in H. Koester and J.M. Robinson (eds.), *Trajectories through Early Christianity* (Philadelphia: Fortress Press, 1971), pp. 71-113.

—'Jesus as Sophos and Sophia: Wisdom Tradition and the Gospels', in R.L. Wilken (ed.), *Aspects of Wisdom in Judaism and Early Christianity* (Notre Dame: Notre Dame Press, 1975), pp. 1-16.

Robinson, T.H., *The Gospel of Matthew* (MNTC; New York: Doubleday, 1928).

Rodd, C.S., 'On Applying a Sociological Theory to Biblical Studies', *JSOT* 19 (1981), pp. 95-106.

Roth, C., 'The Cleansing of the Temple and Zechariah 14:21', *NovT* 4 (1960), pp. 174-81.

Rothfuchs, W., *Die Erfüllungszitate des Matthäus-Evangeliums: Eine biblische-theologische Untersuchung* (BWANT, 8; Stuttgart: Kohlhammer, 1969).

Ruether, R.R., *Faith and Fratricide: The Theological Roots of Anti-Semitism* (New York: Seabury, 1974).

Saldarini, A.J., 'Varieties of Rabbinic Response to the Destruction of the Temple', in K.H. Richards (ed.), *Society of Biblical Literature 1982 Seminar Papers* (Chico, CA: Scholars Press, 1982), pp. 437-58.

—'Judaism and the New Testament', in E.J. Epp and G.W. MacRae (eds.), *The New Testament and its Modern Interpreters* (Philadelphia: Fortress Press; Atlanta: Scholars Press, 1989), pp. 27-54.

Sand, A., *Das Gesetz und die Propheten: Untersuchungen zur Theologie des Evangeliums nach Matthäus* (Biblische Untersuchungen, 11; Regensburg: Pustet, 1974).

—'Propheten, Weise, und Schriftkundige in der Gemeinde des Matthäusevangeliums', in J. Haine (ed.), *Kirche im Werden: Studien zum Thema Amt und Gemeinde im Neuen Testament* (Munich: Schöningh, 1976), pp. 167-84.

Sanders, E.P., *Paul and Palestinian Judaism: A Comparison of Patterns of Religion* (Philadelphia: Fortress Press, 1977).

Sandmel, S., 'Parallelomania', *JBL* 81 (1962), pp. 1-13.

Sayler, G.B., *Have the Promises Failed? A Literary Analysis of 2 Baruch* (SBLDS, 72; Chico, CA: Scholars Press, 1984).

Sato, M., *Q und Prophetie: Studien zur Gattungs- und Traditionsgeschichte der Quelle Q* (WUNT, 2.29; Tübingen: Mohr [Paul Siebeck], 1988).

Schenk, W., *Die Sprache des Matthäus: Die Text-konstituenten in ihren makro- und mikrostrukturellen Relationen* (Göttingen: Vandenhoeck & Ruprecht, 1987).

Schlatter, A., *Der Märtyrer and den Anfängen der Kirche* (BFCT, 19.3; Gütersloh: Bertelsmann, 1915).

—*Der Evangelist Matthäus: Seine Sprache, sein Ziel, seine Selbständigkeit* (Stuttgart: Calwer Verlag, 1982).

Schmid, J., *Das Evangelium nach Matthäus* (RNT, 1; Regensburg: Pustet, 1965).

Schnackenburg, R., 'Die Erwartung des "Propheten" nach dem Neuen Testament und den Qumran-Texten', *SE*, I, pp. 622-39.

—*Matthäusevangelium* (Die neue echter Bibel; 2 vols.; Würzburg: Echter Verlag, 1985, 1987).

Schnider, F., *Jesus der Prophet* (OBO, 2; Freiburg: Universitätsverlag; Göttingen: Vandenhoeck & Ruprecht, 1973).

Schniewind, J., *Das Evangelium nach Matthäus* (NTD, 2; Göttingen: Vandenhoeck & Ruprecht, 1964).

Schoeps, H.J., *Die jüdischen Prophetenmorde* (Symbolae Biblicae Upsalienses, 2; Uppsala: Wretman, 1943).

—*Theologie und Geschichte des Judenchristentums* (Tübingen: Mohr [Paul Siebeck], 1949).

Schulz, S., *Q: Die Spruchquelle der Evangelisten* (Zürich: Theologischer Verlag, 1972).

Schwanke, B., 'Dort wird Heulen und Zähneknirschen sein', *BZ* 16 (1972), pp. 121-22.

Schweizer, E., 'Observance of the Law and Charismatic Activity in Matthew', *NTS* 16 (1969–70), pp. 213-30.

—*Das Evangelium nach Markus* (NTD, 1; Göttingen: Vandenhoeck & Ruprecht, 1967).

—*Das Evangelium nach Matthäus* (NTD, 2; Göttingen: Vandenhoeck & Ruprecht, 1973).

Segbroeck, F. van, 'Le scandale de l'incroyance: La signification de Mt. XIII,35', *ETL* 41 (1965), pp. 344-72.

—'Les citations d'accomplissement dans l'évangile selon Matthieu d'après trois ouvrages récents', in M. Didier (ed.), *L'évangile selon Matthieu: Rédaction et théologie* (BETL, 29; Gembloux: Duculot, 1972), pp. 107-130.

Senior, D.P., 'The Fate of the Betrayer: A Redactional Study of Matt. XXVII, 3-10', *ETL* 48 (1972), pp. 372-46.

—'The Passion Narrative in the Gospel of Matthew', in M. Didier (ed.), *L'évangile selon Matthieu: Rédaction et théologie* (BETL, 29; Gembloux: Duculot, 1972), pp. 343-58.

—'A Case Study in Matthean Creativity: Matthew 27:3-10', *BR* 19 (1974), pp. 23-36.

—*The Passion Narrative according to Matthew: A Redactional Study* (BETL, 39; Leuven: Leuven University Press, 1982).

Shires, H.M., *Finding the Old Testament in the New* (Philadelphia: Westminster Press, 1974).

Smith, B.T.D., *The Gospel according to St Matthew* (Cambridge Greek Testament; Cambridge: Cambridge University Press, 1927).

Smith, C.W.F., 'Fishers of Men: Footnotes on a Gospel Figure', *HTR* 52 (1959), pp. 187-203.

Smith, D.M., 'The Use of the Old Testament in the New', in J.M. Efird (ed.), *The Use of the Old Testament in the New and Other Essays: Studies in Honor of William Franklin Stinespring* (Durham, NC: Duke University Press, 1972), pp. 3-65.

Soares Prabhu, G.M., *The Formula Quotations in the Infancy Narratives of Matthew: An Enquiry into the Tradition History of Mt. 1–2* (AnBib, 63; Rome: Pontifical Biblical Institute, 1976).

Sparks, H.F.D., 'St Matthew's References to Jeremiah', *JTS* NS 1 (1950), pp. 155-56.

Sperber, D., 'Pesikta Rabbati', *EncJud*, XIII, pp. 335-36.

Staab, K., *Das Evangelium nach Matthäus* (Würzburg: Echter Verlag, 1951).

Stanton, G. (ed.), *The Interpretation of Matthew* (Issues in Religion and Theology, 3; London: SPCK; Philadelphia: Fortress Press, 1983).

—'The Gospel of Matthew and Judaism', *BJRL* 66 (1984), pp. 264-84.

—'The Origin and Purpose of Matthew's Gospel: Matthean Scholarship from 1945–80', in H. Temporini and W. Haase (eds.), *Aufstieg und Niedergang der römischen Welt: Geschichte und Kultur Roms im Spiegel der neueren Forschung* (Berlin: de Gruyter, 1985), 2.25.3, pp. 1889-1951.

—'Matthew', in D.A. Carson and H.G.M. Williamson (eds.), *It is Written: Scripture Citing Scripture: Essays in Honour of Barnabas Lindars* (Cambridge: Cambridge University Press, 1988), pp. 205-19.

Steck, O.H., *Israel und das gewaltsame Geschick der Propheten: Untersuchungen zur Überlieferung des deuteronomistischen Geschichtsbildes im Alten Testament, Spätjudentum, und Urchristentum* (WMANT, 23; Neukirchen–Vluyn: Neukirchener Verlag, 1967).

Stendahl, K., *The School of Saint Matthew and its Use of the Old Testament* (ASNU, 20; Lund: Gleerup, 2nd edn, 1968).

—'Quis et Unde? An Analysis of Matthew 1–2', in W. Eltester (ed.), *Judentum, Urchristentum, Kirche: Festschrift J. Jeremias* (Berlin: Töpelmann, 1960), pp. 94-105.

Stone, M.E., 'Reactions to Destructions of the Second Temple: Theology, Perception, and Conversion', *JSJ* 12 (1981), pp. 195-204.

Strack, H.L., *Introduction to the Talmud and Midrash* (New York: Meridian; Philadelphia: Jewish Publication Society, 1959 [1931]).

Strecker, G., *Der Weg der Gerechtigkeit: Untersuchungen zur Theologie des Matthäus* (FRLANT, 82; Göttingen: Vandenhoeck & Ruprecht, 1971).

Suggs, M.J., *Wisdom, Christology, and Law in Matthew's Gospel* (Cambridge, MA: Harvard University Press, 1970).

Sutcliffe, E.F., 'Matthew 27:9', *JTS* 3 (1952), pp. 227-28.

Tagawa, K., 'People and Community in the Gospel of Matthew', *NTS* 16 (1969–70), pp. 149-62.

Tasker, R.V.G., *The Old Testament in the New Testament* (London: SCM Press, 1946, 1954).

—*The Gospel according to St Matthew: An Introduction and Commentary* (Leicester: Inter-Varsity Press; Grand Rapids: Eerdmans, 1961).

Taylor, V., *The Names of Jesus* (London: Macmillan, 1953).

—*The Gospel According to St Mark: The Greek Text with Introduction, Notes, and Indexes* (London: Macmillan, 1955).

Tedesche, S., 'Baruch, Book of', *IDB*, I, pp. 362-63.

Teeple, H.M., *The Mosaic Eschatological Prophet* (Philadelphia: SBL, 1957).

Telford, W.R., *The Barren Temple and the Withered Tree: A Redaction-Critical Analysis of the Cursing of the Fig Tree Pericope in Mark's Gospel and its Relation to the Cleansing of the Temple Tradition* (JSNTSup, 1; Sheffield: JSOT Press, 1980).

Thompson, A.L., *Responsibility for Evil in the Theodicy of IV Ezra: A Study Illustrating the Significance of Form and Structure for the Meaning of the Book* (SBLDS, 29; Missoula, MT: Scholars Press, 1977).

Thompson, J.A., *The Book of Jeremiah* (NICOT; Grand Rapids: Eerdmans, 1980).

Thrall, M.E., *The Greek Particles in the New Testament: Linguistic and Exegetical Studies* (NTTS, 3; Grand Rapids: Eerdmans, 1962).

Tilborg, S. van, *The Jewish Leaders in Matthew* (Leiden: Brill, 1972).

Torrey, C.C., 'The Foundry of the Second Temple at Jerusalem', *JBL* 55 (1936), pp. 247-60.

—*Documents of the Christian Church* (New York: Harper & Brothers, 1941).

—'The Aramaic Period of the Nascent Christian Church', *ZNW* 24 (1952–53), pp. 205-23.

Toy, C.H., *Quotations in the New Testament* (New York: Charles Scribner's Sons, 1884).

Trilling, W., *Das wahre Israel: Studien zur Theologie des Matthäus-Evangeliums* (Munich: Kösel, 1964).

Tsevat, M., 'Rachel's Tomb', *IDBSup*, pp. 724-25.

Unnik, W.C. van, 'The Death of Judas in St Matthew's Gospel', in M.H. Shepherd and E.C. Hobbs (eds.), *Gospel Studies in Honor of Sherman Elbridge Johnson* (ATR Supplement Series, 3; Evanston, IL: Anglican Theological Review, 1974), pp. 44-57.

Upton, J.A., 'The Potter's Field and the Death of Judas', *Concordia Journal* 8 (1982), pp. 213-19.

Vaccari, P., 'Le versioni arabe de Profeti', *Bib* 3 (1922), pp. 401-23.

VanderKam, J.C., 'The Righteousness of Noah', in J.J. Collins and G.W.E. Nickelsburg (eds.), *Ideal Figures in Ancient Judaism: Profiles and Paradigms* (SBLSCS, 12; Chico, CA: Scholars Press, 1980), pp. 13-32.

Vermes, G., 'La figure de Moïse au tournant des deux testaments', *Moïse, l'homme de l'alliance* (Paris: Desclée, 1955), pp. 63-92.

—'The Qumran Interpretation of Scripture in its Historical Setting', in J. MacDonald (ed.), *The Annual of Leeds University Oriental Society.* VI. *Dead Sea Scrolls Studies, 1969* (Leiden: Brill, 1969), pp. 85-97.

—*Jesus the Jew: A Historian's Reading of the Gospels* (London: SCM Press, 1973).

—'Jewish Studies and New Testament Interpretation', *JJS* 31 (1980), pp. 1-17.

—'Jewish Literature and New Testament Exegesis: Reflections on Methodology', *JJS* 33 (1982), pp. 361-76.

—*Jesus and the World of Judaism* (London: SCM Press, 1983).

Vögtle, A., *Messias und Gottessohn: Herkunft und Sinn der matthäischen Geburts- und Kindheitsgeschichte* (Düsseldorf: Patmos, 1971).

—'Die matthäische Kindheitsgeschichte', in M. Didier (ed.), *L'évangile selon Matthieu: Rédaction et théologie* (BETL, 29; Gembloux: Duculot, 1972), pp. 153-83.

Vouga, F., 'La seconde passion de Jérémie', *LumVie* 32, 165 (1983), pp. 71-82.

Waetjen, H.C., 'The Genealogy as the Key to the Gospel according to Matthew', *JBL* 95 (1976), pp. 205-30.

Wagner, G., *An Exegetical Bibliography of the New Testament.* I. *Matthew and Mark* (Macon, GA: Mercer University Press, 1983).

Weinert, F.D., 'Luke, the Temple, and Jesus' Saying about Jerusalem's Abandoned House (Luke 13:34-35)', *CBQ* 44 (1982), pp. 68-76.

Wellhausen, J., *Das Evangelium Matthei* (Berlin: Georg Reimer, 1904).

Wilcox, M., 'On Investigating the Use of the Old Testament in the New Testament', in E. Best and R.M. Wilson (eds.), *Text and Interpretation: Studies in the New Testament Presented to Matthew Black* (Cambridge: Cambridge University Press, 1979), pp. 231-43.

Wildberger, H., *Jesaja* (BKAT, 10; 3 vols.; Neukirchen–Vluyn: Neukirchener Verlag, 1972–82).

Wilkens, W., 'Die Versuchung Jesus nach Matthäus', *NTS* 28 (1981–82), pp. 479-89.

Wilkins, M.J., *The Concept of Disciple in Matthew's Gospel (as Reflected in the Use of the Term* μαθητής*)* (NovTSup, 59; Leiden: Brill, 1988).
Winkle, R.E., 'The Jeremiah Model for Jesus in the Temple', *AUSS* 24 (1986), pp. 155-72.
Wolff, C., *Jeremia im Frühjudentum und Urchristentum* (TU, 118. Berlin: Akademie Verlag, 1976).
Woollcombe, K.J., 'The Biblical Origins and Patristic Development of Typology', in G.W.H. Lampe and K.J. Woollcombe, *Essays on Typology* (SBT; London: SCM Press, 1957), pp. 39-75.
Wright, A.G., 'The Literary Genre Midrash', *CBQ* 28 (1966), pp. 105-38, 417-57.
Wuellner, W., *The Meaning of 'Fishers of Men'* (Philadelphia: Westminster Press, 1967).
Zahn, T., *Das Evangelium des Matthäus* (Kommentar zum NT, 1; Leipzig: Deichert; Erlangen: Scholl, 1922).
Zeller, D., *Kommentar zum Logienquelle* (Stuttgarter Kleiner Kommentar, NT, 21; Stuttgart: Katholisches Bibelwerk, 1986).

INDEXES

INDEX OF REFERENCES

OLD TESTAMENT

APOCRYPHA

NEW TESTAMENT

PSEUDEPIGRAPHA

RABBINIC TEXTS

PHILO

JOSEPHUS

Other Ancient References

INDEX OF AUTHORS

JOURNAL FOR THE STUDY OF THE NEW TESTAMENT

Supplement Series

1 THE BARREN TEMPLE AND THE WITHERED TREE
William R. Telford

2 STUDIA BIBLICA 1978
II. PAPERS ON THE GOSPELS
Edited by E.A. Livingstone

3 STUDIA BIBLICA 1978
III. PAPERS ON PAUL AND OTHER NEW TESTAMENT AUTHORS
Edited by E.A. Livingstone

4 FOLLOWING JESUS:
DISCIPLESHIP IN THE GOSPEL OF MARK
Ernest Best

5 THE PEOPLE OF GOD
Markus Barth

6 PERSECUTION AND MARTYRDOM IN THE THEOLOGY OF PAUL
John S. Pobee

7 SYNOPTIC STUDIES:
THE AMPLEFORTH CONFERENCES OF
1982 AND 1983
Edited by C.M. Tuckett

8 JESUS ON THE MOUNTAIN:
A STUDY IN MATTHEAN THEOLOGY
Terence L. Donaldson

9 THE HYMNS OF LUKE'S INFANCY NARRATIVES:
THEIR ORIGIN, MEANING AND SIGNIFICANCE
Stephen Farris

10 CHRIST THE END OF THE LAW:
ROMANS 10.4 IN PAULINE PERSPECTIVE
Robert Badenas

11 THE LETTERS TO THE SEVEN CHURCHES OF ASIA IN THEIR LOCAL
SETTING
Colin J. Hemer

12 PROCLAMATION FROM PROPHECY AND PATTERN:
LUCAN OLD TESTAMENT CHRISTOLOGY
Darrell L. Bock

13 JESUS AND THE LAWS OF PURITY:
TRADITION HISTORY AND LEGAL HISTORY IN MARK 7
Roger P. Booth

14 THE PASSION ACCORDING TO LUKE:
THE SPECIAL MATERIAL OF LUKE 22
Marion L. Soards

15 HOSTILITY TO WEALTH IN THE SYNOPTIC GOSPELS
Thomas E. Schmidt
16 MATTHEW'S COMMUNITY:
THE EVIDENCE OF HIS SPECIAL SAYINGS MATERIAL
Stephenson H. Brooks
17 THE PARADOX OF THE CROSS IN THE THOUGHT OF ST PAUL
Anthony Tyrrell Hanson
18 HIDDEN WISDOM AND THE EASY YOKE:
WISDOM, TORAH AND DISCIPLESHIP IN MATTHEW 11.25-30
Celia Deutsch
19 JESUS AND GOD IN PAUL'S ESCHATOLOGY
L. Joseph Kreitzer
20 LUKE
A NEW PARADIGM (2 Volumes)
Michael D. Goulder
21 THE DEPARTURE OF JESUS IN LUKE–ACTS:
THE ASCENSION NARRATIVES IN CONTEXT
Mikeal C. Parsons
22 THE DEFEAT OF DEATH:
APOCALYPTIC ESCHATOLOGY IN 1 CORINTHIANS 15 AND ROMANS 5
Martinus C. de Boer
23 PAUL THE LETTER-WRITER
AND THE SECOND LETTER TO TIMOTHY
Michael Prior
24 APOCALYPTIC AND THE NEW TESTAMENT:
ESSAYS IN HONOR OF J. LOUIS MARTYN
Edited by Joel Marcus & Marion L. Soards
25 THE UNDERSTANDING SCRIBE:
MATTHEW AND THE APOCALYPTIC IDEAL
David E. Orton
26 WATCHWORDS:
MARK 13 IN MARKAN ESCHATOLOGY
Timothy J. Geddert
27 THE DISCIPLES ACCORDING TO MARK:
MARKAN REDACTION IN CURRENT DEBATE
C. Clifton Black
28 THE NOBLE DEATH:
GRAECO-ROMAN MARTYROLOGY
AND PAUL'S CONCEPT OF SALVATION
David Seeley
29 ABRAHAM IN GALATIANS:
EPISTOLARY AND RHETORICAL CONTEXTS
G. Walter Hansen
30 EARLY CHRISTIAN RHETORIC AND 2 THESSALONIANS
Frank Witt Hughes

31 THE STRUCTURE OF MATTHEW'S GOSPEL:
A STUDY IN LITERARY DESIGN
David R. Bauer

32 PETER AND THE BELOVED DISCIPLE:
FIGURES FOR A COMMUNITY IN CRISIS
Kevin Quast

33 MARK'S AUDIENCE:
THE LITERARY AND SOCIAL SETTING OF MARK 4.11-12
Mary Ann Beavis

34 THE GOAL OF OUR INSTRUCTION:
THE STRUCTURE OF THEOLOGY AND ETHICS
IN THE PASTORAL EPISTLES
Philip H. Towner

35 THE PROVERBS OF JESUS:
ISSUES OF HISTORY AND RHETORIC
Alan P. Winton

36 THE STORY OF CHRIST IN THE ETHICS OF PAUL:
AN ANALYSIS OF THE FUNCTION OF THE HYMNIC MATERIAL
IN THE PAULINE CORPUS
Stephen E. Fowl

37 PAUL AND JESUS:
COLLECTED ESSAYS
Edited by A.J.M. Wedderburn

38 MATTHEW'S MISSIONARY DISCOURSE:
A LITERARY CRITICAL ANALYSIS
Dorothy Jean Weaver

39 FAITH AND OBEDIENCE IN ROMANS:
A STUDY IN ROMANS 1–4
Glenn N. Davies

40 IDENTIFYING PAUL'S OPPONENTS:
THE QUESTION OF METHOD IN 2 CORINTHIANS
Jerry L. Sumney

41 HUMAN AGENTS OF COSMIC POWER:
IN HELLENISTIC JUDAISM AND THE SYNOPTIC TRADITION
Mary E. Mills

42 MATTHEW'S INCLUSIVE STORY:
A STUDY IN THE NARRATIVE RHETORIC OF THE FIRST GOSPEL
David B. Howell

43 JESUS, PAUL AND TORAH:
COLLECTED ESSAYS
Heikki Räisänen

44 THE NEW COVENANT IN HEBREWS
Susanne Lehne

45 THE RHETORIC OF ROMANS:
ARGUMENTATIVE CONSTRAINT AND STRATEGY AND PAUL'S DIALOGUE WITH JUDAISM
Neil Elliott

46 THE LAST SHALL BE FIRST:
THE RHETORIC OF REVERSAL IN LUKE
John O. York

47 JAMES AND THE Q SAYINGS OF JESUS
Patrick J. Hartin

48 TEMPLUM AMICITIAE:
ESSAYS ON THE SECOND TEMPLE PRESENTED TO ERNST BAMMEL
Edited by William Horbury

49 PROLEPTIC PRIESTS
PRIESTHOOD IN THE EPISTLE TO THE HEBREWS
John M. Scholer

50 PERSUASIVE ARTISTRY:
STUDIES IN NEW TESTAMENT RHETORIC IN HONOR OF GEORGE A. KENNEDY
Edited by Duane F. Watson

51 THE AGENCY OF THE APOSTLE:
A DRAMATISTIC ANALYSIS OF PAUL'S RESPONSES TO CONFLICT IN 2 CORINTHIANS
Jeffrey A. Crafton

52 REFLECTIONS OF GLORY:
PAUL'S POLEMICAL USE OF THE MOSES–DOXA TRADITION IN 2 CORINTHIANS 3.12-18
Linda L. Belleville

53 REVELATION AND REDEMPTION AT COLOSSAE
Thomas J. Sappington

54 THE DEVELOPMENT OF EARLY CHRISTIAN PNEUMATOLOGY WITH SPECIAL REFERENCE TO LUKE–ACTS
Robert P. Menzies

55 THE PURPOSE OF ROMANS:
A COMPARATIVE LETTER STRUCTURE INVESTIGATION
L. Ann Jervis

56 THE SON OF THE MAN IN THE GOSPEL OF JOHN
Delbert Burkett

57 ESCHATOLOGY AND THE COVENANT:
A COMPARISON OF 4 EZRA AND ROMANS 1–11
Bruce W. Longenecker

58 NONE BUT THE SINNERS:
RELIGIOUS CATEGORIES IN THE GOSPEL OF LUKE
David A. Neale

59 Clothed with Christ:
The Example and Teaching of Jesus in Romans 12.1–15.13
Michael Thompson

60 The Language of the New Testament:
Classic Essays
Edited by Stanley E. Porter

61 Footwashing in John 13 and the Johannine Community
John Christopher Thomas

62 John the Baptizer and Prophet:
A Socio-Historical Study
Robert L. Webb

63 Power and Politics in Palestine:
The Jews and the Governing of their Land 100 BC–AD 70
James S. McLaren

64 Jesus and the Oral Gospel Tradition
Edited by Henry Wansbrough

65 The Rhetoric of Righteousness in Romans 3.21-26
Douglas A. Campbell

66 Paul, Antioch and Jerusalem:
A Study in Relationships and Authority in Earliest Christianity
Nicholas Taylor

67 The Portrait of Philip in Acts:
A Study of Roles and Relations
F. Scott Spencer

68 Jeremiah in Matthew's Gospel:
The Rejected Prophet Motif in Matthaean Redaction
Michael P. Knowles

69 Rhetoric and Reference in the Fourth Gospel
Margaret Davies

70 After the Thousand Years:
Resurrection and Judgment in Revelation 20
J. Webb Mealy

71 Sophia and the Johannine Jesus
Martin Scott

72 Narrative Asides in Luke–Acts
Steven M. Sheeley

73 Sacred Space
An Approach to the Theology of the Epistle to the Hebrews
Marie E. Isaacs

74 Teaching with Authority:
Miracles and Christology in the Gospel of Mark
Edwin K. Broadhead

75 Patronage and Power:
Studies on Social Networks in Corinth
John Kin-Man Chow

76 THE NEW TESTAMENT AS CANON:
A READER IN CANONICAL CRITICISM
Robert Wall and Eugene Lemcio

77 REDEMPTIVE ALMSGIVING IN EARLY CHRISTIANITY
Roman Garrison

78 THE FUNCTION OF SUFFERING IN PHILIPPIANS
L. Gregory Bloomquist

79 THE THEME OF RECOMPENSE IN MATTHEW'S GOSPEL
Blaine Charette

80 BIBLICAL GREEK LANGUAGE AND LINGUISTICS
Stanley E Porter and D A Carson (eds)

81 THE LAW IN GALATIANS
In-Gyu Hong

86 WORSHIP, THEOLOGY AND MINISTRY IN THE EARLY CHURCH: ESSAYS IN HONOUR OF RALPH P MARTIN
Michael Wilkins and Terence Paige (eds)